A Bestiary

Aidan Higgins

Dalkey Archive Press

Publisher's note: Originally published in the UK by Secker & Warburg as three separate volumes: *Donkey's Years* (1995), *Dog Days* (1998), and *The Whole Hog* (2000). While each of the three books are here reproduced in their entirety, the text has been reset and repaginated to accommodate publication in one volume.

Copyright © 1995, 1998, 2000, 2004 by Aidan Higgins

First edition of *A Bestiary*, 2004
All rights reserved

Library of Congress Cataloging-in-Publication Data

Higgins, Aidan, 1927-
   A bestiary / Aidan Higgins.— 1st Dalkey Archive ed.
      p. cm. — (Irish literature series)
   ISBN 1-56478-358-8 — ISBN 1-56478-357-X (pbk.)
   1. Higgins, Aidan, 1927- 2. Novelists, Irish—20th century—Biography. 3. Ireland—Social life
and customs—20th century. 4. Kildare (Ireland : County)—Social life and customs. I. Title:
Donkey's years. II. Title: Dog days. III. Title: Whole hog. IV. Title. V. Series.

   PR6058.I34Z463 2004
   823'.914—dc22

                                                            2003070084

Partially funded by grants from the Lannan Foundation and the Illinois Arts Council, a state agency.

Dalkey Archive Press books are published by the Center for Book Culture, a nonprofit
organization located at Milner Library, Illinois State University.

www.centerforbookculture.org

Printed on permanent/durable acid-free paper and bound in Canada.

Contents

Book One: Donkey's Years

Book Two: Dog Days

Book Three: The Whole Hog

Donkey's Years

In Loving Memory

Bartholomew Joseph Higgins
1892–1969

Lillian Ann (née Boyd)
1892–1966

Josef Gustave Moorkens
b. Herentals, Belgium
1897–1952

Niet mijn will, o Heer,
maar de uwe geschiede
Luc. XXII, 42

Genadige Jesus, geef zijne
ziel de eeuwige rust

In the County Kildare the circumstances and appearance of the population located on the bogs, or in their immediate vicinity, are very unfavourable. On each side of those parts of the canal that pass through the bog, the land is let in small lots to turf-cutters who take up their residence on the spot, however dreary and uncomfortable. Their first care is to excavate a site fit for habitation on the driest bank that can be selected, which is sunk so deep that little more than the roof is visible; this is covered with scanty thatch, or more frequently with turf pared from the bog, laid down with the herbage upward, which is superficially assimilated with the aspect of the surrounding scenery that the eye would pass it over unnoticed, were it not undeceived by the appearance of the children and domestic animals sallying from a hole in one side, and by the occasional gush of smoke from the numerous chinks in the roof. The English language is everywhere spoken.

Samuel Lewis Esquire
A Topographical Dictionary of Ireland,
1837

I do not long for the world as it was when I was a child. I do not long for the person I was in that world. I do not want to be the person I am now in that world then.

Alan Bennett

The stench of sensation is like anaesthetic made visible.

Eudora Welty

– Preface –

In the Civil Survey 1654–56 the lands of Ballymakealy, Tirow and Seal-stown are described as merging 'on the East with the lands of Kildrought, on the West with the lands of Griffenrath, on the North with the lands of Castletown and the lands of Mooretown, and on the South with the lands of Ardresse' (Ardrass).

According to the same survey Possockstown (Roselawn) was west of the lands of Ballymakealy. Griffenrath had for long periods been farmed by the Dongans of Possockstown and possibly for that reason came to be so described. In 1643–44 during the wars there were references to Thomas Dongan of Griffenrath, Balligorne and Possockstown receiving special protection.

Richard Talbot, Duke of Tyrconnell who acquired Allen's interest in Ballymakealy, Tirow and Sealstown was brother of Mary, wife of Sir John Dongan of Castletown and Possockstown, and thus had a special interest in acquiring the adjoining lands of Ballymakealy.

Richard Talbot's estates were confiscated following the defeat of the Jacobites and his death during the Siege of Limerick, but his widow Frances Countess Dowager of Tyrconnell succeeded in establishing her claim to the lands of Ballymakealy, Sealstown, Tirow and Oldtown as those lands were part of her jointure.

Bartholomew Van Homrigh purchased Ballymakealy and Oldtown and had to be content with allowing the Duchess to retain the lands for her lifetime.

The Duchess was to outlive all the Van Homrighs and died in 1730 aged ninety-two.

The house called Springfield must have been built by John Clarke who in 1763 granted to John Franklin, then of Springfield, 'All parts of the lands of Ballymakealy, Saltstown and Tirow containing 70A-3R-7P Irish Plantation Measure in which is included the part lately occupied by Richard Hawkshaw Esquire and also that part which John Clarke lately had in his own hands and the whole equals that granted by William and Katherine Conolly to John Clarke except 40A-3R-3P which is on lease to Denis Tilbury (now T. Tyrrell's) together with the dwelling house and all other edifices and buildings on the said lands'.

John Franklin sold his interest to Richard Phillips of the 2nd Regiment of Foot for the sum of £284-3-3. In 1780 Richard Phillips married Dorcas Sheperd daughter of Rev. Samuel Sheperd Vicar of Kildrough and two years later leased it to Richard Baldwin Thomas of Dublin; Ballymakealy, Saltstown and Tirow, then known as Springfield, and held under lease of 15th September 1763 for three lives in Perpetual Renewal at a yearly rent of £80.

The property was then described as 'All that part known as Springfield with the dwelling house edifices and buildings thereon and containing 70A-3R-7P'.

From 1780 onwards, Springfield had a succession of owners. Nicholas Archdall Esq. was succeeded by Thomas Long, a member of the Dublin family of coach-builders, who in 1801 leased to James Langrishe and to his heirs 'all that part of the lands of Springfield containing 47 acres with the dwelling house and outoffices in as ample a manner as held by Thomas Long, for the lives of Christina Clarke née Finey daughter of George Finey and wife of John Clarke, Williamina Baillie wife of Arthur Baillie and Miss Catherine Clarke only daughter of John Clarke survivor of them'.

Catherine Clarke later married Richard Nelson and their interest in Springfield continued until it was acquired by the Earl of Leitrim.

In 1806 Revd James Langrishe, Archdeacon of Glendalough, leased to Francis Walker of Elm Hall, Celbridge. In Pigotts Directory of 1824, Capt. John Bradshaw of Springfield is named as one of the Gentry of the Celbridge area. He leased the dwelling house and outoffices with 33 acres to James Williams in 1833. Williams was succeeded by John Thomas Haughton, son of the late Jeremiah Haughton of the Celbridge Woollen Mills. He occupied from 1845 and was in possession of the house, outoffices and two gate-lodges with 52 acres of land. Jeremiah Haughton was succeeded by John J. Langrishe who died before 1889, when, according to the Valuation Books, his widow Maria Langrishe occupied.

Mrs Langrishe died in August 1898, the last of the family to live at Springfield as the contents of her house were sold by public auction in October 1898.

Subsequent occupiers were Major Hamilton, Captain Mitchell, Captain Richard Warren and Mr Bart ('Batty') Higgins from whom Matthew Dempsey purchased in 1940.

'Springfield in the Townland of Ballymakealy'
by Lena Boylan, *The Celbridge Charter.*

PART I

Kildare

The Great Flood

I am consumed by memories and they form the life of me; stories that make up my life and lend it whatever veracity and purpose it may have. I suspect that even before I saw the light of day on 3rd March 1927 I was already being consumed by memories in Mumu's womb and by her memories prior to mine and by her granny's prior to her, bypassing my mother, stretching as far back as accommodating memory could reach into the past.

My first conscious memory is of our village being flooded, which would have been 1933 when I was but six years old. Our nanny, Nurse O'Reilly – a longshanked rawboned bucktoothed Cavanwoman of indeterminate age who took no nonsense from anybody but her superiors, who knew her place – would have been unable to push the pram much beyond the Abbey on the outskirts of Celbridge, through the water lapping against the wall of Flynn's bicycle shop and flooding Darlington's forge.

I was a year older when the Woolfs drove into Celbridge in style and inquired the way to Marlay Abbey, the home of Swift's devoted Vanessa, country seat of the Dutchman Vanhomrigh, Quartermaster for General Ginkel on the winning side at the Boyne, a bad battle to lose.

The posh London diarist looked about with some disdain ('Grafton Street is not on the level of Sloane Street,' she noted sniffily), noticed the grey sham-Gothic Abbey weathered to look ancient (even Time was deceitful in Ireland) with its sham-Gothic windows blocked up. It was a brief courtesy visit and they missed Vanessa's Bower.

Mumu read, recited, chanted to us (the Dote and I), rarely sang. Where Have You Been, Billy Boy? Billy Boy? Abdul the Bulbul Amir. James, James, Morrison, Morrison, Wetherby George Dupree took great care of his mother, though he was only three. Mumu held my elbows and bounced me up and down on her lap, laughing in my face, bringing my hands together, chanting Clap hands, clap hands till Daddy comes home! Pies in his pocket for baby alone!

'Dead easy,' brother Bun said, strolling about in his CWC blazer, hands in pockets. 'Buck privates.'

Mumu spoke feelingly of 'hard' and 'soft' water for washing and drinking purposes; very conscious of how the wind blew and the changing quality of wind; the soft winds of summer, the cold east wind of spring, the north wind of winter.

Dado held me in his arms at the nursery window, pointing to the wonders of the world without. A goat in a tree, flying fish over a meadow, sailing boats disappearing into clouds. I fidget in his arms, turning like a top spinning, always missing the sailing boat hidden in the clouds, the goat hidden in the leaves, the flying fish hidden in the meadow. All I see are clouds passing over Springfield, cowslip dancing in the meadow, a tree quivering where something living has just flown out of it.

'Ah Da! ah Da!' I cry, twisting and turning in his arms. 'Lemme see!'

Dado holds back his head and laughs at me. He smells of hair-oil, linseed oil, his quiff is parted in the centre like Mandrake the Magician, he wears pointy patent-leather shoes. 'Look A.,' he says, torturing me. 'Can you see it?'

I draw stick-men with straight lines for arms and legs and a circle for the face, with broomhandle hair sprouting as on the gollywog on the jamjar, with vacant expressions stamped on their moony faces.

'Can you do pooley?' Nurse O'Reilly asks us.

For lost things Mumu advises a prayer to Saint Anthony; and the lost things turn up in the strangest places; the half-solid ball behind the hotpress door, the pencil-sharpener behind the mangle, the Yo-Yo in the knitting basket, the cricket bat under the bed, *Ballygullion* under the bath.

A coal fire burns in the kitchen range, the Dote cries because his hands are frozen after riding back from eight o'clock mass. Old Mrs Henry roasts a rabbit in the oven. At Christmas at the back of the church by the confessional (PP Revd Fr Hickey), in the holy crib among the straw, the Holy Family appear to be dead. Saint Joseph crouches forward, staring with a dead man's vacant stare at the dead mannikin in the straw. A coffin is mounted on trestles by the curate's confessional

'The days are drawing out,' Dado announces.

'Where are the snows of yester-year?' asks Mumu.

Out for a spin towards Clane we run over a cat at Barberstown Cross. I look back and see its guts stuck to the road across which a patriotic hand had chalked 'UP DEV!' and beyond it from ditch to ditch another hand has scrawled 'O'DUFFY IS THE MAN!'

'Don't look back,' my father advises, his gloved hand on the steering wheel. 'Never look back.' We drive grandly on.

Lizzy had put his best suit in the oven, to air; the sick black kitten crept in, the oven door was closed and next morning the kitten is removed stiff as a board.

'Got any tickles?'

No.

'No tickles for Aunt Cissy?'

No.

'I just can't believe that!' cries the hearty aunt. 'Cissy will soon find out.'

Now practical fingers probe and dig into me, her strong hands hold me, begin to torture. I am alive with tickles. It's a Chinese torture.

I wet myself, howling with laughter, tumble off the sofa, squirm like a snake on the carpet, wet myself some more, mortified with shame. The hearty aunt is all over me, tickling, laughing, spluttering. I lie dead with embarrassment on the carpet. An amused strange face regards me fondly. My aunty is the famous horsewoman who rode champions, won cups, laid into lazy mounts with a switch, mucked-out stables at cockcrow, could drink Lough Erne dry.

'Who wants a piggyback ride?' asks Dado, down on his hands and knees on the carpet.

I ride on his back. He is an elephant. We are in India, in the Punjab, I hold on to his huge elephant ears. He trumpets at the young Raja in a turban on the veranda. His back shakes, he bucks me off behind the sofa. Now he is a bucking bronco in Texas. I am a cowboy. Rita Phelan sings:

> I'm a rambler, I'm a gambler,
> I'm a long way from home.
> But if you don't like me
> Just leave me alone!

Our cat has a mouse in its mouth. The cat takes it into a corner and plays with it. Tired of play, curving its paw, pushing, kitty bites the mouse's head off, begins to eat it. I hear the crunch of little bones; the tail sticks out and is swallowed last.

'Did you ever see a crow flying and a cat sitting on its tail?' Dado asks.

No.

'Then I'll show you. Watch this now.'

It's a riddle.

On a blank page of my sketchbook he draws a crow on the wing, a black-bird on the wing that Dado calls Crow, and, below, spells out C R O W. He turns over a page and draws a smiling cat with whiskers and spells beneath it C A T, sitting on its own tail. My father shows me the crow flying and then on the next page the cat sitting on its own tail. It's a trick question.

'There,' says Dado.

I am sick.

If I take the medicine and stay in bed and do as the doctor says, Dado promises to give me a surprise present.

'What?'

'I can't tell you what. It's a surprise.'

'Well, tell me what it's *like*. What does it look like?'

'It looks like nothing.'

'It can't.'

My father thinks.

'It's something with whiskers that you keep in a glass cage.'

On the verge of sleep I heard the intruder climb the paling below and jump heavily onto the scuffled gravel, and heavy dragging footsteps slowly cross the gravel and climb the steps and pass through the open front door. Crossing the hall the slow dragging steps came on, ascending the stairs, turning in on our landing, passing the hot-cupboard and now I heard the harsh rasping breath outside the nursery door, which slowly opened, gave inwards. Rigid with fright I sank slowly under the bedclothes, but not soon enough, for the horror had already entered, its huge shadow crowding over the ceiling lit by the wavering blue night-light before Gina Greene's altar. The apparition filled the nursery – the rasping breath, the sound of nailed boots; the puttees and tin helmet, the heavy service revolver in its holster, the baggy cavalry twill worn as if on a scarecrow or a dead man. I heard the glass case being roughly opened and the sound of rummaging as the intruder did what he had come to do. The gloved hands were fumbling at the toys, the breath rasping. He left, making no attempt at secrecy, the slow footsteps dragging themselves along, retreating down the landing, dragging the sack behind, onto the carpeted stairs, then limping across the hallway, out the front door, across the gravel, over the paling.

I heard him scale the far paling and enter the plantation and came up from under the bedclothes to find the glass case hanging open and all our toys and books gone, a note stuck to the glass. Someone was having a good laugh at our expense down in the plantation, dressed as an officer of the British Army in the Great War.

A note in a sprawling slapdash rascally hand was sellotaped to the glass: 'I take, therefore I am.' And below that:

> 'Danger – Stranger!
> HE WHO IS
> (signed) The Evictor.'

If Dado was not exactly our Arts Master he liked to watch us when we were drawing and colouring with pencils and sometimes invited himself into the circle and then would be asked to draw.

He always sketched the same profile of this long-nosed man with elephant ears and centre parting in his oily quiff (himself) always facing left. Then out of the nostrils something was expelled like vertical strokes of rain, a sudden rainfall out of clouds. What could it be?

'Snot!' we screeched. 'It's snot!!'

Mumu would have considered this the very essence of vulgarity but he only smiled a knowing smile. To his cronies and equals he was Batty but to his employees and social inferiors he was M'striggins.

'Wait here,' Mumu would say to unexpected visitors who were always unwelcome, 'just wait here and I'll see if I can get him.'

He smelt of Brylcreem and whiskey and scent, sharpening the point of an incredible pencil and turning a page. He would write us a poem.

'Wait now lads,' he said, narrowing his eyes, touching his nose, thinking it over.

'Wait now,' he said, preparing to expel some scurrilous stuff.

He wrote:

> Miss Hart let out a fart,
> She tied it on a string . . .

But here, alas, inspiration died.

'Whaa din, Da?'

He deliberated afresh; then completed the clinching couplet:

> She kept it in Miss Coyle's house,
> Then let it go again!

Miss Hart, who cut our hair, lived in the village with a sick old mother who wheezed like a Pekinese. She asked awkward questions ('Would you fight your match?'). Miss Coyle was most ladylike and owned 'One Down' the piebald mare, groomed and ridden at steeplechases by Grogan with his cruel hands; but 'One Down' never won anything, not a sausage.

The pencil-sharpener is within a little blue-and-white globe of the world that revolves in my hand as I turn it carefully and there is the pleasant smell of lead and wood shavings as the pencil is sharpened to a point and the wood shavings curl from the globe. Gina Greene does not know how to spell Pompeii but Mumu does and I spell it out to her dictation.

I write out: 'The giant had a tiny hand and he passed me.' And: 'The giant heard the boy laughing in the mountain.' And: 'Some of the Romans in Pompeii started poking spears into the lava balls.'

'Where did you get that, my pet?' Mumu asks.

'I don't know.'

'Spelling improving,' Mumu says, laying her hand on my head. 'Hot head.'

In the drawing-books that Dado buys for us at Woolworth's in Grafton Street in Dublin the Dodo has drawn a menagerie of jungle beasts; these were drawn and painted in when he was our age. They are kept under lock and key in the lamproom which presently will become the Dodo's reference library with *Picture Post* and *Lilliput* and *Tatler & Sketch* and *Illustrated London News* neatly piled and tabulated.

The Dodo had a careful and all-too-selective hand, those white hands he was forever washing and scrubbing and manicuring. He had drawn lions and little hunters in a jungle and coloured them in watercolours to make them come to life with lolling red tongues and dark manes caught in mid-leap over the jungle path at the small hunters armed with rifles, dwarfed by huge trees, all creepers and lianas and pythons wreathed about high branches and monkeys looking down at the little mannikins in khaki shorts, pith helmets, bush-boots and puttees who fired at point-blank range at the lion whose head and out-stretched claws disappear into the puffs of smoke from the rifle barrels.

With coloured plasticine and a nail file and his endless patience the Dodo made a perfect little Robinson Crusoe with a parrot on his shoulder and a fowling piece by his lap, a dog by his foot, his face burnt terra-cotta by the implacable island sun scorching the sand, scorching Crusoe in his furs.

Grogan mucked out the stables, watered the horses, tipped a bucket into the tank full of tadpoles and frogspawn, swirled it about until he got a fill of bad-smelling water, whipped it out, rolled up his sleeves and washed his hands, forearms and neck in axle-grease. He asked us whether we wanted to 'see Dublin'. We said yes; it was a trick he played. He stood behind me with his stubby fingers pressed to my temples and lifted me up so that with slitty coolie eyes I 'saw' Dublin (i.e., nothing). 'Me now! Me next!' Now it was my brother's turn; Dublin was twelve miles to the west of us. All the horses were chomping hay in their loose boxes and Tommy Flynn was taking his melodeon off the big nail in the harness room and the bell was ringing from beyond Killadoon wood, so Clements's workers were knocking off for the day.

The poor and their mongrel dogs were clustering at the front door, stinking up the porch, asking for apples, begging for food and old clothes or anything that was being thrown out, and with implacably lofty bearing Mumu was mounting the stairs to find the Master in the study going over the rent-books and payments for field hands and kitchen staff, and the good news was that he would be down presently.

'God bless you, Ma'am!'

Mumu recited:

> Beware and take care
> Of the Bight of Berin.
> Of the one that comes out
> There are forty go in . . .

Gina Greene recites:

> Little Polly Flinders
> Sat upon the cinders,
> Warming her pretty little toes;
> Her mother came and caught her

>And spanked her little daughter
>For spoiling her nice new clothes.

But who is this Polly Flinders? And who is Gina Greene? Gina lives in the village with all the other Greenes in a dark narrow hovel full of bicycles and dogs and sometimes helps out at Springfield and Rita Phelan (the cat) says that I am 'soft' on Gina, who has long auburn hair done in plaits and a lovely sweet smell and a lovely sweet smile so why wouldn't I be soft on her?

Nurse O'Reilly, chomping with her great buckteeth, recites:

>There was a little man
>And he had a little gun;
>Up to the mountains he did run . . .

No, pipes up the Dote, that's wrong, and recites:

>There was a little man
>And he had a little gun;
>And his bullets were made of lead, lead, lead;
>He went to the brook and shot a little duck
>Right through the middle of the head, head, head.

In the kitchen Lizzy Bolger recites:

>There was a little man
>And he had a little gun,
>Up to the mountains he did run,
>With a bellyful of fat and an old Tom cat,
>And a pancake stuck to his bum, bum, bum.

Having made a disgusting stink my brother rises from his pot, one arm upraised, to cry 'Mafeking is relieved! Hurrah! Stinky, stinky parley voo!'
  'That's not nice,' Nurse O'Reilly says.

The gramophone plays 'Hold Your Hand Out, You Naughty Boy', dust rises and is pierced by spears of sunlight, the heavy record revolves and music smelling of musty herbs issues from the slatted side of the box as a jolly male voice sings in a rollicking sort of a way:

As you walk along the Bois de Boulogne
You can hear the girls declare,
'He must be a millionaire! He must be a millionaire!'

I try to imagine Europe. Joss Moorkens stands with arms folded outside his dugout, waiting for the gas-attack; a train is about to leave a French station, on the side of the carriage is painted HOMMES-CHEVAUX, while a beery voice sings in German. It's the music of Franz Lehar. I try to imagine Vienna. Gay Vienna, city of a thousand melodies.

People are dancing, a carriage is drawn up before a lighted ballroom, Richard Tauber alights in top hat and silk scarf to sing 'Girls were made to love and kiss'. Georges Gautier sings in English, entering the chorus of 'O Bella Marguerita!' like a Riley running downhill without brakes. 'Picking Grapes With You!' 'Betty Co-Ed' follows, then 'The Man Who Broke the Bank at Monte Carlo'. The high strange male voices are all jolly but music makes me feel sad.

A ship under full sail with flags flying from the mizzen waits in the bay as Errol Flynn, smiling gallantly, grinning away under his moustache springs onto a rock and sheathes his sword, leaving Basil Rathbone to expire in a pool. Ronald Colman fights Douglas Fairbanks again, up and down winding narrow stairs in a castle, as I wade upstream and the wind blows in my long hair, I feel the secure weight of my sword by my side. I hear my brother calling. He is cutting quarter-staves in the plantation. I hear black slaves singing. The moon rises over the bay and the ship claps on full sail as a horn sounds in the forest.

I press down hard on my 2B pencil and the lead breaks.
A trapdoor opens at my feet and harsh voice exclaims, 'Villain!'
'On guard!' I cry out in a thin voice not my own.
Then 'The Stein Song' sung by beery weepy German voices. A little boy is flung from high battlemented walls, Rome burns. My father enters, poking into his ear with the end of a match.
'What's going on here?'
'Nothing.'

In the long steam-driven trains of the Great Southern & Western Railways, the first-class carriage into which we were ushered by Mr. Dooley with a formality that stopped just short of obsequiousness, smelled of stale cigarette smoke, trapped biscuit air, dusty upholstery, hair-oil; framed sepia photographs like aquatints were set above the plush, showing hardy souls in long loose bathing-drawers wading in the surf at Lahinch and Parknasilla and gents in baggy plus-fours struck poses on the golf links at Greystones and Delgany. An advertisement for Fury's Coach Tours was phrased with old-fashioned restraint: *'We Lead. Others May Follow'*.

Waggling its wings, a monoplane passed low over Springfield, circled about, and then came in again for a low pass over the front meadow. The daredevil airman Captain Shern, a friend of Dado's, waved gallantly, and flew straight through the telegraph wires, shearing them as if with secateurs. The wings wobbled, the engine coughed a few times, the pilot struggled with the controls. My father leaped off the front step and ran across the gravel, calling back, 'By Christ, I think he's down!'

But he wasn't, for the engine picked up again and the little plane flew out over the plantation, the pilot waving back, crazy in his goggles, heading off for Baldonnel Aerodrome. Dado said he was a gas card.

My three brothers and I, Desmond, Brendan, Colman and myself, well-spaced out gallant walkers, none on speaking terms, arrived at Hazelhatch Station in 'good time', following our long hike through the village. Dado liked to arrive an hour before the train was due. He and the station master, Mr. Dooley, paraded up and down the departure platform, gossiping and sucking Zubes. The tall horse-faced man had a lugubrious manner and stopped when Dado halted to make a point. We watched them both in sullen silence, hating this parade.

So the months passed agreeably enough.

Oh I knew my place all right; was I not that thin-shanked Papist brat? Timid, anaemic, diffident, else why permanently unwell (whooping cough after infancy, adolescent cuts and abrasions became sores that instantly went septic), always difficult to feed (meals were eaten back to front, starting with jelly and ending with soup), always faddy and averse to any change, strange food, timid with strangers (the gent at the garden gate who rattled small change in his trouser pocket and asked, 'Is your daddy about, sonny?'), fearful of nuns and priests (who were scarcely human), fearful of the crumpled little nun who prepared us for First Holy Communion. Fearful ('I do be a-feared,' the Keegans said) of the old deaf Bishop who confirmed us, gave us a stroke upon the cheek, made us 'strong and perfect Christians' (*moryaw*), fearful of big strong Gardai Siochana in blue uniforms on big strong push-bikes with pumps under the crossbar and truncheon at hip, afraid of the 'pinch dark' cellar.

Hidden behind the old cook's skirt smelling of flour or in the currant bushes, that was my place.

'Me fawdur's out but me mudder's a-din,' I lied brazenly.

'Do you want to grow up like your father?'

'No.'

The visitor jingled the coins in his pocket and with a strange lopsided smile twisting his lips handed me a half-crown through the bars of the gate.

But Dado had always told us to say that he was out but not expected back and no one knew where he was; when in fact he was sunbathing in the long grass and him covered in olive oil with nothing on but the handkerchief about his neck and another on his head, knotted at the four corners, himself soaked in olive oil and scalded by the sun.

The visitor went off whistling down the front avenue.

Mumu said that the Keegan boys were just hobbledehoys who had come up from the bogs. But the Dote and I went to school with John Joe and liked Patsy and we wore hobnail boots like them, sucked Bull's Eyes, amazed that John Joe ate his own wet snot; we spoke as they did (dey did) and had inherited their fears and prejudices. We said dis ting an' dat ting, dis, dat an' de udder ting, me brudder, me fawdur, me mudder. We were as they, felt as they, our pals, and Patsy Keegan was my best pal and I felt proud of his strained face and flared nostrils, of the superhuman effort he put into sailing over the hedge and ditch of water beyond, that sneery Neddy had dared him to jump. He was a true champion.

When did you last see a woman wringing her hands or an old fellow wearing vulcanite bicycle clips or nervous black greyhounds on the leash or the inextinguishable fires of wayside itinerants and their washing draped on hedges and bushes and they themselves (The Great Unwashed) none too clean?

I recall: Aladdin paraffin lamps and anthracite and coke and Bird's Custard and sago and tadpoles (pollywoggles) wriggling in the pond at the edge of the Crooked Meadow and cruel hare-coursing and blooding of hounds and the baying of the pack after foxes and twists of hardboiled sweeties in paper bags, a pennyworth and tuppenceworth, and Findlater's men carrying in a week's supplies and being checked by the cook and Wild Woodbines in open packets of five for tuppence halfpenny old currency with farthings in the change and the mad dog frothing at the mouth running in mad circles in humpy commonage near Oakley Park one lovely summer's day returning from the village with fags and brother Bun and I feeling sick and giddy from the first tobacco and the PP's alarming *Diktat* from the pulpit on Sunday and pea-picking for Mumu in the garden and the Bogey Man lurking in the cellar with the arrowheads and the mouldy masks and looking for mushrooms in Mangan's long field with Mumu and the Dodo early one morning in summer and the stink of ammonia in the convent class and the damp poor clothes in the hanging cupboard and the musty smell of nuns and the rustle of their habits and the small turf fire dying in the narrow grate when Sister Rumold prepared us for First Holy Communion and told us, 'You must prepare yourself to receive Our Lord' and the hot smell of the big girls and the provenance of sin – a writhing serpent impaled on the Patriarch's crozier and St Brigid the patroness blushing scarlet up on her pedestal and St Patrick watching with his curly beard – and the purple-shrouded statues at Passion Week and the whispering in the dim confessional and Crunchies in golden foil wrappings and chocolate whirls with whipped cream centres that the Dote and I called Dev's Snots and then Bull's Eyes and Peggy's Leg and liquorice twists and fizzy sherbets and stirabout with cream and brown sugar in the dark after early Mass and servants churning in the chilly dairy and butter pats in the tub and bluebottles buzzing against the larder screen and a snipe rotting on a hook and the cat stink behind the mangle and the sheets airing on the stiffened hillocks of the frozen bleach-green and the tracks of the hare in the snow and lowing cows calving and calves on spindle legs suckling their mothers and mares foaling and stallions mounting with flared nostrils and sows farrowing and ewes lambing and the baldy priest in the awful brown wig saying mass below us at Straffan and the polychrome Christ bleeding with one arm missing at the scourging in the Stations of the Cross that stuck out in little polychrome grottos from the nave and the nun with pinched bloodless lips genuflecting and extinguishing candles with a long snuffer and the lovely byroad by the Liffey to Odlums' and the May procession between the cypress trees along the convent avenue and the gravel biting into my bare knees and I thinking only of the cold roast with lots of salt and the ruffled nun walking against the wind and ruddyfaced Sister Rumold nodding her wimple – like the scuffed lining of a shallow Jacob's biscuit tin or glacé fruit packings – and leaning forward from her highbacked chair in the Holy Faith Convent waiting room and genteely offering Mumu a Zube from a little oval box sprung open in her white speckled hand and my mother in her blandest grandest way (with fur coat thrown open so that the nun could get an eyeful of her expensive Switzer's dress) saying how important education was and the wimple nodding like mad for Sister Rumold couldn't agree more, for the youngest (aged four) and myself (aged six) the middle child were to be taken under her wing the following Monday in the class of Second Infants and Lizzy Bolger had painted her mouth with the reddest lipstick and seemed to be bleeding from the mouth and was coaxing, 'Gizzakiss, ah g'wan!' and the big girls were tittering in the playground and the men were playing Pitch & Toss after Mass above Killadoon front gate and the hay-bogies were grinding along the Naas-Celbridge road and the steamroller belching smoke and stinking of tar and twenty Collegiate College girls in slate-grey uniforms were rounding Brady's corner and two teachers with long forbidding Protestant horse-faces pacing along in front and their shadows flitting along the wall and myself in great embarrassment cycling rapidly by and Satan dining at Castletown (narrated dramatically by the Keegans as if they had been present, carrying in steaming dishes) and the PP sweating and called in after the Vicar couldn't shift His Nibs who sat there sneering and then the PP showed him the crucifix and told him to go about his business and the PP himself sweated seven shirts and died but Satan had gone straight through the floor in a puff of black smoke, leaving a cracked mirror behind as a memento as you can see to this day; all that I recall of those grand times that can never return.

I recall: the bridles and winkers and saddles and stitching and teasers and the stoked furnace going full blast with coal and Josey Darlington beating up sparks in the forge and the farriers and harness-makers of those days and the poor rabbit choking itself to death in the snare and the Bogey Man having breakfast with Dado in the Grand Hotel in Greystones when we were on holiday and the pair of them shaking out their napkins and telling dirty jokes and spooning prune juice into themselves and the suicide old Jem Brady lifted stiff out of the quarry (reputed to be depthless) in grappling irons pulled by the Guards and Nurse O'Reilly lifting up the Dote to view the corpse in its brown shroud in the coffin on trestles at the back of the church by the confessional and the soldiers firing patriotic volleys over the open grave of the patriot about to be interred.

Now read on.

− 2 −

The Keegan Boys

The Keegan boys had us constantly amazed.

They had a mysterious hieroglyphic language, peculiarly their own, utilising their own turds; as my young brother and I were to discover when we became friendly with the youngest brother John Joe, walking a mile to the Holy Faith Convent in the village near the site of an old brewery.

The brothers fought like cats and dogs among themselves; it was their nature, something the poor did. When our favourite, Patsy, the middle brother, was not torturing and tormenting John Joe, he in turn was being unmercifully set upon and bullied out of his wits by Neddy the eldest, a sadist in a cloth cap who smoked fags and played the mouth-organ.

Patsy was held head-down flush to the ground, one arm locked behind his back, Neddy grunting and tittering and Patsy pleading, 'Ah give over!' But the long cruel stringy arms held him as in a vice and Neddy gave off a sour smell of manly sweat, forcing the arm out of its socket.

'Ah Janey,' groaned Patsy, one with the earth. 'Ah be Janey Mack, give over!'

They knew nothing of *'Pax!'* nor any remission of unremitting chores from morning to night, chopping wood, hauling turf, running messages, doing chores about the cottage, each fighting for his own survival. They came out with great cuts of Boland's bread in their fists, chewing, taking gulps of strong tea, masticating the pap. They rolled up their sleeves and made a muscle, the blue veins swelling, throbbing. Neddy made catapults from forked branches and car tyres, set snares, killed what he caught, trapping the rabbit's head under his boot and yanking upwards or dispatching it with the heel of his fist in the nape of the neck. The rabbit made a sound like a sigh. The Keegans were great ones for riding bicycles, mending punctures, performing acrobatics. They went to bed early, for they were up betimes; saying the Family Rosary in the gloaming, all kneeling on the tiles of the kitchen floor, the old man giving out the invocation.

The brothers crouched at sudden stools as if about to burst, used the ditches and fields as open-air latrines, wiping themselves with leaves and grass. Their cottage had an outhouse earth-closet used by the parents and red Mona herself, the sister, but the three brothers 'went' in the woods and fields.

They were always promising to show us something unusual and one day right enough Patsy bade us follow him to see a marvel, and my brother and I followed him across the paddock, over the gate, and there on the slope of the bank by the hedge were steaming turds shat out as curlicues in the manner of stop-start cartoon animation or the stylish effects achieved with marzipan and icing by forcing-bags in Mrs Beeton cookery hints.

'Wha's dat? whaa's dis?' we asked, amazed.

'Bedad tis a furry fuhball match.'

A fairy football match!

Since they owned neither bathroom nor toilet nor pyjamas they stood at the door in their long-johns and pissed in great joyful parabolas of ascending and descending arcs into the yard, bouncing it off the outhouse door and upsetting the hens. Their powerful pee curved out like rainbows under clouds, John Joe's under Patsy's and Neddy's above, and the three pissers smiling to themselves, each holding his mickey with the utmost care and tenderness and delicacy, before they retreated and closed the door and knelt down for the Holy Rosary as they did every evening when the day's chores were done. My brother and I crouched on the roof of their outhouse with two Rhode Island Reds and marvelled at this. Communal crapping sessions in the plantation were to cement a fast bond of friendship between us and the three Keegans, all of us crouching and groaning manfully at stool. It was a token of trust and equality. We covered up and hid our craps with dead leaves, neat and clean as cats.

Casual labouring men passing through left their callingcards in the form of gigantic stools in the bottoms of ditches, in the plantation and even close to the house in the side shrubbery where one was liable to tread in a Finn MacCoolish evacuation left there as territorial claim or territorial insult, gradually acquiring a top-knot of fluff (unless devoured by crows) akin to the grassy mounds that are all that remain to us of the Norman motte-and-bailey defences. Great turds were also left balancing on a cromlech of stones, as a tribal threat, to indicate where those passing through had relieved themselves mightily.

In freezing weather the Keegan boys came out at dusk with jugs and basins of cold water which they threw down on the already icy road between the two lodges, to let it freeze solid overnight, and next morning they had a slide a good hundred yards long and were already using it in their hobnail boots reinforced with brads at the toes.

In those days few cars went by, cyclists kept to the footpath and the turf carts remained at home as Neddy took a long run, jumped onto the slide and went sailing down, calling out, 'Wheeeeee!'

He had a splendid repertoire of styles invented on the spot, which Patsy attempted to elaborate on: arms outstretched as if crucified, arms akimbo, hands in pockets or turning to face the way he came, gliding down backwards, twirling or hands clasped behind the back as if figure skating, crouched down on his hunkers and then slowly rising up again, and then down again – this was 'The Postman's Knock'.

My young brother and I took many tosses, cutting hands and knees but it was great gas all the same. The Keegans spent as much time as they could between chores. Neddy had to saw wood, pile some of it and bring some of it in, Patsy had to cycle to Celbridge on messages for his ma (half a stone of flour, a Boland's loaf, a dozen rashers), and John Joe, bleeding like a stuck pig, had homework.

Otherwise we crept through the plantation, did our business, and had fine times in a yew tree with John Joe who never blew his nose, never had a handkerchief, but always had crusty nostrils or runny snot which he licked up, or rather in, blowing his nose between thumb and first finger like his da, old Ned.

Neddy was a fearless tree-climber and thought nothing of ascending any of the tall pines until he was out of sight and we had to run into the meadow to see him; we saw only his cap come twirling down and heard the harmonica play 'Mairzy Doates' with all the glottal stops out. And there he was eighty feet up, a fore-topman in the shrouds, swaying and hallooing.

The big wooden door of the Abbey stable yard had a lichgate let into it, but both were closed and rarely opened and the outer frame of the big door closely aligned to the wall, flush with it, so that the inquisitive (i.e., myself) could not see in. Such a fortresslike granite bulk with its sham-Gothic windows permanently sealed up just below the battlemented skyline that looked so hostile and forbidding in the setting sun was suggestive of Rafael Sabatini or Baroness Orczy castle-keep-and-moat costume-drama and Ronald Colman and Douglas Fairbanks in acrobatic swordfights along the lines of *The Prisoner of Zenda*, which we had seen at the Metropole, or *Captain Blood* with Errol Flynn and Basil Rathbone, who was wickedness personified, at swordplay on the sands.

Swordplay would take place on these battlements and punitive acts be carried out secretly within the keep and hanged men with tongues lolling out be suspended from windows as dire warnings, like the dead rats I had seen strung up on palings by a farmer, and shrivelled away to skin and bone.

Dado had told me some such story involving a Judge Lynch of Galway town and how he had come to sentence his own son to death and stayed up with him all night preparing his (the son's) immortal soul for the hereafter following breakfast and the noose next morning; how the father hung the son 'with his own hands' from one of the windows overlooking the meandering main street that changed its name three times before it finished, ran out of names; topping him at daybreak. But there again I may have got the details all wrong and all that stayed with me was a dead man suspended from an arched window, swinging in the breeze, gaped at by passers-by.

The small barred Judas set high up in the narrow arched front door of the Abbey suggested a deterrent against importunate charity-seekers. I had seen one such desperate and very determined shawled beggarwoman with babe hidden in smelly folds of the shawl, persistently begging charity as her right; revealing just the crown of the babe's head, she asked charity only for the child. And then waiting by the closed door until it opened again, just wide enough for the nun's hands to reach out with the stale bread and the high meat and the closed door receive the most profuse and insistent thanks of Godblessandkeepyou and invocations to the Holy Mother and all the saints.

And sure enough, by 1952, some years after we had quit Springfield for pastures new, the Abbey and grounds had again reverted to Church hands and the charitable-minded Hospitaller Brothers of St John of God were using it as a community house for the overflow of mentally retarded and physically handicapped inmates from Oakley Park, renamed again and now St Raphael's; later again I scaled the battlements and dropped down to walk by a recently scuffled path, going on the edge, leaving no footprints. Shovels and rakes were as they had been thrown down at the summons of the bell or the whistle for teabreak and the Brother and his mentally defective charges had hurried off for scoff, and were out of sight in the stable yard with a half-wit scullion pouring out generous dollops of strong tea from an outsize taypot before handing around thick wedges of bread and butter.

My first troubling memory is of my younger brother (hereinafter The Dote, for whose sake I would be permanently two years behind at school and indeed would never catch up) grinding his teeth ferociously in sleep. This was dismissed by Mumu as worms but as nothing was ever done about it, the grimly determined teeth-grinding went on, as though my unconscious brother was turning something over in his mind; his embryonic nature expressing itself annoyingly as lead pencil screeching mindlessly across slate.

Dado owned (*owndid* had a more downright positive ring to it, as roundly pronounced by the Keegan boys, *I owndid it, it's mine!*) two gatelodges and third lodge *forninst* Killadoon, all occupied by poor tenants who paid a nominal rent when they could, or no rent at all when they couldn't. The gatelodges with rent-dodgers intact were situated at either end of the avenue, protected by brakes of timber. The front gatelodge or East Lodge was occupied by the Keegans, the oldish couple Ned and Una, the three boys, Neddy, Patsy and John Joe and their sister Mona, the redheaded hot-tempered girl junior to Neddy but senior to Patsy, our pal.

The back or West Lodge was occupied since time immemorial by a genteel single Protestant lady, Miss Coyle, who *owndid* the racehorse called 'One Down', famous for never having won a race. 'One Down' was fed, watered and groomed by Burke, her bailiff, butler and general factotum, in our back stable yard, before Cooney took over the running of the stables. Mr Cooney had left his wife and run off with his pretty secretary, got into the London tabloids, become famous; a story that must not be told.

A wheezing tubercular tenant by the name of Collins occupied the third lodge opposite Killadoon back gate; a bachelor not in the best of health. He paid no rent, contesting that the place was alive with rats and had the Health Board condemn it as being unfit for human habitation, causing the roof to be removed; whereupon he retired in good order into Peamount Sanatorium in the foothills of the Dublin mountains where he passed away soon after, having wheezed his guts out.

All I recall of him was the constant terrible effort to catch his breath. He chain-smoked Wild Woodbines in open packets of five, racked with painful fits of coughing.

The Keegans were responsible for the opening and closing of the heavy wrought-iron gates by the front lodge, responding to the blare of the klaxon halfway down the avenue. Miss Coyle could not be expected to open the smaller and lighter gates by the back lodge, although she might do it as a favour, for she was a lady.

A masterly possessive squeeze of the right hand in its pigskin glove on the black rubber bulb clamped outside the driver's door would be sufficient to bring two or three Keegans running to force open the heavy gates with their shoulders and then stand aside, grinning and saluting as a guard of honour, to calls of 'Av'nin M'striggins!', one of them (generally Neddy) going out to direct the Overland into a clear road. The Guards were already bribed with loads of firewood to stay out of the way, his spies would be on the bridge, and a straight run through the village guaranteed to Hazelhatch Station and a long chat with Mr Dooley before the Dublin train arrived.

Molly Cushen in a gym-slip too small for her is forbidden to play with her skipping rope.

'Molly can give it a few twirls,' the old nun says, groaning. 'But there is to be no skipping or jumping.'

'Listen to what the priest tells you,' says the old nun.

'Do not play with yourself,' whispers the priest behind his cage at Confession.

'What's *adultry?*' I ask.

The old nun's red-rimmed eyes stare at me from within her coif as if she can't believe her ears. She gives the desk a brisk rap with her knuckles and comes down off the little wooden rostrum to stand behind me.

'Don't ask such a question!' she cries, pushing me roughly in the small of the back. 'Don't you dare ask that! Adultery's a crime!'

The big girls are taught in the schoolroom at the bottom of the playground. I walk in procession behind the big girls who sing with ineffable sadness:

> Deep in Thy wounds, Lord,
> Hide and shelter me.
> So shall I never,
> Never part from Thee!

My brother and I leave our bikes behind the spare counter in King's shop where we buy the evening papers for Dado and the *Dandy* and *Beano* and *Hotspur* with the pennies we are given, or we buy three-tier buns.

'Do you mane to tell me you never herd tell of the celly brated outlaw Robin Hood?' Mr King, hands in trouser pockets, asks a customer who gapes at him in astonishment.

It was in the days before bicycles were chained. More than half the parish owned bikes and these were laid or flung indiscriminately by latecomers against the church walls or on either side of the great free-standing bell which could be heard ringing for Mass as far away as Killadoon when the wind was in the right direction, namely from the northeast.

Wielding cricket stumps as broad-swords with cricket pads buckled to our arms as bucklers we clank in heavy armour into a clearing in the shrubbery to fight a duel of honour, while a girl with long brown hair who resembles cousin Honor waits for the outcome, weeping and wringing her hands, in a long conical headpiece like an elongated dunce's cap and a thin off-the-shoulder dress, locked in a high battle-mented tower, waving a small handkerchief.

I hear the girls' cries in the shrubbery and the bamboos disturbed and a high excited voice (my cousin Maeve) calls out, 'He's over here!' While the bamboos are being buffeted I am hidden in a place where no one can find me; I can move like a fox and no one can ever find me. I slip back into the house. Maeve Healy is now coming downstairs in shorts. Mumu says she is a minx, a slithery article, Miss Notice Box. Mumu strongly disapproved of those who 'put on airs,' drawing attention to themselves by showing off; only 'consequential little articles' put on airs.

Lizzy strikes the dinner gong with the padded drumstick and calls out, 'Are yiz all ready yit?' and the Dote comes in his heavy armour through the front door, calling *'Pax!'*

I slip out of my pyjamas and hide behind the nursery door, hearing Dado coming upstairs to say good-night to us. I spring out and bending down open my behind like the little black monkey in the Dublin Zoo, looking backwards through my legs I see Dado's pointed shiny brown shoes approaching and my brother runs upstairs without a stitch but a duster on his head, disappearing into the schoolroom.

'That's not nice,' Dado says. 'Put your pyjamas back on.'

'He's just over-excited,' Mumu says.

'We were only being Fuzziwuzzies,' I say lamely, knowing I have gone too far.

My brother, stark naked with boot-blacked face, is clashing zinc chamber pots together in the shrubbery.

'Get your brother in,' Dado says in a resigned voice.

'If you didn't know you were doing wrong, then you did nothing wrong, pets,' Mumu said, tucking us in.

'We were being Fuzziwuzzies.'

'Of course you were.'

Embroidered like battle standards the banners of Passion Week glisten in royal purple and violent emerald above pews in the packed church in Celbridge and the heavy bell tolls in the yard outside and I smell incense and wood polish and the dense pong of the congregation coughing and shuffling their boots as the officiating priest in gorgeous vestments seems to wade about the altar and sings out in a phenomenally high voice, *'Credo in unum Deum!'* To which the mens' choir responds, *'Et in terra lux perpetua!'* in a deep collective drone. As incense ascends to the roof, St Patrick and St Brigid are shrouded in purple with St Joseph and IHS, IHS, IHS trembles on the banners as they shift and I taste metal in my mouth. The rising incense and the deep drone makes me dizzy, the old priest moves in a dream of sanctity, his heavy vestments held up by two serving novices.

Flowers from Springfield garden adorn the high altar, brought by Mumu in the Overland and kept fresh in buckets of water and then arranged by her and the nuns where hundreds of wax candles burn. I read my prayer-book, feel holy, selected, pure as the driven snow.

Panis Angelicus!

a tenor solo sings out. The tabernacle door is open, the tabernacle empty, a breeze from the habits of the slowly passing veiled nuns touches my face, but my eyes are closed for Perpetual Adoration.

The carbide light makes a tunnel in the dark and I freewheel down the hill past Muldowney's cottage and soon I feel the Holy Eucharist dissolve in my mouth and putting the tips of my fingers together I cross my thumbs and lower my head until my nose touches the index finger and feeling a vague holy love stirring I rise slowly and move backwards from a kneeling position at the altar where I have received Holy Communion, and still with closed eyes, still entranced, I move back to my place.

My brother comes clanking towards me in cricket pads worn as breastplates, an enamel chamber pot strapped to his head.

'On guard, villain!' he cries in a choked voice. 'I'll make mincemeat of thee, varlet! On guard!'

We fight to the death.

We parley; he retreats wounded. We come together, weapons clash.

'Pax!'

We refresh ourselves with Mi-Wadi. Wearing a loose woollen jersey knitted by Mumu in candy stripes but now with the stitching run here and there along the arms, the tops of his Wellington boots turned down, the Dote approaches resolutely for a bout of single combat with cricket stumps as broad-swords. Receiving a mortal death-stroke he falls backwards in slow motion into the clump of bamboos, both hands clapped to his right eye from which blood spurts – a death-blow! He opens a mailed fist to show me his pierced eyeball gushing blood.

'Pax!'

Dado strolls past in his cut-down shorts, a handkerchief on his head, tied at four corners, wearing nothing else.

'Be careful with those stumps. You could put your brother's eye out.'

'Oh we will.'

Pulling back the skin of his mickey, Cox directs a thin jet of piss through the high slit-window of the Convent jax and as it splashes outside we hear the big girls scream. With his shirt rolled up and his pointed bum out for business, Coffey crouches like a monkey above the jax and, groaning deeply, lets No. 1 go between his legs. It splatters on the drain and the stench of ammonia and beasts rises up strong as the wild reek of the Lion House in the Dublin Zoo.

The Dote and I read unsystematically through old Mrs Warren's library, shelf by shelf. We read A. E. W. Mason, Clarence E. Mulford, P. C. Wren, P. G. Wodehouse, Sapper, Rafael Sabatini, Baroness Orczy.

Mumu's heroes were Walt Disney, Noel Coward, Beverley Nichols, Anthony Eden, who was a 'thorough gentleman', and the Emperor Haile Selassie of Abyssinia, who was as black as your boot. Her peerless diplomacy in the nursery:

> Let bygones be bygones . . .
> It never rains but it pours . . .
> Every cloud has a silver lining . . .
> It's as broad as it's long.

She was a member of the County Council lending library wherever she lived. Brother Bun cycled to Celbridge when we lived in Springfield and to Delgany when we lived in Greystones, to borrow more books and hand back the books that Mumu had read or put aside as not worth reading. She could get through four or five books in a week, no bother.

She got through Kate O'Brien, Negley Farson, Rose Macaulay, Norah Hoult, Philip Gibbs, Stefan Zweig, George Moore, Oliver St John Gogarty, Hall Cain, Frank O'Connor, Brinsley MacNamara, Aldous Huxley, Somerset Maugham, John Dos Passos, John Steinbeck, Sherwood Anderson (*Winesburg, Ohio* was indeed a discovery for me), Willa Cather. Of course all were not from the lending library; she read whatever she could lay her hands on, including banned books lent by Helen O'Connor, the doctor's daughter.

With unruffled patience she read Patience Strong, Maura Laverty, Olivia Manning (*The Dreaming Shore*), L. A. G. Strong (*Dewer Rides*), Maurice Walsh (*The Road to Nowhere*).

She had a regular repertoire of sayings, *bons mots* and catchphrases, among which prominently featured: 'A land', or 'a bit of a land', meant an unexpected disappointment, a let-down. 'Donkey's years' meant aeons of Time (presumably Irish, meaning unreliable Time). 'A cock and bull story' meant a tissue of lies. 'Thick as thieves': intense complicity. 'Gas' ('a gas article') meant a merry grig, an amusing person. A 'rip' (or 'right rip'): a bad egg, a scoundrel.

Shooting at missel thrushes in the front field with my new Daisy rifle, the sash window falls on my hand. My father, standing over me, pulls the window up, crushing the top joint of my fingers as he releases it. I am given hot Bovril and bread and the tears dry on my face. My young brother strikes me with a cricket stump and terrified of reprisals runs weeping into the house; staggering in I am punished for making him cry.

I hide under the long table in the dining room. The linen cloth reaches to the floor, and my patience with my elder brother is exhausted. I wait until the family have taken their places and then growling like a mad dog sink my teeth into the white calf of brother Dodo's leg and hang on as he rises straight up with a high-pitched scream. I taste pure venom in my mouth as he staggers from the room.

'Come out of there,' Dado commands. 'This time you have gone too far. You will pay for this.'

My mother holds a napkin to her face. I crawl out, still unrepentant.

Droll old saws and venerable maxims rolled off the lips of brother Bun with the tired precision of a mechanically recorded message, RAF slang parroted out with a line from Shakespeare, from Conan Doyle, from here and there: Press on regardless, steady the Buffs and let the Rangers pass, Mafeking is relieved (heard at a News Cinema), do you use Long Melford (can you box?), skedaddle, buckshee, good show, bad show, bit of a bind, when beggars die no comets fall, a bit dicey, what's the gen?, hunky-dory, not half, jolly good show, dead easy, haven't a clue, mollies, softies, tinkers' gets. Blokes were 'bods'.

He wore heavy army boots and leather puttees, a baggy mossy-green Local

Defence Force uniform with forage cap worn at a gallant angle, carried a heavy Lee-Enfield rifle but no bullets, cycling off down the back avenue to training sessions at Straffan Town Hall, prepared to defend his country against Nazi parachutists to the last drop of his blood, for he was one of the lads.

Get him!

In smart mustard-yellow suiting of Irish tweed Oliver St John Gogarty walked into the garden with Mumu and was taken through the rockery to see her rock flowers. He had arrived in great style in a yellow Mercedes wearing yellow pigskin gloves and yellow calfskin handmade boots. He laughed getting out of the car, saying that yellow was a colour pleasing to God.

Now he walked with his chest thrown out and hands behind his back, one gloved and one bare, smiling at Lizzy who was setting the tea-things outside the summerhouse, the cucumber sandwiches cut very thin and the best china out for the guest.

The yellow Mercedes that stood leaking oil on the front driveway fairly breathed opulence, with leather straps on the bonnet. Of the painter Orpen, whose obituaries he had attended, he said wittily: 'He never got under the surface, Lil, until he got under the ground,' and gave a rich chuckle to which Mumu added her high unhinged laugh, Dado taking his cue from her and laughing too.

Gogarty was a surgeon with his own practice. He told Mumu that he intended to move to America, he was tired of the Celtic chloroform and had no use for Dev: 'A cross between a corpse and a cormorant'. The nineteen Dublin hospitals were lazar houses and the whole country rotten with TB.

From Mumu's bedroom window, opening a slat of the venetian blinds, I watched the great surgeon and wit depart in his yellow Mercedes. A gloved hand out the window waved adieu.

Mumu had told me of his escape from the IRA execution squad led by a Clonskeagh tram driver; how he had escaped their clutches and leaped from the parapet into the freezing Liffey, escaping into the dark, vowing to donate two black swans to the river into whose tender mercies he had entrusted his life.

Despite the lubricious promise of their tides (*Tumbling in the Hay*) I was to find his books disappointing, mere social tittle-tattle in brother Bun's opinion, promising more than they delivered. The debonair specialist would later remove Bun's adenoids, as he had removed W. B. Yeats's tonsils, but cannot have made a very good job of it, for he was to be adenoidal all his life, snoring like a foghorn.

Mumu may have inherited some of old Mrs Warren's taste in reading matter along with her very miscellaneous library. Whose was the much-read volume of Beverley Nicols' *Down the Garden Path* with hand-drawn and end-papers?

She had known Brinsley (*The Valley of the Squinting Windows*) MacNamara through her brother Aubrey, and she knew Crosby Garstin and Percy French and Oliver St John Gogarty, who had an interest in gardens and sent her inscribed copies of his books. She had watched Kate O'Brien taking tea with another lady in the Shelbourne and had brazenly introduced herself to Noel Coward in the same lounge when she discovered him at tea with a handsome young man whom Noel Coward introduced as his secretary. Mumu referred thereafter to dear Noel and dear dear Beverley.

With us who lacked nothing in the way of home comforts, 'want' was a dirty word; servants and nannies were always there, dancing attendance. We lived, as Mumu put it, in the very lap of luxury, and servants attentive to our every wish were at the end of every bellpull, five or six of which were situated strategically about the house, in the upper rooms set into the wall by the fireplaces of white marble, the roaring coal fires.

Our cook, old Mrs Henry from the back road, was one of the old breed of servants – that hardy tribe that accepted lifelong servitude as a bond and contract never to be reneged or broken. If she was too bent and arthritic to be expected to drag herself upstairs at the peal of the bell, Lizzy was there and before the bell pealed twice she would be on her way, adjusting her mob-cap, straightening her black stockings in the long hall mirror below the officers' crossed swords; already clearing her throat for the formal inter-rogative, 'Yessum?'

Old Mrs Henry was too uncouth and humble. When introduced to 'new Gintry' her formal obeisance was more than a courtesy, profound and rev-erential as a genuflection – the courtesy ossified. The smear of blacking on the wizened servile features or across the iron-grey hair, where a hasty hand had smeared it, lending a barbaric touch, the very badge and seal of servility. The smell that attended her entrances and exits was ineradicable.

Of course every effortful trip upward had to be countered by the fretful return downward; indeed twice there and twice back. For after the preliminary foray to ascertain what was required, came the return to base-camp to collect whatever condiments were lacking, then the triumphant return to Mistress with the missing items arranged artfully on the heavy tray, the comb of honey, the gooseberry jam, the jug of cream, the boiling water, the cubes of sugar, the tongs; then the return to kitchen until the meal upstairs was ended, when another peremptory peal of the bell sent Lizzy flying upwards again, scurrying over the damp flagstones past the cellar where we believed the Bogey Man lived in permanent darkness and on via the servants' quarters – under the iron bedstead with its threadbare coverings an outsize chamber was full to overflowing with sulphurous yellow piss – to the warm study or library where meals were taken in winter.

Or up another flight of stairs to dining room or living room on either side of the hall; up three more angular flights to either of the two master bedrooms where meals were sometimes taken in summer, in Mumu's big bedroom overlooking cattle grazing in Mangan's field and the hazy blue of the Dublin hills in the distance.

Of course the poor, whom by divine decree we would always have with us, were suffering permanently from a chronic lack of everything, forever begging and being ingratiating, hands reaching out and always dirty.

'Others won't have your advantages,' Mumu told us. 'Always remember that. You should consider yourselves lucky. Now would one of you give that bell a good pull?'

− 3 −

The Goat in the Tree

Quite honestly, Sir,' pipes up the Dote in an affected fluting English accent, 'really and truly, I'd feel much better after a jolly good hiding. Ten of the best.'

'Is that so now,' I purr, doing the heavy Moderator, the hard Beak. 'Is that so, my lad. Then it shall be done. Down with your trousers this instant!'

My brother raises his eyes to me as if beseeching, beginning to slowly undo his braces. He is the errant son, the lax pupil; I the morally inflexible Pater of Teddy Lester.

'No slackers in this dorm!' I cry.

'But, Sir. . .' blurts the Dote.

'No blubbing, Higgins Minor, *if* you please. We only want plucky lads in this school. Now be a man, bend down and grit your teeth.'

'A jolly good licking,' whispers the Dote, beginning to lower his shorts. He bends, holding his knees, exposing a pale helpless bum.

'Ready now, Sir – lay into it! I need a good birching. I'll take my gruel like a man,' squeaks he.

The whippy bamboo cane cut that very morning smashes down again and again on the desk and splinters into pieces as my brother hops about the schoolroom, rubbing his bum. *'Yarooo!'*

The Beak, grinding his teeth in a fury, has administered the very father and mother of a caning to Higgins Minor, lamed him for the big match. The morning of the big match had dawned fine and clear and the entire school was converging on the rugger field, a Slapton XV versus their arch-rivals.

'Yaroooo!' bawls the Dote, hopping.

The honour of the school is upheld.

I stand on a pile of books, like the boy on the forestool before the drum-head court of Roundheads in the painting 'And When Did You Last See Your Father?' For now it is my turn for punishment. I am honest Arthur Digby owning up to a feast in the dorm. Before me stands the implacable Beak, my brother with a new upraised cane.

He thunders at me: 'Well, Digby, what is it this time?'

'Insub-b-ordin-nation, Sir. Quite honestly, I deserve a jolly good tra-tra-tra-trashing.'

I am afflicted with a painful stutter. The beating-block is rearranged: I step forward, plucky.

'Your old pal,' Mumu says smilingly laying her hand on my head, 'and what does *he* say?'

Bowsy says Da Munts, Da Yeers, Da Lurry, Da Dunky, Da Flure, Da Wurrild, smelling of shag tobacco and the blood of slaughtered beasts and old clothes, and makes all seem both near and far away at the same time, both perfectly formed and twisted, both exact and forlorn, and with him I feel at peace and protected.

Dado told him that the PP had been at him to take my *pipa* away from me, that I am too young for it, it was 'causing a scandal in the parish'. It had to go.

'Now hadn't he a hell of a neck to go and say a thing like that?' Dado asked Mumu who purses up her mouth as if tasting something bitter.

The vapoury blue eyes look askance at me under twitching sandy-coloured eyebrows and always he has something wet in his nostril hairs. He sets me on his knee, offers me a fill of shag tobacco, paring it carefully towards his thumb. I smell an old man who lives alone, who never changes out of his clothes, who never changes.

'Whaa dodey tach yew in skule?'

'Summs,' I whisper.

'I nivver heerd.'

'Dey do tach me summs, Bowsy.'

'Doon an durris mawsh aye doh hulla,' Sister Rumold says.

I march to the door and close it.

'Uskle an fwinnoge!'

I close the window.

'Cunnus taw tu?'

'Taw may gu mah,' I answer.

'You may sit down,' Sister Rumold says quietly. The girls are afraid to whisper. The storm has blown over. The strap lies hidden again in the shallow drawer of her desk on the rostrum where she punishes us. Dicky Hart cleans the Irish off the blackboard without making a sound. We go about our business quiet as mice, counting the hours and minutes until we will be set free.

'Ned Colfer you have me heart-scalded,' declared Sister Rumold, coaxily. Ned smiles a thin sickly yellow smile. She coaxes Colfer: 'You great lug you.'

Ned throws a wild bemused look about the classroom.

'Gradigy suss a hain-a-do! Gradigy suss, gradigy suss, a hain-a-do!' Sister Rumold prompts, clapping her hands softly together as we stamp around the classroom, raising the dust, chanting, *'A hain-a-do!'* An aquatint of a large forlorn collie dog sitting on a quayside watches us marching around the classroom until at a sign one of teacher's pets throws open the door and we can run shouting and screaming between the walls.

'Gradigy, gradigy, gradigy!' intones Sister Rumold beside the open door of the classroom, beating time with her hands, looking amiable now, having told us that we are without exception the laziest and stupidest class she has ever encountered, and that she would prefer to dig drains or be tarring the roads, something like that, rather than waste her time trying to beat some sense into numbskulls.

Breaking ranks and cheering wildly the class runs out into the village. Over the humpbacked bridge, huge brilliantly lit clouds tower up and up, vasty cloud cathedrals; white castles loom.

Eating a Granny Smith (2d.) on my way home I try to imagine Sister Rumold baldheaded with wimple off and black taffeta skirts furled up, tarring a road for the County Council or lifting a pick in an irrigation drain. I cannot.

'The Bowsy stinks.'

'You must never say that of a poor working man.'

'But he does. He *stinks!*'

I thought I was being bright, but I was only being smart. Mumu threw me a very dismissive look.

The desks were scored and gouged and crisscrossed with penknife stabs. We dip our penny pens in inkwells that smell of smelling-salts and ether. The big ink jar is kept in the closet and Sister's pets fetch it for her when required.

Loaded with ink my pen follows the stippled line and writes 'Empty Vessels Make Most Noise' and then 'Necessity is the Mother of Invention.'

The nun who has a red face comes from West Cork and her voice goes up and down. She has a rough temper to match the red face, but when in a good mood she tells us stories of Michael Collins and of her own youth in West Cork. She sucks lozenges to keep her breath sweet but I can tell you that her temper is not too sweet.

The strap is kept in a shallow drawer of her desk, the desk itself mounted on a wooden rostrum a foot from the wooden floor. When her dander rises Sister Rumold slowly stands up and pulls open the shallow drawer where she keeps the strap and without looking takes out the heavy leather strap with lead in it. When we do not know our times-tables or Catechism or Irish, all drummed into us by chanting and rote, she stands behind us and pulls at our ears.

She drags at Colfer's ears as if she intends to wrench them off, lifting Colfer up. He makes a grimace but as though he were in league with her, agreeing to the punishment.

'Will I take the strap to you? Will I now?' she demands of Ned Colfer; her dander and her colour rising.

The angry nun stands behind Colfer and drags grimly at his ears until all the blood drains out of Ned's face.

'Ah be Janey,' Ned Colfer groans, his face now pulled close to the scratched desk, 'ah ah ah!'

'Oh you great numbskull Colfer, open those big waxy ears of yours!' the nun cries, leaning over with the strap in her free hand. She beats Colfer as if beating a carpet, Colfer flinching at every blow.

'Now Aidan Higgins, let me hear you.'

I stand up.

On cold days we sit around the small turf fire and Sister's pets huddle close to her and she tells us again how Michael Collins walked into Dublin Castle with a briefcase marked OHMS under his arm, bold as brass.

A basin of blood stands on a table in the middle of the girls' cloakroom and those who have had teeth pulled are allowed to go home early. Molly Cushen is deathly pale, her face framed by coal-black hair; she holds a blood-soaked handkerchief to her mouth as she goes slowly over the bridge and the wind blows hair into her face.

Being poor at Irish I am not one of Sister Rumold's particular pets. She has changed from the gracious nun who spoke so deferentially to Mumu in the Convent waiting room. I see her now as a pallid nun with a short temper who has it in for Colfer. I feel her standing close to me, her patience growing short, sucking a spearmint. Two desks in front, Colfer holds his hands under his arms; the whole row is getting it, the nun has twice taken the strap to Colfer. His ears are blazing red.

At break the big girls come screaming like snipe into the playground. The days pass. I walk to school.

Three great processions passed through Celbridge. In 1690 the only son of Dongan, killed at the Battle of the Boyne, was carried from the field to the family mansion at Castletown and interred in the parish church by the front gate. The Dongans, Earls of Limerick, were one of the few Catholic families in the Pale to be restored to their estates.

Thomas Dongan was obliged to sell 1,730 acres to Speaker Conolly who had already acquired ten thousand acres of forfeited lands in forced acquisitions in Meath, Westmeath, Roscommon, Wexford, Waterford, Fermanagh, Dublin, Kildare, Donegal and Wales.

Conolly died issueless of a heart attack in his grand mansion in Capel Street, the remains carried in great pomp in the state coach with mourning outriders to the family vault in Tea Lane. An immense concourse of mourners walked behind the hearse, and heard a panegyric to a great man gone.

In 1878 Lord Leitrim's murdered remains – dispatched in Donegal by some of his tenants – were carried via Killadoon with ostentatious display to the ancestral vaults in St Michan's in one of Dublin's poorest districts. Hearing whose funeral it was the people mobbed the hearse, uttering 'fearful execrations', tipped the corpse onto the roadway, vilified the dead man. In this shameful manner he was set upon twice, murdered twice. In Donegal, standing erect in the side-car, he had fought for his life, pulling out handfuls of red hair from the man who killed him.

$$-4-$$

The Bogey Man

A narrow freshwater stream flows out into the sea by the Kilcool end of the south beach at Greystones and after breakfast my young brother (the Dote) and I went down there with buckets and spades, Gina Greene trailing after us.

Blocks of rough-cast boulders the size of removal crates had been dumped higgledy-piggledy below the railway line as storm-breaks. The line – with which I would in later life become so familiar – ran from Rosslare to Dublin, following the coastline from Bray to Dun Laoghaire. In summer the larks sang above a hilly wheatfield. The iodiney smell of seaweed on the culvert, the tide curling in and out, the line of waves breaking along the shore, all that had a disturbing effect on my rural sensibilities and innards before I even knew myself to be Piscean.

Little grains of sand dislodged themselves from the slope of the bank and slid into the stream; I felt the suck and drag under my feet separating my toes and pulling me in. Distant figures were crossing the metal footbridge at Greystone station, where Dado (true to form) was pally with the stationmaster. He seemed to cultivate stationmasters, for he was very pally with Mr Dooley at Hazelhatch.

Then, out of a clear sky, the bolt fell.

The gulls continued to squawk over the culvert, the waves were calmly curling in, the Dote was up to his waist in a hole he had dug in the soft sand; and coming towards us was the very last person in the world that I ever wanted to see anywhere, lunging in our direction with a broken stride. That morning I had been bold and Mumu had told me that she wouldn't smack me but I was a disobedient little brat all the same and she had a good mind to set the Bogey Man on me, to teach me manners. And now he was coming to get me, Mumu had had a quiet word with him; from afar he had me spotted and now I was for it.

The fresh breeze blew from behind him, whipped the tails of his greatcoat, the sort that coach drivers wore in the olden days, and incoming waves curled over the culvert. He wore big brown boots and a wide-brim brown felt hat which he clutched to his head with one hand, the other reaching out towards me, summoning. I watched this holy terror come plunging towards me like a meteor; unable to cry out or run away, I awaited my fate.

The Dote was preoccupied in his hole, now submerged up to his shoulders, still patiently digging. A single figure on the metal footbridge seemed to be looking in my direction but the quarter of a mile that separated us might have been the width of the Atlantic Ocean and all the pebbly foreshore of shingle the terrain of the Bogey Man and those whom he would punish for their misdeeds were corralled into it. His method of punishing would be uniquely his own, uniquely horrible. I imagined that he would run upon his victim, fix his lips to my lips and blow all his foulness into me, his badness, as you would blow up a frog by sticking a sharp thrawneen through its skin. The victim would be filled up with that foulness and expire on the spot.

I sank down into the bank as it approached and tried to make myself invisible. But what a hope!

Arriving by the stream and not even bothering to break his stride the Bogey Man leaped across to my side, the tails of his greatcoat spread out behind him; confronted with the spectacle of me cowering there, abject, he halted in his tracks. Bending down as if to verify the truth of this emaciated creature who abjectly cowered before him, he brought his twitchy face close to mine and the smell that came reeking from his stomach was hot and savage, a compound of stale porter, shag tobacco, hyena cage, burning slack, an open cesspool wriggling with fat white worms, rotting fungicide in a winter wood, as if he was decayed or had beshat himself.

He asked in a breathless panting voice if I had ever been to London? Or seen the King?? Did I know Gamage's of Holborn??? I shook my head, pinned to the sandbank by his brown anxious eyes, his panting breath, his shadow, his vileness. For I had never been to London, never seen the King riding out of Buckingham Palace in his coach with the Queen by his side. All I knew or feared was that it was foggy there and Soho lay underground and race-gangs knocked the points of railings and filed them down to dagger sharpness and gangsters from the Gorbals – the very worst, the hardest criminals – concealed razor blades in the peaks of their caps, for slashing the faces of opponents. And they fought in gangs in the underground city always obscured in thick fog. These undersized taciturn dangerous men were undernourished and would think nothing of slitting your gizzard if you as much as looked sideways at them. They were very touchy.

'Then you know nothing,' spat the Bogey Man with a gush of fetid hyena breath right into my face, dismissing me.

With upraised hand he seemed about to swipe me across the face but glancing furtively around he quickly touched my knee with a claw scratchy as a badger, brought himself upright, preparing to move away.

'You could do with some fattening up,' he called back in a hoarse broken voice.

I watched him pass out of sight, plunging through the wet sand of the foreshore as if in a quagmire, pounding along until he had rounded the blocks of cement and disappeared off in the direction of Kilcool. Little grains of sand escaped with the sound of a sigh and running together collapsed into the fast-flowing stream and my heart (that had stopped beating ever since the Bogey Man had first addressed me) could begin to beat again.

The Dote called to me from his hole in the sand (where he was now up to his neck) and held up a crab. Gina Greene had tucked up her skirt and was slowly wading in our direction along the edge of the sea.

Dado said that Greystones was a place where Protestants came to die, like old horses put out to grass when their useful days are over. Mumu said he shouldn't say such things, but Dado only sniggered, a silk cravat knotted about his neck like Freddy Brown, and rustled the *Irish Times* at her.

In a silken kimono of vivid Japanese lozenges inset with dragons and wearing plimsolls on her bare feet Mumu left the Grand Hotel each morning when the sun shone, going by the esplanade to the south beach for her morning dip. Her woollen bathing costume of horizontal blue-and-white stripes with midnight-blue trunks that reached to near the knees but left most of the back bare could be seen crossing the shingle below the ice cream hut and the turnabout where the trains reversed for the journey back to Dublin. Flinching she cautiously entered the sea to perform a stately breaststroke. After breakfast Dado drove to the golf club for a morning round.

The distinctly posh aromas of the Grand Hotel overwhelmed me, always overly sensitive to smells and their significance: the intractable odours of fine furs, tobacco and violets, velvet brocade and polished woodwork, the wholesome smell of furniture wax mixed with the coarser aroma of roast mutton; carpets and drapes, perfumes trapped in an airless vacuum where uniformed hotel servants bore trays of afternoon tea, drinks. A plush and satin parlour, cloth of pearl and coral, a musky chamber. The effluvium of plenty was strong here; an aura of privilege and opulence.

– 5 –

The Bowsy Murray

Grogan (breezily): 'The hard Bowsy! How's the form?'
The Bowsy Murray (gravely): 'Hardy aul day.'

The Bowsy was crippled with the arthritis. Yet he had a positively Homeric way of mounting and dismounting from his trusty butcher's bike, low slung and very prone to punctures with a black-painted hand-tinted sign slung between his legs, from the crossbar on which was inscribed in white lettering:

J.J. Young, Victualler
Celbridge 4.

The act of throwing a stumpy-booted and gaitered leg athwart the low saddle was a grave gesture both ceremonial and heraldic, man and machine (wrapped in symbolic flame, suggesting Mercury) emblazoned on some obscure escutcheon invoking Subordinacy, Humility, Obeisance, Homage, Destiny, *Victualler*! He threw or rather cast his weary leg across the accursed saddle (he was afflicted with piles) with all the easy grace of long custom. He stank like an ancient Irish battle long lost. The triumphant victors having given three rousing cheers and stumped off, brandishing their bloody weapons, to dine in high style that very evening off the finest plate, served by henchmen and lit by ranks of wax candles dripping from Georgian silverware; the defeated left dead on the cold field as wolf-fodder, crow-bait and spoils for pillagers.

The Bowsy was a strong stumpy little man who got about, when not awheel, with a pronounced limp (on which more anon); about his middle a broad leather belt with studs to augment coarse country braces or what he called galluses and, tucked into the long-johns (combs), a labouring man's collarless cotton shirt known as Grandfather, never washed but worn until it could walk off him. On his broad cranium the same cap worn in all weathers all its long natural life, a greasy sweatsoaked affair crushed in his hands and wrung out when confronted with the Gentry, who were always out and about.

He habitually wore a bloodstained blue-and-white striped butcher's apron tied behind, dirtied with gristle and mincemeat and snot (for he contrived manual emissions of snot while in motion and some of it came back on him, in high winds) adhering to it, a seal of his worth. A sack was thrown over the shoulders in foul weather or snow, more token than actual cover; and when it was teeming with rain, and don't forget we're in the Midlands, he arrived agleam in black oilskins with tam o'shanter like Skipper, the herring fleet captain, as if he were a fish (a flounder) or had come by water, so drenched was he. But always cheerful, always cheerful, leaving his puddles behind, and not a word of complaint, never a word.

He cycled miles in all weathers on his stiff delivery bike, stubby *pipa* clenched between stumps of broken brown teeth; soaked in sweat, running with rainwater, to deliver the meat and sausages and silverside and black and white puddings that were the staples for the not-so-well-off so addicted to rashers delivered safe and sound into the hands of the poor recipients.

Neither he nor his trusty machine was 'able' (as he put it) for the slight gradient on the front avenue, so he was obliged to dismount and push it the rest of the way. Every Saturday afternoon regular as clockwork he arrived with the sirloin of beef wrapped up bloodily in yesterday's *Evening Mail* and, like Olympic athletes passing on the flame, conveyed this safely into the hands of old Mrs Henry, for her to tell him that it was 'a nice piece of meat', and carry it off to the larder; hardly in the larder door before she came hurrying back to do the honours, offer him a bottle of Guinness to slake his thirst and beg him to be seated and take the weight off his feet, with which he gratefully complied and always with the same formality, washing his hands in coarse soap at the scullery tap while Lizzy set to work with a corkscrew, so that the hero full of village gossip, saddlesore and battlesore, could blow his nose into the sink and sit on a kitchen chair, to stink up the kitchen as he indeed made himself 'at home'. Mumu confessed that she thought the world of the Bowsy Murray, and Dado said the Bowsy was no fool.

With a dextrous turn of the wrist old Mrs Henry took the poker to one of the covers on the range and had it open to feed in more coal from a tilted scuttle, stoked up the fire and made it go roaring up the flue, before setting the big sooty kettle on the hob. Lizzy told the Bowsy that he was being treated like a prince and the Bowsy, pleased, looked down complacently at his stumpy little legs outstretched to the blaze. He wore leather gaiters winter and summer, liked to pour his own pint, keeping his little finger crooked as if he were taking tea with a grand lady, not porter with the cook. He drank tea and Guinness *together*, taking a mouthful of bread thick with butter, then a swig of tea, munching away at the sops like a cow chewing the cud. He put his thumb through the handle of the cup and swallowed as if from a goblet.

Now he took a good long swallow, drew his fingers through his walrus moustache and brought up a low rumbling belch from the interior of his stomach.

'Nutten lika gude suppa tay.'

'The Bowsy just let out a rift,' I informed Lizzy Bolger.

Mumu called a belch a rift; rifting was rude, but it was all right if you covered your mouth with one hand and said Excuse me or Oh-I-do-beg-your-pardon in a genteel voice.

Old Mrs Henry sliced off generous cuts of bread and I put the poker through the bars of the range and when it was red hot laid it across the bread spread with brown sugar and made a game of noughts and crosses that in the mouth tasted of treacle; for I ate only dry bread, was allergic to butter, put sugar on all my food.

'That stomach of yours must be wan mass of worms,' old Mrs Henry said, sniffing. I saw loose yellow hair about her crumpled ear.

Screwing up her eyes and tilting the big empty teacup this way and that in her hand she prepared to read the tayleaves, the backs of her old working hands speckled like a bird's egg, flecks of amber in her tired old duck-egg blue eyes, strands of white in her grey hair. She wore brown worsted stockings that went halfway up the calf, held in place with black garters that were always slipping down. She had a comforting homely smell off her like an open tin of biscuits.

I smoked on the sly with shag tobacco that the Bowsy had pared carefully into his calloused palm with a clasp-knife, giving it to me mixed with a Wild Woodbine ground in the heel of his fists that he swore would give me a grand mild smoke.

Meanwhile old Mrs Henry saw dark strangers, journeys across black water, good or bad fortune on the way.

As she read the headlines of the *Evening Herald* she moved one finger below the line of print; her lips saying the word before she pronounced Aby-ssinnia! She used a hairpin to underline more difficult words. The Italian soldiers were slaughtering Fuzziwuzzies in the desert, the naked tribesmen armed with spears and Mussolini's son machine-gunning them from an aeroplane.

'An dey oney poor bloody savages,' the Bowsy said.

Lizzy lowered the clothesline. It was a long bar held in place against the ceiling by a rope looped about a stanchion near the famous mangle; the nursery was above this and in bed at night I heard it squeaking and gibbering down like the damned screaming in distant Hell.

I walk on uneven paving-stones that sweat, down the corridor below a line of dusty bells, past a whitewashed wall covered in drawings of Spitfires and Lysanders and Stukas and Dorniers drawn in pencil by myself and my three brothers. In the kitchen old Mrs Henry and Lizzy Bolger are cleaning and plucking beheaded pullets killed that day. With their feet in feathers and their hands bloodied they pull out entrails, winking and laughing like a pair of witches, their reddened hands methodically plucking feathers. I smell cold guts.

'Where's Ma?'

'Yewer Mammy's run off with a sailor,' Lizzy says, leaving a smear of blood on her forehead.

'No.'

'Yewe'll see soon enuff, Mister Smarty!'

I run from the cackling witches.

A barrel-chested sailorman with red hair pulls steadily at the oars, smiling at my mother who sits facing him in the thwarts. She is dressed for a long journey. The sailor has gingery hair and bottle-green eyes; behind them a ship rides at anchor. My mother is leaving without a by-your-leave, without a goodbye kiss, without a backward glance. Up anchor at full tide and away! A rowing boat approaches a wooden jetty by moonlight, in silence but for the soft whirr of Ger Coyle's projector and I imagine that I can hear oars. A mysterious passenger shrouded in an overcoat, with face shadowed under the brim of a hat, bends forward, gazing steadfastly at the rower. The prow touches the jetty, the passenger rises, begins to turn, but before I can see the face the film ends. The film has no beginning and no end. A hunter enters a cave after a bear, savages run down a jungle path. Who is this traveller?

Mumu is leaving us. Choking with misery I lie in the long smothering grass.

I sat on the Bowsy's leathery lap and asked him to tell me again about his time at war.

It was like this (said he): 'Dim Jairmans made mate adim.'

One Sunday following a bombardment lasting a week he advanced with his platoon with bayonets fixed across a hill covered in corpses that had bloated up and gone black in the sun.

'Did you ever,' he asked old Mrs Henry, 'hear tell of the Vimy Ridge?'
She never had, had never set foot out of Ireland, as her mother before her.

The men killed in the shelling had lain there and the stretcher-bearers
couldn't reach them, swelling up and slowly turning black.

'Lost in action,' said the Bowsy, looking at me with his blue bemused eyes,
'so dey do till the next-a-kin. But glory be to God summa dim lads wint out
over dim failds in bits an' paces.'

He told it to us all again (it was like Dado and the time when *he* escaped
from hospital, letting himself out the window on knotted sheets; the to-
be-continued tale of his mistrust of surgeons. The Higginses were all like
that, Mumu said, afraid of the knife.): The explosions that would pull your
bowels out, the scream of pain, someone had bought it. He took a terrible
blow on the chest over the heart (here the Bowsy struck his heart) and the
air over Vimy Ridge began to turn grey with little grainy black spots falling everywhere. He lay stretched out amid the corpses. 'Our lads an' their
lads, God help us'.

Presently his officer was staring down at him asking, 'Anything wrong,
Gunner Murray, are you hit?'

No, Sor, nothing exactly wrong, Sor, only the air of Vimy Ridge was turning mauve and his boots began to fill with blood.

He was carried behind the lines on a stretcher; from field hospital by
troop-train across Belgium to a ship preparing to leave; the wounded Irish
were returning home. After a slow voyage (dodging U-boats in the Irish
Sea?) they reached an unknown port at night. The Orderly who had sat
with the wounded stood up and said: 'Okay, Paddies, home. All you lucky
blightahs for Blighty! Any of you perishing Paddies got relatives 'ere?'

'Where are we?'

'Dublin.'

Dublin! Glory be to God, he was back home.

He was put into an ambulance, carried in a stretcher into Mercer's Hospital. In the field hospital the surgeons couldn't find the shrapnel inside the
Bowsy but in Dublin he would be examined by specialists. Sir James Ware
walked through the wards followed by a retinue of internees making copious
notes. There was a hole in the Bowsy's chest, covered in a sort of cobweb of
filmy skin that blew in and out as he breathed; dark blood from near the heart
had pumped out.

Sir James Ware examined him and made a mark with an indelible pencil
near his heart (the Bowsy indicated where and Lizzy and old Mrs Henry
stared) and told the Bowsy not to go and rub it out. They should X-ray at a

certain angle, Sir James said; the X-ray showed the piece of shrapnel lodged near the heart. Sir James Ware removed it.

The Bowsy left hospital for home. He became a gamekeeper on Lord Portarlington's estate at Emo Park, where he was a gun-bearer to King George VI, a guest at shooting parties, who always asked for the Bowsy.

'Did you know the King, Bowsy?' I asked him, inhaling his smells, tea, Guinness and shag tobacco, his long-sweated-into working clothes. 'Did you spake to dey King?'

'Shure I knew him as well as I know your own Doddy,' said the Bowsy, shifting my hot bottom on his lap.

I looked at the mottled hands of the soldier and slaughterer who had walked with his platoon one Sunday across Vimy Ridge; had stood and received orders from Lord Portarlington; had handed a gun to the King of England in the hide.

Here the Bowsy took out a stubby pipe from his overall pocket, struck a safety match, touched it to the bowl, sucking his hollowed cheeks, going Mmmm, mm, mmm, holding up the match for me to blow out.

One unlucky day in summer he was walking alongside a hay-bogey and didn't the load shift and the lot came down on the road, but a pitchfork went through his right knee. Nothing would persuade him to go into hospital to have it seen to; he had enough of hospitals and surgeons. For nine years he suffered on and off; at the end of that time a Dublin surgeon had crippled him for life.

('Don't go *near* those buckoos!' cried Dado.)

But the pain had come back too often, he couldn't sleep, putting his foot on the ground was like putting it into a furze bush, he decided to have it seen to. The choice was between two surgeons, Dr Chance or Dr Cherry. 'I took a chance on Dr Chance,' the Bowsy said with a heavy sigh. ''Twas the wrong choice.'

'How long have you had these?' the surgeon asked, tapping his varicose veins with the stethoscope. 'We'll whip those lads out too.'

The Bowsy drew at his pipe and stared into the fire. 'He was whippen everting outa me.'

He was given sedatives and a hundred injections, put to sleep and operated upon; to wake up a cripple. He wasn't to know this until later. Convalescence was endless; after five weeks he demanded his clothes back, he was signing himself out, returning home, he had work to do, his Lordship would expect to see him. Dr Chance told him: 'You go out that door at your peril, Murray.'

He dressed, walked out, took a bus, took a train, walked three miles to

Emo Park, where all was in disorder. A thick country buck had replaced
him, doing the rough work, feeding the pigs. The Bowsy's temper had
become short, the pain hadn't gone away, he was limping about. One evening while sitting there at supper the sucks began screeching.

'What ails the sucks?' he asked the country buck. 'Didn't yew fade dim?'

The country buck looked shifty, brazening it out. 'Yarra why should I fade
dim, isn't wanst or twiste a wake enuff for dim sucks?'

That did it: the Bowsy rose up, he was as strong as a gate, his rage when
it came was terrible, he was livid. The country buck spat on the floor and
scraped it with the toe of his boot. 'Why should I din?'

The Bowsy broke past him in one lunge ('Iffa he hadda touched me he
was a dead man'), the clasp-knife already open in his right hand, and went
for the screeching sucks, intending to slit every throat in the stye. The blade
entered the side of a suck's neck; but didn't the Bowsy slip and the knife
jumped out of his hand. The suck was bleeding and screeching in terror
but the Bowsy had come to his senses; he let the country buck help him to
his feet.

A silence fell on the kitchen but for the sound of the fire. I slipped from
Bowsy's grasp and stood up.

'The sucks is skraatchen! The sucks is skraatchen!!' I screamed at the top
of my voice and seizing the long deal table by its middle part with superhuman
strength toppled it over with the Boland's loaf, crockery, a two-pint jug of milk,
butter and jam, the Bowsy's cup and saucer (he had risen in alarm, was holding fast to his half-swallowed glass of porter); all crashed in a loud satisfactory
manner on the flagstones of the kitchen floor, a noise greatly augmented by
a high keen from cook and Lizzy's unhinged screeching, all of which was so
much music to my ears as I fled from the scene of the crime.

'Ah cummere to me now me old shegoshia,' Grogan coaxed me in the yard,
and his cruel cat-stretching hands reached out.

'Don't be at him, Grogan,' Lizzy said. 'Yewer always at him. Lave him be
– he's in disgrace.'

She was on her way to the bleach-green with a tub piled high with washing;
had set it down to catch her breath. But the cruel torturer's hands held me in a
vice. 'Now we'll see who's strong,' Grogan hissed into my ear, doubling me up
in a fierce wrestler's grip, with my head upside down between his knees. 'Ever
hear tell of the Irish Whip? Or of Dan O'Mahoney of Ballydehob?'

The blood has gone to my head, I feel faint.

'Let him go, Grogan. Let him be.'

In bits and pieces I fall onto the gravel from Grogan's smothering grip and run after Lizzy into the bleach-green where she has begun to hang up big sheets on the line. Rita Phelan came singing onto the bleach-green with more washing.

> Kiss me wanst and kiss me twisst
> An kiss me wance agin,
> It's been a long, long time,

sang Rita, holding up washing.

'Daffala does have me heart-scalded,' Lizzy told Rita.

'Now yewell catch it hot on the BTM, young fellah-me-lad, so you will,' Rita said spitefully.

'Don't care.'

'You will when your Doddy comes home.'

'Won't.'

'Will, cry-babby!'

'He's a caution,' Lizzy said.

Ah, Dado!

I had not seen them set the table on its legs again and clean up the mess on the floor or Bowsy clap his sweaty cap back onto his matted hair and hoist the empty bloodstained basket on his right arm, bid old Mrs Henry and Lizzy the time of day and stump from the kitchen, but from Mumu's window in the window embrasure behind the drapes I watched him cycle off down the front avenue, cranking down on the stiff pedals, one shoulder crooked, the skirts of his coat fluttering, going easy on the gradient. J. J. Young (Victualler) was a mile away in the village. Cattle and sheep were driven towards J. J. Young from all quarters of Kildare, sheep and pigs and lambs, lowing and bleating and baaing and grunting, their fate already sealed when paper money had changed hands in some dim and dirty pub. And then they had only to wait for the Bowsy to arrive, with a grimy bloodstained sack about his waist, a crowbar in one hand, the butcher's knife in the other, sharpened to razor keenness on the whetstone.

I tried to see the Bowsy (Gunner Murray of the Irish Fusiliers) in puttees and wrinkled uniform, a tin hat, carrying a heavy Lee-Enfield rifle out of which a bayonet sprouted in an alarming way, a heavy pack on his back, gone to fight for King and country (the wrong King and the wrong country), the same gamekeeper and beater who had driven hares and pheasants towards the King, or handed him his gun, the King whom he knew as well as he knew my own father, Dado of the Knotted Hospital Bedsheets.

The Bowsy herded them into J. J. Young's yard with its ominously sloping drains. Soon blood would run down those slopes. Did he whistle through his teeth as he approached to stun with crowbar or slit throat with butcher's knife, as he did habitually while waiting for his tea to cool? Sometimes I heard what I took to be the sounds of their distress mixed with the church bells Protestant and Roman Catholic that came jumbled together on the wind, the irate highpitched screeching of stuck pigs in the village a mile off.

Wisdom of the Bowsy Murray:

> You can't bate a good strong potta tay.
> You can't bate a good supp tay.
> Nutten like a good potta tay.
> Tay does be a rale drug.

Wisdom of J. J. Young, Victualler:

> Of course when you're dead the kidneys are no damn use to you.
> Turkeys are down on last year.
> > They do say the bowels of Strongbow are buried above in Dublin City.

The upended carcass of a buff-skinned pig was slit up the middle to expose its rosy entrails and red innards, suspended from a hook so that its trotters hung down and its snout bled into the sawdust alongside the decapitated body of a speckled cow. Rows of dead poultry and bloodied game hung from smaller hooks; a sad array of fur and feather amid the chill stench of entrails.

A great stag's head protruded from the wall above the chopping-block, its glazed eyeballs sad and weary. The office was a cabin under the roof, reached by spiral steps; Mrs Young ran the business from there and kept an eye on all movements below, handing down change to J. J. Young.

J. J. Young was a tall taciturn man with a beaked nose. He wore the blue-and-white striped butcher's apron tied about his waist and a set of carvers in a leather pouch like sixshooters in their holsters; for had he not once saved me from the rough lads of Tay Lane who went off to steal kindling from Killadoon and had menaced me, or pretended to, on the brow of the hill, on their way home?

I had always considered J. J. Young's to belong to a peculiar and even fabulous end of town, quite unlike the grandeur of Castletown gates at the other end. Little donkeys that brought the turf carts from as far away as Birr were hitched to the disused mill windows with sacks of fodder hung from the bars. The fire from Darlington's forge lit up the houses opposite (like a stage-set when the electricity failed) where gossipy women stood about with folded arms. The forge furnace lit up the betting office where Nurse O'Reilly put down cautious bets of tanners and bobs and half-crowns from the tips she received from Grogan and Burke, who were in the know, or said they were.

A penny-farthing bicycle, peculiar and out-of-place as a giraffe, was suspended outside Flynn's bicycle shop as a sign, and around the corner of Oakley Park demesne wall was the thoroughly peculiar Death House near St Mochua's from where the rough lads set out on their marauding expeditions.

The kind-hearted J. J. Young had laid his hand on my shoulder and enquired had I got the collywobbles. His wife was nodding down from her eyrie, smiling and nodding (I used to think that she had no legs or body, just a nodding head) and J. J. Young snapped the twine on the parcel with one jerk, as he might wring the neck of a pullet, and handed it over to the customer who stood at the open door, gaping back at the red single-deck bus that had come off the bridge and was stopping before Breen's Hotel.

'Dus dat buss gwantah burr?' he asked.

J. J. Young said that as far as he knew it did and (to me) not to mind those fellows, referring to the Tay Lane toughs who had come back laden down with kindling. I should not worry too much about them, J. J. Young said, giving me the benefit of one of his rare sad kind afflicted smiles.

– 6 –

The Great Wall of China

But 'in the heel of the hunt,' Mumu would say, meaning when all was said and done, they didn't go and sneak on me; they said nothing. Grogan told me that it took Lizzy, the Bowsy and young Henry (who had come in from the fields) to get the table on its legs again, and that I must have the strength of ten men when my dander was up. I told him I was strong as an ox.

When I strolled into the kitchen there was a silence.

'Up Dev,' I said.

'Yule cotch it hot when yure Doddy hurs of duss.'

Who sailed in but Mumu, who had been alerted by the commotion belowstairs.

'One fine day that rotten temper of yours is going to get you into trouble, Sunny Jim,' said Mumu frostily.

I retired behind the mangle where the cats made their stinks. It was my glory-hole, Mumu said. I smell the dirty mangle water in the bucket squeezed and wrung out of sheets; the rollers exude black grease that comes out in thick globs. Lizzy gets all flushed at the mangle, her stockings coming down, her hair in disarray, groaning and sighing at the hard chore, slowly at first and then in a rush at the end, dragging the handle, manhandling it, sweating.

'Let him stay there and cool off, Mrs Henry,' Mumu said.

'Oh but hasn't he been bold, Mrs H.!'

Ba, ba, ba, I thought to myself; womanly loyalty! Sour milk!

'No supper for yew,' said Lizzy, putting her oar in.

'O'Duffy's your man,' I said.

'Cheeky.'

I wanted to run away from home, to China. I would prefer to be walking along the Great Wall of China, looking about me with slitty eyes, flouncing my pigtail. I did not love Mumu any more because she was Dado's sneak, nor old Mother Henry who was a lickspittle, nor Lizzy Bolger who was deceitful when it suited her, I did not love any of them any more.

Then I heard the klaxon blare at the gate and presently the sound of wheels crunching over gravel and slowly entering the yard and even more slowly backing into the garage and the sound of the garage doors being banged shut and then my father was wiping his feet on the back door mat and walking away from us towards the study, calling out, 'Anyone at home!'

'Here,' I whispered.

They were silent before him and I was not punished. After supper I escaped into the shrubbery, riding at full tilt on a little wild thing, a pinto, myself a Pawnee brave on the warpath.

Rogation Days meant heat and offerings. The warmth of the sun and the closeness of the cloudy days sickened me. I walked slowly through the Crooked Meadow and saw a cock and hen pheasant on the bank; my sandals were covered in yellow pollen.

− 7 −

The Bareback Rider

Mulligan's Field, where film shows were given periodically in a marquee, was out on the Dublin Road before you come to Sir Ivone Kilpatrick's gate. Faded old four-reelers made even more indistinct by the daylight filtering through canvas, showing jumpy episodic sequences of cowboy films, a ghostly Joe E. Brown reduced to a grin in *The Six Day Bicycle Race* and even ghostlier Charlie reduced to bowler hat and black moustache in *The Rink*. Fossett's brought their circus there.

Lizzy Bolger took my young brother and I with her pal Rita Phelan; the two girls powerfully scented wore alarming scarlet lipstick for the big occasion. The stained canvas of the marquee smacked against its braced supports, sinking and rising as if taking great breaths as the wind dragged at it. The band, up on a makeshift platform of planks, played old circus tunes. The trampled grass gave off smells of the damp earth. We sucked boiled sweets from paper bags handed around by Rita Phelan. A white-faced clown with a bulbous red nose and orange hair stumbled across the ring in outsize boots and baggy pants to trip over the low barrier and fall into the lap of an embarrassed countrywoman sitting in the first tier of wooden seats. He began to bawl, rubbing his eyes and pointing, calling her his Ma. The crowd roared laughing.

Obscene was the stare of this clown now joking with the audience, codding and raising his painted eyebrows, as he cocks one leg. Obscene the angle and position of the flower he carried. He walked with a slowness amounting to criminal intent, his gestures licentious and provocative in the extreme.

He lifted one foot, then the other, to examine the soles of his big boots for dog turds; he had wet himself or done it in his pants, drawing out his striped clown's trousers, opening his mouth wide to stick out an astonishing tongue. He shouted at the band, who brightened up to call back at him. He was everywhere, held it all together with his coarse innuendos.

A circus man in a blue boiler suit held a zinc bucket near where the animals made their entrances and exits; the Lion Tamer doubled as Strong Man, bare to the waist he cracked his whip to make the jungle killers lay back their ears, and Rita Phelan sucked in her breath. The great lioness emitted a bloodcurdling growl and slunk along the bars while the lions sat up on tall tubs and yawned at the audience. The Lion Tamer lay down on the lioness and feigned sleep; then he kissed the lioness. More fellows in blue boiler suits ran in and dragged the cage out and in came the performing dogs, pissing with excitement, followed by a lady dog-trainer in riding britches fairly bursting at the hips. The dogs were all over the place.

I followed the jauntily swaggering hips of the trainer; but it was the bareback rider coming next who was to sweep all before her. The band, brightening up again, played her signature tune, and in she came. First she circled the ring astraddle two trotting white ponies, her actressy eyes catching the light, she held her bare arms out for applause, I watched her spine and rounded knees as she jumped through a blazing hoop.

She was all movement, all mystery, struck no poses but those of her craft, beautiful beyond compare. Now two quick-stepping white ponies with dusty pelts and red plumes circled the ring; she left one dusty back for the barrier and left it for the other broad back, facing forward, then backwards. Following her progress in a smaller circle the Ringmaster was speechless, strode in a tight circle with his long whip folded, as if witnessing perfection itself, never taking his eyes off her as she leaped through a whole series of hoops.

Under the swinging electric bulbs the marquee looked less shabby, the ponies whiter, brisker in their trotting as a heavy shower of rain pelted at the canvas and an ostler stood with his mouth open, holding under one arm a bucket of sawdust and lion dung and finished a long yawn.

And now she jumped from the dusty back of the pony for the last turn and the Ringmaster had his arm about her waist and his whip upraised for applause, and then he swept his hat off and ran after the ponies who were galloping out by themselves. From their short jogging legs to their nodding plumes they were all joggy movement, advancing in time to a music out of Time (the excited trumpeter was on his feet, holding what appeared to be a red chamber pot before the mouth of his instrument, blowing like Tommy Dorsey) and the top of the marquee slapped against the high poles, and the lights fixed around the ring were shining on the top hat of the Ringmaster and the eyes and teeth of the bareback rider. The young equestrienne seemed to drift; she walked out to the centre of the ring, bowed, ran off.

Wild horses came in at full gallop with a handler being dragged off his feet, pulling at the traces for dear life. The handler went 'hup-hup-hup!' and the big speckled horses tore around to the music, the band could not keep up with them. 'Hubbledebay!' The lions, pulled in again, dragged their fur against the bars of their cage and pissed violently, and Rita Phelan again hissed between her teeth, hot as a furnace on the high wooden plank. All passed, the animal too. 'Allyoop!'

Disguised now as the Strong Man in leopard skin which left half his chest bare and exposed a hairy male nipple, the Lion Tamer came back, on his feet Roman sandals, on his powerful wrists leather thongs with buckles. Arching his back and puffing out his cheeks he lifted an impossible weight previously carried in by four men, two of them ostentatiously staggering; raised one arm with ponderous slowness to display an awesome underarm forest.

The bareback rider now dressed all demurely in a shabby raincoat sold raffle tickets between the rows of seats. During the intermission, when Lizzy and Rita puffed their fags outside, the Strong Man had changed into a dark blue suit with thin white stripes, ox-blood shoes and an open-neck white shirt, and talked to the bareback rider by the entrance, flashing his white teeth, resting one hand on the small of her back and killing himself laughing. Under the shabby brown raincoat she wore a tulle skirt and Wellington boots. I saw again the pleated underskirt pressed to her thighs, rising and falling as she stood facing the wrong way on the pony's back, turning up her wrists and looking about with bright eyes, deep into her act, untouchable, pulled hither and thither by the music, by the ponies, by the Ringmaster's languidly twirling whip, by the turning Earth itself.

Then the band stood and played the 'Soldier's Song' and the lights were being taken down and we went out and I heard a tractor belt humming and there was the Strong Man on the steps of his caravan, talking to the bareback rider, now in headscarf and fur-lined bootees. They would travel all over Ireland together with Fossett's Circus. Rita Phelan asked me had I liked it. Had I Hell! The bareback rider! The bareback rider! Where would you find her equal in tights today?

− 8 −

The Protestant Gate

Would you two lads like a spin?'

The Overland had a richly purposeful odour of leather and mahogany and Dado, a very indifferent driver, in wide-brim tweed cap and pigskin gloves with the tops rolled back, now with a casual touch of his fingertips on the rubber klaxon had summoned the

Keegans (as genii out of a bottle) to throw wide open the heavy front gates, with a resolute blare of the horn.

He drove it in a highbacked lofty manner as if controlling a dromedary with a touch of a bamboo cane; the yellowing side-windows (not glass but some material before Perspex) sagged and flapped in the breeze of our passage as Dado let her out, the speedometer wobbling at fifty and the floorboards heating up. It was grand airy motoring in high style and the Dote and I rode on a howdah, looking down benignly at our native bearers.

Dado drove us to a sweet shop on the road to Clane, where in the early winter dusk we saw the lights of CWC shining like an ocean liner out at sea, the castle of the Wogan-Browns by the Gollimockey stream, visible over the low hedges.

A black dip-stick with white calibrations down the sides was wiped in an oil rag, one of Dado's discarded shirts, and thrust firmly into the petrol tank, Dado having unscrewed the cap with its silvery winged Mercury, for he never knew how much petrol was in the tank, or whether she was dry, ordering sixteen or more cans from the village pump. A spare can was strapped to the running-board.

And so we would set out grandly. There were few cars on the roads. Dado drove the sky-blue Overland at a stately pace through Clane and Sallins, like Baroness Blixen driving to the Muthaiga Club in Nairobi, the guest in highest places, friend of big game hunters and titled people, Sir Northrup McMillan, Eric von Otter and the Prince of Wales.

But it is not of the Overland's travels around Kildare, now speeding, now crawling, for Dado refused to buy a driving licence, preferring to bribe the Guards with parts of trees chopped into logs, that I would speak; but of the enigmatic posture of Protestant gates. Postern gates.

I am thinking now of a certain gate in the townland of Donycomper opposite the Catholic cemetery. An imposing front entrance leads into some hidden Protestant estate. A wide gateway – more doorway than gateway – of some smooth hard expensive pale wood, birch or beech finished with layers of tongue oil, meshed with cast-iron cross-pieces and wrought metal scrollwork fastened with many nuts and bolts and latches and padlocks and rivets and deadlocks, faced the road with an inflexible Protestant gravity. This formidably wide gate was permanently closed, like an Anglican church, leading no doubt to tonsured lawns well and truly mowed by grey-faced Protestant gardeners, by scuffled driveway where a severe lady walked absently under a wide-brim sunhat, carrying a trug, followed as absently by the half-closed eyes of large somnolent comatose pedigree hounds; all would be protected by inherited wealth in that hidden demesne where I had no right to be.

It was – to borrow one of Mumu's formulations – the 'very epitome' of Ascendancy stuckupness, a very Protestant entrance which refused entry, but gritted between clenched teeth: KEEP OUT!

It was formidable as the striding giants of yore in their seven-league boots, to a nipper in shorts and openwork sandals soiled by cowshit that I had trodden in, yellowed by field pollen and dandelions and buttercups, who liked to consort with the snotty-nosed brats of lodge-gate tenants very lax at paying their rent; impassable as the 'grim eight-foot high iron-bound serving man' mentioned by John Donne. The gate was shouting out in imperial fashion, 'Clear off you bally Catholics – these are *Protestant* grounds! Take care! Off with you now or by Christ we'll set the dogs on ye!'

And already we hear the deep baying of the killer pack. Oh dear God didn't we take to our heels and off with us down the slope; before us the shell of the mill, then the humpbacked bridge; the Liffey pouring out through its five arches and old Granny Greene herself sitting outside her doorway, smoking a clay pipe, driven out by the turf smoke, getting a breath of fresh air before venturing back into the dark warren where all the Greenes lived in the dark.

'Lowry Maher floggin' de bar!'

'Burst the goalie!'

'Frig the fecker!'

Mumu referred disparagingly to those beyond the Pale as 'fishwives' and 'guttersnipes', hooligans and Yahoos. She never joined us on those carefree Safaris for boiled sweets and Liquorice Allsorts. The Dote and I, sons of bigots – as befits those lucky ones born into privilege under the right auspices – read P. C. Wren's *Beau Geste*. Our proud parents would tell us how a fortune had been taken from the ground by a resolute Higgins.

Bisbee and the vanished copper-mine towns (haunt of ghost-town buffs) adjacent to doomed Tombstone near the Mexican border of old Sonora was where my grand-uncle Tom Higgins had made his pile in the 1860s. Now all had gone back again into the ground. Waste dumps, headframes, test holes, open pits, abandoned copper camps and railway stops dot the region; a timely reminder of mining's fickle nature, there under Mule Mountain.

– 9 –
Zeno's Café

Two European gentlemen sit facing each other diagonally across the carpet in deep leather-bound armchairs that smell of hot hide, their legs stretched out luxuriously to a heaped coal fire roaring up the chimney.

One is grossly corpulent with protruding boiled eyes who wheezes like a Pekinese while puffing away at a thick cigar. This is Fatty Warnants, the Belgian envoy to Ireland. Pale and bloated as a toad and sweating profusely, one chubby hand folded across its fellow and both resting on the immense tweedclad belly that rises and falls with each stertorous breath, whilst wallowing in the depths of the armchair like Mr Verloc, sate Fatty Warnants who ran the armaments business *Fabrique National*, supplying armoured carriers and FN rifles and ammunition to the Irish Army.

Fatty is a friend of Zeno Geldof, another Belgian, who owned The Broadway Café in O'Connell Street, known to Mumu as Under the Ocean because it was below the Ocean & Accident Assurance Co. Warnants is a friend of Joss's and Zeno Geldof, the Moorkens' fishing tackle and firearms shop in Upper Abbey Street not being far from Zeno's Café.

The three friends met in July each year at the Belgian Embassy in Ailesbury Road to celebrate the National Day for the King of the Belgians. A formal invitation was sent out: *L'Ambassadeur de Belgique a l'honneur de vous faire savoir qu'une Sainte Messe . . .*

Fumes of black tobacco drifted over their heads to collect near the ceiling and through this acrid smokescreen they boomed away at each other, above our heads, eavesdropping behind the sofa. They seemed to be clearing phlegm from their windpipes or gargling (in fact they were talking to each other in Flemish).

The Flemish larynx was a darkly constraining sound-box that emitted unheard-of gargles and groans, signifying God-knows-what; the gorilla-speech of grunting Calibans. They spoke as the Bogey Man spoke, in intense and compromising vagaries, that or muttering incomprehensible gibberish; for this was how men communicated on the Continent – this dark talk would give you the shivers. And the women of Belgium, how did they talk? Quacking like geese? Oh horrors! *Bedlam*!

The drawing room seemed to have shrunk, congested by the dense fumes from Fatty's thick cigar and Joss's bulldog pipe. The Dote and I hid behind the sofa until driven from the room by fits of the giggles; we were obliged to crawl hurriedly away, in stitches.

The two gentlemen were silent for a moment, but halfway up the stairs we heard them resume their dark Calibanish grunting. Flemish swirled around the room, mixed with tobacco fumes, suggesting distant places and savages, as Lizzy Bolger came with eyes out on stalks starting from her head, white as a sheet, summoned with the drinks tray by a strong yank at the bellpull.

One of the Moorken girls of Herentals and Antwerp had married a Lieutenant-Colonel Edward Ghys who had served in both wars. Another sister – Emilienne who was called Tante Mil – had married Albert Buyle, the director of a radium factory at Herentals. The Schelde at Antwerp, where Joss's family were born, is wide and pushes a great tide onwards.

Fatty had a French wife called Cleo; his real name was Gustave. Yet another Gustave.

When you stood at the urinal of the Grafton Picture House in the steamy atmosphere of gurgling pipes and the antiseptic tang of air-sweetening cubes dissolving at your feet in the piss and looking up at the shadowy forms of male and female pedestrians passing overhead, distorted in the rhomboids of thick glass, you would suppose yourself to be in a submarine.

When we walked up the white marble staircase of the Capital Cinema under the pictures of the stars, Robert Taylor and Spencer Tracy, Lana Turner and Merle Oberon, to the ticket office where complimentary passes were handed over by a female attendant in a purple uniform and pillbox hat with strap under the chin, her face made up like a mask, it was like being in a palace.

Sometimes on a winter's night we heard the sinister drone of Dorniers and Heinkels passing high overhead. Ours were no match for these. Lysanders and Avro Ansons (motto: 'Small But Fierce') took off from Baldonnel, flew out over Celbridge, over Killadoon wood, hid in the clouds until the danger had passed.

– 10 –

Wurung

Looking longingly once more through *Paris Salons* etc., and feasting my ravening eyes again on the shadowy nude ever stationary who never turned to face me under the studio skylight, I chanced upon some elongated Art volumes devoted to the Pre-Raphaelites and opening one at random was shocked to encounter the par-boiled eyes of the Bogey Man fixed steadfastly upon me.

He was sitting with a moony-faced woman with goggly gooseberry eyes who might have been his wife or sister, dressed in a windswept cape and bonnet. They were seated close together for reassurance and warmth in the stern of a ship just leaving for foreign parts, perhaps Australia. Wrapped in travel rugs about their knees both were staring as if mesmerised back at the receding quayside and the land they were leaving, staring straight at *me*, as if accusingly.

The unsettling windy daylight that suffused the painting suggested a port of departure where floods of tears might be in order and not far off; redolent too of a hospital forecourt where patients assembled, still weak in the legs, resistance still low, bidding adieu to doctors and nurses who had looked after them. The picture reeked of convalescence, as if tilted by sickness (no one there looked well); it was called *The Last of England*.

I asked Gina Greene to go with me into the cellar and hand in hand with candles lit and wavering in the fetid updraught we descended sixteen steps by mildew and cobwebs into the stink and darkness below. To the arrowheads and mouldy masks of dragons and racks of empty wine bottles discoloured and hazed up, and there around the corner in the furthest recess was a damp sack by the wall, where he must have slept curled up like a dog. But of the Bogey himself there was no sign. The cellar was empty.

He had sailed away with his sick wife or the mad sister to the Antipodes, the hot continent of extraordinary creatures, buck-jumping kangaroos and sandblind upupas and leaping wombats that would come as no surprise to a pair as strange as they, perhaps already living in a shack in the Outback, in some remote place like Dajara or Wurung on the Flinders River near the Gulf of Carpentaria, far away, far away. Perhaps they had started a tannery there?

– 11 –

The Hand & Flower Press

Mumu, herself a voracious reader, had turned the Dote and myself into bookworms. The initiation came when we were six weeks in bed with measles in a darkened bedroom (we were moved to the Dodo's for a view of the Dublin hills) and not allowed to read. She read Hans Andersen to us; it was a revelation. Mrs Warren's library was there to be read;

all Dickens with Boz and Cruikshank illustrations in a matched set, Scott's *Waverley* novels, which I found dull. P. C. Wren, Baroness Orczy and the rest in shelves that reached from floor to ceiling in the study. The first discovery of our own was Clarence E. Mulford. For some years a 'present from town' was invariably another two Hopalong Cassidy novels at two shillings each from Eason's in O'Connell Street, which Dado would bring back home in the bus, to find us waiting at the gate.

The packages were not to be unwrapped until we reached the house; I imagine so that Mumu could witness our delight. Hopalong and Mesquite Jenkins and Red Connors were our Wild West pals. Our next discovery was Sapper, all the Bulldog Drummond stories. We too became voracious readers. Dado did not read books but had on order a quantity of Irish and English newspapers in addition to the huge American newspapers that came from Los Angeles with his dividends.

The Dote and I were addicted to 'Mutt and Jeff' in the *Evening Herald* and 'Mandrake the Magician' in the *Evening Mail*. We had no dictionary in the house but Mumu could explain the hard words until she pretended to be stumped by *'Crime passionel'*, by which time I had begun to put aside childish things. I was in the pram until no longer able to fit in it; would always be two years behind in my schooling, because the Dote had to begin with me and I was 'held back'. When already into puberty I beshat myself with excitement and Mumu ran a shallow bath and cleaned me as if I was an innocent again, handing me a large sponge when she perceived my embarrassment, to cover my shame.

Lizzy asked the Dote what he wanted to be when he grew up. The Dote answered stoutly: a crow. Mumu said he was stubborn as a mule, he dug his heels in and would 'go far'.

She said; 'Wanted: a detective, to arrest the course of time.'

'Steady the Buffs and let the Rangers pass,' said brother Bun, just arriving.

As a lad I was much given to melancholic brooding and bucolic reverie, oft sunken in apathy and sloth, addicted to daydreaming on or around lewd subjects, never in the best of health, wandering about in a dream, chronically anxious, chronically constipated, spending hours in the lavatory. It was my long puberty. Ah, puberty!

Mumu said that some girls were 'low', without going into too much detail. The big hot girls on the back road smelt of tea and jam; mouths daubed with lipstick seemed to bleed.

They coaxed: 'Ah, gizzakiss! Ah do! Ah g'wan!'

They threatened: 'I'm gona tell on yew so I will!'

They kicked football with us in Killadoon, screeching in the tackles or squatting on the embankment to watch us play, Patsy Keegan urging the kicker to 'burst the goalie'.

'I'm black out wiff yew!' Rita Phelan screeched naggishly at Grogan.

Even before I was assailed by dirty thoughts or unchaste desires, I felt a blush coming like a wave that must bear me along with it; the Cattle Trough Guilt had me blushing to the roots of my hair as fleshly temptation strode into view in the shape of two dozen hefty Protestant girls with fresh complexions out from the Charter School. Rounding Brady's Corner, chattering like starlings, with a few teachers pacing behind, out for an airing to Odlum's crossroads and the Hill of Ardrass; and all their Protestant shadows flitting by along the wall and the chattering and giggling risen to a crescendo as I appeared on my Raleigh, mortified as sin and already blushing. Sometimes I would turn about and pedal back up Springfield front avenue as though I had forgotten something, and cycle down the back avenue to see the tail-end of the crocodile passing by Miss Coyle's cottage. Tail-ends were *Verboten*. My confessor urged me to pray for the grace of holy purity.

Dado warned us that we would 'ruin' our eyes by too much reading. We were blinding ourselves. He himself had no interest in books but did much browsing in newspapers. His heroes all tended to be stereotypes of himself – Gordon Richards who had ridden more winners than any jockey alive; the diminutive brave Irish fullback Con Murphy; the skinny runner Tommy Coneff of Kildare; and the even skinnier boxer Jimmy Wilde, the ghost with a hammer in each hand.

He spent much time gaping vacantly out of windows, revolving a spent match in one ear, then the other. In those rapt vacant times perchance he was invoking and evolving the fabulous creatures so colourfully involved amid the flora and fauna of his stories of Finn MacCool and Jack Doyle and Dan O'Mahony, famed for his Irish Whip. He had a repertoire of yarns that involved giants, ogres, hobgoblins, monsters, not forgetting the resident fairy that was to be seen – if you were quick enough – in the rose bushes by the summerhouse.

He spoke often of the olden days and of 'Aten Matches' or eating contests between a couple of legendary trenchermen pitted against each other, in consuming legs and (if up to it) thighs of 'dunkeys' roasted over a spit for the occasion. When one contestant could eat no more he gave his opponent best. The champion said to fetch in the mother (mudderdunkey said Grogan in the re-telling) donkey and he would eat some of her too.

I know that in our heroic ages, the apocryphal time that may never have existed and certainly not as we imagined it, in those lost and forgotten times, when the hindquarters of a Wicklow deer or Irish elk were served up, the bravest warrior present had the right to the thigh, it was the champion's portion and woe betide any man present who laid claim to it or gainsaid him; for then both would seize their swords and go at it hammer and tongs in a 'fight to the death', Dado repeated with relish.

These were not Grimmlike tall tales and folk yarns about greedy German giants, I see now, but rather folktales reflecting fears or tremors boding ill, passed on from father to son, my father having heard it from his father as he from his, so that those terrible times of famine would not be forgotten.

When Mumu asked me to pass her the big scissors I carelessly tossed it to her as she lay propped up on pillows on her bed covered with newspapers, their sheets buckled and scattered amid *Good Housekeeping* and *Woman's Own,* and her boobies loose in a thin-strap nightdress. She threw me a quick censorious look.

'That's very rude. You mustn't throw things at ladies; you could rupture my breast.'

I heard 'rapture' and 'my breasts' and had a sudden twinge of Old Adam and instantly assumed The Guilty Look. For in our family I had two faces: The Guilty Look and The Bear's Face, one developing from the other, compounding chagrin and intense embarrassment at being found out.

Eau: Faiblesse devant les tentations.

One Sunday after Mass in Straffan I took a bundle of London newspapers into the rockery for peace and quiet, in order to study the long sinful legs (ungirt was unchaste) of the variety girls without any inhibitory checks in the *Sunday Dispatch*.

Among the books in the study I had come upon *Paris Salons, Cafés and Cabarets* by Sisley Huddleston and spent much time poring over a monochrome nude posing in a shadowy studio. On the orderly shelves of the Dodo's reference library I found neat piles of *Lilliput* and in them stark-naked English ingénues photographed by Douglas Glass in a field of English wheat.

'With yourself or with others?' questions the priest from behind the wire grille partition that separates us. I see his tilted profile, hand to brow. He does not look at me. The nuns told us that the secrets of the confessional are 'sacred', and in any case always forgotten by the priest the moment he steps out of the confessional. I smell the sacred wood and the priest's hair-oil. I have been pulling my wire again, while 'entertaining immodest thoughts'.

I take a breath; falling back into deep abasement. 'Wiffmeself Fawdur.'

The priest shifts in his seat, the face comes closer, the whispery voice asks, 'How many times?'

I must not let this sin catch hold of me. For my penance would I say three Our Fathers and a Credo. Did I know the Credo?

'Yis Fawdur,' I whisper.

'Go in peace then, my child,' the priest murmurs. 'Say a prayer for me.'

The little Judas slides shut.

And now, trembling as if in the presence of something sacred, summoned by a surreptitious joy, I quickly undress and already stiff slide feet first into the tepid brown water in the ditch that embraces me. Eel-like I push it into the yielding mud, fornicating with the bank that bulges up at me in an obliging feminine way. The muddy water of the stream shat into by cattle holds me fast; the roaring in my ears is the circulation of the earth's blood, I smell the fresh trampled grass where the beasts have come down to drink and I am one with them and all creation shitting and shameless. Fibrous white stuff floats out of me and I see my rapt face reflected in water like the moon in clouds.

Drained by self-abuse I crawl from the ditch like Crusoe from the wreck, to dry myself with a linen pocket handkerchief and dress by a bed of nettles.

The Hand & Flower Press! The Hand & Flower Press! A fig to the fiction of holiness, to all lay priests!

I began to cultivate a taste for meditation and vague daydreaming.

A definitely risky word was 'suspenders' (suss-spend-ers) that hissed like a snake, even if Dado wore men's suspenders to hold up his socks with little clasps that clipped on like ferret's teeth. Whereas Mumu, ever coy, wore a lady's suspenders fixed onto a hidden corset that required much artful wriggling and bodily contortions with a quick catching of the breath in order to bring stockings and garters of crushed strawberry into alignment, that brought a gratified flush to her powdered cheeks.

As with halitosis or the toadstool reputed to be poisonous (emitting a sudden puff of decay when trodden on unawares), another unsettling word that sometimes cropped up in my reading was 'chastity' (chas-titty), ogling me, invoking the somewhat shameful spectacle of shy Mumu nipping up her tweed skirt to adjust the slipping garter, revealing a guilty border of corset with fancy stitching and lubricious lace-bordered trim of fine crochet-work in off-white already suspiciously stained; the buff and subtle dove-grey overlaid by some heavy usage, depicting the god Pan and a primordial scene in full rut in broad daylight, shamelessly copulating.

The bedroom was far away, the chamberpot always in use. When Mumu got out of bed for her ablutions (and she was to spend years in bed when her nerves went against her) and went off in her Japanese kimono of writhing dragons and sluttish slippers to the bathroom to cut her corns, I saw the soiled and discarded corset thrown down on the bed and felt uneasy in its presence. It had a strong purposeful female presence all its own; a clinging gluey smell, sweetish – the disturbing spent whiff of warm plasticine.

– 12 –

Kitted Out for Killashee

The Dote and I were fitted out with:

2 Dark Grey Suits, 1 extra pants,
4 Shirts - 2 grey and 2 white,
2 Grey Pullovers - V neck (long sleeves),
3 pairs Pyjamas,
3 pairs White Socks,
3 pairs Grey Stockings,
12 Handkerchiefs,
3 Hand Towels,
1 Bath Towel,
1 Laundry Bag,
Dressing Gown, Slippers, Toilet Requisites,
Clothes Brush, Shoe Cleaning Materials,
1 pair Walking Shoes,
1 pair Light Indoor Shoes (black, laced),
1 pair Brown Sandals,
1 pair Wellingtons,
1 pair Blankets,

3 pairs Sheets,

3 Pillow Cases,

Rug or Eiderdown,

3 Table Napkins,

Breakfast Knife and Silver Fork,

Silver Dessert & Tea Spoons (All engraved

with pupil's initials), All articles of clothing

to be marked with pupil's name and, in addition,

the number '26' on articles for the laundry.

FOOTBALL: Green Jersey,

White Togs,

Green and White Socks,

DRILL: All White - Woollen Jersey,

Twill Pants (short),

Drill Shoes,

all procurable at

'Our Boys', 24 Wicklow Street, Dublin.

I write 'L.D.S.' on each page top of my lined theme book, meaning *Laus Deo Semper*, Praise God always. When the page is full I write 'A.M.D.G.' at the foot, meaning For the greater glory of God. So that all my work, full of errors, is always in His honour. I miss Springfield: the Place That Never Changes. Our serious Catholic education begins.

Sunday was visiting day but Mother Mulcahy advised Mumu not to call for a fortnight, to 'allow the two boys to settle in'. Dermot Doorley from Longford would show us the ropes. The Christmas vacation seemed far away. Our Lady's Bower felt cold and austere. I thought of Haffner's peppery sausages bursting open in the pan, Dado crossing his legs (in plus-fours) and shaking out his napkin at supper. We marched through Killadoon wood with the Keegan boys, all Republican Irregulars, chanting:

> I stuck my nose up a nanny goat's hole,
> And the smell, it nearly blinded me!

Walking backwards in a dream, staring up at the sea-green dome, the daydreamer Glynn fell with a weak little cry into the goldfish pond. He wears teeth-braces and is very vague. Madame Loyola gave him a special exercise book for him to compose his stories. He wrote ('I had been forestalled . . .')

of Knights at the Crusades, ancient times. I saw only a jackass looking over a gate as it begins its atrocious bray.

We wear coarse jerseys of sackcloth on play-up days and our faces turn strange colours as we struggle in the thick grass. The Dote wears a loose cardigan of greengage and candy; he unknots his school tie, laces up his football boots, totters out into the playing-field.

At Christmas Springfield appears to have shrunk. We put on grand airs before the rustics; wear ties, become proper little gents, snobs. Prigs.

A fire was lit in the nursery and as a treat (for it was the last day of the holidays) we were served tea and scones with Mumu hovering around, all solicitude, our trunks packed and Dado already backing the Overland out of the garage. We prayed that the Guards would be out cycling on their big black bikes, so that the unlicensed Overland could not pass through Sallins, Clane or Naas, and we would miss the sad church bells of Clane, the fancied temptations of Manzer's. I had discovered Sir Arthur Conan Doyle and was immersed in *A Scandal in Bohemia*.

Finicky about food and who served it to me, I would starve in Killashee, for I would not eat buttered bread and was reduced to licking toothpaste to kill the pangs of hunger. Coldsores on my lower lip went septic and I was picking at this in class where Madame Ita Magdalen was raging, had instituted a reign of terror. She made Hugo Merrin and myself wear leather gloves in class, a stigmata like dunces' caps. Madame Ita Magdalen had russet coloured cheeks like Bramley Seedlings with the hoary aura of apples about them, a down of fine white hair visible in slanting sunlight. For evening devotions she wore a veil over her wimple.

Madame Patrick Clare took us for walks through the sunken Pleasure Grounds, down hundreds of steps to the swimming pool long out of use, emptied of water, with clumps of dead leaves and crow droppings. We walked along the path covered in moss and overhung by rhododendrons. Madame 'Paddy' Clare was a stout calm nun, but the tall and angular (and often angry) Madame Ita Magdalen was a storm. Culprits were told to stand in corners, then outside the classroom, then put in solitary confinement in the dark store cupboard opposite. Jolly visiting priests called for half days, asked that some of the boys put on the gloves and box for them, at which Madame Ita Magdalen flushed and showed her great horse teeth, taken by the spectacle of footwork and feint as blows rained down on bare boy-flesh and the stoutly perspiring visitor looked as if he might put on the gloves himself and try a few rounds with Madame Ita Magdalen, who had put a coy hand up to her face, discovered blushing like a bride. The boxers fought in a hypothetical sort of ring formed by the desks pulled back in the classroom where Madame Loyola (who 'took' French) had written on the blackboard:

> *un petit ruisseau comme un ver, la forêt*
> *en automne, la mer iodée et tumultueuse,*
> *les ports.*

Madame Ita Magdalen's face had a saltpetred fuzz of fair hair over a maroon complexion that flooded with dark blood like the wattles of a turkey-cock when her dander was up. At the head of the table in the refectory she sat between her pets, lashing into her lunch; a great engine of resentment was being stoked up as she cleared her plate of gristly meat and turnips and spuds, taking great draughts of water from the jug, and then putting away a sago pudding with prunes; a repast that might have ended not with a prayer but with a resounding belch.

But no, for she was sucking in her great herbivorous buckteeth and rolling up her napkin to fit it into its plastic ring and rising to say grace, indicating that the meal was over.

'All in!'

'All out!!' went the bells and whistles.

Walks were 'off', Scarisbrook was ordered into the mop cupboard. There was a distinct impression that boys if left to their own devices could only get into trouble, would get out of control. Mr O'Neill the Games Master ran up and down blowing a whistle. Domination was a kind of sexual play. The huge fat priest heard confessions sitting on a chair at a prie-dieu, the sinner perfectly visible, kneeling with bowed head, murmuring his sins. The whole school walked in silence up and down the corridor, as punishment. I thought, these thwarted nuns might have found their true vocation in a field hospital or leper colony.

I wouldn't eat butter, which I associated with cows and lactation, the softness and sickness of womankind. Meat had to be cooked to a cinder or I wouldn't touch it. ('Don't play with your food!') I blushed to the roots of my hair when I felt the Cattle Trough Guilt swooping down over me again. 'Immodest thoughts' tended to involve the darkly attractive Molly Cushen with the deep silky voice who lived up Templemills way near the weir.

Running water was an aphrodisiac before I knew the meaning of the word: the flushing of the nuns told me something before I could put two and two together.

I pronounced Thames as 'de Tams', and the class tittered.

Madame Ita Magdalen said we were no better than savages and the whole class was put in detention. Imperator Basil Fogarty had read aloud an account of ancient Rome for the whole school at lunch and our class had been caught up in a game of make-believe in the long grass of the playing field, where slave struggled with slave, caught in nets, and cruel Caesar gave the thumbs-down sign for the victim to be dispatched, whereupon Madame came out (gone the colour of a turkey-cock) and blew her whistle for the entire school to go indoors. She said she would not have us behaving like savages. Anthony Scarisbrook showed us the discoloured and enlarged veins of his wrists where Madame had punished him with the stick. 'It's not right,' he said. He would write home and tell his parents, so he would. But all our outgoing mail was read and censored; we were held in trust never to say or write anything derogatory about Our Lady's Bower, ever. We were honour bound.

We hear of Eck, Hus, Zwingli, Euclid, the Diet of Worms. We walk the corridors in silence, it's punishment for the whole school, Madame's pets are encouraged to sneak on us. Madame takes out the stick, sucks in her buckteeth, goes white in the face. Speaking is forbidden at lunch and supper; we retire to bed in daylight, where speaking is also forbidden. In Madame's classroom a reign of terror begins. I am sent into the dark cubbyhole where the mops and brooms are kept. Madame says I have a bull neck. 'If I have to spend all day,' Madame says up on her rostrum, drawing in her breath, 'if I have to spend all week, you'll get this right.'

I am struck on the back of the head with the tin edge of the ruler, which does nothing to help me remember French irregular verbs.

'No surrender!' cries Louis Noonan.

Wednesday night is bath-night. We wear full-length bathing drawers in the bath and are forbidden to lock the door, it must be left wide open. Madame shows us how to soap ourselves and cover up again. Sometimes oh God in she rushes to empty a bucket of cold water over the bather. Madame comes from Kerry and could kill you if you did not know your French verbs. Louis Noonan says we should all march out down the front avenue, with drums playing; a revolution!

Madame storms in, mounts the rostrum, takes a handkerchief from her habit and with both forefingers together delicately blows her nose.

Platters of thickly buttered bread are set out on the refectory tables; the light shines on the glasses and silver, all engraved with pupil's initials. I can see the trees in the Pleasure Grounds, silently I beg permission to rise, walk to the kitchen entrance where an old nun hands me a plate of dry bread and a small portion of jam to spread on it. If she forgets to come, I am too timid to complain, and go hungry to bed. I drink cups of water in the dormitory, it is still daylight outside, I hear the birds, lick paint off lead soldiers and hope to die.

Basil Fogarty reads *Hiawatha* for both classes; Hal Hosty sings 'South of the Border' and Madame goes red with embarrassment again; bending low before the altar, the stout wheezing priest (who hears our confessions and the nun's confessions) strikes his breast and intones, *In principio erat verbum, et verbum erat apud Deum,* and Eric Sanderson rings the little bell. The whole school sings the *Veni Creator.* Madame wears a veil over the shell of her coif, which she raises to receive Holy Communion on her tongue. Mother Superior (Mother Mulcahy) looks just like Eugene Pacelli; she comes every Friday to read reports and give out class cards. She gives us a spiff. Madame Loyola beats us; we are hidden away in Our Lady's Bower, Killashee, Naas, County Kildare. It has no end; the long term engulfs us. We sing:

> This time ten weeks where shall we beee?
> Outside the gates of misereee!

Ten weeks: an eternity.

My young brother and I are in a class together under Madame Loyola. When we go up a class we will be under Madame Ita Magdalen. And then God help us. Our class

Pat Rogers,	John Quirke,
Jim Morris,	Cormac Brady,
Liam Lynch,	Hugo Merrins,
Eugene McCabe,	John Glynn,
Eric Sanderson,	Tony Sweeney,
David Hogan,	Peter and Aiken Austin,
Ted Little,	Jimmy Donnelly,
Michael Cuddy,	Pat Pullen,
Frank and Joe O'Reilly,	Pat and John Markey,

Aidan and Colman Higgins.

Subjects taught as prescribed by the revised Primary
School Syllabus. Optional subjects: Piano, Riding. Fees
to be paid in advance.

In the melancholy matter of so-called self-abuse the Piscean preference
has always been to do it in water, take the *soi disant* wriggling beast Thing-
amajig in a cattle-trough in August and September heat. Above me the
vaulted sky of Clare's madness.

Alongside the cattle-trough stood the ring-pump which brought ice-cold
water up out of the ground. A galvanised wrought-iron chute was bent and
attached by wire to the mouth and water pumped into the trough. Heifers
and polly bulls with dusty polls stood in liquid dung and laid their heads
across each other's shoulders, rolled their oily eyes and beshat themselves
and then dipped hairy chins into the icy water that held my member as in
a vice. They slurped it up, making a noise like suction pumps, ignoring the
desperate exertions of the pale nudist (Crusoe hauling booty from the wreck)
with his tool stuck into the mossy side as if into female pubic hair. And meanwhile what was the Dote up to?

Why, adding to his stamp collection, fiddling with tweezers. Having
saved up sufficient pennies and tanners he had taken out a subscription for
Wide World and began an intense study of its contents. He had progressed
in one hop from *Wizard* to *Wide World*, from Clarence E. Mulford to Charles
Dickens. He was reading *Martin Chuzzlewit*, then it was Henry Williamson's
Chronicle of Ancient Sunlight, then Tolstoy's *War and Peace*. There was no stopping him.

– 13 –

A Day at the National School

Out on the Templemills Road opposite The Grove and the squat
Methodist Church stood the National School, a much-dreaded
institute long renowned for the punishments meted out there
by the Brothers. The lads of the Convent trembled at the notion of ever
attending; for if the nuns were severe enough with the strap, the Brothers
were savages altogether with the stick. The Dote and I, all atremble, were

dispatched there. For one trying day we suffered under the thumbs of iron disciplinarians and begged that we never be sent back.

The windows were high in the long classroom and the supply of daylight and fresh air limited because of the tall demesne walls opposite and the stand of trees beyond and, and in the place of torture, the huffing and snuffing of a score or more of uneasy hobbledehoys who stood with hands behind their backs and shoulders against the wall, for a spelling test. Some of the lads we had known in Convent days were now big strapping youths.

We, with Killashee behind us, kept out of the playground at first break, sat on the river-wall and threw heels of our sandwiches down for the fish. Our new schoolmates catcalled and mocked our high and mighty accents until a handbell was rung and we were told to close our books and stand along the wall for a spelling test.

'Stand out there, Ned Colfer,' the teacher called, 'and let's hear you spell "patriotism" for us. Pay-tree-ah-tissm.' Pulling a woeful face (for didn't he have a woeful stutter?) and swallowing a frog, Colfer prepared for humiliation.

He had shut his eyes the better to concentrate, to show he was trying.

'Now Ned, take your time. Don't rush it. We have all the time in the world. Pay-tree-ah-tissm.'

'Pat-pat-pat . . .' stuttered Colfer, gone red as a turkey.

'Take your time, Ned,' purred the teacher, smooth as silk, reaching for the stick.

'Put-put-put . . .'

'Pit-pit-pit . . .' stuttered Colfer, sweating.

The teacher stood up, stick in hand, looking grimly determined now.

'Pot-pot-pot, ppptk!' Colfer swallowed and stopped, his eyes still closed.

'Very well then. Now Colfer, you can surely spell "stupidity"?'

'Stew-stew-stew, ssppssspppk!'

The cane crashed down on Colfer's inky desk, scored with penknife cuts and abrasions, causing him to jump and his eyes to fly open. Now he was for it.

'Stand out there until I stew-stew you, numbskull. You're the straw that broke the camel's back. Stand out there!' Ned Colfer awkwardly held out a trembling hand at face-level. The teacher brought it down and steadied it, measured his stroke, lifted the cane high. Colfer chewed his scummy lips and got all tightened up, with eyes closed again prepared for punishment.

I heard the crows squabbling in the trees and the murmur of the river running out under the knots in the floorboards and wished myself far away. Colfer had curled up his fingers to take the blows and now both hands were under his oxters and he had his head down as the teacher unrolled an old worn well-used map of Ireland all wrinkled and torn to point out County Kildare with the stick which I expected to see spotted with Colfer's blood.

'Can anyone tell me how many counties there were in the Pale?' Clever brother the Dote, looking around at the numbskulls who had not raised a hand, cautiously raised one of his.

After a serious consultation that evening our kind parents, easily persuaded by our begging ('We don't ever want to go back to *that* place!'), had agreed to send us to Clongowes Wood College, where our two elder brothers had gone, and Cousins Syl and Pompey. Mumu came to tuck us in and convey the good news; that very night she would write to the Rector, Father Fergal McGrath. The fees were stiff, so we would have to work hard. We said, 'Yippee!' and did handstands on our beds. Smiling Mumu tucked us in and told us to say our prayers and be good boys.

We would miss a term. But a tutor would be found in the village to prepare us for the Jesuits. Presently the prospectus arrived. We would be kitted out at Our Boys in Dublin, in hardwearing mustard-brown matching herringbone tweed two-piece suits, feeling very grand indeed after two fittings, standing grave as statues before a long mirror.

– 14 –

The Temptress, the Eely River

I had thought always of her as The One.

She travelled to and from Dublin by bus. I didn't know her name. Perhaps she was a trainee nurse doing her intern? On one memorable occasion she had sat beside me and I breathed in a ferny scent of hair and flesh that was stronger than cosmetics. When she moved the scent became stronger. She spoke to a friend, craning back, telling of stockings she had purchased at Garnett's in Dublin, and I listened.

I had seen Mumu lift her skirt and seen the mark of garters where they gripped the thighs but never had I seen a young one lift her skirt, and never kissed a pretty Prod, and this one was so pretty, and I wondered what it would be like, to kiss her. I saw her skirt raised above her knees as she showed me the Garnett's stockings and spoke of mesh and size (so difficult to get during the 'Emergency' when everything was rationed) and kneeling down in adoration before her I was permitted to kiss those warm odorous thighs so obscurely craved. You may kiss me there, she whispered to me. Just once, just there, no higher. I fancied that something venturesome peeped out at me from half-closed mischievous eyes; and I did. Her calmness unsettled me; I was too shy to look at her, much less speak to her, I who was too young for her.

When she stared out the window I saw her reflection watching me in the glass, where lights shone and people with parcels had gathered to wait for the bus, and I encountered a glance both moist and disturbing, a quick feminine glance that sank into me before I could turn away. I thought of her walking in the wards and speaking softly to sick ones. The texture of her Proddy skin was glazed and clouded as if greyish-blue smoke tinged her living flesh, lent it a down of dusk. Then my furtive and craven Catholic eye fell to the bulge of her amply rounded thigh, to the grey-blue tracery of fine veins at her wrist where bare skin showed in the vee of her gloves, and the teasing bulge of her garter. She wore a small lady-model wristwatch which I imagined would show a different sort of Protestant Time; corn-coloured hair was cut to the shape of her face, brown-skinned, and the same blue veins throbbed at her temples.

'Actually I did,' she told her friend.

Her breath told me what she had had to eat. Actually I didn't, actually I wouldn't . . . actually I just might. She glanced up at the parcel on the luggage rack where the advertisement said, 'We lead, others may follow'. And a hobbledehoy with flaming ears lifted it down before she could stretch up for it and she thanked him, dipping her eyes. She rose up, preparing to go, and I let her out into the aisle.

I had felt embarrassed when sitting next to her in an untoward intimacy of odours and intake and exhalation of breath, and imagined that a sort of counterfeit intimacy had sprung up between us and been wordlessly shared, even if I could not bring myself to speak to her. She for her part had probably been relieved that I hadn't. I followed her, Dado at the front of the bus making a great show of letting her go out first before him, doing the gallant. Her calves quivered in high heels as she walked away, going to a girlfriend who came with her bicycle, holding it by the handlebars. She had a neat feminine way of mounting, thrusting herself forward on the pedals and then subsiding onto the saddle. She began to move off, pushed by the friend who walked alongside. As she went a sense of evening accompanied her and the pain which I had hardly felt at first kept on growing. As she went away a part of my unformed life went with her.

Heavy rolls of the evening editions were being hurled from the roof of the bus with the bicycles stacked there lifted down and the driver had stepped into Breen's to slake his thirst. She, sadly departing, waved back. She combined blonde and brunette elements of two film actresses I secretly desired: Priscilla Lane and Evelyn Keys.

Oh but she was evermore The One!

Shriven by the handsome curate whom we call Father Basilica, who was a novice in Rome and cannot forget the Holy City (it features in every sermon and the great basilicas are named), and feeling very pious, I carry a prayer book about with me, the squat size of the *Mickey Mouse Annual*, and take it up the fields in order to pray undisturbed and to commune with nature. It has a white laminated cover of horn or ivory with IHS embossed in silver, shooting out static flames, with a purple book-mark to hold my place.

I kneel rapt in prayer before the frog-infested pond near the fox covert and watch the frogs rise and sink with outstretched skinny arms, leaving trails of bubbles as they go, kicking up powdery clay from the bed of the pond, or breaking the surface to slowly open the portals of their wise old eyes as though it were the first day of Creation. They are the image of nude old men, bald-headed with their mickies wizened away to nothing, floating through clouds, they sail up and down for air, jerking spasmodically with long obscene hind legs. They burrow into the powdery clay that rises up like smoke, digging themselves in until only their bums stick out.

The tadpoles devour each other indiscriminately, feeling no pain, working up from the tail; two or three of them stuck together, feeding, the middle one half-eaten by the end one, and only the head of the foremost one remaining. Rita Phelan calls them pollywoggles.

A labouring man with his coat off in the heat, wearing what Rita calls 'galluses' (his braces) looks over the hedge and discovers me kneeling by the pond.

'Grand day out!' he calls.

'Grand!' I simper, feeling very silly, a right eejit.

His red-faced brother discovered me a week later, the heat wave continuing unabated, kneeling naked and poring over one of the Dodo's

Lilliputs with English girls in the nude up to their bums in an English wheatfield. A coarse amiable voice called out in derision as I crawled into a bush, dragging my shirt and shorts in after me. I watched him cross the field when I was decent and dressed. He wore big hobnail boots and carried a blackened billycan; without breaking his stride he jumped the ditch into the next field, striding onward, whistling, not a bother on him. I heard a cuckoo calling in the Crooked Meadow. Where I stood was the limit of Dado's seventy-two acres; beyond lay Matt Dempsey's land and Major Brooke's land again, where the hare-coursing took place, the killing on the slope.

'That Phelan girl is a right h,u,r,e,' Dado said, sucking in a morsel of gristle in his teeth.

I kept my eyes fixed on my plate.

'May I replenish?' asked brother Bun in a fatuous way, holding up the carafe of water. 'Do you use Long Melford, Sir?'

The days press in. In an aimless sort of way I cycle about, without any design or purpose. A donkey starts to bray, drawing in terrible lungfuls of agony; a haycock begins steaming. I feel the bridge wall vibrate. Two hundred yards away in the shallows two young women of surpassing beauty wade in their bathing costumes below Straffan bridge. Water invites, the whole earth breathes; I sink ever deeper into shame and abasement. Confession is torment. I tell my sins to Father Basilica. My sins are always the same, dirty thoughts.

I float with the current that drags me down, pulling at myself, swallowing water, half drowning, sinking ever deeper into shame and abasement.

Behind the fretted baize in the wired-up and domed valves of the wet batteries a red light pulsates, electrical discharges begin to squeak and gibber, bubbling away with static, and a throaty seductive female voice calls out voluptuously, 'Hello, hello, we're gonna play roly-poly today!' and is instantly cut off by howling frictional electricity, spluttering and gurgling with the hydrogen gas being emitted from sulphuric acid. The heat is sweltering. The word 'stall' excites me.

The river is full of eels, Josey Darlington tells me. He is working in the forge for his father the blacksmith. Two pretty cyclists pass Sadlier's Harness Parts and ride onto the bridge where a breeze makes their thin skirts fly up. I see their shadows pass on the bridge wall opposite, hear their startled cries.

Dado tells Mumu that Rita Phelan is a brazen hussy.

Stunted Grogan the cruel stretcher of cats has started going steady with Rita Phelan. Rita is his moth; Grogan is no Molly. Mumu says they are well met.

Whistling between his teeth Grogan curry-combs Sally the mare, mounted on a small footstool to reach her spine.

I ask whether Sally likes it.

'Begob she loves it,' Grogan says, whistling tunelessly, and feeling hocks and tendons, pushing the bay's flanks.

A huge inquisitive horse-eye regards me.

'Whoa there, me beauty!'

Sally's hooves strike the cement ramp with a ring of steel and sparks fly.

Dado collected two free balcony passes in the booking office halfway up the grand stairs at the Capital and retreated down to the street as we passed in through the purple curtain with our bags of fudge, going by the framed photographs of Hollywood stars, Robert Taylor, Spencer Tracy, Ida Lupino, the usherette going before us with a torch into the dark, leading us to our seats, and into the middle of my most secret and fulfilling dream come true: the secret island under the sea! *Bahama Idyll* starring Madeleine Carroll and Sterling Hayden is in Technicolor, both have blonde hair and are very tanned, the sea is absolutely blue. Even the title intoxicates me: *Bahama Idyll*! Idyll means lounging about in the sun, Bahama is an atoll in the Gulf of Mexico. In an office in a skyscraper in the big city (Chicago or New York) Madeleine Carroll removes her stockings behind a screen. With strained anxious faces they approach each other in a cave under the sea. We see it through to the end. It begins again. The curtains part and lights like an Aurora Borealis flood the screen and the film, which we have seen from the middle, begins for us.

Something light as a feather tickled my bare hairless leg in my first pair of longers and instinctively I had one hand to it as it reached my knee and drew out not a woodlouse, spider nor a cockroach but a small house mouse which I dropped over the balcony rail without second thoughts. Not a sound came from below, where some matinée idlers were coughing in the poorer seats, utilising the toilets.

We chew fudge and observe Madeleine Carroll move behind the screen to unzip her garter and begin to remove her stockings again, while Sterling

Hayden, for modesty's sake, waits on the other side of the screen, and the Dote is whispering, 'This is where we came in.' Reluctantly I follow him up the dark aisle with the little spotlights under the steps where the usherette points her beam. We pass out by the curtain and Dado is waiting for us. Gallantly he asks whether we have been any trouble to her. 'Oh none at all,' she says. She wears an extraordinary bellhop uniform in purple with a purple pillar-box hat worn at a rakish angle with a strap under her chin. Dado has been across the street in the Gresham Bar where no doubt his cronies, the lounge lizards, congregate.

I think that Dado's cut-down trousers are not as smart as Sterling Hayden's but about Madeleine Carroll's shorts I cannot even begin to think. I get sick in the bus going home in daylight. Mumu asks us what we saw and did we like it. We tell her something about *Bahama Idyll*.

'It wasn't like *Coral Island*,' I said.

Mumu had the cards set out for Pelman Patience.

'I have a crow to pluck with yew, mister!'

Patsy fixed me with an implacable glare and took a step closer, rolling up his shirt sleeves to demonstrate the stringy muscles of a labouring man's son. His face had gone a curious colour, pinched white about the nostrils.

Patsy's face changed colour with his moods.

'Don't I have yew now!'

The sudden blow – when it came – arrived from far away, striking me high up on the chest, knocking all the wind out of me.

'Don't!'

'I have yew now!'

'You haven't, you know.'

Patsy raised his fist as if to repeat the blow, then put his arm about my neck and wrestled me affectionately to the ground.

I strip naked, roll in dry horse-dung, swallow frogspawn, crawl through the wheatfield. The roan stallion prepares to mount the bay mare. Drawing back hairy black lips to expose great horse-teeth in a terrible grin, the stallion mounts from behind. Awash in sweat, the pair of them seem unusually naked, stripped to necessity, stuck together in a field of rolling hillocks. Like angels struggling to fold their heavy wings they go dancing over the hillocky field, kissing and biting through manes of hair, snorting and whinnying.

Brother Bun squirts cold water over me from a garden hose. He is dressed in a black bathing costume that sags and reaches halfway down his freckled legs and I see the limp outline of his little willie outlined in the damp cloth. Silently I chase him out of the garden, over the paling, down the front meadow, over the paling onto the front avenue, across the second paling, into the paddock; he slips through a five-bar gate and runs bleating away. I take a breather at the gate, watch him run away from me, and my great anger subsides, subsides.

The brazen hussy puts a thrawneen into my mouth and dares me to race her to a knot in the centre.

'I dar yew and I double-dar yew,' she challenges me.

Her breath steams in the cold air, her nostrils flare as she clamps her mouth on the thrawneen and begins ravenously eating it. I see her approaching eyes, her working mouth, I bite the thrawneen short and give her best, it hangs from her mouth with my spittle on it. She makes as if to strike me.

'Take a coward's blow!'

We stand face to face. She reaches out and touches me.

'Give us a coort. Ah give us a squeeze!'

She turns on her heel laughing. I smell her cheap perfume and her lipstick. For me she feels nothing but contempt. The frozen pump behind her is trussed up like a madman's trousers.

She and Grogan slip into the hayshed. When they reappear an hour later Grogan looks pale and drained. Is she his moth?

Josey Darlington pulled the eel trapped in his night-lines out of the Liffey. Dragging the hook from its obstinate black jaw he threw it up the bank where it thrashed in sudden convulsions.

'It's desperate hard to kill an auld ale. It's desperate killing wonna dim lads. De oney way is to spit tobacco juice down its nick. Be careful. They'd bite the hand offa you.'

The river, gathering speed as it neared the weir, suddenly dropped from sight. Swallows were dipping for insects. 'By my sowl . . .'

Neddy Keegan broke the necks of rabbits under the heel of his boot or with the hard heel of his hand with a karate chop. Old Mrs Henry sawed the heads off cockerels with the carving knife and gave the heads to the cats. The fowl seemed to take the sudden effusion of blood in their stride, as a fact of life. They went on scratching for food, rooting about and clucking, making that droning sound in their throats that my brother and I called Years-Gone-By.

The eel began to slither back towards the river, but Josey kicked it away, cursing. He took out his knife and snapped open the blade. The eel coiled itself without a sound about the clasp-knife as Josey dug, grunting, at its neck; bones and tendons were severed and blood splattered on the grass.

– 15 –

That Noble Pile

Measurement began our might' pontificated Yeats, the Protestant tenant extraordinaire and poet-with-tenure at Thoor Ballylee, humming to himself, up his winding stairs.

Home was where? Home was what?

For the inheritors of forfeited estates and lands it was a surrogate home, a place they would have to get used to; for the very poor, the defeated, home had become a torture-chamber. For the adventurous, it was the place to set out from; for the unadventurous, it was the place where personal property was secure, where one sat down and supped in peace.

Cottages, lodges, bathing houses and temples sprang up about the estate.

Four times a week her Ladyship met the poor of the area and gave them free food, i.e., the kitchen waste with scraps from the dining room table. To eat well gave a sense of power. Indoors and out her forbidding manner and commanding presence induced awe in those undernourished and weak with hunger. The childless chatelaine had her own ways; one did not presume to take liberties.

She was said to be 'kind and generous' to the poor; but what does that mean, if she did not offer to abate her high lifestyle by one jot or tittle to help lessen that poverty?

Fraternity cannot be when it is but a disguise to salve conscience; it becomes a condescending philanthropy, a fake charity dispensed with the left hand.

In any case Anglican high charity for the lowly Catholic oppressed would always be suspect, a dubious altruism tinged with self-interest, left-handed charity, dexter charity. 'Charity,' as my dear mother was never tired of repeating, 'begins at home.' The first unwritten rule of the law of survival is immutable: 'Look to your own.'

Lady Katherine and Lady Louisa after her no doubt accepted the poor Catholic villagers as they were: namely, unwashed, evasive, shiftless, fractious (when it suited them), quarrelsome, superstitious, light fingered, polyprogenitive, impertinent, pushy, deferential, scatter-brained, abject and dumb with embarrassment in her presence. She was a practical woman and saw things clearly, would not tolerate cheek from employees or wastefulness in the execution of their duties; she liked to have her own way, and thought to save the poor by good example, cleanliness, order, punctuality, cheerfulness, good manners, good sense. She wrote: 'They went through quietly . . . The poor people will find that we are their best friends at last.'

She begged them to put away the pikes, to listen to reason.

Absurd monumental groupings or emblematic fancies wrought in bronze, marble or granite, such as the enmarbled callisthenics of the Laocoon, Cleopatra's Needle on the Thames Embankment or the Albert Memorial in Kensington Gardens are silently intimating something or other like a person pulling a face or a face partly averted while shoulders are being shrugged.

If the Wonderful Barn at Leixlip was built as a repository for grain it was also put up as a threat, the winding stairs and narrow windows part of its defensive system. The preposterous Obelisk was commissioned by the widow of the Speaker Conolly to 'adorn her estate and to honour her husband', after a winter of famine and frost. It cost her £400, with labour at a halfpenny per day. There was something freakish and even threatening in these oddly conceived monuments and follies, with enigmatic elements in their convoluted structures; in some obscure way all were casting long threatening shadows, shadows cast by good King Billy, the victor at the Boyne, signifying 'The Spoils of War'.

Even the sphinxes over the front gate were odd, as if the head and upper torso were modelled on a human model, even if her Ladyship (Louisa) had wanted to put up two couchant stone lionesses (the ones who do the kill while the lions sleep) facing each other; or perhaps she wanted to go the whole hog and have dragons. They were half-human half-beast and halfway to being gargoyles, grim or grinning, hunched up, sticking out their tongues.

Below them Tom Conolly had kennelled his hunting pack and somewhere in the stable yard the bear was chained, ready for the bear-baiting days when the dogs were pitted against him, rearing up and growling, cheered on by the gentry.

The Death House near St Mochua's in particular was freakish, the sort
of monument that might have been erected over a battlefield; but the victory at the Boyne refuted, turned aside and 'On Yonder Rock Reclining'
sublimated into 'High Anglicanism Enchained'. The Great Lord and the
Great Lady, held in a chill classical pose for all eternity in the Death House,
threw an even greater shadow: 'The Malign Presence', all dragon lines and
killing points.

In her heart of hearts, in her Protestant bones and coursing through her
central nervous system was the deep-seated conviction stronger than any
prejudice, that the Celbridge Catholic poor were beyond saving, as a hayfield
so long subjected to torrential downpours that it had gone rotten, reverted to
humus (regard the sorry chapters of their unfortunate history).

On May 21st, 1798 Lady Louisa wrote:

> This last week has been a most painful one
> to us. Maynooth, Kilcock, Leixlip and Celbridge
> have had part of a Scotch Regiment
> quartered at each place and every day
> threatening to burn the towns. I have spent days
> in entreaties and threats, to give up the
> horrid pikes. Some houses burnt at Kilcock
> yesterday produced the effect.

Celbridge was always in danger of being attacked by rebels coming from
their camps at Timahoe and Donadea. A company of the Derry Militia
arrived to protect Castletown House and eighteen of them snored on the
floor of the Long Gallery. Colonel Napier of Oakley Park moved his family
in with the Conollys.

With a firm hand she wrote:

> June 1, 1798. There have been skirmishes in this
> neighbourhood; two hundred of
> them forced through our gates and passed across
> our front lawn at three o'clock on Saturday morning
> last but they went through quietly. We are happy
> in being able to preserve Celbridge.

Tom was on the side of the property-owners. He and other prominent
landlords formed the Yeomanry Corps to act as a home guard to help

maintain law and order. The regular troops were posted along the coast to prevent any attempt at invasion by the French. The rebellion, even if averted in Celbridge, cast a gloom over Castletown as the Conollys had relatives on both sides. If Tom Conolly opposed rebellion, Lady Sarah Napier of Oakley Park, sister of Lady Louisa, was a committed rebel, and Lord Edward Fitzgerald, nephew of Lady Louisa, was a leader of the United Irishmen in Leinster; twice informed against, he would come a cropper: the twice betrayed one became the noble corpse.

The big houses of Kildare had begun to burn. Lady Louisa took to walking through the fortress at night, for she slept lightly, walked silently about, checked the doors, heard the eighteen Militiamen snoring and farting in their sleep, hardly a reassuring sound. The flushed face of her huntsman husband at the far end of the long table was no more reassuring.

She thought to herself: 'May the giving hand never waver. If I sit down again to such sumptuous fare and remove the lid from one more brimming soup tureen, the first guest I pass a plate to will be the Devil. One of these evenings we'll sup with the Devil.'

Some such notion may have passed through her Ladyship's practical head. For the Williamite victors the consuming of grand dinners had a symbolic force; for was it not a further confirmation of a conquest already complete? the ritual aftermath that involved the handing out of medals? While the people of the countryside starved in their mud hovels the rich ate their fill. (Captain Ernst Junger of the Wehrmacht dined one night in 1942 at the Tour d'Argent, and noted in his diary: 'One had the impression that the people sitting up there on high, consuming their soles and the famous duck, were looking with diabolical satisfaction, like gargoyles, over the sea of grey roofs which sheltered the hungry. In such times, to eat, and to eat well, gives one a sensation of power.' It was into the third year of the Nazi Occupation and Paris had begun to feel that they would never go. Paris was no longer Paris but stunned, atrophied; the average citizen lived on very thin rations and was half-starving.)

In Madrid Generalissimo Franco, Spain's Caudillo for forty years, had signed death-warrants over his after-dinner coffee, before strolling to the long windows of the Palacio, to admire the gushing fountains before him.

Ruling and holding were done with a heavy hand (for property-ownership is akin to murder) and rulers must be ruthless if they wish to stay in office; others' (prostrate Spain) deprivation whets the appetite with all the purposeful lust of profiteering.

Lady Louisa stirred the brimming soup tureen and thought that others' hunger added a subtle bitter flavour to their own rich repast. *L'art de la civilisation consiste, à allier les plaisirs les plus délicate à la presence récurrent du danger.*

When Tom Conolly returned from hunting in the late afternoon he washed and changed and went down to dinner. Each guest had his or her individual servant standing behind the chair, which was put in place and lifted away as the guests sat and rose again. On occasion they were served up as many as seven meat dishes, with the best wines, followed by elaborate desserts. Scullions bore away the dirty plates in buckets down to the kitchens one hundred yards distant.

Around five in the afternoon the ladies left the gentlemen to enjoy their port and cigars while they retired to the drawing room for coffee and tea and gossip. At about six the card tables were brought into the Long Gallery and backgammon and quadrille played, for nominal stakes, until ten o'clock. Elsewhere in the great room the guests played billiards or the piano, read or wrote letters. Just before bed the servants came quietly in and laid a light supper upon small tables. Thus replenished the guests retired to bed, a fire lit in the grate and hot-water bottles warming the four-posters.

At ten next morning breakfast was served in a small parlour where their host and hostess were waiting. A meal consisted of chocolate, honey and breads baked in different colours for variety.

At one infamous meet a stranger rode with the Killing Kildares. No one had remembered him taking a stirrup-cup before they rode off, but it soon became apparent that here was a matchless rider. Tom Conolly jumped everything in sight with the stranger a stride behind; and so it went on all morning, jump for jump, at some of which more cautious huntsmen turned aside. Until they came to an impossible jump at which Tom Conolly drew back and watched amazed as the stranger in ratcatcher on the sweating black stallion sailed over.

Tom Conolly invited him back for dinner at Castletown.

He sat next to Lady Louisa as composed he had sat on his horse, now washed and brushed, with not a splash of mud on him. He joined the gentlemen for cards after and proved to be as good at cards as he was at jumping ditches – until he made the mistake of dropping a card (it was the ace of spades); or perhaps that was in the design too, for else how would he have identified himself, at the heel of the hunt?

'By the way, the name is Satan.'

It was old Nick in full hunting pink.

The blushing young serving-wench from the village stopped to pick up the dropped card, having begged his pardon and curtsied nicely. She reached down her hand and was shocked to see that the guest had removed his riding boots and wore no socks over cloven feet, and had a close whiff of brimstone before she screamed; for what young thing waiting at table would expect to be serving Satan himself between soup and grapes! He touched his sybaritic lips with the serviette and coughed behind his hand, saying politely, 'No more for me thank you, Lady Louisa. I am full to the muzzle. You see before you a lover of beautiful things. I knew your Christ once.'

He gave a short barking laugh as he threw back his head, whereupon the terror-stricken maid crouching at his feet keeled over backwards in a dead faint at this atrocious blasphemy. Nor could the mouldy old Vicar shift him, for he would not budge an inch but sat there, impervious to prayers and insults, grinning mischievously as he drew on a long cigar. He appeared to be in his element.

The portly, red-faced Parish Priest – for *he* had been summoned when all else had failed – having drenched the unwelcome visitor with holy water to no avail, showed the cross on his rosary beads, and with fearful execrations IT vanished in a puff of acrid yellow smoke into a crack in the floor, leaving the shaken priest to 'sweat seven shirts and die', as the Keegans graphically reported, as if they themselves had been present at these strange proceedings. 'As true as God,' Neddy said, blessing himself.

Welcome and unwelcome visitors had come up the front driveway between the lime trees that turn coppery in autumn. The heiress Katherine Conolly, daughter of Sir Albert Conyngham, had been no beauty, and survived her husband, buried in the preposterous mausoleum on Tea (or Tay) Lane. She was succeeded at Castletown by William who married Lady Ann Wentworth, daughter of the Earl of Stafford. He died two years later, leaving Castletown to his son Thomas, who married Lady Louisa Lennox, daughter of the Duke of Richmond, when he was four and twenty and she was fifteen years of age. She was to survive him by two score years and more. She was a homely looking lady. For 'she continued to perpetuate his memory' read: by threats, overt and sly, she continued to remind her tenants and dependants on which side their bread was buttered, and who was buttering it.

As the estate was self-supporting, it required brewers, bakers, weavers, carpenters, dairymaids, stable boys, gardeners, coachmen and masons in its upkeep. The estate was run by a land steward and a farm staff of up to five and twenty men and boys working a six-day week, rising each morning at six o'clock (her Ladyship rose at eight).

Butlers received remuneration at the rate of thirteen pounds old currency per annum, cooks twelve, coachmen eleven, gardeners ten, kitchen maids and cowkeepers three pounds to keep body and soul together. They were fed by her Ladyship. It was ever thus; the heiress graciously accepted two rich inheritances as her right. It was like that in those times for those people; the rich had the ball at their feet.

Castletown House commanded one hundred grand rooms to accommodate whatever guests were invited. Drawing rooms and dining rooms, kitchens, bedrooms and four-poster beds, a print room, all were there for their pleasure. The servants' quarters had an army of servants awaiting their pleasure, for 'the quality' expected only the best.

This stately residence originally had two hundred and thirty windows but one had been blocked up in deference to Buckingham Palace's two hundred and thirty windows. For three weeks' work in 1783 the window-cleaner's bill came to three pounds ten shillings.

Only the richest and blackest of natural-born Protestants had ever occupied the manse. Peacocks strutted across the gravel and the black rabbits gambolled on the river banks below; above them a flag flew, a sky for the favoured.

The great Palladian manse laid out over extensive acres had been the brainchild of William Conolly, the poor son of a Ballyshannon publican from Donegal. The plans were conceived and carried out with no regard for cost – thanks to the wholesale appropriation of forfeited land in the six counties – by the Italian architect Galilei, as an appropriate country seat for the Speaker of the Irish House of Commons.

Judicious interbreeding had brought revenue but no progeny; Speaker Conolly was to die without a son; Lady Katherine barren as Lady Louisa after her.

Lovell Pearse, designer of the Irish Parliament House, is credited with the details of much of the interior; slate, stone and fine furniture were of Irish manufacture and the silverware from Irish mines. It was said to be the largest eighteenth-century house in Ireland – a veritable Xanadu on the plains of Kildare. The façade was four-hundred feet long by sixty feet high in granite cut from Hazelhatch quarry, flanked by curved colonnades and outbuildings, messuages and curtilage assigned to their use. It was this noble pile that met the eye of the rebels on a morning in May 1798 and fairly took their breath away.

Before them an immense granite façade towered up into a cold moonlit sky full of icy stars, massive as a fortress or a grey military barracks forever braced against them and their puny likes; an impenetrable Protestant breast of iron three feet deep, four hundred feet long and sixty feet tall, with a flag flying brazenly at the masthead and a hundred or so full moons racing and skipping pellmell athwart every window.

− 16 −

The Names

Behind any text of any value lurks the subtext. 'Here's I: Sunny Jim.' Old Thady Neales boasted in 1729 that his ancestors had come to Celbridge when it was Kildrought in the reign of the first Elizabeth, about the time the Dongans had acquired (that resonant word) Castletown and all the others had followed, mongrels after the bitch in heat,

the Dutchman Vanhomrigh*
the Napiers
the Clements
the Prices
the Baillies
Thebold Donnolly**
John Maunsell***
Chief Justice Marlay
Fisher the nailer
Tilbury the glazier
Carberry the brewer
Martin Lacey
Elinor Sadlier
Hinzell
Charles Davis
Annesley

*The agent of General Ginkel, Earl of Athlone and Chief Commissioner for Revenue in Ireland, whose only daughter Esther fell in love with Dean Swift, who repudiated her; whereupon she 'embraced Bacchus'. Took to the bottle.
**who changed the name of Celbridge House to Oakley Park and bought the house and lands from Colonel George Napier.
***who in 1813 purchased the estate for his son Richard so that it remained in Maunsell hands for over a hundred years.

Lumley

Dignam

Finnerty the dyer

Carter

Finey*

Ahern

Cotter

Tyrell

Kane

Stephen Coyle

Kevany

Russell

Rourke

Doyle

Dease

Darlington

Dempsey

Tisdell

Hart

Sutton

Fenaughty, who looked after Tom

Jeremiah Haughton

Clancy

Talbot

Cotter

Hannan

Dunne

L. W. Flowers

Blake

John Wynn the baker

Dr Robert Clayton, Bishop of Clogher

Richard Nelson of Maynooth

Thomas Croker, lawyer of Backweston

Ann Rives, Dr Clayton's niece

Arthur Maguire

Louisa Staples, wife of Admiral Packenham

*(George) who built Mulligan's House in 1750 on the site of 14 mud cabins along the road to Maynooth.

Thomas Conolly of Castletown
Revd Henry Lomax Walsh, Prebend of Swords
Mr Waters, Vicar of St Mochua's
Hugh Hill
the Fordes of Donashcomper and Simmonstown
William Kirkpatrick who married Mary Carr in 1809
Sir Ivone Kirkpatrick who died in 1964
Mr J. Bruce Bedin of Wilmington, Delaware

Barry the auctioneers
Gleeson
Leslie Young
Eric Murray
Van Lonkhuyzen
J. J. Young, Victualler
Mr Edward Williams, teacher
James O'Neill, teacher
William Gibney, teacher
Ellen Wall, teacher
Miss Fennell
Boylan's Garage
Londis
Allen
McDermott
W. M. Callender

to mention only these. In a will made out in 1561, 'all these lands of his (Sir James Alen of Saint Wolstan's) were the gift made to him by King Henry VIII of most noble memory, up to the dissolution of the monastery or priory of Saint Wolstan's; his principal place by the New bridge in the Countie of Kildare called Alenscorte, otherwise Saint Wolstan's.'

The Alens, as likewise their neighbours the Dongans of Castletown, were Catholic and had fought on the losing side for King James (James the Shit) in the Jacobite-Williamite wars. When the Normans arrived in 1170 they had found much of the land under grass.

My own Family Tree had sent out sprouting roots here and there down the years. Of those, Aunt Ada (Mrs Frank Lynch) lived in Dun Laoghaire but ended her days with her daughter in England. Hilda Boyd (Mrs Perren) lived in Buenos Aires all her married life. Herbert Boyd and his wife Nora lived in Dublin. Their son Bill, of whom little is known, lives somewhere in England. Aubrey Boyd (the detective manqué) lived in Montreal; his daughter Aideen (Mrs Ron McKenna) lives in Abbotsford, B.C., sending 'very chatty letters each Christmas' to Mrs Margaret Moorkens the widow of Captain Gus, holder of All Ireland High Jump record as a youth, Captain of Terenure Bridge Club and chairman of Irish Firearms Dealers at the time of his death; son of Gustave senior, my parents' go-between.

My Aunts and Uncles are as follows:

1873 – 1915 Mary Jo. Higgins married Patrick Newman
1881 – 1936 Margaret Higgins married Peter Newman
1882 – 1916 Thomas P. Higgins married Ciss Foran
1885 – **** Norah Higgins died as a child.
188* – **** Jack Higgins
1887 – 1969 Bridie Higgins married Michael Connolly
1888 – 1963 Molly Higgins married Charles Smith
1889 – **** Anna Higgins married Dr Vincent Delany
1890 – 1970 Bart Higgins married Lilly Boyd
1892 – 1971 Nora Higgins married Jack Healy
1894 – 1963 Tess Higgins married Mjr Hugh Stevenson
1897 – 1987 Gertrude Higgins married Andrew Moore
Grandfather:
1835 – 1897 John Higgins married Margaret Carroll
Great Grandfather:
c.1810 – 1879 Patrick Higgins married Hanora Flanagan. Patrick was a farmer, near Boyle.

May their shadows never grow less.

The Diocese of Kildare appears to have been founded towards the close of the fifth or the commencement of the sixth century by St Conleath or Conlaid, who erected the Cathedral and became first Bishop. The first English Bishop was Ralph of Bristol, consecrated in 1223. The first Bishop after the Reformation was William Miagh.

— 17 —

A Longford Wedding,
Suicide of Josef Moorkens

In one of the heavy family albums Joss had drawn the Angel of Mons in a HB pencil, as good as any you would find in a magazine; an angel with huge wings kneeling to offer the bays to a fallen hero, while overleaf Dado in his best hand had inscribed an elevating thought lifted from Shakespeare:

> Give thy thoughts no tongue,
> Nor any unproportion'd though his act.
> Be thou familiar, but by no means vulgar.
> The friends thou hast, and their adoption tried,
> Grapple them to thy soul with hoops of steel.

On the verso were protective sheets of semi-transparent tissue paper so that the angel and the Shakespeare thought appeared through gauzy veils, and there was Uncle Jack the roustabout receiving a tin of petrol, now just handed off the wharf for the *Whoopee* and Auntie Nora belting another fag on the quayside and Honor and Maeve pulling faces at the camera, and a commemorative photo of Mumu-to-be and Dado-to-be posed as bride and groom on the driveway before Melview soon after their wedding day.

The bride wore a wide-brim hat with a conical crown, a smart going-away outfit that made her hips flare out, white calf-length little boots with high heels and pearly buttons down the side; in one hand she held a folded parasol and smiled her sweetest secret smile for the camera, for Batty, as if holding an invisible nosegay.

The groom displayed a manly pair of calves in checkered woollen stockings tucked into plus-fours cut in the loose baggy style made popular by Bobby Jones, and two-tone brogues with pointed toes, a tightly fitted two-piece suit of houndstooth tweed with vent, a bow-tie at a gallant angle, a small curly-brim derby balanced on the crown of his head, with centre parting above a conspiratorial smirk (for who knew what lay ahead?).

The new groom's ever-impatient right hand was about to throw open the little latched side-door of the Hillman; the camera had caught him in the very act of opening it for the new bride to ascend, all scented and smiling and ready for the great journey to begin. The hood was lowered and a large trunk commodious as a wardrobe lashed to the rumble seat. On the side of the trunk facing the camera a careful hand had painted in block white lettering

MR & MRS B. J. HIGGINS
SPRINGFIELD, CELBRIDGE
CO KILDARE

A spare can of petrol was strapped to the runningboard and the newlyweds about to depart to Mulrany for their honeymoon. The crank-shaft hung docile and ready between spoke wheels. My progenitor is probably informing my mother-to-be that he will presently give her (the car) a few darts, to warm her up. He knew nothing of the workings of the internal combustion engine; as ignorant of that as he was of the workings of his own interior, dosed with tea, balls of malt and Epsom salts for a curative. He drove with old-world panache, his jaw out, arms rigid on the steering column. Ahead lay seven anxious barren years. The Dodo was still an angel in Heaven, waiting to be summoned (I was to arrive nine years later).

But the groom's impatient foot is already on the runningboard. And off they go to Mulrany. I turned over another gauzy page and saw a sepia print of the pair of them in a jaunting-car with a bit of blood between the shafts. In one gloved hand the triumphant groom holds the reins; from an inside pocket he dramatically withdraws a large service revolver for the sun to shine on the long dangerous barrel and oiled chambers. Lillian Ann straightens her back and her eyes sparkle as Bartholomew James cocks the Browning. Did you ever, he asks waggishly, ever in your life see such a large revolver, Lillian Ann Boyd? Oh no indeed she never had, oh never.

Brandishing the loaded revolver and with whip aloft in its bracket, my ardent father drives the high-stepping pony at a spanking pace down the Battery Road through Longford town. He was deep in one of those daydreams that can overtake even the shallowest of men; akin to being in the midst of the most tumultuous of parties. Lillian Ann is aglow, luminous with happiness.

British Army troops from various regiments had been garrisoned in the cavalry barracks at Longford over the years. But he protects her from the murderous Black and Tans who career about the back roads of Ireland in Crossley Tenders, intent on humiliating and shooting down innocent Irish.

The Sherwood Foresters was a name that kept cropping up whenever Mumu mentioned Longford and Melview and Jamestown or Battery Road. The Sean Conolly Cavalry and Artillery Barracks, Lower and Upper, had been occupied since 1899 by a succession of regiments that began with the 90th Battery Royal Artillery, then came the 6th Battalion Rifle Brigade that saw service in the South African War. Then came the Royal Army Service Corps, maintenance staff only; then the 5th Battalion Royal Irish Regiment that saw the Dardanelles. Then the Sherwood Foresters, cheered on by Mumu, the King Edward Horse, the Unknowns of 1917–20, before the 9th Lancers and the 13th Hussars. Last but not least came a Company of the East Yorks who were to hand over the barracks to the Irish Army.

Another picture is thrown on the magic-lantern screen by a shaky hand. A line of ashen-faced Tommies in tin helmets and baggy khaki uniforms, carrying heavy packs on their backs, go into action with bayonets fixed, having beshat themselves and risen in absolute silence from a trench deep as the grave, urged on by their ashen-faced officers, and begin to cheer – their mouths wide open and not a sound issuing; they stumble forward for King and Country into the German gas that drifts in a sinister way slowly towards the English lines; their weakening cries founder in the toxic fumes. Poison gas drifts across No Man's Land, creeping over the barbed-wire entanglements, into the shell craters, deep into English lungs.

Josef Moorkens, my uncle by marriage, the brave Belgian volunteer well under-age, will soon swallow German gas, as he prepares to go into action with the second wave of Belgian troops, slapping his pockets, carrying parts of a machine-gun that will never be used that day. On his long feet, puttees, polished boots laced up; on his face a dreadful expression, for he fears that he may be going to his death that morning. On his head a peculiar potty-shaped helmet with a ridged backbone down the crown.

All is silent but for the whirring of Ger Coyle's projector (for we are watching a private film show in the back lodge with Miss Coyle serving up buttered water biscuits which I will not touch).

But look again!

Here he is large as life, standing with folded arms, his legs planted wide on the duckboards, now helmetless (it rests on a sandbag within easy reach), enjoying a pipe. His dark eyes stare fixedly out at me. In the sepia background the Box Brownie has picked up trees with their heads blown off, shell holes filled with water, a torn-up waterlogged wasteland: Flanders Fields! On the back of the curling sepia print a hand (Joss?) has written in faded-blue ink: 'view of a mudshow after bombardment 20–12–1916'.

Speculation about a dead person only begins to be legitimate after the ascertainable has been ascertained as far as possible. Take the death (by his own hand) of my uncle Josef, the go-between when my parents were courting ('Bart will follow on bicycle') as a case in point. Mumu, slightly psychic in her quiet way, for it wasn't all nerves, as she was slightly hysterical, had in a nightmare seen the corpse of a naked man laid out on a cold slab in a windowless room that was very chilly, though the corpse was sweating. She confided this to me some years later in Doran's snug in Baggot Street.

The slab had been cold as ice when she touched it. The corpse was stiff as a stone statue but sweating and she could not look at the face. Two years later Joss gassed himself. It was the last in a series of bungled trade and business projects that had failed him; this was, to use a favourite term of Mumu's, the straw that broke the camel's back – something to do with sub-standard materials supplied in a building contract gone wrong. Entering the first finished house with gas connected up to the mains, Joss had lain down to cover himself with his overcoat, put his head into the oven and turned on the juice and drank it in. This was two years after Mumu's nightmare of the sweating corpse.

His eldest son, another Gustave, the spit and image of his tall father, had been led by a Civic Guard into the Dublin Morgue to identify his father. When he stepped into the cold windowless room he had entered my mother's nightmare; for there was the long dead man sweating on the slab; when they pulled back the sheet he recognised his father. Mumu's dream was out.

After the seven barren years she gave birth to the Dodo who was to inherit her hazel-green eyes, her withdrawn and secretive nature, her reserve, her morbidity (was it a morbid shyness? 'Mortified' was a habitual term with her; crushed with mortification, with embarrassment; in her expectation, people rarely if ever came up to scratch).

As to the Dodo, he is a complete puzzle to me, an enigma. Was it relevant that Mumu's brother Aubrey, whom I had never met, followed people about Dublin silently on rubber-soled shoes, unseen and unheard, overheard confidences and indiscretions, taking notes; that being the way of another secret nature? I knew nothing about the Boyd side of the family, apart from what I have inherited from my mother, her secretive side.

In the big heavy memorial album interleaved with tissues reposed the pencil sketches of houses in snow and harbour scenes, modelled on the nuns' coy ways with themes and slushy poems and elevated thoughts, all seen through a sort of mist or haze. Brinsley MacNamara, who had famously shared digs in Dublin with Mumu's brother, had inscribed one of his own poems that began:

> Her shoulders shone
> As though polished by the admiration
> Of a thousand eyes . . .

Dado wrote in the same slapdash hand that he had used at the Agricultural College where he had kept notes on sheep drench, yaws, foot-and-mouth disease, crop rotation and stock feed.

Old photos that Time had bleached out, turned sepia, were glued fast onto the thick pages and constituted a faithful record of parents and grandparents posed and arranged as stuffed figures in a waxworks; grave be-whiskered men of substance in stiff cravats that made their jaws protrude. Spats over polished brogues, paunches spanned by half-hunters secure in fob pocket, waistcoats stretched to bursting across the well-filled stomachs of stout paterfamilias. Some casting demented looks, fixed stares (from holding an awkward pose to accommodate the time-exposure) directed at the shutter; frantic-looking ladies in hobble skirts and unbecoming hats, holding fans, umbrellas, parasols in chubby hands, holding themselves rigid and upright as Victorian dolls, squinting.

When Ger Coyle touched a lighted match to the fuses of the long fireworks that hung on the railings in front of the house, they went whooshing up over Springfield to spread themselves out abundantly in the sky like luminous flowers spending themselves with matchless effulgence, for Mumu, enchanted, to cry out, 'Oh isn't it just lovely!'

As indeed it was.

– 18 –

Starlings Invade the Nursery

One fine morning in June Dado entered the nursery, barefoot in his pyjamas, the day being already well advanced and the sun well up and shining on the ceiling in thin layers through the reflected slats of the venetian blinds.

He had marched in to inform us that the sun was shining and it was high time to be up and about. Going up to the nearest green venetian blind he remarked, 'It's a bit stuffy in here, lads. I think I'll just throw open a window.' And with that he gave a sudden short pull to the cord that rolled it up and down, and as he did so his pyjama trousers slipped down below his knees. The rear exposure was sensational, something I had never conceived of, the hairy crevice and billy-goat's matted danglers and dingleberries, though he had the trousers up about his waist, held with one hand, in a trice. The blind rattled down again as he knotted the cords of his pyjamas, flannel pyjamas striped blue-and-white like a butcher's apron but faded and bleached with washing, with a great rent or gash in the groin.

Scarcely yet fully awake but alerted to strangeness and abominable effects, I averted my eyes from whatever fresh horrors might be in store as he turned to face me. He drew down the sash window and a stream of fresh air flowed in, and with it a single starling. He moved to the second blind and just as he jerked down the cord a second starling flew in via the open window, followed by a third and fourth. Others came in as the second window was thrown open; there were eight or nine stares flying about the room, knocking against pediment and in a flustered way against the frieze of bathers and donkeys and bathing huts towed into the sea, the repeated motif confusing them even more, though birds cannot see pictures; as if they could make their escape that way, out over the false sea.

They flew about the room, making no cry, just the rustle and flutter of agitated wings like silk rubbed briskly against silk. Until one of them found the second open window and flew out, presently followed by the others, to the great amusement of the Dote who was just waking from a deep sleep. Mumu, in a summer frock, now appeared with fresh orange juice, and was told of the miracle, the four-and-twenty blackbirds, which I made much of, attempting to block out what I had inadvertently been privy to, the forbidden fruit which in the years to come (and how soon) would be taboo, the fruit of the loins and the closed bedroom marked:

Strictly Private
Keep Out

and the shameful dossier marked 'Marital Secrets', all of that.

Dado glancing down and perceiving the great opening or tear or rent or gash at his groin and the vision of sun-scorched shanks, hurried from the nursery in order to change into his sunbathing outfit immediately. His slashed shorts were the cut-down trousers of a suit; with their fashionably frayed edges they were three decades before their time, when idleness and lolling on beaches became the rage. 'Batty' Higgins, like Albert Einstein, had tried to simplify his life as much as possible; in his case, by doing very little work. With stained rug and linseed oil he was off to the long grass of the orchard for some intense hours of 'getting a colour up'. His skin wouldn't take the sun and he first turned the colour of rhubarb, then the purple of peony rose or the wattles of an enraged turkey-cock. Being more or less permanently idle did not fret The Narrow Fellow in the Grass; for idleness suited him, with some light scuffling of gravel. No odder farmer refused to farm in Kildare. Was he a *Waster?* Certainly he had spendthrift ways, sucking the juice from an orange and throwing the rest away, discarding packets of cigarettes (Players No. 3) with a few cigarettes still intact, which had made secret smokers of myself and the Dote. It would have come as a great surprise to him that Kildare land values multiplied; the forfeited lands given away after the Battle of the Boyne would be worth £300 an acre in 1990. Dado was born on a small farm at Newtown-Forbes. Great-uncle Tom, the LA millionaire, had bought Melview and provided for them all. Dado was left it by his grandmother in 1921 and soon sold it to Margaret Newman and moved to Springfield, which he purchased for £5,500, a good price then. It would go for £25,000 less than thirty years later.

(If his animus against 'nancy-boys' was more pronounced than his animus against 'corner-boys', his animus against 'Jew-boys' was greater still. He had a strong streak of racial bigotry in his nature, and was not alone in this, in Ireland.)

– 19 –

Mistress Mumu & Old Jem Brady

Mumu, sucking a Zube, had many terms of disapproval for those whom she disliked; 'obnoxious' was one of them, an obnoxious one (a Yahoo) was beyond the Pale. 'Etiquette' was a strong term of approval; it conveyed sound morals, backbone. 'Gone West' meant (of an object) irrecoverable, lost irretrievably. If someone was 'all over you', it meant they were being smarmy and insincere; 'insincere' was the most damning of all terms in her high lexicon of disfavour.

'Few and far between' was one of her beady-eyed selective terms for weeding out worth from dross; few and far between (as far as she was concerned) were the rare ones, the hearts of gold. Essy Brady, the dumpy daughter of old Jem, had a heart of gold. When Mumu brought her flowers from Springfield garden, or apples, wasn't little Essy profuse in her thanks. Mumu, it must be admitted, liked nothing better than playing the gracious lady, and old Jem was most deferential in her presence, standing hat in hand before her.

Then one spring old Jem Brady began to go queer in the head. Dado told him that there was a colony of rats in the hayshed and old Jem said: 'Of all the birds in the air I do hate a rat,' which was to become a stock phrase in our family. As with the old standbys: 'Is that a dadger I see forninst me? Tell me this, do you ever open a book at all? If the blood isn't in first-class condition, out march our friends the pimples.'

He had a colony of rats in his own head and couldn't get rid of them. By summer he had become very strange, off somewhere on his own. Then, early one morning with heavy dew on Noonan's wheatfield, he resolved to do away with himself (the Guards traced his footsteps through the morning dew). He threw himself head-first into the quarry, said to be depthless, and sank like a stone through the lilies.

The Guards dragged the quarry hour after hour; on the point of giving up they decided on one last trawl before tea, and let down the grappling irons once more. This time, up came the drowned man clutching lily pads and weeds, his eyes and mouth open, filled with mud, his white hair muddied too, for he had left his hat on the bank.

The corpse was washed and set in a coffin on trestles at the rear of the church near the PP's (Fr Hickey) confessional. The Keegan boys told us that he was dressed in a monk's brown habit, with holy scapulars about his neck and his rosary beads entwined around his hands. He was buried in Dony-comper Cemetery with all the other Bradys and Coyles and Russels, and Mahoneys and Cotters and Aherns and Tyrrells and the rest.

'Fend for yourself,' Mumu said with a resigned look. 'Charity begins at home. Everyone for themselves.'

Mother Machree was far away.

Thereafter the blue light hovered over the surface of the quarry depths in wisps of early-morning fog as we tore past on our bikes for eight o'clock mass. The Keegan boys (our authority on faith and morals) said his soul was suffering in Purgatory and would be there for maybe thousands of years, doing penance for having taken his own life.

– 20 –
Because We Are Catholics

B ecause we are Roman Catholics we eat fish on Friday and attend Mass on Sunday and church holidays, whereas Protestants such as Helen O'Connor and old Doctor Charlie O'Connor and their English nephew Derek Chapman do not believe in the Virgin Mary or go to Mass.

They go to a different church with a different outside and an inside that I have never seen and a different spire and different religious ceremonies and a bell that sounds different to ours, and they do not bless themselves or dip their fingers in the holy water font when entering the church and they wear different clothes and speak in a different voice in a different part of their throat and the Protestant complexion is different from the Catholic which can be reddish like baloney or very pale like cheese or yellowish purple like a fungoid growth.

Old Mrs Henry and Bowsy Murray and Lizzy Bolger and Rita Phelan and Grogan the groom and the Darlingtons and the Keegans are all Catholics and go to Mass every Sunday. The Bowsy Murray blesses himself before he eats and when he is finished eating and when he hears the distant sound of the Angelus bell coming on the wind from a mile away in the village he stands up as if in church and draws out his rosary beads from his coat pocket and kisses the cross and begins murmuring his pater nosters with his lips moving and the walrus moustache too, with his eyes closed, and he ends with an arthritic dip of one stiff knee in the sketch of a genuflection and again kisses the cross on his beads but in an absentminded sort of way as though he and God were on familiar terms. And then he opens his eyes again, pocketing his beads, surprised to still find himself standing in Springfield kitchen with old Mrs Henry, as if he had been up in Heaven for a while and come down again.

Old Mrs Henry said that the Bowsy was a very devout man and that if e'er a man will go to Heaven, it will surely be the Bowsy, who attends evening devotions in summer and goes on retreats and is a member of the Men's Sodality.

But those who take their own lives cannot go to Heaven. So my uncle Joss is damned, as is old Jem Brady: a blue light now hovers over the quarry as confirmation that he is indeed damned, or so claim the Keegans.

Dado is both a practising and a non-practising Catholic at the same time; he practises his religion rather as he drives his car, absentmindedly, erratically.

The flowers on the Straffan high altar came as like as not from Springfield garden and as often as not Mumu prepared the floral arrangements. It was her way of attending Mass, *in absentia*, on Saturday when nobody was about.

Calm and impersonal in a dream of sanctity the priest was saying mass and turning back the heavy pages of the Bible and joining his hands and genuflecting and murmuring the Latin.

Dado preferred to arrive late and take his place halfway up the choir-loft stairs with the other malingerers, sending us ahead as his representatives. He kept a display handkerchief stiff as a starched serviette in his breast pocket and another in his cuff, which was removed to brush off the wooden step and spread to kneel on, on one knee, hiking up his trousers and putting his face into the palm of his hand in a gesture of symbolic abjectness (Emperor Charles V humbled in the snow), closing his eyes until the little joined sanctus bells rang forth to announce the consecration over. The priest's distant mumbled Latin was virtually inaudible and the sermon listened to with half an ear.

Thus Dado was both attending and not attending, half-present and half-absent, both damned and saved. Although it was probably the fears of eternal damnation rather than the notion of setting us a good example that drove him there in the first place. It was a way of getting up an appetite for lunch.

The sternness of duty did not appeal to him; it was a Proddy virtue unknown to Catholics. It seemed to me that the polychrome Christ in the Stations of the Cross that lined the nave rather resembled the Dodo's figure of Robinson Crusoe baked brown by the sun at Mas-a-tierra (he had come off it 'scarcely articulate', the prototype of all castaways). Christ had lost one leg (or was it one arm?) at the scourging. I saw that as true duty performed well: the scourging heathen laying it on, grunting; the swooning Saviour taking it, biting his lips. Dado, sorry to relate, was a pastmaster at limp performances of duty. He admired bravery and courage in mettlesome men (Uncle Jack riding the Shannon waves in the *Whoopee,* throttle fully open, Major Graham jumping into the Liffey and not able to swim a stroke), because it was something he was deficient in himself. He was a born avoider of responsibility.

He was not the sort of man that could be challenged to a duel; for he would have denied any intention to insult. He could not defend his honour because he had none to defend. For would a true-born gentleman, chivalrous and brave, defend himself with a spade against an opponent squaring up for a gentlemanly bout of fisticuffs, even if footless with the drink? (In later times, with Springfield sublet, subtenant Ball had attacked him while scuffling the front yard.) When he played me at draughts, wrong moves could be taken back.

'I didn't mean that. Take that one back.' Unpalatable reality had somehow to be circumvented.

– 21 –

The Bad Smell

Dado could be very dismissive ('cutting' was Mumu's word) and caustic in his references to 'that Jew-boy Jack Ellis', disparaging him in company, even though Jack Ellis had sold him a suite of furniture at discount and I suspect lent him money when American funds were slow to arrive. Because that good-hearted man, who happened to be a Jew, helped him when help was needed, Dado had it in for him.

When we heard the priest murmuring the *Laus tibi Christi* we knew that the Mass was ending; soon he would be warning us of the wicked spirits who 'wander through the world for the ruin of souls', and it was time for us to descend the choir-loft stairs and join Dado on the gravel, putting on his cap and motoring gloves and saying, 'Off home with us now.' The car was parked nearby, all the spoke wheels thoroughly baptised by local dogs, who had it in for the Overland.

Dado donated generously at the collection with a wad of folding stuff dropped into the collection plate at High Mass after the sermon in St Patrick's Church. He did not care to make his Easter Duty locally, because the priests 'knew too damn much' about him already; so he made a general confession maybe once a year in the Carmelite Church of St Teresa in Clarendon Street in Dublin, into the accommodating ear of a Carmelite monk who didn't know him from Adam, behind brown drapes. We sat in the hushed church, with just a handful of the faithful praying by the high altar or doing the Stations, and all the votive candles burning on the stand for all the sins confessed, and we could hear the murmur of the monk shriving Dado and the sound of a harp in Johnston's Court. And then Dado came out of the confession box and went up near the altar to say his penance and then we all went out into Grafton Street and he handed us a half-crown each for presents. After a word with the commissionaire Mr Shakespear outside the Grafton Picture House, he told us to wait on the bench in the foyer and he went round the corner for a ball of malt at the Sign of the Zodiac. And when we had waited maybe an hour an unfrocked clergyman with rotten teeth came in and sat between us and said rotten things in a low but penetrating voice, like a rat whispering dirty which we didn't catch and wouldn't have understood had we caught. Presently he got to his feet and shambled out. As a dog will leave its doggy smell behind in chair or kennel so he left his sinful smell behind. A bad smell.

We sit there quiet as mice near the ticket office, a narrow wooden cabin with a small glass window, and talk in whispers. *A Hundred Men and a Girl* is showing with Deanna Durbin and Adolphe Menjou. Mr Shakespear walks up and down and controls the queues, balcony on one side, stalls on the other. One memorable day we saw *The Wizard of Oz* at the Grafton Picture House and then most of *The Thief of Bagdad* (with Conrad Veidt and Sabu) at the Capital, all complimentary tickets. Harris's Music Shop is opposite the Grafton, a dim neon-blue grotto with Hohner mouthorgans laid out on display under glass and a Jewish assistant (who is perhaps the owner), suave and sinister as Conrad Veidt himself.

The blue convalescent neon light of the music shop we dared not enter unaccompanied is repeated in Jack Ellis's underground toilets, where the urinals smell of hospital, and pedestrians can be seen in shadowy form, passing over head on the thick opaque glass. But that is not all. 'Soon It Will Be Their Turn' hangs there between the Gents and the Ladies. What do they want of me, this speechless company standing huddled together, wringing wormy-veined hands and staring out at me with their afflicted eyes? Behind them immense clouds rear up. Is it a cyclone or duststorm on the way? A bunch of dirt-farmers with no time to read or educate themselves, doomed to poverty. Are they Mormons or Dukebors or Okies? They stand silent in the depthless pearl-grey atmosphere of oncoming afternoon, mistrustfully eyeing me.

One of Dado's great heroes was the boxer Jack Doyle, who later in his career became the all-in wrestler passing himself off as 'The Gorgeous Gael'. Cartoonist Tom Webster had much fun at his expense, dubbing him 'The Horizontal Heavyweight', because of the number of times he was knocked out in the ring.

It wasn't because he was knocked out so much that made him a hero in Dado's eyes, but because he had married Movita, herself a knockout and stunner who had been in *Mutiny on the Bounty* with Charles Laughton and Clark Gable. Dado was very impressionable where good-looking women were concerned, particularly when associated with wealth, or what looked like wealth. Dado was a puritan affecting to be a swinger, which made him a hypocrite as well. The famous Doyles appeared together at the Theatre Royal with the Royalettes in *Something in the Air*.

Some years later in London, from the upper deck of a double-decker bus bound for Shepherds Bush, I would see the Doyles below me on the footpath outside Mooney's pub at Notting Hill Gate. The Gorgeous Gael now wore a leather eye-patch like Peg-Leg Pete. He had a lowly job as bouncer in Mooney's. Thus had the mighty fallen.

– 22 –

Flotsam

Nothing done by Nurse O'Reilly in dusting and airing the bedroom or bed-making and sheet-changes or removal of chamberpots or replacing of jaded flowers or general freshening up could ever quite dispel the stuffy sickroom smells that still clung to pediment and blinds and skirting-board and eiderdown and puffed up pillows, which smelling salts and 777 sprinkled on the clean sheets or the regular Hoovering of threadbare carpet had attempted to banish without success.

The big white chamberpot had been removed and in its place came a sort of portable lav shaped like a footstool in inlaid mahogany which concealed the invalid's potty behind an angled trapdoor and could be closed up when not in use or emptied when full, which now made its appearance with a dreadfully complacent air of permanency at the foot of the bed. The invalid's potty removed from its container and draped with a hand-towel would join Dado's chamber from the middle room where he slept, a chamber generally a third full of startling orange pee, at the head of the stairs, and both pots in due course carted off, emptied and washed in readiness for new stinks.

Mumu's periodic absence in the bath offered an opportunity to freshen up the bedroom. Mumu in kimono and slippers made great ceremony and to-do of an elaborate long immersion in bath salts and foam, after the water had been heated up, and recharged in mid-session with boiling water carried up by Lizzy and taken by Nurse O'Reilly and tipped in after much, 'Are you ready now, Mrs Higgins?' and calling out and banging of doors and sounds of running feet. During which time the fresh garden flowers were arranged and the venetian blinds drawn up tight as a drum and the sash windows thrown open top and bottom, and all neat as ninepence against the reappearance of the invalid, scented and pomaded, declaring herself to be a 'new woman', to climb into bed in her dressing-gown and turn her face to the wall, the blinds having been drawn again and Nurse O'Reilly having removed herself, backing out, closing the door silently, as upon a dead person.

As elsewhere alongside the other beds an upended apple-crate stood beside the high double bed reared up on its castors where Mumu slept alone now, Dado having been relegated to the small middle room above the front porch, facing out to the distant hills and the Hellfire Club on the summit.

The apple-crate did service as a narrow bedside table with cretonne tacked on and two shelves turned inward to carry night accessories and invalid stuff required; bromides, Milk of Magnesia, Milton antiseptic, Eno's Fruit Salts, Macleans, a comb, a brush with brown hair stuck to it (it was 'coming out in fistfuls'), a glass of water, a half-peeled orange, polar bear mints and Vaseline, hair-slides, lipstick, nail file and buffer, and a fat black novel (its jacket removed) glistening like a slug, a bookmark protruding midway through.

I picked up a dog-eared page at random and read with a creepy reawakening of the flesh – a forbidden excitement returning (as immersed stark naked in the cattle-trough I fornicated with its mossy side, harkening to the souse of the sea) – for just then and there in that place (a German hotel) a man (who was perhaps a soldier on leave or a sailor off a boat) overheard a couple enter the room next to his and begin to undress. The man listened and heard the soldier presently say that all he wanted was a big bun, to which the woman responded with a slap and a laugh, saying that she thought she could supply that all right, and after a while 'crowed with pleasure' at whatever the fellow was doing to her, engorged in the woman or vice versa.

It was a novel entitled *Flotsam*, translated from the German, one of the banned books supplied by Helen O'Connor. With blazing face I threw the novel down and fled from the bedroom as if the jaws of Hell had opened wide, and some of Satan's hellish cohorts were in full cry after me.

(A coal fire stacked with damp slack was roaring up the chimney and black tobacco fumes rising upward clung to the ceiling of the living room where Fatty Warnants sprawled in one of the squat leather armchairs (sold at discount by Jack the 'Jew-boy' Ellis of the Grafton Picture House in Dublin), wedged in by his own grossness, puffing on a fat cigar; opposite him sat Joss, of whom one could see nothing behind the smokescreen but immense leather gaiters stretched straight out before him in highly polished boots; and the pair of them gargling and gulping and snorting away in Flemish.

So that's what it was to be adult; to smoke like a chimney and stick out your great boots and gaiters and exchange opinions in an incomprehensible tongue. I thought of trenches and dug-outs and Belgian troops mustering on a station platform, awaiting a train that would carry them on leave to their pleasures or to the Front to their deaths, for the entire Belgian Army had been virtually wiped out on the first day of battle. So I turned the heavy pages of the great black album.)

A press of people in winter clothes blocked the main entrance to the GPO under the pillars. Near the bridge sat bloated bronze ladies with sleepy eyes, their nipples punctured with bullet holes from the time of the Troubles. County people were hurrying for the last bus that left from Arran Quay, their children sucking ice cream cones and crying. The last bus departed in daylight during summer, after which no more buses ran, for the 'Emergency' left everything in short supply. Dado brought home strange brands of cigarettes – Passing Clouds and Capstan and Balkan Sobranie – kept for him by Dermot Morris his tobacconist who was also his solicitor; as well as Craven A and Gold Flake and Player's No. 3 from Miss Nairn at the Grafton Picture House, in exchange for apples and plums from Springfield. The Dote and I were given pocket money for sketchbooks and Windsor & Newton watercolour paints and Dado bought us two Hopalong Cassidy novels from Combridges. Sitting with his back to the balusters of O'Connell Bridge, a legless beggarman played 'The Isle of Capri' – my tune – on his harmonica, vamping. We had saved up to buy new mouthorgans at Harris's Music Shop and Dado had embarrassed us by talking of crops and the weather like a true-born countryman to the posh Jewish salesman. For Dado spoke to all men as if they too were farmers; as he spoke in a special knowing way to all women and embarrassed us again before Miss Nairn in the Grafton café by asking what was there to eat, for the lads; and when Miss Nairn had replied, 'We have nice ham,' Dado had said, very well then, we would all have the nice ham.

On the Liffey embankment a rebel hand had painted in white capital letters that dribbled 'DOWN WITH THE IRISH RULING CLASS, LACKEYS & GOMBEENS OF ENGLISH IMPERIALISM!'

The neon Bovril sign still bled all over College Green.

Gulls flew over the bridge, letting loose their plaintively sad gull-cry *Woe! Woe!!* in a stink of diarrhoea.

It was Spring as we set off for home again with the two new Clarence E. Mulford's in our bags, wrapped up by John Sibley himself, and were we not happy as the day is long? Oh that Mesquite Jenkins, that sprinting and deadly nakedness!

Maria Montez's eyes had flashed dangerously; she wore a transparent dress and her dander was up. Sabu had curly lips and rode on an elephant. A trapdoor opened. Below, sewers, rats, nameless filth, where a hideous fate awaits. Streets are obscured in ground-fog and an old Italian plays a violin. Two fellows listen, one says, 'Luigi has found it!' Luigi is blind. I try not to cry but feel sick in my stomach (the ice-cream in Woolworths, the hair stiffener at Maison Prost, the smells of the city) as melancholy overwhelms me.

'Any excuse for swigging in bars,' Mumu said.

She refers scathingly to 'lounge-bar lizards', and I see Dado drinking whiskey with a curious scaly creature who wears a midnight-blue suit, the trousers with razor-sharp creases, black silk socks and black patent-leather shoes that you could see yourself in. They sip some green concoction from long-stemmed glasses, sitting with legs crossed on tall bar-stools in the Royal Hibernian Hotel. The LBL is smoking a cigarette in a long amber holder while eyeing my father through the smoke with slitty dark eyes and I wonder can it be the 'Jew-boy' from Harris's Music Shop.

I loathed my skinny feet, detested the sandals worn out of shape, drank chilled wellwater from the ring-pump like a cowboy, cupped hands dipped as a bowl, a dipper. I saw the Overland leaving the front yard, going down the back avenue. A courting couple had come a short way up the front avenue to disappear into the plantation. I thought to tell Grogan but remembered that I was not a sneak, not one to snitch.

Old Mrs Henry (who is not my friend) spreads my favourite homemade blackcurrant jam on hot soda bread and silently offers it to me, and I as silently refuse it. I write on the drawing wall: 'The man was smoking on the beach.' I draw him smoking. Then I wrote: 'The sun comes up with colours and the man wakes up.'

I asked Mumu at table what 'flotsam' meant? Was it like loathsome? Well not quite, she said, and fiddled with her napkin. What was it then? Mumu said it was a mess, something spilled out, sort of floating away, that sort of thing.

But this made it no clearer to me.

'Why do you ask? Have you been reading it?'

'Some of it,' I admitted.

Why did the soldier ask the strange woman for a fat bun? did he not get enough to eat in the barracks? Was it because he was hungry? Was that it?? These were questions I could not put to Mumu.

Mumu had gone very red and said it was quite unsuitable reading for a chissler and would I please stop reading her books. It wasn't appropriate, she said in a frosty way that made it plain to me that the subject of 'flotsam' was closed.

The hungry soldier had said to the unseen woman: 'All I require is a big fat bum.' The words lit up in neon lights, tantalising, riveting, fishy.

The unseen woman responded, 'I think I can supply that all right,' and had 'crowed with laughter'.

– 23 –

The Bracing Air of Sodom

Aeterna Non Caduca

Sunday was visiting day at CWC and the cars of the doting parents began to converge soon after lunch. Castle servants were sent out into the playing fields to inform the Line Prefect of a call for Higgins. It was on formal occasions like these that the more theatrical of the Jays came into their own.

The flamboyant became more flamboyant, the eccentric more eccentric (hands folded into the wings of the soutane, a fixed smile on the pale face), the twittery ones became more twittery, the flaky ones flakier, the ingratiating ones more ingratiating, the serious ones more serious, the dancy ones more dancy, as gnu astray amid a herd of exotic gazelle, so 'The Dog' McGlade and 'The Frog' McCarron and 'Lugs' Hurley and 'The Razz' O'Byrne strolled amid the school blazers and the frocks and high heels and demi-veils and the serious pipe-smoking fathers of lawyers and barristers and architects to be; with some of the lay teachers such as 'Horny' Ward (Physics & Science) and Mr Cullen (History & Geography) dressed in hairy tweeds, with 'The Dandy' (the handsome French teacher, reputed to have 'laid' Nurse Redmond behind the bicycle shed) or 'Bats' Brannigan the Arts Master in paper-bag brown overalls such as worn by storeman or car-park attendant – all these exotic creatures were disembarking from the Ark.

There would be the three Line Prefects, the Spiritual Father, Father Minister and the Rector himself, perambulating through the Pleasure Grounds and by the First XI pavilion or taking tea in the castle with the ever-loving mothers; the mothers and sisters in their finery lending a welcome unfamiliar feminine touch to the proceedings of an institution resolutely male as Artane or Mountjoy. This casual parade of prosperity and wealth, with Bentleys and Overlands and Rileys and Buicks parked bumper to bumper on the driveway before the castle where the CWC flag flew, was a reassuring sight for all concerned, to be sure, there by the Gollimockey stream.

The visiting hours were as ritualised as the older forms of Jesuit punishment dating back to the Inquisition and torture and execution at the garrotte in a public square. Or the victim put to the question in private torture apartments and brought forth to be executed in public with a great show of pomp and circumstance to drum taps and hooded processions in the days of the *autos da fé* in Murcia, Oviedo, Sevilla, Cartagena or Cadiz. For they (the Jesuit Fathers) 'had not got where they were by hiding their lights under a bush,' Dado said with a dismissive sniff.

The penal docket issued in class was in Latin, the number of pandies (usually four to six on alternative hand) specified by the Jesuit Father or lay teacher, folded and handed to the offender who took it to the office of one of three Line Prefects situated far apart in different quarters, each of them known by reputation for varying degrees of leniency or severity, gentleness or sadism.

The procedure was that you knocked on the door and were called in, presented the docket, watched the pandy bat (some were slim, some fat) being removed from a drawer or inside the soutane. You took your punishment on either hand, thanked the priest and withdrew. Some pandied heavily, breathing hard; others lightly, going through a formality. In winter you warmed your hands on the radiators. There was no horseplay.

The pandy bat was a sort of *sjambok* slick as a spatula that imparted sudden deadening pain, felt in the head as in either hand, turn and turn about, pain travelling through the nervous system.

In order to reach the Line Prefect known for soft punishment beyond the baths and the whirlpools of Charybdis it was necessary to pass the lair of

Scylla, namely, the Prefect of Studies, a notorious flogger of boys whose door was always threateningly wide open and himself inside on the q.v. for fellows tiptoeing by with punishment dockets in their hands, holding their breaths. You were likely to be called in and punished on the spot.

Stout Tom (he of the florid complexion) roamed the corridors to punish any boys found outside classrooms, waiting in a sort of intermediary zone between punishments not yet formulated or for the master within to cool off and summon the culprit back in. If caught by the Prefect of Studies, your fate was decided there and then; Father Tom decided what was the apposite punishment and began laying in without a word spoken. Those habitually sent out to cool their heels outside a classroom were dealt with in the appropriate way – the choleric Prefect of Studies rising on his toes when pandying, really laying into it. Woe betide you if he found you on one of his bad days. His choleric nature was to get the better of him in the end; watching CWC defeat Belvedere in the Senior School's Cup proved too much for his ticker and he keeled over at Donnybrook and was dead before the ambulance arrived. I was in the infirmary when the news came.

The bracing climate of the institute of higher learning that was the great Jesuit monolith CWC set down on the plains of Kildare – where the wind seldom abated but was always busily blowing around the old turreted castle of the Wogan-Brownes – plus the more or less constant supervision that was *de rigueur* with the Jesuit Fathers (some of whom now teaching had after all been model boys themselves and must have had some inkling of what might be going on there under their noses) had produced a simmeringly overwrought tumid atmosphere that was a cross between racing-stable and bordello, in the tumult of indoctrination and inter-disciplinary pursuits as laid down by the blessed Ignatius Loyola.

But hormones were hormones, that was not to be gainsaid, and boys would be boys, more's the pity, and required sharp watching all the time.

After two years of Killashee and the neurotic nuns, we had gone there at reduced fees, the Dote and I; from 1942 to 1946 I passed painfully through successive grades of Grammar, Syntax, Poetry and Rhetoric, having arrived too late (too old) for Rudiments; enduring a boredom that was acute.

CWC: Hothouse of Frustrated Desires.

The tall handsome Higher Line tack (Prefect-in-the-making) Phillipa lusted after Mitch of the Lower Line, who pined in turn for Sonny the exquisite soprano in the Third Line who sang a heartrending *Veni Creator* from the choir loft at Benediction.

To avoid detection and ridicule, the Black Sow (who was much admired) lay supine on the floor of a deserted classroom (it was 2nd Syntax, where I had often suffered) during all-out after breakfast, to practise on her French horn; emitting vulgar fortissimo farts and what sounded like the doleful mooing of cattle *en route* to the abattoir.

CWC on its lush acreage of good arable land was divided, as was ancient Gaul, into three parts, in an ascending scale of learning: viz., the Third Line for ages 12–14, the Lower Line for ages 14–16, and Higher Line for ages 16 to 18 or 19; each Line or House taking in around a hundred Catholic boys.

Myths and legends, as in prison, were rife. Was it the bracing climate, hormonal eruptions, the temptations of the flesh or the strictness of the Jesuit regimen – the niceness of an overt jurisdiction which afforded every freedom, and none at all? We were in permanent distress in a cage of our own devising.

The Dodo (OC 1931–37) was still remembered! He too had become part of a legend. Like 'Spike' O'Donnell (thought to be murderous in his ungovernable rages), the 'Baa' Keegan and the indomitable Fahy, small but fierce, who when crossed in love fought a hated rival in a duel with hatchets behind the Lower Line pavilion, all for the love of a Sow. Fahy was fierce as Finn MacCool, so the legend ran, with his dander up.

It was said of the Dodo that the subjects that failed to interest him – Irish, Mathematics and Science – he refused to study. And special rules had to be made for him; he was exempted from all rough games and punishment; and this, mark you, in an institution that believed in both – games in the bracing cold to curb the rebellious young Adam; frequent punishment to curb the wills of demons – working on the assumption that a good beating never harmed any boy, always a debatable point when dealing with out-and-out neurotics.

Under immediate threat, the docket in his hand specifying the punishment to be administered by a Line Prefect far away on duty, the Dodo had fainted.

Exposed to the permanently drenched and windswept playing fields he had promptly caught pneumonia; when the echoing corridors resounded to the busy pandy bat at work (Father Tom with a scowl on his face was doing the rounds) the Dodo would be safely tucked up in bed in the infirmary, a coal fire burning in the grate and matron on her way with Horlicks and buttered biscuits.

Fearfully I crouched at stool like a madman in Katanga awaiting revelation, for the jax roof to be removed and God speak to me direct! On the inner door of my box a wit had written in pencil:' 'A man without a woman is like a fish without a bicycle,' and I thought of the wooden cleats of rugger boots that resounded like drum taps on the parquet floor of the changing room (or a chorus girl's high heels) when Dog's Hole ran out for play-up in scandalously brief shorts (her daringly raised skirt): the earthy stains of contact sport suggested venery.

A thick gob of semen the size of a sheep's eye was stuck fast to the door; it began to slide downward as I watched. A naked male figure with arms outflung and widespread legs showed off the balls of a stallion and a careful hand had pencilled below: TB AMAT BF and I guessed who they were, lurking in the darkness.

The love-notes arrived by circuitous routes and in curious forms in the long term when resistance was low and whole classes dreamed of the bared thighs of boys who had become girls overnight, the sows. (There were two in 2nd Grammar.) The girl was the good-looking boy made up in the December play who had become a real boy in the dormitory again; an easy lay, a good ride. Shower-nights were electric with promise. The short towels were tulle skirts thrown over the shower stall; the gush of steam suggestive of sauna and Roman orgy. Cold fumbles in the scrum were reenacted by gingery Doorley against the tittery Black Sow under her towel as she ran for bed, when the Line Prefect's back was turned, more interested in young McLoughlin who had strained a thigh at play-up and needed massage.

Looking out of the Lower Line library one dreary afternoon when shop had closed and rain had made play-up impossible, whom did I espy but the same pretty Dog's Hole followed by the Black Sow (two much desired blondes who apparently fancied each other) emerging from the storeroom opposite where pingpong tables were stacked, where they had been comparing vaccination marks.

Certain Lower Line tacks had dry-bangs (a ride without the trousers removed) with passing Third Line sows pulled into the deserted library while the chapel filled for evening devotions. The two lines moved slowly by either wall, coming from the Third Line quarters, and spies were out to watch who was coming.

When full the school chapel held three hundred or more and the Higher Line Prefect knelt behind on a small rostrum, leading the prayers. The Stations of the Cross ended with a prayer for peace.

The persistent drill of prayer combined with the iconography of bared flesh and bleeding wounds, the insistence on abstinence and suffering, had become an aphrodisiac itself; the long hours spent in religious devotions from an early call (6.50 a.m.) to late prayers, sapped resistance, patience, will-power, sapped us. Catching tantalising glimpses of sows and the favoured ones secretly desired and ignorant of such adoration, wedged between rows in chapel, now kneeling, now standing, now singing, now silent, now devout, now half smiling, now definitely tartish (notes were being passed) or thought-fully picking her nose, did nothing to help; nor did the sudden vision at study, six rows in front, of Holland perched whorishly back from the seat of her desk, the Lady on the Swing.

Third Liners with high unbroken voices were lusted after by lusty Lower Liners with their contraltos and tenors, who were in turn lusted after by mature Higher Liners with their baritones and basses announcing in no uncertain manner that soon they would be out in the world and free to impregnate real girls if they so wished.

All joined together to sing 'Daily, Daily, Sing to Mary', and Paddy Court-ney and Bot O'Toole (who was English) were smirking behind their West-minster Hymnals at Pierre Daly, the tall prefect standing in the front row of the Higher Line pews. For his ears alone they sang loud and lewd 'Daly, Daly, sing to Mary!' watching the quiet wing threequarter with the long spidery legs who was so hard to bring down in a tackle. Was Mary one of the laundry slovens who did the beds, finding a note under Pierre's pillow ('I'd love to ride you'), signed Pierre Daly? They might just as well have sung 'Eskimo Nell' or 'Roll Me Over in the Clover', they sang with such gusto and *élan*.

The cubicles in the square were often defaced with drawings and graffiti, to be whitewashed away by lavatory attendants who were rarely seen, to be defaced again, for it was natural (at Declamation Father Kelly declared that it happened in Pompeii).

Strands of barbed wire stretched above the high wall as if we were indeed in prison, though half the Higher Line had once done a bunk under it and decamped to the Liffey in preference to a dull debate held in the gym.

Entwined initials and hearts oozing blood and pierced by daggers were whitewashed out over and over again, as were coded solicitings in chalk and pencil. Many generations of adolescent youths had ejaculated and slashed against these slates. The college was old, but those Graeco-Roman practices were still older.

To slash (to piss), to take a box (to crap), to spoon (to court), to sow (to love), to sigh, to sin-o; it was nature, as was tossing off, pulling one's wire, getting one's hole, going out with, getting a horn, getting into; and the graffiti, the epistolary flourishes, but the capricious synonyms adopted to lull suspicions and conceal whatever flutterings and hankerings might be festering in the breasts of some three hundred adolescent boys over a period of five years in the long ferment endured and suffered through three months of isolation in the long term in the depths of County Kildare away from the refreshing if disturbing company of any females and obliged to make do with these pseudo-girls with names like 'Titch'. It was the little language of lovers, qua Swift's *Journal to Stella*. All was temptation in flowery dells, in term-time, as in a penitentiary.

Meanwhile one day in the stinking gym, didn't Handlebars Hastings go and treat us to a regular tirade of abuse, twirling his waxed moustache and pacing up and down as if on the parade ground. His grown son helped laggards over the wooden horse and attempted to pacify the old man, an ex-British Army drill sergeant shell-shocked and irascible. He went for a lad called Billy Roche. Roche complained to the Rector and a token apology was offered: he had been thinking of a different Roche altogether.

Redhead McGivern inscribed Fairy Moore's name (Michael) in lovingly elaborate Gothic script on the fly leaf of Fairy's missal and surreptitiously passed it back as the Third Liners filed past the Lower Line tables in the refectory under the wooden rostrum where Father Minister (it was little Micky Kelly) presided over the tables with a twinkle in his eye that could be seen at the far end of the refectory.

The Dodo had opened the batting for the CWC XI. Once dug in – and his remorseless strategy was one long patient process of digging in – he was extremely difficult to remove, scoring nothing but staying on and on, blunting any attack, until all the other batsmen had departed and only the Dodo remained, walking in slowly, carrying his bat through a whole innings.

He became such a fixture at the crease that the attack wavered before such obduracy and gave way, no bowler was able to remove him. But he refused to score runs, take chances, and partners were run out halfway down the pitch. The Dodo refused to budge, raising a batting glove, Wait! No run, partner!

He played a ghastly game, making up his own rules, slowing it down to a dreamlike pace; collar about his chin, white CWC cap down over his nose, glaring at the bowler as if through a visor in a suit of armour. Jabbing and poking, levelling the crease about him with the tip of his bat, picking up straws, rearranging pads and gloves, studying the field placements, leaving his crease as the bowler ran in – Wait! a mote in the eye? The umpire (Harrison of Notts, the school coach) eventually gave him out in order to see the last of him. It was not a joyful performance.

'Iggings,' Harrison marvelled, scratching his head, 'blimey wot a blightah!'

Fidgeting and scraping at the crease, 'gardening', ever and anon taking fresh guard, continuously adjusting his batting-gloves, the peak of the white cap, the shirt collar up about the bridge of the aquiline nose; surreptitiously fixing his protective box, the Dodo stood his ground, implacable. With sly Ranjilike leg-glances and glides he wore down the attack, tickling it into submission long before stumps were drawn. An explorer poring over a map of unknown terrain would have hardly applied himself so assiduously, so tenaciously, 'coldly heroic'.

He kept judicious records of the time spent at the crease, in default of scoring runs, holding up the game until the opposition capitulated, noting questionable or 'wrong' decisions; for 'Wrong decision' appeared often in these private Wisdens of his. Crouched at the edge of the white mark, at the edge of the dream, after taking a guard of middle-and-leg, tapping the white line with the tip of his bat as the bowler ran in to deliver a bouncer.

The fast delivery sang past his ear.

Then the affronted stare, the careful re-examination of the field placing, the resumption of preliminary tactics of preparation, the fiddling, the digging in, the tap-tap and nervous back-lift of bat, bracing himself visibly for the next delivery, for all this would go down in the book: 'Received two bouncers'.

When finally removed by some phenomenal 'shooter' he waddled very slowly back to the pavilion, unpeeling his batting-gloves as he went, ignoring the incoming batsman for whom he had no word of advice, approaching the silent crowd as though a wrong had been done him and for whom applause was somehow superfluous.

D. J. B. Higgins c. Hayden-Guest, b. Blood-Smith . . . 4 was set down in the score card. The Dodo, having removed pads and protective box, donned his First XI purple blazer and cravat, washed his face and hands, combed his hair, and sauntered into the score-box to gaze down sadly at the action on the pitch below, Blood Smith high-stepping into his next torturous delivery.

When questioned about his dismissal he would open his hands, raising a 'quizzical' eyebrow, then the hands together again in a limp silent gesture more expressive than words, a mime that can only be described as liturgical. Words failed him; he had run out of patience.

His strategies for survival were all negative.

He had fainted away when about to receive pandies – the leaded leather disciplinary strap – and thereafter was excused punishment by Father Minister and wrote lines instead, as though he were an English schoolboy – a unique dispensation in CWC. He spent much time indisposed in the infirmary, well muffled up, just his nose showing. A model pupil in most respects, he was quick to pick up a virus. No one bullied him; he did not put on the gloves in the gym or wrestle on the mat, he was beyond all that, it was not his field.

One Sunday at visiting time Dado arrived in the Overland well stocked with food for our hamper and we walked in the Pleasure Grounds with the Razz O'Byrne. As behoved an absent-minded genius – for he was a Greek classical scholar of distinction – the Razz's black soutane was liberally smeared with chalk-marks where he had wiped his hands when grappling with difficult Greek on the blackboard. The oily eyes of a bullock peered from behind his small bifocals. He clasped his hands behind his back, folding the wings of the soutane and walked along wrapped in thought. Other Jesuit Fathers walked there by rhododendrons just coming into bloom, in the company of parents whose boys were under their care. Our parents had known the O'Byrnes in Longford and had the utmost respect for the Razz who had famously knocked the stuffing out of an anti-Christ Spanish Nationalist when he cursed him and spat on his cassock. (The Razz had been a novice in Salamanca, a *novillero* in the great Bullring in the Sky.) Whereupon the Razz (so ran the CWC legend) had torn off his dog-collar, spat on his hands, squared up to the impertinent anti-Christ, spat on the ground at his feet, and said, 'Nobody spits on me! Come on, you pup, you're up against Gerry O'Byrne!' and laid the fellow out with an almighty haymaker in the breadbasket.

One Missionary Night the Razz had shown his long-promised footage of the Spanish Civil War in a small room behind the gym, packed for the occasion. A rooster crowed silently and flapped its wings and then soldiers in forage-caps were brandishing rifles and stumbling up a hill, giving the clenched-fist salute, and the great stone cross was slowly falling from a church dome in slow motion and a long line of refugees with their children and possessions were making their way along an endless road and fingers were pointing to a clear sky out of which the bombers would come in formation and in Madrid on a balcony draped in flags General Franco was haranguing a silently cheering crowd below.

The Razz had been on the side of Franco, because Franco was against the Reds and so must be on the side of God (and the Pope agreed). He had confidently identified a Republican corpse on the battlefield, a close-up of the dead face covered in flies, projected on the sheet, as a mountain range near

Malaga.

Father Gerry O'Byrne, SJ, was a scream.

Dado spoke to him familiarly as though to an old friend who had shown up again. The Razz spoke of atrocities in Spain, the violation of nuns and the torture and murder of priests by those forces on the side of Satan.

He said he had no objection in the wide world to CWC playing cricket matches against Protestant, Presbyterian, Methodist or even Masonic schools, but disapproved of the game on principle. 'It's a garrison game, Batty – an English fancy, and we should have nothing to do with it. We have our own games.'

Here spoke the hurler on the ditch.

Dado must understand, the Razz urged with some warmth, clutching his arm, that 'all those fellows with double-barrel names' (Gifford-Clark, opener; Blood-Smith, medium-pace offbreaks) were nothing but the illegitimate off-spring of titled English families who had discarded them and sent them over to Ireland to be brought up as Masons and Methodists. 'You had only to look at those fellows to know that.'

Dado nodded his head sagely, being as big a bigot as the Razz himself.

That very evening we had a treat in store.

The Dog McGlade was giving the spiff! When the Dog climbed into the pulpit he was frequently carried away by his own rhetoric; and the longer the sermon the shorter the study time. Dado said that he would certainly stay to hear the Dog; he would sit in the back of the chapel where he would not be noticed. Anew McMaster in his prime could scarcely hold a candle to the Dog McGlade at sermon time!

The sacristy door swung open and out came two gorgeous altar boys followed by the Dog scowling down at his boots. Dipping one knee and pressing it down with both hands he genuflected as one long-accustomed to genuflecting, moved to the pulpit, adjusting his surplice, black highly polished boots visible beneath the cassock. Firmly grasping the white marble balustrade he pulled himself up Father Mappelwise; the noble head presently appeared over the lectern. He laid aside his missal, set out his notes, unstrapped and discarded his wristwatch (a flurry of excitement here, time was to be of no consequence), hoicked up his surplice, cleared his throat and prepared to launch himself like a high-diver into yet another of his justly famous Sea Sermons. For the Dog was obsessed with the sea.

Combers were surging onwards towards a distant shore, pounding the boulders to smithereens where gulls were tossed by the wind (the Dog was off!), seacoasts threatened by a storm, mariners imperilled by raging billows, the valiant helmsman notwithstanding. The long watches, wind-shifts, swelling surges, torn sheets, tidal stinks at moonrise (no heaving embonpoint, for women never appeared during the ecstatic course of these spiffs; they knew their place and remained indoors out of sight), and the packed chapel shuddered to its foundations, to the very rafters, to the fine oaken beams, to the Evie Hone stained-glass windows above the high altar; observed by half-naked he-men in skimpy togas – the Apostles – and a Saviour in a loin-cloth brief as decency would permit, as rendered in oils by Sean Keating (RHA). Judas Iscariot was said to be based upon one of his (Sean's) deadly enemies.

Holding onto the pulpit now drenched with spume, aghast at what he had stirred up, and as if standing on the very poopdeck, tilting and heaving into a raging tempest or Force Twelve gale, the Dog, swaying with the movement of the ship, indomitable, wind-whipped, chap-lipped, drenched in salty spray, hair on end, took the chapel by storm. He invoked wrath, wrack, sea-bladder (sniggers, here), crosswinds, monstrous tides, *more* onrushing combers (his flash word), muscles strained to the limit and beyond, fortitude tested to breaking point, as his oratory rose to new heights of theatrical panache, arms thrown wide.

And then slowly subsiding, modifying his address, bringing us back to reality, the hands now joined, then a delicate blowing of the nose and handkerchief replaced in sleeve; leaning forward he stared piercingly into the body of the church. He was finished.

The whole school, cowed, knelt now with eyes closed and heads bowed, prayed for succour, for the success of the forces of Christ in Europe where the war still raged on. The silent congregation was drenched in spume, by spent combers, awaiting their deliverance (Dado having dipped one knee in token genuflection and quietly departed before the Dog had gotten into his stride).

The Dog McGlade never gave anything less than his best. His oratory had the formal majesty of an organ voluntary.

It was a raw winter's day at the end of a wet week towards the latter end of a wet year, term-time in mid November, another Sunday, visitors' day again at CWC, and we were expecting Dado.

He arrived in the Overland at the hour he had promised.

We had sat a Latin exam and partaken of a soggy lunch. Now we sat in the back seat of the Overland, parked facing in to the moat, the Gollimockey stream, eating blackberry tarts and drinking Bulmer's cider. With curtains drawn we were in a sort of tent, looking through the cuttings from newspapers that Dado had brought us. Mutt and Jeff in the *Evening Herald*, Mandrake the Magician in the *Evening Mail*, Cruiskeen Lawn in the *Irish Times*, with miscellaneous news items that had caught Dado's fancy. The pincer movements of Panzers in Russia, an American airman kneeling to be decapitated in Japan.

Dado had come early as promised; the Overland was stocked up with provisions for our tuck-box, homemade cakes and apples from the orchard. Dado smoked a cigarette and questioned us about the exam.

Thornley sat beside me in class. He had an unclean mind, and could make his tool stand up at will, a ferret stirring in a sack. The General was casting our theme-books around and Thornley whispered, 'Star in the east', glancing down at my fly-buttons undone. 'Playing pocket-billiards again, old son? Pulling the old wire, eh?' he gave me a nudge.

'My son,' whispered Father Perrott, with drawn face white as a sheet, through the wire lattice from the darkness of the confessional, wrung from the depths of his compassion.

A white figure dressed for rugby in the briefest of white shorts flitted by on high studded boots over the gravel to where a cutting wind whipped around the castle walls.

'Looking shagged,' murmured Thornley in my ear (my bad angel), his bitten grubby fingers pointed to where the loved one was shivering in thin rugby togs, sulkily avoiding all bodily contact far away. 'Little balls of fire'.

Father Kelly was everywhere at once. He had come to CWC after years in Australia, with advanced theories on coaching; the College XV and subs were to be given chops at supper, fed up like a hunting pack. And with good results; the historic day was about to arrive when CWC would finally defeat their old rivals Blackrock College (Dado's alma mater), thanks to Father Kelly's coaching.

Father Kelly was running alongside the attacking backs, threading his way through the forwards, digging the heel of his rugger boot into the ground, pointing, blowing his referee's whistle, scrum-down! He was taking no chances. The team was trained to a hair.

'Soul of my Saviour,' I sang feebly with the rest, not feeling pious but a perfect hypocrite, 'sanctify my breast.'

'Little gains,' our Spiritual Father (Father Adare) intoned creepily, 'little gains, little losses.' He had encouraged the whole School Sodality to even *earlier* rising; up at crack of dawn in winter was not enough for the brave soldiers of Christ, who were now required to rise at 6.00 and wash in cold water, to be in the Sodality Chapel not later than 6.50 a.m.

'To seek,' prayed Father Adare unctuously, 'to strive, to gain, and not to yield,' making a deep obeisance before the open tabernacle. A voice of manifold reason, though other baser promptings might still prevail.

It was rumoured that the Black Sow had shown her tool to Marshall, her Lower Line lover, on the castle stairs.

Early Mass in the Sodality Chapel in the castle tended to be a cosy affair. Father Adare made religion sound warm and tame; piety piled upon piety sounded safe, if also dull as botany.

A small toadlike bald visiting priest made it sound dangerous as a lobotomy, and put the wind up all his hearers at the Annual Retreat, three days of silence and meditation. No love-notes were passed in chapel now. The retreat wore on, from which Third Liners were being excused. Thornley, the ferret in the sack, my bad angel, no longer engaged in piggyback rides in the empty Lower Line library with desirable Third Line sows dragged in off the corridor and submitted to a quick dry bang with trousers on; he had had no emission stains on his flies to cover with a book while dipping a quick genuflection and leaving chapel with eyes modestly lowered. As a Tack he had come in last and it was his privilege to leave first. He spoke of nothing but screwing, getting his hole.

Now the confessions were full.

Spooning, sowing (Dutch *zog*, German *sau*, Latin *sus*, Greek *hus*, *sus*, female pig; sodomy), making sheep's eyes, passing notes, feel-ups in the scrum, 'bad' thoughts and attendant surreptitious acts were definitely 'out'. Unseen, aloft behind us in the choir stalls by the great organ, the tenor Waldron with a broken arm sang 'Stabat Mater'. The clear voice was an asphodel in the wind, pollen blown, intractable amber; it came on a joyful wave-frequency of incorruptible uncompromising (it was a dead language and couldn't change) uncontaminated Latin. The voice, still ascending, seemed to drift from afar.

. . . mater dolorosa, juxta crucem lachrimosa . . .

Father Perrott, ghostly pale, clutching the wings of his soutane, glided into the confessional and took his seat, drew the curtains, pushed open the Judas, prepared to hear the worst.

'Now, my son,' he whispered, 'what have you to confess?'

Give or take, let all slide; all turned to impurities in the end.

*   *   *

Captain and crew of the good ship *Loyola* were Rector, slim Father Jim; Prefect of Studies, stout Father Tom; Father Minister, little Mickey Kelley; and the three Line Prefects, Father Weft, Woofe, and weeshy Father Ween. Trim Father Adare was Spiritual Father of College and Community.

Among the latter were Warrandance, Fr Warranty, Fr Colloney, Kilfenora, Tooey, S. Pettigoe, Errigal and the venerable Fr Durance, who was as old as the hills. The lay Brothers Boyce and Stack were in charge of refectory and toilets.

– 24 –

The Price of Land,
the Great Lord,
the Gollimockey Stream

Included in the old parish of *Donaghcomper* were the townlands of Rinnawad, Ballyoulster, Commons, Coneyburo, Coolfitch, Elm Hall, Loughlinstown, Newtown, Reeves, Straleek and St Wolstans.

The original parish of *Kildrought* (Celbridge) contained the present townlands of Aghards, Castletown, Celbridge Abbey, Crodaun, Kilwogan, Moortown, Oldtown, Thornhill and Oakley Park.

Many miles of rough-hewn limestone walls standing over ten feet high and three-and-a-half feet thick at the base and twenty inches at the top and surmounted with broken bottle shards, not infrequently green Guinness bottles set into cement, built by Catholic labour to hide the prosperous owners who had paid out the lordly sum of a half-crown per perch to protect their Protestant privacy, are a feature of County Kildare as distinct as its towers and follies, as also found around the grand estates in County Kilkenny.

In the time of Ludlow and Orrery the forfeited lands had been portioned out to Cromwell's officers and soldiers who had signed up to fight on credit and would have to commute arrears in pay in exchange for land and property; they and their descendants would have all of that, the good weal in perpetuity. One million acres had been set aside to meet the Adventurers' claims, three-quarters of the prize was theirs by bailiwick. By May of 1652 Ireland lay prostrate before its foes; the Statutes of Kilkenny would deliver the *coup de grâce*. The extreme misery of the Irish race was pressed down hard and running over. (An artificial drain – quite erroneously called the Gollimockey by generations of inkstained CWC boys – had been laid down by the Wogan-Brownes to feed into the moat; whereas the little Gollimockey stream, a small meandering tributary of the Liffey, flowed close to the left of the back avenue or what the English prefer to call 'drive'.)

After the Boyne bloodbath the Unprofitable Land ('Mountain & Bogg') went for a penny an acre or was given away; profitable land went for four shillings an acre.

Rent per plantation acre, in pence

c. 1660	30
1683	40
1725/6	53
1752/3	67
1755/6	200
1815	360

The Napoleonic Wars may have inadvertently contributed to the 1815 increase.

With uniformed outriders and postillions the Great Lord rode out with the utmost elegance in his splendid vermilion-and-gold state coach (a plushy parlour in cloth of gold and coral, a musky travelling chamber), down from his town residence in Capel Street onto the northern quays, and on out via Ormond Quay, Wolfe Tone Quay, Parkgate Street and the Department of Defence, and so on to Chapelizod. The spanking greys and the golden coach more an object of bewilderment and wonderment to labourers who uncovered, and to passing gentry who formally saluted the Lord Justice (one of three), the foremost man of his time. Awed (the gentry) by the £25,000 per annum income, the high style, the panache (was he not the son of a poor Ballyshannon publican in County Donegal? an upstart who had made good?). He was his own man.

Dado must have inherited some of grand-uncle Tom's nature, for he liked nothing better than to dispense largesse; a gold ring for a grandchild, the head chef from the Shelbourne Hotel hired when he entertained lavishly at Springfield. Mumu, with a hangover, read Ethel Mannin (*Too Late Have I Loved Thee*), the liniment and smelling-salts by the bed, Eno's, Milton, Negley Farson's *The Way of a Transgressor.*

Mumu had an unforgiving nature. 'I *detest. . . .*'

She had a repertoire of disparaging terms. 'A right common little article, that one. Common as dishwater.' By her high bed on the upturned apple crate, a powder puff, lipstick, nail scissors, hairpins, the articles of her toilette.

The Boyds did not know where Auntie Ada had come from (she had married a man called Lynch by whom she had three children); her appearance (wistful, peakily pretty) was unlike any of the other Boyds. She introduced herself apologetically: 'You see I am the common one of the family.'

'Sod that for a lark!' burst out brother Bun, pal of buck privates and the common man.

'A little bird told me,' Mumu said mysteriously.

Well, that was the mysterious Aunt Ada; a wistful, pretty little wren's face under peek-a-boo dark hair, anxious eyes. She watched the Dodo batting in the nets at Springfield, old Keegan in hobnail boots, belt and braces, in his shirt sleeves, bowling long hops.

As batsman (stone-wall opener for the College XI) the Dodo had a composite model in mind; the dour unemotional Douglas Jardine whom no attack could trouble, and Ranjisingh with shirt billowing like a sail. He and brother Bun (who kept wicket) were on the College XI and on vacation time were picked to play for North Kildare CC near Kilcock, turning out with old Jack Wallace (phenomenally slow twisters), young Wallace (fast and erratic), Barney Parr and the Pig Menton whose big brother Brendan could clout sixes into the Grand Canal.

The Menton brothers too had been to CWC, and all knew the slang which did not change from generation to generation; in the generations before us, in those endless terms, they learnt it all.

Now touching the matter of floating a debased currency, Swift in his *Drapier*

Letters said that if Wood's halfpence ever became currency, it would take 240 horses to bring Mr Conolly's half-year's rent from Dublin to Castletown and require two or three great cellars for storage.

'Whatever you undertake,' wrote a kowtowing petitioner, 'God prospers.' Parents took to naming their children after him or his lady, hoping to inherit some of that luck, if nothing else. The birth registers record William Conolly Conyngham, William Conolly Coan, William Conolly McCauseland. To ensure a twofold patronage his man Finey christened his daughter Williamina Katherina.

The records of Springfield can be traced back to 1734, five years after the death of the Great Lord of Celbridge. In those days the North Salt holding belonged to Castletown, as did most of Celbridge, all prosperity emanating from the Great Lord. Springfield remained in the Castletown books, leased out to various families until the 1840s when it was purchased by the Earls of Leitrim (the Clements family), owners of Killadoon estate, who continued to lease out Springfield until 1906 when a Major Hamilton bought the house and seventy-five acres of grazing land. From then until the present day there have been a series of owners but it is in the same place marked 'Springfield' on the map of County Kildare drawn by Lieutenant Alexander Taylor of His Majesty's 81st Foot Regiment in 1783.

Back in 1734 it had been first leased by Speaker Conolly to his agent George Finey – 'for the lives of John Finey,' Christina & Williamina Katherine Finey daughter – all that part of Ballymakealy, Saltstoun & Tikkow 111 acres.'

In 1763, 'Lease renewed to John Clarke, husband of Christina Finey for the life of the said Christina, Williamina Katherina Baillie (née Finey) and John Finey.'

In 1763, 'John Clarke of Dublin to John Franklin of Springfield – all parts of the lands of Ballymakealy, Saltstoun & Tikkow.'

In 1763 (1773?), John Franklin to Lieutenant Richard Phillips 2nd Regiment of Foot – for £284.7.6. lands as above.'

In 1780, Richard Phillips of Springfield married Dorcas Shepherd, daughter of the Revd Sam Shepherd, Vicar of Kildrought 1735–85.

In 1782, Richard Phillips to Richard Baldwin Thomas, gent, lands as above.

1786, Lands as above to Nicholas Archdale Esq.

1789–95, Leased to Thomas Long Esq, the famous Dublin coachmakers.

1801, 'Thomas Long released unto James Langrishe & his heirs.'

1806, Revd James Langrishe Archdeacon of Glendalough to Francis Walker of Elm Hall, Celbridge.

1817–26, Leased to John Bradshaw & Arebella his wife.

1833–45, John Bradshaw to James Williams, lands as above.

1845–54, Leased to John Haughton and Margueretta his wife.

In 1850 they held the house, offices and lands (52 acres) from the Earl of Leitrim, who had bought Springfield from the Castletown estates in the 1840s. John Haughton was the owner of the Celbridge woollen and flour mills.

1868–1906, John Langrishe leased the property and the family remained at Springfield until 1906.

1906, Springfield and 75 acres bought by Major Hamilton. Major Hamilton sold to Captain Mitchell who sold to Captain Richard (Dick) Warren nephew of Major Darling of Sallins who sold to my father Batty Higgins for a rumoured £3,000, house and three lodges with 72 acres of prime land; this must have been soon after the end of the 1914-18 war.

Some three-score years on, following the birth and upbringing of four sons, Dado sold out to Matt Dempsey the popular horsebreeder of Griffin Rath who fathered nine children there, for a rumoured £5,000, the house and lands with two lodges. Two score years later Dempsey sold out to Alistair Campbell, an Aer Lingus airline pilot, for a rumoured £14,000, house and 12 acres. Alistair Campbell had two daughters reared before he sold out to a Dr Anthony Walsh, a gynaecologist, who converted the old kitchen into a surgery. Dr Anthony was the pale gynaecologist who had practised in a private hospital in Clane but dearly wanted to set up at Springfield on his own, having made his fortune in a Baghdad hospital seemingly staffed exclusively from Dublin, performing kidney transplants during the Iran-Iraq war.

The Iraquis had an anti-personnel bomb that burst twenty feet up, causing fearsome back injuries to troops who had thrown themselves flat.

If a doctor got one kidney operation in six weeks in Ireland he would be lucky; but in Baghdad Dr Tony was getting four or five a week. When he found that the Iraquis were removing the kidneys of Iranian POWs he swiftly removed himself from Iraq. Know your friends.

The house and lands now changed hands for £150,000. The Campbells moved to Bath. An electric blanket ignited and the house caught fire. It was believed locally that the Bank repossessed.

A misfortune far worse than fire was to follow.

Young Morgan Sheehy, Managing Director of Ove Arup consulting engineers, the largest in the land, had his eye on it, and soon had bought it for his Texan wife Libby to do as she pleased. Texan gigantism was given a free hand. Sunken garden, power showers and Filipino servants were installed, a stand of old trees cut down to open up the view and the inner harmony destroyed. The character of the changes – such drastic surgery – was to disfigure what had been there before. By raising 'internal specifications to an exceptionally high degree' – in the orotund jargon of the selling agents Palmer McCormack – the character of the house had been too drastically altered and disfigured; the hasty over-liberal hand had done its work. By 1993, Ove Arup & Partners were seeking substantial reimbursement for work done on Springfield that had been charged to the firm. Morgan Sheehy died of a heart attack, aged forty-two; his widow flew her six children back to America.

Offers in the region of one million punts were being sought for the 'lavishly refurbished' Georgian mansion outside Celbridge.

Refinement and good taste are hard to come by; a heavy price must be paid for improvements, in one way or another. When overwhelmed by the sheer weight and preponderance of vulgarity, thick as buttermilk, newly on display in a plug-ugly modern state, the pet-food manufacturer's land of doped livestock, winter fields reeling with slurry, high cholesterol counts and human cardiac cases who had brought such misfortune on themselves by overfeeding; not to mention FF forcing-beds, Cokes and over-chilled Budweiser, pie-in-the sky, and all Irish citizens now fairly bursting out of their sausage skins with newfound prosperity and consumer insanity at Crazy Prices shopping mall in grey Portlaoise, well – something must give. Enjoy your day!

So in a sense all had come full circle.

American money had found the place and American money had lost it. As Arizona copper in Old Bisbee near the Mexican border had made it possible in the first instance for my improvident begetter to buy Springfield and its grazing land, so in the latter stages of give and take had Texan push and persuasive collateral helped to mar its Georgian charms – fragile enough perhaps – and even more so than Dado's wasteful ways.

The grandiose improvements – a new (and superfluous) entrance gate by the East Lodge with monumental granite piers alongside the former front gate, the sunken garden, the seven bedrooms with *en suite* bathrooms and power shower cubicles, the golden taps, the Filipino servants, the large adjoining glass conservatory – had done nothing much to improve any-thing, rather the contrary. The foolhardy attempts to convert Springfield into a minor Dallas mansion had not come off. William Conolly, the son of a Ballyshannon publican, who had raised himself up by the straps of his boots, would have been rightly appalled.

Just prior to 1990 agricultural land in County Kildare fetched £1,500 an acre, whereas building sites near services in sought after areas fetched £15,000 an acre; at present building sites near services fetch over £30,000 an acre in the Clane area, probably more in Celbridge and Leixlip.

Bisbee produced more than eight billion pounds of copper, worth about two billion dollars when it closed for good in December 1974. It had been named for the San Francisco Judge DeWitt Bisbee, the investor who never laid eyes on the camp.

– 25 –

The Dodo, his Habitat

Time stood still in the stable yard at Springfield; time stood still in the garden where the pediment of the sundial was cracked. Dr Charlie O'Connor was a regular visitor; he wore a fur coat down to his ankles and was seldom sober, driving about the country roads at ten miles an hour.

Dado continued to play gold at Lucan and Hermitage, the fees would somehow be found. My improvident parents dined and wined well at the Spa Hotel but had begun (however unobtrusively) to live in elegant poverty. It was a matter of honour to keep up appearances; the four daily papers continued to arrive as did the seven Sundays, the Bowsy brought Young's side of beef each Saturday as usual, Findlater's men continued to arrive. My father remained calm; my mother held her own counsel.

Then one terrible night he woke her to announce that all their money was gone. 'It's all gone, Lil,' he groaned, and turned his face to the wall. The third-born (me) and the fourth-born (the Dote) could not go to Clon-gowes after all.

'Oh that bloody fool!'

Springfield was sold and we moved to Greystones in County Wicklow by the sea, where we were not known at all.

On the instructions of the owner
FOR AUCTION
SPRINGFIELD PERIOD RESIDENCE
CELBRIDGE
Suitable for Stud Farm
Ideal Hunting Box or Small Racing
Establishment
Inner yard with stabling for 9
Cattle yard with Dutch Barn &
ties for 40 Cattle. Attractive
flower and vegetable gardens.
Fee simple. Rateable Valuation
on Buildings.
SEEN ONLY BY PREVIOUS APPOINTMENT.

Both Mumu and the Dodo had nervous breakdowns.

The weakest ones seemed destined to go to the wall, be afflicted with every ill that flesh is heir to; and for such unfortunates, so numerous, Dado had a dreary formula of invocation as tried and tested as the Litany of Loredo:

'Not looking well . . .'
'Not looking at all well . . .'
'Looking bad a month ago . . .'
'Shocking-looking a month ago . . .'
'Now looking really bad . . .'
'Looking terrible the other day . . .'
'Not looking herself (himself) at all recently . . .'
'NEVER LOOKED WORSE!'

This miserable antiphony of dire forebodings rang constantly in my ears and coloured even the alternative viewpoint, the response always less insistently stated, as the short uncertain summer precedes the long killing winter:

'In *powerful* form the other day!'
'Looking great!'
'Never looked better!'

Temporary states of well-being were merely aberrant lapses from the norm (why does it seem so Irish?) of ill health and never to be trusted on any account; weak as flies in winter the people crawled about, burdened with life.

Sudden let-downs and chapters of disappointment led inevitably to nervous breakdowns, coming in various forms and when least expected – again maladies peculiarly Irish. The condition of one's interior and the conditions of the air were discussed incessantly with a sort of rapt interest and intensity. Whoever heard of an island people stuck with such a vile climate go on about it so incessantly? Do the Eskimos speak of snow and ice? Do the Bedouin complain of heat and desert? No, not them.

The Dodo was set in ritual.

The ritual poke at the fire at specific times, the ritual heavy sigh, the staring fixedly at a stain on the tiles where milk had boiled over and left a hardened scum, all was ritual. For a nightcap (which he made for himself, Mumu long abed) he liked a glass of hot Ovaltine, set on its saucer before the fire; more ritual.

He liked to stay up late, listening to AFN with Hope and Benny wise-cracking; this was his sole participation in any human communication. His laugh (a snigger) was a donkey braying far off, choking on it, indistinctly heard.

Gassy smoke spat out and sucked up the chimney in the updraught, to be dispersed in the darkness. A sudden viridian jet came at right angles, aimed at Dodo's fat ankles. He did not yield, but crouched as close as he could get to the flames. All was in order: the pot of tea warming at his feet, the jar of homemade jam, the wireless knob within easy reach of his soft prehensile hand. He liked to work to the distant throb of subdued dance music: Sinatra singing the ineffably mournful 'Moonlight in Vermont', Hoagy Carmichael's 'Star Dust', Perry Como warbling 'It's Impossible'.

His favourite programme was *Hi, Gang!* with Ben Lyons (plumply unc-tuous), Bebe Daniels (sprightly sexy) with Vic Oliver (plummy Jewish, a gad-about-town) serenading the Marshall Plan in close harmony:

> Gee, Mr RoozyFelt, it's swell of you,
> The-way-yore-helpin'-us-taw-windewäaaar!

He liked the American Armed Forces Network of news and entertain-ment programmes, relayed like a game of baseball or American football, split up into playing periods, the rapid-fire crosstalk of rivals on the air. The fast wit induced a snigger now and then. The wide-open vowels of the newsreaders suggested the wheatlands and prairies of the Land of the Free. The vowel-sounds were assertively open – NÖWOW for 'now', ÖWWER for 'hour'. From six to midnight the Dodo was glued to the wireless, buffeting it when the reception was poor (a storm on the Irish Sea). On weekends he monopolised the set. Mumu would not dream of interfering; she listened only to *Mrs Dale's Diary* when the Dodo was away at work.

The Dodo was mean to Mumu, cruel like a lover; excused and forgiven like a lover. Smirking at his manicured nails he shared a joke, his head wobbled, his shoulders shook. 'He-he-he-he!' went the Dodo.

'He has a lovely smile,' Mumu said, 'when he cares to use it.'

The Dodo used it very sparingly.

If her cooking did not come up to scratch he flung pots and pans about the kitchen, hissing imprecations between his teeth. He had begun to withdraw into himself, to close up.

He never used my Christian name, it was 'Hey, you!' or 'him' or 'That fellow'. Once (after the bite under the tablecloth) I was 'the rat'.

He had no friends in the wide world, confiding only to a small pocket diary wherein were scrupulously recorded the many wrongs done to him. The Dodo was a card.

It was a rare smile right enough, when the Dodo cared to bring it forth. The head wobbled, the eyes twinkled, the lips curved into a smile of almost beatific coyness; and shaking all over like a fat jelly the Dodo went, 'Hee-heehee!'

'Piece of cake,' said the Dodo between compressed lips. With hazel eyes revolving in his head and one ear pressed anxiously to the wood; the Dodo fairly drank in 'Blue Moon', '(Blew Hooo!), I hear you calling'. He was always at his fingernails, trimming and buffing and manicuring.

Now that he wanted to speak, he found it was too late; he couldn't do it, couldn't articulate. He had lost the words; it was years since we had spoken to each other. (We had never spoken to each other.) Living in the same bungalow, eating at the same table, silence had always reigned and been accepted as quite normal, quite natural, if that was what he wished. We would have accepted anything he did (if he wished to sit on top of the wireless that was okay), no matter how peculiar.

The Dodo had grown corpulent, bulky about the hips, taking short womanly strides. That secrecy of his, the rare soprano giggle, the simper were all womanly.

'*Do you hear?*'

I looked over at him; had I heard aright, had he indeed addressed me? He was fixed rigid on the edge of his chair, wringing his hands. His profile told me nothing, gave nothing away. He looked as posed as the jumper on the high parapet, the suicide leaper gazing down into the void; he would not look at me. All his life he had avoided eye-contact and hand-clasps. I strained my ears, waiting for him to speak again. He sat there rigid, his tea untouched, and something pinged in the air between us, faint as the sound of telegraph wires over a ditch. Some alarming message was humming through the wires, over the frozen ditches; somewhere a hesitant hand reached slowly out, lifted a receiver, and an ear heard, a muffled voice spoke.

I did not speak, leaning forward in the same attentive pose as my brother, bookends both, a couple of stone caryatids. He would not look directly at me, I was receiving that oblique glance he had for others. His close attention seemed to be directed at a cone of violet coal-gas that had fired out and curled back through the bars of the grate, turning a vivid green as it emerged, fiercely ejecting a funnel of brilliant white smoke. It spat poison gas.

'*Hear it?*'

Silence but for the spitting gas. It fanned out, sucked itself back behind the bars again, subsided. Unconsumed slag, eaten with fire from within, fell into the heart of the flames. It was very hot in the living room, too hot, our faces glowed.

'Hear what?' I asked him.

For reply the Dodo made an indistinct sound in his throat, heaved himself upright as he pushed back his easy-chair and went in an awkward scurry out of the room. He had taken the red-hot poker with him. I heard him scuffle out, heavy on his feet; there came a cold gust of night air down the chimney, another from the doorway and the Dodo armed with a poker had vanished into the night.

The Dodo and I had been sitting for some hours before the fire, in an unbroken silence; nothing unusual in that, we never spoke to each other, had become virtual strangers. One day he had closed up, and after that all we could get out of him was grunts. He did not seem to approve of us. He had been sitting forward in his easy-chair, staring into the heaped-up fire of slack that burned in the narrow grate.

Cartridge paper had been tacked down on the table behind him and upon it another of his severely perfect designs in a hard pencil; T-square and set-square, ruler and eraser, callipers and marking ink, mapping pens and sharply pointed pencils cut down to a classical third, all were meticulously set out. The drawings would remain there tacked down with drawing pins for as long as the Dodo required his final design; the table was no longer available to the family, as with the wireless after working hours through the week, or all weekend if the Dodo wished.

That seat was his and when he entered the room he claimed it. If he found it occupied he would look astonished and whoever sat in it would defer to him, give him back his place.

The pot of tea and buttered toast, untouched, were still warming in the fireplace. He studied every evening after a day in the quantity surveyor's office on Stephen's Green; working steadily and neatly for his final examination, not tolerating anything short of perfection in himself, and flying into a great rage if his papers were shifted or disturbed in any way. Indications of his displeasure were conveyed to Mumu who passed the message on. She cooked for him, did his washing, mended his socks, ironed his shirts. His life had been arranged in a formally set pattern from which any deviation would be intolerable as we, who feared him, were left in no doubt. At home in Caragh ('Friend' in the Gaelic), a disintegrating summer bungalow on Kinlen Road on the very outer perimeter of the Burnaby in Greystones among Protestants, and fully occupied all the year round, the Dodo spoke only to utter heartfelt curses, spitting out our dear Redeemer's name: JEEeeeezus Christ! The Dodo was of the stuff that your silent psychopathic murderer is made, the one who suddenly takes a hatchet to his frustrations. Oddly enough the terror merchant Hitchcock had lived briefly just down the way.

On this particular evening that I speak of, he was not working, but sitting forward in his weekend pullover and leather slippers, staring into the fire, fetching up deep sighs at intervals and studying his hands, appendages that always seemed to fascinate him, judging by the amount of attention he lavished on them, as though they were insured like Betty Grable's legs.

The fire had spluttered again and sent out its licks of blue flame and my 'Hear what?' was still echoing in the living room.

I stayed put.

In a while I heard the Dodo come back in and the catch on the front door clicked to. He came and sat down again, replacing the poker. He was breathing deeply, white in the face, sweating. Silence . . . reigned again. Then the pale hands were extended once more to the flames, the soggy toast, the knobs, to 'Moonlight in Vermont', to 'Star Dust'.

The ever-silent Dodo leaning forward on the crushed cushions of his collapsed easy-chair was a dead ringer for – whom? Where? The sledded Polack on the ice?

He had made himself very remote and austere, like a Great Lord, hardly condescending to see his tenants or hear their grievances. He spent much time in the Godlike occupation of trimming his fingernails and cultivated a haughtily languid manner to impose his will (silently) upon inferiors, foremost among whom were numbered the Dote and myself, coldly subjected to this freezing authority, which I see now as an unconscious parody of Dado's loose paternal control.

The laugh that was suddenly wrung from Mumu was high-pitched and hysterical. Neither she nor the Dodo were given to spontaneous laughter. Of course silence between kith and kin was not uncommon in those days before television, in the country, where you amused yourself as best you could to pass the time. The Dodo's solitary amusements were as sterile as his lonely sports; the distant figure pacing up and down by the irrigation ditch in the gloaming, poking at the rough with an iron in a fruitless search for a lost Dunlop. His patience was phenomenal.

He had some theory about the mastication of food, so many chews per mouthful, the lower jaw moving in a slow lateral manner like a ruminant. And how unnerving when he ceased chewing to glare! If he caught you looking at him he glared at you like a basilisk; you had no right to stare. If he required anything at table he cleared his throat twice *Err-humm!* with a rising interrogative inflexion, and pointed with his chin at the object required, water-jug or butter-pats, salt-cellar or pepper-pot. A treble clearing of the throat followed by the Err-humm at a more peremptory pitch that admitted no refusal, meant: May-I-have-your-best-attention! A heavily ironic Err-H U M! testily signified: Birdbrain! A pointed and testy AHhem! meant: Cut-it-out! Don't try-me-too-far! If our attention could not be gained by these means (if one flatly refused to look at him), the Dodo was finally reduced to speech.

'*I say!*'

'What does he want?' Dado asked, looking up and down the table. But Mumu always knew what he wanted; her motherly instinct told her, and pepper-pot or mustard was handed across. Our brother was retiring into silence. One fine day all communication between us would cease. After that there would be only the grunts.

In his own home, as in the depths of a burrow, the Dodo lived his own peculiar life as if it were normal, like some exotic species of nocturnal beast that is rarely seen and whose odd habits are not understood. His workroom (the former schoolroom where our first tutor Mr Barrett had put the famous question, *What animal with four legs lives in a stable?* To which the Dote, hardly breathing, stoutly responded, 'A rat!' to make a show of us, Mumu feared) smelt pleasantly of turps and oil paint. He was putting the finishing touches – the lettuce – to a meticulously accurate copy of 'The Boy with the Rabbit'.

Oh that inexplicable blackout choler of his – what did it mean? What portend? What did it hide? What hurt conceal? What grievance long brooded upon? During seven years of detention in two strict boarding schools he had become withdrawn, reverting more and more into silence, choler, accidie. In the family circle he had become dumb, torpid, and was putting on weight like a Galway hooker clapping on full sail. Certainly he was no longer the Don Budge of the Centre Court, as of yore, in the days of Kay Stammers and Alice Marble, in impeccable flannels and headband winding himself up to serve one of his extraordinary complicated services, rigid as a medieval siege engine. The service ball was thrown high in the air, squared at, recaught; the Dodo once more realigned himself, cast up the service ball (two other spares bulging in his pockets), squared at it, recaught it, all aflutter, crying out 'Deuce! . . . Thirty-fifff!! Vantage!!!' In a lather of sweat he disputed the score, retrieving high volleys from the top of the ten-foot high beech hedge, or from the orchard beyond. The Dote and I were reluctant ball-boys, slipping away into the orchard or into the shrubbery when the Dodo's broad back was turned. Mumu sat on the terrace by the summerhouse, knitting, smiling, smoking, waiting for Lizzy to bring out the tea. The missel thrushes sailed down from the beech tree into the yew.

Alone, when all had retired, the Dodo bowled into the cricket net for hours at a stretch, aiming at a single stump, sometimes knocking it out of the ground. Each delivery had to be retrieved, twenty-two paces for the length of the crease and then as far as the rockery wall for the run-up, under covert observation from the Dote and I up on our bird-killing platform with Rolos and air-rifles and one of the cats. The Dodo went pounding down the crease below us, his shadow racing after him. Nothing seemed to discourage him. The sun high and the shadows sharp, Voce comes in to bowl. A heavily-built man, he pounds in, propelling himself at the wicket. The batsman (Ponsford of Australia in a baggy green cap) stabs at it, and spectators applaud an easy catch in the slips (where Hammond waits, the safest pair of hands in Gloucestershire) and the Dodo with his shirt out comes running down the pitch with both arms upraised to indicate a virtually unplayable delivery. Ponsford, bat under one arm and cap in hand, shakes his head, begins the long walk pavilionward.

W. H. Ponsford, c. Hammond, b. Higgins. . . . 77

Every evening after work he walked the path by the big beech hedge, a sort of penitential tramping up and down for an hour or so after work; until he had worn the path polished as linoleum. On winter's nights he exercised by moonlight and the path shone under him like a stream.

The Dodo, who had no friends, liked to keep in touch with the old Alma Mater. He had collected piles of CWC Annuals next to *Lilliputs* and *Picture Posts* in his reference library, familiarising himself with the progress of former classmates out in the world at large and photographs of Imperators and teachers who still remained; Mike Clarson (Maths), The General (History & Geography, which for some reason was taught as one subject), Horny Ward (Physics & Science), Brannigan (Art), Father Gerald O'Byrne (Ancient Greek). College, that time of infinite boredom and drudgery for me, is not a time I look back upon with much pleasure; but for the Dodo it was different, for he must have persuaded himself that he had been happy there, in a way, protected from punishment.

One day the hard decision had to be made.

The Dodo submitted himself to a place in the country where he was to spend some time under observation and work on the farm. Hard manual labour would settle his nerves, it was thought; Dr George Sheehan gave it as his considered opinion that this would be the making of him.

Mumu wept for a whole day after agreeing that he should go. On the day of his departure she took to her bed fully clothed in the early afternoon. Or rather she took to *his* bed, in the narrow boxroom between bathroom (where a tap having dripped for months then ran for years) and the bedroom I shared with brother Bun who had become very partial to pints of porter in the pubs of Greystones, for Springfield had been sold to Matthew Dempsey, a farming neighbour who had put in a concealed bid. The Dote was working for the architect Berthold Lubetkin in London.

Mumu patted the place beside her on the blue-and-white counterpane with its design of poultry that had come from Springfield with us. She wept quietly and miserably as if she intended to weep for a long time, because her heart had been broken, her hair loose and hairpins falling out, her nose and eyes red with crying. She was inconsolable and drew me to her and tried to kiss me, her face on fire, all blubbery and smelly (urine and Baby Power) and weepy, and I held her roasting hand and wished myself far away. She asked, weepingly, what would become of her darling? Would they be hard on him, the rough fellows, was he in good hands, would they understand his needs, his withdrawn nature (she could not bring herself to say his silence), his troubled being? Would the doctors understand? Fondling my hand, would they, would they? And did I understand the humiliations he must endure? He would have to perform hard manual work that perhaps he was not able for, he would have unfamiliar faces about him, rough fare at table, rough horseplay and jokes, and he would have the electroshock shot into him, and how could he endure that?

Dado had driven him there that morning in the Overland piled high with enough clothes and provisions to take him to the North Pole.

From this ordeal he returned even more taciturn than before, leaving immediately for the officers' cadet course at Cranwell. Not for him the slogging about in the infantry – ignorant buffs all – nor rattling around in a tank, nor sick as a dog in a destroyer, nor even sicker down in a submarine. No, no, it was up in the sky for him, up in the cold air by night, wizard prang in the wild blue yonder – nothing but blue skies for him, 'Stars Fall on Alabama'.

¡El Zopilote Mojado! ¡Contralador de la noche fria! ¡Sereno del aire frio! What is it a sign of when you find a centipede in the bath? A single bat at eventide?

For the mentally disturbed, the room they find themselves in must always be the same room, filled with the identical furniture as recalled by the suffering mind and the all-too-familiar dreaded accessories instantly recognised. The torment, identical as before, is resumed in a new place that is an exact replica of the old, detestably familiar. What takes place there, in the suffering brain, the 'seat of all ideation', occurs and recurs as in the original torture chamber and may not be spoken of by the sufferer, because it is literally indescribable.

So the heated study of a home called Springfield was shifted intact (in the Dodo's troubled head) from a mile outside Celbridge on the wet byroad to Naas and set down intacto in the Burnaby at Greystones less than fifty miles away and now called Caragh on Kinlen Road in the Protestant enclave. So that all his (the Dodo's) torments could begin anew, with not a stick of furniture out of place, not a familiar stink abated, each fire the same fire and furthermore, to lend it the veracity of a true nightmare, the invariably wetted slack thrown on with a hasty and liberal hand by Dado himself without a word.

The study (or library) at Springfield with the heavy curtains drawn and the door closed, two Aladdin paraffin lamps with elongated glass globes lit and the coal fire augmented by wood aglow made all hot as a furnace, hot as Hell. The Dodo crouched forward on the very edge of the commodious but uncomfortable and smelly leather armchair (sold at discount from Jack Ellis's warehouse) and extended his soft white hands to the blaze, palms out, then the backs, gently closing the fingers into a fist before opening them again into a fan, in a reflexive manner which with cats, the Dote and I called 'feeling the fires'.

Poor-quality coal would give way to wood as trees were felled and wetted slack give way to damp turf as World War Two (known euphemistically as the 'Emergency') dragged on. If WW2 was not Ireland's war, not quite real for the Irish, so the Dodo's shift from Springfield to bungalow bliss in the Burnaby at Greystones was equally an illusion. One of his open leather-work slippers held the front door ajar, which meant that he was off playing golf; *that* was an irrefutable fact. Mumu's 'Would you ever take a look at the door and see if your brother's off golfing?' when decoded, read: 'Is his slipper in the door?'

The so-called living room was a low-ceilinged stuffy room smelling of coke and heated leather. A pot of tea and buttered toast warmed at the narrow grate, but of my brother there was no visible sign, apart from these comestibles and the guardian slipper holding the front door off the catch. The slipper-in-the-door prevented it closing and was also a silent order that supper should be on the table in the kitchen when he returned and removed his spiked golfing shoes in the porch to step into one slipper and limp or hop into his cramped bedroom (no room to swing a cat) and step into the second slipper, to make his way into the adjoining bathroom for his ablutions and to take the nailbrush to his nails.

The Dodo playing cricket, even opening the batting for CWC, seemed always to be at practice. Similarly on his lonely forays over the outer nine at GGC, he was at practice again.

Now he made his way resolutely across the untended garden and the path he had worn by the vegetable patch; moving with short rapid mincing steps, hips and shoulders going, an odd galvanised way of progressing. A limp canvas bag (bought from stout Scuffle in the hut by the railway station) held a miscellaneous set of mismatched hickory-shafted clubs, wielded most incompetently by my brother.

He played alone over the deserted outer nine, away from the clubhouse, lifting his head, splaying his shots, cutting great divots, hurling clubs about, cursing his Maker.

The Dodo's golf was all practice: six or more practice swings followed as like as not by fresh-air shots, wild shanks followed by even more atrocious language; the Dodo played a very blue game of golf designed for himself alone. A distant misshapen figure with arms locked rigid, stuck at the summit of a cranked swing, unable to bring the club-head down. The Dodo was carving his way up the long eight.

Once, in a snow-fight near the ring-pump, I, having had the effrontery to throw a snowball that had caught him below the knee and filled the turn-ups of his grey trousers, stood my ground in the ditch below him and received a coldly dismissive glare from angry hazel eyes.

'Take that out, at once!'

I had cravenly obeyed, the Dodo towering forbiddingly above me with folded arms, Montgomery of Alamein.

Once the Dote and I had filled a biscuit tin with field mice and put it in his bed by the hot-water bottle; he would let them loose when he turned back the sheets. But this affront to his dignity he kept to himself, at least there were no repercussions.

Silent, torpid, crouching over the fire, he drew out a clean linen handkerchief from his trouser pocket, trumpeted into it thrice, studied the results (prone to nosebleeds), folded it and put it away. I suspect that he could bring on heavy nosebleeding at will; it was one of his tricks for getting into the infirmary. A regular splashing in the back of the classroom announced that Higgins senior was having another nosebleed, and should take himself across to Matron.

The wireless knob was within easy reach.

The reception was poor, the batteries dying. Uttering low heartfelt imprecations the Dodo fetched it a buffet, it was not going to best him. On 3rd September 1939 he had strolled in flannels into the kitchen to find the Dote and myself with old Mrs Henry sitting before a roaring fire and had coolly informed us that Chamberlain had just declared war, and sauntered out again. Old Mrs Henry blessed herself and said, 'God save us all then!'

Presently the nagging jeery voice of Lord Haw-Haw came from Berlin, the BBC news jammed with accounts of deaths and bombings, information from spies working in Britain.

The Dodo began to study Morse code at the Atlantic College in Dublin, taking a room in Mespil Road. He had volunteered for the RAF, for night-fighters; the Dodo was above all earthly things and on the side of Gubby Allen and Lord Burghley, Don Budge and Hammond, against Lili Marlene and Goering and Eva Braun and Goebbels and Julius Streicher and Alfred Rosenberg and von Ribbentrop.

'That's what he's set his heart on apparently,' said Mumu. Von Ribbentrop was only a champagne salesman, she told me in her most withering and dismissive manner. She preferred Anthony Eden who was a real gentleman.

The Dodo waited for his call-up papers.

He went off to Cranwell Cadet School, walked through blitzed London in the blackout, saw Pat Kirkwood's long legs and wide smile on the stage when she sang to the troops, 'Oh Johnny, oh Johnny, how you can love!' He sat in the stalls in his RAF officer's uniform at Rattigan's *Flare Path*. For if Mumu loved English royalty, the Dodo loved England, home of Hobbes. When questioned about night-flying he had this to report: 'It's a worrying sort of activity, actually. You are always conscious of the need to get home.' This was a long speech for him, stating the terms of survival.

Of the war itself, which left so many million dead, many of them non-combatants, I recall only the bombs dropped on Dublin by one Dornier or Heinkel that had been chased from the English coast or had strayed over the Irish Sea, rather as a hen menaced by dogs will lay eggs in out-of-the-way places; the shock-waves travelled down the Liffey and through Killadoon Wood to wake all the pheasants and set them shrieking, seconds before Springfield's nursery windows rattled in their frames. Thirteen miles to the west the blast had demolished houses on the North Strand in a trench a thousand yards long. Diplomatic notes flew but to little avail. The status quo remained the same for German combatant and Irish non-participant. Both knew well enough how the wind blew. Dev had been stubborn about the ports, dug his heels in, would not let them go.

If on looking back I (too young to know) could remember only the beginning, the Dodo's dramatic announcement, then he himself (non-participant extraordinaire) had perhaps mislaid it. For the war had ended before he could take off on a mission into the black night.

When he came home on leave, Mumu (whose nerves had gone against her and who was to pass the war in bed) bravely rose up and washed and dressed herself in fur coat and demi-veil to perch on the edge of a wheelbarrow, the Dodo in his RAF pilot's uniform and daredevil forage cap angled on the wobbling head, one hand resting on her shoulder; and on the prudish lips of both (so alike!) the *ghosts of smiles*.

When his leave expired Mumu resumed her life in bed, for an existence without him wasn't for her any life at all. She would prefer to be dead, did not wish to live. Her voice had become fainter, pitched higher; she was becoming him.

On Monday, June 2nd, 1941, the *Irish Times* (price 2d. Saturdays 3d.) headlines were dramatic:

GERMAN BOMBS WERE DROPPED ON DUBLIN

GOVERNMENT PROTEST TO BE MADE
IN BERLIN

DEAD NUMBER 30;
INJURED OVER 80

Investigations having shown that the bombs dropped were of German origin, the Chargé d'Affaires in Berlin is being directed to protest, in the strongest terms, to the German Government against the violation of Irish territory, and to claim compensation and reparation for the loss of life, the injuries suffered, and the damage to property. He is further directed to ask for definite assurances that the strictest instructions will be given to prevent the flight of aircraft over Irish territory and territorial waters.

The four bombs were dropped in the Ballybough and North Strand areas and twenty houses completely demolished. A further bomb was dropped near Arklow on Sunday morning, but no lives were lost.

From within the relatively secure confines of the Vatican City, Pope Pius XII sent out Whitsuntide greetings to the world in a deeply ambiguous message of goodwill and mixed metaphors – a gloss on Pope Leo XIII's encyclical, *Rerum Novarum* ('the Magna Carta of a Christian social endeavour'). His Holiness spoke of deep furrows and grievous disturbances, both in nations and in society, 'until the years finally poured their dark and turbulent waters into the sea of war, whose unforeseen currents may effect our economy and society'.

Goods were created by God for all men and the natural right to the use of material goods provides man with a secure basis of the highest import on which to rise with reasonable liberty (sic), 'to the fulfilment of his moral duties'.

The Pope urged the need for the cooperation of all.

Failure (common to all human activity) should not make mankind forget the inspiring message of the *Rerum Novarum* (issued in 1891 by Pope Leo XIII) which 'tomorrow, when the ruins of this world hurricane is cleared, may be the outset of a reconception of a new social order worthy of God and man and will keep living the noble flame of a brotherly social spirit. Nourish it; keep it burning, even more brightly; carry it wherever a cry of pain reaches you,' the Pope concluded.

The war in Iraq had ended; Crete fell to a German air armada. The British cruiser *Sheffield* entered Gibraltar in a damaged condition; the destroyer *Kelly* went down carrying with her Lieutenant Commander Lord Hugh Beresford, to the inexpressible grief of his mother the Duchess of St Albans and the sister-in-law, the Marchioness of Waterford.

It was a busy Whit.

Between 12.30 and 1.30 a.m. on Sunday, the day after the *Luftwaffe* had bombed the North Strand, unknown planes were heard passing over Dun Laoghaire, proceeding in a northerly direction. 'Searchlights were observed.'

Later that morning, shortly after 10 a.m., two tenement houses collapsed in Old Bride Street, Dublin, killing three persons and injuring fifteen others. Among the dead were Mrs Brigid Lynskey (30) and her five-month-old baby, Noel, and Samuel O'Brien (72), a pensioner of Messrs Guinness.

The precise cause of the collapse was not known; it was believed to be due to a combination of factors – the old tenement houses were shaken when the bombs fell on Dublin on Saturday morning, and a heavy lorry had passed the building shortly before the collapse.

My mother stayed in bed for two years.

She became obese, inventing a nervous disorder that would keep her with the too-much-loved eldest son: claustrophobia. She had *claustropho-*

bia and could not attend Mass any more; crowded places did not suit her, crowds distressed her; no place where she had been happy could be visited again. Her few friends were reduced to an irreducible minimum. The house was a 'disgrace', she was ashamed of it, the housework was beyond her. Her manner became distant; she spent hours staring out the window at the clouds. A priest came once a year to give her Holy Communion.

Dr George Sheehan, a good family friend of long standing, came with his black bag and a heavy old panting Labrador. The animal came wheezing into the bedroom after his master and collapsed on the threadbare rug, its design (peacocks) worn off by time. The collapsing dog shook the room, the grey-haired Dr Sheehan reached out his hand for the patient's fluttering pulse and asked, 'What seems to be the matter, Lily?'

He examined her but could find nothing wrong and retired, baffled. The war raged on to the tune of Melachrino's strings, *Forces Favourites, Hi, Gang!* and the rhumbas of Edmundo Ros.

My mother stayed in bed.

My father tolerated it. This was her choice, he could not gainsay it. She was happy in her own way, he said. From her sickbed she dominated him and the household where little housework was attempted any more. Her voice became fainter and fainter. Dado had an offhand way with the bills, impaling them on a wire skewer and forgetting them. Creditors called and were palmed off with farfetched promises of sudden wealth, debts cleared. Then for six months my father dreamed winners. He broke the local turf accountant who called and begged for time to pay. In his experience the bookie had never known of such horses winning at such long odds.

The war, which would come to an end before the Dodo could go into action, continued to rage on.

There was nothing *organically* wrong with Mumu, Dr Sheehan said; her nerves had gone against her, that was all. To be well again she must rise out of bed, get on her own two feet, find outside interests.

One bright day in spring towards the end of the war, my father, urged on by no fewer than three doctors – a nerve specialist had been summoned from Dublin – persuaded Mumu to get out of bed, with much coaxing and promises of a table booked for dinner at a nice hotel by the sea.

'All right,' she said, doubtful but resigned, 'all right then . . .'

None of her clothes fitted; a suitable ensemble had to be let out and a day wasted.

'She's perking up again,' Dado said, glad to see any sign of improvement.

'She'll be right as rain,' said old Mrs Henry.

'Now Ma'am,' said Rita.

She left her bed, seemingly excited by the prospect of an outing. A hired car called. She was weak on her pins, could barely walk, being very obese and short of breath, but managed to get outside the house, marvelling at the bright colours of spring, the birdsong, the refreshing breeze. All teeming life lay without.

But when she saw the sea she flatly refused to go on. Dado coaxed and promised but Mumu would not listen to reason. On she would not go for all the tea in China; no argument could shift her. My father had to tell the taximan to turn around. Mumu went back to bed.

A week later she confessed to me: 'I just couldn't go on, Aidan. Something stopped me. It was the sea that separated me from the Dodo. Do you understand?

Then followed that numb slow time when my mother refused to leave her bed, refused to be cheered up or even to read, her spirits sunk, her voice gone, sleeping away the days, a resentful unconscious deep-breathing inert apathetic living mound.

What did she want?

What did she think or see? Wings tipping over the waves, the sun in splendour on the water, the tide flowing in and all grief forgotten, the Dodo in his night-fighter giving the thumbs-up from the shining cockpit, saying it was a piece of cake and performing the Victory Roll for her?

She saw only the angel in the Dodo. Bed offered no comfort or rest.

'I'm dead tired,' she often said. 'I'm really tired out . . . exhausted now.'

In that sluggish time, when my mother had ample opportunity to sleep and dream away the days, dream away her life, she had a nightmare of Joss dead.

He had been the go-between from Belgium when she and my father had conducted their courting; and had himself married the next youngest of six – was it? – sisters.

Mumu celebrated the end of the war in her own way, by rising up out of bed. The Dodo was in Scotland, now studying to be a Land Surveyor. My parents moved from Greystones to Dalkey, a change before death.

– 26 –

The Course Record

NAMES					H'Cap	Strokes
A	A. C. HIGGINS				3	—
B	G M Rowe				8	—

CARD No .... DATE ....
COMPETITION **GRAND HOTEL CUP**
100 METRES = 110 YARDS (Approx.)

STROKES

OUT	30
IN	36
GROSS	66
H'CAP	3
NETT	63

Hole	Title	Medal	Forward	Winter	Par	Index	A	B	0
1	Burnaby	277	264	263	4	18	3		
2	Garden	455	446	431	5	8	4		
3	Ridge	400	393	393	4	1	3		
4	Oozler	160	151	141	3	10	3		
5	Spinney	374	360	346	4	3	4		
6	Narrows	321	315	306	4	5	3		
7	Dolly	148	128	112	3	16	3		
8	Mill	449	437	449	5	12	4		
9	Rookery	127	125	121	3	17	3		
	Out	2711	2609	2562	35	Out	30		
10	Big Tree	364	362	315	4	2	4		
11	Farm	327	263	312	4	14	4		
12	Pigs Hollow	177	168	151	3	9	5		
13	Campbell's	286	284	255	4	15	4		
14	Sugar Loaf	377	366	325	4	6	4		
15	Crow Abbey	339	334	318	4	7	4		
16	The Bell	202	194	190	3	11	3		
17	View Rock	284	276	279	4	4	4		
18	La Touche	334	329	320	4	13	4		
	In	2690	2568	2465	34	In	36		
	TOTAL	5401	5175	5027	69				
	S.S.S.	68	67	67					

STABLEFORD

POINTS	

PAR

WINS	
LOSSES	
NETT	

FOR OFFICE USE ONLY

BACK NINE	
LAST SIX	
LAST THREE	
LAST TWO	
LAST ONE	

Please repair pitch marks on greens and replace all divots

Competitor's Signature ....

Marker's Signature ....

ALTERATIONS TO SCORES MUST BE INITIALLED

It was a lovely summer's morning when Geoffrey Rowe and I played in the Grand Hotel Cup. Dado appeared beside the eleventh fairway to ask how the lad was doing. Out in thirty and five under, going strong. I four-putted the next green, which had been enlarged by running a hand-mower over the fairway and the pin placed in it. Thirty-six home gave a gross sixty-six that could have been two or three shots better. It won best gross.

– 27 –

On the Isle of Man

On Christmas Day 1951, my first Christmas away from home, a colourless, windless, sunless grey-Manx day at the tail-end of an idle year, I found myself sharing a Christmas goose with a stone-deaf glutton in a boarding house on the Isle of Man.

The choleric grunty feeder with perspiration starting from every pore, uttering the deep heartfelt groans of a sated carnivore, was none other than my old Barton Cup teammate, J. D. Parsons, the Plantigrade Shuffler in person. We had teamed up as an unbeaten foursome combination of flair and lively opportunism, the Shuffler ever in storms of coughing and pipe-drill, rolling in putts from all angles across sloping greens. One of our foursome opponents had been a one-armed Dublin golfer by the name of Hamlet, from Stillorgan, with a stout sweating partner from Galloping Green, a pair defeated one summer's day at Foxrock.

We ate in silence but for the grunting and chewing of bones in Beverley Mount boarding house on Woodbourne Road where my destiny had now taken me; to this salubrious watering-hole in the middle of the Irish Sea, a resort popular with workers from the Midlands and the North of England. A tall monkey-puzzle tree in the narrow front garden blocked out the light. The summer cruise in the Indian Ocean had proved impractical, or perhaps my employer-to-be had totted up the cost. Suffering from obesity and 'incipient alcoholism', delicately phrased, he had chanced upon *The Fallacy of the Hopeless Case* by Dr Alexander Howitzer and was putting himself into Dr Howitzer's hands in a sanatorium for sad cases near Douglas. The cure went on behind high stone walls, with a gatelodge and keepers; straitjackets and sedation supplied on request. A barren Indian woman was trying to have a child, a fellow with curvature of the spine was trying to walk straight; Dr A. Howitzer took them all in; succour was his forte. Malingering would not be tolerated; the treatment would take ten weeks, fees a hundred pounds a week with a down-payment of fifty on signing.

The heavy Xmas fare proved too much for me, after a vegetarian diet of Galtee cheese, eggs and milk. The next day, with profuse apologies to landlady Mrs Crowe for hardly touching her goose, stuffed, roasted and basted to a succulent brown, I resumed my ordinary of vegetarian omelettes.

The Plantigrade Shuffler had gone to Trinity College where he had graduated as an architect. Brother Danny had lost a leg on Anzio Beach, emigrated to New Zealand, practised as a doctor, visiting the islands, until lost at sea (the missing ketch *Joyita,* an unsolved marine mystery), possibly eaten by cannibals, the Shuffler thought. As the eldest son he was obliged to take over the running of the family business – a footwear factory in Athlone in the dead centre of Ireland – and be answerable to his martinet of a father, old Parsons, a bigoted old Protestant gent who was down on alcohol (to which both his sons were addicted) and Roman Catholics ('No truck with Papists!'), few of whom owned property in the Burnaby, an enclave within an enclave in the Greystones population of out-and-out Protestants. 'Up King Billy!' was the blazon on his banner.

One morning the flag of Greystones Golf Club stood at half-mast to signal the passing of old Parsons and the course was closed until lunchtime, though the bar was open. The will was in the hands of the trustees; the home in the Burnaby and the footwear factory in Athlone, with £66,000, was the Shuffler's *if* he remained on the wagon for a year, testified to by a reliable witness. It was a stipulation with which he could not comply; in practice it was impossible.

Thrice a week he drove to Athlone in his Mini; then home, rattling over the cattle-trap under the arched entrance of *Greystones Golf Club (Members Only)* that was a sign for the favoured, by the eighteenth green and up the ramp by the Pro's hut (old Martin), over the moat and under the lowered drawbridge and into the castle yard, the bawn, to the merry sound of bells ringing and bugles calling and a flag flying to announce the safe arrival of the inheritor, and old Mrs Martin (quick to move her hand from the till) opening the first chilled Dutch lager of the day and the members telling each other 'The Shuffler's back!' As the thirsty *castellanus* returning from the wars.

He was a card, deaf as a post but merry as a grig. He dined in the Grand Hotel, the Railway Hotel, the Clyda, The Horse and Hounds in Delgany, making great depredations among the stocks of Dutch lager. Coming and going like the wind, no sooner gone than back for another one; no sooner that drink finished than off with him again, visiting all the posting-houses on the road to ruin, crying out, 'One for the road!' He was a solitary drinker, even in company, for his deafness kept him apart. He drank at the bar of the Grand, at Lewis's near the convent where the Sharps and the Jacksons sat around the fire, drinking brandy with Charlie Reynolds the

Garda Sergeant, served by Patsy who was thought to wear a corset to keep his figure trim; on to Danns and the Clyda Hotel *en route* to Delgany and the Horse and Hounds. He drove back at speed through Greystones, via Trafalgar Road, Victoria Road, Kimberley Road, Eden Road, Whitshed Road, Portland Road and Erskine Avenue, so that you would hardly know you were in Ireland at all. On one famous occasion he drove across the eighteenth green in his Mini; and he the Vice-President of the golf club!

Now I was to be the minder or golfing companion, a vegetarian imbiber of soft drinks and holder of the course record (it was a lovely summer's morning), hired to play golf once a day over Braddan public links and to see – to testify to the testy trustees – that he had stayed on the wagon for one whole calendar year.

Thrice a week he walked to the sanatorium for his infrared treatment, for doses of salts and invigorating pep talks from Dr Howitzer.

We flew in on a grey sunless day.

The details of our arrival, the unpacking of the golf bags, the signing in, all is obliterated from my mind, as the endless wearysome nightshift in the extrusion moulding plant is obliterated, as the details of punishments in three schools are obliterated, swept away.

J. D. Parsons, the Plantigrade Shuffler, *nuestro amigo,* (you should have seen him lining up a putt!), deaf as a post without his hearing-aid out on the course, indomitable batler, the pipe-drill, the tics, the daring recovery shots from deep bunkers, the sunny smile, the gleam of honest perspiration, the extraordinary Waa-waaa-waa of long-drawn upperclass consonants (being deaf for so long, since the age of sixteen, it must have been an aural recall of the posh accents of English fellows at TCD, gone all wonky in the airwaves, distorted by the passage of time, become a parody of what it had attempted to respect – he spoke as Bulldog Drummond and his gang must have spoken, the club drawl).

'The cure takes ten weeks. Perhaps by then I'll have developed a taste for tomato-juice,' he sniggered.

The Plantigrade Shuffler rarely looked you in the eye and then only by accident, busily lipreading, nodding his head; scuttling into the bar, into the Gents, into the changing room, a deaf man's extra-loud vocal chorus booming inanities ('Playing to single figures!'), his hearing-aid worn under the arm (the battery buzzing, very loud when he drank soup, if plugged in), the plug in one ear, a sort of harness.

'Hello, Joe, you're looking well.' Joe Mulderry, the poker player, looking like death warmed up). 'Hello, Freddy. (Freddy Quinn, his inseparable side-kick). Looking well.'

'Hello, Des.'

He had a furtive abstracted smile, looking down at his shoes, over his paunch, standing at the end of the bar in his accustomed place, rarely sitting, his feet crossed when he began to feel comfortable (after the sixth Dutch Lager), a pedagogic way of making points with the stem of his pipe. The refill, the tamping down with finger, the match lit, the quick insucks, the very flushed face very serious now, sound of sucking in air, bubbling of pipe, waving of match to extinguish, puffing out clouds of smoke, rolling over on the convex rubber soles of his expensive brogues. 'Has Beppa been in?'

Then the short abstracted puffs followed by a storm of coughing, bent double at end of bar, red features gone purple, hand to paunch, pipe stem waved about, fiddling with hearing-aid, to crackling of static, storms of coughing.

A delivery so rich and rare, so *rubicund* it sounded posh, put on, faked, never heard on earth before, was in fact intended dead seriously and so accepted by those who had become accustomed to his eccentric ways at the golf club.

An evening out was an occasion for a loud braying of indiscretions heard across the bar or the length of a dining room; and every evening was an evening out for the Shuffler, imbibing quarts of Dutch lager, topped up with gin, wine and cognac.

'The Shuffler's a scream,' they all agreed at the club where he was vice-president.

The Shuffler dining out made a real pig's nose of it. The hearing-aid batteries were constantly giving trouble, bubbling acoustics with every mouthful, the battery on the table before him, loud compliments paid to the ladies, Bep and Bimp in stitches, wasn't he a scream! He was an unconscious clown, master of the loud devastating *non sequitur,* and all thanks to deafness. A rum cove was the Shuffler.

'Bep been in?' The Shuffler asked between one hacking cough and another, waving his pipestem about to clear away the smokescreen.

'Not yet, Mr Parsons,' spoke out old Mrs Martin over the bar counter. Astonishing blood-red lipstick daubed across her mouth gave her the alarming look of a whore from *Les Fleurs de Mal.*

Perhaps this unregenerate boozer had his old man, dead but still operative, to thank for the state he found himself in? Old dead Parsons was still clamped to his back by the inflexible terms of the will, as Sinbad the Sailor had the Old Man of the Sea clamped to his back. He had been a martinet in his lifetime and continued to rule from beyond the grave. Having undermined his eldest son's belief in himself, when a qualified architect had become the manager of a boot factory, he had seen to it that his wishes would be honoured posthumously.

The Shuffler was a *softened up* drinker rather than a hardened drinker, rendered all round and wobbly by prodigious intakes of Dutch lager and the resultant flatulence.

The caddies kept an eye out for him, recognising the wheels slamming over the cattle-grid at the entrance gate, the car door banged shut almost before the engine died and the Shuffler already surrounded by caddies calling out to be hired. The going rate in those days was half a crown a round with tips optional, a wing.

Who strolled in then but May Fitzgibbon and Dorry Oulton followed by Joe Mulderry and Freddy Quinn, the two pallid poker players of smoke-filled rooms.

Hello Des!

Hello May! Hello Dorry!

Hello Des!

Hello Joe! Hello Freddy!

All agreed that all were looking remarkably well.

The general consensus of opinion in the bar was that he (the Shuffler) was a hoot.

A hoot.

Endless visits to the Gents to empty his bladder; storms of coughing announced his return to the bar where he preferred to stand at the serving-hatch. His amiable gossip revolved around golf, the condition of the course, the health of the members, all old friends like Joe Mulderry, Freddy Quinn, John Sibley, John Thullier, Norman Dickinson, Dr Ian Moore, Harry Duggan, Harry Jervois, Major Frank Stone, Captain Simon Pettigrew. The Right Revd Riversdale Colthurst had a plain scraggy spouse who wore a tea-cosy on her head. The Honorary Club Secretary had been gazetted from England and the Rutland Halberdiers; Lieutenant-Colonel Howard Cornwallis Lewis (retired) was a pompous ass. He liked to be addressed as 'Colonel'. It was my pleasure to slaughter him in singles, leave him to go spluttering off down the hill. I nicknamed him Humphrey Chimpden Earwicker.

The Colonel liked to begin the day with a prodigious military evacuation in the club bog. He shat like a Lewis gun. Loud groaning stools were his speciality, with devastating sound-effects, an early morning military barrage with rising stenches finished off in the grand manner with multiple flushings and vigorous application of stiff bumf, the toilet roll sent fairly spinning, like the unrolling of banners.

Then, with much bluff H'RRrrummphing and clearing of the windpipe he stepped out to wash his hands, scrub his nails, comb back sparse bracken-coloured hair, straighten his club tie, put himself to rights. Whereupon he lit up his briar pipe and emerged pristine, set off upstairs to his cubbyhole off the boardroom, his cramped office quarters, to formal acknowledgements of 'Good morning, Colonel!' from staff and whatever amiable member might be about at that hour, looking for an early game; glancing upward at the broad back ascending the stairs in a cloud of good-quality tobacco fumes. He and I had never seen eye to eye.

This testy military type was all the more formally an officer because of never having seen action. When the Right Revd Riversdale Colthurst (Army Chaplain) had laid a complaint against me for 'driving into him' over the hill at the 11th, the Colonel was pleased to formally acknowledge it. 'Higgins, we have just received a complaint from one of the members. Should you care to offer some explanation, ahem, we await your reply. The matter will be brought up at the next General Meeting.'

Acid correspondence passed between us. He surprised me with football stockings off, warming my frozen feet at the coal fire in the bar; that kind of conduct would not be tolerated.

'Good morning, *Colonel!*' was balm to his gilead. He was to die in harness, of a heart attack at Bray GC, collapsing on the 14th green, muttering his epitaph ('I'm finished!'). This by way of captious aside. We are on the isle of Manx cats, not Bray.

The daily ritual of a round ('to reduce obesity') was to continue from the first day, no matter how inclement the weather. We played for the usual stakes – a half-crown for a win, a tanner for birdies, dykes and oozlers, half stakes on the bye, loser pays for the first round of drinks, non-alcoholic beverages preferred.

Sometimes we returned to the Peverel Hotel for our refreshments; we were remembered, the barman greeted us.

The Plantigrade Shuffler's round agnostic cheeks glowed a duller purple as he laboured up the slopes of Braddan public links, where hills and gradients abounded, following the high arcs of his drives, struck with determined grunting. Addressing the ball well teed up, the curvature of his spine became more pronounced, paunch matched by hump, that gave him a simian look. Everything about him was curvilinear, from round cheeks to paunch, and like the Dodo he too seemed to totter forward on convex soles. The backs of his hands were hairy and as he struck the ball he grunted, following its course with some body English.

He was all roundy, the spine rounded upwards towards the neck, the neck bulged upwards towards the skull, the skull curved into the inflamed face. The very strokes he struck were perfect arcs, hit with a half-swing from rounded shoulders with a grunt, and looped too was the parabola of the shot, the Warwick dispatched briskly on its way with much topspin.

Above the sea on the exposed Braddan Hills we followed our drives, one sixty or eighty yards ahead of the other. The days were wretchedly cold. One morning I struck a seabird on the fairway with a low drive, my hands frozen, and had to dispatch it with a sand-blaster.

After lunch I was free to continue my roaming about the port. On the milder days the sky over Douglas turned the flesh-pink of yew bark cut with a knife, a roseate island light. I stepped into the pulpits and read from all the bibles. In St Kyran's Roman Catholic Church (Mass & Daily Communion 8.00 a.m. Daily) the door sighed shut behind me and the street noises abated. A band of diffused coloured light filtered down through the stained-glass windows above the fourth and fifth Stations of the Cross. The wind was humming in the apertures of the long windows above the altar, the noises from outside reduced to a low innuendo, a distant buzzing. It was the first week after Epiphany.

On 10th January 1952 we went to the Christmas panto at the Empress Theatre and I heard the panto girl sing 'Pale Hands I Loved Beyond the Shalimar' (where are you now?), and was much taken with her. I wrote her a fan letter and she agreed to an assignation at two-thirty next day at the Manx Museum.

We began walking out. The nights were so freezingly cold that not even a Manx cat would venture out of doors. We walked the roads sparkling with quartz around the Braddan Hills under an amazing canopy of stars, and she told me that was the Liverpool boat sailing for Liverpool and those lights were not an ocean liner coming in but Lamona Asylum, where the

Plantigrade Shuffler (having gone off his head) was to be consigned on January 21st.

He asked me to spit in his face and I obliged, for why gainsay him if he imagined himself to be Christ, and he an unbeliever?

Frescoes of angels were painted on either side of the confessional. The angel on the left hand had a sly eye and a prudish 'o' for a mouth, with elbows held stiffly by the side and the palms of the hands extended outward, just below the shoulders, in a frozen cataleptic arrested gesture. In graphic capital letters below on a scroll blowing free in the winds of Heaven was inscribed MISERICORDIA.

The angel on the opposite side held a formidable key diagonally across its chest, the angelic brows drawn together in a severe manner, while on a companion scroll was printed ABSOLUTIO. On the half-door of the confessional a brown card was pinned to the monk-brown curtain:

Rev Theo. Craine, PP

On the evening of the 20th January the great Naturopath gave a talk to which his patients and members of the public were invited: 'Out of This World to Soft Lights and Music'. It was snowing. The Plantigrade Shuffler and I dined at the Perivale with my panto girl and a friend. The Shuffler was drinking again. He said that the sanatorium was surrounded by a bad cloud, and he was moving back to the hotel. It was to be the end of our silent evenings sitting around the fire. At four-thirty in the morning I was woken by Tom Crowe laying his hand on my shoulder, to whisper that a policeman downstairs wished to speak to me.

I found the Plantigrade Shuffler in an exalted state of madness. He had set fire to the bedroom curtains and might have burnt down the hotel. They were talking of certifying him. He had become Christ expelling the buyers and sellers from the Temple. The sergeant and police doctor converged on us. I refused to sign any papers. They told us that we were going for a short drive, it would be for the bet. In the squad car my now deranged employer was squeezed between two huge constables in the back seat, looking like mad preacher Casey offering his wrists for the handcuffs in *The Grapes of Wrath*.

We swept up the curved driveway of Lamona Asylum and piled out. Two inmates carrying a bucket stacked high with dirty washing set it down in order to gape at us. A door in an ivy-covered wall sprang open and half a

dozen wild-looking internees in white coats approached us. Me they unerr-
ingly picked as the mad one. 'You've got the wrong man,' I said. The Shuffler was undergoing transformations, now he was a middle-aged matron
about to bear a child; he was shaking his head with a sweet maternal smile,
telling them his time was not quite up. They placated and coaxed him and
drew him in with them and closed the door and that was that. I went back
to the boarding house and told the Crowes. Mr Crowe kindly booked me
onto the first flight to Dublin. I said my goodbyes. I said I would contact the
trustees. There was a sister somewhere. It was all most unfortunate I said.
We must all hope to be saved they said. We shook hands. A cab came and
took me to Douglas Airport, for a flight to Dublin.

On the day he mailed off his mad thesis to Dublin (one copy sent registered to Professor Walton at TCD, one to Professor Erwin Schrödinger
at the Institute of Advanced Studies, the first never acknowledging it, the
second most alarmed by it) he was fairly flying, a spring-heeled Jack full of
helium. Walking to and from the post office he seemed to be high-stepping
it through a quag or trying to make himself ultra heavy, so as not to fly off
the Earth itself, rising vertically until hidden by clouds; stamping down
on the pavement as if to increase his weight, assume the leaded boots of a
deep-sea diver.

The Plantigrade Shuffler had formerly walked with the rolling gait of a
sailor, but now it was the wound-up clockwork *locomotor ataxi* of the habitual
boozer, the hard drinker's roll, *en route* to the pub named The Hair of the
Hound, or the Consul on his way to El Farolito, Casanova incarcerated
with the rats.

Neither of us was quite normal; given the state I was in I couldn't see how
disturbed he was, behind his habitual twitching and eccentric behaviour; if
he was going off his head I couldn't see it. I had read the thesis but it hadn't
conveyed much sense. He had proved or attempted to prove that pain is
palpable; more than that, an objective part of us like an appendix or a pip
in an apple, that could be seen and presumably removed, like a cancer. I
didn't see what he was getting at; for an unbeliever, a sceptic such as he,
it seemed to me a very roundabout way of admitting Original Sin, about
whose existence I had little doubt.

Besides, I was myself deep into studies of madness. Thomas Mann's
Der Zauberberg in the Lowe-Porter translation, Wyndham Lewis's *Blasting
& Bombardiering* and a large tome illustrated with schizophrenic paintings
made by disturbed minds in institutions for the insane, entitled *Wisdom,*

Madness and Folly. Huge coloured spheres were bounding towards a distant horizon or bouncing towards the viewer and about to burst from the page.

In my own days of destitution and misery which were soon to come upon me, brought on by undernourishment and the pull and stress of a purposeless existence which had become more and more distressful to me, I was to experience something similar; a sense of doom allied to irrepressible gaiety, akin to Herr Mann's pleura-shock, first mauve and then purple, as the hooks go in. A sort of extreme miserable bliss, or blissful misery *in extremis.*

And then?

Dado had resumed his endless pacing from sink to window to command an angled view of Kinlen Road and then the long silent stare out, the abstracted pacing to and fro; the circumspect belch followed by subdued fart told of the eventless passage of Time.

Tyres on gravel, the front wheel of the heavy Raleigh pushing open the yard door, signalled the precipitous arrival of the Dodo back from a day at the office in Dublin, the train to Greystones, the bicycle ride home. A short silence meant he was removing his bicycle clips at the back step, the sound of the flange banged back and the door rattled to its foundations, told us that the Dodo was home again. Everybody opens a door in a characteristic and revealing way, revealing as thumb-prints; the Dodo *fired* open the door and propelled himself into the kitchen, anxious to get in a few holes of golf before supper, or dark, depending on the time of year, before 'Moonlight in Vermont', before the stars came out to play. A rattle of lids on the electric stove told that he was checking out the supper, the silence meant he was changing for golf, following by pissing and flushing and banging of bathroom door; then the slipper in place, then silence, out. A quick sighting of the Dodo carrying his limp canvas holdall and assortment of clubs; head down, puffing out his cheeks, with short fussy steps crossing the path he had worn between the trellised enclosures and out into the back field near the rugby club, and away to the back nine. He was not a member, he was trespassing, resolute in his pleasures as in his work.

No monkey-wrench ever tightened bathroom faucets in any Higgins home, that's for sure.

He had not remarked upon my leaving nor on my return. Life resumed its even tenure as before. He moved like a stout middle-aged woman in a hurry in a hobble skirt, progress impeded by the enveloping heavy cloth. I thought of the *tenue* of the other, which had been extremely odd. He seemed to be filled with helium which was lifting him up and he slapped down his feet as solidly as possible in order to stay attached to the gravity from which his madness was trying to free him. A chemist's window blazed with the display of an outsize bottle of azure blue.

To cut a long story short, I was back safely again in my little pink padded cell, hearing the taps dripping all night long, before you could say *dementia praecox*.

Of the outward flight I have little or no recollection, although it was the first time I had flown anywhere; or for that matter on what airline we travelled – Air Man? Manx Airways? for insignia a black cat sans tail sitting up pert and smirking on outstretched tail of crow in full flight; nor can I recall the small island airport where we landed, neat as Menorca.

Of the return flight I recall only the plane tilting over Bull Island and a horizontal line of grey cloud like grey moiré lifting as we came in over Dublin and how it rose up (silently, no orchestra in the pit) like the safety curtain at the Gaiety rising on Paulette Goddard and Burgess Meredith in *Winterset*.

And needless to say I flew in no wiser than I had flown out, and certainly no richer. A week or so later I was summoned by one of the trustees to luncheon at a gentlemen's club on Stephen's Green. An excellent wine was broached. I spoke of a child drowned in a fountain on the esplanade, falling through thin ice and hidden as the water froze solid again, and how they came and found the little dead one, like looking through a window. At the coffee and brandy stage we were the best of friends, the kind-featured trustee in the starched collar and I, and diplomatic feelers were extended. 'As to remuneration for any inconvenience suffered, I think we should . . .'

I held up one hand. I told him they didn't owe me a penny. I was sorry for the man put away, and hoped he would be out and about soon. We shook hands on the steps.

Some time in the following year I had a letter from the Plantigrade Shuffler. He thanked me for what I had done for him. He had put in his time, stayed dry, come into his inheritance, and £66,000 was a tidy sum in those days. He seemed to be in the best of spirits, spoke of another fourball in the Spring, when the greens were cut and rolled. No cheque was enclosed. Life was real, life was earnest, and God was good.

PART II

London

Ealing

Nothing is easy in a strange place, at first.

It took me some time to become acclimatised to factory ways and life at Fordhook Road with the frightened French couple who were dreading the end of the world.

Nor was finding Ealing Common as easy as at first surmised. From a perusal of the Tube map I found it named there but be damned if I could find it. I had done the Stations of the Cross many times as a penitential exercise; now I was doing the outer circles of Hell. And Elizabeth Bowen's neurotic mum had it perfectly right: London had a smell of its own.

When I did eventually make it overground at Ealing Common, coming up out of the bowels of the earth, I found a pleasant enough area disposed on either side of the Uxbridge Road, leading east to Acton Town and west to Ealing Broadway, which I had visited several times on the Tube, before taking the next east-bound connection Londonward. A butchery and bakery and cake shop and newsagents with awning were tidily arranged around the mouth of the Tube, out of which came dead air smelling of coke. Fordhook Road was to be my home-base for the foreseeable future. A neighbour with brush and pan was scooping up fresh horse manure, while glancing up at jet skylanes streaming in towards Heathrow, as if this was manna from Heaven – the hot turds carefully collected and carried through the house to his roses at the back. Was this an omen?

My quarters – one room with bed and use of bathroom-cum-toilet – were neat as a pin. I shared digs with Kevin O'Sullivan, a whilom golfing crony of Delgany, who worked at Firestone manufacturing huge tyres for the African market.

In those days the street-criers were still to be heard, ringing their bells and calling their wares; selling and buying ironmongery and odds and ends off horse-drawn drays. Voices from an English rustic past of Cobbett and Jefferies; a past which I had heard echoes of on the Isle of Man. Manx street-criers ringing handbells and uttering strange calls, incomprehensible Manx cries.

London town, when I eventually reached it, had a strange smell all its own. A smell like nothing else on earth – a stale spent smell with its own peculiar murky daylight, unchanged I dare say since the young Konrad Korzeniowski saw *a rusty sunlight that cast no shadows* some forty odd years before, when he had settled himself in digs near the Thames to write his first sea saga, *Almayer's Folly*. Nothing had changed essentially in the interval.

Perhaps it was the dusty miasmic after-stink of the Blitz – that horrific hammering – that still lingered on the air of the early 1950s when I first set foot there, before the end of the smog?

I had sold my golf clubs to a man in Hammond Lane Foundry, paid for a single ticket on the packet steamer sailing from Dun Laoghaire to Wales, boarded the London train and stayed on it until it steamed into Euston, went down steps with great misgiving, bought a ticket to Ealing Common, boarded the Tube and spent several hours shuttling to and fro, mostly underground, but always ending up at Ealing Broadway.

True to my obsession I spent long hours underground, as if bribing Charon to ferry me across the Styx, but could not see the further shore. I had been briefed by brother Bun who had been working for years at the British Film Library at Brentford; and now here I was shut up in a succession of onrushing Tubes.

At last, exhausted, I took the right connection, found Ealing Common when the automatic doors slid wide, stepped out onto the platform a new man. Crossing the Uxbridge Road with a light step I found Fordhook Road as the map had suggested, and the digs brother Bun had put a deposit on in the house so hoovered and polished by the middle-aged French couple who were anticipating the end of the world, a rain of atomic bombs.

Next morning I presented myself at the Labour Exchange and accepted my fate as a factory hand in Ponds Cosmetic Factory in Perivale at the lowly remuneration of seven pounds a week in the old currency, out of which thirty-five shillings would be deducted for rent. I would walk to work.

I prepared myself for a diet of Quaker Oats and milk, tinned beans, Take & Lyle honey spread on sliced loaf, washed down with Nescafé. The work in the stores was not arduous but a 6.00 a.m. shift meant rising at 4.45 a.m. In the factory I wore a brown boiler suit and laboured there for nine months, developing a taste for Watney's Red Barrel ale and Senior Service cigarettes, saving twenty pounds.

It was scarcely an auspicious beginning in the Greater London labour mart, in the footsteps of so many of my countrymen. With Jeffries (a baker laid off) and Tom Davies and Mr Brogan the chargehand in his white coat, and Vic Webb (ex-Army) with his limp, and the dull torment of working on the conveyor belt; beyond a certain speed which I considered inhuman I flatly refused to go, and let the stuff pile up, let the ganger curse, let Minny have kittens.

White froth from the cider factory was blown into Ponds' loading yard and fell like apple blossom or summer snow. At a break from the conveyor belt a group of girls in purple overalls had found a piece of smoked glass and stared through it at an eclipse of the sun and Milly Ashbrook remarked that at the next eclipse none there would be alive. It was July 30th, 1952, in my beginnings. The Bristol lorry driver gave me a present of rhubarb from his garden. He had a pleasant nautical Bristol accent, a seafaring burr, one arm tattooed with a cross and 'Father, Mother, Christ, Forget Me Not' in florid script amid the hair on his forearm.

Belisha beacons were spilling an overflow of ruby light onto the pillars of the Midland Bank on the Mall when I walked again across the Common in the near lightlessness before daybreak and the long-distance lorries were starting up on Hanger Lane.

My next foray involved digging up a back garden in Swiss Cottage, and poor shaly cindery soil it was too; that part-time job did not last long, at remuneration of a half-crown an hour. Then I worked longer hours for a hard seven months for better pay at Punfield & Barstow extrusion mouldings plant out by the Great North Road, reading *La Nausée* and lunching off two thin chops and tinned peas in a transport café. The chargehands here were Bob de Palmo and the whistling German, Martin Muhl, who boasted of the time he had worked flat out on a twelve-hour nightshift with his shirt off.

I sweated it out with Monk the Jew and Blizzard the Jamaican, as black as your boot, who paid extra rent for being black in a white area. Basket the Pakistani and Doody the moody Corkman were on my shift. I had digs in an upper room on Abbey Road, above Wholefart and Angel, a pair of huge decayed floozies who chain-smoked in their bathrobes and ran endless baths, occupying the bathroom – which was also the toilet – for long periods. I alternated day and nightshifts, working eleven and twelve hours. Some diehards were prepared to work an hour overtime, regulating polythene in semi-automatic presses while being stunned by a deafening night-long cacophony on maximum amplification, deluging the exhausted workers who didn't appear to mind the pounding percussive beat. It was like being flogged.

Through one of the Musgrave sisters I found piecework that I could do at home; painting Geordies the size of your thumb, in kilts, as a movie promotional stunt that would drive the sanest person mad. For a time I held down a part-time job as swimming-pool attendant at Marylebone Public Baths; but I saved nothing.

'Use your loaf, mate,' was the embattled war-cry of the weary factory hands
and shift workers. Meaning: Wise up, get smart, fiddle.

In 1956 I was either working as a factory hand in Ponds (Cosmetics) in
Perivale with Jeffries and Davies and old Bert Pollard or as a trainee extrusion moulder with Basket and Blizzard in Punfield & Barstow (Mouldings)
at Burnt Oak on alternating day and night shifts. I recall the nausea of the
long nightshift and staying awake when working the semi-automatic presses
and the incessant barrage of Muzak from the amplifiers – 'The Yellow Rose
of Texas' and 'Be My Life's Companion' firm favourites, until they were
coming out of our ears.

As with the Muzak and the howling headlines of the *Daily Mirror* so it was
with my sandwiches, no matter how carefully prepared, no matter what I put
into them, they all tasted the same, an unappetising mush.

Khrushchev and Bulganin – 'Mr K & Mr B' in the overly familiar parlance
of the tabloids – had arrived on a state visit in the Soviet cruiser *Orzhonikidze*
which had anchored in Portsmouth harbour. Commander 'Buster' Crabb
the intrepid frogman had swum under it in his flippers and never surfaced
alive again. The body was later recovered with not a mark on it. The Soviet
diplomats kept their lips diplomatically sealed, the Cold War tactics of not
showing your hand.

Farewell the Davall Clock Factory, adieu Cider Factory, the Enna Infants
Bath Factory, trio viewed so oft from the loading-bay, a view of the last fields
of England. Farewell thin anxious Minny organising labour on the factory
floor, Mr Lambert in his blue suit striding to and from the office, farewell old
Bert at the shredding machine, Ted Heavens in the stores, farewell early shift
and nightshift, Nescafé and Quaker Oats, farewell the *Daily Mirror* and Yana
('Britain's Singing Bombshell') and the girl with heavy menses who fainted
at the conveyor belt and her sleepy sister with hand impaled on the carding-
machine in the Lipstick Room, farewell lovely pay-days and the present of
handkerchiefs and the Christmas bonus in the pay-packet.

I was one of the blokes pulverised by a tediousness that could not be contained but somehow had to be endured. It was all a 'bind' (Cockney slang for
the intolerable chore) in brother Bun's adopted huff-snuff Limey lingo.

The English factory hand, your average pieceworker, is likely the most
miserable of all working men on the surface of the globe. The centuries-old
stoicism of the footsoldier in English lines that never broke, no matter how
savage the assault (Malaparte remarked upon this), lives on in a vulgarised

form in the bloke or bod you see before you, drowning in his *Daily Mirror,* forever accepting hand-outs, cutting corners, saving his face, bellyaching at his sorry lot, putting in overtime, lowering a few pints at his local, 'supporting' this soccer team or that, a broken-down knacker's-yard animal, a crock with all the stuffing knocked out of it. Brother Bun had found his spiritual home not far from Ealing Broadway in the company of contentious Gorblimeys, the miserable sods of Ailing.

P&B manufactured objects as diverse and various as collar studs to aeroplane parts. One worked, quite literally, by the clock. Fifteen semi-automatic presses thundered away twenty-four hours a day, never silent and stopping only to accommodate a new time-cycle installed by the clever engineers; and the fifteen operators kept their eyes glued on the clock, a large oval one-handed chronometer that ticked off the seconds, 39,600 of them in a nightshift that seemed endless to the operator.

One kept to fixed pressures and time cycles, producing, say, four articles per minute, per shift schedule as ordained by the graph hung outside de Palmo's office. It was common practice to force up the pressure and extrude two seconds prematurely. In order to achieve a four-a-minute cycle, say, you were allowed two seconds for opening, two seconds for closing – opening again on the tenth second, extruding on the twelfth, closing on the fifteenth and repeating this cycle four times every minute. But by opening on the eighth, extruding and closing as instructed, it was possible to close on the thirteenth instead of on the fifteenth, opening again on the twenty-first to close on the twenty-sixth instead of on the thirtieth, gaining two forbidden seconds on every quarter of a cycle. So we slaved away, opening, extruding and closing twenty-eight thousand times instead of the regulation twenty-four thousand. This was piecework put into practice and a little private gain hard won against the odds; the carrot of private emolument dangled tantalisingly just ahead of the whip of the capitalist employer, P&B (Mouldings) of Burnt Oak.

To see Monk (the Jew) or Blizzard (the Jamaican) wipe clean the platters of polythene that had been subjected to heat and severe pressure was to understand the 'hidden agenda' of the system, the ethos of the Dark Satanic Mills; the little bit on the side was the factor that made the whole thing work. And I recalled (in the endless nightshift one had ample time for such trolling back) how old Mrs Henry (God rest her soul, for she must be long gone to her reward) wiped a plate clean with a sort of dogged earnestness, with slow loving strokes (for she herself was also trolling back into her own past, before my time) as if it were a baby's bottom. The care and attention she lavished on our dirty plates was the same loving care that she had lavished on the Dote's dirty face (tears that grimy fists had knuckled into his eyes) and thrice dirty bottom, dutifully, lovingly wiping both clean, as she would my own tear-stained face and beshatten bottom, although strictly speaking it was not her job to clean either end of us, her place belonged below, in the kitchen. She did it, out of the goodness of her working heart, to spare us embarrassment with Nurse O'Reilly, that martinet, or Mumu, that grand lady.

At the end of a shift and without even a shower to clean us, we departed from the premises of Punfield & Barstow as if soundly whipped, to doze all the way home in the smelly Tube.

In Wall's ice-cream factory, putting in overtime, I worked in cold storage for an extra ten bob a week, fifteen pounds per week in twenty-three degrees below freezing, putting in forty-eight hours. And furthermore, in a heat wave in July; though the last thing any of the blokes or bods craved was an ice cream, least of all a Wall's wafer, after the vomit smell of the factory floor. Black men lay out on garden benches, seemingly decapitated.

These were some pockets of the labour mart in the Greater London area, the equivalent of Fritz Lang's grim *Metropolis* and not the romantic lies of Carné's *Le Jour se Lève*. In those years not long after the end of the war, the cessation of hostilities; being some account of my time locked into the system – mocked by Beckett as 'the great big booming buzzing confusion'.

Those days of factory labour are now mercifully obliterated by Time, the great fixative and cure-all. Muzak was piped in day and night through eleven-hour shifts and rained down on the heads of passive labouring subjects; it gave me a lifelong aversion to so-called pop music, which I associated with servitude.

– 29 –

Tea With Mr Spender

'Porchester Terrace,' I told the taximan soberly.
One could hear the loud bottle-party from the street. The host was nowhere to be seen, the lighting dim in one room, completely dark in another, both crowded as jails. Presently out of the darkened room

sprang lean flamenco dancers in tight black dralon trousers, cummerbunds, about their narrow waists, awash with sweat, gruesomely active, their flies stained with emissions from dancing with the girls in the dark.

In they strutted, gesticulating and rolling their eyes, showing the base-metal fillings in their teeth. A Mr Guy Tremlett and a Mr Rory Bagshot introduced themselves. Did I know Riley and Jebby? asked Pigshot or Bigshot, perspiring like a pig. No, really? Not know old Jebby? Never heard of Binky? Their interest waned, was dissipated. They showed no interest in the girls who were drinking cheap red wine out of cups. They had eyes only for the enflamed flamenco dancers with the indecent stains; a right pair of sodomites. No drinks were being offered; one brought one's own bottle.

'I'll snap it off!'

'Damn your yellow eyes!'

An Andalucían song began to whine on the hidden turntable and from the kitchen down the hall came host Peter Upward bearing a plate of spaghetti bolognese, followed by a trim young slip of a thing carrying two mugs of wine. They sat back to back like book-ends, Upward applying himself to the food. From the manner in which he ignored her it was evident that she was to be his that night.

'It was to be either flamenco or booze,' Upward explained, wiping his lips with a tissue. 'So we decided on flamenco. Didn't we, kitten?'

Kitten rubbed her back against his. A tall brunette in tartan slacks stood in a corner with two dull fellows.

'Jean love!'

'Murty!' a strangled voice said.

A middle-aged man went by with a stunned girl in tow. She wore Italian sandals, a tight gossamer-green dress. The dancing girls in the darkened room were screeching, pissed as cunts. They were being agreeably tortured by the young flamenco dancers, ravening and raging, and all dead ringers for Tom Maschler.

'Who, if I cried,' intoned a cor anglais voice, 'would hear me among the angelic orders? None, I fear.'

'Structure,' articulated a thin voice behind the sofa just vacated by the host who was clutching his kitten on the darkened dancefloor within.

'May I?' I asked the mossy green dress, greatly daring.

Couples glued together circled the floor more or less in time to the gluey music issuing from the darkened room where the flamenco dancers were having a ball, their stamping feet sounding like hoofs. I danced close with the mottled man's discarded girl, grasping her resolutely about the hips and girdle, moving slowly, now trapped this way, now that, breathing her scent, feeling her supple spine through the conducting agent of thigh and leg, floorboards.

'You'd never guess whom I had tea with last Tuesday,' she murmured, breathing Martini fumes into my face.

'I would not,' I said.

'James Joyce,' she said. 'Don't hold me there please.'

'Don't quite get that.'

'No?'

'Absolutely no.'

'Oh but it's *true*!' she said, giving me a sweet lopsided smile, and all the honesty of her greenish eyes. I could smell her lipstick.

We circled slowly. I could smell the lipstick mixed with the Martini above or below a delicate sweat, her personal aroma. She was rotating, thinking, absented.

'Not likely,' I said. 'No. Hardly possible. He's been dead some time. Since January 1941, I believe. Buried in Zurich.'

'You don't say.'

We danced about. The room was hot and airless, buzzing with partytalk.

'Oh I'm sorry,' she said, holding her head back, watching my lips as if lipreading, for what would I say next to disappoint her? 'I mean James Stephens. Last Tuesday I had tea with James Stephens.'

'I'd like to believe you,' I told her.

'You don't – why ever not?'

'He's dead too, unfortunately,' I said.

'Never heard that.'

We were hardly moving, cornered in a clot of sweaty dancers. Then it cleared a little and I steered her backwards, feeling that supple but unsober spine. The same Spanish song whined from the inner room. We danced around, the mottled man observing us.

'Oh but I *am* a fool,' the green girl whispered in my ear. 'It was Stephen *Spender*!'

'Much more likely,' I said, 'considering.'

'Considering? Oh! Isn't *he* alive?'

'Absolutely,' I said.

I could see the green girl taking tea with Mr Spender in a tearoom near the British Museum. She showed him a notebook of handwritten verse. Spender bent forward. The music stopped. A fellow who had announced that he was in publishing asked the green girl for a dance. Rolling her eyes like a doll she was swept away into the shouting throng.

'Structure,' the same voice insisted behind the sofa.

'I must say . . .'

'May I get you a drink?'

'Do forage around.'

I stood next to the mottled man. Very soon I was privy to unwanted confidences of an intimate nature. Most girls who went to bed with him, he said, conceived, and all who did brought forth daughters. But he couldn't make the green girl (apparently her name was Jean) come.

'Come to bed?' I asked obtusely.

'Have an orgasm.'

'Ah-ha.'

'Perhaps it's my fault?' he suggested.

All those who conceived by him bore daughters. Middle-aged and thin on top, with teeth in ruins, they still wanted him, wanted it, and he old enough to be their father. I heard his intestines rumble and groan and a blast of decay issued from his troubled interior along with sundry unwanted confidences and the stink of cheap vino. His breath was foul.

'Can I take her home with me?'

'Tee hee,' tittered the troubled mottled man.

A tall tease with long black hair down her back and a startling white face like Juliette Greco sailed by, very disdainful, very soignée, in the grip of a fellow with double vents. They danced at arm's length, stiff-kneed, with teeth braced in open hostility.

'Ivy Compton-Burnett,' an intense voice sang out, 'and Jack Yeats are my all-time favourites!'

A heavy hand fell like a claw on my shoulder.

'Know Shropshire?'

'No thanks.'

The tall girl in tartan slacks was going home. The host was nowhere to be seen. Unable to restrain himself after the closeness of the dancing he had taken the kitten away with him to an upstairs bedroom. And at that moment the flamenco dancers, the Maschler-clones awash in semen, burst from the darkened inner room, pointing long quivering fingers at each other's drenched flies and shouting, '*Borrachos! Borrachos!*'

I had no coat to collect; I had nothing to collect, it was time to go home.

'Moscow Road,' I told the taximan.

— 30 —

The Attic

The last Tube had certainly gone, sucked away into the foul-smelling tunnels, and the stations chained and padlocked for the night. Outside it would be cold; remote stars shone over Truss City.

Narrow stairs smelling of dust led down; I could not tear myself away from that warm attic.

'Stay if you wish,' you had said. 'There's a spare bed.' So I stayed, though not in the spare bed.

My own room stank like a larder, for I cooked and washed there, slept there too; it was squeezed between the high end-walls and cramped as a coffin. No sunlight could ever penetrate into Prince Edward Mansions. My landlady was French – another French landlady! – and believed that all the Irish were dirty in their habits. The place was a warren of admonitory notices and prohibitions of one sort or another: don't do this, don't do that. Madame Sagaison (may she rot in Hell) looked for pubic hair in the bath, stains in the lavatory bowl, puke in the hall. A drugged girl was sent weeping away. No questions were asked. In the near vicinity, two lobotomised patients, one a young woman, threw themselves from windows to their deaths.

I dropped my key down the elevator shaft. Madame Sagaison opened the door resentfully, dressed in pink slippers and gown; was this the time to come home? The morning milk came up in the lift. Movements late at night were frowned upon. The rent was more than I could afford but I liked the area of Notting Hill Gate and Kensington Gardens.

In the daytime the thick carpet creaked; she was standing outside my door, breathing heavily, expecting the worst. The Irish were lazy too, good-for-nothings; an abject race. She was French. But I paid my rent on the nail. So I was allowed to stay. I stayed. It was the first night in Truss City with you, a city transformed. In the night it began to snow.

I walked a station platform under the city, numbed with happiness, felt the dead air of the trains blowing on my face, unmindful of the squalor of King's Cross. Above ground it was still dark but below in the murky warmth the early shift-workers were already heading off for the factories. An obstinate crew, not young, set in their ways; their clothes the colour of mud.

A life of factory work, interrupted by war, perhaps a stint overseas, had worn them down. Then they had their country to serve or die for but now they had only themselves and they were lost, whether they knew it or not. They resembled, if it was anything living, old horses. Broken-winded work horses, their usefulness at an end, nags fit only for the Great Knacker's Yard.

I was with them in the deepest station under Truss City, under the Zoo, Queen Mary's Gardens and the Toxophilite Society. They were bound for Northfields and Osterley, Fulham gas-works and the dreary stations to the West. Factory hands, oil-darkened, clutched *Daily Mirrors* and factory-fatigued eyes stared at the pin-up, the girl-for-the-day, a sultry brunette with little on, sulking by the sea, well calculated to send the circulation up. Hers the swelling haunches of a brood mare; a long shank of dark hair, thighs invoking stalls and hard riding, tumbles in the hay. An expansive bosom was tightly clamped into the twin cups of a minute bra. There was high summer in her haughty gaze. Young, full, with parted lips, she stood provocative and near-nude on a pebble beach, her toes splashed by a cold sea, and pouting bore their hot scrutiny point by point. For she was their lost summer – the one they never had. In all that avid and packed repleteness she was lending herself, giving herself over to the gross pleasures of multiple exposure, reproduced twenty-thousand times, a hundred-thousand times, three million times, held fast in grimy fingers, breathed upon, stared at, devoured, enjoyed by proxy down there, down on the murky platforms under the city, the readers dizzy, nauseous, reeling from bed into this place where no air stirred but dead air, blown through the darkened tunnels by onrushing trains. The hot levelled gaze said, 'Just you dare, mate.' The cajoling pose (one deep breath and all would fall off) said 'Try!' If the opened centre-spread was their morning feedbag, she was their hay. 'Yana, Britain's Singing Bomb Shell!' gushed the caption.

The light that flooded the carriage did not seem to belong to life proper. She was theirs for the morning, with that bold dire stare, held fast, breathed over, desired, dreamed of, prized by famished eyes, stripped, enjoyed. The air was not clean, light changed on a raised sign, the name WIMBLEDON was lit up and hydraulic doors sprang open down the entire length of the train, a beautiful rapt face flew by. I stepped into the grimy carriage and sat down opposite a corset advertisement. Tread the rubberised surface, grasp the moist pole! The doors clamped shut all together, half-opened again with a monstrous mechanical sigh, then clamped finally shut. The train shuddered down all its length and the empty platform began to flow past and the advertisements became blurred and I was flowing along towards Bromley and Upminster, Uxbridge, Hounslow West and its howling dogs, lovely odd places no doubt, out there somewhere. The galloping train rushed through the tunnels, bored through space, *Würde, würde*! pushing dead air before it, bearing me along the District Line in fine style.

I was travelling, it now occurred to me, studying the Tube map, in altogether the wrong direction; but this did not seem to matter much, it was a good joke. Misery and hopelessness was a good joke; even Rayners Lane, with or without the possessive, was a good joke. I was alive at last, sudden contact humming in me. Study the map, consult alternatives, go back, try again. Go on. A murky sort of light beyond the racing glass indicated that day was about to break, rise up again over Truss City.

The cause of it all slept away whatever remained of the night in her high attic. The covers of the spare bed were not disturbed. You lived high up and clean like a bird; there one could breathe. For me you represented freedom. The W-framed attic with its deep window embrasure was the secret play-house that a child might build in a tree.

'Can I come again

'Of course, if you wish.'

When I changed trains underground the *Daily Mirror* girl by the sea looked like a rubber doll. I held onto another sweaty pole, sat on another worn seat, studied the same Tube map. Where are ye bound for, sad shufflers? Waterloo and City lines, dirty white for Bank, the city, brown for Bakerloo, black for the North! I found myself now travelling backwards in elevated spirits on the yellow Circle Line, heading straight as a die for Hounslow and its maddened dogs. A carnival mood had taken hold. On I went.

Above me a day hard as iron was breaking, as I stepped out, breathed snow. It was snowing on Moscow Road. Leaving behind me the acrid stench of the cage and the touch of hard shoulders, I felt my shoes crunch in thin snow. The outlines of buildings loomed up with windows lit here and there. Two Indian girls in saris were laughing and attempting to catch snowflakes in their open mouths.

I returned to Prince Edward Mansions, rising up in the elevator to Flat No. 8 like Jupiter Tonens. The milk delivery was outside the door. My room stank of monkey, the alarm was just about to go off. I changed into my working clothes, warmed a saucepan of milk over the gas ring, spooned Nescafé into a mug, prepared for another working day at Ponds.

It was at a South African party at 18A Belsize Lane attic to which I had not been invited that I became friends with my future wife, Jill Damaris Anders. I had come on the suggestion of Michael Morrow, an inveterate party-goer; it was a party for friends, with slivovitz from the Yugoslav Embassy laid on. In attendance were: the Pinkers, the Harringtons, oily Tom Maschler (briefly), Pat Godkens and the two inverts from the flat below, Chris and Luther. There was dancing in a very confined space. Michael Morrow and I sat back to back on the spare bed and drank slivovitz and smoked Balkan Sobranie. We stayed on after everyone had left; eventually we spent the night there, head to toe in the spare bed like Mr and Mrs Bloom. I did not get a wink of sleep.

I waited five weeks before phoning. Again I visited on my own, found the door open as before, the phone in the hall, the number on the dial; when five weeks passed I had plucked up enough courage to phone the Yugoslav Embassy. A friend wanted to know something about the French Cameroons. It was merely a tactical ploy, moving crabwise like a dog. I was invited around for a meal. It was then I must have stayed the night. You were my unknown mistress. In you I was to find both mistress and wife; rarely are both united in one person.

Your life, as narrated by you, was to me in the highest degree fascinating.

The pederasts in the flat below liked to talk to you while in the tub, scrub your back in the communal narrow bathroom shared with the Pinkers, and photograph you as screen siren of the 1940s pouting over one naked shoulder at the camera. Luther from the island of Mauritius spoke French, was black as a pot; his philosophy was simple: 'Life is a rugged path which we try to make smude.' The islanders dreamed of buried treasure, dug great holes in the beaches.

Chris, who moved the false teeth of his lower jaw like a pike, taught art in a school at Crouch End.

They were a loving couple long together, and good company for you, in whom they both confided.

There had been a third, Lonny, a gentle boy who had died young. His mother had come from Natal for the funeral, and you had collected flowers on the heath for a wreath and a man had exposed himself.

Everything was photographed – the gentle departed one smiling on cue at the piano, the two pederasts cross-eyed with lechery, the Harringtons posing artfully; it had all taken place in the confined spaces of your attic with the long window embrasure, before my time.

You were Balance. Libras can be both tyrannical and conciliatory, blowing hot and cold; don't try to reason with them, logic is not their forte, nor patience. On her small turntable she played Jacqueline Françoise, and composed lapidary verse.

Inhabit and bring
To the pale shell your
Body as an offering
And a promise of life.

In a rubber-goods shop down gloomy Goodge Street, into which I ventured with extreme reluctance one grey afternoon, I was sold large brown horsepills the size of Bull's Eyes which a sallow-complexioned dispenser of condoms assured me would do the trick; at least nobody had returned to complain.

There had been dancing in the confined space between two beds and Eonie Harrington fell into my lap. There I danced with you, call it dancing, held you within arm's reach and saw close up the clown's face. Sure I must perish by your charms.

I had been introduced to her by Michael Morrow from a bed in the Mile End Hospital ('This is my South African friend'); she had brought him sketching pads. I had come with Mad Meg, bringing Player's cigarettes. Mad Meg, sensing trouble, had hurried me out of the hospital and into the Coach and Hound.

– 31 –

Billy

Boys in the garden were blowing up frogs. Figs rotted and fell from the fig tree, all the fronds of the palm trees rustled in the breeze. The scent of pine, roses, dry earth, the watered garden at sundown, pepper trees, bougainvillaea and syringa all summer long fill the tumid twilight air and the pigs are screeching in fear, held down by African butchers; she and Fiona Doran ran with hands over their ears but still heard the frantic screeching. A bad smell of death wafted up from the tannery when the breeze blew from the wrong quarter.

Miss Weir her piano teacher assured her that she had 'near-genius'. They played games of forfeits. The Everett sisters drove by in their phantom Buick. Hoarsely, with feeling, Miss Weir sang the Burial Song from *Aida*.

Boarding school was a time of prolonged physical discomfort. The girls of Kaffrarian High wore unbecoming blue uniforms 'always damp and smelling of laundry'. Billy played the lead in Anouilh's *Antigone* in an amateur production in the King Town Hall in aid of the Red Cross and was photographed by the local newspaper, staring pensively from a papier mâché castle window at the mess backstage.

The fellow who played opposite her – could it be Reg Gasson? – had struck a classical pose, pressing the back of one hand to his brow in a gesture of anguish. He wore grey worsted tights and the press photograph in black and white showed a large stain at the crotch; evidently nerves had got the better of him.

Billy worked in Bat Whitnell's law office in East London and dreamed of London, England, and the West End stage. The Reverend Herron thundered out his Hellfire sermons but a ghost stood between Billy and brother Lloyd; Elwyn had crashed his Miles Master when he was eighteen and his sister twelve.

Now Nells was in love with her.

His hair was trimmed short like a convict's. He sat behind the wheel of the truck that was piled high with furniture and cooking utensils *en route* to Kidd's Beach for the summer vacation. The sun shone through the skin of his large protuberant ears, lighting up the blood vessels. Tongue-tied, he stared through the insect-smeared windscreen, mashing the gears, too shy to speak to her or look her way, seated beside him, he humming to hide his embarrassment, the overheated engine panting and stalling. He pitched the bell tent a hundred yards from the sea. They heard the deep grunting of baboons in the thick shelter that grew down to the water's edge. Shadows on the canvas at night, the oil lantern swinging, incey-wincey spider climbing up the spout.

Then: Sunset over a vast hot landscape and the beginning of hot nights with trains shunting, the squeal of hot metal getting into motion again, hiss of escaping steam, the mournful bellowing of cattle (now it was their turn) on their last night on earth and the hollow Baptist bell banging away into the small hours.

She and Stephanie Weir with skirts hiked up about their waists climbed the picket fence into forbidden ground, saw light shining in the ground floor of the Stewart's house and Syd the diving champion naked from the waist down and hands active at hidden crotch, engaged in 'some secret male thing', so they crept away, mystified. She was the youngest, and only daughter in a family of three, one of whom died in an accident. Her parents had wanted another boy; the old man called her Billy. Done your homework, Billy? Been to the dubs, Billy?

Her parents were not hitting it off, they rarely spoke to each other, old Jonathan Carl spent much time in the office. The home atmosphere was distinctly chilly. Spirit mediums were consulted. A glass serving-dish broke neatly into four parts, a chair moved itself a fraction, ectoplasm curled from the wall, a dog barked at the framed photo of the young pilot with crewcut and cheery grin, framed on the sideboard of the living room and observing every meal served with much sighing. Her mother never laughed, her father rarely smiled. A partner lost company funds and a pile of debts accumulated; Jonathan swore to work even longer hours, every tickey would be returned to the investors. Gauche suitors invaded the house. Her mother went sighing from room to room.

Thousands and thousands of needles of rain struck her face and shoulders, scattering over the public baths where she swam lengths alone; then home in the rain to a deserted house and a meagre supper in the fridge. As she prepared for bed she heard again the evening commotion of pigs and a terrible smell wafted itself up from the tannery. Her brother Elwyn had to kill himself larking about in a Miles Master that went out of control and exploded on a hill. Gone were the days when her mother, erect by the open patio door, sang:

> I gave my heart to one man,
> Loving as only woman can . . .

As soon as Billy came of age she sailed for London on a Union Castle liner, embarking at East London with her best friend Fiona Doran, daughter of Dr Doran. The last she was to see of her father for some years was the old man standing on the dockside holding up bunting made from a number of handkerchiefs tied together, growing smaller and smaller on the quayside, calling, 'Goodbye, Billy!' She and her friend Fiona wept their hearts out on the rails.

– 32 –

The Ice-Cream Factory

The ice-cream factory was vast: a brown windowless bulk somewhere beyond Willesden junction. Trucks assembled in the loading-yard at night in the heat wave. Because it was nightwork and there was overtime, I had ten bob extra again for working in cold storage. It was difficult to stay awake, even in the freezing bays.

A tall shell-shocked worker threw a fit in the canteen. One night on the loading-bay a small coloured man went berserk, shouted, 'Fuck your sister!' at a huge dull Irishman who backed away; he was given his walking papers on the spot. The gates opened, a Black Maria pulled up, factory guards led him out, a small insubordinate figure walked away, a free man. Down-coming tins jammed in the exit points and had to be knocked free, bursting open on the cement floor and the stuff pouring out. The factory itself smelt of vomit.

I worked in the freezing areas, drawing good wages, but exhausted all night, half-asleep on my feet and all sandwiches tasted alike. In the garden, during the night break, exhausted black men in white overalls were laid out on the benches, as if headless and armless. I was saving up money for our first holiday on Inishere. The regulations said I had to be clean-shaven; the freezing cold stung my face.

When the two heavy doors were thrown open high up by the ganger an Arctic scene offered itself to my eyes: snow and fog, rime and mist and the bays iced up.

Palsied with the cold I stopped the run, started another line, sent it out, blowing into the iced-up intercom. The ganger cursed me. It was soft as shit. 'Try an' stay awake, matey.'

On weekends Mick Swords of Tipperary caroused with friends in the West End, walking back to Shepherds Bush after the last Tube had gone. In Kensington Gardens he saw a fellow mounting a whore who drank from a bottle. Irish whores, Swords swore, were the worst, the most inept. 'Dormant fucken rats'.

It was a sort of underground place reared up into the sky, spewing ice cream and smelling of lost hopes and vomit. You came with me once to the gates. You were aghast at the squalor. 'Do chaps work there?'

'This chap does.'

You were staying with your friend Pat Godkens on Campden Hill. Our marriage banns were posted. A keen young priest was giving you Catholic indoctrination at the Church of St Thomas More, not far from our old quarters at 18A Belsize Lane. We were to be married there; since a wedding in a Registry Office seemed as impersonal an act as, say, purchasing a dog licence.

We walked in Holland Park by your old office in the Yugoslav Embassy, by white statuary laid out on the grass like corpses of Holland House. The husband of Pat Godkens was a beast, you confided to me. He drank double gins, overfed and overweight, overbearing, a mother's boy. Silence was called when the Prime Minister spoke on the radio. Eden spoke on Suez.

– 33 –

Galustian & Co.

An unknown mistress possesses a unique charm, Bayle avers. But while the charm of novelty yields progressively to the knowledge of character, bliss comes only with intimacy. First it's victory; afterwards comes pure felicity, provided one is dealing with an intelligent woman (a very Froggy rider).

'The nicest feeling,' you admitted in my narrow bed in the murky room (daylight slanted in, meagrely apportioned, fresh air not at all), 'is waking up in bed at the wrong end of town. Finding yourself in strange territory, and going home in a taxi.' Where we found ourselves now was home, had to be home, at 18A Belsize Lane (her eyrie, at the topmost attic on one of the topmost hills of North London) or No. 8 Prince Edward Mansions (my coffin at Notting Hill Gate); home is where you start from.

To get to work you took two buses to Kensington High Street and walked to the Yugoslav Embassy through the poplar blossoms blowing like snow from Holland Park. Wherever you walked extraordinary climatic conditions prevailed.

Two fat men met, wheezing, on the stairs and embraced under the portrait of Tito. You brought back booty, slivovic and Balkan Sobranie from Embassy parties which occurred quite frequently.

Your life before me teemed with admirers. Some of them still hung in there, phoning HAM 348 at awkward hours, breathing heavily. You neither encouraged nor discouraged them. Vuck Eisen lived around the corner, strikingly handsome, homesick for Rijeka. Admirers abounded, phoned or hovered near, just out of sight.

By night in that first summer we swam in the Women's Pool on Hampstead Heath and I covered you in flowers. Members of eccentric religious sects came floundering down the hill with arms outstretched, calling out incomprehensible incantations. A small 'combo' composed of alto sax, guitar and harmonica played Satchmo numbers (had he just died?) all night long under an oak tree. We obtained the signature of Josh White after a concert at Burnt Oak. 'Hey! Gimme a raincheck!' signed *Josh White*. He promised to play at our wedding but never showed up. Josh never showed up to sing 'John Henry'.

In winter you walked in fur-lined bootees and a short tartan tweed skirt of Royal Stuart on the damp or frozen earth as if it pleased you. You said you liked the cold days and the last leaves dropping from the trees. And now you wore a white angora poloneck with tartan slacks.

'She has a really soiled face, that Jeanne Moreau.'

Many of your judgements were incomprehensible to me. I just couldn't see that. Jeanne Moreau had a lovely face.

'I must have fruit!'

You went shopping by West Hampstead station where the Punch and Judy show was performed near the pub where Ruth Ellis shot her lover and the price of vegetables lower. You kept a ten-shilling note in the vee of your glove, put aside weekly for fruit, which seemed extravagant to me, the Mick paying out three pounds for renting out one room sans daylight or air, told that I had the palate of a dog, that I must experiment, open up. Ever try avocados? persimmons? pawpaws? yumyums? Never heard of them. The Cockney greengrocer smote his mittens together and boasted that all his market produce came fresh that morning from Covent Garden. 'Ain't got no dud 'uns 'ere, Miss.'

I frequently felt at a loss; your past was becoming more real than my own. I, the sombre cooker of dull spuds and carrots, my staple diet spaghetti bolognese in a darkened room that stank of cooking, unwashed clothes. I lived poorly then. Once I had invited you to dine there; once only.

You had a clown's sad face.

You were not prudish (*'Je ne regrette rien'*). In a dream you sat on Orson Welles's great lubberly lap and looked close at his blubbery Rosebud lips, his sneering mouth – well then, a mouth capable of sneers. (Wasn't 'rosebud' a sneer?) You thought him mean and told him so. 'You're so mean,' you told Orson, 'it's coming out of your ears. Can't you feel it?'

Orson jerked his head back, opened his mouth wide ('like a cave'), beckoned to someone. 'Get her!' Throwing back his great head he gave a rich expansive laugh. He was not fooling you. 'He watches you craftily to see how you take it. His eyes are inquisitive.'

Orson Welles was no fool.

Even your dreams were rich and fanciful; perhaps one day I too would appear in them with Orson Welles? You marched down Rosslyn Hill past the George IV, our local, heading for Chalk Farm with a Spanish basket a third full of fruit and vegetables.

Did I know Gascoyne? Did I know Derain?

Were these more exotic fruits, gascoyne and derain?

You were driven down to Sussex to meet George Barker and who sat next to you in the friend's car but Gascoyne who did not utter a word. Appearing at Barker's door he took a naggin of Scotch out of one pocket and handed it to Barker without a word, then another naggin from another pocket and handed it over, walked in, sat down and not a word.

Not a word out of him all day, just drinking Scotch and looking from face to face. On the way back to London he ventured two remarks: 'That's supposed to be a good field for mushrooms . . .' And: 'There's an underground river there.' He had given up writing poetry and painted pictures that were like Persian miniatures. He had threatened to blow up Buckingham Palace. Gascoyne was perhaps a little unhinged.

Your former boss had been a priapic Persian.

A handsome brute, most amorous, by the name of Haig Galustian.

'Nothing miniature about him.'

He had designs on her; the day began with a chase around the office. He was deadly serious and carried an erection like a spear. He was most persistent, hot and hasty, never had a South African girl. One or two orgasms and an English girl was finished. 'You cannot begin with me,' she told him. He was slung like a stallion. The races continued. He was operating in something shady, munitions or arms deals. One set of files were top secret; he had the key. One day he phoned, instructing her to burn the secret files at once, the duplicate key was hidden in such-and-such a drawer. If the police came, she was to admit nothing, he was out of the country, the files never existed.

It was a hot day and she had been sunbathing nude in the garden. She burned the secret files, raking up the charred remains and buried them, waiting for the police to arrive. An hour later Galustian phoned to say it was all a mistake. Too late, the files were destroyed.

He was hot and hasty.

She shared a flat with two other South African girls. The thing to do was to have a black lover. Nirodi Nazunda had a skin so black it was almost blue, sat stark naked on a rug and was greatly admired by the girls, when in walked an even prettier brunette, Diane Liebenberg.

Billy was going out with a cad from the FO. She had to lie naked on the bed and say, 'I want to be focked.' He was hard to please, cruel, overbearing, took taxis everywhere.

When the two queers moved from the flat below a tall shy admirer moved in, with terrible halitosis. He ate nothing but fish, painted nothing but fish, and the flat began to stink of nothing but fish.

Meanwhile I searched through Islington for a lost earring, dropped when we came out of Collins Music Hall where a stripper was pushed naked on a bicycle across the stage. Pauline ('Take 'em Off') Penny wore nothing but a fixed smile and the gallery hooted. You laughed at the serious nudist on the bike, but I never recovered your lost earring. You had a habit of losing things.

Leaning perilously out of the attic window, naked as the day you were born, you called down to the milkman four storeys below, to leave Gold Top Cream. 'Milkmin!'

I lay between the blue sheets and marvelled. The sheets were fresh, the room aired, fresh air blew in, there were flowers in a vase. I had bought a secondhand wedding ring in Kentish Town; we were to be married in late October. We had breakfast with fruit. Anthony Stanger of the FO with his kinky tastes was a thing of the past, with the blue-black bucknaked West Indian, the priapic Persian who had given you a going-away present of a black French corset, very fetching on, and you had wept buckets.

In the National Gallery on Trafalgar Square you stood under the giantesses of Paolo Veronese, the most flittering light of the old Venetian school, under the huge torpid sprawl of brown-skinned lethargic propagators whose oaken-hued limbs were as the wide branches of great oaks, whose breedy boles were their well-fleshed haunches, whose spread hair was as the colour of beech leaves stirred by a serene breeze in autumn, whose ophthalmic eyes (the sleepy eyes of born breeders) were bursting from their sockets, as if stunned or drugged, drugged with life, with sensation, staring out from the boscage above the door where a sleepy gallery attendant was trying not to doze off.

So had I worked as a store-hand in Ponds (Cosmetics) at Perivale near the Great West Road, then at Punfield & Barstow (Mouldings) as an apprentice extrusion moulder on day and nightshifts near Willesden junction, while you worked for Haig Galustian, and in the Yugoslav Embassy, then as the personal secretary of Randolph Churchill who paced to and fro with a hangover, unshaven and unkempt, dictating on his feet. Then we were both taken on as trainee puppet operators by John Wright in Hampstead. He had rented a room in the corner house of Professor William Empson, set up a marionette stage and we practised how to operate the puppets before a wide mirror in cramped dusty quarters, as we would later in Mlini in the stifling Adriatic heat of August.

Your fond dream of a career on the West End stage had come to nothing. An interview had been set up with John Gielgud at the Old Vic. You had a drink in a bar to steady your nerves and told the barman where you were going. He said 'Read hit to us 'ere, luv. We'll be yer h'audience.' So you delivered your audition piece in your best Antigone voice to the morning boozers and it was a total fiasco. The boozers just looked down at their pints, cleared their throats, shuffled their feet, and you knew it was no good. You marched out of the bar, threw the script into a refuse bin, and shortly after that went to work for the priapic Persian, began running.

I moved into 18A Belsize Lane while we were being trained as puppet operators. The arrangement was that the company would go ahead in a newly acquired custom-built Bedford truck; we would visit my parents in Dalkey and rejoin the company near Dubrovnik towards the end of summer, at Mlini.

In the meantime you told me the story of your life.

The to-be-continued tale of the wife to be. We were married in the Church of St Thomas More on November 26th 1955. Best man: Hubert Mary Bermingham, B. Arch. Music (an organ voluntary by Telemann): John Beckett. The words were extremely bawdy; we had just the airs.

– 34 –

Your Life Before Me

Jill Damaris Anders was born on 21st October 1930 at 2 Raglan Street in King William's Town in the Eastern Province of South Africa, within sight of the Amatola Mountains which stood up to the west as a reminder of native cruelty and barbarity, short rations, prisoners inhumanly dispatched. Born of a Welsh mother and a German father under the tricky astrological sign of Balance (Libra), when lawyer Jonathan Carl Anders was already an old man.

He was a notary or family lawyer who made out deeds of possession in a miniature script as he sucked little black pastilles to keep his breath sweet for clients. He wrote in the neat precise hand of another age – fussy, industrious Samuel Pepys. Debit and credit, profit and loss. He wasted nothing, ate the core and pips of apples.

He wore a stiff wing collar, a choker, and button boots well polished; and had a distinct look not of Pepys but of General Jan Smuts, that thorn in the British side. I saw him ever in a vapoury daguerrotype fumed and framed in oaken leaves with cannons going off in the background and natives being impaled. He would have been a patriot in whatever country he found himself. German settlers, Lutheran missionaries, were all around; there was even a village called Berlin not too far off. As vain as he was deaf, he would not wear a hearing aid or ear-trumpet, being obliged to shout at his clients over the pipe tobacco he had spread to dry on his desk. He was a sweet-natured old man, a gentle soul. All his life he had worked hard. In his middle and even late eighties he was putting in eight and ten hours at the office, as he had when aged fifty; still shouting at his clients, still with mounds of tobacco out drying on his desk, still deaf as a post. He was the best Pop in the whole world and she was his beloved Billy.

Her moody mother had no pet name for her and showed precious few signs of affection, let alone love. Billy with her amiable clown's face, who tended to drop things when nervous, was merely 'my girl' – addressed with a cutting coldness.

We sat on a public bench in the sun and watched the kites fly. Below us in the Parliament Hill Fields the ground fell away to the ponds surrounded by willows, poplars and copper beech.

'Pop had me too late.'

'Why too late? You're here, aren't you?'

'He'd turned sixty when I was born,' you said. 'That's too late. Anyway he wanted another boy.'

A small Oriental person was flying a silken kite, a blood-red tar-black dragon with glistening scales, a good twenty feet long with a mouthful of dragon teeth and fierce glazy eyes. It lifted in the sudden breeze and went wobbling and jerking up over the stand of trees, swelling mightily as it ascended, filled with air, while its owner, running backwards and clutching the cord, shrank away to nothing, a mere mortal.

'It's too late.'

'Too late for what?'

'To be a father,' you said, smiling now at the frantic antics of the dragon-keeper, 'at sixty.'

'Pish, pish.'

'Yes, yes.'

'Not in Ireland. At least not in the old days.'

'Well for God's sake look at Ireland!'

'True.'

Now the dragon was far up and still rising on the thermals, its tiny owner calmly unreeling a mile of line that curved and bellied away from him, up and up to where the mighty dragon was butting its head bloodily against a low cloud.

Presently we would go down to Highgate village and into the Flask where Hogarth had once caroused, sitting snug with a covey of wags. We passed Gaels with scorched faces at fierce hurling, strong country boys (looking demented in crash helmets) roaring out the Holy Name as they whirled and pucked in a lather of excitement, sending the dun-coloured ball down the field to where a pile of discarded clothes served for goalposts.

'Now Tom avic, into him!'

'Now Tom Malone!'

Tom Malone with white hair and a pale-green ganzy was smooth as oil, hard as teak, wriggly as an eel, pucking goals from all over the place, no holding him.

'Up Down!' you called, but no one heard.

They didn't hear you; they were back in Kerry, in Kilkenny, in woody Kildare, pucking and blaspheming. The sun was sinking behind all the horizons of the heath and Truss City had vanished into a dim grey haze below; now it was just a glow in the sky off towards Neasden and Dollis Hill. Tomorrow for sure would be a scorcher.

Now the hurlers were struggling and swearing mightily near one of the makeshift goals, upraised hurley sticks of ash smacked fiercely together.

'Oh Jaysus you eejit!' a voice called in agony.

'Blood will be spilt,' you said.

We walked down past the ponds.

– 35 –

The Pond

I lay on the moored raft and watched the white blossoms drifting off the poplar trees that grew around Hampstead Pond. Through slitted eyes, peacock-twittering, the stagnant brown water resembled a motionless river. The causeway was a bridge. Serious men fished there with gaffs and waders as if after fighting salmon in a running stream.

When a swimmer dived off the raft, it tipped and brown water washed over it. For a time I was alone there. An odour difficult to describe arose from the bed of the disturbed pond, a blast from an upset stomach. Girls in tight costumes swam in the dirty water, breaststroking, holding their heads high, Professor Empson among them with something foul (snot? emission?) caught in the forks of his mandarin beard. He did not know me; I closed my eyes. The sun was hot in Hampstead high summer. The raft began to tilt. I opened my eyes.

Professor Empson was breaststroking back, stately as a paddle-steamer, and a plump girl in a yellow costume was hauling herself aboard. She had left a wake of scent on the water, now it was on the raft. The sun shone on the oiled sunbathers, poplar blossoms drifted by in the breeze, carried on the surface as though the pond-water was moving. The plump girl had stretched herself out on the damp boards. She lay there calm as a leaf, caught in a fluid sensual dream; her diaphragm heaved mightily with every breath.

A rowing boat was putting out from the bathing place, the little lido among the trees. At the end of the duckboards of the wooden jetty the sunbather ostentatiously immersed in *Malone meurt* (purchased in Paris) sat still with feet submerged, staring down at extremities that appeared to be severed below the knees.

The raft tilts again. At the end of the wooden jetty the cadaverous reader of Beckett stares down aghast at his reflection without feet below the knees. The sun shines. It shines on sticky sunbathers oiled and creamed with Nivea; a rowing boat is pulling away. The oarsman pulls easily, not to disturb the swimmers or the moorhens hidden in the overhang. As he comes on I see that he strangely resembles Ussher who resembles the dead Cavé, the friend of Dégas. The boat leaves a line of bubbles behind.

High up in the azure an unseen jet fighter bangs through the sound-barrier and (as though there were some casual connection) more blossoms are shaken from the poplars that line the pond. Turning in mid-pond and casually shipping his oars, Ussher-Cavé now begins retrieving something with a grappling-hook.

I lie there letting time drift. Impressions offer themselves, briefly focus and slip away again; the raft rocks, brown water washes over it. The plump girl, heavy as a stove, has dived off. A line of bubbles shows where she has gone under: her hands surface, then her head. Her scent lingers, sweetly cloying, not pleasant. Professor Empson breaststrokes in his stately way through the filth. A tall auburn-haired beauty in a red dress is crossing the causeway with a towel under her arm. She waves to me.

I leave the raft, letting the water receive me; not only filthy but tepid, both bidet and toilet, the used bathwater of thousands, hundreds of thousands over the years. Trapped water; the blossoms are scum. As I touch the jetty you appear above me, having undressed in the ladies' section, hung up your red dress, covered your purse. You stand adjusting your rubber bathing-cap; your face changes subtly with the hair hidden.

She leans forward, poised to dive, taking a deep breath. The boatman is closely examining a dripping object. She launches herself from the jetty above me, passing like a swan over my head.

Now in the Oxo-tinted pond I am holding you up, lifting you above the scum, the mire, and you are laughing. Laughter comes so naturally out of you, childlike and hopeful. Do clowns laugh? No matter. We are in the shadows, in the chilly water; as I sink you rise, held up by the waist. Aloft in the air you are laughing. My head is below the surface but I can feel the laughter in my hands, your laughter, as if it were the best joke in the world, the world gone from us and we are slipping away. *Do as I bid you and you will find out my form. There are no pure substances in nature; each is contained in each.* We are slipping away. All around us the scum, the spent blossoms floating on the dark Oxo-brown water. The raft is empty; we are the last. The boatman watches us. He has a weather-beaten face, long countryman's cheeks, and smokes a pipe, looking thoughtful. Noble it is to decay growing wise, as metaphysics wears out the heart. We were happy in a drugged manner; supposing Balance and Pisces can ever be happy together. It was a start.

In the dingy purlieus of Camden Town I'd bought a second-hand trunk the size of a wardrobe, weathered oxidized green as if recovered from water. The shopman, dingy as his premises, hove it onto the pavement to demonstrate that it could take hard knocks. I had some trouble getting it aboard a bus – Crusoe lugs his painted chest across the Ox Mountains – passengers had to force their way past it. We were preparing for the Adriatic voyage.

Your dream: an open matchbox contained a miniature Field Marshall Montgomery, a little figure that rolled its eyes when you tilted the box. The real Montgomery stood on a knoll nearby, with rolled maps under his arm, looking over your head in a far-sighted military sort of way. When you put down the breakfast tray your dressing-gown fell off. 'Make me warm,' you said, climbing into bed. Your life before me was full of admirers.

— 36 —

The Ghost of Elwyn Anders

My poor parents had not yet moved, or been forced to move, from Dalkey to Dun Laoghaire, in their slow but remorseless progression downward. They were still living in Dalkey, on the fringe of respectability in Breffni Mansions, prior to their last move to squalid underground quarters at Haigh Terrace.

Dado had aged. That morning we surprised him mowing the grass by the Georgian granite steps as we came in the gateway, to be welcomed like royalty.

They occupied the upper floor while a family who never appeared had rented the basement flat. The double flight of granite steps led to the hall door, then more stairs to their living quarters, too many steps for my overweight mother.

Mumu too had aged. With long white hair combed down over her shoulders she was sitting up in bed in a woollen cardigan with all the stitching gone along one arm. My recently acquired spouse received that pointed stare as of yore, and for you a sweet smile, and you heard for the first time Mumu's high sing-song voice asking rhetorically: *'Is this Jeel?'*

Mumu's bedroom was a large bare room devoid of carpet or family suite on the bare boards; all that remained was one uncomfortable high-smelling leather armchair, strategically positioned facing the high bed, the last of the suite sold at discount by Jack Ellis the much maligned Jew. In a corner a great mound of old newspapers reared up, high as the hill of Tara, mostly back numbers of the *Irish Times*.

Three long windows overlooked Dublin Bay. When I threw open one of them the sea with its smells entered the room. The wind boomed all around the house; yachts were tacking towards Howth, the line of the granite harbour wall stretched away to the northeast. Now the invigorating smell of new-mown grass was in the bedroom. From where I stood it would be possible to follow the course of the mail boat arriving and departing. We had flown in.

Dado, acting the butler, now carried in a tray with tea and gateaux. They fussed over the preparations; was it strong enough, there was no cream but would milk do?

'Of course,' you said.

'Is it all right?' Mumu inquired anxiously.

'Perfect,' you said, your legs crossed in tartan slacks, a black beret, high-heeled black boots, a grey high-neck pullover, a wedding ring. The angle of the beret had been nicely judged and stopped just in time.

Dado was taking all this in, this was how the international set dressed; he was more accustomed to stocky broad-beamed types with the complacent rumps of brood mares. Horsey women.

'Anders,' Dado said, looking at his tea-leaves, head tilted judiciously to one side. 'Now what kind of name was that?' He was seated like a garden gnome on an upturned orange crate as if on a throne. You had given him a present of a gold tiepin with turquoise inset and he was wearing it already. 'Is it German or where does it come from?'

Dado knew where it came from right well, for I had written many letters from London and he was thoroughly *au fait* with his new daughter-in-law's background.

'Sugar?' offered Mumu, dispeller of mystery.

'My father is German and my mother Welsh,' you said, crossing your long legs.

'Now are you satisfied!' cried Mumu, smiling at her daughter-in-law who sat with legs crossed and beret removed, quite at home, eating gateaux from a saucer.

'We put on no fine airs and graces here, my dear.'

Here Mumu threw Dado one of her most withering looks. He was staring at you and wobbling his head and seemed to be quite taken with you, as with all sirens and tall good-lookers; at least I hadn't landed myself with a flibbertigibbet.

They had made up twin beds for us in a room without furniture or carpet. We pulled them together and threw open the windows to let the strong sea-air and all the aromas of the sea and garden flow in. There were cut flowers in a bowl.

'Oh this air!' you said, naked at the window. 'It's not true. It's just like Hermanus, only stronger. I grew up in this kind of weather.'

Billy was quite a specialist in air.

Odours of seaweed and brine all night long, of new-mown grass, odour of drifting space. All night long the house swam through space as dogs barked in the quarry behind the town. The Dalkey night was hectic with moon-maddened dogs barking their heads off at the full moon sailing resplendently over the quarry. We were home.

Next morning even before I had opened my eyes I recognised the distinctive sound of my progenitor's arbitrary stop-and-start method of mowing grass without a catcher attached, conserving his strength and trying to make enough noise to waken us. Sunday church bells were ringing all around and from the kitchen the aromas of breakfast were wafting.

When you appeared dressed at the window Dado called up that breakfast was ready when we were, but to take our time, and already he called you 'Jilly'.

We drank draught Guinness in a rundown Dalkey bar. Out in the bay in a rented rowing boat we watched the church spires sink and the Wicklow hills put on more bulk. White clouds drifted on the breeze as I dropped the lures over the side for mackerel. The silver sank like shot into the green depths below us, but were the mackerel running?

'I had a peculiar dream last night,' you said. 'A dream that Elwyn had come back.'

You told me your dream.

It happened at Jan Smuts Airport. 'He was flying in on such a lovely day.' They were there waiting, all the Anders, and one can imagine in what a state. You saw the glimmer high up like a silvery fish in the blue sky over the burning Rand. The Anders family watched it come in as if it were an ordinary flight arriving at Jan Smuts.

She didn't know what to expect when it touched down – would it burst into flames and a winged horror come bounding out, a black Elwyn racing towards them, screaming, '*It's me! It's me! I'm back!*'

It circled, made its approach run, touched down, taxied in quite normally. The steps were pushed up, the door opened and the passengers began alighting.

'I recognised him by the way he walked. He wore a tall hat but carried no hand-luggage, no briefcase even, nothing. Waving, if you please, an outsize stetson! It was Elwyn alright, my long-lost brother whom we hadn't seen in fifteen years, had come home. He was all grainy and colourless like a photo that's faded, walking among the others in a kind of mist. It was most odd and disturbing. On this strangely bright unreal day to see my dead brother come towards us, not hurrying, carrying the stetson and smiling, coming up to us waiting there at the barrier. My mother had begun weeping already.

'He came right up to us. I was so happy to see him, grinning from ear to ear and holding this outsize ridiculous stetson.

'My mother was becoming smaller and smaller, weeping with happiness, her eyes shining. Elwyn spoke all our names. Mom and Pop, Lloyd and Sis.

I was still his little Sis. Did we embrace, shake hands? I forget. Mom just kept on weeping and shrinking, Pop was growing younger and younger the more he looked at Elwyn who was saying very little, just grinning away all the time as if this was the best joke in the world. He'd brought no luggage because he wasn't staying, apparently.

'In photos his nose turned up, but it didn't really. He was very calm, took my arm and then *I* was crying because he was back.

'We enquired where he had been all these years? He clapped the stetson right back onto his head, onto the airman's crewcut, tilting it over one eye and winked, those bright devil-may-care eyes amused and observing us. "Oh, I've been around," he said. He was a real grinning devil.'

You had the collar of your donkey-jacket up about your neck and the beret down over your ears. It was cold out on the bay. A beam of sunlight lit up Howth Head. Below us, deep green water and stuff streaming down. I felt the strong drag of the tide on the lures down on the bed of the bay, pulled at the oars, facing you, reduced to just a nose and amber hair emerging from the donkey-jacket. Water and air were cold, the tide on the turn; such opaque peace!

'What happened?' you asked Elwyn.

He rolled his eyes.

'I got too cocky and over-confident, you know. I lost control and went into a high-speed stall at an altitude too low to pull out of. After three hundred hours flying time you think you can do anything with the crate but you can't. You can't fly the kite upside down. You have to learn to talk upside down in a Miles Master. Your Adam's apple comes up into your throat and you can't get the words out.'

He was laughing and rolling his eyes in a droll way, making a joke of everything, even his death. His loving mother had carefully kept the SAAF heirlooms, the medals mounted on black velvet, the Flying Logbook, his wings and dress uniform, and a school exercise-book preserved from the time when he was aged ten.

He had crashed his Miles Master on a farm called *Donkerhoek* (dark corner) not far from Bloemfontein in the Orange Free State, which was not a free state.

She didn't know the name of the krantz in the Amatolas where British soldiers were thrown during the frontier war, known as the Kaffir Wars in the history books. In the country of the clicking Xhosas, Kreli (1820-1902) was Paramount Chief of the tribe during the first part of the nineteenth century. Her loving Pop never spoke of the war or the English POWs thrown from the krantz, except to tell her that it was there he had learnt to eat the whole of an apple, core and all, so he must have been hungry.

'I was only twelve then,' you said (now mysterious as an oracle seated in the stern of the boat, with the hills behind you; you disguised, suffering, speaking in tongues). 'When he went missing. In the dream he would have been, let me see, thirty-one . . . supposing the dead age, which is hardly likely. They are always at whatever age they die at; isn't that right? They always remain the same. But I hardly knew this joker. I'd loved him much and he me, I suppose, I being the youngest and all that, the baby. Mom loved no one else but him, as she made clear enough to me. Certainly she didn't love *me*.'

Dead brother Elwyn had once attempted to teach maths to his Sis, but it was a total failure. You can take 1 away from 2 but where has it gone, where is it? He was patient, he said: 'It still exists somewhere in some form or other. Nothing ever disappears.'

Nothing he said or did could surprise her; she expected that of him, surprise packages, delights. He thought he had control of the Miles Master but he hadn't. Hold onto nothing; nothing lasts.

I rowed to new fishing grounds off the Forty Foot. To one side, among the grey boulders, a corpulent nudist was going in on the sly, crouching; with a male head but female appendages, just lowering itself surreptitiously, flinchingly dipping its androgynous extremities into the now-swelling-riptide, bobbing up and down before the quick total immersion and being jeered at by some wheeling gulls.

A year passed, a cloud going over. My mother found that she could not take the steps and they moved again, going underground at Haigh Terrace, for a cheaper rent. They were going down.

– 37 –

From Fiume to Old Ragusa

We had come from Ostend by train, watching pilgrims embarking for Lourdes. A heavy woman was carried aboard from an ambulance. Her face turned purple with embarrassment when the wind lifted her skirt and exposed unsightly maroon bloomers to the gaping crowd of idlers at the ship's rail.

We passed from winter and rain in Belgium (stations with names from the Great War, hard rain on the restaurant-car window in Köln) into high summer after the Alps. The white butterflies *Kohlweisslinge* dipped and dodged over a shallow clear river where Austrian cattle waded; we changed trains at Köln and again at Ljubljana and reached Rijeka in the early hours of the morning. The tourist office was open. It was not yet seven and they were selling steamship tickets near the harbour. A brown skeletal porter in a loincloth was most persistent and took our baggage away. Shabby soldiers in baggy uniforms were being drilled by a furious little officer. Jill wept with exhaustion and frustration and the strangeness of it all. I bought tickets and we went on board, eating tomato sandwiches on deck when the ship sailed, and you went below into the cabin, shared with two huge German Fraus.

After interminable hours of heat and sea the sun sank and the moon appeared. The Dinaric Alps looked like a mountain of ashes. I dozed in a canvas chair on the open deck, listening to the pleasant sound of the prow cutting through the water. The other passengers sat silent as ghosts all about me. The air was clammy, I smelled pine forests. In the middle of the night a storm came up and raged for an hour. Then all became still again.

We entered Dubrovnik, old Ragusa, around six next morning. We were going on to Cavtat and Mlini, climbing hundreds of steps in the great Adriatic heat of high summer, to where the Puppet Master waited in duck shorts; to Epidaurus in the old dispensation.

On a small pier in the middle of nowhere between Rijeka and Dubrovnik the steamer was offloading melons and machinery. A young woman stood and watched. She was brown as the dry earth she stood on with one good leg and the other a wooden stump to the hip and a kind of sarong about her waist but nothing else, barefoot she observed me while breastfeeding a small brown infant covered in flies.

It was close and humid and when she moved the strong shape of her showed through sweat-soaked cloth. When she spoke to the infant she showed gums the colour of yew bark.

She put the child down among the water melons, took one up, tested it with her fingers, cut it quickly in two with a kind of panga and approached me on the rail. She might have been rolling and fornicating on the dusty ground, so sweat-soaked and dusty was she. Streams of sweat poured down her face and torso as she offered me the fruit, lactating freely (waters tumbling down from Lahore), saying something in her own language which I could not follow but had a nearer whiff of her reaching up with ancillary tufts drenched and she was chewing some sort of nut that stained her teeth and lips.

Then she went back to the child, picked him up and set him to one of her bursting pomegranates, set him to suck. She watched me eating the water melon. When the steamer cast off with a thick black plume of smoke rolling back from the stack and a merry ringing of bells from the captain or helms-man, she stood on the pier and watched us depart, the child still sucking away for dear life, covered in flies, dreaming the day away. It was somewhere down the coast there, miles from anywhere known. Our puppet tour would take us to Sarajevo where Wright was to be fêted by the Yugoslav puppeteers and fondly embraced by a bearded, homosexual puppet man. We were offered slivovic and Hadji Bey Turkish Delight.

PART III

South Africa

'Mourning airs of forgotten childhood, mingled with premonitions of one's last end.'

Images of Africa (1971)

The Shore of Africa

The approaches to a new continent are ever prescient. When we took the plunge over the Equator, flying fish sank to starboard, porpoises surfaced aft and every evening the sun went down in formations of cloud, furnacelike, dramatic as Doré's illustrations to Dante, in old Mrs Warren's library that became ours. Such lovely leewardings must lead somewhere. The first sight of Africa low on the horizon on the port side, a dim white skeleton coast; a mirage that goes.

We toured Europe with the John Wright Marionette Company from August to November of 1956, beginning in the great heat of the Adriatic near Dubrovnik (oh Mlini, ah Cavtat!), touring Yugoslavia and Germany, before the North Sea cold of Holland; refitting and rehearsing in Amsterdam for the coming extended tour of South Africa and both Rhodesias.

Early in December 1956 we sailed on *Die Waterman* for Kaapstad. My diary reports: '20th Dec. 1956, Cape Town. Prancing airs of the Cape of Good Hope. Table Mountain looms over us, balancing on its summit a single white cloud. It's a hot day in high summer here. The passengers crowd the rail. A blinding glare comes off the sea in Table Bay. Here everything is on a grander scale (even the swallows are bigger).'

Blossom, Le Roux, Zebra, Power, George are our stops along the way. The ostrich farms; a lady in a picture hat stands before an easel on Mossel Bay.

On December 24th two engines pull a long line of carriages through the Blaauberg Mountains in a long train travelling on the Garden Route from Cape Town to East London in the Eastern Province. Wheatlands go right up into the foothills of the mountains which are lime blue; the horizon seems very far away, bright and luminous. Jolting over the points on the bridge above the Zwartkops River, passing New Brighton location outside Port Elizabeth at dusk, lines and lines of hovels give way to arid land where the dark relocated race remain invisible in the native hut called Heart-of-the-Beast. An African internment camp sprawls featureless in the growing darkness; nothing can be added and nothing can be taken away from the African shanty town. Most mournful aspect. Where huts end the barren land begins again. Clatworthy, Funeral Furnishings All Parts.

But wait, life is here! In the twilight, clinging high up on the wire fence like bats, naked picaninnies stretch out their skinny hands towards the lighted carriages that glide slowly by, the dining car passing last. They are the colour of dust, chanting 'Hippy! . . . hippy! Hippy!'

Happy Christmas in Sud Iffrika!

On December 25th I wake up on the upper birth of a first-class carriage in a long train travelling on the Garden Route through the Drakensbergs to meet Billy's parents at King.

Prancing airs of the Cape of Good Hope. The train is stationary out in the veld and I feel the warm air coming through the carriage window and all along the track the crickets are going like wildfire.

Then the long train begins to move again with much creaking and groaning and pissing off of oil and steam and jostling and colliding of bumpers. Onward from Hex River, Mossel Bay, Plettenberg Bay, to Port Elizabeth, to East London, to King William's Town by the Amatola Mountains.

To good old King, to good old King, where I am to meet Billy's aged progenitor (who was in the Boer War) and anxious progenitrix, which fills me with foreboding.

We arrived by night in an immensely long dark train pushed by two steam engines belching flames and smoke, that went snaking around corners, one end emerging into open country, the veld, with the other end still out of sight, negotiating rocky curves. On leaving Cape Town days before we may have passed through De Aar, Graaf Reinet and Adelaide before East London, and now we were drawing into King William's Town, Billy with her head out the window and telling me, 'There they are!' and already in floods of tears.

Her parents were waiting sedately among Africans in striped blankets under an illuminated clock in a darkened station where great wooden crates marked KWT in stencil were being trundled up and down alongside the now stationary train – was it the end of the line? It was a scene from another age; the night departure of the troops for the Sudan in *The Four Feathers*.

Since all handsome young heroes arriving from overseas were variants and eidolons of the dead airman, Gwen Anders became coquettish at once; a peck on the cheek was in order, I was after all her new son-in-law. The old man was making a great to-do of fondly embracing his long-lost Billy. He drove us slowly and carefully to their high bungalow on the edge of town; next morning I would see the open country, the veld stretching away into the distance where a line of hills rose up, all trembling in the sunlight of the Cape.

They speak odd languages here, echoes of other languages; your Afrikaner (Boer, pronounce 'boor' or 'bore') with his kitchen-Dutch, not duden-Deutsch, but a sort of strangled Low German (the strongest word is '*braaivleis*', before '*veld*', and '*coon*'), the lowly 'Kaffir' (their fated body-servants forever) utters his clicks; the English-speaking settlers speak in their pinched way, afraid to open their mouths: 'Mai wiff. Pseude-Iffrika.'

Ireland would fit comfortably into the Transkei if they rolled it up, maybe smaller than the great Drakensberg Range, the Great Karroo or the Orange River basin, where we swam naked and saw the weaver birds nesting, where the sun shone all day long, the water free of bilharzia and crocodiles.

Meals tended to be a little formal, with much play of starched napkin (touched to the lips, fiddled with, adjusted under the chin for soups), and one did not dress too casually, certainly not go barefooted, like a picaninny.

'If you accept the hospitality of a country,' said lawyer Anders over the breakfast table, fixing me with his steadfast honest-to-God old watery blue eyes with the vapoury anxious stare of a hare or bream, 'then you *cannot* write against it. It wouldn't do.'

We digested this morsel of common sense.

He was German down to his buttoned boots, believing that one representative male white voting citizen simply did not go out on a limb or go against Judge and Jury; and most certainly did not disobey the law of the land – particularly if the land was South Africa and the laws Dr Hendrik Verwoerd's.

He let it be inferred that any rational bias of his against integration was an impartial bias, for white after all was white and black distinctly black. I could detect Bible bigotry in this – the drunken helotry of the Old Testament – but did not wish to argue the point.

'It would be a grave discourtesy.'

He did the needful, pouring out the tea.

Gwen smiled at me. She was quite content to treat 'them' as subhumans, her black domestics were semi-wild semi-trained black pets kept in kennels – the smoke-blackened cement hut at the rear. They understood orders if the orders were simple enough; this she contrived by addressing them in a slow distinct manner and by dropping the definite article. That was as far as

African progress should be allowed to go.

The old paterfamilias, heaving a sigh, having folded his napkin and put it into its plastic ring, rose now to indicate that breakfast was over. We had partaken; he had spoken, we were free to disperse.

He disapproved of the amount of wine and beer we had stocked in the ice-box but we were overseas folk after all and had our own customs, beer after breakfast being one of them. He and Lloyd, the son with the gun, voted for the United Party led by the absurd Sir de Villiers Graaf up on his white charger; the token opposition with the token liberal jackass in charge.

It was a party that could always be relied upon to defer to Nationalist will when it was a matter of closing ranks and all Blankes worth their salt voted wholeheartedly for white solidarity or voted in fear of outright black majority. Dyed-in-the-wool liberals – pseudo-liberals in the secrecy of the voting booth – such as Jonathan Carl who displayed the anti-intellectualism of the sincere Positivist to whom all explanation is suspect, were for the status quo at all costs.

Old man Anders was ninety if he was a day, having served in the South African War, but still remained in full possession of most of his faculties. Suited and cravatted as if the denizen of a previous age, he sat stiffly in his rocking-chair on the patio, facing his surviving son, with the temperature already risen into the high nineties, and both invisible to each other behind generous open spreads of the *Cape Times* which they rustled at one another in lieu of polite conversation, the deadly daily commonplaces.

Brother Lloyd had married Elaine Tutt, one of the East London Baptists, having bought a revolver to scare off a rival suitor.

The rocking-chair tipped, the big pages rustled stiff as palm fronds, a faint breeze wafted through. Barefooted and in khaki shorts the tolerated visitor from overseas, an awkward son-in-law under an African sunhat, sneered at Sir de Villiers Graaf and read Gibbon in the shade of the fig tree out of the atrocious heat of mid-morning, sipping ice-chilled Lion beer, hearing African voices passing by on the dusty road below. Up the way were the blue Amatolas and the krantz down which British soldiers white as sheets, as ghosts, were pushed to their deaths by order of cruel Kreli of the proud Xhosa nation. Down the way was the King tannery with stinks as atrocious as the heat.

But, lo, an African postman glistening with honest sweat came ambling up the path, taking from his postbag a neat package which he held up and called Bwana Higgins. It was a rare find. Basil Fogarty, a Scot with a bookstore in Port Elizabeth, had traced and procured the unprocurable – an American first edition of Djuna Barnes' 1938 novel *Ryder* (Horace Liveright of New York). He had laid his hands on a novel I had been after for years (Hi, Basil, if you're still alive!). The postman, who knew his place, handed it to his Baas, who handed it to his guest; the old German jaw most resolutely set.

'You must respect our ways.'

So I began again, jobless.

For two years we had toured South Africa and both Rhodesias, from Windhoek in Namibia to Worcester in the Cape; from Humansdorp to Plettenberg Bay to Louis Trichardt in the Transvaal; from Blantyre back down to Eshowe and Port Shepstone, saving £200, old currency, to salt away in the British Kaffrarion Savings Bank in King. In all we played in over two hundred towns and dorps.

– 39 –

Touring with the Puppets

John Wright's Marionettes
National Theatre Organisation 1957 tour

22-27 Jan. 1957	Cape Town	Town Hall
	Wynberg	Town Hall
	Woodstock	Town Hall
1 Feb.	Bellville	Communal Hall
	Rondebosch	Town Hall
	Paarl	Town Hall
	Somerset West	Town Hall
	Stellenbosch	Botha Hall
	Wellington	Town Hall
	Worcester	Hugo Naude Centre
	Robertson	Town Hall
	Swellendam	Town Hall
	Riversdale	Town Hall
	Mossel Bay	Town Hall
	George	Town Hall
	Oudtshoorn	Drill Hall

	Graaf Reinet	Town Hall
	Cradock	Town Hall
	Somerset East	Town Hall
	Kirkwood	Church Hall
1–2 Mar.	Uitenhage	Town Hall
	Port Elizabeth	City Hall
	Grahamstown	City Hall
	King William's Town	Town Hall
	East London	Selborne College
	Durban	Wesley Hall
	Pietermaritzburg	Rowe Theatre
	Estcourt	Town Hall
	Harrismith	Town Hall
	Bethlehem	Town Hall
	Kroonstad	Town Hall
	Vereeniging	Town Hall
1 Apr.	Van der Byl Park	Rec. Club Hall
	Johannesburg	Technical College
	Pretoria	Grootkerk Hall
	Brakpan	Town Hall
	Springs	Town Hall
2–3 May	Benoni	Town Hall
	Krugersdorp	T.H.
	Roodepoort	T.H.
	Randfontein	T.H.
	Germiston	T.H.
	Boksburg	T.H.
	Heidelberg	T.H.
	Standerton	T.H.
	Ermelo	T.H.
	Bethal	T.H.
	Middelburg	T.H.
	Potchefstroom	T.H.
	Klerksdorp	T.H.
	Kimberley	T.H.

	Bloemfontein	T.H.
1 June	Smithfield	P. A. Venter, Hairdresser
	Burgersdorp	*Albert Times*
	Queenstown	Venetian Blind Centre
	Molteno	Town Clerk
	Steynburg	Pretorius & de Kock
	Tarkastad	Tarka Distributors
	Indwe	Ko-Op Handelsvereniging
	Elliot	R. H. Thompson
	Matatiele	Central Pharmacy
	Harding	O. T. Bowles, General Dealer
	Margate	Ports Limited
	Port Shepstone	A. Ross & Co.
	Scottburgh	*Scottburgh News* Agency
	Ixopo	Mr Ross, Ixopo Hairdressing Salon
	Ladysmith	*Ladysmith Gazette*
	Greytown	George's General Store
3 Aug.	Pietersburg	de Bruyns Shoe Store
	Tzaneen	Lenel Shoe Store
	Potgietersrust	Impala Winkels
	Groblersdal	Corrie's Hairdressing Saloon
	Bronkhorstspruit	Town Clerk
	Brits	Transvalia Meubels
	Koster	Harmonie Cafe
	Rustenburg	Uitspan Cafe
	Lichtenburg	J. J. Smit, Hairdresser
	Kuruman	Model Bakery
17 Aug.	Van Zylsrust	Primary School Hall
	Askam	Hostel Hall
20 Aug.	Gochas	Hostel Hall
	Stampriet	School Hall
	Aranos	Primary School Hall

	Leonardville	Pretorius Cash Store
	Gobabis	Headmaster, High School
27 Aug.	Windhoek	Messrs Nitzsche-Reiter
	Okahandja	Mnr E. Gelhar
	Omaruru	Mr Gloeditsch
1 Sept.	Uskos	Mr F. A. Jensen, Turnhalle
	Kalkveld	Mr Christies, Dealer
	Outjo	Headmaster, High School
7 Sept.	Grootfontein	Mr Zechokke, Nord Hotel
	Tsumeb	Club Hall
	Otavi	Mr Mutavszik
	Otjiwarongo	Mrs L. Kunze
	Swakopmund	Mr Clajus, Faber Hall
15 Sept.	Mariental	Mrs U. Massman, Charneys Hotel
	Keetmanshoop	Dr Burger
	Karasburg	Volkswinkel
	Ariamsvlei	Principal, Primary School
	Upington	Café Royal
	Keimoes	Pietersen se Modewinkel
	Kenhardt	Voortrekker Cafe
27 Sept.	Williston	Amandelboom Cafe
	Calvinia	J. W. van Staden, Auctioneers
	Van Rhynsdorp	Town Clerk
	Clanwilliam	J. J. Louw, Municipal Offices
1 Oct.	Citrusdal	P. de Villiers, General Dealer
	Moorreesburg	Handelsvereniging
	Riebeeck West	Mr Kruger, Municipal Offices
	Tulbagh	Mr J. H. Theron, Tailor

	Ceres	P. F. de Kock, General Dealer
	Wolseley	Mr Groenewald, Central Café
	Laingsburg	Die Scriba, N. G. Kerk
	Ladysmith	C. H. Wessel & Son
20 Oct.	Beaufort West	General Hairdressers
	Loxton	Town Clerk
	Carnarvon	Central Café
	Victoria West	Karroo Printers
	Britstown	Mrs Sarel Daneel
	De Aar	Brits en Roos
	Hanover	du Plessis & Keun
	Richmond CP	Ruchof Koffiehuis
	Middelburg CP	*Die Middellander*
	Colesberg	v.d. Merwe & Bezuidenhout
1 Nov.	Bethulie	Attie du Plessis, Hairdresser
	Aliwal North	Kruger's Hairdressing Salon
	Zastron	N. J. de Wet, General Dealer
	Wepener	Frasers Limited
	Maseru	Secretary, Memorial Club Hall
	Ladybrand	Central Café
	Ficksburg	H. B. Kruger, Hairdresser
	Senekal	Springbok Outfitters
	Winburg	*Winburg Post*
	Ventersburg	The Town Clerk
	Welkom	Manie van Rooyen, Radio Shop
	Odendaalsrus	Sonop Limited
	Bothaville	Venter & du Preez
	Heilbron	A. Howell, Vermaaklikhede

	Sasolburg	Secretary, Amateur Dramatic Society
21 Nov.	Volkrust	Metro Café
	Newcastle	Newcastle Hairdressing Salon
	Glencoe	Stey's Electrical Service
	Vryheid	Empire Theatre
	Wakkerstrom	Uitspan Café
	Carolina	Miss Welman, Butows Chemist
28 Nov.	Barberton	C. H. Coertzen
	Nelspruit	Central Café
	Lydenburg	Die Scriba
1 Dec.	Belfast	C. J. J. van Vuuren
	Witbank	Coalfields Trading Store
	Delmas	Delmas Radio Shop

The South African tour ended at Delmas, about which I remember nothing. Our 1957 itinerary took in over 150 towns; *en route* here and there we encountered the full force of Afrikaner bigotry, the laager mentality in whose language the strong words were *Voortrekker* (helot), *braai* (bigot), *veld* (patriot), *kaffir* (a racist jibe). The only English word on their lips was deployed as an expostulation – as one might say 'Fiddlesticks!' – 'Shame!' as in 'Och shime min!' All words were spoken in their language with relish, assurance and familiarity, as of something you could not take away from them; the hard ring to it echoed their innermost convictions: *This lind is ours min*. Well certainly it was a lovely land of gorgeous vistas, if only the blight of apartheid could be removed from it, the scales dropped from bigoted white eyes.

The 1958 tour of Southern and Northern Rhodesia began on February 23rd at Umtali in torrents of rain. We were all injected against cholera, smallpox and yellow fever. Crossing Beit Bridge we travelled as far north as Kariba Dam. Scotch 26s. a bottle and all the African loaders weak with bilharzia. We played:

Bulawayo
Fort Victoria

Gwelo
Gwanda
Chipinge
Umtali
Salisbury
Kariba Dam
Livingstone
Victoria
Lusaka
Broken Hill
Mufulira
Kitwe
Zomba
Gweru
Que Que

to name but these. I recall: baboons grunting in the baobab trees at Wankie, the tintinnabulation of the diamond-doves in the suffocating heat, the air-conditioned bar in the Baobab Hotel, the early departure for Victoria Falls, flamingoes in a lagoon at evening, elephants cropping the treetops on the way to Kariba Dam, and the lioness running before us in the headlights of the Bedford truck. The Arab dhows tacking across the fast-flowing Zambesi at Tet, the bad-tempered monkey on its perch, at the end of its chain.

In the Rhodesias they speak yearningly of the Yew Kai or 'good old Yew Kai'; landlocked Afrikaners never speak of Holland as home. The tour ends somewhere south of Salisbury. Exhausted, tired of the company, we are going back to Johannesburg, to begin again. Goodbye John and Jane, Margaret and Tim. Adios vile Brink, our Afrikaner driver with bloodshot eyes and stomach ulcers. Brink by name and brink by nature, the bane of kaffirs and munts. *Hasta la vista*, cackface.

– 40 –

The Child of Storm

Our first son Carl Nicolas was born on the fourteenth anniversary of the Hiroshima bomb, 6 August 1959, named after careful old Jonathan Carl and reckless Nicolas Chamford (1741–94), the friend of Mirabeau, in Johannesburg at ten minutes past ten of a winter night, the seasons being reversed there.

Next morning I brought mother and son home to the spotless apartment, the new cot looking out over the distant mine dumps of Bez Valley. Mother Superior would not dream of parting with the swaddler until the father had disbursed a cheque; for this after all was lawless Jo'burg. Amigo Trevor Callus, intemperate poker-player on the green baize of Adamczewski's Bellos Guardo, drove us home at a stately forty miles an hour in his racing DKW. In the top-floor apartment neat as a pin, the fridge was stacked with Mateus Rosé, fine Rioja and champagne from the Pa Petousis off-licence to fitly celebrate the storm-child's homecoming.

I saw a white angel-child in Jill's arms on the deserted station platform at Blaney. The low white walls reflected a positively intractable heat and even the African porters had taken cover. I bade my travelling companion adieu – a surly soldier – collected my baggage and alighted.

I hadn't seen my son, aged eleven months, for a month during which I wound up our affairs at Johannesburg and said goodbye to friends. Carl Nicolas no longer recognised his father. The white angel sat on my knee and suffered himself to be embraced in the roasting car with the smell of heated leather. Beads of perspiration stood out on his forehead, but he did not recognise this over-familiar fellow with goatee who seemed to know his mother, now making a balls of gear-changing and telling her husband some bad news. Her old Pop was far from well; I would have to sail alone and they would follow when they could. I buried my nose into the sweet-smelling hair before me.

Under the fig-tree's shade in the great heat of King I read Gibbon and watched my son crawl at speed down the sloping lawn, heard the high-pitched screeching of African women passing on the road. Child-bearing is the lowest form of creativity, said Plato sourly; but Plato was wrong. In the cool of the bungalow we drank gin and tonic. The trunks were packed. The black nanny adored the crawling child, grandfather had recovered and a date for sailing was fixed. My son began to recognise the man in the shade.

Our ship, the *Warwick Castle*, was already berthed at East London docks. It had sailed in convoy to the Middle and Far East, ferrying Hurricanes and Spitfires with medical supplies and condoms for the Allied war effort.

In a garden-flat in Ranelagh I would begin to support a wife and small son on a modest stipend paid monthly by the publisher Calder who had accepted the first book of stories, most of them written during the two-year puppet tour.

Soon we had moved to Nerja in Andalucía where I finished my first novel. It was a new beginning, another life; for we live again through our children and, as the first was to be joined by two more bouncing boyos, I was to enjoy three extra lives and be thrice-blessed. The first, the child of storm, a hot-tempered Leo as befits the fire sign, was carried in state (there was no elevator) to his high home on the fifth floor back, above the double line or honours, guard of jacarandas shaking their little bluebells all along Isipingo Street above cosmopolitan Hillbrow.

PART IV

Dun Laoghaire

The Gentleman Rider

Flaky distemper fell from the low ceiling and lay as a greyish slush on the damp linoleum that had perished and buckled here and there, by the door that would not close, under the draining-board, around the dented and seldom disinfected bucket that had no handle, before the stove with its coating of thick grease, as Sharpe the taximan moved in the room above. He was their landlord, and the rent was low.

In the cold basement flat below, the old somnambulist, sodden with tea and porridge, stared out over the soiled half-curtain with its design of cornstalks and sheaves of wheat. In the narrow patch of earth outside finches flitted among cabbage stumps and valerian withered on the granite wall near the postern-gate; and then a tabby cat appeared on the path and birds flew out of the apple tree and the cistern upstairs began to choke and splutter.

My father heaved a sigh, turning away from the window to walk slowly in creaking cricket boots over the faded surface that sweated all winter and entered the room off the kitchen where he slept. A barred window admitted some light, the pavement was level with the top of his head, he could follow pedestrians from their knees down going by. At one time it might have been the larder. He made up his bed. It had no sheets; a narrow bed that sagged, covered in soiled and threadbare rugs, a poor man's rest. He threw on his overcoat and muffler, prepared to sally out.

My mother was waking in the shadowy front room in stale air. A low table on which were scattered miscellaneous objects stood by the fireplace where she had burned papers. A single uncomfortable leather armchair was piled with newspapers. The damp stain had come back on the wall. The ship's clock from Irish Lights – a hand-out from her sister Evelyn, Joss's widow – stood on the sideboard; the sorry sideboard itself had come second hand from Andy Hand of Cumberland Street. It was Autumn 1961 and the clock hands were three-quarters of an hour slow.

Through the persistent drizzle of impressions and half-impressions filtering their slow way sluggishly through his (Dado's) morning brain, one effacing the other, interspersed with yawns, farts, rifts, sighs, the sound of the hour came from the bell tower of the church on Royal Marine Road. In Monkstown, Glasthule, Sallynoggin, Killiney, Dalkey, Kill o' the Grange and Cornelscourt it was nine o'clock where he stood among fifty thousand others preparing to face the day in Dun Laoghaire, the old Irish royal dun, now a place of church spires and dog turds. In No. 5 Haigh Terrace underground it was still 8.15.

Dado crossed the dark hall to Mumu's room. He needed money to fetch milk and bread for her breakfast. She brought out a purse from under the mound of pillows and from it extracted a half-crown which she handed across in such a way that her hand did not touch his, saying: 'Mind you bring me back the change. Not like last time.'

Their roles were reversed. Now it was she who managed the money, the dole, such as it was, and issued the orders, such as they were, for him to obey. Poverty had chained them to each other and this ritual. Whereas before it was she who had been the solicitous one and he the strict one, now it was she who was strict and he solicitous. She had had to 'put her foot down' as to who should visit and who should not ('I don't want that one in the place. Don't talk to me about that fellow!'), Aunt Mollie but not Aunt Gerty. The flat was 'too shabby'; it was a disgrace, she hadn't the heart to clean it, and would be just as pleased if no one came. So no one came.

Corcoran, the retired publican who was interested in antiques, called and was turned away. Mumu had never needed friends and now towards the end of her life she had none except Mrs Bowden, a widow who worked in the Irish Sweepstake offices at Ballsbridge.

'Are you finished with these?' my father asked, pointing at the pile of newspapers on the armchair. My mother hid the purse under her pillow. Yes, she was finished with them, there was nothing in them. She watched him collecting them, folding one upon the other, pressing them down, He read nothing but newspapers and he read them thoroughly, omitting nothing, competitions in the London tabloids, sports items, lists of runners at racetracks.

A languor and weariness seeped up through the worn carpet, coming out of the floorboards. This had happened before; this would happen again, with modifications. The very air was tired. My mother turned her face to the wall. Footsteps made a hollow sound passing by on the pavement outside. A man and a woman shape passed. People were on their way to work. My father left the room.

What kind of a day would it turn out to be? Good or bad, wet or fine, ordinary or exceptional, a great sum won at long odds, a few hours of forgetfulness in the bars? Snuffling up his nose, my father retired to his room, piled the day-old newspapers on another great pile already mounted there, hid the half-crown in an empty Player's packet, took a florin from its hiding place, put it in his pocket, pulled on a pair of woollen gloves. There was hoarfrost on the window. News items of general interest were impaled on great nails, what he termed 'buck nails.' The window gave on to a terrace that led to the Mariners' Church and the grey harbour, the mail boat docked at No. 2 berth. My father had been down that morning shortly after seven o'clock to watch the passengers disembark. Three or four times a year he would see someone he knew; it made the day for him. The habit of going there had become a ritual for him, this small indomitable man with bowed back and vague eyes and wavery talk. Sharpe had been summoned to drive us the few hundred yards to Haigh Terrace on our return from South Africa with grandchild. But on that raw morning no one known to him had disembarked. Sharpe had a few fares. My father returned, lit the gas oven, left the oven door open, the only heating available. The kitchen warmed to a humid body heat as he prepared porridge; it was like attempting to warm an igloo. He ate his porridge, plugged in the electric kettle (a handy present from his daughter-in-law), went back to his room to change into his only good pair of shoes. Other figures passed the window, huddled against the cold wind blowing off the harbour. He changed out of his cricket boots. Now the passers-by were walking above his head, as he bowed down to tie the laces. Above his head the school groups from CWC, the crossword puzzle that almost won the big prize, the charm-contest that had ('Dalkey Man Wins jackpot!'); spot-the-ball competitions. He had received his cheque on the stage of the Savoy Cinema. The DJ had asked: 'How do you pick the pretty ones?' He had answered: 'I married a pretty one'; that went down well.

'That bloody fool,' Mumu said, bitter as corrosive acid.

Once well-off, he had lived improvidently; now he had nothing but the old-age pension and the rent that my brothers paid between them. He collected the pension in Glasthule where he was not well known, or not known at all, whereas in Dun Laoghaire he was known. For getting through the winter, those interminable winters that he hated, a sack of low-grade coal or turf came with the pension. He burnt it extravagantly and then went without heating, opening the gas-oven door, turning the gas half on, sleeping half-asphyxiated, sending out great droning snores.

Whatever he won he spent immediately; that was his nature; given a little he became a spendthrift. Money burnt holes in his pockets. He liked the open-air life, out in all weathers like a cab-horse.

The brilliant unsurpassable past and its retinue of cronies, good fellows, yachtsmen and ladies in white, flowed by, borne along by the Shannon and waved to him from the white deck, calling out, 'Batty!' My mother was among them, waving a parasol.

In return for light gardening duties in a Glenageary home he had the price of a suit off the peg from one of the seven married sisters, all well-off; he being one of three sons, the odd one, the mollycoddled boy.

In my father's family there were seven girls and three boys. Margaret who married a Newman, Anna who married a Delaney, Bridie who married a Connolly Fagan, Nora who married the famous athlete Jack Healy, Tessie who married a Stevenson, Molly who married a Smyth, Gertie who married a Moore; and the lads Tom, John and Batty, my father, who married Miss Lilly Boyd, whose father was the Peace Commissioner at Longford. Her brothers were Aubrey and Herbert, her sister Evelyn who married Josef Moorkens of Hertenfels in Belgium, the go-between. And was there not an Aunt Ada who married a man called Lynch who had a grey son called Herbie who played with the Dote and I in those endless summers in Springfield in the long ago? There certainly was.

Kind sister Molly bought him new shoes, the ones he was wearing. His friend Corcoran stumped up twelve pounds for a winter overcoat; he was fitted out. He accepted charity in the spirit it was offered, did not complain of his lot, wore the collars of one shirt, the cuffs of another, the body of a third (the tail of the latter cut up to make the former parts), wore another as an undershirt, for he was thin and felt the cold. For the same reason he washed irregularly; the narrow bathroom with its peeling walls and cold water was not very inviting. He never took a bath. In the toilet the cistern was out of order, the chain wound about a wire scrubbing brush; you flushed with a handy chamber pot. It would do.

For most of his life my father had dressed casually, tight cord jackets with single or double vents (true mark of a racing man or a bounder), thin-stripe good-quality shirts, ties that stood out from the chest when secured by a tiepin, three inches of cuff on display, gold cuff-links (when he had them), a handkerchief up one sleeve, a display handkerchief in the breast pocket, highly polished tan brogues with pointed toes and perforated uppers, a centre parting in the quiff, a dandy's socks, a whiff of eau-de-cologne. He never wore a hat.

A short, amiable, nimble gent who was sometimes – to his great delight – mistaken in public for this or that professional jockey, Smirke or Quirke, which he accepted as a compliment. After all, he had ridden in his day, been a gentleman rider. Lifted his elbow at the Horse and Hound.

Often he spoke of the great jockeys of his time: Joe Canty, Martin Quirke, Morney Wing, Dinnie Ward, Martin Maloney and Charlie Smirke ('a Jew-boy but a great jock'). For him they represented the golden age of racing, at a time when he himself had money, money to burn. His time was the best and only time. And those were the jockeys he had watched going over the jumps and galloping on the flat. He had seen Steve Donoghue win the Irish Derby at the Curragh in 1916. Donoghue and Smirke had each ridden three Epsom winners. Dado and Mumu saw the Irish Grand National at Faery-house every Easter Monday, once in the snow. My mother in a cloche hat and a fur coat, my father peering through binoculars.

In August they drove in the Hillman or the Overland for the Galway Plate, drank whiskey in the Great Southern Hotel and walked in Eyre Square, drove home late to Springfield, none too sober, to the roaring fires.

At Jamestown uncle Jack Healy had bred and trained racehorses. At Springfield he sucked raw eggs, the diet of athletes. He had won the Liverpool Grand National in 1938 with a horse called Workman, T. Hyde up. Mumu's other brother Jimmy rode thrice in the Liverpool Grand National, coming second once, third the following year. But was there a brother Jimmy? Was not that rather Jimmy Brogan? Search the records for the amateur champion jockey Jimmy Boyd.

Dado himself, once an amateur rider, had always dressed like a swank. Nowadays, with the going a little harder, he still dressed like one. A dark suit, patent-leather pumps, the relics of his dancing days. When the patent leathers wore out he wore my old discarded cricket boots, two sizes too large, which he stuffed with wads of the *Irish Times* as undersoles. The paper shredded as he walked, bits of newspaper erupted from his heels, making him into a winged Mercury. Walking about the flat, farting, he shed stale old news, the stamp scandal, the fellow who absconded with the funds.

Another more resourceful breeder more methodical in his ways took over the running of Springfield and other racehorses were exercised over the seventy odd acres; Ringwood Son and Cabin Fire flew over the jumps where One Down had faltered and Grogan had come down.

My father spent much of his time in the men's bathing place at Hawk Cliff in Dalkey, a fair walk for an oldish man. He gossiped with the swimmers in the summer, kept an eye on Corcoran's clothes in the winter. Corcoran, retired publican and reformed alcoholic with ideas about physical fitness, swam in the icy winter sea, did exercises in the buff on the cement ramp. He had a bald pate which he daubed with brown boot polish, bought my father an occasional packet of Player's, instructed him how to bid at auctions, further to his interest in the antique trade, for he was too shy to bid himself, or did not want to be known ('Too damn cute', Dado said), a silent man with a shaky hand ('The jigs', Dado said), a speech impediment.

'That fellow would drive you mad,' Dado said. 'He's cracked himself. Who else but a madman would want to jump into the sea? Do you know what temperature it is? Forty-two degrees. Corcoran's mad.'

The undercover bidding at auctions was not done on a percentage basis, my father (no businessman) neither asked nor was offered remuneration other than packets of Player's, for after a lay-off of about fifteen years Dado had begun to smoke again.

'Corcoran's stingy,' Dado said. 'Tight with his money. And he has pots of it. Keep it and you'll always have it.' I suspect that Dado had hoped to inherit some of it, if only by outliving Corcoran, though Dado was at least ten years Corcoran's senior but always spoke as though he himself would live to be old as Methuselah. His credulity, when it came to base human responses, was matched only by his ignorance; his faith in people had the naive quality of primitive superstitions. What he firmly believed had a charming inaccuracy about it, an arrested stage of knowledge or ignorance like the mythical basis of the heavenly bodies as seen through pre-Copernican eyes. He was gullible to the furthest extent imaginable.

'The bug,' Dado croaked, coughing to demonstrate it. 'I've got the bug.'

It (pneumonia) was 'going' in Dun Laoghaire; in due course he would catch a 'dose' of it, be laid up. About the workings of his own constitution (marvellously healthy when you consider how little he ate) he knew about as much as he knew about the language of the Copts.

Still, ever optimistic, he bought tickets in the Irish Sweepstakes, as he had done all his life; half-shares once, now quarter-shares. He lived in hopes.

'By the living Jaysus this year my luck will change, I have the feeling,' he said, staring fiercely at me with his weak blue eyes that were always watering now in the cold. The *Arcus senilis* had spread, vague hopes swam there, vague dreams of prosperity at the eleventh hour, all addled together.

'Begod it can't get any worse,' said he, laughing.

'Mind your language,' Mumu said sharply. 'I'm sure Jeel isn't used to such language where she comes from.'

'Grow up woman,' Dado said with a devastatingly vulgar sniff at the door.

'Very trying,' Mumu said, shaking her head. 'That fellow is very trying.'

'Trying' was one of her dismissive terms.

She was jealous of his attentions to my wife, had mistaken his inbred courtesy for incipient senility; so in the ashes of their old love there was still a little fire. At all events she resented the gallantry displayed for my wife's benefit.

Mumu came by bus to see her grandson, changed at Appian Way, with a rice pudding in a plastic bag, with love, with fondness, making that journey across town to see us all, to give us her fondest love.

We had called on them once or twice a month, hardly more than that, from Ranelagh with two changes by bus via Merrion Road to Dalkey, generally on Sundays. And at two or three o'clock in the afternoon we would find them still in bed in separate, dark rooms with the shutters drawn, the light already beginning to wane and a foghorn sounding mournfully out in the bay.

Dado, dressed and spruced up, brought out the tea and plates, mentioned a new lightship or floating lighthouse that was to be moored on the horizon on a sand bank; of its usefulness he was highly sceptical, as he was of all services in the public sector or any improvements from any Fianna Fáil government (the new car ferry would ruin the three yacht clubs), for had he not been to Blackrock School with Éamon de Valera and beaten him in the 880 yards.

'A killer,' Dado said, 'that fellow's a killer.'

'Talk about what you know,' Mumu said sharply.

'My dear woman,' my father said, 'my dear woman.'

Truth to tell, I had grown very tired of these barbed exchanges and wished they would end. A foghorn moaning out in the bay, the low-kilowatt bulb already on in the afternoon, the feet of pedestrians passing above eye-level above the half-curtain, the great damp stain on the wall, my mother bringing out a Monument Creamery Cake from the cupboard where scraps of food were hidden away, my father in creaking cricket boots fetching a lemon for our tea. So was ending a long and latterly acrimonious associa-tion, at the beginning of which I tottered across the nursery to be received into the open arms and scent of Mumu who assured me warmly that I was a little dote.

From her lair my poor mother stared at me, as though I were far away. The room stank of women's old stale things, cheap perfumes, old clothes. A stoop-shouldered man coughed in the vegetable garden that was restricted as a prison exercise yard. He wore a cloth cap, a muffler about his throat, a sallow face like the tubercular Collins who had died in Seamount Sanatorium. Perhaps he was a war-veteran, gassed or shell-shocked? He had a closed and miserable air about him, and no civil word for anyone. My mother said that he watched her at her toilet behind the half-curtain, but that was impossible, for the half-curtain reached up to the lintel. An apple tree with dark rain-saturated boughs kept out the light. The garden was planted in cabbage, the apple tree yielded bitter cookers, the tall granite spire of the Mariners' Church rose above the granite of the garden wall which had a postern door let into it, used by the surly fellow in the cloth cap. He was a roomer in the flat above Sharpe. The church had been built in the early 1700s by convicts hauling the stone from Dalkey quarry.

The auctioneer's notice for the sale of Springfield, discoloured with age, was impaled on one of Dado's buck nails. The four sons had scattered to the four winds.

The grounds of the Marine Hotel were infested with cats. They stared through the railings at the stout old lady with white hair walking painfully by. Mumu had put on considerable weight, her ankles were swollen, she advanced with a pronounced roll, uneasy on the slopes above Moran Park.

There was the bowling green popular with English summer visitors, there was the pond with its ducks and geese.

My mother's health was poor, she did not look after herself, she liked a drop, injections for pernicious anaemia kept her alive. 'Without those lads,' the doctor had warned her, 'without those, Mrs Higgins, you wouldn't walk the length of this room.' Sometimes the injections were painful, though she never complained; she drank JJ green label to put a little fire inside her, spent hours in Woolworth's in the winter, for the warmth. I had seen her in the bookie's with her face pressed close to the list of runners, the lens of her spectacles criss-crossed with innumerable fine lines, an intricate spiderwork of fine white lines delicate in texture as the lines in Pavel Tchelitchew's *Inachevé*, but no good for her failing eyesight. It must have been like walking through a snowstorm; she was living in a twilight world at the end of her life. How could the good God be good if He overlooked or ignored the fate of the Jews, for wasn't He a Jew Himself? How could He let that happen, then? And if there was no justice to be expected in Heaven, what hope had we? Ask His Mother, I suggested.

Mumu felt the cold.

For a while she blinded herself wearing her sister's cast-off reading glasses, her eyes grown huge and froglike and confused. Study the list of runners in the Turf Accountant's, fancy the chances of certain favoured jockeys (Piggot, Scobie Breasley, Joe Mercer), slap a bob on the Tote, win a bit, lose a bit, drink when you can, avoid people, endure life. Grief brought to numbers cannot be so fierce.

The foghorn in the autumn, the leaves rotting off the trees, Cork Road, Tivoli Road, Ulverton Avenue, Corrig Road, Oliver Plunkett Road, the Orphanage, and one day like another, winter turning into spring and spring into summer, and that into autumn and then the winter again, delayed daylight shining weakly on the Muglins, on deserted Bullock Harbour, filtering at last into Haigh Terrace and into her stale-smelling lair.

One dark would be just as another dark. A patch of white out at sea meant gulls over sewage, 'stormwater' drifting out or in on the tide.

Dado retired at eight to rise at two in the morning and make himself a pot of tea, drinking it alone in that morgue of a kitchen, sleeping the thin sleep that the old sleep, awake at seven in the morning in the dark, and then down to the railway tracks, the barrier, like a crow in a cold field ploughed up, watching his travelling fellow-countrymen, the Irish back from England on their holidays, the tired faces coming through with poor baggage.

On the pond below the Mariners' Church leaves and scum had gathered, bloated white bread, geese, reflections of bare branches, iron railings and the trembling image of a granite wall. A breeze passed over it, the images changed, shifted, the bowling green lay deserted, clouds were reflected in standing water, life was passing, opportunities wasted; a tracery of leaves and feathers, the hair of the dead drowning there.

Dado passed down the hall and let himself out with a yale key. Opposite was the Marine Hotel with its granite bulk and scuffled gravel, the cat-infested grounds. He went on, huddled into his raincoat, resentful of the interminable winter that 'took it out' of him, weakened him and made him anxious for his health. Mumu had a touch of bronchitis.

She had had herself photographed on a public bench at Salthill, squinting into the sun; in a capacious handbag the letters I had posted in Johannesburg. She has watched the old *Dun Aengus* beating out towards Aran, the last landfall before America.

They had stood on the pavement outside the Monument Creamery and called to us, standing on the platform of a No. 8 Dalkey bus inbound for the Pillar, holding up their grandson, to please come soon again. My father tapped the window when we had taken our seats, Dado nodding, smiling, to please come soon again, and Mumu waved and nodded, come soon again.

At Booterstown we had seen the twenty-foot model of the TIME ale bottle, an illuminated beacon for thirsty travellers by the sloblands and the sign of Kinch.

From draining-board to kitchen table five anxious creaking paces, glare out through the half-curtains (a yellowish flaw near the shocked-blue of the iris); from there to the open bedroom door five-and-a-half slow, anxious creaking paces, snore through the nose, break wind circumspectly, draw away, pull away, be patient.

My gull-eyed father put down a sliced pan loaf and a pint of milk on the sideboard by the clock that was still three-quarters of an hour slow at the last reading and began slapping his pockets in a crafty way and frowning, saying (lying again!),

'You won't believe this, Lil, but that bloody bitch has given me the wrong change again.'

He was a tanner short. Two tickies.

'No, I don't believe it.'

Dado, a true Stoic, accepted good or bad fortune as it came, like a gardener who instead of watering his plants, waits for rain, confident that it will come sooner or later (as it certainly would in Ireland). He devoured the tabloids, a lifelong and insatiable consumption of bad news; his was an insidiously lazy mind. O Angel of Time, you who have counted the sighs and the tears of mankind, forget them and hide them away!

Dado's expressions were these: 'a rip' (an exasperating person) or (more forcefully) 'a right rip': impudent bitch. 'Dough' (the American inheritance, or money in general). 'The wind always blows cold over graveyards.'

Mumu's expressions were: 'a lug' (a thick fellow, stupid), 'slushy' (romances), 'ructions' (rows), 'biddable', 'barging', 'farfetched'. 'Thick as thieves'. If someone was 'all over you' with flattery it only meant they were smarmy and insincere.

Brother Bun's expressions: 'a bit dicey, what's the gen?' 'Hunky-dory', 'not half', 'jolly good show', 'haven't a clue'.

− 42 −

The Hospital by the Sea

That morning the bell had rung early, someone kept a finger on it. I put on a dressing-gown and went down the chilly passage to hammer open the stiff rainsoaked door of our garden flat. There was nobody there, though the gate into Charleston Road stood wide open.

I shut the door and returned to bed and must have dozed off for this strange dream came to me.

A World War II Sunderland flying-boat was blundering slowly through clouds at no great altitude and being fired at by persons on the ground armed with antiquated rifles. There came a shout from the door: *'Here she comes again!'* I ran out and took up one of the heavy rifles, a Lee-Enfield that I recalled from Local Defence Force days at CWC when we had fired them at the range.

I could see the shadowy bulk of the Sunderland flying through clouds, it had a white fishlike belly. If I hit it I knew it would explode, as a whale hit with a harpoon that carried a charge in its head. But as I fired, the recoil strong as the kick of a mule, the dream ended. I didn't know whether I had struck it or not; allowing for the trajectory and altitude I had fired ahead of the flying-boat, passing high up through clouds white as snow. If I had fired well ahead of the white belly, it was me the bullet struck.

Some warning there, a premonition, I felt uneasy, bad news was on the way. An hour or so later the doorbell rang again. I opened the door this time to a motorcyclist in black leather and a crash helmet, taking a telegram from his bulging satchel. He said, 'Higgins'. I said yes I was and he handed it across; it was brief:

'MA GONE TO HOSPITAL × COME OVER × DA × DUN LAOGHAIRE'

The hospital was by the sea.

It stood near the harbour and the three yacht clubs, near the railway station. St Michael's was a bleak-looking edifice in grey stone. The Dalkey bus dropped me near the gate. Clouds hung low and I could see my breath in the air. Before midday it was already twilight. In the damp the snow had turned to slush and the slush to water soon after it touched the ground, forming irregular puddles in the hospital car park. Nothing kept its shape. The name of the hospital was reflected upside down in puddles of water. I saw the lame man going by and called to him but he did not hear me, chose not to hear me.

It was late autumn, in as far as there can be an autumn after no summer; for me it was already winter. Everything was grey, lead-coloured, not a stir of air, the low clouds releasing a drizzle of snow.

A resident medico beckoned me into a small well-heated room near the grim reception hall. He told me in effect that my mother was dying; her lungs were gone. We 'could but hope' was his way of saying there was no hope at all, but I could call him at any time. 'Any time,' he repeated firmly. I thanked him and we shook hands. I went up to her. She was in St Cecilia's Ward, the ward for the female dying, near the service lift. I walked past the curtains and saw that she was certainly dying; her caved-in features and leaden colouring did not belong to the living. Her lower jaw had sunk. They had removed the bridge and the flesh of her face had begun to collapse as the bones came through.

If she lived through it, she would most likely be paralysed; opinion varied as to the severity of that paralysis but none was sanguine. It was better, perhaps, that she should die knowing nothing and feeling nothing. The nuns were looking after her. They were dressed in white habits and moved silently about the ward. In that hushed room the light was going. They moved past the windows, wimpled and pale-faced sentinels of twilight, ghosts of this gloomy, fatal world. They did not represent the world, to be sure; they were the sexless gate-porters into the next. My mother was in good hands.

She, a great student of obituary notices, had feared death; first with religion and then without it, she embraced it again towards the end of her life. It's a strange Catholic fear, the fear of death, very Irish, in a religion that harped on agony, last things. A little light, a last feeble glow of intelligence about to be snuffed out, a little hard-won breath, and then it would be the end.

It was hard-won all right, pulling her down. She was dying with each heartbeat; her sorrows and pleasures shut up there for seventy and more years would die with her, she brought her past with her. Something of me too would die with her; I was watching part of my own death. It did not seem to belong to me, yet it was mine. Will my own death be like that, for another?

Brother Bun materialised out of the shadows and stood by her bed. The Dote had come briefly but had returned by boat to London; he would have to return again to be there at the burial. The Kerry nun had let it be known that the nearest and dearest should be around, time was short, and where was the husband? 'Ah, let the unfortunate man rest,' murmured the compassionate brother Bun. Her favourite was absent, circling the hospital, wrestling with his silent demons; his love was too great to attend.

For now the long-brooded-upon, the long-feared had caught up with her at last and soon there would be no more light, no more thought, no more injections or pain, no more breath; she was going out, knowing nothing of this, advancing step by step in darkness, going out in deep coma. She would know nothing of what had finished her – the cerebral haemorrhage, the night stroke. I took her hand.

She was hardening already, tending towards the inertia of matter. I could not think of her dead, gone, any more than I could think of myself dead; but nonetheless it was only too apparent that she was going. Long ago in the garden at Springfield she had sat on the rug and read Hans Andersen to the Dote and myself as red pulpy berries fell like drops of blood from the yew tree full of missel thrushes. She had been a beauty in her day, and a local poet had composed a sonnet in her honour, the beauty sitting on a public bench on the Mall. Rhymester Jim McGinley had inscribed his little book of doggerel to her, Lillian Boyd. Printed on poor quality paper, it had once been an object of wonder to me. Jim McGinley's verse was printed in the *Evening Mail,* which seemed to me a female newspaper, reserved and rather dull. It ran the 'Mandrake the Magician' strip which the Dote and I followed with the closest attention. The magician's cold shaved features would never change or age, he was always Mandrake, his coal-black shiny hair was slick and the precise middle parting was like Dado's. Cloaked, he was my father in tails. He had a gigantic Negro with thick lips who went about dressed in leopard skins as body-servant. Dado subscribed to four morning papers and two evening; the *Evening Herald* was masculine with the head of a Crusader stamped on red as banner on the front page. The Dote and I followed the adventures of Bud Fisher's 'Mutt and Jeff' and Inspector Wade and Donovan. Inspector Wade was another eagle-nosed type, also with centre parting, and a quiff like bow waves which we attempted to imitate. The *Herald* was hot bread just out of the oven; whereas the *Mail* was a glass of cold milk.

All of that happened in the long ago; and so remote in time it seemed to belong to someone else's past, not mine, when the three of us sat under the oldest tree in the garden and the yew berries fell about us, disturbed by the thrushes feeding. The smell of freshly cut grass, the smell of the lime on the tennis court, the odour of grass decomposing behind the stand of bamboos, this belonged to my childhood, and my sweet-faced mother reading patiently to us there in a voice that breaks my heart. The straight white guide lines were for mixed doubles at tennis and Billy Odlum, stout as Billy Bunter, playing in braces and falling heavily; and they were the lines I must follow out in the world, the guided world that the nuns and the Jesuit Fathers spoke so often about, the world I had never found. The bamboos whispered of the advantages and pleasures that awaited me there; the stand of silver birches behind the summerhouse said the same.

She had reared us gently. Taught us to like books and paintings and suchlike, art, all the things that my father rather despised in his heart; he had the horses and the farm – those other bright fanciful things were beyond him. My parents were kind; putting our interests before their own, they had pinched and saved to give us a preparatory school and then college education which they could ill afford; an education that dropped off me like water off a duck's back. I took only what I wanted from it, the residue and hard drupe of my exasperation with it, and myself in the toils of it; boarding school for the sons of the privileged is a sort of penitentiary. From it I learnt the strange art of making myself invisible and travelling free on public transport through Dublin and London, as if I were already an old-age pensioner, in my middle twenties. The Jesuitical fiction, those pious lies, telling of the world's essential order and goodness, may have dropped off me like water but had made me an invisible man.

I looked now into the caved-in closed eyes and wished for her that she should not survive, not continue to suffer, but rather depart in sleep; the bad colouring and stertorous breathing, the white hair soaked in sweat and arranged in an unfamiliar way, made her a little strange to me, and I had not seen her in a nightdress in many years. I wished this for her who so dreaded death.

The previous year had been a year of deaths; too many too near to her. She had lived with my father in that damp place below street level, poorly enough towards the end, and had got at him, taken out her resentment on him, the last man able to defend himself, for he had no guile, no hidden resources, whereas she had her boiling resentment – if her life had gone wrong it was all his fault. Everything he did (and he did little) and everything he said (and he said much) annoyed her, yes and beyond all endurance. She was dying, as women sometimes die, of their man's equanimity.

The days refused to change, the living living and the dying dying. Funeral cortèges passed slowly through Glasthule, the shiny complacent hearses laden down with flowers, of the death-fleets owned by Creegan and Fanagan (both CWC), moving in the narrow way by the pedestrians doffing their hats to the unknown one who had passed out of life, was free as air, or who knows, plunged in Hellfire for all Eternity. Was it Eudora Welty who remarked on the ominous feeling that 'attaches itself' to a procession, as hinted at in the story of the Pied Piper of Hamelin? Droves of the dead went 'in all directions', my mother said, prone to exaggerate when her stronger feelings were aroused. She meant the ceaseless activity of the living into life and the dead into the ground, where she herself was now heading. Dun Laoghaire itself, formerly Kingstown, the ferry-crossing to England, had something of the River Styx about it, the boat train packed with commuters drawing out for Westland Row, tired Irish faces gaping from the carriage windows in winter, the level crossing passed, rain on the tracks, the gate closing like the end of one of those prodigious watery yawns that bring out a tear and a groan, and my father huddled into his thin coat going home.

Your dear father, she said, disassociating herself from him; your *dear* father, meaning that abject fool.

He still loved her in his way, but that was also too late; the life they had shared together had gone sour on them, they had drifted apart over the years, as I from them, as my three brothers from them and me. We had never been what is called a united family.

At five that morning the tide had begun to go out for her.

It was the turning point, entering the third day of deep coma. My father had been visiting her day and night, haunting the hospital. He had seen her at eight that morning and was convinced that she would not survive the day. It was her last day. Sunday in Ireland.

The streets were deserted, the sky grey and overcast by mid-morning, threatening snow. As I was shaving, the bell sounded. My father had come to say that she was sinking fast, not expected to last the day.

'Oh she's very bad,' he said, shaking his head. 'Very bad. I'm afraid she's going on us. Get over to her quick. I'll try and get the other fellow.'

The other fellow was the Dodo, who had flown in from Scotland but was not visiting the hospital; he was kept informed of progress. He had cultivated a princely hauteur that was most unbrotherly. I told Dado to stay where he was and try to rest. He was worn out with worry and grief; if anything happened I would phone. He needed rest. I built up the fire and he sat before it in his overcoat. Then I left. It had begun to snow. At Ranelagh Circle I recognised a heavy figure emerging from the newsagent's with English Sunday papers tucked under one arm. The Dodo! He pretended not to see me and turned quickly away, going by the wall with short, rapid, fussy steps, a furled umbrella in one gloved hand. He would not go to the hospital, only near it, to feel he was somewhere near her, but he could not bring himself to watch her dying, and he couldn't talk to me. Some intuition had warned him that she was dying that morning. I let him go. There's love for you. I too turned away. A crosstown double-decker would take me via Appian Way to the Dalkey or Dun Laoghaire bus stop.

I reached the hospital before eleven. The house surgeon told me what he had to tell me. I went upstairs to sit by her bed until she died.

When I reached the curtained bed I did not know what might await me – a death's head, my poor mother transformed by dying into some kind of horror. A dull heavy breathing came from behind the curtain and told me that she was still alive, just about. I stood by the bed. A nurse came with a chair. I sat down.

For two days death had been harrying her, drawing closer and closer, and now it was very near. It was doing terrible things to her; she was holding on with all her remaining strength, mumbling with pinched-in and discoloured lips,

For me? Is it for me this time? Me?

Unmistakably it was for her; death was already stirring in her. She had been relatively passive for two days, two days of more or less quiet dying; now giving way to this internal turmoil that would end it. Her spirit was now engaged; before it had only been her body fighting with the blow, the hard night stroke, now it was her spirit – the weary breathing of a stubborn pilgrim ascending a penitential hill, a stony way. A bird lost at a window.

For me? Is it this time for me?

The bridge of her nose was bruised on either side where the useless spectacles had pinched, or it was the mark of when she had fallen in George's Street, one windy night when we had been out drinking hot toddies with the lame man in Mooney's bar.

Now she was ascending a steep hill, going on at all costs, puffing at it. It took all her strength and more but she was obstinate, going at it, her nose pointed, my poor mother wearily persisting, her eyes sunk, her mouth collapsed, looking bitter and deprived, attempting the last impossible hill.

Who may say what humiliations can be borne, what the body can endure, what the mind can stand? I sat by her, held her hand, called to her (and it was here that brother Bun entered the ward and approached diffidently), felt her pulse where the feeblest lymph fluttered and ebbed away only to come fluttering back again, as if uncertain of its welcome, the blood that had given me life. I put into her unconscious hand her own rosary beads of mother-of-pearl, listening to her hard breathing, intermittent snoring, and wished this indignity ended, her troubles over. Her cheeks sagged and filled, loose on the bone, and a little white froth or scum had accumulated at the corner of her mouth. This sac wavered, agitated by the air brought up painfully from her lungs. It soon dried out and another began to form. Each breath dragged up with such painful and persistent effort disturbed the bedclothes where she lay on her side, offering to us her final agony.

Then another followed, hard as the preceding one, harsh as the one that followed, and the little scum wavered on the dry breath issuing from collapsed lungs, torn up from deep inside her. All this interspersed with sighs such as a child might give, uncertain of what was happening. Then silence as though she were listening, harkening to something. She had begun her death. I held her stiffening hand where *rigor mortis* had already started. Her hair was damp with the terrible effort of giving up her life, as all about her the ghosts moved, whispering. A moth was burning in God's holy fire.

It had become quiet in the ward, a feeling of the Sabbath prevailed, the minute hand moved around the dial of the ward clock and the hour hand dragged itself after; time went by sadly and slowly. The nurse on duty made an entry in the Day Book and went past, disturbing the close air, her starched uniform rustling. The ward was warm and full of nuns moving about at their business silently. On the table by her bed stood a bowl of water with a white towel over it, cotton wool, a glass tumbler, a black leather Prayer Book, a priest's crucifix. She must have received Extreme Unction.

The thin gusts of snow blown against the long windows soon melted and ran down the panes of glass, but it was close and humid in the ward. My mother was the only one dying. The gob of spittle hovered in the corner of her dry mouth and an old arthritic nun with a mushroom complexion inside her white coif came and laid a white and speckled hand on my mother's forehead and her fingers lifted her eyelid. *Leave me alone*, the hazel eye said; *I am soon leaving you.* That famous fixed stare. Her eyes were fixed on something moving within herself, something reflected there. World-weary flesh, unbend; eyes, look your last. I was offered rosary beads.

I took them in my hand but declined to kneel, for I wanted to watch her while she was still alive, so that if she opened her eyes it would be me that she would first see, as she had been the first person I had seen in my life, without even the light of intelligence to inform me it was Mumu looking down at me over the end of the cot and begging to be recognised.

But Mumu's eyes would not open again, ever in this life. The dutiful sisters were kneeling around her now saying a decade of the rosary. They went at it sing-song, a patter long learnt by heart, drifting with it, telling of the termination of another life soon to be ended, that bulk of sins (Mumu and sin did not go together) at which their prayers were pointing, prodding, urging *Sanctify! Sanctify!* as a thurible swung to and fro by a server with his mind far away – more lullaby than dirge, pleading and lamenting in high sweet voices.

Oh now, thought I, if she who so dreaded all this mumbo-jumbo were to open her eyes! They wanted to hurry her away, make all decent, change the sheets, put up the screen. *No more sensual fret*, they chanted, lost in their dream; *relieve her of her hard cross, oh Lord!* But her eyes did not fly open. The difficult breathing went on. Now it would pause, as if she were listening, harkening, then continuing as before. A heavy sigh fetched up, then another breath taken, then the subdued rattling in the throat, a snore, then another breath pushing out her cheeks, and the pitiful effort to live began anew.

Ledge by ledge she was climbing, turret by turret, looking in all the windows. *Relieve her of her sad cross*, the chorus of nuns chanted, staring at her. *Lead her to the light*, they murmured. *Take from her her hard burden! Let her have respite from her hard labour, oh Lord!* To one side of me brother Bun shifted uncomfortably, his adenoidal breath snoring discreetly.

But she was still down at the foot of the hill. Grown cynical in the face of innumerable setbacks, a deeply disappointed woman, I daresay, she would carry her cynicism and disappointments with her like banners or campaign medals for valour, into whatever region she was bound for, eyes tight shut (and here the laboured breathing faltered, as if she was following my thoughts; it carried on a little way, faltered again, slower and then, quite abruptly, stopped).

'She's going,' the old nun announced, falling forward on her knees and dashing holy water into my mother's face. They began the prayer for the dying.

It was most urgent now; the nuns raised their voices (the thurible swung faster, sending up clouds of incense), hunting my mother's wilful spirit hither and thither, trying to tell her that it was not like that, that it was not like that at all; but it was eluding them, rising up through the smoke of the incense. The snow was melting down all the long windows of the warm ward, the nuns' breaths going together as if to help her on her way. It seemed like something I had witnessed before, though performed in a manner more accomplished; this was a botched rehearsal for something that had never happened, would never happen.

And true enough the harsh and troubled breathing did begin again, hesitantly at first, uncertain of its welcome (for her spirit in anguish had just flown over the Abyss), and then resumed as determined as before, rasping and wheezing now – the obstinate effort to scale the impossible hill. The candle in her limp hand tilted at a dangerous angle, dripped candle grease on the sheet and holy water rolled down her cheeks like tears.

Nonplussed by this turn of events, the old nun came to observe, felt her pulse. The breathing was weaker but still persisting. Mother Superior made a sign and the nuns left the bedside to go about their chores as silently as they had come. Then she too followed.

I looked at my brother who raised a sigh. Then at my mother, who had only been pretending to die. Her humour had always tended to be on the grim side, rarely if ever aimed against herself. Was this another of her grim jokes? One directed against herself? She was obstinate and set in her aversions, had not anticipated much; now she was dying at her own pace and in her own way. The prayers of the nuns had not touched or even reached her and they would never reach her. She had always scoffed at nuns – their dubious piety and questionable humility, holiness; nuns and male hairdressers, barbers. Like slugs, she had said.

The pleas of those who have turned away from the world in order to pray for it – their lullaby could not touch her or reach her (drops of holy water rolled unheeded from the sunken cavities of Mumu's eyes). The candle had been snuffed out and taken from her; it would not be much longer now, this was the pause before the end.

Presently the old nun came back, watching her suspiciously, as if my mother might leap from bed and run from the ward; she felt her pulse, whispered something to the young nun who looked after my mother. Then she went to another part of the ward where a strong female voice was calling. I held her hand. It lay limply in mine, life was all but extinct there. I liked the young nun's calm countenance and unhurried ways and asked her name. She told me that she was Sister Alphonsus Ligoura, Sister of Mercy. I sensed a different sensibility; nuns with hair shorn and vanity gone were distinctly different. I had found a prayer for the dying by Cardinal Newman on a card by the glass bowl, the wadding and heavy crucifix, and asked Sister Alphonsus Ligoura if she would be kind enough to read this prayer. 'If you wish,' she whispered. She knelt down and I with her, below the mound that was Mumu dying, and she began to read it in her white voice: *And my Guardian Angel whisper peace to me*, the white Sister of Mercy read in a white voice bled of all inflexions. She finished the prayer and looked at me. 'Again please,' I said. And my mother, her face discoloured, her breath going ever slower but resigned to it at last, down at the bottom of the hill, harkened, heard the prayer whispered by the nun.

I was handing her back her copy of Hans Andersen that she had read to us: the Dote and I stricken with measles in the darkened bedroom, or out and about on a rug in summer, and Mumu, young then, dressed in a summer frock with Japanese prints, took the book in hands that were not discoloured, saying brightly, 'Enough for one day I think.'

It had a pale-blue cover and no illustrations, the dust jacket lost. Enough for one day. The tormented breathing stopped, this time for good, and she had gone upwards out of her ailing body (clutching Hans Andersen to her breast), past the unavailing prayers of the Sisters of Mercy, past the falling snow, the accumulated slush. Slowly from the corner of her mouth some pale matter flowed.

Now the nuns were back in a flurry of kneeling and relighting of the candle, the candle lit and thrust into her dead hand and the Prayer for the Dying set out after my mother.

When they had finished they blessed themselves, rose up and moved off, the old Kerry nun and another nun hid the bed with screens, I could hear them whispering behind, church gossip, technical stuff.

Inside the ward it was warm. Only my mother was cold. Outside the snow whirled away, over the pubs where she had liked to drink whiskey, out over the yacht basin and the harbour, out over Ireland's Eye. The old Kerry nun offered us a cup of tea. It seemed to be the custom; I did not want it but took it without milk or sugar and swallowed it scalding hot. The old nun questioned us about the family. I told her that I was married, this was brother Bun, brother C. was in London but would be present for the funeral, and brother D. (the Dodo) was hovering around in the vicinity. She offered no comment on this, was small and bent and reached only to my shoulder, had rough manners (the way she had lifted Mumu's eyelid) but no doubt a kind heart.

'Was it your first?' she asked me.

'Yes,' I said, the tea scalding my insides.

'Ah, that's hard then. For it's worse when it's your own poor mammy. But sure God is good and He will be good to her, poor soul.'

'Yes,' I said.

Behind her the nuns filed silently by; the curtains blew inward and I saw a darkness of shape as if thrown down on the bed. I had not been able to weep. Going out, I looked for the last time at where she lay. Her mouth had fallen open and she was all dark and angular and stiff. When a thing lies still, it will be still forever, is a truth that no man can deny. Death had fixed her in this inimical pose – dark and punished, she no longer resembled my mother. The jaw had fallen in, the brown lisle stocking stuck out, I saw it all before the curtain fell.

'Go on now,' the old nun said at my elbow. 'Don't be needlessly troubling yourself. You can do nothing for us here.'

'I suppose not,' I said.

I let the curtain drop, blotting out the face that was not my mother's known face; that dark and monumentally stiff figure.

'She had her wish anyway,' I said.

'And what was that?' the old nun inquired, smelling of mould-mushroom.

'To die in Ireland,' I said.

The old Kerry nun gave me a crafty sideways look and the hand that she offered me was almost as cold and unreceptive as Mumu's.

I thanked her and left with brother Bun.

Outside it was cold and overcast. The snow had stopped falling. I felt some relief; pain and decay, fishing just below the surface; decay and pain, it was like leaving the dentist's following an extraction, some decay in the system had been removed. And now that it was removed one was glad to be rid of it. Something of myself had been removed with some pain and now I was free to go on without it.

The water in the harbour was still and the colour of lead, and there were the masts of the yachts bobbing on their moorings and there was the gutted church. I waited for a bus to take me back to Ballsbridge, from where I would take a taxi home.

I found the old man sleeping in his overcoat, the sink blocked with his endless tea-leaves, the electric kettle out of order, my wife and child away, no light, no fire. No matter. I made him tea and brought it to him, told him what had happened, that she was at peace, that everything that could have been done was done, that the nuns were great. He sat wringing his hands and staring at me.

All had been done and everything was over.

He had grown old in a few days, now he was an old man.

He lived in his overcoat, a gift, dreaming of summer like the flies, only emerging from winter-long hibernation to lead a summer existence hardly more purposeful than theirs, setting out each day for Hawk Cliff to join Corcoran, keep an eye on his clothes, watch him dive into the sea. He expressed a wish to see her.

'Later,' I told him. 'They said to come later. They are laying her out now.'

He stared at me in horror.

'Drink your tea, Da.'

Later on we would both go and see her; see how she was. I tried to recall some verses by the recluse Emily Dickinson; how was it they went? A death-blow is a life-blow to some?

> A Death blow is a Life blow
> to Some
> Who till they died, did not
> alive become –

Who had they lived, had died
but when
They died, Vitality begun.

My peevish elder brother was nowhere to be seen, on or off the premises.
The Dodo, unknown to us, was flying south; squawking on the wing.

− 43 −

Mortuary Chapel

Dado and I, a little the worse for wear, visited the mortuary chapel after dark on the day she died. A young nurse led us to a wooden shed to the rear of St Michael's Hospital. She went ahead of us and unlocked the door and stood aside for us to enter. She had a small watch pinned to her bursting chest. We went in, my father with bowed head as if being punished; gallantry itself with the ladies as a general rule, he had nothing to say to the pretty nurse with her chestful of breasts and her robin's bold eye.

An open coffin stood on trestles to one side of the altar. We stared at what was in it: my dead mother, his dead wife, in her blue shroud. She was alone there in the silent chapel, calm and composed; nothing would ever touch her and she would never come back, dressed in the cerements of the grave. She had been a beauty in her day and now her looks had returned. I, who had a lifelong dread of touching a dead person, kissed her forehead. It was cold as winter stone. The Ice Queen received my homage icily; she was hard as granite yet gentleness glowed from her; with her beauty, her good nature had returned, her mouth was no longer bitter. The strained and worried look that she had worn for so long had gone; I had never known her, as her expression − disdainful, frigid and yet sweet − spoke to me.

No one had ever known her. The petty annoyances of her life were over and done with − husband and sons who loved or didn't love, couldn't love, it was all the one to her. I had the feeling, looking at her there, so sedate and still, yet so sweet, that one is always being observed, under constant surveillance. Underlying theme of the overlying earth that would presently serve as blanket; soon she too would be anonymous as earth. She who had such a mistrustful nature had spoken dismissively of 'cock and bull stories' and 'tissues of lies'.

Now it was someone else who watched and guarded her, and from under her closed eyes she still watched me. We said our silent prayers and prepared to go. My father hesitated between the coffin and the altar and, raising his right hand as if addressing a living person, said, 'Goodbye now Lilly!' saluting the stone effigy in the coffin. He went out then with head bowed, not looking at the nurse. She locked the door behind us. Crossing the moonlit yard we entered the hospital again. He stopped in the corridor, and the place was a warren of corridors, to say: 'I can't believe it. Fifty years married and look at her there.' His voice echoed down the corridor where an old nun dressed in white was coming towards us.

'She was a beauty in her day, you know,' he said.

'She's a beauty now,' I said, watching the nun coming on.

'It would have been our Golden Jubilee this year,' my father said. 'We'd have both our names in the papers. She said she'd never live to see it, but I don't think she meant it.'

The old nun came up and spoke to us. They all agreed that my mother was a beauty; the Child-of-Mary blue shroud suited her. The Sisters of Mercy would be going down through the night to pray for her. Going out I tipped the doorman half a crown.

'I'm sorry for your trouble,' he said.

It was freezing again, a cold night with the moon flying fast through white clouds, and the wind whistled down the hill from the direction of Dalkey. Across the narrow way light shone in the shop selling funeral items, wreaths and printed requiem cards, hire-purchase terms, artificial flowers in domes of glass, tributes to the dear departed – the usual forlorn objects that one seldom notices when passing by. Stained glass, blue shadows, arpeggios, funeral organ music, mental somnolence. Mother dear, goodbye!

One may hope: Never again all this agony of life. Certainly it's not supportable on a hedonistic basis; it is only supportable, if at all, when one digs down into oneself. And then? And now? Soon for her, poor dear, would begin the 'barehead life under the grass'.

Mumu would belong to the earth soon and it belong to her, and the past also, and not only her own past but all past, it was there waiting. She had existed as part of the seminal substance of the universe that is always becoming and never is, and had now disappeared into that which produced her, coming out between my grandmother's legs. Many grains of frankincense on the same altar; one falls before, one falls after, it makes no difference.

'Thou art a little soul bearing a corpse,' quoth wise old Epictetus. St Paul called the human body a seed. It was sown a natural seed; it was raised a spiritual body. Some things are hurrying into existence, others hurrying out of it, and of that which is come into existence a part (Mumu) is already extinguished. Everything is only for one day, both that which remembers and that which is remembered (I had stood with Mumu in Doran's snug in Baggot Street in my warm Menswear overcoat and thought I would never die as Mumu, Powers in hand, told me of the sweating corpse that was Joss in the morgue). Persephone protect her; and Xochipili, the Lord of Flowers.

The sad signs of approaching spring that my mother had waited and watched for were all about us; the earth hardening in April, the birds nesting, swallows on the way, soft days when her corns ached, announcing rain. She had moved about more easily then, burdened with too many clothes, the wintry load. Spring in Baggot Street.

The auguries of summer at Springfield had been the corncrake grating rustily in the upper field where a hare decomposed in the well at the ring-pump and grass sprouted through the perished boards and cuckoos were calling in the Crooked Meadow. Then the mated starlings, the same pair every spring, with an oily sheen to feathers that resembled fish scales, returned to nest in the wall of the rockery between the broken limestone and corrugated-iron roof of the shed.

Kick over a stone and out come familiar grubs.

We were hardly into the steaming pub when whom did we run into but one of Dado's cronies, a man by the name of Larry Ball, with drink taken. He seemed unmoved by news of my mother's death. Hearing of my travels from my father, proud as punch, he informed me that he, bouncing ball, had sailed twice round the world.

'Ah Larry,' Dado said, ball of malt in hand, holding him with his watery blue stare, 'if she was here well Lord knows she would be laughing with us now.'

Stout and wheezing, with soiled protuberant boozer's eyes, Larry Ball was packed into a worsted grey suit. He had a blunt mottled complexion and the cloudy eyes of a cod, and sat with stout legs wide apart, mopping his brow.

Magnified prints of racing yachts lit from above showed them running before the wind; Howth, as ever, lay in sunshine. The soiled protuberant troubled eyes studied me (I could see a dull question formulating in that gudgeon's eye). So this was the artist of the family. The mournful music came from tapes behind the bar: *Sundays and Cybele*. It had been played while she was dying, while I drank gin in Mooney's and spoke to an aunt on the phone, while the snow was still falling, now it still played and she was dead. Nothing had changed in the bar. She had died on Sunday. But who was Cybele? one of those dying and resuscitating female Mediterranean divinities who carry towers and temples on their heads?

'Ah God now, Batty, the world has changed a hell of lot since our young days,' roared Ball, looking at me with deep misgiving.

We left gasbag Ball sunken in gloom when the pub closed and bought a bottle to take home. A great deal of handshaking went on. My father was by this time in a maudlin state, inundated by the past and no one to share it with, Ball waving a meaty palm and disappearing towards the taxi rank. We went home in our own taxi, I built up the fire, brought out the bottle, put on the kettle, and my father sat before the blaze, glass in hand, his eyes watering. I have his hands, he has mine, depending on how you look at it. My wife was asleep in the front room, our child tucked up in his cot.

On the morning of the funeral I lay in bed covered in coats. Rain had fallen or was still falling. I heard a car pass on the road. The sound came clearly – the slap of wetted tyres on wetted asphalt, a savage mangling of gears at the corner and the pitch of the engine rising. It passed, and the sound died away. I heard another approaching at a dangerous speed, all out, driven by a maniac, slamming into a gear-change at the corner, the driver impatient, taking it too fast. I felt it inside me, the wet tyres shuddering at the sudden braking, the whine of the engine risen, ready to burst through the walls, scatter my thin morning sleep, pierce my eardrums, the fan-belt screeching, '*Oxte! Oxte!!* Awake!' A fearful blast of sound, like pent-up rage released in damaging blows. I was tightened up, waiting for an accident to happen.

Then something immense and airborne almost lifted the roof off the house. I saw its shadow blunder across the wall, onto the cornice, and whip away as the whole house shuddered. It went on into silence. The roots of my hair stood up, for it wasn't any car driven by a lunatic or a jet airliner flying too low through cloud, but her own unhappy spirit that had plunged past, looking for Hell or Purgatory, before disappearing for good and all; and I recalled the dream, the spectral bomber.

My father had woken and was calling for us to rise. Quinn's black funeral limousine was coming at nine sharp. My wife would come with us, a friend would look after our child. We followed the hearse to Glasthule Church; it was low sprung, packed with flowers, the lights on inside illuminating the coffin, looking almost festive, so that people stopped to stare at it going by. That was the evening before, the Removal; this would be her last journey among the living.

After the Requiem Mass we rode in high style behind a liveried chauffeur to Deans Grange Cemetery, following the flower-laden hearse. Out of the main traffic it picked up speed, threading its way through the lanes. There were other hearses there before us and groups of mourners standing before plots or walking here and there in the barren fields of the dead. We were directed to the wrong grave, under a yew. Four rough fellows, gravediggers in Wellington boots, came stumbling across, waving their hats and calling out, 'Higgins! Higgins!'

The open grave was on its own away from the congestion of headstones and crosses (as if in deference to her claustrophobia) and deep – eight feet of opened earth, livid clay, a plot in semiperpetuity. The brand-new coffin would not be brand-new for long, down there in the dampness of earth. It was cold, a cold exposed place, with groups of dark-clothed figures gathered around open graves or moving away. There was snow on Three Rock Mountain. Few, as she had predicted, were there to mourn her. The Dodo was not present; Swift had not attended Stella's funeral, the woman who may or may not have been his wife; and Wilde had refused to leave prison to see his dying mother. The Dodo, holding fast to his own inexorable nature, had kept away. One may assume that all three had their different reasons. Fearing a nervous breakdown, the Dodo wrote in his neat and precise hand, he had thought it best to leave immediately after the Requiem Mass, and I did not see him again. O be thou damn'd, execrable dogge!

Thereafter, per brother Bun, he wintered in Tasmania, home of the waddling duck-billed platypus and Tasmanian devil on that remote island off the end of Oz in the Tasman Sea at the extreme rim of the globe; returning to Largs in Scotland each spring for the golf (more shanking and hooking and missed putts and blue language, no doubt). The Dodo returned home before the swallows dared.

Mumu had died on Sunday 16th October 1966 in St Cecilia's Ward of St Michael's Hospital in Dun Laoghaire, formerly Kingstown, and was buried on 20th October in Deans Grange Cemetery outside Dublin. There were many buried there who had gone before her. She was the first of us to go.

– 44 –

Sedna

It was said of Henry Cavendish the famous scientist that he had probably uttered fewer words in the course of his life than any man who lived for fourscore years and ten. No doubt he had his own reason for being silent (as Crusoe on his island hidden behind his palisade and terrified of encountering savages), immersed in his work. The Dodo too had been immersed in his studies when qualifying to be a quantity surveyor, in his lifelong silence, his separateness, that long intransigence – even Crusoe had.

Certainly he was most retiring and reticent; you wouldn't meet a quieter fellow outside an enclosed order of monks. He had addressed to me his brother, not more than a hundred words in his entire life; not that I saw much of him after the time in Kinlen Road and my stay in Clonskeagh Fever Hospital where malnutrition and scarlet fever had laid me low.

Our paths had not crossed in ten or more years when he came down from Scotland for his mother's funeral. Like the war that he had missed, the combat missions he had not flown by night, so with Mumu's funeral; he came as if to attend, but in the event did not, could not face it, but turned aside. He hadn't anticipated the coffin lid being off and when invited (silently) by one of the mutes to pay his last respects, he had turned away, gone out into the yard, and paced about, troubled.

He had not changed, merely put on weight, grown into a corpulent middle-aged man still awkward on his feet, a Buddha wobbling on an insecure base, moving on convex soles like a penguin, the creature that flies in its sleep, or a toddler learning to walk. He was still keeping his distance, keeping his trap shut, addicted as ever to prolonged Trappist silences interspersed with heavy sighs and sorry eructations of wind in his gullet, as though he were somewhere else, thinking of something else. I had the unsettling impression that he was far away, sipping his gin and tonic with a shadowy version of myself, though we stood side by side in Mooney's bar, listening to *Sundays and Cybele,* silent as ever. I had nothing to say to him. But oh hadn't he such a lovely smile, if he cared to use it. Not that he, so sparing of his benevolence within the family, had ever cared to use it on me.

His head wobbled as if loose on an insecure base (Buddha nodding), a

Black Baby bowing on its plinth on receiving a penny for the Foreign Mission and the saving of heathens.

When had he begun to go all silent? Was he a silent boy already at Killashee? I had never actually touched him; for you would no more touch the Dodo or shake his hand then you would pet a python. He was broody and inaccessible; that unapproachableness was his deepest lair, his high nest or Secret Place (a child's cubbyhole), his covenant with himself.

What could I say to him, after the long silence of those years? 'Once I was set upon by two surly louts in a bar in Drim. They seemed to think that I was an undercover Brit agent sent into Connemara, drinking bottled Crusaders in the heartlands of the Provos. They frisked me, claiming to be Provos. What do you say to that?'

Silence. The head wobbled, the ghost of a smile quivered at the corner of the thin lips. He continued to sip gin. Once had I not asked him for a loan of a thousand pounds (Irish). I needed the return air-fare to Texas. I wanted a stake to take me to Austin for one semester at the University. But did I, by any chance, get it? No. Had he even answered my letter? No. Would I mention that here? No. Would I ever in my heart of hearts find forgiveness? No.

Brother dear, I could have said, laying a placating hand on his arm, hear me now. Never had I felt less welcome than in that faraway bar on the western seaboard on that drenched peninsula where all old Irish grievances fester. I was drinking bottled Crusaders with an authentic Englishman, an ex-British Army Tank Corps man by the name of Foss. They took us for a couple of Englishmen and gave us the hard eye. Maybe they were armed at that, maybe they had a mind to shoot us. Who can say? The youth of Drim took home good money from the Japanese canning factory and reeled into the bar already high on potcheen.

'Provos,' I told them, 'I spit in your eye.'

Taken aback, the blood-brothers-in-arms (James Joyce's 'sanguinivorous bugaboos') exchanged swift eye-messages before beating a retreat to the far end of the bar where they put their heads together to mumble their mouths in the Gaelic.

Were they proposing to shoot us out of hand? Our boon companion, the fair Contessa Rosita (who had a smattering of the old tongue), now threw discretion to the winds, her dander up. She marched down the length of the bar with her hair on end to formally accost them.

'I know what you're saying about us, you fuckers, and I don't much care for your tone. If you want to make something of it just follow me!'

Over to the door she marched, flung it open on the wild black night without, daring either of the bold boyos to step outside with her. The lads looked shifty and went all silent. Outside! No thanks.

They backed down. Johnny O'Toole said later that they were pirates; but how was one to know? Maybe they were armed and high on potcheen before they came in. What do you think brother-of-mine?

He folded his wings, heaved a heavy sigh, voided a few knotty evil-smelling turds, held his silence, by way of response.

Silence (the deep silence of incertitude). The Dodo continued musing, staring into his gin with a reflective half-smile graven on his thin lips. He would slip away before the funeral cortège got moving.

We had somehow assumed that he was in the second hired funeral car *en route* to Deans Grange Cemetery, when in fact he was already on his way to Dublin Airport. Oh he was a strange fish: none stranger in our waters. Communication with the Dodo was like trying to fathom a new and unpredictable chess opponent; the hidden strategies would reveal themselves in time.

That voice of his – when it came, propelled into reluctant speech – was faint and mournful as the distant foghorn mooing out in the bay, with neither lung-power nor willpower behind it. He was a strange one.

The Dodo had grown stouter and older, wore a good-quality suit on his back, and walked – or rather rolled – as I had remembered from Springfield days, the path by the beech hedge; awkward child or shackled somnambulist or sleep-walking penguin tottering on the cement ramp at the Dublin Zoo.

A great Anglophile, he followed the cricket tests and rugby internationals with the closest interest, kept meticulous records, rugby programmes from Lansdowne Road, cricket score cards from Phoenix Park, Trinity College and Rathmines, sets of Wisdens. He had a room for his files and records which he kept locked. The shelves reached from floor to ceiling, the files went back ten or more years, the place stank of Jeyes Fluid.

After the moves from Springfield to Greystones, to Dalkey, and then the nadir, the Haigh Terrace garden flat, a damp underground warren, the files were dumped in tea-chests where the contents went mouldy on the damp tiles. One day I dragged them into the garden, doused them in petrol and set fire to the lot – saving one diary from the bonfire.

It was bound in bottle-green leather, the dark green of the old corked Guinness bottles and also the green of the smelling-salts bottle which Mumu kept to hand; there was a loop for a slim pencil that was missing. The *School Boy's Notebook* compiled by Marc Ceppi for the year 1934, contained much useful information and 'many tables helpful for his work and play'. The author of *French Lessons on the Direct Method* had brought out a list of Sovereigns on the English throne – a stale breath of the past – a table of Latin, French and Greek verbs, some 'strong' German verbs, mensuration formulae, a handy table of logarithms, a list of possible careers in the Colonial Service and Indian Police, or anywhere in his Majesty's armed services spread throughout the world.

Since leaving CWC in 1937 the Dodo had subscribed to the college annual. It hadn't changed its format or editorial policy in the intervening years. The same smooth-faced Imperators and Prefects gazed complacently at some goal out there in the real world of Law and Finance and Engineering and Science and Shell Oil.

It was typical of the Dodo, given his withdrawn and evasive nature, that he didn't subscribe directly but sent a postal order to Mumu towards the end of each summer to buy it at Smyth's on Stephen's Green. I open a page at random:

August 9, 1934, Thursday.
Woke up at 6.30 & roused Ma and A. & went to look for mushrooms in the field opposite. Got a good few at first. Got tin can from lodge people after. I brought some to Mrs Coyle (in bed).
August 11, Saturday.
Half Quarter Day. Cardinal Newman d. 1890. Hammond 302 not out. Very hot.

The long field was still damp with dew at six-thirty in the morning of 9th August 1934, sparkling with light. Among toadstools, thistles, cowpats, spiderwebs sagged on the tussocky grass, going with a checking motion in the breeze, throwing off drops of moisture and lightness. White pupae were hidden in the still centres of grasshopper cocoons. Mushrooms, counterfeit fairy-rings, and the sun shining over the river; the resurrection of the body! It was the twelfth anniversary of the Battle of Liège and two days before the fortieth anniversary of the death of Cardinal Newman, when the three of us went out looking for mushrooms, Mumu aged forty-two, the Dodo sixteen and I seven years old, walking to and fro amid thistles in Mangan's field bounded on four sides by walls, with Killadoon wood facing the Charter School. I remember the dewy field and the search for mushrooms; spears of grass shone, puffballs went sailing downwind, we trod in liquid cowshit.

We had come in by a five-barred gate near Brady's corner, the gallant Dodo throwing it open for Mumu to walk through, saying 'Thank you, Desmond.' Was he not the perfect gent in his purple cricket XI blazer?

Oh he was. Yes he was.

Our No. 8 went bowling merrily downhill at a good lick by Dun Laoghaire harbour and out by the Top Hat Ballroom and the pond and bandstand at Blackrock Park heading for Rock Road and Booterstown. All the windows were thrown open on the lower deck and some kids from the Coombe were singing glees. A strange whitish emulsion of afternoon light filled the lower deck that had become a fish tank where sprats darted; the kids had stopped chewing bananas and were in constant movement, pulling at the seats, looking out the windows, and their brazen mothers had got them quiet and now they sang glees in high sweet voices. The poor of Dublin had little enough to sing about, but they sang glees. The sour whang of the unwashed came from them, returning home after a day at the sea, at Bullock Harbour or White Rock, and nothing could diminish their high spirits.

So those were the songs of praise sung at your passing: *Sundays and Cybele* and glees. You could not be disappointed any more. Your final presence – leaden, serene and descending – had intimated: *Take heed of what you see, my son; for as you see me now so shall you one day be.*

You had changed, become cold and austere, become Sedna the Earth Mother who lives under the ice. White birds flew to unknown coasts over your head and the Aurora Borealis danced in the sky. But you saw and heard nothing but the roaring in your ears, down among the walrus herds and the seal herds and the big fish; you yourself had become one with the deep fish, you *were* a deep fish; half-fish, half-human, my little soapstone mother. We had buried you on a grey autumn day, slightly head-first (you were always impetuous), dropped a framework of wreaths on top and left it at that, no thumping of clay on the coffin lid. Not many attended your last obsequies. It was almost nice to be going to earth before the winter. The grave, *das Grab,* in the old Gaelic dispensation it was The Dark School. You were reduced – no, refined – to that; you had learnt to prop up the earth with a stone. Hands long still in the grave . . . oh look at the clouds!

Farsoonerite Fears, Preverbal Chaos, Undertow of Time, the Mulligrubs

'To return to childhood haunts is to retreat into a land which has since become unreal and hermetically disturbing; a paler shade of grey prevails there.'

Ronda Gorge & Other Precipices (1989)

i

The sullen art of fiction-writing can be a harrowing procedure; an inspired form of pillaging. The writer has never scrupled to beg, borrow or steal from other sources, languages and times when occasion seemed to demand it; as I have had to 'borrow' money from my father, as my three sons borrowed from me in turn – the commodious *vicus* of recirculation that keeps the world turning.

'Borrow' may be a misnomer; say rather, put to better use, refined and improved out of all recognition. Both *Balcony of Europe* (1972) and *Scenes from a Receding Past* (1977) are out of print, and will remain so in my lifetime. I have freely pillaged from both for sections of this present work – bold Robin Crusoe ferrying booty from the two wrecks.

The transported elements of these 'liftings' now serve different purposes – as Crusoe had to cut down a great hardwood tree to make a plank – so too the castaway's necessities when conveyed within the stockade contrived a cave-dwelling from the side of a hill.

They have become my own stories again.

In an ingenious technique of survival Crusoe had to multiply whatever meagre resources lay to hand, *multiply himself* – in direct and open disobedience to his father's wishes, always working against the well-intentioned paternal advice to stay at home – and would be transformed into a fully manned and armed encampment if the dancing savages ever returned in greater numbers to smoke him out. Significantly the first word he teaches his man Friday, in the command structure of language is . . . 'Master'. Me Master, you slave. Carping reviewers, those journeymen ever hasty in their judgements and not too prone to split hairs, have objected to the prevalence of lists in the Higgins *oeuvre*, still emerging and changing, which they took at best to be an indulgence and at worst as a poor imitation of James Joyce's worst excesses (Lestrygonians; organ: Esophagus. Technique: Peristaltic). But hold your hearses, carpers.

Lists or catalogues of proper names can be ambiguous – and sinister – as processions, be they military, religious, funeral or Klu Klux Klansmen burning effigies by night, preparatory to hanging some unfortunate next day. Eudora Welty, the Natchez Trace yarnspinner, instanced the Pied Piper of Hamelin luring the children into a cavern that opened and closed on them. I took the notion of lists from Rabelais, via Urquhart two centuries before James Joyce. Crusoe was obliged to keep lists in his head, ink being in short supply on the island. A chronology, arbitrary as our evolving history, intro-duces Ur-Provos into Connemara somewhat prematurely; logically they were still merely a misty, reflective gleam in the eyes of their fond parents. The sap risen in the tree-to-be, flies astir in the Irish ointment, gangrene growing in the wound.

Now at the risk of spoiling old work for new readers, it must be admitted that the four apathetic spinsters of *Langrishe, Go Down* (1966) were my broth-ers and myself in drag, subjected to a sea-change and all the names altered except the dog's. The real (once living) Langrishe sisters were a pair of prim spinsters who occupied Springfield before old Mrs Warren. Rumour – the greatest of all whores – had it that they were partial to a drop and had to be helped up the front steps and possibly tucked into bed by the yardman who acted as postillion, on returning home inebriated from social calls and, who knows, uncertain of their whereabouts, (as at public readings I myself have sometimes been introduced as the renowned author of *Langrishe County Down*). Horses for courses.

As a spell or curse might be cast or hurled in a fairy tale, the four old biddies living in the country have, hey presto, become the four-fold mystery of myself and three long-lost brothers. (Joyce thought that a brother was 'as easily forgotten as an umbrella'.) For the purpose of this bogus autobiogra-phy, bogus as all honest autobiographies must be, I have changed them back into my own brothers again, nettle-shirts and all. Wasn't it Orwell's conten-tion that autobiography is only to be trusted when it reveals something dis-graceful? I have attempted, by stealth, to discover the snake in the garden.

I am writing of a time of Aladdin oil-lamps when all lay in darkness outside the charmed family circle; of the time before television, before bicycles had to be chained up; so much has changed within one lifetime. I was hoping to catch some lost cadences of my mother's voice – an echo reaching back into the previous century, to the voice of my maternal grandmother; into the true darkness before my time.

ii

All subject peoples must deem their natures to be – however obscurely – biologically inferior. All Paddies are patsies at heart. This assumed base inheritance induces doubts as to the cast of one's countenance and produces a characteristically uneasy stance before superiors who now encounter the shifty eye, the cringing look and evasive response. Doubts as to one's exact whereabouts and precise *raison d'être* for occupying (polluting) that particular spot, must linger in the breast. Why that particular space in that particular time and why me? And all further progress impeded by certain distinct doubts as to the rights (disputed rights) to be there in the first place, even if under the most adverse circumstances and restricting conditions imaginable; a set of galling tallies and intolerable limitations guaranteed to produce stasis; the haven (purely Irish) of exquisite inertia.

Accidie was the disease of monks, a lay version (as a long wet winter produces slugs and weeds) being the mulligrubs – the celebrated Celtic shiftlessness or civic inertia.

Joyce's term for such negative capability was 'farsoonerite', in the sense of copious alternatives, all negative. I'd-sooner-do-this than that, I'd-sooner-be-there than here, the Irish way of prevarication.

Neville Chamberlain's disastrous foreign policy of appeasement to Hitler was decoded as 'umbrology'; a neat neologism for the act of nervously fiddling with a rolled gamp while taking umbrage; prevaricating diplomacy, dithering.

The imagination of a people long oppressed tends to produce, down the ever-narrowing lanes of possibility, curious and wayward simulacra, shadowy substances, deceptive substitutes – the 'hoax that jokes bilked', in Finneganese. All our hopes and fears are joined together in an inexplicable way, our weaknesses with our strengths. The Celtic imagination was *bestowed* upon us by centuries of occupation. Bite, aginbite! Sting, inwit, sting!

Natures wrung by obscure abstract hatreds must come by the most devious ways to understanding, if needs be via mayhem (with us almost a family affair), and all in the name of thwarted love.

As a pale shadow cast in weak sunlight, fear has always been my constant companion. Fear, the basis of all nastiness. The lengthening shadows of King Billy (pronounced bully) and his henchmen, the bounders and bouncers, hovered over my cot.

Prototypal Irish hospitality with its compulsive amiability, the cottage as open house, a place for quarrels to be settled as vociferously as possible, the clamorous argument fairly bawled out, is highly suspect. Such twisted pseudo-liberality must indicate something other than mere friendliness; it suggests fear and uncertainty. A hundred-thousand welcomes is excessive, in all conscience; *Cead mile failte* is an awkward formulation, more an attempt to put the visitor at his ease. For the giver knows right well that there is almost nothing to offer, the larder bare.

'*Mi casa es su casa*' say the open-hearted Spaniards a little speciously, an old grandeur still duplicated in the stilted formality of their epistolary style. My house is your house; but one was not supposed to take this offer too literally. The over-generous host, fallen on hard times, begs the favour that the guest overlook this temporary poverty. The good heart must stand as collateral against the empty larder. The giving hand would never waver, at least theoretically; convention would have it so.

It is a beautiful form of courtesy. The true civility is to be generous with what you haven't got. King Ferdinand and Queen Isabella spent years on horseback campaigning against the Moriscos; they had no home to go to, it having been taken away from them by Bobadilla. The Spanish royals were poor as church mice. They had started the fashion of offering the freedom of their house, quite forgetting that they had lost it and had no royal largesse to offer; all that remained was Spanish *dignidad*. The Spanish and the Irish, with miserable histories not too dissimilar, are much alike in their fervent phobias about open homes and giving hands that must never waver. The fear and uncertainty that underlie such token hospitality is an Irish Catholic neurosis which can be detected behind the wish to please so evident in the works of 'Frank O'Connor' (a Cork civil servant by the name of Michael O'Donovan), the Monaghan bogman Kavanagh and in the broth of a Borstal Boy himself; here again the craven urge to please, to be amusing at all costs. Behan of course carried the notion of the Stage Irishman to its logical conclusion; legless incoherence and wild abuse terminating in fits of projectile vomiting.

The Stage Irishman, the butt of all butts, represents the nadir of the above stasis in a petrified form; a sort of Irish Aunt Sally, a sorry figure in the stocks, a bad joke.

iii

I was ever a prey to ogres and demons.

In that cold echoing vault of a Georgian mansion, every room creaking and groaning upstairs all winter in storms of wind and rain, they were threatening to come down the chimney, drop into the freezing nursery where my young brother and I lay shivering: to fall upon us as their meat, their allotted prey and gobble us both up. Huffing and puffing and covered in soot they had us at their mercy, Dado having gone off boozing with the Bogey Man who lived in the cellar with the arrowheads and empty wine bottles gone mouldy; Mumu having run off with a soldier.

The roof demons were pastmasters of disguise and transformation and could transform themselves at will into many kinds of horrors, now reduced to the size of toads or eels to force themselves down our throats or by puffing themselves up, fill the room as elephants or elks.

Liebnitz has most ingeniously suggested that the function of monsters is to help us recognise the beauty of the normal. To learn is to submit to have something done to one. Everything is already known, provided you know where to look for it. Prejudice is a state of mind brought on by experience. Or, if you wish, 'common sense is the deposit of prejudice laid down in the mind before the age of eighteen' (Einstein *dixit*); distance being the perquisite of happiness. One can only love one's neighbour at a safe distance, *pace* one of the Karamazov brothers.

Perhaps every child's animistic view of the unknown world which they unaccompanied must enter fearfully, is the truest view of our world and the cosmos at large which we are likely to be vouchsafed?

Just because that world-view is so circumscribed by a desperate and anxious love and need for mother and assured home; *just because* it is so saturated with fear lest something (a slithery demon! a goggle-eyed ogress!!) or some dark enemy come swiftly to snatch it all away; *just because* so threatened, might not it be all true?

Even if it is, as it must be, fear-ridden as the morning noon and night of Prehistoric Man fairly gibbering with terror and afraid of every step he takes and – most alarming of all – with a name for nothing. Existing perpetually in that preverbal chaos, in the limitless darkness of nameless fear (the Earth unnamed!). Earth as the unknown, the nameless ground he stumbles across; with his timid will and perception stalked by another Unknown that shadows him, continues to multiply itself, never defining him – it (the Other) the arch-enemy, a dark hole, a Nothing where an incalculable Time runs away (look, no hands!) from him or drags him down, pulls him under.

All this must the child suffer.

What year of storm saw a gravid speckled cow dead a day or two, with stiff uplifted legs and stillborn calf half-emerged from under its tail in a mess of blue guts, killed by fright when struck by lightning near Sadlier's shop that sold harness parts there by the bridge?

A river flows through the village; an old humpbacked stone bridge bisects it, a five-arch stone bridge of picturesque Irish antiquity.

A ford of stepping-stones led across there before the bridge was built and there is another by Castletown estate on the road to Leixlip. In lawns sloping down to the Liffey the cock pheasants strut with gorgeous tails erect, cocks of all walks. A rare breed of black rabbit colonised the river bank and grazed there where the cock pheasant and its mate patrolled as masters of all they surveyed. The narrow gravel avenue led to the Batty Langley Lodge, a loony-looking artifice, a consternation of singular shapes as though her Ladyship had taken leave of her senses or had caused it (the peculiar-looking gatelodge) to be erected both as charming whimsy and overt threat. With Wonderful Barn and Conolly's Folly these large and ostentatious monuments stood as souvenirs with clout and undoubted cachet, casting their rapacious shadows.

Every race to its own wrestling.

No matter how miserable its history, every race on earth sees itself, fitly and properly, as exemplar of the entire human species, its prototype and paradigm; the *mere Irish* being no exception. An English Pope on the Vatican throne had granted an English King sovereignity over the poor little magic nation dim of mind called Ireland for short, so oft short-changed and cheated; and the Second Henry gave it to Strongbow who having portioned it off, handed Kildare (follies, ruins, rich grazing and all) over to Adam of Hereford, the Norman knight who had brought Kildare to heel – ground Celbridge under his spurred boot, dug in the rowels. Thomas de Hereford built the Corn and Tuck Mill of Kildrought early in the thirteenth century and his new tenants, walking as if on eggs, brought corn to be ground and wool to be woven and got the place going.

In 1202 Adam de Hereford founded St Wolstan's monastery; and so the community and the village began to develop around the church, the castle, the mill.

Many townlands in the Celbridge area owe their present names to prominent Norman lords and knights who had settled there. Oldtown and Newtown, Parsonstown and Griffinrath, Posseckstown and Barberstown with

Simmonstown, to name but these. In Ireland, go where you will, you are walking into the past. Stone effigies hunched up in the niches of Catholic graveyards are silent representatives from that past; the long-dead ones staring back at the living with round shocked afflicted stone eyes.

An awkward squad of soldiers in mould-green baggy uniforms fired a volley over the freshly dug grave of some brave patriot at Donycomper where I stood by a cypress tree that wept in the rain. Nurse O'Reilly stood near, her face darkly flushed.

Less than ninety years before I was born the bog people of old Kildare were reduced to living underground in the bog itself, from whence the carters with their turf-carts and small donkeys carried loads off to distant Dublin, and came back asleep in their empty carts. To the mid-nineteenth century the bog people of Kildare were living at a bare subsistence level, poorer than the nomad tribes of northern Norway. The Irish peasantry knew hardship as they knew their bogs, they were intimately acquainted with both, being residents of sod-hovels on the very bog itself. The Stoics and the Romans after them believed in signs and omens, unable to envision a world without cruelty and inequality.

The Anglo-Normans of Kildare planted as Agronomist Soldiers and builders of castles, constituted a hard-headed fighting stock not too given to hair-splitting or abstract thought, were content enough to live out their lives on confiscated lands, behind high estate walls protected by broken shards of bottle-glass, hidden away behind masking ambuscades of 'Protestant beech', an enclave within an enclave. In the secret recesses of their inherited estates they asked each other: 'Are not the requirements of the rich greater than those of the poor?' Not hearing the forlorn echo: 'Aroo adin, Maaaster? Havoo nara crust for us?'

All hidden and secluded places pleased me. Behind old Mrs Henry's voluminous warm petticoats, where reaching back she could secure me and press me to her, for I was only skin and bone. Or behind the mangle under the sheilamaid where the cats made their stinks, or in the orchard or in the shrubbery, the attics or stables, or in the plantation where I could keep the house under close scrutiny and watch the comings and goings in and out – the Bowsy Murray smelling of entrails and carrion cranking up the avenue on his butcher's bike, a sack thrown across his shoulders and an old weather-beaten hat clamped down on his head, arriving punctually with the Saturday roast, a bloody side of beef wrapped in yesterday's *Evening Mail*, Mumu watching him closely from her niche in the bedroom window.

We cannot allow our hopes to rise too much, since history has branded us as malcontents. Flat unaccented blurred speech distinguishes the Joe Soaps of hereabouts from those of, say, the Kingdom of Kerry, whose strong reflexive diphthongs have powerful Gaelic roots.

All my life have I had vivid and disturbing dreams of Springfield; dreams disturbing as nightmares pulling me down. Perhaps it was the memory of the fragile front door thin as cardboard set into the portentous porch with its stained glass – a door that any determined lawless boot could kick in, which caused the ever-circling ever-returning revenant such uneasiness?

Duties and land taxes and labour levies were anathema to him (Dado) who hid in the long orchard grass when the Taxman called every five years or so from Dublin. Major Brookes of Pickering Forest hid in a bush on his own front avenue, where our land steward Tommy Flynn surprised him when calling with a spayed collie bitch for her Ladyship. He saw the curl of smoke rise from the bush before the carriage sweep and, looking in, saw the Major complacently smoking his pipe.

'Glory beta God,' said Flynn, 'what are yew doin' adin the bush, Major?' By way of response the Major only laid a finger to his lips, admonishing silence. Mum was the word. The Taxman was about.

'The great body of the people were of pastoral habits,' wrote Samuel Lewis. 'A hearty, affectionate, loyal race of men fresh from nature's hand; uncommon masters of the art of overcoming difficulties by contrivances.'

In 1980, on my return from years in London, the Irish population register had shown an increase for the first time since 1841 or just prior to the last (and worst) Famine when the uncommon masters of overcoming difficulties were reduced to eating not only their own dogs but their own dead, with gallows-meat cut down after a public hanging, of which there was no scarcity. This had become their ordinary, as testified by Lecky the historian and poet Spenser, no friend of Ireland. The Irish were actually living in Ireland again; the outflow of immigration had ceased, for the time being.

But best of all was to climb the high demesne wall and drop silently down into Killadoon wood with the Keegans and their dogs and follow the path by the pond to the river, trespassing through Clements's land and now forninst us a private very Protestant river owndid by those unseen damnably peculiar ones; a brown stream dangerously deep-swirling by with treacherous currents in which poor Catholics like us, none of whom could swim a stroke, would surely drown. Aroo in din? Aroo dare?

It was a thoroughly Protestant stretch of river there by the bend with the disused cemetery hidden under weeds and the back lodge with suspicious

Proddy lodge-keepers ever alert and ready to expel Catholic trespassers from these hallowed precincts; as once a haggish virago had erupted from the lodge, screeching, 'Git outa death gordon dis minute!' at us innocently gathering walnuts under the great walnut tree.

The river became if possible even more Protestant as it progressed, flowing by Mulligan's house opposite Castletown gates by Christ Church on the site of the old kennels for Tom Conolly's pack of hounds brought over from England. The 'silly tiresome boy' had been the son of the Earl of Stafford, and had contrived to keep the 1798 insurrection out of Celbridge, as he might have kept out the plague, prevented it from spreading.

Hereabouts the river poured in a red flood most purposefully through the Anglo-Saxon lands, flowing dark brown with its sunken weeds streaming bold as battle standards, while along the peaceful banks the pheasants still strutted, while the black rabbits of unique breed scuttled into their burrows; until emerging again as a Catholic river on the far side of St Wolstan's in Dongan's land once more, full of abandoned things bloated by long submersion, bicycle frames and water-logged boxes for Irel coffee and parts of beds, a sorry-looking horse skull and a broken sofa; to flow on towards Lucan and the Strawberry Beds and Harold's Cross greyhound track at Chapelizod and then Guinness's brewery with a line of barges tied up on the quayside with wooden barrels being stowed on deck by strong men in their short-sleeves; and then under all the bridges, to go out stinking horribly of diarrhoea past the Customs House and Ringsend, to empty itself copiously into the bay, a drunkard running to vomit up intemperance.

I'd watched it start out at Straffan, before the dams at Golden Falls and Poulaphuca stopped the flooding, as a shallow narrow but clean Catholic stream flowing sedately through the Pale with its pinkeen and small pollock and gudgeon and trout, flowing through Protestant lands and changing colour as it went entering the confiscated estates and flushing darkly as if thoroughly embarrassed as it advanced with a rush of blood to the face but still all swelling with pomposity as it (no longer 'she') rounded a bend shat into by cattle, until it flowed between the embankments beyond Kingsbridge Station, now Heuston, to emerge again as an unclean Catholic river, to go and discharge itself – now dark as cascara or porter – most frothily into the choppy waters of the bay.

From the yew tree the Dote and I watched the comings and goings in the garden from our high platform of barn doors lashed together as a raft and provisioned

Crusoewise with Rolos and apples and armed with Daisy air-rifles, repeaters. To unwelcome callers (i.e., all callers) we were simply Not at Home.

With us in our tree-house we had a cat to devour the kill, the poor missel thrush dropped at point-blank range. We were dead-eye-dicks like 'Red' Connors, legendary rifleman of the Bar B-Q ranch with Hopalong Cassidy and Mesquite Jenkins, roisterers of the bunkhouse and the corral, relishing our grits and side-meats and beans and coffee around a campfire out on the prairie or the range under the stars, hearing coyotes.

Strangers walked about the deserted garden and orchard, passed into the rockery, sampling pears and plums, mystified as to our whereabouts. My father was that strange hop-o'-my-thumb or how-do-you-do; an absentee landlord *permanently in residence.*

I myself never wished to leave the big garden with its interleading paths under the rustic arbours and rustling palm trees, passing the cracked sundial and tennis-court with wormcasts on wet days (of which there were so many) and the hedgehogs in summer, those strange slow-moving creatures with the faces of bats creeping out of hibernation in the beech hedge; never wished to leave the walled rockery where the monogamous starlings returned to their wall-nest every summer. A place of teeming bees and wasps and the aromatic odours of the tomato plants in the greenhouse; all of that never-to-be-relinquished world.

But how futile now to affect to be that other gormless imbecile that was me once, younger than my own grandchildren (Paris, Yanika, Oscar Sand) today; or to pretend that the hand which writes so confidently in its late sixties can be the selfsame hand that wrote with such uncertainty at six.

I am a different person now. The me then and the me now, co-existent in two such entirely different worlds, are two entirely different beings.

Deans Grange Cemetery
Blackrock, Co. Dublin

Grave No: 53-V3, St Brigid
Lillian Higgins, age 74, 5 Haigh Terrace, Dun Laoghaire
died 16th January 1966.
Bartholomew Higgins, age 74, 11 Springhill Park, Killiney
died 28th September 1969.

These are the only two interments in this grave.

Dog Days

For Zin,
on the sunny side of
the street.

. . . in the hoax that joke bilked.
James Joyce,

Finnegans Wake

PART I:

First Love

– 1 –

The Happy Hours

First love, then the pharmacy.
E. M. Cioran

In those never-ending summery days of endless dalliance in the dunes, never-ending but brought to a decent close only with the coming of dusk, in the cool of the evening with the sun going down at last, when hand in hand we wended our slow way home along the railway track that ran parallel to the shore, until we came to where the little stream flowed out into the sea, all was tranquil.

Our unchained bikes were propped up against the broken fence, one lying on top of the other as if engaged in rapt and silent copulation, the heavy Raleigh model on top, the dainty female model underneath. From there we cycled alongside the south beach, to make our not-so-different ways home.

Drained and sated by her and the sea I cycled back to the broken-down bungalow on Kinlen Road on the edge of the Burnaby, still tasting and inhaling her homemade lobster mayo on my positively tingling fingertips.

Meanwhile Philippa with inflamed cheeks fairly cauterised by persistent kissing, made salty and sticky with seaspray and tangy fish scales, was being slyly admired by the lecherous Scuffle from his little cabin or observation post by the railway station. Portly and wheezing he saw and admired the twin dimples of her bum ('my boh'hum') as she flew by, offering him an alluring last glimpse of her fareyouwell behind fairly moulded into ice-blue poplin slacks which she had run up herself, the clever thing, on her mother's sewing machine; tight-fitting slacks out of which her buttocks were fairly bursting, as she flew by, showing off deep dimples.

Philippa wore nothing much at her ironing. She was more a small brown wren than she was a wagtail, darting from her bush, twittering, flitting from point to point, racked with nerves, troubled by foddering.

When she applied lipstick she puckered up her Clara Bow lips to get it even, a little red purse for her small change. Once she had a boil on her bottom that had to be lanced by Dr Wylie, for whom she must have obligingly raised her shorty nightdress and lain on her stomach to be lanced.

My brown hedge-warbler stood at the ironing board in her bra and panties and sang a little song under her breath, running the grace notes all together with trills and runs, rumpily ta-thumping and ironing carefully dampened skimpies while throwing me a fiery look of disfavour; wasn't I the really low one!

Her plump rump, let it be said, was twice the size of her bust and deeply indented with dimples provocative as nipples, beslubbered with kisses.

She had been a late baby; later again a Montessori instructress; hers a complacently lazy mind. I read Herrick to her, lent her *Fanny Hill.*

But she was beyond corruption. *Coitus interruptus* became our *modus vivendi;* it had in it elements of the carnal, as we came to our pleasures by ways circuitous, that were our own ways.

'Naughty!' groaned stoutly perspiring Scuffle, clasping himself manfully under the service counter on which were scattered the dismantled parts of a bicycle and repair kit, French chalk and inner tubing.

To every crochet its quaver; for look you now she has dismounted to purchase something, some essentially female thing, from Johnston the chemist. Tampons, underarm roll-on, mouth detergent, creams, pills.

But a late date on the harbour wall? Not on your life. I must be out of my mind. What did I take her for, indeed! One of the slack-mouthed local trulls, common little tarts, or what? Who did I think she was? Whom did I take her for? She, the refined lady sixteen summers my senior, thirty-eight to my rising upstart twenty-three and not long out of college, at that. We met in the little seaside resort.

Philippa might just have resembled Murphy's Celia in being ('for an Irish girl') 'quite exceptionally anthropoid', when it suited her. She was a Montessori mistress and mine too, in a way, all nine stone six ounces of fragrant womanhood, come what may. Every licence allowed by lissom lady, from oyster-kissing to manual masturbation, but full frontal assault and penetration was rather frowned upon and the cunt proper definitely *verboten.* These were her strange ways; just so much and no more, be satisfied with what you got. Her religion (was she not a practising Catholic who went to confession and took communion?) forbade it. She would not brook it, could not go the whole hog.

'Be good.'

Where does that take us? Where does one go from there, messmates? Who declared that it was possible to wear away the night with all importunity, just by kissing and plain touching, without consummation – Doctor of Divinity John Donne? Or John Webster?

We were stuck together naked as limpets for hours at a stretch, clenched tight as clams in the windy dunes, lost in the bracken, in the ferns, in the long grass by the faraway beach; until I had almost worn away her patience, her resistance; until Mother Nature herself, grown even more benevolent, had succumbed, become emblem all incandescent and azure above and pulsing here below, to dazzle our eyes and senses and the little port-resort acquired a new and alluring character, became transformed in our honour. Butterflies born in the sun flew about all the livelong day.

Betimes (secluded away together in those hidden places, in transports of joy in sea coves or lost in the bracken) my longing for the bitch was so intense, and never to be gratified, that my teeth ached. A drowsy numbness took hold of all my senses. I wanted to eat her; or, failing that, take a hatchet to her. I had a permanent hard-on, my hot imagination brought on promptings bad as that of the Aboriginal slavering away in the burning bush and frothing at the mouth. Or primitive men anywhere in the fastness of the world at any time, far worse than being afflicted with a hernia or severely ruptured; for 'well-hung' suggested nothing so much as freshly slaughtered game sizzling on a spit.

Philippa Phillips was my meat, all of her 63 kilos; all, all of a piece. My portion; we were made for each other, despite the discrepancy in age. Our prolonged gymnastics were necessarily restricted to an empty train carriage or a pine copse on the slopes of the Big Sugarloaf in winter; but in summer with all the freedom of out-of-doors we reverted to savages.

Could that be what Yeats – who himself came late to wedded bliss – had in mind when he wrote of 'The fury and the mire of human veins'? We know that the beasts of antiquity bred on the run, their glans encrusted with blood and excrement.

But a rendezvous after supper on the Greystones harbour wall was stretching it a bit. To watch the sunset! Not on your Nelly! Favours were favours, boons were boons; this was compromising.

I stood alone on the harbour wall to watch the red sun rise up out of the sea. Gulls were squabbling on the breakwater. Then a pack of scurvy eager mongrel dogs came trotting down to reconnoitre, to make an inspection, informally lifting a casual hind leg with ease born of long practice, to piss quickly on posts, car wheels, low walls, lamp-posts, sniffing the results, canine sprinklers getting the day going.

The familiar shrill whistle of the four o'clock train coming on the breeze announced her arrival. She was approaching me through all the tunnels as I waited by the station on my heavy Raleigh, right toecap to kerbside, and the piggy small hostile eyes of the obese Scuffle observed me from the hut.

She appeared suddenly and visionlike amid all the flustered commuters pouring forth from the station.

Philippa Phillips stood out brown as a nut after a fortnight in Rome on Montessori business, dressed in a clinging summer frock with uplift bra. On her brown legs were Roman sandals laced up the calves to dimpled knee rears. She smelt of summery things, boxed tennis balls in mint condition because never used, cut fruit and freshly ironed cotton and linen. A difficult menses sometimes left her wan and bedraggled. She rarely if ever initiated moves but softly returned my ardently bold kisses in a slow hesitant manner with closed eyes, that drove me mad. On the night train we engaged in upside-down kissing against the grain of her pulpy lips, I playing the hard-hitting Donald Budge to her gentle Kay Stammers (this was before grunting became fashionable on the court). She returned my hard services ('you are lustier than I') with careful slow lobs of her own. My return smashes fairly took her breath away. Her own breath was always sweet. Do what you can; you learn as you go along.

Where from there? Well, first to tea with Mother; then with me into the bushes. No sooner out of sight than naked and clinging together in a long kiss, my manroot reversed, her hands defending her breasts, the large nipples already erected, brown as walnuts. And then the old refrain: 'No, no, we mustn't!'

She was a late arriver at life's feast, a middle child, the misunderstood one least loved, least favoured, leastways by her crotchety mother. Her old pater was already adrift into senility. The stern crewcut blond brother, Reverend Father Philip Phillips, SJ, was built like the young Gary Cooper, off converting heathens in some Ugandan mission station.

And Phil herself, what of her? She tried me sorely with her precepts and possibilities, her nays and her ayes ('Now you are being perfectly disgusting'). Her midwinter face was powdered chalk white as a Kabuki doll. Prim rosebud lips of Clara Bow, hands and feet most delicate and refined, a gentle musing voice – she did not question much; most things amused her – rounded limbs, rounded calligraphy, nut-brown hair rounded on curlers; modest scents, *contained* personal odours, nice airs and graces; her own shy stratagems to entrap and enslave. But no harbour wall, *if* you please.

Once and once only had we attempted and attained bungalow bliss at Much Ado, the humble abode falling to bits, gaining surreptitious entrance to my tiny pink bedroom, like the interior of a mouth, hard by the kitchen sink. It had formerly been a lumber room or storage place for cleaning materials; by reaching out you could touch either wall from the centre of the cell. I had rigged up some bookshelves and there was my library, the Shakespeare, the Schopenhauers, the Huxley novels in uniform edition, *Antic Hay*, Burton's *Anatomy of Melancholy*.

Into this pink cell crept the three of us, the two of us and the dog, little Kurt. Philippa was undressed in a trice and had slipped between the clean aired sheets that I had taken from the line, doped with verbena, while Kurt with a contented deep sigh stretched himself out on the rug and industriously began to lick his prick, groaning and worrying as he transferred his attention to his haunch and rump, gnawing after fleas, while I was after his mistress.

Brown as nougat Philippa lay obligingly on her stomach and I lay on top of her with my hard-on wrapped in woven white cotton bathing drawers tied with a drawstring, serving as a primitive contraceptive device (since there were no balloons to hand, which in any event were forbidden). I cupped her crushed breasts in both my crossed hands, holding her secure, whispering soft words of appeasement, fastened my teeth into the odorous nape of her neck as a ferret might secure its victim, a rabbit stiff with fright, and pinion it against the end-wall of the burrow, kill it with fright. Not that Philippa was in the least alarmed by this overt display of hairy male force.

In the ramshackle bathroom a defective cold tap dripped wastefully away. Shivering and groaning the dachshund watched what was going on in the bed, then sprang on to the coverlet and curled up at our feet, an heraldic beast, our protector, while Philippa continued to whisper sweet nothings into the pillow and I to pour semen while frantically biting her neck, her short hair. I had mounted my rod, and tried casting it shallow waters. If one starts drowning . . . if you start drowning . . . .

Suddenly we stopped drowning at Kurt's warning growl deep in his stomach to alert us that someone was approaching. And sure enough there came the sound of hard bicycle tyres spurning the gravel and the yard door being yanked open imperiously.

We heard the Dodo (for it was none other) hurl his machine into the toolshed, then the kitchen door was rocked to its hinges and rapid fussy footsteps oddly feminine tripped across the buckled linoleum.

Making a face and naked as two plums, Philippa held the little trembling beast tightly against her warm breasts to quieten him, telling him to hush in a soft whisper, to hush up, it was only the Dodo returning from his office in the city; at which Kurt showed his fangs and bristled all along his spine, like a hedgehog closing up.

Quietly and in orderly fashion we dressed and let ourselves out the back way, softly through both doorways, on tippytoe over the gravel, Philippa dishevelled, Rory affecting calm and brave little Kurt vigorously wagging his tail in token of his approval that we were away.

Badger, badger! Holt, holt! Hasten, hasten! Horn, horn!

Sometimes it was 'Sweetheart', sometimes it was 'Skunk'; but the King knew her not.

– 2 –

Sirius Rising

On moonless August nights in the dog days, with Sirius rising, in blossom time, in the happy blossom times, our bliss was complete. For then we had the whole of Kilcoole beach to ourselves and could cavort in our skins in the surf to our hearts' content, run from the dunes into the sea to kiss and embrace there, Philippa icy cold who a moment before had been roasting hot, splashing through the shallows as the tide flooded back in.

We swam through a phosphorescent sea that silvered her all over with gilded scales like a trout silvery and resplendent that I could ardently embrace, vigorously towel dry, she squirming, then eat her (her bush the garnishing), telling her she was MY trout, my mare, I was both the poacher and the groom, the ostler whistling between his teeth, rubbing down the foddered mare Cabin Fire. I was rough Rod, up early to muck out the stables, groom the fidgety mare, curry-combing and plaiting, whoa there my beauty!

I'd lent her Herrick's bawdy love poetry to his mistress Julia ('On Going to the Bath' dog-eared for her attention), hoping to get her into the mood, but not at all, her susceptibilities were tender and tentative as the horns of a snail. I told her that her nipples were as 'strawberries half-drown'd in cream' when she wore white cotton. The bawdy verse of Dean Prior's Vicar was as water off a duck's back. Philippa considered 'Love perfumes all parts' in questionable taste. And what of it if he *had* taught his pig to sit with him in the garden and down his pint like a true-born gent, what was it to *her*? She was no great reader, this outsplashed lady, a siren sprung dripping from a canvas by Delacroix straight into my bed.

The incoming surf made soft sounds of systole and diastole like a sigh or series of small sighs one following the other to rattle the pebbles, running them in and out again, as if playing a game, before withdrawing with calm regularity in a sudden seething respiration on the shore. A wet cling, as in an embrace, the lips glued to other lips, the hand in the small of the back, then the parting exhalation, like a contented sigh.

Semen and seaweed smell of the nocturnal sea, the spumy splash and plash of the surf's inswell that hit us as we went in, in the nip, holding hands, Philippa quick to dip down, to hide her shame. We swam out together.

'I wonder if old Major Storey is watching us in the dark? Got his night-binoculars trained on us?'

In the moonlessness she emerged covered in gooseflesh, to be embraced and run along the shore, a white moth, a pale female shape drawn in light brown chalk on a blackboard, pounding along in her pelt. Night Stalker!

In the endless days of that phenomenally hot blue summer that burnt up the fairways of Delgany and Greystones we went in the nip in full sunshine on Kilcoole sands too hot to walk on with bare feet and ate cucumber sandwiches and fruit, sunbathing in the dunes hidden by seagrass, Pan and captive Nereid covered in pollen, gone the colour of autumn leaves. 'Make me come slowly. We have all day.'

It was none too easy to warm up that flesh of hers, to inflame a libido so placid and conforming; for the nuns had got to her and reformed her. That sweet smile on lips I had bruised was only a token acquiescence, deployed until the sticking point was reached, the hard chastity belt that she wore all the time under her clothes and even when stark naked, doing what she was not supposed to do, with tissues near. She had a core of unassailable virginity, wiping her hands. The order to stop, to disengage, was whispered hotly into my ear.

'Now you're being disgusting again!'

Stew me! What rash expenditure of spurting semen! She aroused me and made me randy as a billy goat with her calm refusals, and how gladly would I have impregnated a whole screaming convent of randy hysterical pubescent schoolgirls, beginning with Mother Superior, blushing Sister Philippa with only rosary beads about her waist, fainting with desire. 'Get brutal with me, Rod lad.' Her long stint teaching with the nuns of Leeson Street had left her torpid in her fleshly appetites! Only her pious spirit gave a feeble glow; the rest was fallow ground.

I laid my hands on her bare whaddyoucallit, bit her, wantoned her, *gored* her.

'I'm sore. You made my breasts sore. You made them very sore, you beast you.'

'Sorry,' I mumbled in a beastly furtive way into my muffler, for it was winter, and we were hidden away in the firs on the slopes of the Small Sugarloaf on a bracingly cold day.

'What are you mumbling about now?'

'Nothing.'

'Horrid beast.'

'That's me. I'm your horrid beast.'

'You horrid thing!'

Her breasts were freckled like wrens' eggs, rarely seen and as hard to find; enhanced (when finally exposed) with large nipples the size of conkers.

Yet all that summer we had wrestled in the dunes, in the nip, in the sea, in the ferns, on the railway siding, on the embankment, I as eager to have what she was so purposeful to defend. We walked and sunbathed and dipped our inflamed parts in the chilly sea that made her nipples erect, as it caused my manroot to extend itself in an even more purposeful manner. I fingered her and she me, we came together. Who *mounts* the meek? (Quarles). What power is it, which *mounts* my loue so hye? (Shakes). My wiggywagtail.

Until I lay exhausted alongside her, failing to get inside her, the pair of us naked as salmon on the seashore, panting. Touch again her flesh, get her going, until I sapless, spent, he by her. We were inseparable; she took it out of me (gingerly fishing my cock from my flies as if handling a viper become python).

Philippa's constant companion about Greystones was Kurt her little German sausage dog always trotting along briskly obedient at her heels. The elongated low-slung animal conveyed the impression, as do all that breed, of shameless canine nudity combined with shattered nerves. Kurt was indeed a nervous wreck; the collar and identity disc suggested S&M practices.

− 3 −

Stolen Kisses

She was shy as a postulant. The thick dark bush came as a great surprise, that hot hairy bun that she kept warm and secret between her legs, as the two smaller buns under both arms rounded as one of Tiepolo's androgynous angels (did I detect a whiff of incense?). Philippa was full of Mother Nature's feminine juices, fairly brimming over. I counterfeited a proper Romantic anguish and laid hold of her, stuttering my importunity: 'Oh I have such desyre to know thee, Philippa! I'd know thee carnally!'

'You may kiss the small of my back,' she said primly.

My urgent and pressing adoration required much strenuous outdoor bussing and fondling even in winter frost and snow and in the remotest places (the remoter the better because there I could go further), between the railway tunnels, on the side of the Big Sugarloaf. We hiked to Greystones from Bray and from Bray to Greystones by the cliff walk to see old movies at the Roxy and Royal and Stanley Illsley and Leo McCabe in plays by Giradoux and Wilde and walked home in the moonlight to dip in the nip in Greystones harbour or by the culvert on the south beach away from the huddled forms of Major Storey and his wife, inveterate night-fishers on their camp-stools, and Philippa phosphorescent in the spumy spray whispered 'You are lustier than I.'

– 4 –

Philippa's Aged Parents

Philippa's parents were old as the hills.

To a quite marvellous degree old Paul Phillips resembled the Boer War hero General Jan Smuts. Same goatee beard, stiff cravat and look of unflinching rectitude. They were dead ringers. Stiff too and forbidding in manner and mien was old Mrs Paula Phillips, an elderly lady of dignified demeanour all powdered up to sally out, impress the neighbours with her edifying example. She had made it plain that she disapproved of me laying siege to her elder daughter. Threw me a leery look.

Moving at a slow and stately pace she made her way around the corner into Trafalgar Road and so over the footbridge – humpbacked as so many things in Greystones, the seaside resort where Protestants come to die – spanning the railway line and thus to the church for evening devotions. She was somewhat humpbacked herself, stricken by the years.

Muffled up in monk-brown bombazine with a veiled pot-hat impaled with an eight-inch hat-pin on her haughty head of old hair pulled tight in a bun, on her feet buttoned boots from a previous era, a plaid shawl draped about her bulky shoulders, she carried a short furled umbrella with amber holder, a prayer book in the other gloved hand; and so accoutred advanced puffing and panting and prodding the footpath in an ill-tempered way with the savagely pointed ferrule. Crossly she advanced, ruffling her drab feathers, a Rhode Island Red unable to settle before a dust-bath, to calm her nerves. She had a hen pheasant's eye.

She was a restless religious discontented woman and nothing in the world could please her. I could detect no trace of Philippa in her except perhaps a certain disdainful twitch of the nostril, sometimes.

– 5 –

The Bouncing Balls

The Ball brothers were well oiled as ball bearings; they liked a drop. Having lost a leg on Anzio Beach Captain Andy limped for the rest of his life, until lost without trace with the crew of the ill-fated *Joyita* in the fastness of the Tasman Sea. The little ketch had been found a month later a thousand miles off course with a shelter arranged aft as if a solitary survivor had hung on there until provisions gave out and he slipped over the side to join his companions in Davy Jones's locker where an unkind fate had sent them months before.

'Knocked on the head by savages,' Brandy drawled through dense fumes of Three Nuns. 'Or maybe eaten by cannibals.' Hahahahaha!

Many's the time I'd partnered or opposed battling Captain Andy in singles and friendly fourballs about County Wicklow and Dublin from the Grange to Portmarnock. He reeking of Bushmills, chain-smoking, stumping fiercely off the first tee at ten in the morning and out onto the dewy fairway.

Once in a mixed foursome with Ena Wilkinson and prim and proper Dolly Oulton, Brandy was passing water in one of the corrugated iron shelters with foreskin retracted when he was stung painfully by a nettle, on his cock. Andy split himself laughing.

The British Army officer and hero of Anzio DSO and bar stumped about on one artificial leg, listing to port and starboard, too proud to use a stick, pickled in excellent Scotch and perspiring profusely.

Both brothers sweated heavily, oozing alcohol from every pore. Brandy kept one stabilising elbow on the bar counter, wiping his overheated brow with Kleenex, ever anon relapsing into sudden storms of coughing that bent him double, purple in the face, giving the death-rattle of a smoker's cough to end them all. The clubhouse wet-wit Joe Mulderry declared that it was Brandy who deserved the bar, whatever about the gong. The male members guffawed and slapped him on the back while Captain Ball smiled a bleak smile. Hor-horr-hor! They were a mouthy lot, proud of their club wit, such as it was, the dopey idiom of village gossip.

Mulderry was Managing Director of Polikoff Rainwear and drank like a fish, could probably have drunk the two Balls under the table, for he was truly pickled in strong spirits and drank all the time; whereas Brandy had to remain sober some of the time, in order to manage his boot factory with any degree of competence.

Capillary vessels had erupted and burst in Brandy's blazing cheeks now gone purple, like so many drunken asteroids in the night sky, a kind of alcoholic fireworks display. He had the snouted appearance of a hedgehog, the snubby nose with delicate nostrils, damp nostril hair showing when he struggled with his pipe; the little bloodshot eyes dark as sloes, with an oily, shifty sheen that was the booze speaking.

He stumbled about in his rubberyblubbery way, as if on convex soles, topsy-turvy as a spinning top running down, beginning to keel over. Heavy intakes of alcohol had made him the way he was, uncertain on his pins (loco-motor ataxy), freighted down with gallons of Dutch lager, his morning tipple to get him going, then quarts and firkins of good-quality wine and spirits to get through the day and lighten the evening and night, propping up the bar in storms of coughing, four or more sheets into the wind when he knew he had had enough at last, stumbling hastily from the bar. Then the slam of the car door below, the engine racing, accelerating off over the cattle trap, and as like as not ending up in Lewis's or the Clyda ('One for the road!'). The Guards (Charley Reynolds) turned a blind eye; licensing hours were flexible, serious drinkers could be accommodated as long as they gave no trouble, and the brothers Ball were a victualler's delight. Brandy was regarded with affection by all who knew him. He was a card.

Mellowed by prodigious daily intake of spirits Joe Mulderry had the yellowed complexion of a wizened mummy long put away into some dusty catafalque; doubtless the internal cells had atrophied, kidneys and lungs in dire straits.

− 6 −

The Undertaker of Aungier Street

Wilmot Wilkinson, he of the twisted lip and the florid complexion (florid as behoves an undertaker, an onerous and dirty job, like refuse collection, that has to be done) was on fire with copious libations of Bell's whiskey and loaded down with all the sour accumulated grief of the day that had slowly seeped into his very soul. And an undertaker's soul must indeed be a grief-sodden one, for his working days are endless, he trades in grief, does business with the recently bereaved, the widow-of-a-day, the wifeless husband; they take their toll. Morticians only become drunkards out of sympathy for their suffering clients.

Coming home on the last train, much the worse for wear (what with Bell's and hand-wringing and apt condolences) to solace his sadness he sometimes picked up stray sluts parading along the damp platform at Bray station and shagged them silly all the way through the tunnels. For a few quid they obliged – working-class girls with easy morals, smelling high as badgers in their setts.

He emerged dramatically and drunkenly from a first-class non-smoker, unsteady on his pins, speechless and footless, hitting the open gate with his shoulder and falling.

Risen again, helped to his feet like a boxer in the ring, he made off into the dark, staggering away down the sea road, much to the amusement of Willie Doyle the ticket collector who was keeping an eye on the slut now slinking to the ticket office for a single return to Bray, the final run back to the terminus, a fiver richer.

Sometimes aboard too would be the coldly sober unfrocked clergyman whose mind, greatly disturbed, was a teeming riot of filthy images and leaping devils going about their business of torturing souls. He had rodent teeth brown to the roots and a fund of filthy stories which he liked to void into the appalled ears of single women travelling alone, frightening them out of their wits, his vile breath steaming forth as out came the filth. For him it was perhaps a form of confession that included absolution. Maybe it gave him some relief, like a stiff smelly stool.

– 7 –

On Being Whirled Away

With her customary caution Philippa deplored all 'underhand dealings' and 'back-stairs intrigues'; she was one of life's late arrivals. Her movements were both shy and seductive; very composed, she had a pale face. Pimply Prudence, her plain sister, spitefully called Philippa 'Lardy-Face', whereas it was *she* who had the lardy face. She was jealous of our happiness, if it was happiness; for Philippa was my troubled love, as all first love must be.

Philippa had a prudish little 'o' for a mouth but a voluptuous body; the games mistress transformed under the shower, steaming.

In the morning sun the larks sang as they spiralled up from their nests in the ripening wheat and we sunbathed in the nip behind cement blocks that made a sea wall at the point of the south beach where the little stream flowed out.

In the evening sun on the slope of the wheatfield she confessed – and how much it must have cost her! – that in the event of the old love ever returning, she would have to drop me 'like a hot brick'.

I knew whom she would drop me in favour of, I knew whom she meant, having seen them going out together. He came before me. Oft had they canoodled in the back row of the balcony at the Ormonde Cinema. With his false teeth removed the false poltroon protested that he felt ashamed to kiss her; but she said that she didn't mind, he should go ahead and give her a kiss. So he clamped himself on to her and gave her a long clinging, lingering slobbery loathsome toothless *kuss*, the rascally Kraut, so he did.

Where?

In the back row of the balcony.

Who?

Kurt Klingsore.

But who is this Beau Brummel, this hole-and-corner upstart, this balcony groper? tell me, tell me. None other than Klingsore whose roly-poly sister Ena is the wife to the lean mildewed Wilkinson, the man with the twisted lip (from rather close shaves), undertaker of Aungier Street where it always rains; it just pours down on the mourners assembled there.

Well, I did not exactly whirl her off her feet. I had no money (a great want); was I not poor, lived from hand to mouth on handouts, like Murphy. But the quiet fishing village cum seaside resort had become transformed into a little paradise fit for us. The space occupied by PP, where she lived and breathed, whirled me away. She simply whirled me away. Or was it love that whirled me off?

Mind you, she was no raging beauty, no *femme fatale,* a handmaiden in the Great Court of Love, at which she was an indifferent participant. Yet she was not my type, that's possible.

Though virgo intacta she had the body of a breeder. Breedy breasts and wiggywagtail bum, with her mother's suspicious eye in the undergrowth. *She* would have had kittens had she seen rough Rod the cocky groom run alongside her daughter and the pair without a stitch on them and Rod with Bronze Age erection that only grew stronger with running and air and total immersion in the iodiny sea. Rod wanted to stick it up her accommodatingly big bum.

But oh dear me no, she just couldn't oblige (her priest had extracted a promise). No, not her; oh she just couldn't, not after confession, in the summertime, in the summertime, in the glimmer time, on the harbour wall.

She was somewhat pigeon-toed, or perhaps it was knock-kneed, depending how you look at it; it gave her a hip sway, a nautical swagger. I found the in-turn, the dimpled backs of the knees, the sway, very attractive, it suggested a sort of fainting submission to a sufficiently brutal approach. She was certainly a bit of a flirt. It was all part of her brown-skinned charm. She wore summer dresses cut straight across the bust, with her arms and back bare; on request offered me undepilated armpits to lingeringly kiss and would obligingly raise her skirt or lower her panties in semi-retreats (overlooking the White Rock, overlooking the railway line beyond the tunnel) to expose her all so that I might fondle her.

'I desire you, Philippa.'

'If we were married you could have me every morning like porridge.'

'Maybe I don't like porridge.'

'Then I'd be your All-Bran, your Wheat Flakes.'

Her defensive strokes were immaculate, her strategy hard to disarm.

'Do me up the back, lovey. Zip me up.'

Only the terns and mews that laid their eggs on the beach and circled screeching over Philippa's head as she went in her pelt into the sea knew what was going on in the dunes, between dips, on our private nudist beach at Kilcoole. Peeping Toms crept along the path on hands and knees, hunkering up to take a quick dekko (heraldic beasts extending dexter paws) and then softly down again, gliding along the sandy path like snakes, like eels, like lugworms. Or, upright, strolling by, whistling to indicate innocence of intent, or standing stock still, appraising horizon in a rapt and studied fashion, as if no impure thought had ever crossed their filthy minds.

Apart from these annoyances we had the beach to ourselves (Major Storey and wife as blurs in the distance in the heat haze, indistinguishable from the cement blocks that guarded the railway line), to eat our tomato sandwiches and Marmite, fruit, Cadbury, in peace. On good days her flesh was on fire.

Philippa was brown as one of Gauguin's odalisques, brown all over but for the soles of her feet and the palms of her hands. Once by a reservoir near Lucan a fox had broken cover to trot down and drink, observing us craftily from the far bank, its muzzle in the water, observing Philippa tearing off her panties, Edwige Feuillère succumbing. 'I'd be your slave and doormat.'

As a girl she had gone roller-skating at the Bray rink and noticed a tall self-possessed youth who was Garrett Fitzgerald home from boarding school.

Once as a grown girl with drink taken, in puce ballgown and imitation pearls, she had shimmied up the long drapes of the ballroom of the Grand Hotel in Greystones to touch the pelmet with her fingertips and slide down to the applause of dancers hardly less sober than she.

I accompanied her up in the little elevator cage at Brown Thomas above the ladies' lingerie department, to change her mother's lending library book on the first floor.

Below us the metal canisters conveying small change flew back and forth along their wires, crashed into the sockets. They were packed with silver and coppers like Mills bombs or hand grenades.

Once a month in winter I took a bath at the Railway Hotel (our cold tap ran summer and winter but we had no hot water) opposite the station for sixpence, cycling there with a bath-cube in my pocket for a shampoo that left my hair stiff and matted as the dusty coat of a Kerry Blue.

Josey the golfing barber cut my hair, demonstrating Jimmy Bruen's peculiar golf swing ('a swing within a swing') in his emporium near Scuffle's hut. He cut my hair for two bob with the same clippers used on corpses whom he laid out neat for interment.

From the stoutly perspiring Scuffle I bought a No. 2 wood known as a brassie in those days. I paid him £2 and kept it for years. Until I sold my clubs and took the mail boat to England.

− 8 −

The Grafton Picture House and Restaurant

All was different then. A courteous time of 'dating' and 'walking out' together and a courting that meant darting forward to open doors or pull back chairs for ladies. Such Hollywood-inspired gallantries were commonplace in the days when bikes (not to mention daughters) could be left unguarded and unchained against area railings.

It was all Pond's face cream and powder puffs for pretty girls in chiffon and womanly women in starched taffeta.

'I knew you fancied me by the way you stared at my lips.'

'Oh any excuse.'

Philippa wore a bison-brown velveteen overcoat with a dotey sprig of something scented in the lapel and a sort of cowl or hood about which she draped her Switzer's silk scarf, a fashion borrowed from Maureen O'Hara in *Sitting Pretty* where she was the very prim and proper American housewife wedded to Robert Young, a hubby much given to pipe-drill and quizzical looks, a coy little smirk playing about the corners of his curly lips.

We saw Deborah Kerr and Robert Donat (ever looking ill) as drab wife and dispirited city clerk with a permanent cold sitting silently at breakfast, gazing with loathing at his soft-boiled egg in *Perfect Strangers*; the drab couple who later are transformed by war and become gallant, he in the Royal Navy and she in the WAAFS, coming together at the end. In the balcony of the Capital with all its ornate boxes I felt Philippa melting, her overcoat slipped back on the seat and the place warm as a sauna with its cigarette fumes and body heat.

Old Paul Phillips rustled the pages of the *Irish Times* at old Mrs Phillips who was turning the pages of the *Catholic Standard* and wondering what her eldest daughter was getting up to with her young Catholic suitor, a most unsuitable match, she felt, eructating, wheezy, troubled with indigestion.

We walked out together to the tune of 'These Foolish Things'. We were teamed up in the mixed fourballs at the Greystones Golf Club; as members of the Irish Film Society we sat in the balcony of the De Luxe in Camden Street and saw Edwige Feullière in *Le Blé en herbe* at a Saturday matinée. Philippa was in the Ladies, applying powder and lipstick, freshening up for nice tea at the Grafton Restaurant upstairs. For she knew that the bold Rory would eat her up in a first-class non-smoker all the way to Greystones through the tunnels, if we had a carriage to ourselves, as private as a closed *fiacre* to the Bois.

We walked through the Green to Grafton Street and mounted the steps of No. 72, a mock Elizabethan edifice that stood opposite Harris's music shop with mouth organs and mandolins on display in the window with squeeze-boxes like cash registers arranged on their sides on purple baize.

An elderly retainer with frizzy grey hair twinkled out at us, squeezed tightly into the ticket office that was cramped as a confessional and made of the same sombre dark wood suggestive of penitence. *South Riding* was showing. We ascended the carpeted stairs and into the lovely eating emporium above the vestibule where I helped to remove her overcoat and scarf and hung them on the wooden rack. By the faint illuminations of the little table lamps with maroon shades and tassels Philippa studied the menu.

One who had come there often to eat in the 1940s has described it well: 'Its bill of fare [is] hallowed in one's memory. Consisting totally as it did of variations under a theme of different names, all nearly amounting to exactly the same thing.'

Why, he could have been describing our cavorting by the shore and tumbles in the hay, more properly speaking, bracken. The menu of the day went unchanged down the years, offering:

> Tasty Tea, Evening Tea,
> Tempting Tea, Afternoon Tea,
> Savoury Tea, Snack Tea and (in awestruck italics)
> *The Gourmet's Tea.*

'Will you chance the Tempting Tea?' I suggested lecherously, pressing her foot. Thoughtful Philippa bit her lip. An anchovy on a slice of toast was added to whatever you had with the others; but this exotic fare was reserved for gourmets only.

> The sombrely illuminated room [wrote the traveller in time], its tall-ceilinged interior resembled the galleried hall of a great country house [in Westmeath, perchance?]. There was a screen in a darkened corner behind which an elevator brought food up from the kitchen below. Upholstered chairs and banquettes upon which to sit under the lofted imitation beamed ceiling. The recessed wide sills of the fake Tudor windows and mock mahogany furnishings.

The waitresses were up from the country and emerged slowly from behind the screen to hover over our table, pencil and pad poised to take the order. It was like a picnic in a wood, served by dryads.

'Oh I'll just have the usual,' I said.

The traveller ends: 'Such was the solemnity of this place's marvellous strange peace.'*

The toilets were situated in the basement below the vestibule. Between Ladies and Gents hung a bizarre man-sized poster blue-tinged as with leprosy showing Doukhobors or Okies cowering under great storm clouds that tower up above the dry prairies. An enigmatic caption read: SOON IT WILL BE THEIR TURN.

I stood at the urinal and marvelled as pedestrians carrying parcels walked above my head; the soles of their shoes pressed down on the rhomboids of thick glass and up above there was a whisper of rain.

*J. P. Donleavy, *Ireland in All Her Sins and Some of Her Graces*.

– 9 –

An Aged Barber

It was when *The Best Years of Our Lives* was running for ever and ever in the musty old Metropole and Sean O'Faolain, editor of the *Bell,* was demanding bananas on his breakfast cereal and the war was on. I was seated in a barber's chair in an underground emporium in O'Connell Street near Nelson's Pillar where the trams started for Dalkey and Palmerston Park from the heart of the Hibernian metropolis. You could get a short back and sides for two bob with a sixpenny tip thrown in. Maison Prost on Stephen's Green and Suffolk Street were the posh places where you paid more.

My mother used to say that barbers were like slugs, they led such unnatural lives. The old one who was clipping my hair would have been born around 1870; now with bad halitosis and fallen arches, moving slowly, wearing the white smock favoured by barbers and dentists. He had behind him a long unhealthy underground working life in electric light with never enough exercise or fresh air in the People's Gardens in the Phoenix Park, putting in long hours for poor remuneration, always on his feet, in the days when trams still ran and the elevated Bovril sign was spilling its stupendous cinnabar neon gules all over College Green.

The old barber was clipping my neck and blowing the hairs away and wheezing into my ear some pleasantries about one of his more famous clients who had come puffing down the narrow wooden steps off the street, as I had. A broad fat man in an Inverness cape, with a cane and a wide-brim black hat, and quizzing-glasses depending from a stylish black cord. The Gargantuan subsidence of elephantine buttocks supporting the vast bulk of the great public debater who had disputed matters of moment with Shaw and Belloc, written *The Man Who Was Thursday* and the Father Brown stories, almost put paid to the barber's chair. Some years before, he (G. K. Chesterton) had monumentally occupied the very seat on which I sat being tickled by short hairs down my collar.

One fine May morning I was walking west along Waterloo Road when whom should I see approaching on the same pavement but a small-sized, brown-faced man in a pale serge suit and tan brogues, hatless, a miniature lariat serving for a tie, that gave him a look of Hopalong Cassidy. He glanced at me as he passed by. It was Frank O'Connor.

Years in the States had imparted a Yankee swagger to Mr O'Donovan, formerly of Cork City, who wrote for *Holiday* magazine and the *New Yorker* under the pseudonym of Frank O'Connor, whose early work my mother had venerated – *The Saint and Mary Kate.*

One grey onyx-and-opal day so typical of Dublin weather, I was waiting to book a ticket for *Winterset* which was about to open at the Gaiety Theatre with Burgess Meredith and Paulette Goddard, when the very lady, Chaplin's leading lady, passed through by the stage entrance, with a sweet smile for the waiting punters, and for me.

Alistair Cooke was writing a script for Chaplin as Napoleon in exile on St Helena, working on Chaplin's yacht, and watched Paulette Goddard in a bathing costume; he said she looked 'trim and shiny as a trout'.

On the stage for the Maxwell Anderson play she brought a touch of glamour, a suggestion of an exotic world outside Dublin and the musty drapes and the safety curtain with old advertisements for Virol and Eno's Fruit Salts.

It was a time when I yearned to get out of Ireland but lacked the neck, the gall, the courage to walk up the gangplank of one of those foreign vessels tied up along the quays near Butt Bridge. Famous ones had passed through, trailing clouds of glory. And I was stuck there.

Oh, clay.

– 10 –

The Old Flame on Butt Bridge

Years roll by, as roll they must.

One grey Dublin day didn't I find myself back, twenty-five years on and now the father of three bouncing boys, passing over Butt Bridge (itself strangely deserted) when who should appear out of the nowhere abracadabrawise but a familiar famished face and form dressed more or less as before who made as if to walk past me without a nod or smile of greeting nor any sign of recognition whatsoever: the Old Flame!

She cast a look of sour aspersion in my direction as if to dismiss me, a low fellow trying to trick her, pick her up on the middle of Butt Bridge; she hurrying on, outraged honour engraved in every quick motion of her rump.

'Phil! What's got into you? Don't you remember me? Rory.' This drew her up short; adrift and at a loss (was there even a suggestion of widow's peak?); halted in her tracks but conveying the impression of hurrying away at top speed. Ah but those shy subterfuges still scalded my heart. I had heard that she had married G. F. B. Ball, 'Brandy' to his intimates, former Captain and then Vice-President of the golf club where Philippa was Lady Captain. Brandy owned a footwear factory in Athlone; he had died of the drink, leaving most of his money to a sister in Taunton.

And still we were meeting on bridges; for had not our very first rendezvous been on the little humpbacked bridge over the duck pond in Stephen's Green one greyly overcast day like this one, when she had come strolling to meet me there?

Who said that first love has this in common with last love, it is again involuntary? What aches a man is to go back to what he remembers, wrote Faulkner. As you taste it you destroy it, say the wine buffs.

'When he performs all joy deserts him,' Ernest Ansermet mocked the anxious Stravinsky on the podium, conducting a performance of one of his own works that he knew by heart but was unable to take his eyes off the score. Nervous as a child on the first day at school, Stravinsky had pushed his music stand up against the rail in order to count time.

At my entreaty she advanced starkers into the dark waters of Lough Dan, thought to be bottomless. The mountain lake engulfed her as she cautiously advanced to be dismembered inchmeal; legs first to go, then the hips and mound of Venus, the dimpled rump and cleft, then the belly and bust (all centre and no circumference, as Celia's); until all of her was severed up to the neck and only the poor flustered face floated free on the dark unruffled surface of the lake (the sun having retreated behind a cloud and the lake become darker). The face still smiled bravely back at me as the water closed about her neck. 'It's warm as toast in!' inanely sang out the decapitated head afloat on the darkening surface, as she launched herself and began a ladylike circumspect breaststroke out into the lake.

'I'm coming!' I called, dropping my trousers.

Closing my eyes and drawing a deep breath in I went after her and struck out bravely for the further shore.

Istanbul, anyone? Who's for Venezuela? Buenos Aires? Montevideo? All the seas of the world.

PART II

No. 11
Springhill Park

– Preamble –

Time . . . attenuates memories.
Byron, *Journal*

My father is in an old people's home down the way. He pisses his pants like Molloy, grumbles like Malone, crouches over the electric fire (two bars), sets his pants on fire, burns pills in the grate. The birds sing. Spring is under way.

> The doctor gives him a week or two. He just about holds on, mind almost gone. Now they call it cancer. He would be in pain but for the drugs. He has your letter but probably doesn't understand it & will hardly reply. The operation caused the symptoms to spread all over, & to the mind. Person & events have become confused & interchangeable for him. He says you were fitted with false teeth when you were here but lost them, & himself and Jimmy Martin looked for them but didn't find them. He told me he was taking the boat. Next day he said he slept it out. He gets up at night & tries to get out the window etc. & is a danger to himself & others. In Duns they would cage him in bed. His paranoia & aggressiveness increase with his helplessness.

A letter from my brother.

– 11 –

My Father Dies

A third of our life-span is spent in sleep. Two-thirds of the Earth's surface lies underwater, as three-fourths of Connemara lies less than a hundred feet above sea level; so a good third of one's address book contains addresses of friends gone to another country, ex-friends, suicides, dead friends (the truest) gone to the other country from whence none return.

In Ireland we are always walking into the past. Even a thoroughly flat country such as County Kildare, my home county, opens willy-nilly into the past. A curious past without Renaissance or Reformation, without flag or proper government, without national identity or street lighting, without an effective police force until Sir Robert Peel in 1829 introduced the peelers.

It was a dark hole then.

The laws had not yet been committed to writing; there were no written records until the seventh or eighth century. 'Thus separated from the rest of the known world and in some way to be distinguished as another world,' famously declared King Henry II's amanuensis and historian, Giraldus Cambrensis, the wily Welsh fox.

The Dutch historian Huizinga considered his work to be a kind of poetry, a kind of dreaming; historical understanding would be akin to a vision. He compared the wigs of English judges in capital punishment days to the dancing masks of savages; for when they donned the death-cap it performed a similar function: transformed the wearer into another being. He wrote: 'There is not a more dangerous tendency in history than that of representing the past as if it were a rational whole, dictated by clearly defined interests.'

Stoutly argued, Dutchman, but where does it leave the poor mealy-mouthed Irish? Still in the lurch? Cromwell put his black curse on us. He wanted to drive the entire race back to their primitive origins, have them crawl about on hands and knees on the foreshore of Kilkieran Bay, become seal hunters and scavengers living just above subsistence level, revert to savages, barking mad.

I saw a scarecrow striding manfully downhill by the Dargle stream in County Wicklow near the Mulcahys' summer retreat. Pheasants are calling in a piny wood and cattle with dungy hindquarters slowly wending their way, without herdsman or dog to direct them, towards the byre. A little boy lost or being punished weeps bitterly by the rainy outskirts of Rathdrum.

In days gone by a man would sometimes allow his horse to choose the way. No more; now no horse, no way. (Just going for a ramble threw Johan Huizinga into a kind of trance; he did his thinking while walking.)

History?

Pâté de foie gras stuffed with rat poison, a servant sharpening knives, a shout in the street. Albert Speer locked away for twenty long years and three fat keys turned thrice – for Spandau Prison is within Berlin, and Berlin was within the Wall, a hundred miles inside the GDR – noted in his secret diary a thought from Henry James: 'Next to great joy, no state of mind is so frolic-

some as great distress.' And amended this rather finely with: 'There are situations in which fear and hope become one, mutually cancel each other out
and are lost in the dark absence of being': (*Verloren im Dunkel der Seinsferne*).
Speer knew whereof he spake. The real city lies all about him but he cannot
see it, any more than its strolling citizens can see him, nor Hess, nor Baldur
von Schirach; all three must serve out their sentences, but Hess will never be
released.

One day in the sixteenth year of his long sentence he had a brief opportunity to furtively embrace his wife, but he did not avail himself and let the
chance slip; fearing, if caught, to get some of his guards in trouble; or else
himself troubled and his will weakened by penal years gone and others yet
to be undergone. He didn't do it; didn't stir.

To retain his sanity he undertakes immensely long imaginary walks.

Crossing the Spandau exercise yard with Rudolf Hess, who may be mad,
he hears a cock crowing over the wall in the city, and the exultant cries of
excited children at play. He walks across the garden he has planted, uprooted
by the Russians every third month, walks on right out of Spandau Prison, out
of Berlin, over the Wall, walks through the GDR like a man sleepwalking,
walks out of Germany, out of Europe, crosses the Bering Strait as evening
falls. In time he has traversed a distance equal to the perimeter of the Earth
itself, finds himself in Kars, in Turkey, as night falls. He has been there
before, on his holidays, he knows the place. Now on the slopes of a mountain
a tent has been pitched, a lantern swings from a pole, two figures sit peace-
fully by the fire, himself and a guard. Above their heads hums the immense
firmament blazing with stars. Will he always have a guard as his constant
companion?

A lawn mower is being pulled and pushed back and forth through scutch
grass behind the Balcony in Killiney, a house rented by the painter Harper
and his Yorkshire wife Pat. I heard it one misty morning as I climbed Killiney
Hill. A mile off, over another hill, my father was dying of cancer.

With a sudden squealing of brakes a red single-decker bus (No. 59) makes
a tight left by the Sylvan Café. Someone has painted in big white emphatic
capitals on the wall:

NO!

A fog of freezing air blows dust and papers by Regan's Pub and in the airless lounge a tall Mayoman with incipient jigs raises a double brandy to his

rubbery lips, twisting his mouth to ingest the draught as though swallowing cyanide at eleven o'clock in the morning.

Out of the clinging mist that swallowed up Dalkey Island in a trice comes a donkey pulling a trap carrying tinkers and their possessions, redheaded children hanging on for dear life, the angry father standing and hurling abuse at the little fast-trotting donkey and lashing at its spine.

They sweep past Regan's, a blur of nomadic faces seen for a moment before vanishing down the hill. The pub in Killiney, the only one, is called the Druid's Chair. My father informs me that in the olden times it was the headquarters of a convention of Druids.

I enter the park, look down into the seaweed beds. Behind the Druid's Chair a white horse stands fetlock-deep in lush grass with a jackdaw perched on its back. Young Mrs Harper in scarlet hot pants strolls along the footpaths under hawthorn and cherry, a figure in a Pre-Raphaelite painting. Down a step in a shabby snug in Dalkey village a betting man circles his fancy with a ballpoint on the list of the afternoon runners at Leopardstown. He has put a few bob on Royal Braide.

The dense white mist, thick as cotton wool, rolled in from Dublin Bay and covered Dalkey Island. A lone blackbird sings in the clinging mist below the obelisk: *'Aujourd'hui! Aujourd'hui!'*

In the seventy-eighth year of his life my father is dying of cancer. The surgery has been too much for him. He shuffles forward as if on snowshoes, stopping frequently. He might as well be on crutches; it would be something else to complain about, take his mind off himself.

'It isn't right, Rory. It's not *right.* I can hardly walk. Never thought it would come to this.' A shake of the head, and he shuffles forward, stops again. I beg a lift of a passing motorist and we are conveyed down in style to Fitzgerald's.

My old man had been a keen horseman in his day, golfer, breeder of grey-hounds, a backer of horses, a dreamer of winners (for a whole month in the Burnaby he had dreamed winners, almost broke the local bookie, who had never known such rank outsiders come romping home at such long odds), a rider of women, too, by all accounts; or so he liked to imply.

He holds a hot toddy in both hands, warming them, and stares at me with his vapoury duck-egg blue eyes. 'Do you tell me so now?'

Above the low lintel of the sunken Gents a notice is tacked up: MIND YOUR HEAD. My fingers tingle. The face in the mirror looks strange. In monstrous mime it (the face not mine) conveys the message: *One day you too will be old and helpless as he. And how will you like that, Mister?* Eh?

The Earth pulls towards it all falling bodies. The Gnostics believed that the angels put the same question to every dead person: 'Where do you come from?'

My father was dying piecemeal. His wandering mind couldn't hold on to any subject: they slipped from his grasp. His thoughts wandered about in vaguely concentric circles, loosely adrift like clouds. Choice seemed both endless and tiresomely circumscribed.

At No. 11 Springhill Park in Killiney a goldfish tank of unclean water turning toxic stands at the stairhead leading to my father's cramped and chintzy room. At the bottom of the tank a dying goldfish lies upside down with its intestines hanging out. My old man's mind is elsewhere, fretfully mulling over the extinct past and its retinue of cronies long gone but still gabby and full of gassy life, going on with their stories, in my father's mind. He has not much strength left in him, extending both hands to the red glow of the electric fire pulled close to his chair. His fingers open and close, taking in the heat, a cat feeling the fires.

Sometimes he, the ever-extravagant one, the big spender, chooses to forget that he is destitute, on the dole, asks to be booked into a hotel or into hospital; anywhere away from the regime of Mrs Hill, the ex-nurse who runs the place, referred to as 'that Presbyterian bitch'.

He examines the contents of his pockets, bulging with letters and newspaper clippings, stubs from the Malta Sweepstakes. His liquids have been severely cut down, alcohol is not permitted on these premises. In the toilet he kneels before the flushing bowl, dips in his cupped hands and drinks. I had brought him a noggin of John Jameson and this we must drink with him, he insists. Always and ever the big spender, the good fellow, the buyer of rounds. He hides the bottle under his pillow with other contraband, putting one over on the officious bitch.

When he leaves the room she will come poking around, making up the bed, fluffing out the pillow, emptying the pisspot, throwing open the windows, confiscating the whiskey.

The old ones assemble below in an airless living room, pick over the magazines long out of date, gape at the TV, doze off, passing the time until another square meal comes around again. A stale spent smell permeates this establishment presided over by the ruddy-faced and brusque former nurse, Mrs Hill. She encourages the feeble old ones to take some fresh air; the gardens of Killiney are in their gorgeous May bloom. And why not take advantage of it?

As my wife and I were leaving she stopped us at the foot of the stairs. 'Have any – mmm – arrangements been made?'

I was shocked as by blasphemy or an obscenity; but the ex-nurse knew her job and had read the signs correctly: my old fellow wasn't long for this world. He would die alone amid strangers, making jokes, joshing, letting them know that he was a great man once.

No such arrangements had been made, no coffin ordered, no grave plot booked. Dr Duffy the kidney expert was in sporadic attendance. With close-cropped fair hair and manicured fingernails Dr Duffy halted at the top of the stairs, with his fingernails taps the tank of now greenish stagnant water and the sick goldfish stirs, turns over slowly, giddily dying. 'Hmmm,' Dr Duffy murmured to himself and passed downstairs with his medical bag in hand.

'Evening, Doctor. Grand day.'

'Evening, Mrs Hill. It is indeed.'

Everything was in apple-pie order at No. 11 Springhill Park.

– 12 –

57 Beskidenstrasse

On 27 May 1969, a bright sunny day with wind (Watt's weather) in Dublin Airport, a perfect day for flying, said my wife (our middle lad James got sick all over the expensive Hollywood tan brogues of Mel Ferrer, immersed in the *Irish Press*), and we all boarded an Aer Lingus flight for Heathrow where we would join a Lufthansa flight to Berlin Tempelhof.

A swinishly stout German couple pushed their way to the head of the queue. We descended through thin cloud at Bremen, thicker cloud at Hanover, and touched down from a clear blue sky at Berlin Tempelhof at 1400 hrs, where Peter Nestler's own secretary, Fräulein Barbara Weschler (in thick pebble spectacles) awaited us, holding aloft a banner with this strange device:

PROFESSOR O'HILLS, WE ARE DAAD!

We had arrived; another life had begun. The Berlin air was effervescent and smelt of pine, *everybody* spoke German, Fräulein Weschler simply could not do enough for us, she was ours to command. Herr Nestler's big car would be at our disposal, and he himself would drive us around. The lighthouse would be found for Herr Professor O'Hills and his lovely frau and grand kids.

After a month of searching, a fine mansion was indeed found in Beskiden-strasse in nookshotten Nikolassee near Krumme Lanke.

Zbigniew Herbert from Poland, seldom sober, lived with his titled wife at the far end of the long tree-lined road. Mando Arravintinou from Greece was over at Wildpfad. We were amid the more distinguished DaaD *Gäste* in Berlin.

The wooded surroundings were full of squirrels, strange birds made their calls at night, the Havel lakes were near. In Krumme Lanke French divers searched the Oxo-dark lake bed for wreckage of a Lancaster bomber shot down by Günter Grass's anti-aircraft battery during the *Kriegsjahren;* the crew had baled out long ago or been eaten by the little fishes. We settled in.

Towards the end of September the message arrived.

In the wooden postbox by the gate of No. 51 a postcard lay face up with my younger brother's distinctive calligraphy: 'Father died yesterday. 29.9.69. C.'

At the corner self-service I bought a bottle of Jameson and accepted heavy Deutschmarks and pfennigs in change for paper money from mil-dewed fingernails. *'Danke, mein Herr . . . vielen Dank.'*

'Yesterday' in Killiney was already three days gone past in Berlin, gone already into Time onward rushing at vertiginous speed, carrying us along.

Today in Dublin my father, grown mysteriously young again, the hand-some suitor for the hand of Lilian Boyd, rejoins my mother, even younger than he, in beatific bliss for all eternity in Deans Grange Cemetery. In the great metropolis of the dead among whom was numbered Brian O'Nolan alias Flann O'Brien held in high esteem and affection by my fussy mother, all three lying there until Resurrection Day, made one in God.

I walked through Jochen Klepper Weg, broke off some flowering branches of linden and carried an armful into the mansion now lit up like a ship. I put the flowering shrub into a vase, measured out two generous libations of ten-year-old Jameson and sat in the sunroom to offer a silent toast to my departed gentle progenitor: 'Upriver always, Da!' That which we are must cease to be, in order that we may come to pass once more in the body of another. *Padre,* be still, and exist anew! (A page was turned, an old man sighed, leaves fell from the linden tree. Tracery of leaves, tracery of leaves.)

Upstairs it was uproarious bathing time. My sons were having hysterics, all three of them like seals in a Germanically large and accommodating bath, with the windows thrown open on the incessant birdsong in the garden and surrounding woods, the air inside permeated with the scents of bath salts and unguents and Pear's soap and flowers. Your glass of wine stood on the edge of the handbasin. You were soaping them and washing their hair and sang

'Frère Jacques, Bruder Hans' in an inspired Esperanto mixture of German, Spanish, French and English, and they were laughing their little heads off. To learn is to submit to having something done to one.

What I would hope to convey, reader, is movements from the past (movements of the hidden heart), clear as sand in running water; the strange phosphorous of a lost life nameless under the old misappellations.

There are days when we scarcely know ourselves; days when we do not properly belong to ourselves; assailed by the strangest of feelings and moods that are perhaps forebodings of our last end (in the form of stupendous sundowns), with cattle bawling in descant, and the Connemara hills of Gorumna and Lettermore (formerly small islands) reflected inverted, standing on their heads, in tarns gone lapis lazuli as the sun goes down, as if gallons of Quink had been spilled into them, and upended swans feeding at the bottom, at this going down of the sun again, and the Friesians bawling to be milked and two seals hunting salmon under the bridge on a strong incoming tide. What clarity of the firmament blazing and dancing above the pier at Bealadangan! The small Starres do reel in the Skie.

Mysteries: revealed truths which we cannot comprehend.

You can see it any day you like in the streets of Dublin.

Incredulous recognition of long-lost friends on all sides. Some of it of a theatricality which must be suspect, the fervent grasping of the hand while loudly expressing disbelief in the lost one's corporeal presence, while pumping the hand up and down. "Is it yourself that's in it, avic? It can't be! I DON'T BELIEVE IT!' Manus, Finbar, Paddy, Ronan, Damien, Rory, Danny, where *were* ye? A-roaming in the gloaming? These strange encounters are so common that they must be regarded as a feature of the place; characteristic of a small capital regularly depopulated by centuries of emigration, in an expiring light.

On 16 June of 1978, the year I am recalling, the voice of the Hound Dog Man was howling over the city, where I found myself drinking hot rum in Agnew's of Anglesea Street near the quays, a pub popular with bus drivers and conductors. A conductor toting his leather satchel and clipping apparatus stood before me with eyes half-closed, holding on to my arm, and his scummy lips sang 'It's a dr*ee*em, oney a dr*eee*mmmm' and he humming like a radiator.

'Whossa greatest singer inna worrld?'

'Alfred Deller.'

'Izzyonnacharrts?'

'No.'

It was Bloomsday and my eldest son's eighteenth birthday, the thirty-third anniversary of the destruction of Hiroshima. It was a lovely blue morning in 1945 when the cylindrical bomb with its packed canister of unholy death came drifting down out of the sky on its little parachute like a child's toy, to explode over a city fragile as if made of papier mâché and some 200,000 Japanese civilians with a great cry gave up the ghost.

– 13 –

Los Alamos

Robert Oppenheimer weeps.

Grounded American airmen are ordered to kneel to have their hair and their prayers cut short by one fierce practised swing of a razor-sharp ceremonial sword; the head falls to the earth as the neck opens to spurt arterial blood some distance and a terrible cry hangs frozen on the dying lips and the lungs have stopped functioning. Drenched troops begin 'shogging' (edging) to their night across a hill in Scotland. They had taken up their positions in the wet cornstocks and tried to sleep, trying to keep their powder dry; Major Hodgson rides along a mucky lane, lost in thought, not knowing that the Protector had decided, after some prayers, to attack at sun-up, send in his shock troops, the Dragoons, show no mercy to prisoners. He (Hodgson) hears a cornet crying in the night, crying for his mammy, for he knows that his hour has come. It is the night before the Battle of Dunbar. Major Hodgson fiddles with his tobacco pouch, coughs, his mount limps, having over-reached in a gallop out of trouble. He does not like the feeling that is growing on him. Someone is watching; someone is waiting; know your enemies.

The harvest moon (tee-tum, tee-tum) wades deep among the clouds of sleet and hail (Carlyle).

The nuclear physicist is sobbing his heart out. He has had mushrooms for breakfast and quarrelled with Bohr. He too has a sense that something very bad is about to happen, but Oppenheimer will not let Bohr know what his feelings are; Bohr is an idiot.

The Pentagon had already authorised the priming of the second knock-out bomb. The next city scheduled to get it in the neck is Nagasaki: they will make a clean sweep of wiping out hundreds of thousands of innocent civilians whose only offence was to be born Japanese and call Nagasaki home. It would be home no longer when the second annihilation bomb came drifting down out of the clear sky.

In the heart of the elemental chaos let loose, a dead sun shone fiercely but briefly (candle flame extinguished in mine filled with methane fumes), stronger than the true sun of midday, the Life Giver.

But this was the Life Taker (Oppenheimer had wept) and before the tarry incendiary rain had begun to fall, the double atomic thunderclap had echoed hollowly off Heaven's doors.

But the Americans had already begun to prime their second bomb. The ground war had been conducted without mercy on either side, with grenades and flamethrowers to choke the foxholes in islands and jungle from Guam to Guadalcanal – names that seemed sticky with soldiers' blood, the dead, the wounded, the dismembered, and those set on fire.

The enemy, Nips or Japs despised and feared, were seen as subhuman, against whom every barbarity and atrocity was permissible; vengeance would be wreaked in full measure by the stronger, deaf to all entreaty.

The logic of total war demanded the infliction of intolerable pain, the more atrocious the better; and in this sense the two bombs were perfect, the fruit of the Manhattan Project that had caused Robert Oppenheimer to weep. They were named as if after beloved domestic pets, Little Boy and Fat Man, and the first B-29 bomber was named after somebody's mom, Enola Gay, homely as blueberry pie.

The Fat Man was in fact Churchill whose V-sign was the fuck-you finger insult denoting cuckoldry; as the rival swastika was the crux desecrated, a torture wheel whereon victims were broken.

At Los Alamos in the desert of New Mexico the Americans, Nils Bohr and the other clowns, made the Trinity Test at 4 a.m. Far away in a filling station a woman saw the sun rise, and half an hour later it rose again, the proper sun rising at the proper hour. The theoretical physicists were screwing their wives like monkeys, carnally committed by nerves and anxiety.

'Why are we all having babies out here?'

In Hiroshima and Nagasaki it would be better for the women *not* to have babies, not just yet.

The fellow who ascended the tower to plant the Trinity Test atomic bomb, closely observed by the wives (already pregnant) of the Manhattan Project specialists Bohr and Oppenheimer, heard ring in his ears the triumphant Waltz and Serenade by Tchaikovsky played over the Tannoy. The Los Alamos valley was thirty miles wide, green on the near side, with orange rocks moulded by sun and water. One observer had noticed a yellow halo about the mushroom cloud which he likened to the haloes about the heads of holy martyrs in paintings by Grünewald; when he might as well have compared it to greenish gangrescent pus on cotton wool covering a war wound.

If the Axis had discovered fission before the Allies, then God help us all. Hitler had his own musical fancies and selected what seemed to him appropriate fanfares to precede Reich network announcements of striking victories in the field as Czechoslovakia, Austria, Poland, France, The Netherlands and parts of Scandinavia fell. The invasion of Soviet Russia, code-named Barbarossa, would be 'child's play in a sandbox,' he told Keitel: he had chosen Liszt's *Les Preludes,* found by Funk and a splendid example of Reichian *Poshlust* matching the splendour of Goering's uniforms, Speer's architecture and Party bombast in general, to be the Nazi victory fanfare or war dance.

Hitler himself had dreamed up the Stuka's diving screech to terrorise the bombed ones below. When he appointed himself supreme commander in the field, *Oberkommando der Wehrmacht,* designed his battle pennant, he saw only what he wished to see (war was all maps, spread out on a thirteen-foot table, a huge block of marble cut in one piece; a matter of straightening out bends, throwing in fresh divisions; the names of places, Maikop, Sochi, Sukhumi merely distractions), heard only what he wished to hear, and kept his soft manicured hands clean in choice chamois gloves. He had thought up a grenade-throwing machine constructed along the principles of the lawn-sprinkler, but its functional purpose was suspect, for it flung grenades back into its own lines, not that this would much inhibit its inspired inventor.

Orders came from on high; he was not prepared to give up ground, the bends in the front must be held at all costs; the enemy position must be overrun. The enemy must be out-flanked, out-tanked, out-gunned, out-produced on the home front (munitions in the hands of Speer), out-man powered (Schacht), out-ball bearinged. Raus! Raus!

'At all costs!' It should have been stitched in scarlet into his white silken battle pennant with its swaggering dangerous swastika. Face us at your peril!

Now, at the corner of Harry Street and Grafton Street where once the grand old picture house and restaurant stood (Nice Teas a Speciality), I wasn't thinking of Harry Truman hiding behind the long drapes in the Oval Room. This President would have dropped forty atomic bombs on the holy city of Kyoto but had to make do with two, one for Hiroshima, one for Nagasaki.

'Forty years on dis earth,' declared the bus conductor with a desperate sincerity, positively foaming at the mouth, 'an' e'll be remembered frevver!'

Now the flower-sellers were offering bunches of *sempervivens,* sometimes called immortelles, the little flowers of the Andes, outside the Dublin Savings Bank. The Sign of the Zodiac stood opposite, now in new hands.

In the old days the draymen from the famous brewery at St James's Gate came there to tether their heavy dray horses to the railings and let them chomp away at clumps of hay with their big herbivorous buckteeth, pissing like waterfalls on the pavement.

In clumped the weary draymen in their clayey boots, calling for foaming pints. They stood at the bar counter and gazed up with proper reverence at the stained-glass windows above, where the heraldic beasts stomped and ramped in their spotless stalls.

PART III:

Ballymona Lodge,
1985

– 14 –

Aboard the SS *St Columba*

One murky morning in mid-January I entered an icebound Euston station in a London under snow. The Holyhead boat train was running late but the *St Columba* was waiting in Wales.

I travelled there with a young couple not on speaking terms. When they got on the train at Crewe they were already reduced to sign language. She offered him sandwiches, a thermos, fruit; he would accept nothing from her hand but stared out the window with pursed lips. He didn't know her. Having waited until she was finished and tidily repacked, he helped himself. They ate separately, methodically chewing and swallowing, looking out the window into Wales, pretending that the other was not there. They were having a tiff. Presently we reached Holyhead and there was the SS *St Columba* moored to the quayside.

As a heavy hose discharges dirty water, Muzak was being pumped indiscriminately into every nook and cranny of the broad ferry, soaking into each corner of the renovated lounge, into the toilets and into the luridly lit Cardiff Arms Park bar which was doing a roaring trade as soon as the security cage was unlocked; as into the Lansdowne Road bar where a wild-eyed Kerryman paced to and fro like a caged beast.

It must be said that the Irish *en masse* in transit in close, overheated quarters are not an attractive sight; shabby as itinerants, their children already running wild as mice, miscegenation upon miscegenation.

To ram the message home a patriot's hand had daubed in black paint shiny as tar the divisive equation IRA + INLA = FF? How damnably unnerving to be among one's own at last!

Soggy sandwiches purporting to be ham and cheese were on display behind glass guarded by young slovens in soiled overalls. On the boat deck the baggage master inclined an ear to the whisperings of an overexcited woman that caused his cod's eyes to bulge. The silent pair who had got on at Crewe were *still* not speaking but as black out as before, trailing about on their own with mulish obstinacy as we moved through a darkening sea, apparently proceeding in the wrong direction, into the Channel and open ocean; a sensation familiar to train passengers in foreign lands where trains enter a station only to retreat the way they have come.

My *compañero* Paddy Collins the fractious painter and man-about-town and his late companionable octogenarian friend Arthur Power, assuredly no sailors, had once for a dare sailed over the Irish Sea to Wales from Dun Laoghaire harbour in Arthur's twenty-two-foot yacht that had previously sailed no further than the Kish or Howth Head. With slop pail on masthead as primitive radar equipment they had sailed for Holyhead, a problematical landfall. Coxman Collins was alarmed by what they encountered.

Vast ocean-going liners honking mournfully proceeded through the Channel on set radar courses, sending out wakes strong as tidal waves. The small yacht grew smaller and bobbed about like a cork on the swell, Arthur green to the gills retiring below for forty winks. Every conceivable shape of vessel moved through the Channel day and night.

They could have been sunk at any moment; they were nothing on the radar screens. Arthur slept on and did not appear on deck until Wales was sighted, a headland and Welsh cattle in a morning mist: Holy Island. Collins moored the yacht, threw himself down on the beach and was out like a light. Then they had to face the tricky return voyage.

They made it somehow and sailed into Dun Laoghaire harbour with dewy shrouds in the early hours with all the spires rising up into a pearly Irish sky and the dogs barking a welcome home. A solitary Chevrolet was parked by the pier and binoculars were trained on the intrepid mariners. 'One man at least didn't want to see us back.' Who was it but the cuckolded husband smoking his way through packets of cigarettes, running the window up and down. The buggers were back. As they glided in and made fast to the moorings the big car glided away.

St Columba docked in darkness. A taxi took me to Breffni Mansions through a light fall of snow. I had not phoned and did not know what welcome to expect, or whether the Master was at home. I rang the bell. After some delay (for Paddy now was old as Arthur then) he came downstairs and opened the door, invited me in. I toted two heavy bags.

'I'm staying a month.'

'You are?'

In the event I only stayed the night; we were to fall out before the eventful evening was over. I found two Marquis de Riscal in the Off Licence.

'Shoot the corks off,' Collins said.

In his irascible old age much annoyed him; I had forgotten just how much he needed to be the centre of attention. Patricia came into the house, returning from a bar where she said she had been insulted. I spent an uncomfortable night in a spare bed in the room where he worked amid the smell of turps and oil paint, listening to the lamentations of the gulls. He had been insulting in Normandy and now worse nearer home, the home I was looking for, wherever that might be.

Patricia was up early brewing coffee.

'You shouldn't have to take this from him, Rory, you his oldest friend.'

'I won't any more.'

I took a taxi to Merrion Square to lay claim to my new inheritance, the first *Cnuas,* Charlie Haughey's government grant for needy artists. I found the Arts Council people in carpet slippers with their feet up on radiators. The paymaster was in his office upstairs; the first cheque could be issued immediately.

From there in the ice and slush I took another taxi to the Trustee Savings Bank in Grafton Street opposite the flower-sellers and the *sempervivens* and opened an account; then a third short taxi ride took me a place I knew in Harcourt Street, a small hotel run by country people, with old wooden floors squeaky as the Musée Rodin. I booked myself in and was assigned the same top room I had been in before, No. 23 under the roof. Margaret from Offaly, the maid of all work whose chores never ended, showed me to my room. My posh accent baffled her; she probably took me for a Frog.

'What nationality are ye?' she asked, turning the key.

'Irish, the same as yourself. I've been out of the country for years.

'And now you're back?'

'I am.'

'It must be grand to be back.'

'Certainly.'

Bad weather followed me about like a faithful hound. In my long absence the plain Dublin girls had become plainer but to compensate for that the pretty ones had become even prettier. They moved delicate and cautious as cats on the icy pavements with scarves about their mouths like yashmaks, joky Boy George headgear and stripy leg warmers.

Bay Leaf French-style restaurant had become an Irish-style antique shop. There was a proposal for all-female graveyards. Shelagh Richards had died in her sleep, aged eighty-one. O'Casey had fancied her as a young girl. At the Arts Club W. B. Yeats asked: 'Who's that girl with the head like a lion?'

'The buses still running?' says I to the taximan.

'Just about,' says he to me.

'Still snowing?' says I to him.

'Annywan with half a fukken brain wouldn't drive today. Fukken ice
– *hard*!' says he.

'Are we in for it?' says I.

'I'd say we were,' says he.

A couple of years later my irascible old friend took his leave of the waters
and the wild when widow Patricia and daughter Penelope scattered his ashes
from the banks of the Garavogue. A young piper played a lament, Anthony
Cronin read some of his verse, a swan took off, the risen breeze blew ashes
back and I may have swallowed some grey particles of thighbone or cranium,
taken like communion wafers, as nourishment on the way.

Prior to that the widow twice over had looked into the coffin of her first
ex-husband and been taken aback by his tiny size; neat in a bow-tie he had
strangely shrunk. John Ryan had shrunk in his casket, became an effigy, a
totem. Is that the fate of all dead husbands, in the widow's mind – to be perceived as effigy?

Country people creep about this hotel where the floorboards creak and the
children of the owners run free and shy as foxes, freezing when you encounter them. In the dark airless bar the serious imbibers thoughtfully swallow
dark pints of stout pulled by sullen barmen. No television (a mercy) but piped
Muzak all day until the bar closes and then some more until the last toper
collapses. The dulling pressure of circumstances presses down.

The pay phone, full of coins, was torn from the wall by vandals, Tom
the barman tells me. The other phone is in the office. This is the Hotel of
Creaking Floors, what can I do for you? A female guest complains of no hot
water in the bath, no curtains in the bathroom, no bumf for the loo. I am
reading, appropriately enough, Werner Herzog's diary of a walk he took
from Munich to Paris in the depths of winter to save the life of Lotte Eisner.
'Sorrow was gnawing in my chest.'*

My room overlooks the rear of old disused premises once the home of
Edwards and MacLiammóir, both now dead, whom I remember well. The
house too looks dead, its windows rotting away. The snow has gone; now it
rains, a purposeful drizzle. All is dripping and falling away. I have phoned my
brother, will look around Wicklow town for winter quarters; having decided
against Wexford.

---

* *Of Walking on Ice (Vom Gehen im Eis)*.

'Don't hit that man!' cried one of the lads armed with snowballs as I came a cropper outside Blazes, the two feet suddenly gone from under me on the icy pavement.

EEC Eurobarometer reveals that the Irish are a little less gloomy about the future than a year ago, while the majority remain pessimistic all the same. Forty-five percent believe the world situation will disimprove this year. They are not as downhearted as the Belgians, of whom only 12 percent believe that matters will improve, while 51 percent believe the contrary.

Given optimum choice, purely hypothetical of course, optimists outnumbered pessimists in West Germany, Italy, Denmark and Greece; whereas the spiritual suffering of the Swedes knows no bounds and must be unmatched in any other north European country: their social services the best and their suicide rate the worst (the Russians beyond the Urals are beyond the bounds, the Finns remain enigmas). By the first third of the coming century all Sweden will be controlled by a few companies and life become a sort of Swedish Ford plant, which may account for the present high suicide rate.

Women are slightly more constipated than men and the young in the 15-25 age bracket more so than those older than them. Eighteen percent of the Irish fear world war, as do 25 percent of the Dutch. The former Boomtown Rat Bob Geldof is again fundraising for the starving Ethiopians, he himself made rich through his philanthropic activities (Band-Aid).

Sufficient to say it's time and weather like this that bind us together as a nation, make us what we are, lackadaisical daydreamers hardly able to put on our own socks. They say of days like these, with a sweetly dying inflexion, 'Isn't that a *miserable* day?' almost with affection. As if such days were not a constantly recurring misery here in Ireland, among the time checks, weather forecasts, jingles and advertisements.

A *very* cold north-to-northwest airflow covers all Ireland. Sharp early frost, sunny spells, scattered showers of hail, sleet and snow, some possibly heavy and prolonged but dying out during the evening. Frost becoming widespread, sharp and severe. Moderate to fresh and gusty northwest winds, strong in some exposed areas at first. Maximum temperatures 2 to 5 Celsius. Further outlook: Very cold. Severe frost. Isolated wintry showers dying out. Rain or sleet extending from the southwest.

Sunny spells!

'Fukken ice – *hard*!'

Morning train to Wicklow (it's the train for Wexford). Check out of here. Pack.

– 15 –

The Return

Wearing a dead man's cast-offs and with his Spanish hunting bag slung over my shoulder – gifts from Annmarie Suchman a widow of Santa Cruz – I hauled my baggage down to Reception, checked out of the Hotel of Creaking Floors, phoned up a taxi to take me to Westland Row station, now Pearse Street station, named for the patriot and martyr, to catch the morning train that would deposit me at Wicklow station, if it was still operating, where my brother (not seen in ten years) would surely be there to meet me, if all went well. But you never know.

I was looking out for winter quarters, a quiet place to work in, now that I had a stake; but such was my present dreadful anxiety that I was still considering Wexford. Was there no room for me in the world? It was the year after Richard Brautigan had shot himself in the Montana woods. He and his buddies, a gang of moon-mad Midnight Cowboys high on angel dust, had gotten too darned fond of shooting out the bunkhouse lanterns.

Grove Press my American publisher also published Brautigan and I had taken to his hip fiction in Spain. My old *amigo* Deck had phoned my office in Austin from Santa Cruz in southern California across God knows how many time zones to tell me that he was dead, had blown himself away.

I spent Christmas 1984 with the Decks whom I had last seen twenty-one years before; after I was through the fall semester at the University of Texas at Austin where I had been hired to teach Creative Writing, don't make me laugh, an occupation or pastime recondite as falconry.

After Santa Cruz I spent a week in London with my three sons and one estranged wife, before crossing to Dublin on the *St Columba* in the depths of winter, a bitter winter it was that year, that murky day in mid-January.

Dublin was icy, the whole city frozen up; walking on the hard-edged slush was perilous.

I was the only passenger to get off at Wicklow station. It was not the same station I had passed through thirty-seven years before when on vacation with Conal Cullinane. By a low bridge the train had crossed a shallow weedy river and by rights should have drawn up at a seaside station, but the sea was nowhere in sight; we were in the country. The portly stationmaster in uniform was disappearing into his cubbyhole and the switchman (it was hairy O'Hills) had left his signalbox to light a fag and stare down at me, then a signal dipped and the train already out of sight tooted its horn on the way to Rosslare.

I stood on the edge of the platform with all my worldly goods at my feet, the 'lifer' released for one day from the penitentiary in the grand old Russian movie *The Ghost That Never Returns*.

The signals had changed, the switchman went in and some linesmen in Day-Glo came shambling along the track, smiting the sleepers.

'Is this Wicklow?' I called down.

'You're bang on there, boss.'

'It doesn't *look* like Wicklow.'

'Well it's been here a long time.'

'It must be Wicklow.'

I took my bags in both hands and walked out of the station. There were a few cars parked by the kerbside but I did not see my brother's, nor did I know what make of car he drove, something modest certainly. Then, close to, a car window was rolled down and my brother's face looked up at me, grimacing.

'Hello there. Get in. Shove your bags in the back.'

I got in, stowed my baggage.

'I shouldn't be here,' my brother said, letting in the clutch.

Stay, Time, a while thy flying!

'How's that?'

'I'm late for a meeting already.'

He drove in a jerky fashion down the hill a few hundred yards, turning left into a car park among low-lying offices. He said I could wait there; he would not be long. I said that I preferred to wait in a pub. He said he would drive me to the Grand Hotel but I wouldn't like it.

'Why not?'

'An awful place.'

So he drove me there. There was a long curving bar and a big fireplace with a great log fire burning in it and chatty curates pulling pints for a few late lunchers.

'I'll be grand here,' I said.

'I won't be out much before four.'

'That's all right,' I said.

– 16 –

Santa Cruz

In Santa Cruz (the Holy City of Oz) on Monterey Bay in northern California the acolytes of High Tech speak in intense and compromising vagaries. Terms once used for 'mind-expanding' drugs are now applied to computers: expand your mind through software, get wired to God! Get with it, man!

A haven for hippies for more than a decade, mall rats panhandle in downtown Pacific Garden Mall, while in the surrounding redwood forests dropouts, drifters, renegades and tree-people live in abandoned cabins and almost literally 'hang out' in tree-houses.

Digital data with mind-bending capabilities is yours to play about with, and the information purports to be the key to the whole new world, a mystical universe where magic comes alive.

Dr Timothy Leary begat Geneen Haugen who begat Allan Lundell who begat Howard Pearlmutter who begat Steward Brand who begat John Lilly who begat Robert Dilts, a Santa Cruz software engineer working on a series of seminars on computer engineering.

In the drug era, people realised it was possible to reproduce the brain, but it was too hard to control. With a personal computer you can reprogram your own brain and you can be in control, it was thought. If you want a message from the high-technologists, it's the exact equivalent of what the ecologists are saying. If you look at ecology and you look at computers, the same rules obtain, the same messages emerge. We're in a direct feedback loop here. Right? Neat.

We're in a loop in history, man. The world is being recreated and we're right in the middle of it. People have a lot of power right now. Right? That's why it's important for us to spread the possibilities on the higher side of force. Trippy spiritualism. Right?

Some people are computer freaks from the age of seven. Some are happy to stay that way. When in doubt, man, punt.

All that stupendous coastline aquiver in the luminous air has a very Spanish look to it, first appropriated and stamped there when Father Juniparo the Franciscan monk walked there, saw what he saw and liked it. He was the right-hand man to Caspar de Portola, Governor of Baja, California.

Robert Louis Stevenson lived there for four months in 1879, a century after the Spanish development had started, and found a world of absolutely mannerless Americans, whereas the Spaniards and Mexicans were doing all things with grace and decorum.

In the darkness the wind chimes sound on the balcony and the seals are barking in the bay and around the wharf. Anastasia's voice became plaintive, repeating my name over and over. I cooked you two eggs sunny side up, you drank three cups of coffee and left by taxi in the dark, near to tears again. You were flying back to Austin, Texas; I to Copenhagen via Dublin.

A sound like a car horn stuck or a factory buzzer going is the sound of an early goods-train pulling out of Santa Cruz. It's 7 a.m. I am lost in the land of illusion, formerly Brautigan country.

The airport van which took me from Santa Cruz to San Francisco was driven by an ex-Marine. I was the only passenger and we got into conversation. He told me he had married twice, had two daughters; one studied English, the other, law. The first has no knowledge of the world: 'iniquity is outside her range'.

He served on a heavy cruiser in the Korean war. 'You gotta study your enemy. Unless you know your enemy you're dead.' His recommended reading: Philip Wylie's *Generation of Vipers*.

– 17 –

Dream-Houses

My brother Colum, the Dote of Yore, had worked under the architect Lubetkin in London in the Tecton offices. When I arrived he and his wife had been living fourteen years in Co. Wicklow, renting a place at Three Mile Water and working as site architect for the modern village Cooney was building for his wife. Now he was head of the Planning Department of the Wicklow County Council and was building his own house on some land he had bought in Dunganstown East. Patiently as the laying down of petroleum deposits or the snail that moves about with its house on its back, my brother was building his dream-house on a hill.

He had qualified as an architect, as had Max Frisch, Aldo Buzzi and Saul Sternberg before him. He was a person of great patience who showed a

marked preference for well-made things, a bit of old craftsmanship, nothing
gimcrack for my brother, whose character had been formed early.

Mumu had knitted him a mealy-coloured Jersey in fawns and browns
like the markings on a thrush and this he wore until it fell off. He dressed
himself with the slow solemnity of a priest vesting; it was all ritual, the order
in which he dressed – the knitted socks, the boots, the underpants, and so
on, and last came the Jersey, slipped over his head with a struggle to get the
arms free of stitching that had unravelled; this with the priestly pride of the
kissing of the alb before he slips it about his neck. Daily for years and years I
had watched my brother dressing, standing by the bed opposite mine in the
nursery. He had a special intense look of concentration. He preferred that
mealy Jersey with its yellow specks to all others; it was like the *Mickey Mouse
Annual,* a Christmas book shaped like a squat box that we asked for every
Christmas, having worn out the previous copy by intensive reading.

That early determination of character (sometimes known as 'thickness'
or obstinacy by Mumu) had manifested itself when the Dote took out a subscription for the *Wide World* magazine from money he had saved up, doing
chores about the house, running messages, patiently accumulating enough
pocket money, not spending it on Rolos.

When he began collecting stamps he bought a stamp album and tweezers,
consulted Dublin philatelists, shaking his savings box, a small red pillar box
with a slit for the pennies. He probably preferred saving to spending.

When he had read systematically through a whole shelf of the novels of
Dickens, he turned to the two shelves of Scott's Waverley novels.

My brother was thorough in all he did. Hereabouts none called him by
his Christian name; he was Mr O'Hills to the Beltons and the Cullens and to
Jim Phelan, the father of nine. Dim-witted Hughes had brought him a blinded
jackdaw to look after, intuiting a hidden compassionate nature; the lamed
and broken had an appeal.

On my first day he came three times to the Grand Hotel: once to deposit
me with my bags, then to say the meeting would delay him, until at half-past
five he condescended to take a drink – a half of Guinness. He invited me to
sup with them.

The nameless low-lying abode was on Dunganstown hill just off the
narrow byroad, guarded by earthen embankments, so that you would pass
and not see it from the road, for no chimney stacks were visible, no windows
revealed any interior, no name (Ard na Greine was popular all over Ireland) graced the gatepost. But it was in there all the same, crouched down
and hidden by its earthworks and plantings of saplings – a cross between a

Russian dacha in the woods and Robinson Crusoe's ambuscade built into a hillside, not intended to be seen.

It had the functional look of Crusoe's makeshift compound, thrown together with material that came to hand; part stockade, part granary, a homestead not drawing attention to itself, like its owner.

All this I would discover on subsequent visits; on the first night I saw only the interior, and that was strange enough.

There was a touch of the rough rustic about it. The *russkaya isba* of Russian log house made of great logs of dark wood that could rot in time; one thought of snow falling and serfs crouched over dying fires. Here was a shabby variant of Marxist André Lurçat's *'maison minimum'*, the house-of-few-things, a simplified plebeian dwelling place.

I thought again of the prototype, of the marooned one, Crusoe and how he had put together a dwelling place ramshackle yet strong from the parts of two disintegrating shipwrecks; of the Tule tree-house 2,000 years old in Mexico, a functional abode that could contain whole communities of simple folk who dwelt there like birds and bees in Cowper's 'boundless contiguity of shade'.

This functional austerity, an austerity so much a factor in my brother's character and reasoning (use what you have), brought to mind the house that Wittgenstein, a true lover of the austere and unadorned, had designed for his sister; said to be nothing more than supporting walls and beams. The alcoholic Flann O'Brien, homeless in his own home, dreamed up slaphappy subterranean dwellings. Giacometti had a dusty grey studio filled with narrow forms and piles of old newspapers.

I remembered the great yew tree in Springfield garden, the oldest there, spreading its shade over the tennis court, a feeding place for missel thrushes and blackbirds all summer long.

Up in it my brother and I had constructed a tree-house – a raft (actually a stable door) in the sky, hauled up by ropes and warped about thick branches; on to which we took our provisions, cats, Daisy air-rifles, reading matter (*Hotspur* and *Beano, Dandy*); and if we stayed still nobody need know we were there.

We could have stayed there forever.

Elizabeth Bowen has written: 'I had heard of poverty-rotted houses that might at any moment crumble over one's head; but this one seemed to belong to those edifices more likely to collapse not through decay or inherent faults of construction but because, alas, all building materials are perishable as our own bodies and like them fated to fall to dust. The walls seemed thin as rattan and the roof joints groaned as if they could already foresee their end.'

The purity of their seclusion was unimpaired by either telephone or television and as my brother wrote few letters and his wife I suspect none at all, their seclusion was total, kuskykorked up tight. And since they had no telephone I came unannounced, greatly to the dismay of Stella Veronica, for visitors were few and far between. The Mini was angled in under the lean-to and my brother advanced to break the glad tidings. I brought two bottles of Marquis de Riscal, not having seen them in ten years.

'We have a visitor.'

In the shocked silence that followed there came an appalled whisper:

'Who?'

'Rory.'

She gave herself up for lost, vanishing, vaporised into thin air, pleading a sudden headache; at least she was not in the narrow galley kitchen nor in the living room. Perhaps she had fled upstairs, both hands clutching her temples? My brother found a corkscrew with some considerable trouble and I opened one bottle with practised ease, to let it breathe.

The Russian cats – fabled creatures oft mentioned – were strays found on building sites and befriended by my kind-hearted brother, taken home and permitted every freedom of the house, sleeping on their double bed and walking across their table, 'laws unto themselves' as my brother put it.

My brother and I dined off our laps by a dying fire like characters in a Gogol novel, served silently by the unseen wife who remained invisible throughout the frugal meal but for the white nun's hands that passed condiments through the serving-hatch.

We sat by each other in the ingle of a fireplace cramped enough to be thought Tudor, the low chimney-breast decorated with small tiles painted by the owner, seemingly at a time when chimneys had just been invented.

An arras of careful drape of cotton batting made for a snug retreat close to the fire. The chimney opening was low to the ground and drew badly, sending out puffs of smoke from the flue. A few briquettes smouldered in the grate. It was a constricted hearthside, the easy-chairs were uncomfortably low and we crouched about the fire that was slowly expiring, while the Russian cats flitted about upstairs in the privacy of the gallery and glared down at me through the banisters.

'This is a really nice wine,' a precise white voice enunciated from the galley.

Presently stewed apples and custard would be served out with Swiss roll and tea.

'When will it be finished?' I enquired.

'Not yet, nowhere near,' my brother said. 'It would be wrong to say it's half-finished.'

'Well, dream-houses never get finished. Look at Gaudi's La Sagrada Familia in Barcelona – God's *casa* still roofless in the Ramblas.'

After supper, wedge of Swiss roll in hand, my brother offered to show me over the premises. I was first taken into the kitchen, narrow as a trawler's galley, from which the hostess had fled, perhaps up the uncarpeted wooden stairs, and was even now hiding under the bed, uttering silent screams.

But no. The bedroom was confined as a Union Castle cabin; one could barely stand upright in the centre of the narrow way. The inset dormer windows were just beyond reach, pitched at an awkward angle into the sharply sloped roof.

It became stifling hot in summer, stuffy and impossible to ventilate in winter. The half-tame rats ran races above their heads and pissed on to the bed, my brother told me. He would have to do something about it sooner or later; perhaps knock out an opening to let in some fresh air, but of course that would admit the cold too.

Great feculent piles of old newspapers, magazines, periodicals and folders bulged from a shelf low down, while more of it showed under the bed. The high cabin was partially masked by a hessian runner. We went downstairs again and I was shown the bathroom. An old-style bathtub squatted on stout little legs on a wooden dais, the bath itself piled high with old grey washing that looked as if it had been seeping there for days or maybe weeks.

'The wash,' my brother breathed into my ear, as if admitting to something shameful.

Dostoevsky had defined eternity, Tsarist Russian style, as a bathroom full of spiders. But where was Stell?

I was in for a surprise.

My brother pushed open an unpainted door without lock or bolt to secure it that gave into a carpenter's rough shed open to the elements, with apertures for windows not yet in place, smelling of putty and cement, with a single unshaded 40-watt bulb that lit the grey figure who sat bowed down on a kitchen chair set into the bare earth. She was gazing raptly at the soil at her feet, hands folded in timeless resignation on her lap, as if beholding the very foundations, the roots, the worms, the teeming decay. The pose was pure Whistler's Mother but painted by Sickert.

'Oh hello Rory! Long time no see,' said Stella Veronica, unsmilingly, still staring at the earth.

My brother quietly closed the door on this eerie apparition.

It shook me, taking me back to the time when we were poor in Greystones. My brother had written from London, asking me to call on Shell and 'cheer her up'. She came to the door of the parental home in Greystones harbour, a rubberised 'hotty' clasped to her stomach, invited me into the chilly parlour, the closed-up room where none but guests were taken, and played 78 r.p.m. records. I told her to put on bonnet and shawl and took her to Lewis's Hotel just up the way where I bought her a Gordon's and tonic with my last half-crown, served by Patsy the barman who was reputed to wear a corset.

With a wristy twist betokening long familiarity I now uncorked the second bottle of Rioja while my host attended the dying fire and we sat warming ourselves about it, recalling old times in Celbridge and Greystones. Until gradually, slow as the incoming tide into Greystones harbour, whilst still remaining out of sight but throwing appropriate remarks from various quarters, now from the gallery above (as if dressing herself, preparing to go out), now from the atrium (as if adrmiring her husband's watercolours of Greystones and Bray Head, all framed by himself), now near the front door (as if about to take her leave), now (very muffled) from the bathroom (oh horrors!), now (plucking up courage, getting ready to make an appearance) saying something witty through the serving-hatch with a silvery laugh quickly cut short – until at last Stella Veronica shyly parted the arras and joined us about the fire, accepting a refill.

They showed me their drawings in pencil, each compulsively drawing the other's face, the loved face, or their own, as if drawing distant hills, always the Sugar Loaf big and small, Bray Head and Greystones harbour, generally in winter when the front was deserted. And Stella Veronica's oil paintings and papier mâché busts of heads done twenty years previously; for all these were mementoes. And they repeated the names over and over, familiar as the beloved landscape, Val Hinds and 'Bunch' Moran.

My brother told me that when the cowboys had departed and when their botched work had been corrected, he found himself hammer in hand on the roof at midnight, knocking nails into the slates; until one of the Russian cats that had climbed up the ladder after him put its paw on the nail-head and stared into his face, intimating that it was time to down tools, call it a day.

'It showed more sense than you,' I said.

The closed-in life they led seemed to suit them; they did not need friends any more than they needed telephone or television, giving all their love and affection to the walls and strays that came their way (the cats, the blind jackdaw, the badger that ate its way through a wall), and the pets kept dying off, until the overgrown garden had become a veritable pets' cemetery.

The room I sat in, all the rooms of the house, looked as if they had never been swept or cleaned. They had one of those old-fashioned hand-manipulated carpet-sweepers that housewives used before electricity and Hoovers came; but somehow one could not see Stella Veronica in headband and apron getting into every corner, washing and dusting, setting the place to rights. It was like a child's tree-house, and dusty naturalness a part of its charm. The scale too seemed off kilter, better suited to a couple of dwarfs in a fairy tale. If she was too timid to ride a bike (oh the brakes!) Stella Veronica could hardly be expected to clean a house; and her husband, who didn't notice, really didn't care. In such a peculiar functional dwelling as this one, notions of clean and dirty hardly applied.

Cordially invited to spend the night (but where? between them, pissed on by the rats?), I declined, saying that I would try the Grand Hotel whose off-season rates were reasonable. When we had finished all the wine and the Swiss roll and said all we had to say my brother drove me back at breakneck speed along the narrow twisty roads. The headlights failed twice, but he drove on at unabated speed. He had bought the Mini second hand for £1,000 and she had never given him any trouble, touch wood, yet.

'Why bother about style if reality is already two-thirds illusion?'

Brother Colum had always carried common sense to absurd lengths: that was the way he was made, the way he thought. To the slapdash and the meretricious he opposed an inflexible will.

Together with Stella Veronica he had cycled into Soviet Russia, to Leningrad to see the collection of early Impressionists.

On sagging telegraph wires suspended on crude poles swallows the size of partridges went *weeedy-weedyweed!* just as at Springfield in the 1930s when we were children.

– 18 –

Cycle of the Hours

The lyrical Gallic gloom of Marcel Carné's *Les Enfants du Paradis* and *Hotel du Nord* were very much to brother Colum's taste.

On the grey penitential stones of Greystones harbour my brother and Stella Veronica undressed on either side of a rowing boat winched up above high tide, discreet as the sheet drawn across the room in Capra's movie *It Happened One Night*; the sheet separating Clark Gable from Claudette Colbert.

Stella Veronica ('Shell') was the youngest and prettiest of five pretty daughters, namely: Derithea, Conchessa, Fanchea, Gilliosa and Stella – and brother Gilmar (who rarely ventured out of doors) there to protect their honour. As soon as they arrived in London they married strong bony men with bank balances and jobs in the City and bachelor apartments around Wimpole Street.

The emaciated cyclist and architectural student Colum O'Hills pursued her wordlessly at first, throwing lingering looks before accelerating off as though borne on fragile diaphanous wings to supper in Kinlen Road on the fringes of the Burnaby.

Shell, still single, had the sticky eye of a pollen-glutted bumble bee that can neither sting nor stay nor fly away, fixed with longing for my brother, the ace cyclist.

He, burning midnight oil and applying himself to his studies, travelled to and fro by train, from Greystones to Westland Row and thereafter on foot to Earlsfort Terrace. The evening brought him back again to the bicycle shed and Willie Doyle and Kinlen Road. After supper he brought out his papers and studied by night.

One morning, foodless, he fainted in the urinals of the university. Coming to he found himself alone and on the flat of his back, with seagulls squalling and fleecy clouds passing overhead; he did up his flies, got to his feet, left the urinal.

His hands turned faint blue and then duck-egg green after diving off the harbour wall at low tide, a tortured corkscrew that attempted to copy the famous diver Eddie Heron, followed by long immersion in the cold sea. A knightly display of valour put on for his ladylove who watched breathlessly from behind drawn curtains in the Mulvihill home abutting on the harbour. Then (by this time they were talking) she was handing him his threadbare towel on the harbour wall smelling of fish. She was soon to be seen on his crossbar, my brother inhaling the meadowsweet and columbine of her flaxen hair, in his seventh heaven, flying past the Eden Hotel or parking outside the Ormonde Cinema.

The starved anxious whippet face was that of Pierre Batchef the hero of *Un Chien Andalou*; Stella Veronica was Dita Parlo, the child-bride and waif on the barge in Vigo's *L'Atalante*.

In the days before they were married – when he had qualified and moved to London to work under Lubetkin – the cyclist faithful unto death phoned long-distance and when he was connected burnt her initials (S.V.M.) on his wrist with his lighted cigarette, as he heard her dear distant voice through his exquisite pain, come all the way to London, as knight of yore encountering his beloved swooningly attempting to press past him on narrow turret stairs presses burning lips to her inside arm, that intimate place, causing her almost to faint, her eyes closed; he begging a boon, to know what trial or tribulation he should undergo to earn her love.

The terms of the marriage contract were not binding enough for Stella

Veronica: *till death do us part* did not go far enough; she wanted them to include eternity too, which she hoped to spend with her grey-faced young husband. My brother stubs out his lighted cigarette on his wrist as the dear voice whispers sweet nothings for his ear alone, all the way from Lewis's Hotel (S.V.O'H), my brother sobs.

His attic in Buckland Crescent, Swiss Cottage, had a stink hard to describe – coal-slack and perdition, rank as a dog kennel. In those Dostoevskian living quarters under the rafters my brother worked as one condemned to it. And there began his conquest of the great grimy city immense in extent with its millions of inhabitants, that spread itself about him in all directions.

Head clearance was adequate if you happened to be no taller than five feet eight inches. Certainly it had a strange odour all its own, a stink of poor man's clothes mixed with stale cooking smells, a dire musty pong that belongs to unremitting poverty – at one time it had probably been the maid's room.

Smells were long trapped there. He lived on oatmeal porridge, Heinz beans, cheese, rhubarb and Bird's custard, bread and milk, the beginning of his vegetarian regime. Which was more or less my own diet in far-off Ealing Common, in a room rented from a French couple who feared that the end of the world was nigh.

I sometimes called to borrow small sums of money, and pound notes were produced from the battered cardboard suitcase he kept under his camp-bed. He cooked his morning porridge on a single gas jet; heating was supplied from a single-bar electric fire.

To ventilate the attic and liberate some of the more offensive stinks long trapped in it he raised the skylight a few notches to admit the muggy heat of August or the freezing foggy air of December that penetrated into the lungs like poison gas in No Man's Land.

In a London heat wave he lifted his work-chair on to the zinc table and stuck his head out the skylight and worked there undisturbed even by the constant drill of traffic. He was his own overseer, with his pencils and reference books and T-square, his own cook, banker, manservant, tutor, librarian and supervisor, his own man. And he loved Stella Veronica Mulvihill most dearly and intended to make her his wife.

And so he did.

'Why is my blood turning blue, Colum?'

Stella Veronica's finger joints are wrapped in dirty rags like little mummies and secured with cellophane which binds these rags too tightly.

'Shell doesn't believe in breathing.'

– 19 –

In the Hall of the Mountain King

S tella Veronica's moody brother Gilmar was an indoors man. He said that everybody spent their life indoors, except perhaps the tourists who walked about the streets. I never spoke directly to Gilmar, for his distant manner did not invite such approaches. I heard him in another room playing 'In the Hall of the Mountain King' on the hand-cranked gramophone.

When it stopped Stella Veronica asked 'Are you listening, Gilmar?' speaking in the same low conversational tone she was using with me, to find out whether he was listening at the door.

Do the habitually silent ones endure a constant tumult and commotion, a disturbance of the suppressed emotions akin to the disturbance of tinnitus, a Bay of Biscay nausea? Sarah O'Donnell, toothless as an old woman, who had lived all her life on Inishere, used to complain of constant noises in her head. Day and night she had the din of tinnitus in her inner ear.

The mother crept about the house, quiet as a mouse, venturing out for provisions. She rolled an orange under her bed before she got into it, to find out whether a burglar was hiding there; she would surely know if the orange didn't come out the other side. All the mad Mulvihills were like that, creeping about, a bit cracked.

Gilmar seemed to be fascinated by the O'Hills, the four brothers living on the edge of the Burnaby in a cottage only intended for summer use.

'They never go out. They spend their time looking at themselves in mirrors,' he told Stella.

When the Mulvihill daughters refused to feed him any more he took to dossing down in the deserted rugby club (now Hickey Field) where my brother fed him scraps from the O'Hills' meagre larder.

We, the grand O'Hills of the swanky Burnaby, were no better off than they, the poor Mulvihills of the harbour. We all moved about on bikes, summer and winter. Stella Veronica herself spent much time indoors.

Sometimes Gilmar, sick and tired of the house and gazing at himself in the mirror and playing 'In the Hall of the Mountain King', would primp himself up and lacquer his tennis shoes for a rare public appearance, posing on the steps as if anticipating applause.

When Gilmar broke out into the open after years indoors in the damp harbour house or living like a dog on scraps in the deserted rugby club it was to take up a very precarious peripatetic life awheel as unlike the sedentary life which he had led before as you could imagine.

He took up with his friend Alan Foster who had walked out of the office of his father's shipping firm in Dublin after one day's work there and had decided there and then never to return.

They went cycling around England together, knife and fork tied with coarse twine to the crossbar, the togs and towel clipped on to the back carrier.

Until Foster met a rich Australian who was looking for a gardener to look after his many lawns. So Foster took the job and went to Perth to mow a rich man's lawns. He wrote back that he was made for life, and asked Gilmar to join him. But Gilmar wouldn't go.

He continued his own cycling about the roads of England, with his bare necessities on the carrier, and many out-of-the-way places from Minehead to Exeter and from Perranporth to Portland Bill saw him, not hairy because he could not grow hair on his face, but wiry and tough like an itinerant, and they heard his songs, a sort of mockery of Irish ballads, the diddley-diddley shit become solemn as he sang 'Come Back Paddy Reilly' or 'Phil the Fluter's Ball'. Until he went too far, or the itinerant life became too much for him, and he was sent into an institution for his own good, to get a change of clothes; a place where he could be fed properly.

His friend Noel Ferns from the haberdashery near the bridge visited him there.

Gilmar asked him, 'What do you think of snow?'

'I hear it falls from the sky in winter, Gilly.'

'No, no, you got it wrong, Fernsy. It comes up out of the ground.'

– 20 –

Some Suggestions for Brightening Up the Home

I sat in the back seat of the Mini and smoked roll-ups and Colum sat sideways on in the driver's seat, chomping methodically on soggy cheese sandwiches prepared by Stella Veronica, staring into the damp car park, a tarred area near the sea.

'Why not move into one of the many B&Bs dotted about the town?' my brother suggested, pulling an extraordinary face.

We had considered a mobile home propped up on bricks, in the lee of a dripping pinewood near Three Mile Water, looking over the valley. It was actually a Dublin tram cut in half, hauled there by tractor. We had looked at it; it was a good deal less grand than the railway carriage at Rethondes on the edge of the forest of Compiègne.

We stared out at the deserted car park and the grey sea over which grey wintry clouds moved.

'I knew a man once who lived on a canal barge moored in the Surrey docks. As the Thames rises and sinks twenty feet twice a day on the tide, it was like living in a lift,' I said.

Colum took up his bottle of milk and swallowed some of it, rolling back his eyes the way hens do.

The canal barge *Humbaja* was long and narrow and constructed of unusual material (aluminium) by two Italian brothers who had previously concentrated on manufacturing ice cream. In summer the condensation produced an inch or two of water in the galley; it was an object of terror in the Camden dock when it came off its moorings. In it my former free-living friend traversed the weedy waterways of England, passing through hundreds of locks *en route* to Humberside.

In his cups and strapped for money he bartered *Humbaja* for a smaller vessel; and that for a smaller one again, until he sold out for a push-bike and then it was shanks's mare and the towpath.

'Chekhov once slept in a second-class railway carriage abandoned on a disused track,' I said.

My brother still chomped on his sandwiches and looked out on the unappealing view, the low sea, the empty car park, a tar barrel that served as a skip, wheeling gulls.

'The view from the Infirmary,' he said.

On the stroke of 6.30 a.m. in came Mick the yardman smelling powerfully of anthracite and abattoir in boiler suit and hobnail boots to give the fire a poke and refill the coal scuttle, and another Infirmary day began in bed at CWC with gossip and regular meals and dozing with glamour puss 'Dog's Hole' Maguire, 'Titch' Fennelly and Donal Crosbie in adjoining beds.

Outside the rain fell in sheets. We had beaten Blackrock in the semi-final of the Senior Rugby Cup at Donnybrook and the sadistic Prefect of Studies 'Boozy' Barrett fell dead of a heart attack.

– 21 –

My First Arrival

My first arrival into Ireland was my entry into life proper, head-first between my mother's chubby legs in a Dublin nursing home. My first view of nature was at Springfield in the big front bedroom with a view of distant hills, the cows in Mangan's field and Killadoon Wood.

A day or so later, 4 or 5 March, I was bundled into swaddling clothes and woollen cap and bootees, clasped in my mother's loving arms in the leathery-smelling back seat of the Overland proceeding at a stately pace out of the city, through Lucan and left before the Spa Hotel on a narrow byroad to Naas.

At Springfield my two elder brothers impatiently awaited the late arriver, five years after brother B, seven after brother D. Another two years elapsed before the squalling of brother C would complete the quartet.

Soon the four of us were living in uneasy proximity, until brothers B and D were packed off to boarding school, first Killashee Prep School with a French order of nuns, and then Clongowes Wood College with the Jesuit fathers.

Brothers A, B, C and D were conceived and born in the order: D (the silent, the fingernail trimmer), B second (the bucktoothed), myself third, giddy me; then sound C bringing up the rear.

The four of us were to convene at Springfield; old Mrs Henry from the back road was taught to cook some rudimentary dishes by my mother; there was Lizzy Bolger as maid of all work and Gina Green was called in from the village for emergencies (unexpected guests from down the country). Nurse O'Reilly was there to look after my mother 'when her nerves went against her'.

We lived in a Georgian mansion in increasing rural dilapidation as the years rolled by and with them my father's fortunes, as property and real estate in Los Angeles were sold off and no more fat cheques came rolling in.

Between us and the brown River Liffey reared up the high boundary walls topped with bottle glass that marked off Killadoon estate owned by descendants of the infamous Lord Leitrim; a grand Protestant estate into which Catholics were unwelcome except as day labourers on push-bikes or moving manure by wheelbarrow.

– 22 –

Wicklow Town

Wicklow town is situated at the mouth of the River Leitrim at the foot of Ballyguile Hill some twenty-two miles south of Dublin. Vessels can enter the harbour at any state of wind or tide. Ships of 2,500 tons can discharge cargo. In 1641 General Sir Charles Coote had his soldiers set fire to the church where the townspeople had taken sanctuary on what is now Melancholy Lane. On Gallow's Lane public hangings took place of the 1798 rebels, including Billy Byrne.

The great cable-layer Halpin was born there. He retired there, having laid some 25,000 miles of cable, and died in his home at Rathnew. The little town was granted a Royal Charter by James I in 1613.

On the second Sunday after I took up residence I walked out on the back road past the Columban Missionary Convent and the new golf course and the bungalows my brother built for Cooney, his boss, a three-mile walk to Wicklow town. Robins were singing in the low hedges and a little girl was feeding hot gruel to a pup at a gateway.

'Am I going right for Wicklow?'

'Straight down. You'll see a big town in front of you. That's it.'

I went down. And there it was.

Cords of wood on the quayside were waiting to be shipped off. The Leitrim Bar was by the river.

Penetrating into Cooney's wood, a young fir wood very piny underfoot, I couldn't find the path leading up to the knoll and came out again, causing a lemony guard dog to bark and keep on barking as I passed by.

Distant figures, larger than life, were walking about in a purposeful way on the new golf 'track', toting buggies behind them, past bunkers, far away. The winter greens were spiked and sanded, the air blew cold from off the sea.

I had my photocopying done at Flitterman's drapery and shoe shop. They were closing, unable to get insurance against burglary, after five break-ins in the past year. The criminal fraternity was prospering.

Meanwhile up in Dublin, in the Horseshoe Bar of the Shelbourne Hotel on Stephen's Green, in amiable juxtaposition sat Randal, Count MacDonald of the Glens, the Honourable Garech de Brun, heir to Guinness millions, and Lord Henry Mountcharles whose forebears had stood shoulder to shoulder with or near enough to William of Orange, King Billy at the Battle of the Boyne, the upshot of which upsets and disturbs the body politic to this very day. The young Lord Mountcharles lives in some considerable splendour at his ancestral seat at Slane Castle, the grounds of which are let out for rock concerts.

In Wicklow I stayed three days and nights in the Grand Hotel and then signed an agreement to share a modern bungalow with a single lady, one Dervorgilla Doran of a ripe 44 years, who had converted a run-down County Council cottage with outdoor toilet into a comfortable home in the Japanese style, Ballymona Lodge. I rented it for a year. I was assured that the owner would be away most of the time. There I would find the quietness that Julien Sorel knew in prison. There I would become quieter than humus.

I would also be required to feed and exercise a large black Labrador of two years, the guard dog Blackie. Solved, for the time being, 'the torment of no abode'.

Tommy Cullen has suggested that I buy the cottage abutting on the cemetery near Three Mile Water.

'It's owned – oddly enough – by a Protestant lady, a Mrs Hall. She is being driven mad by her relatives and would let it go for £2,000.'

'I'd have the Hughes family as next-door neighbours,' I said. 'They're mad already.'

'You could sell it in two years and make a profit £2,000. That's not bad.'

'Homeless' must be one of the saddest words in the language: the condition of houselessness. Pity the homeless. Some bright suggestions from well-wishers for my new abode:

(a)   a B&B in Wicklow town;
(b)   a Dublin tram cut in half;
(c)   a run-down cottage by a cemetery.

Bizarre.

Melancholy Lane is named for the massacre of Wicklow townspeople, men, women, children, grannies and dogs burned alive in the church by order of Sir Charles Coote. The 'mere Irifh' need expect no quarter; no sanctuary for them in their own church; a wailing throng were driven in like sheep to the slaughter, the door barricaded up and the place ignited.

Coote had no more compunction about getting rid of them than if they had been a nest of rats to be pitchforked. The screaming congregation in that fire are very remote from us and refuse to be focused in the mind's eye; themselves as carbonised by Time as the fifty-four luckless French prisoners asphyxiated in Kinsale in January 1757.

I could no more imagine them in their last agony or as blackened heaps in a gutted church now being rained upon, open to the elements, than I could imagine Davies the tramp in his heyday driving the first Baby Ford ever seen in Wicklow down the main street to the consternation of dogs and townsfolk. It must have caused as much rumpus as did Faulkner's dashing Major de Spain in his new red EFM with cut-out blaring, passing and re-passing the Mallisons' house in Jefferson, Mississippi.

St Patrick himself thought twice about landing on Irish soil after his coxswain or steersman or whatever he was, one Manntain, had all his front teeth knocked out by stone-throwing and catcalling natives who ran along the shore, wild as troglodytes waving sticks and defying them to land. Now he has a church named after him there. The mate, was he?

The Murrough or 'plain by the sea', where I set off one day walking the fifteen miles to Greystones; the Black Castle, Paidin's Rock, the three lighthouses, one functioning, are all sweet landfalls in the Land of Nod.

− 23 −

Interrogatory

Here's the author and co-tenant and the bane of his life, Dervorgilla Doran, at parley. 'I always thought it would be right for a writer,' she said.

'You've got one now but is it the right writer?' I said.

'I might even begin to write here myself,' she said.

'Oh I shouldn't do that, Dervorgilla.'

'Why not?' said she.

'It's not you,' said I.

'No?'

'No.'

'You'll look after the house for me?' said she.

'As though it were my own.'
'Don't get too fond of that idea.'

Her three sisters, all raging beauties, were, in order of appearance

Parma Pipina Assumpta,
Caterina Perpetua Emeraldina,
Dolota Bobolina Ubeda

(for mother Doran pregnant with her third daughter had been reading the great Russian masters). Dervorgilla was the fourth and last-born daughter.

Mrs Agatha Doran was a stern matriarch.

Thirty thousand condoms have been imported into the country since 1980. The anti-condom lobby fears that 'soon the floodgates will open'. Fourteen thousand Irish emigrated to Britain during the 1940s and 1950s. The official figure in 1985 was down to 6,000; today it would be more like 30,000.

A weak winter sun all day with smoke drifting over Clinton Binnions's field. The school bus passes the gate at four, a package of toys arrives for Dervorgilla from Japan, addressed to 'Ballymona Edge'.

Dervorgilla and Rory co-habiting were as separate and apart as it was possible to be within a small area, the feminist lady being very insistent upon 'one's own space' *pneus* flew back and forth, as with Frederick the Great and Voltaire in Sans Souci. 'Shall we go over the books tomorrow?' began and ended with Rory writing out a large cheque, always double what was anticipated, rent being frequently asked for and paid in advance, for Dervorgilla protested she was 'strapped for money'; meek Rory never questioned her strict accountancy. The bungalow was shipshape as a yacht, pristine from stem to stern. Dervorgilla left me a note:

'Air-locked taps in a disconnected water-supply can do damage. Advisable to keep a small supply of fresh water as reserve.

When the water is cut off, be careful not to draw too much in bathroom as pipes may air-lock (or burst?).

Should this occur, the air-lock is easily removed. Use hose (from patio), connect other end to air-locked tap. Switch on both taps when water supply is renewed, to force water up into air-locked pipe.'

Dervorgilla with her flaxen hair cut short and her quietly assertive manner, leans on her friends as on a ferminist sorority, and puts me in mind of those formidable early feminists who would brook no obstacle. Women of the stamp of Lady Hester Stanhope, the young Baroness Blixen (wasted by venereal disease but still managing a coffee plantation in the Kenya highlands, shooting lions), Freya Stark the octogenarian traveller and linguist learning Persian in her extreme old age, Mary Kingsley travelling alone in West Africa.

'Where is your husband?' they asked Mary Kingsley.

Her clever reply was calculated to disarm.

'I am searching for him.'

Bluestocking and suffragette with something of the later briskness of the kennel-maid slopping out at 6 a.m. are mixed with positively militant qualities, or better still, the sterner piratical backbone of the pirate queen Granauile who sailed to London and spoke with the Virgin Queen as an equal, in Latin; these her innate qualities.

'My Lord, you know what you were before I made you what you are now. Do my bidding or by God I will unfrock you,' Elizabeth had addressed one of her froward archbishops; that was pure Dervorgilla. If she was determined to have her way, she got it. But in my brother she had met her match. He was beholden to nobody, was immune to coercion and threats, refused to take bribes, was endowed with the patience of a galley slave.

Planning permission was required for the mobile home brazenly parked in the paddock, and planning permission Dervorgilla would not get. They both dug their heels in. The mobile home was a fixture in the paddock with Dervorgilla's friends coming in and out. Every time he saw it my brother ground his teeth.

'Would you mind telling her that that thing is illegally parked there and will have to be moved?'

'And who will move it? The County Council won't annoy her even if it's contributing illegal rents and contravening God knows how many laws.'

Dervorgilla began a vendetta against my brother. She conducted it rather as the Boer farmers waged guerrilla warfare against the British Army by stealth, knowledge of the terrain and superior cunning.

'Your brother's an impossible person to deal with. Did you know he is greatly disliked around here? Why is he doing this to me?'

It was a striking feminine ploy. Dervorgilla wanted my brother's guts for garters. She had met her match: a will obstinate as her own. My brother must have been the confirmation of her worst fears, being even cagier than herself.

– 24 –

The Bum Bailiff

Polyphiloprogenitive Joe Fallon the needy, breedy father of seventeen, or was it nineteen? I was never sure, any more than Joe himself, prematurely aged by breeding, honorary bum bailiff and permanently disgruntled odd-job man about the place, has been summoned by phone from Bavaria to give a final trim to the lawn. He performs this service with the utmost ill grace; I see the set face under the battered hat going to and fro behind the spluttering mower chewing up stones.

The dispossessed one never meets your eye, nor does Matty Doran: Biddy's quiet man cannot rid himself of the stink of pig slurry, of servitude, working a fifteen-hour day at harvesting. He works for Herbst the German.

Mylie works for the German too and is another one who will not meet your eye. Perhaps direct eye contact implies social equality, might even constitute a challenge, a threat. 'Take that bold look off your face,' my father used to say, giving me a poke in the back; 'get back into the house, you little brat.'

With those three it's not so much subservience or shyness or cringing before social superiors, but more a matter of reserve, of manners, slyness, country cuteness. Joe Fallon can never set foot in the old homestead again, unless invited in; the Council cottage has been transformed beyond recognition into a modern bungalow, no more the old shabby place with outside toilet constantly occupied. There he had brought up almost two score children, fed them, set them up in life.

The nearest he gets to it is the kitchen porch, Blackie's quarters; he must never presume to pat the Labrador on the head any more than he would presume to shake Dervorgilla by the hand. Blackie would have gone for him, as the loyal animal goes for the unhappy postman darting from his van; as he would go for all such intruders.

Jim Phelan, father of nine, salutes me from the mobile home roof and addresses me as 'Sir', which makes me feel uncomfortable. 'The Finisher' is Dervorgilla's nickname for Phelan. It was Phelan she called in to finish the job when she had exhausted herself working on the drains and walls, injuring her back again with the jack-hammer; until she had worn out all her helpers and the boyfriend had fled back to Australia.

Joe Fallon the erstwhile owner and she the grand single lady, a speaker of foreign languages, secure and sedate in herself and her possessions, her cushions, are poles apart socially and could belong to different races. The man who once owned the cottage and the acre-and-a-half of land, now works there part time as her handyman. The man who once owned the property outright now trims her hedges, cuts her lawn and scythes her paddock, rakes the gravel and humbly accepts mugs of tea and biscuits from her hand, and acts as a sort of unpaid overseer or bum bailiff when she is off in foreign parts.

Many an acrimonious aside did he make to me, addressing my ear, to the effect that he had been badly diddled in the transaction and made a fool of; the day after he sold for £6,000 he could have £17,000 in the open market, as was known to the party that purchased, her smart Dublin lawyer and the tricky estate agent. They all knew that and laughed behind his back. He had been badly taken in.

It could of course be said that he himself had never recognised what he had or the possibilities of the place; the grand view over Binnions's long field and the rolling hills beyond. For Joe the run-down cottage and the bit of land that went with it was all that he might reasonably expect in the way of worldly bounty, his due here on this earth. And all it represented was so many chores, his wife endlessly big with another child, the endless feeding, the endless upkeep of property already falling to bits.

A field was a field for all time and nothing more than that and he need not expect anything grander. Whereas Dervorgilla had to travel to Japan to see what could be done at Ballymona and at no great outlay (£2,000 down payment secured the property). She, so often strapped for money, saw what could be done and she did it; transforming the place by stripping the walls back to the brick, digging drains, installing a bathroom and modern kitchen, knocking out windows to get a better view.

What would the likes of Joe do with a view? Views were beyond anyone with so many children to rear.

When Dervorgilla had let out Ballymona Lodge to other sub-tenants, Ned Ward had acted as her bum bailiff, arranged the letting and collected the rent. When Dervorgilla returned he handed over £1,000 in cash. A commission had been mentioned and a few hints had been dropped, bum bailiff now feeling very foolish; but nothing came of this and Ned did not care to press the point. He received not a penny for his trouble. He swore that he would never do it for her again. 'Dervorgilla watches the pennies.'

Biddy Doran (no relation) the cleaning-woman comes twice a week with her two brats. She tells me that the Wicklow people are an unfriendly lot, unlike the Wexford people; wasn't she herself born and reared there and intended to return? She ran a stationery shop in Gorey, 'before Lara came along', as she coyly put it. Then along came Laurence with the snotty nose, the image of his da and 'stands just like his granda'. Biddy had big ambitions for him and probably saw him as a doctor or lawyer. She wanted to get him out of the fields.

Matty's existence is all drudgery or near enough to it, labouring from six in the morning until nine at night for the German, overtime paying his taxes. While the well-off Herbsts are off skiing in Switzerland with governess and the two kids, Matty is bringing in the Herbst harvest and Biddy feeding their cats and dogs.

— 25 —

Fumes

Apall of rank Virginia tobacco smoke hangs in the Periwinkle Bar, enfolding all in its mysterious embrace, dense as a gas attack by the Boche on the Western Front. The Periwinkle is a bar of some decrepitude patronised by the disorderly youth of Wicklow town. On the morning I slunk in it was deserted but for an English visitor downing an imperial pint of lager and his small daughter hanging on to the pinball machine that was firing off coloured lights. Some friends arrived and began to talk in their strange fractured English.

'Yew git outah bed inna mawnen an luke aught d'windah an ooow d'yasee?' (Pregnant pause, rolls eye, gulps lager.) 'Nuffen. Nabaddy!' No work, see. He's got into the routine now and stays in bed until 11 a.m. Early rising is not on (Hockney would not have approved of this slackness). 'It ain't flash, see. Wot's the point?' The will to work has gone.

There's a power of grim dark pubs in Wicklow town. But grim and dark as they are they are not as grim and dark as those of Carraroe in remotest Connemara beyond Gorumna or Newbliss on the Monaghan border which was too grim even for the bold Dermot Healy and thus must be adjudged *the pits*.

I myself go to the Leitrim Bar by the river, a pleasant stroll past the Garda barracks and over the low bridge. Arc of a rainbow above the harbour where a long freighter from Bilbao is offloading a cargo of slag, waiting to take on logs, packed into a great pyramid on the quayside.

The Leitrim Bar is usually deserted when I arrive in the morning or around midday with my provisions in plastic bags, for a few drinks before I phone Sadie for the taxi back.

See here.

A pool table, vapid radio music to make you dizzy, a TV screen in the public bar for the horses, a view of the stormy sea outside the door, with a rostrum for live music in the lounge to be avoided at all costs. Dowling himself serves me a half-Guinness and Jameson chaser, way-out 'ham' sandwiches smothered in mustard, here's health.

Da Dowling is the father of eight in this breedy corner of our fair land: four redheaded sons will carry on his name and no doubt the Dowling breeding propensities. He spent the morning rolling empty iron lungs into the yard; he is his own cellarman, after being a butcher for most of his working life in Birmingham. Three years ago he entered the bar business and hasn't he got it made?

Clear sky again after three consecutive overcast days. Walked into Wicklow by the back road, past a yard with two savage Alsatians that attempt to tear down the gate to get at me. Snow on nearer hills. Called on Dervorgilla's cleaning-woman Biddy in Herbst's gatelodge. Toys and tricycle strewn about the entrance. Large TV screen adding its heat to already overheated living room, the young Roddy McDowell in racing silks. Two brats nagging each other and tormenting the cats that glide in and out. The Quiet Man takes his grub in the kitchen. The German Herbsts are about to depart for a skiing holiday in Switzerland. Biddy will feed their cats and dogs.

Am advised by Butler the chemist not to buy expensive eye-drops, Optrex will do the trick. As he is making out the prescription he gives me a penetrating look. 'Don't I know you?'

I retire to Healy's Bar for some peace and quiet. Am I or am I not the same person I have always taken myself to be? And in that case who am I? It is better to be precise than to be imprecise; for you can be imprecise in many ways but only precise in one way, the correct and only way, or so a Chilean nuclear physicist once told me in Texas. Only in such discipline can we hope to find freedom, if it exists. How many facts does a life story require? What is fact and what life story? No, it is not enough to live; you need to know as well.

The butcher with bloodied hand and forearms, as if he had just beheaded Mary Queen of Scots, recognised me stepping fastidiously into the sawdust and called out 'You're the pork-fillet man!'

Woke this morning to hear my name called, and raising the slats of the venetian blind what did I see outside but my brother's greenish visage under the rim of his porkpie hat pressed to the streaming glass. He was *en route* to the office and had stopped by on a business call, and yes thank you he would accept a Nescafé. Why not? He wore a soiled muffler and wool gloves as his only concession to winter and the perishing cold that he as a vegetarian must have felt acutely; as acutely, I thought boiling the water, as he felt everything that might touch his solitary vexatious nature.

My brother was not what you might call a sharp dresser. His new hound's-tooth tweed jacket that had been bought off the peg for £40 in a Dublin haberdashery was identical to the one he had discarded, having worn it daily for fifteen years; Identical even to the pen and pencil protruding from the breast pocket, the tools of his trade.

Would I ask neighbour Ward whether the screeching of the power saw at the farm on the Blainroe crossroads could be heard in his place (Ned's). And if so did it disturb him? Did it constitute a nuisance, in a legal sense? The woman who was objecting lived at the crossroads and claims that she couldn't talk to her friends; she couldn't hear them talk, and was 'almost weeping' – this imparted with a shake of the head and a titter, the stock response which my brother has for all human foibles and the distress that sufferers seem to bring upon themselves.

I said I would ask Ned. I didn't hear it myself, being around the corner and protected by a stand of saplings.

Tuesday, 8 January
Streams of water invade the waterlogged fields. Cycle to Brittas for milk and mulling wine. I see surf breaking on a deserted beach and the tide out as I pedal up the hill under the cawing crows in the tall trees coming into Brittas and passing the dim-wits' summer quarters now closed up. A beardy puck-goat glared at me over the low wall at Three Mile Water where the twisty road ascended towards the little cemetery. The puck-goat is old Hughes himself. My brother's first home was in Cullen Cottage where he had as neighbours the extended Hughes family, some of them with their wits seriously astray; gone crazy as hares from sheer misery, like Faulkner's Bundren family burying the granny.

There were all-year-round dim-wits at Three Mile Water and a summer contingent to be found in the holiday homes outside Brittas, supervised sipping their soft drinks in the dim recesses of McDaniel's in the daytime.

The Hughes family disperse themselves in mobile homes raised up on breeze blocks and are to be seen toting shovels, cutting up wood on the saw-horse, mooching about or gaping over the low wall at passers-by.

In the boggy place a silent mongrel watches me fly by. January proceeding; dark by 4 p.m., bright evening star; lit wood fire at five, night comes down early. At Cullen's shop Una dragged herself out of the *Irish Press* to tell me that yesterday's cortège was for Alec Stone's father who died in his eighties. Tommy attended the funeral; she tended shop.

The storm promised by the weatherman last evening is even now approaching the western coast and will reach the eastern by midnight.

At 1 a.m. it struck with dramatic force and blew all night. Next morning a strange bird with drenched feathers was preening itself on the fence.

My brother says that he doesn't understand Aristotle. Happiness, not goodness, is the end of life. We choose happiness for itself, never with a view to anything further; whereas we choose honour, pleasure, intellect, because we believe that through them we shall be made happy.

Cyril Connolly maintains that this is a restatement of Santayana, who said that happiness is the only sanction in life and where happiness fails 'existence remains a mad and lamentable experiment'.

Connolly added the rider: 'The heart is made to be broken, and after it has been mended, to be broken again.'

– 26 –

'Cash' Murphy Appears

It is virtually impossible to move about unobserved in the country, particularly on foot, where your every move is observed and interpreted. Dervorgilla told me to be sure and lower the venetian blinds in the room of my new home when I venture out, for the poachers who pass unseen through Cooney's wood keep a sharp eye on Ballymona Lodge. So I do all that when I walk out or go by bicycle: lower the blinds, double lock. Keep wits alert.

I cannot say 'Stay!' to Blackie the black Labrador who is young and foolish and follows me everywhere, to the beach, to Brittas, to Wicklow, causing an unprecedented uproar at the butcher's and upsetting the local dogs. If I want to go out unescorted I must do it surreptitiously, on the sly, like a thief, creeping silently about the house, watching until Blackie dozes off in the patio and I can slip out, tiptoeing on the grassy verge, not on the gravel, slipping out on to the road and left by Ned Ward's cottage, closed up, past the baying Alsatians until I come to Blainroe crossroads and sharp right by Kilpoole tree nursery, safe now; and down the hill with the first gladsome sight of the sea risen high above the trees, and a stocky fellow leaning on the gateway with his back to me, apparently watching the farm machinery working on the slopes below.

'Hello there,' said he to me in a familiar way.

He is a high-coloured rough man with wild blue eyes, bursting out of his skin but full of cool cheek. Why did I go on the lower road? wasn't the other shorter? why did I do that now? I said that I preferred this way because it was quieter. He asked me what I did.

I wrote radio scripts for the BBC; I was a radio writer, I said. I felt him watching me as I walked away. He knew who I was, the new tenant of Ballymona Lodge, Dervorgilla's guest; he knew that as well as had the two poachers in the nuns' grounds. They all seemed to know. I felt rather a fool, telling him this.

'Fancy that now,' said he.

'Cash Murphy,' said Ned. 'Have nothing to do with him. Cash is as mad as a brush. Lock up when you go out.'

Mad as the mist and snow was Cash Murphy. Lock up your daughters and your spoons. His redheaded brothers were all villains, Biddy told me. Redheaded villains.

One day he jogged by in a rhubarb-red tracksuit; another day he staggered out of a gripe, carrying a large pane of glass, presumably stolen. This mad red burglar would steal Dervorgilla's cushions from the mobile home the night I had the Laits for dinner; Cash would also remove the sparking plugs from the car parked by the front door. Ann Lait was the auctioneer who told me of Ballymona Lodge.

Walking the back road I felt I was less likely to encounter him. If he saw me setting out for Wicklow he knew he had me, with hours in which to empty the bungalow and mobile home, take what he pleased: stealer of cushions and auto parts.

When Dervorgilla (batting her eyelashes like a coy geisha) had explained what she wanted, Cash nodded, gallantly stripped off his shirt, spat on his hands, blessed himself and knocked the creosoted fencing posts into place with powerful blows of a sledgehammer, displaying a goodly ripple of the manly muscle that had so enchanted Dervorgilla; and the undulating fence rose up like a dream.

Dervorgilla had got the idea from the clever Japanese, designers of miniature rockeries, stroll gardens and the like, who speak of 'borrowing' the garden. You are led by a winding path which, with short side-spurs, carries through the entire garden and back to the starting point. You must take sightlines into consideration, redesign the lie of the land, pulling as it were the valley into the living room, as in a Bonnard canvas the rumpled sheets of a double bed resemble clouds and vice versa, or Turner's interiors resemble tempests.

The fence must be of uniform height but it undulates to match the valley which it confronts and to which it conforms, the slope of the land continuing into the house, seemingly containing not only Binnions's long field and grazing Friesians but Clinton himself, a shadowy figure in the cabin of his careering agricultural machine flinging out feed while manfully struggling with the controls.

Binnions's herd of newly milked and apparently newly washed Friesians stroll majestically on to the sparkling morning field with the aplomb of a cast of stout Restoration ladies powdered and primped in velvet and lace coming fully costumed on to a brightly lit stage, disturbing a flock of feeding crows that scatter above them, announcing more rain on the way.

A 'vigorous depression' is approaching our shores. Hardly a day goes by without another murder being done, and in the most public of places; and vile knee-capping punishments, more often than not the knees of innocents. Polymath Sean V. Golden has left Brixton and is *en route* to China on academic business. He is a friend of Ned Ward's.

'Cash' (so-called because he never has any?) has the gingery colouring of MacMurrough's footsoldiers, gone from the fields into the first line of battle, fearless wild opponents, open-air men who know the traps and indentations of the land as they know their own hovel. He has been barred for life from McDaniel's who rather go in for family parties and discourage drunkenness on the premises.

When his dander was up he had the strength of a hundred men, John Stamp the barman tells me. 'Cash is highly strung.' When in a red fury he reverted to type, became battling Con of the Hundred Battles, became Finn himself. What possible use would a hero like that have for Dervorgilla's precious cushions, the covers 'lovingly sewn'?

– 27 –

My Second Arrival

My second entry into Ireland some half-century later also occurred in the depths of winter and was no less upsetting and nerve-racking, except this time I knew what to expect.

Again the uncomfortable journey over water, the darkening way, apprehension about the welcome awaiting me, palpitations in smoke-filled low-ceilinged lounges, Lansdowne Road bar and Cardiff Arms Park bar, and crowded companionways, the groaning bulkheads, the vomit in the scuppers, the children running wild, the wash of waves without, and always the muggy air of the interior of the ship. The SS *St Columba* wallowing through the murk was due to dock at No. 2 Pier, God willing, more power to Him.

My parents had lived out their last years in a squalid basement flat in Haigh Terrace near the Garda Barracks in Dun Laoghaire and my wife and I were separated when I stepped again on to the gangway and the cold winter air struck me in the face with flecks of snow, for it was snowing again. Freezing air gushed up from the harbour below while a skinning wind blew from the northeast with scuds of icy snow falling out of a freezing sky as I stepped on to terra firma.

– 28 –

The Haughty Horsewoman

Brother Colum has had a run-in with a haughty horsewoman. 'Hi there, you!'

So sang out the haughty horsewoman, rising in her stirrups to get a better view of the miscreant grovelling in his miserable potato patch.

'Barked' might be nearer the mark, from the throat of her so massively astride the big grey gelding, pointing with her whip at my brother who a moment before had been bent over the assiduously manured drills but had obligingly straightened up with a meek smile, and every appearance of craven shiftiness. 'Stop doing that!'

He was a little late in getting down his British Queens but he could swallow his pride and after all what were a few more minutes lost in the vast aeons of Time lost already; and who was this imperious lady ordering him about like a coolie in a paddy-field?

'The weather's been unseasonably warm of late, and to tell the God's truth so am I,' tittered the brother in his lackey's tenor, giving a suggestive hike to his working trousers that adhered to his thin shanks, white skin visible through layers of repair. 'Swimming weather.'

The haughty horsewoman stared down speechlessly at him as if examining a bug or turd. Her wide-flanged nostrils flared and her constricted bosom heaved.

'Don't you dare get bolshy with me, you impertinent upstart! Don't try me too far!'

'Oh no, ma'am, certainly not,' said the brother, reverting to type and cringing.

The proud rider was darkly flushed and it became her. The whispery voice had sounded subversive in some creepy unspecified way that she could not put a finger on; she suspected that he was mocking her.

'Pah!' she spat out. 'Out of my path, peasant!' and spurred her great dappled steed onward.

February snow on nearer hills, ice in Blackie's water bowl. Dublin householder (this from *Irish Times*) shot intruder dead with shotgun kept under bed. In the old days pisspots were kept there but mother Ireland has modernised herself wonderfully, with power showers and *en suite* shower rooms.

Of the annual 10,000 break-ins and burglaries more than half involve violence against the person, but it is not advisable to shoot an intruder, even if he is armed.

Now some sums. It costs the state £22,000 per annum to keep an Irish person in an Irish prison, where they will certainly acquire bad habits. If not already TV addicts, as the heroin habit, they will become addicts in the Joy. Benzedrine to kick-start the Joy day, Seconal to end it.

Of the half-million dogs on the island, how many worry or kill lambs and gravid ewes at lambing time? What does that cost the farmer in dead livestock? What does it cost the dog-owner? (Many won't buy a dog licence.) I can live on less than half what it costs to house a person 'doing time'.

The Irish Sea is half a mile off, hidden behind Cooney's wood. On disturbed nights you can hear it muttering to itself, tossing and turning in its disturbed sleep. It is a most consoling sound and lulls me to sleep.

By the open gates of the Columban Missionary grounds I met a broad-

shouldered bigbeamed water-eyed farsoonerite farmer in shitcaked Wellingtons who was knuckling the ducts of his weeping red-rimmed eyes with a
rawboned hand.

'Hard day!' said he.

I asked how the lambs could survive in the freezing snow. He told me that
they were hardy enough and would survive.

Passing through (trespassing) the Missionary grounds on my way to the
Nuns' Beach a month previously I encountered two rough-looking poachers
who said they knew who I was and where I was staying, and this, mark you,
on only my second day of residence at Ballymona Lodge. The tom-toms had
already announced the arrival of Rory of the Hills.

– 29 –

Lambing Time

From Blainroe crossroads comes the high whine of a power saw
chewing up planks. Beyond it stands the Approved Stud whose
yard, ever awash in pig slurry and liquid cattle manure, would turn
your stomach.

I prefer to walk the back road by the new golf course, arriving in Wicklow
via the Green Hill. Male and female figures attired for golfing march this
way and that, pushing or pulling buggies, replacing divots, recovering from
shallow bunkers, lining up putts on spiked greens, replacing flags and striding towards the next tee. It looks a purposeless sort of open-air activity that
you might not think to associate with pleasure, unless you played the game
yourself. As with other pleasurable activities (chess, copulation, fly fishing),
it looks ludicrous until you give it a try.

At Blainroe crossroads were some cottages crowded together in cosy famil-
ial juxtaposition, two of the cottages accommodating the copious overflow of
old Fallon's ever-active loins, ten stall-fed daughters and seven redheaded sons,
milk-stealers and lurkers in hedges. I called one day with an order from distant
Dervorgilla; she would like the lawn cut and the hedge trimmed. I was directed
to the middle cottage, which throbbed with stereophonic racket. When the
door was eventually opened I saw the huge TV set straddle the floor before
which flushed daughters and bawling babes sprawled, sucking and chewing at
the fast food that never left their hands. Talk about the fury and the mire!

The fields around are in frantic stir at lambing time, placentas blowing
about like refuse and the newborn lambs eager at the teats, two of them lifting

the patient ewe off her feet. The ewes are worried, seemingly confused by the struggling outline in the sac that is feebly trying to break out into the air. If the ewes by accident find themselves on their backs, they cannot get on their feet again, piteously bleating; and are defenceless against the grey crows for twenty minutes after giving birth. The parturating ewes have no inkling of danger as the predators hop close to pick out the eyes of the newborn lambs.

'Don't forget that the grey crows have to feed their young too. It's our fault for domesticating the sheep,' so says Ned Ward, dog-slayer and authority on country matters.

Wild sheep are a hardier breed better able to fend for themselves, more akin to the wildebeest that breed on the run when harassed by lionesses on the teeming Serengeti plains. *Their* young must start running as soon as their hoofs touch the earth, for the lions have their young to feed too. The Great Butcher has generously provided a larder for all; the grand cycle of creation has slaughter at the centre of it.

Strychnine to kill the grey crows is laid in a freshly killed rabbit, and fixed as bait in the fork of a tree. The mongrel 'Rags' finds it, devours the rabbit and with it the poison, races home howling to die in his own backyard. The wife is frantic, but the husband knows the cure; he takes 'Rags' by the hind legs and whirls the little dog around his head, as though he would throw him a mile. 'Rags' howls loud and long, expecting to have his brains dashed out against the wall; his master, the hammer-hurler, has gone stark mad. The dog vomits up the strychnine in sheer fright and recovers. Strychnine has therapeutic effects, being a tonic and stimulant if taken in moderate doses.

The mistress of 'Rags' herds a little flock of those who are 'wanting', i.e., not quite all in it, not right in the head, up the hill from the holiday home and takes them into McDaniel's, where they get very excited ordering up Deasy lemonade.

– 30 –

A Bat at Evening

Nature will return, my brother firmly believes, because we have too much. Too much of what? Why too much of everything, too much surplus, or what we don't need and very likely don't want.
He is joyless, or joyful in a strange way. A bat at evening.

Statistics show that in the west of Ireland one in every four people over the age of sixty is afraid to go to bed, but sits up all night saying the rosary with a loaded shotgun to hand. They are afraid to take sleeping pills lest they be murdered in their sleep. Three or four gangs are operating, robbing farms in remote areas of Roscommon and Mayo; thuggery is rampant in Sligo and Donegal and the young ruffians are slipping over the border. The old people take pep-pills and hardly ever pull off their clothes, afraid to sleep, their nerves shattered.

All who suffer so are neurotics. The importance of politics in one's life can hardly be overrated; but today you cannot buy a loaf of bread without being in some way involved in politics.

American Presidents Truman, Eisenhower, Ford, Kennedy, Nixon, Johnson, Reagan were ever apt to prate of 'our freedom', and the 'free world', meaning capitalist democracies; Reagan visiting his homeland (Ireland) in a bulletproof raincoat like a G-man, Nancy with terrific facelift smiling bravely by his side.

Politicians live in another world. In any case politics concerns itself only with the things that can be talked about; you have to figure the rest out for yourself. The nostrums of X and Y are as incomprehensible to me as Hubble's evidence of an ever-expanding universe, baffling as the quantum theory. *Twice* as baffling.

In *Image* fashion magazine the names of the owners of beautiful homes featured are suppressed for security reasons. Stamp, the young barman at McDaniel's pub in Brittas refused to give me a figure for weekend's takings, saying he would be an eejit to do so. An attempted robbery by the Dunne gang down from Dublin had been frustrated by the Special Branch. But the takings are stolen the following Monday and a week later Stamp's two-stroke motor-bike disappears. He tells me that he and a friend are saving up to open a nightclub.

Laragh Inn near holy St Kevin's Church was sacked by the Provos as punishment (revenge) for the drug-dealing that allegedly went on there – a sort of knee-capping of guilty property by this illegal organisation so keen on retribution, tit for tat. The Provos claimed that it was the headquarters of a cartel of known drug-pushers, one of the ringleaders well known to me personally.

Ned Ward makes miniature hurley sticks for the American market. The cartoonist from Disney Studios draws Irish leprechaun cards of elfin awfulness. On the patio of Ballyhara Lodge the Japanese Zen priest took deep breaths, looked out over Clinton Binnions' field; never before had he known such serenity and peace.

Ten peacocks parade about the renovated grounds at Kilpeddar. The former mucky yard has been transformed into a paved courtyard with swimming pool, the plastic porch of the Queen Anne mansion replaced by a granite Queen Anne porch, the bell tower good as new, in distinctly German taste. Years of Irish neglect and rot, bad management and eventual bankruptcy have given way to Germanic *Ordnung*. Regard the Regency mirrors, the Boissy and Georgian fireplaces, the stucco plaques by Creedons, the Curragh oatmeal carpets with thick pile, the Anatolian rug as table cover on the heavy glass table made by local blacksmith Harry Page, the pale-pink chairs of Italian baroque.

Brother Colum and Gilmar Mulvilhill – once Gilmar overcame his reluctance to venture out – were great ones for taking the air and hiking about and they knew the fields and seasons, the ditches and hedgerows and copses of trees around Greystones and Delgany as well as poachers get to know their particular terrain.

Gilmar had cycled around England and into Devon to sing his maudlin Irish ballads and come-all-ye's in rural pubs until his health broke down and as John Clare before him he found himself in an institution for the insane out of which he was never to emerge. He got to like it in there. His true friend Ferns visited him on Sundays. He knew no other kind of life than the one he knew now and didn't have to worry about himself ever again. Institutional existence with sedation pills and regular meals suited him down to the ground. Nineteenth April, a lovely washed-out blue day as if rinsed; the itinerants' piebald ponies stand out on the headland most surreally. The growth starting despite the chill wintry air and first swallow flies over Magheramore beach. A dead seabird shot on the sand.

On the bridge *en route* to the Leitrim Bar, the tide is coming in and young lads with lines out for crabs are using lumps of pink meat as bait. The crabs pulled from the river crawl about in the grass; the tide continues to come in. A bumble bee with wet wings crawls across the patio, attempting to take off from the lower step; it cannot and crawls in circles as if drunk, stinging the dry clods of earth I had turned the day before.

'Sheshudda knocked it down,' says Joe Fallon, limp father of seventeen, a gloomy bugger if ever there was one. His old Council cottage is now the modern bungalow Ballymona Lodge of unthinkable cleanness and ladylike neatness.

He prods up and a new spud with a brown and broken fingernail. 'Rubbish. The soil's no good.' Unable to bring himself to look me in the eye he shuffles off, halts to say 'Summer end', staring at the overcast sky. What can he mean? Clinton Binnions could have objected to Dervorgilla digging her drains so close to the fence; but he never objected. Fallon objects to everything, a true farmer.

Twentieth April, Hitler's birthday; an Arian fascinated by fire.

Elderly men with polyps in their bowels require careful watching, close observation; and President Reagan is one such. This is the latest prognosis of his physician in the White House. The President's bowel movements will require careful watching and must be closely analysed to determine what course of treatment is best.

In Spandau Prison in Berlin two prisoners remain, one of whom will never be freed. Albert Speer, with none else to talk to, talked to his shadow; for Rudolf Hess, the lifer, is off his rocker. He may not even *be* Rudolf Hess. Who then was it crashed the Messerschmitt in Scotland? Who was the *Über-Hess* making the peace-feelers?

Years later he told Speer that the idea of the flight had come to him in a dream of supernatural forces. A fortnight after he had defected, Speer sent flowers to his dying father without however revealing the sender.

Great flocks of crows pass overhead each evening at nightfall, coming from their feeding grounds along the coast, heading for their nesting places in the wooded valley. Always there is one straggler, an ageing crow last to leave the wheatfield after the main body has departed from the communal scoff-patch. As it flies on into the darkness of late February the safety of the communal buzz must seem to recede and recede as the old crow struggles onwards.

Crows live nine times longer than man, says Hesiod.

Outing to see friends in Thomastown in Kilkenny. Saw a stoat with a young rabbit in its jaw near Baron de Breffni's castle. Spoke to a traveller on the platform of Thomastown station who had seen a white owl near Bagenalstown.

Dublin in April rough as Reykjavik, wintry chill in late April, and sooner or later you meet a madman in the street.

After many years' absence and strange adventures (Cyclops, Scylla and Charybdis, Circe's cave, the singing sirens) Ulysses returns home jaded and saddened. He is not recognised; only the dog remembers him (I have forgotten its name); home seems strange to him.

Ulysses himself did not recognise Athena at first.

Robinson Crusoe marooned on an island defends his home, dug out of a hillside, with a wooden stockade of pointed stakes; primes his muskets, sharpens his cutlasses, affecting to be a fortress fully manned, and prepares to sell his life dearly against the man-eaters who paddle in from another island.

From an armchair in the living room I can see a line of hills maybe twenty miles off across the valley. Hundreds, maybe thousands, of crows pass over at dusk. This will be my home for the predictable future.

– 31 –

Anastasia and the
Seven Dervorgillas

Dervorgilla, two-faced as those stone heads on Boa Island, gave me her sworn promise that she would be out of the house during Anastasia's ten-day visit from Texas; she would do the decent thing and make herself scarce, stay in the mobile home and only avail herself of the kitchen for meals. She would keep out of the way. But did she? She did not.

When Anastasia arrived there seemed to be about seven Dervorgillas in residence, strolling from room to room and immutably present like Lady Brett Ashley in Hemingway's great novel. Ballymona Lodge was contracting; with one of the Dervorgillas seated in the kitchen brewing up Earl Grey while another strolled in the garden with trug and secateurs; soon to be joined by a third in bikini for sunbathing, with Ambre Solaire, sunglasses and paperback, *The Quiet American* by Graham Greene, a novel full of lies. While a fourth Dervorgilla emerged radiant from the bathroom, after enjoying a long souse, to be joined by a fifth Dervorgilla face-creamed and in dressing-gown, phone in hand, all prepared for a long gossip with a friend in Ballinaclash. Two more Dervorgillas occupied the master bedroom, discussing us in low voices. There could be as many as four Dervorgillas gossiping together in one room at one time, and no room for myself and the truly quiet American whose drunken Russian grandfather had broken his neck after a fall from a loft in Tiflis.

We took to walking on Magheramore and Magherabeg with Blackie, walking to bars in Wicklow and coming back by Sadie's taxi with Blackie whining and slobbering.

'This won't do at all,' I said. 'I didn't invite you here to share a house. We'll take a train.'

I questioned Biddy about the car-hire situation in Wexford and was given the name Mylers.

'Absolutely no hassle,' Mylers' man assured me.

I phoned my namesake hairy O'Hills in Wicklow station and was given train times; soon we were seated in Sadie's van *en route* to freedom.

On the third day we would return the mud-caked hired car to Mylers together with keys and road maps. There were some extra expenses and the £60 quoted had become £100; I had paid out a similar amount at Lawlor's Hotel in Dungarvan.

I saw a familiar face at the wheel of a Hillman Minx proceeding at a stately pace along the seafront; what was Seamus Heaney doing in Wexford in midweek, and did he drive a car? Somehow Seamus did not seem the type; a push-bike and a long Oxford muffler would be more his style.

We walked along the seafront at Wexford and passed a number of low shebeens until we came to a narrow one with the name *J. Banville* emblazoned over the door in flowery grot. SMOKE CAPSTAN said a slogan on a tin plaque with gruff male hail-fellow-well-met straightforwardness. Player's *Please!* piped up the companion scroll in a softly appealing feminine voice, cozening, teasing.

'Shall we try this?' I asked Anastasia.

'OK.'

And in we went. It was a narrow functional sort of a chilly place such as were to be found everywhere in Ireland at one time but now are on the way to becoming extinct. Modest unpretentious places with Formica and ringboard, not exorbitant to imbibe in, if not particularly agreeable in themselves, fag-smokefilled drinking crypts. A rumpled clean-shaven bullocky man in crumpled snuff-coloured two-piece suit that sagged at the wide seat as if it belonged to a bigger man was leaning across the counter, thoughtfully picking his dentures with a spent match and studying the racing columns of the *Irish Press*, a low paper established by Dev and only good for starting fires. He did not appear to have backed any winners today.

Seeing patrons entering he straightened himself up, stuck out his welterweight's underslung jaw in an oblong face as if kneaded in grey putty or knocked out of shape in the ring. Brush-cut hair stood up stiff as hog's setae on the crown of his bullet head.

'What can I do you for you folks?'

He enquired our wants in a low sincere voice, the modulated tones of a sacristan or undertaker's mute; he had not expected customers at this hour. Half-imperial pints of Guinness with Jameson chasers, right you be.

The publican's name was etched or stencilled athwart the fly-blown semitranslucency of the bug-smeared glass

J. Banville
Licensed Vintner

Banville (supposing it were he) served us our chill half-pints and shots of
Jameson, placing the former carefully on the Guinness mats supplied by
St James's Gate and giving the cold counter a perfunctory wipe with a damp
rag.

'Are you Banville himself?' I asked civilly. 'By any chance?'

'Well, you could say that I'm *one* of the Banvilles. It's a common enough
name hereabouts. Are you looking for him?'

'You wouldn't, by any chance, be any relation to *the* John Banville, the
Kepler and Copernicus man?'

'Not that I know. What does he do? Is he an astronomer or what?'

'You could say that.'

He returned to his *Irish Press* and resumed his browsing up and down the
racing columns as the draught Guinness, black as the Styx, went clammily
down into our interiors.

The outer aspect of the port of Wexford – the drenched seafront, railway
sidings, squalling gulls, the huge backsides of rusty freighters no less alluring
and equally uninviting, were visible through the blurred panes. I called for
two more shots of Jameson.

We did not prolong our brief visit. When waiting for my change I
attempted another bold cast.

'And how are the boys of Wexford who fought with pike in hand?' I asked
jovially. 'Any slight improvement in the general bowel condition?'

The pugilistic crown of hair positively bristled with hostility and the
lower jaw took on a truculent slant as Banville shovelled over my small
change.

'Gone across to England or joined the Provos,' groaned the disenchanted
publican. 'We have our own internal emigration you know, like typhus.'

'How's Wexford business generally, then?'

'This town is dead. It died two years back.'

We thanked him and took our leave.

'The wrong Banville,' I told Anastasia. 'Absolute camel. Our man within
is the sort who licks his fingers to turn a page.'

In the returning train (whose windows as lips that were sealed, wouldn't
open) Anastasia complained of feeling the cold, her hands were cold, so I

said put them in my pocket (like a warm muff or a hot brick at the Opera), my trouser pocket, which she obligingly did. And soon, between one thing and another, she began to warm up, and had to retire to the Ladies to regain her composure, and returned looking radiant and sat beside me, and gave a sigh, and I said, 'You're looking rodent.'

She offered me her small devil finger and said 'Smell that', which I did and recognised what it was and said 'Lobster mayonnaise' with relish, just like Blazes Boylan. And Anastasia gave her small tinkling laugh that invoked sleigh bells and reindeers with antlers and a couple eloping in a sleigh piled with bearskin rugs across icy wastes.

And then, as on a *tabula rasa*, came a converging valley of bare brown trees gone purple in the waning light and an estuary with swans upended, arses in the air, as pretty as can be.

On the journey down to Wexford we had shared a carriage with Narbonne rugby supporters over for the match in Lansdowne Road who were travelling in the wrong direction, and had a poor meal at Lawlor's Hotel in Dungarvon and never dined there again, having found the Moorings, where we dined on Saturday, the day of the match. I thought it was only a pub by the water but the owner threw open a door and showed me a lovely restaurant and said 'We're chock-a-block but I'll try and fit you in', and we had a good meal there with good Rioja and Anastasia looked very Russian. We had watched Ireland play France in a very dirty (fouling) drawn game at Lansdowne Road and we lay on the bed and drank Smithwicks and smoked pot and then crossed to the restaurant and it *was* chock-a-block.

And the following night we returned and had a tiff and Anastasia withdrew herself and all future favours in a most frosty Russian manner and walked back to the hotel through snowdrifts eighteen feet high with packs of wolves howling in the nearby woods and was fast asleep when I returned, having stayed up drinking with Alex the owner by the great fire.

She didn't hear my knocking. The cheeky receptionist phoned up. 'We have your husband down here in Reception, Mrs umm Mills and he says he can't get in.' So you opened the door and climbed back into bed, the single bed, and I saw the clasp-knife by the bedside table and we made it up and got back into the double bed and you wept (again) and said you were being silly and you were sorry.

One of those days was my fifty-eighth birthday and we walked about Dungarvan and admired a line of snow-capped hills and, meeting an old woman who had lived there all her life, I enquired the name of the hills, but she didn't know the Drum Hills. Then we drank frothy beer in a pub in

Youghal open to the elements, and then we were on the road again and you drove like a fury up the backsides of huge lumbering pantechnicons thundering on and leaving us their wakes of mud and water and the wipers were going and you pulled out and pulled out again, overtaking in one of your black Russian moods that was a continuation of the first mood begun in the Moorings by the fire where we drank brandy. And you broke a long silence (during which I feared we might be killed under the road monsters travelling at high speed before and behind us) to say that you would not and could not wait all your life, that you would meet someone else and have a child by this other man, this someone else, this nameless one.

Then, following another silence, staring grimly out the smeared windscreen at the wake that the lorries were spewing back at us, you said, No, you said, no indeed, you would not wait. He would not show up. You would have no child by him.

So we reached Wexford station and returned the mud-caked car to Mylers (still sans apostrophe) and spoke to the taciturn Banville and took the return train to Wicklow, and all the Narbonne supporters had returned to Narbonne after the dirty game in Lansdowne Road, the drawn game. So we reached Wicklow station with frayed nerves, having splashed out maybe £300, and walked down into the village for a last drink at the Forge and I phoned up Sadie for a taxi and she said she would be there in a jiffy.

Sadie Dolan was as good as her word and transported us back to Ballymona Lodge. Dervorgilla was *in situ*, smiling a cat's smirk (didn't we find the single bed a bit *cramped?*) and loyal Blackie wagging his tail, delighted to have us back. The bungalow shrank again as we walked in. Back we certainly were with Blackie and the seven Dervorgillas.

— 32 —

Silent Love

Anastasia Ranoch lived at Oakmont Boulevard in Texas with two thoroughbred Skye terriers black and dusty like a pair of ambulatory hairy mats who spent their day barking through the fence at the grackles that infested the trees all tropical in the terrible Texas heat that came from the desert. These two and a male budgerigar called Martha who masturbated himself on a little plastic bell thoughtfully supplied by his mistress who walked barefoot about the house in slashed shorts as short as shorts could ever be, for Rory.

She had studied the Red Indians on graduating, had spent time in prison (trespass on a reservation), liked to dress in battle fatigues, and held the rank of major in President Reagan's secret army of PhD graduates specialising in a study of industrial diseases with findings perhaps useful for waging chemical warfare. She refused to let me see a photo of herself in uniform but could fly and travel at reduced rates if she wore it.

She looked very Russian in the photograph on her American passport. In strange hotels she kept a clasp-knife by her bed. She had had a bad experience in love.

On her last day at Ballymona Lodge she woke me at 8 a.m. to listen to a blackbird singing its heart out in Cooney's wood, a music that would have delighted Messiaen and delighted Rory and we made that which must not be spoken of (whisper it), were obliged to make t'nelis evol. Then we walked for the last time in the balmy air up the Columban Missionary avenue and were saluted by two nuns coming down from the convent.

The station was closed up but a Mohawk in black leather, leaning against the station wall, with a ring of spits about him, like a grasshopper evolving from the spittle, informed us that 'your man' – Hairy O'Hills – 'is somewhere up the line.' Michael Dolan, husband of Sadie, said he would drop your bags in later and we went for lunch in the Grand Hotel.

> Turkey and swedes
> Apple pie and ice cream
> Coffee and Hennessy

An old Hitchcock movie *Young and Innocent* with Derrick de Marney was on in the public bar of the Leitrim where we had another Hennessy. The train left Wicklow at 5.05, reaching Connolly station 6.05.

Outside Bus Arus I left Anastasia for her dreadful long hike through space back to Oakmont Boulevard and the Skye terriers.

'Can't I cry now?'

> Dublin–Gatwick
> then Gatwick–Houston
> Houston–Austin

I took the next train back to Wicklow, feeling like a toad, watching a stupendous sunset over Kilcoole, phoned Sadie and was back in Ballymona Lodge by 7.30. A breast of turkey in the freezer, a bottle of Bordeaux a third depleted, and Dervorgilla snug abed in the mobile; at least the lights were off.

A fat bluebottle, eager for dung, lit on the wicker chair, flexed its hind legs briskly and flew out. I was wearing Anastasia's green socks; she had taken some pebbles from Magheramore back to her bedroom in Oakmont Boulevard as a memento, another bad experience in love.

Home to Texas!

Texas is home of strange allergies, and grackles, those coal-black Golgotha birds that can't sing and can hardly fly, but spend their time in the low thorn trees, shitting on the roofs of cars.

What is there to record of that time in May at Oakmont Boulevard? The fireflies in the Rose of Sharon bushes, the two Skye terriers barking at passers-by behind the high fence, the death rattle of the grackles in the live-oak, the snail tracks on the fly-screen, the thermometer climbing until it had registered 110 degrees in the midday shade, the hawks flying before the storm.

Black and dusty grackles cranked themselves across the sun-drenched garden and I knocked one down with a rolled *New Yorker* that fell on the stiff pseudo-grass, the Astro-turf fouled by the terriers.

– 33 –

The Worst Choice

The worst choice of ales and beers in Europe is sold in Ireland at the highest prices. Over-refrigerated Budweiser, perhaps suitable for Texans in summer at temperatures of well over 100 degrees, is popular. Irish lager, like its English counterpart, is but a feeble imitation of the fine Pilsners brewed on the continent. Irish ale is weak and watery and full of gas, real ale unheard of.

Tommy Cullen has a shop at Brittas.

When four intruders waited in their car with the windows down, listening and waiting, he loaded his shotgun, crept down on the driver's side, put the barrel through the window and told the man, 'You have five seconds to get out of here.'

They took off over the roof.

No use feeling foolish if armed men break in and find you unarmed and defenceless. Tommy keeps the shotgun under his bed. The area around Brittas is all firearms, burglar alarms and guard dogs, as you can find out at night, when the prowlers are abroad, setting off the guard dogs and the alarms.

Blackie goes a-roaming again. Roaming the roads will be the death of that dog. What's the significance of the big black dog that follows the traveller everywhere?

– 34 –

Davis and Demons

The young pine wood that the dead Cooney had planted as his memorial makes its sounds all night, bird-call and breeze, the risen wind batters it, the poachers pass through unseen with their silent dogs. Retired to bed with windows closed behind the venetian blinds I am not thinking of ghosts and demons of the night but of flesh and blood raiders masked in balaclavas and armed with shotguns who come in cars to coast silently over the cattle-trap and arrive at my doorstep; a blow of a crowbar and they are in. Blackie is knocked on the head.

Sanguineous bugaboos move by night in stolen cars and all those who sleep the sleep of the just are their allotted prey.

The guard dogs bark all night. Any suspicious noise on the road brings Blackie out of his kennel to bay; and he sets off the others, beginning with Dr Meenan's dog; a chain reaction gets dogs barking as far as Herbst's yard and beyond.

Last December in Santa Cruz the seals lay about the pier and barked all night like dogs when I was making free of the Suchmans' drinks cabinet at four in the morning, playing Bach sonatas for violin and harpsichord, No. 5 in F Minor for preference, listening to the seals barking.

Dervorgilla's binoculars pulled the valley and distant line of hills closer. An almost Bavarian landscape was revealed on this lovely summer's day with the patio woodwork creaking in the sun, jackdaws scoffing in a tod of ivy and the first swallows of summer spurting by after rising insects. Why is it one takes the summer days of other countries for granted but never an Irish summer? Is it because they are so rare? The prancing air of Cape Town with outsize swallows flying over the harbour, the High Rand day of Johannesburg where I lived for two years, the dry heat of a Karoo winter's day, sandy Prussian day of Berlin, Bavarian day in Munich with the *Föhn* blowing, the Copenhagen day and Andalucían day all were known to Rory in his years of travel. But Irish summers were strange and unexpected and only the summers of my distant youth (1933) seemed fixed and abiding. The changing countryside and its changing people were unfamiliar and outlandish as Reykjavik or Watseka, Illinois.

Clinton Binnions is putting up electrified wire in his field, to define the grazing grounds of his sportful Friesians that have never known of the slaughterhouse and cavort about, butting each other and pretending to be alarmed by Ned Ward's white setter who runs at them in mock attacks. Have the Friesians infected Clinton with their skittishness or has he infected them with his? Ireland's only swimming farmer.

Sunday, 30 June
Cycled back from Brittas with Blackie weaving all over the road to find a note from brother scratched with key on silver foil of cigarette papers.

> I will call at about 9 a.m. tomorrow
> in case you need a lift to the station.
> I think it is tomorrow you go to see
> the King? Colum.

Nelsons came for dinner. Dorothy's cat face, beatific smile of pure exhaustion, pale and overworked. They are saving to buy a semi-detached house in the vale of Shanganagh. Trouble with publisher Cashman, working on second novel. Hot Dublin scandal: woman at hen party found herself last in line for powder room. Famous lesbian was pleasuring all who came, in a queue, gratifications digital or oral. Schsshters!

Myths begin in Ireland as shaggy dog stories; famous (though perfectly ordinary) personalities become legendary beings. Perfectly ordinary individuals in the entertainment, sports and communications trade became regular folk heroes overnight, names to conjure with; famous almost by accident, become legendary beings. O'Hehir the sports broadcaster with his frantic soprano screeching, affable Gabo, moanin' low Bono and the Band-Aid man Geldof, all pure buffoons in their various ways, as tall, white-bearded Noel Purcell before them. Since nothing much could be said in their favour they were elevated to the lofty status of Great Irishmen of Our Time.

In a derelict three-storey house overlooking the river on Leitrim Place near the pub lives bachelor Davis. His condition appears to be one of extreme destitution; he shuffles about in a greasy overcoat, his gooseberry eyes watering, grey arthritic hands ingrained with old dirt. Yet the Davis family were well-off once; he drove the first motor car through Wicklow. He lives alone, a needy bachelor; the house was broken into and the family silver stolen. Behind a high untended hedge Davis lives out what remains of his life; you would take him for a tramp.

I crossed the river by the low bridge, saw crabs tumbling past with the outgoing tide; and so by the yard of empty Guinness barrels, iron lungs waiting to be collected from Dowlings riverside hostelry.

In the Leitrim Bar I am civilly served a shot of Jameson by the redheaded son of the former butcher who has two shops on the main street. Looking out the window I see the sea breaking over the low wall and the shell of the old station, its platform and loading sheds long disused, where I had arrived for a week's holiday around 1949. The station had moved inland since; it had stood there once with the solid look of permanancy peculiar to railway stations, when I stepped off the train, aged about twenty-one years. In an August heat wave Conal ('Bruiser') Cullinane and I paddled over the horizon. We could see fathoms down into the clear green sea.

You can look at something a hundred times and not recognise it: namely, the ruins of a railway station long abandoned by the sea.

– 35 –

The King and Queen of Spain

Monday, 1 July

Ned called at 8.20 a.m., brother Colum at 9.15 to take me to the station (the County Council offices being just down the hill). The gold-edged invitation card from the Department of Foreign Affairs stated that

> The Taoiseach and Mrs Fitzgerald request the pleasure of your company at lunch in the Iveagh House at 1.00 p.m. in honour of Their Majesties the King and Queen of Spain on the occasion of their visit to Ireland.
> P.M. Informal dress.

In my case very informal. The only suitable apparel I possessed was at the cleaners, an Aran baínín jacket dyed black, sans buttons and lapels, a present from a man in Shamley Green, Surrey.

I had seen a jacket in the window of a high-class haberdashery in Kildare Street opposite Dáil Éireann. Slip it on, said the suave outfitter, who praised the fit and hang, as good as tailored, made for me. He was prepared to knock a fiver off the retail price; so I made out a cheque for £100, thrice the price I had ever paid for a jacket, this one of handwoven Donegal tweed. Colours from our countryside. Joy and health to you when you wear this, said the weaver's tag. I said I would keep it on.

A crowd of idlers had gathered about Iveagh House and Gardai and plain-clothes detectives were positioned along the railings of Stephen's Green; for the state visit of the Spanish royals was common knowledge since they had appeared the previous evening on *Today Tonight* TV bulletin and had been introduced to an enchanted nation by Mr Brian Farrell, constricted in dinner jacket and bow-tie.

They had already paid a courtesy visit to President Hillery at Arus an Uachtaran in the Phoenix Park and exchanged pleasantries about the climate. King Juan Carlos then made a long speech in Spanish out of which emerged, as flotsam on the flood, *Irlanda, España, Armada, Iglesia, Americana*; to all of which Queen Sofia listened attentively, smiling sweetly when she deemed it appropriate. Toasts to both nations were proposed and drunk.

Going in in my camouflage I was among men in dark suits and stout elderly priests in black standing by the bar with drinks in hand amiably chatting with all the aplomb of men of the world accustomed to such formal occasions when clergy and laity commingled pleasantly as the gin and tonic in their fists.

State visits and cultural events flush out the pushier type of prelate, as sporting events always flush out a rash of priests to take the best seats as their God-given right or throw in the ball at Gaelic games and then present cups to the victors as smoothly as they offer ciborium and consecrated host to the faithful with their tongues out for it. Standing on windy hillsides at coursing matches they cheer on the greyhounds and watch them tear the hares asunder; as if there were a close kinship between the May altar and processions and rituals in the open air and the GAA and blood sports in general, accepted as an appropriately healthy and natural masculine sort of activity fit for strapping Gaels of all stripes.

The stout elderly and now thoroughly flushed clerics who stood by the serving-hatch were no doubt former Salamanca novices who after ordination had got up into the pulpit to preach Franco's cause against Godless Communism. They congregated in the bar as though such lay premises were familiar as their own sacristies. Such processions and rituals had been going on in Ireland ever since the Eucharistic Congress in 1932.

I questioned a flunkey as to the correct protocol for addressing the King. 'Your Majesty.' Pure gold! The clang of sword unsheathed, the taunting challenge, lances upraised against a blue sky, pennants aflutter. Lucia Joyce doted on the weak Windsors, would jump on any bus bound for Windsor, wrote to the King of England: 'Majesty.'

There would be no delay; just a quick handshake and pass along into the dining room where place-cards were on every table.

Never had I been presented to royalty before, much less shaken the hand of a King and his Queen. This one did not require to dress up to be a King. In his hand he held no sceptre, on his head there was no crown, about his shoulders no ermine-lined cape festooned with medals; yet his whole appearance was manifestly kingly. This was the Spanish King who had marched alone into the Cortes already assembled and informed his Generals that the Putsch was off, they should remember their oaths of loyalty to him. They could go home.

The winding reception line went down a short flight of carpeted stairs and rose again on the far side, where the royal pair would presently appear with the Fitzgeralds. Mrs Fitzgerald smiled from her wheelchair as though it were perfectly natural to smile up from a wheelchair to a gathering of stout elderly priests lining up to shake the kingly hand and look humbly into his eye, encounter that parboiled Bourbon stare. Mr Haughey, former Taoiseach and now Leader of the Opposition, was immediately ahead of me in his double vents, always smaller than expected, blowing his nose with circumspection into a spotless linen handkerchief. Ahead of him shuffled the old priests who had studied in Salamanca and sided for the Roman Catholic Church and Christ and their Order and Franco.

And now Mr Haughey had reached the King and did not 'make a leg' but bowed his head as if receiving holy communion and I heard his low deferential murmur as he took the King's hand. Then I was face to face with the King. I had written that he looked constipated on the Spanish stamps; for such *lèse-majesté* one could end up in the stocks. But had el Rey Juan Carlos I read it? Beneath the immensely high Bourbon forehead the eyes of a keen yachtsman stared at me.

'*Su Majestad,*' I murmured, timidly pressing the King's hand. And then to Queen Sofia: '*Su Majestad.*'

'You've forgotten me,' said an amused voice from below as a gracious hand was extended from the wheelchair.

'No, I haven't,' I lied, and reeled on, propelled by the elderly priests now made ravenous by rich cooking aromas, into the high-ceiling chamber miraculously fragrant, a place as cool as the Alhambra with a breeze blowing through. I was seated at a table with the political correspondent of the *Irish Times* and a Cistercian monk who was editor of *Crux*.

The menu had ingeniously amalgamated the colours of the two flags. A gazpacho soup, turbot and chillies with new Irish potatoes, chilled Spanish white wine, a sorbet with coffee and cognac, and you would not get as good at Restaurante Hermanos Macias in Ronda. The King sipped red wine and stared thoughtfully away into space, no doubt going over the lines of his speech, staring over the heads of the old priests now lashing into the good fare; the high-domed forehead dominated the table. Garrett Fitzgerald was charming Queen Sofia who was laughing. Then the Taoiseach stood up and made a speech in fluent Spanish not once consulting notes; to which King Juan Carlos responded in stilted English.

The priests applauded. Mumm champagne was served up and the dining room stood for toasts: Spain and Ireland, the King and Queen. The battle of Kinsale was tactfully avoided; whereupon the royals departed. Equerries were already packing, flight times checked; the royal entourage was heading west. The *Irish Times* man and I finished off the Mumm. It had been a splendid luncheon party.

− 36 −

The *Camarero* Miguel Lopez Rojas

You do not presume to pester or bother a King with idle questions, much less volunteer information or engage in backchat; one does not question Kings, who have no tactful responses to such impertinence. If he should come calling to your house *you* stand.

I had wanted to tell the King that at least one of his subjects – Miguel who worked long hours in the Bar Alhambra in Nerja – was on his feet from ten in the morning until two the next; had been his loyal subject years before he had ascended the throne.

One fine summer morning in Nerja I was having coffee and cognac when there came the throbbing of mighty engines passing close in to the Balcon de Europa. Stepping out into the heat I saw the immaculately white and spick-

and-span destroyer bristling with long-barrelled guns passing close in as if to warn or impress the watchers. The entire ship's company in white were drawn up ramrod stiff on deck, saluting the flag, hands and faces brown as teak, come perhaps from Alicante or Cartagena and now heading in for Malaga.

Franco the fox dared not come all the way from his lair in Madrid, not on the high winding road from Almería for it became progressively more dangerous and could be mined or blocked with dynamite, and man-made avalanches send motorcades into the sea. For the last leg of the journey he was coming by sea, out of sight in his air-conditioned cabin. The dictator who had made Hitler wait and kick his heels while he took his siesta was a small, portly, choleric man who nursed his phlebitis, took his pills, nursed memories of north Africa and the Rif, the fight for Malaga and perhaps the names of those executed by his orders.

I told Miguel that the Caudillo was passing. By way of dismissive response he narrowed his eyes and spat in the dust.

All dictators have this in common: they take little mincing steps, fussy as goats. Perhaps their jackboots are killing them?

– 37 –

Epistolary: 1974–78

I have come upon some letters my brother wrote me eleven years ago when he was living at Three Mile Water, before Dunganstown East. He wrote to me from the wilds of Wicklow, where he was digging himself in.

> CULLEN COTTAGE
> THREE MILE WATER
> NEAR WICKLOW
>
> 14 Oct. 1974

Dear Rory,

A few lines, as promised.

Shall I begin it? Now actually 14th Dec. Time did not permit a second line until now. Working like shit in the office & in my own time on office work to the detriment of my own affairs. I work late in the evenings & rarely have a lunch hour with the result that I calculate I work a six-day week for the price of five. It's daft. Why do I do it? To avoid falling below a certain minimum level of incompetence I do both my own work & that of my three 'assistants,' who I, in fact, assist. I got rid of one, psychopathic as well as incompetent, who wouldn't do what he was asked, but not for that reason but only by saying either he left or I did. (Back to Ludlow Road, or worse – charming prospect.) Although any reasonable organisation would have been glad of the opportunity to get such a person out, this character was simply passed on to someone else eventually, the first two on whom it was tried declining. So all the architects have to contend with this & adopt the attitude of not having the staff so that the work can't be done, generally concentrating on their own affairs, owning pubs & chemist shops about the city & drawing £4,000 a year; which is a great pity as the work is useful & pleasant & simple enough to be capable of being done without any assistants, but there is so much of it that it takes a lot of time & I keep struggling to get on top of it, which is in theory possible but I can never quite achieve.

I have brought home work this weekend & was up until 3 & 4 o'clock last weekend. The purchase of the land for the house is complete but there is no opportunity to design it. I suspect, incidentally, that it was bought just too soon & prices are now going down . . .

CULLEN COTTAGE
THREE MILE WATER
NEAR WICKLOW

30 March 1978

Dear Rory,

So that is where you are (wherever it is), if you are still there?* I have not verified your position on the map. I would do so if there was any chance of going in that direction; but there is not, as my house building struggles continue & do not show much evidence of coming to an end. I can, perhaps, see a minimum that could be done to make it habitable, at which point we could move in & finish the rest afterwards. It is not how I would have liked to go about it, but probably that will happen. It is necessary to move in at a certain stage to prevent the interior fittings being stolen. However as it is a considerable minimum & I work slowly I could not say when this might be. I

---

* I was sharing a house, a model Irish cottage, with Rosita at Beladangan across the causeway in Iar Connaught.

am in the difficult position of knowing, perhaps too well, how things should be in theory without having any practical experience of how to carry them out in practice. I remember seeing Werner Schurmann building his house & thinking I could never attempt such a thing, but am doing all right, as far as it goes. At the moment I am still only at the stage of taking down & rebuilding defective work which I paid local cowboys to do, & this is more tedious than building it in the first place. They were unable to make an opening of the correct size for a door frame or window frame, leaving gaps of up to two inches which they were unable to fill in such a way as to keep out the rain. The roof also leaks, for which I have myself to blame because although I knew there was such a thing as an exposed site I did not take it very seriously, assuming that a fairly steep roof pitch would shed water in any circumstances. Unfortunately the site is probably more in the category of very exposed, being elevated & by the sea, & the rain is capable of being driven from the eaves up the roof & over the ridge rather than flowing downwards in the manner one would expect. When driven like this for a day or so in a gale it can find its way in if there are any mistakes. I have come to detest the wind, which has also blown scaffolding off the roof, breaking rooflights, & taking nine square feet of aluminium sheet off the top of the chimney & left it in a ditch a quarter of a mile away.

All of which is very tiresome in every sense. When not working I sleep, & then insufficiently. I received a copy of your book, with thanks, but my only reading these days is the paper, during meals, & so out of touch that of the two works you mention as influences I have not even heard. Therefore, as a paper reader, I have seen & enjoyed your pieces on Ireland. They are vivid & exact, such as the pipers like 'demented bees,' a description which is quite audible. Also Ben Kiely's praise of the introduction to the short story anthology, which I would like to see some time. Cuttings, as always, are enclosed, possibly of no interest except the obituary of Heidegger to which I draw your attention with reference to my remarks about his influence on Beckett: Being can be addressed not expressed, waited for (!) not spoken for . . . that seems clear enough?

C.

DUNGANSTOWN EAST
WICKLOW

13 July 1978
Thursday

Dear Rory,

Thank you for yours of 22 May. Is it such a time ago? It seems like a few weeks. These long Summer days seem shorter than the others. I go in the garden after dinner, presently it is after 11 & another day is gone without much to show except a lot of grass cut. This year I determined to cut it before the seed had a chance to form since neglecting it in the last few years for house painting with the result that even the vegetable patches were attempting to revert to their natural state, which is that of a meadow rather than a garden. I have been cutting our meadow with a scythe, or half an acre of it, a pleasant occupation when the swing of it is acquired, which has taken me a few years & I now fly along like a character from a bad novel by John McGahern. I suppose what is wrong with him is what Marinetti objected to '. . . memory, nostalgia, the fog of legend produced by remoteness in time, the exotic fascination produced by remoteness in space, the picturesque, the imprecise, rusticity, wild solitude, corrosion, multicoloured disorder, twilight shadows, weariness, the soiled traces of the years, the crumbling of ruins, the taste of decay, pessimism, phthisis, suicide, the blandishments of pain, the aesthetics of failure.'

Hoping you own ills have gone away.

C.

Rather than face the boredom of driving his Mini on motorways across England my brother took the side roads and by-ways into Wales, heading for the Holyhead ferry. He fell asleep at the wheel and crashed. It was a bad crash out of which he was lucky to come alive. This was some years before when I was living in London.

He wrote to me from a hospital in Wales. Later, on the mend but still on crutches, he summoned me into Wales to get him out of hospital and we travelled back by train, and then took a bus to his hutch in Ealing where he insisted on cooking lunch.

Assembling the components of this dull but nutritious meal (we were spared cabbage) my brother sailed about the kitchen on his new crutches with all the nonchalance and *élan* of those intrepid early aviators who flew channels and oceans as if they were mere ditches. As if he had been doing this all his life; as in a sense he had, and overcoming all obstacles by sheer obstinacy. His resourcefulness, like his patience, was endless. All his life he had consumed stewed apples and Bird's custard for the motions and Swiss rolls for a treat; which was another form of constancy, of loyalty to his obligations, his life.

Colum and Stella Veronica returned to Ireland along the motorway in their Tin Lizzie and my brother had his hands clawed off by one of the wild Russian cats rescued from the building sites, who did not care to travel in a Mini box.

– 38 –

The Dodo in London

In those trying times my estranged wife Jane and I were cooped up on the fifth or topmost floor of a five-room walk-up cold-water rent-controlled apartment above shops on Muswell Hill Broadway in north London.

Our flat was the highest of the highest building on the highest hill surmounted by a little tower overlooking Alexandra Park and the Palace, adjoining an ABC cinema complex that was later demolished.

The ceiling of the flat immediately below us was leaking and then systematically pulled down by a clever Cockney, until it was on the living room floor and the landlord liable for repairs. After twenty years of ding-dong our marriage was coming to an end; as were many others in a building always leaking and in need of running and immediate repairs.

In the hazy blue distance lay Potters Bar in Hertfordshire, Hatfield and the way north. The kindergarten and Mrs Kanji was just below; a fifteen-minute bus ride took my middle lad to Barnet Art College and beyond that Havendon Wood and open countryside, a haven for lechers in the wheatfields.

From the wrought-iron balcony at the rear you could see down to the playing fields of Crouch End and the noble dome of St Paul's.

A landing covered in a threadbare runner bisected the apartment from front door to bathroom in the back; the rooms led off this, three narrow bedrooms, a more commodious master bedroom, and a living room lined with books that overlooked the broadway and its incessant traffic.

There the Dodo, not seen in years, paid us an unexpected flying visit, travelling by train from Largs on the Firth of Clyde. I had not set eyes on this odd relinquent of mine since our mother's demise in Dun Laoghaire some years before, when he had flitted in and out, not attending the funeral as he thought it might be too distressing for his finer sensibilities.

To what now did we owe this singular honour? *Tiens!* He just happened to be passing through *en route* to Paris and needed a place to lay his weary head for the night, and what could be more natural than to beg a favour of his younger brother? He had phoned my wife to ask whether we could put him up for the night; and she could hardly refuse him. It was high time he paid us a visit; the lads must have grown big as trees.

When I heard the buzzer go I pressed the release button and a disembodied distant voice squawked down below amid the din of the broadway that swelled in a crescendo as he pushed open the street door and now he was coming up. I opened the apartment door and waited for him to appear, not having seen him in seventeen years.

The bloody old Dodo was coming up, the old rip, a rare visitant indeed; I was curious to see how Time had dealt with him. He halted at the mezzanine below, rang the bell, cleared his throat; the door was opened by Mrs Fisher and my brother addressed her in that unforgettable fluty mooing voice without maleness or resolution or lung-power in it; an odd buttery, neutered voice on the stairs, a whispery gush of sibilants.

'Does Mr Rory live here by any chance?'

Top floor, boss! Go right up! Right on, squire! They're in!

Breathing stealthily through his wide-winged nostrils the Dodo slowly ascended the last flight of uncarpeted stairs that stank of dog piss (the Barraddas yappers), grasping in his right hand a golf driver without its covering. He appeared from the waist up, had grown corpulent and was now a veritable Mycroft Holmes in girth, wearing well-cut expensive tweed suiting of grouse-moor twill.

He had the face of a Roman emperor, a fleshly face set into its final form – an odd mixture of my father's weak face and my mother's in a certain mood. This would be his final face, the visage he would take with him into the grave. He had brought no presents; had he not brought himself all the way from far distant Largs, a perilous journey southward! Step in, step in, whoever you are.

He bore no malice, shook no hands. He entered nodding as if he knew us well and had come here many times before and been welcomed as a true and valued friend.

The Dodo perched himself on the very edge of the sofa and accepted a gin and tonic, holding the driver like a mace between his knees. He was heavy and monumental as a graven image; a non-smoker he could remain silent without any embarrassment. He was puffed after the climb, one hand masterfully reposing on his knee, The Great Condottiere.

Who spoke of the density that people seem to possess as we keenly observe them? He kept his eye fixed on me, his mother's hazel eyes alight with some secret mischief (her humour had always been rather bitter), as if it was some private joke that I couldn't share. His head wobbled on its broad axis. This was his easy social manner; he was at his ease in any company, among the golfers at Largs where he was regarded as 'quite a local celebrity'.

Was he intending to play golf in Paris with one club? And were the partners or partner male or female?

When supper was announced he marched to the table in the kitchen with measured tread, always a good trencherman.

My sons were in stitches; they had not expected such a strange uncle. He consumed his *babotjie* with a steady and methodical chomping, and when the meal was over announced that now he was off to the West End; he had booked a seat for a play. He was flying on to Paris in the morning; at what hour did we rise?

Next morning I took him to the bus stop. Adieu, happy landings, keep the head down, watch that shank. He shook all over to indicate silent mirth as he stepped aboard the W7 for Finsbury Park and was whirled off down the hill. I hoped that was the end of him. He had never been much of an older brother; indeed nothing fraternal existed between myself and that cold slab I call the Dodo.

– 39 –

The Classic Cinema
in Baker Street

Coming out of the Classic cinema into the gloaming, the late afternoon summer light peculiar to Baker Street and the purlieus of Madame Tussaud's – there was a pleasant pub opposite that I occasionally frequented – who do you suppose I saw strolling ahead in black leather jacket but Lindsay Anderson, and walking behind him my brother, unknown to each other, the last two people I would have thought to see there but the two most likely to travel distances to see a Welles movie, particularly *The Magnificent Ambersons*.

In those far-off days before marriage I was working in an extrusion moulding plant in Burnt Oak and reading Sartre's *Nausea* over lunch (two thin pork chops and tinned peas) in a transport café on the Great North Road. I introduced my brother to Anderson and they repaired to a coffee joint on Marylebone Road. I took a bus going south to the Bayswater Road, then another going west to Notting Hill Gate, then the Central Line Tube going to Ealing Common via White City, still full of the strange emotions that the movie had evoked.

I had first seen *Citizen Kane* with Philomena Rafferty in a repertory cinema near Marble Arch; my brother, ever contrary, dismissed it as a young man showing off. But what showing off. He professed to be an admirer of *The Great Gatsby,* the novel not the movie; a novel about 'the huge incoherent failure of a house' and a dream (Daisy).

Welles had died working at his desk late on the night of Wednesday, 9 October a few hours after Old Parr and I would set off downhill into the pitch darkness, followed by the curses of the mad Finn. Two years later his ashes would be flown to Malaga in an unmarked blue urn in the safe keeping of Beatrice Welles, his daughter by Rita Hayworth; to be immured in a wall on the bull-farm of his *amigo* Antonio Ordoñez near Ronda. An unmarked urn set into a brick wall without a plaque marks his last and most secret resting place, perhaps known only to Ordoñez.

Twenty or more years previously I had watched him (Ordoñez) working the bulls in a *corrida* with Jaime Ostos and El Viti in the bullring by the Alameda Gardens. Years on I lunched at the Restaurante Hnos. Macias (*Un Típico Rincon Rodeño en un Marco Incomparable*) with my last love Alannah near the Ronda bullring. Our waiter said that Ordoñez had semi-retired but was still killing the bulls; it was in his blood. One of his old picadors had been in the previous night to take a bowl of soup.

Orson Welles's Xanadu – Hearst's San Simeon – was the frightening castle of a fairy tale, with its hall of mirrors, its echoing corridors and wide flights of shadowy stairs, its fireplace the size of a barn, the wifely boudoir a doll's room, the inmates shrinking away, observed coldly by the sinister butler who knew where all the bodies were buried.

A strange clear late afternoon light even at 8.00 p.m. on 6 June 1972, my sons kicking football on the patch below the flats, brother Colum in Carmarthen West Wales general hospital. Rather than go on the motorway he took side roads into Wales, fell asleep at the wheel, crashed into a wall, came to hearing a South African voice asking for an ambulance; he had a broken leg, jaw and teeth and is now on crutches. He comes by train to London tomorrow, wishes me to accompany him from Wales.

Muted whirr of the pet hamster on its treadmill down the corridor and a recorded voice in my ear explains in German that all the lines into West Berlin are overloaded. A dry whirring in my ear as the phone rings in an empty flat in Schwabing.

– 40 –

Mornings in the Dewy Dell

In my years in Muswell Hill I drank in the pubs around there and in Highgate village or walked through Highgate Wood and Ken Wood and Hampstead Heath to the various pubs of Hampstead to Harry's bar on the hill, the Coach & Groom.

V. S. Pritchett says that you can knock on any second door in London and find people there who have travelled the world, and I have found this to be true of casual acquaintances encountered in pubs. Morning drinkers in London always have interesting stories to tell, taste buds lubricated and tongues loosened by the first pint of the day, *memoria technica* clicking into action.

One fine summer morning I descended the fire escape and got on to the pathway that joins Alexandra Park and Highgate Wood, formerly a railway line, now the dewy dell, and made my way to the rustic Royal Oak, a Courage house deserted at that hour. Presently an unshaven geezer came in and immersed himself in the *Daily Mirror*, with the first foaming pint of the day to hand, best bitter a thirst-quencher with salted peanuts.

I read in the *Guardian* that the headless corpse of a man had been found sitting bolt upright in the passenger seat of an architect's car parked opposite the main gates of Highgate Cemetery. On his way to work the architect had seen something peculiar on the nearside seat, which at first he took to be a log of wood put there for a joke; but when he got into the car he found a male corpse minus the head, apparently removed from a coffin in the nearby cemetery. But why leave it in his car? Why dig it up anyway?

More morning drinkers began to filter into the public bar for jovial banter. I fell into conversation with a ruddy-faced dapper little man who introduced himself as Geoffrey Hogg late of Norwich and the Norfolk Fusiliers (were they the famous Buffs?), the father of six bouncing daughters, an admirer of the poetry of George Herbert and the music of Elgar.

'Trooping the Colour is based on illiteracy. Even so I could cheerfully wake up each morning to the strains of a military band.'

Here the amiable Hogg gave a strange high-pitched laugh. I wondered whether he was by any chance related to the man who had wanted to or had cuckolded Shelley but didn't think it proper to enquire. Perhaps he was. He told me that he had lost a translation of *Table Talk* in the Great Yarmouth flood. We spoke of Charles Lamb and his attempts to give up smoking, both he and Coleridge throwing their pipes away on Hampstead Heath, when it was country, and returning next morning to look for them. We spoke of De Quincey and his drug addiction.

'Did you read about that corpse found in the car in Highgate?' I asked. 'I wonder who put it there.'

'That would be Farrant up to his tricks. He drinks in the Prince of Wales with the Welsh witch. When we were introduced by Darcey Farcey he gave me a most peculiar handshake. A sort of manual French kiss.'

'That would be Farrant.'

Nothing could put a dampener on Geoffrey Hogg late of the Buffs; he fairly exuded sound common sense.

The lone imbiber in the Alexandra had been a film projectionist in Mozambique. He told me that when the natives couldn't pay their taxes, Salazar had sent out his bombers from Portugal and bombed the village, having warned them to get out; he wanted to teach them a salutary lesson. They came in with their taxes. Salazar had put manners on them. 'Well, you can't run a dictatorship along humanitarian lines.'

Had I not been there with the puppets, come by road from rainy Blantyre out of what was Rhodesia; crossed the Zambesi at Tet, saw a monkey chained on a platform in a yard at evening, discovered that sparkling Portuguese rosé in the bubble-shaped bottle with the decorative label? Mateus Rosé, a good name for some profiteering lecher. Mateus Rosé cost ten and sixpence, or two for a guinea. In the days when newspapers cost a penny, a gin and tonic half a crown and there were eight in a pound, a quid.

Those were the days when Jane and I lived high up on Muswell Hill Broadway; when I couldn't extract royalties from a tight-fisted publisher; when our marriage had begun to break up; when I drank like a fish and my work went off the rails.

— 41 —

The Finn

In early October of that year I had a visitor staying. Testy Old Parr arrived from over the Irish Sea for a short winter break, dossing down in the mobile home in the paddock, filing the chain off Dervorgilla's bicycle, for which I would have to stump up £5 later. We cycled to McDaniel's for a drink.

Dole boys were bashing balls about the two snooker tables that were rarely unoccupied and a gross spillage of lurid colours and stereophonic dialogue spewed from a monster TV screen raised on high. The place was commodious as an aircraft hangar and as unappealing. As we seated ourselves in the ingle, John Stamp took an armful of elongated wedges of dried turf and piled them up into a great conflagration under the stuffed fox that stared down with blind glassy eyes. You had the choice of being roasted in the ingle or frozen by the counter.

John brought us hot whiskies and halves of Guinness. A leering hairy lank fellow came to sit opposite us, sniggering into his drink, presently identifying himself as a Finn, and certainly an unsober one, disposed to be offensive. I had no wish to bandy words with this sallow fellow nodding into his drink. He had reached the stage of insobriety where he wanted to be offensive and presently had dismissed us with contempt as bourgeois and even – compounding the insult – *petit bourgeois*. He invited us to step outside.

No thanks.

As we left we heard him phoning the Garda barracks in Wicklow. We took off without lights into the pitch darkness, soaring off down the long hill. I took my bearings from the faint starlight that showed between the trees not meeting overhead. Old Parr followed.

Next morning we were on the road again, tyres pumped up, heading for Lil Doyle's, turkey sandwiches and gin.

In the afternoon as darkness was falling we entered Healy's pub in Wicklow town and were set upon by a local drunk who became even more abusive than the Finn. He enquired where our yacht was moored. He said he would take it offa us; he was going to take everything offa us. He took us for Englishmen, I in my Blue Peter and Old Parr, who was certainly an Englishman (with an Irish mother from Ballina), born in India.

Old Parr swirled his Guinness about in the glass to bring up a head, but offered no comment, staring sagaciously at the row of bottles confronting him. His tufted grey locks were standing on end as though he had seen an apparition.

'The same again?'

'Why not.'

– 42 –

'Cash' Up for Sentencing

Didn't Cash get off light,' said Ned Ward.
'How's that?'
'A thirty quid fine is nothing to Cash.'

Cash Murphy had appeared briefly in court to answer charges, to be fined a very nominal amount by a lenient Justice of the Peace and given several months in which to pay it. The Guards said that Cash's house was a regular Ali Baba's cave of nicked property, among which were Ann Lait's car parts and Dervorgilla's cushions. His defence had been a bare-faced lie; his mammy *wasn't* dying.

A few days later I passed him on the steps leading from the butcher's shop to the harbour where a freighter from Bilbao waited to take on a cargo of timber.

Out of great misery comes great joy. Dervorgilla's cushions were returned to their rightful owner and the covers thrown straight into the washing machine which thundered away day and night on its rotors. She had insisted that the place be kept in apple-pie order and would not agree to Biddy cleaning once a week as I had suggested. She had backed away from me as from a leper when I approached smoking a roll-up; all the rooms but mine were non-smoking areas.

– 43 –

Year Ending

Clinton Binnions advances slowly in green Wellingtons amid his placidly grazing herd of Friesians who hardly deign to take notice of him as he strolls among them, slaps a meaty hindquarter ('Thou art mine, goodly lass!'). The sea-swimmer, horse-rider, tennis player who makes his own wine now claps his hands; and slowly they rise up and amble offstage, swishing their tails. Binnions, abstracted, hands plunged in pockets, his thoughts far away, follows them off the field.

I was thinking today that my father, dead these sixteen years, was like one of those minor Shakespearean characters – Rosencrantz and Guildenstern – who are killed offstage and never rejoin the action but take a curtain call at the end when they appear half out of character (already actors on their way home), bowing deeply to the audience, with complacent smiles.

Saw a rare thing on tonight's RTE station: a Finnish film on Elias Lönnrot. Reindeer pull a sledge at top speed across the snow-plain, a cabin full of wild dancing girls throwing up their skirts to expose naughty linen petticoats. Doesn't he figure in one of Borge's fables as a figure of doom?

Made sortie out for wood. Phone rang twice; I did not answer. Dervorgilla is due mid-September, has been away since Sunday, 23 June. Her mail has begun to arrive already. Am thinking of moving on when she returns. A van goes by, on the side is inscribed SADIE DOLAN.

I recall Paddy Collins in his dark den in Delgany gatelodge near the Bell Hole, abuzz with house-flies thickly clustered. He said they didn't bother him, he quite liked them, as company. He made trips to Dublin on the bus to relieve the monotony; was lionised by the ladies in the Arts Club. 'It's Paddy!'

Crusty epistle from Old Parr rusticating in France, where Massif Central will find him. 'Abandoned language almost entirely, took to hand signs, rubbing belly, tipping thumb towards the mouth. Swimming in lakes, wine-tasting. Parry is bound for the Great Barrier Reef.'

25 September (Yom Kippur)

Woke before alarum with finger on stop button. Ambitious young David Hockney had tacked cautionary precept above his bed, for his eyes alone to see as he woke: *Get Up Immediately!* Seems to have worked in his case. Motion in shed as kettle boils, out of delicacy for sleeper whose bedroom abuts on bathroom. Mist obscures valley almost to door. Both windows wide open, post van brings mail for Dervorgilla.

Ned Ward came at midday to say Gardai had told him that farmer had shot a bitch and her two ever-straying pups who had been worrying his sheep. Dervorgilla on her back on sofa engaged in long telephone conversation. She goes into hospital tomorrow.

30 September

Phoned Stevens Hospital and got on to Dervorgilla. Operation tomorrow, she needs transistor and Chopin piano tapes. Convalescence with the Grennans.

Ned went to see corpse of setter bitch and pups shot a week ago. Pheasant shooting season begins tomorrow.

2 *October*

Biddy called with clinging daughter Lara with thumb in mouth in company of little Siobhan Herbst, with exophthalmic eyes and brown skin, daughter of little Orson Herbst. Biddy screeching 'Mind your new dress!' to fractious daughter, on her worst behaviour.

Phoned Stevens Hospital. Dervorgilla sounded weak, requires roll of film.

3 *October*

Dental appointment. Mini crashes over cattle-trap, flurry of gravel and crunch of brakes. The brother!

'I've only got ten minutes to spare!'

Accepts glass of chilled white wine, chomping at his sandwiches, always the same, then rushes me to Matthews's surgery.

Afterwards to Periwinkle for hot toddy and cloves. Fug of tobacco fumes and TV hubbub. Asked for it to be turned down and I would accept a second hot toddy. Boozer with purple face, scum of Guinness on lips, wipes lips with back of hairy hand, staring fixedly at me, then up at TV screen, its racket moderated.

'Izzy 'n Amorican or whah? Ah fukkim!'

Brother takes two gins and lime, then off to dig in garden; his compost heap needs some attention. He allows himself little free time but finds it refreshing to dig after a long day in the County Council office.

He is famous for his refusal to accept bribes.

4 *October*

Another dental appointment at 2.00 p.m. Downpour woke me at 4.00 a.m. Lightning over hills, moon scudding through clouds. Storm reaches crescendo, abates, then comes again. I lie listening, comatose, warm and secure as Cooney's wood is buffeted by gale for an hour. Late for appointment.

Recalling (under the needle, to piped Muzak) Stella's unlikely account of her dental appointment 'at nine' in Westland Row some years ago. She wondered: Was it a.m. or p.m.? Went in the morning, street deserted but for man who opened his overcoat to expose himself naked to her. She bashfully looked aside, saw two rats copulating in the gutter. Query: Do rats under observation couple in broad daylight? Are there dental surgeries in Westland Row?

5 October

Ned Ward visited Dervorgilla in hospital. Injection delayed, in much pain, stoical, brave.

7 October

Aerogramme from James: 'Jane met us with a deep tan. England seems unusually dull and pseudo after Spain. *Yo busco trabajo.* Carlos singing out of tune as usual.' Died this week in Deya on the island of Majorca that vain poet Robert Graves (1895-1985), sometime *amigo* of the Kerrigans, buried in Deya Cemetery with hat and cape. Died too that acid man Geoffrey Grigson, poet.

Through D.'s binoculars saw what I took to be large deer stalking through far-off meadow; turns out to be a pair of cavorting horses.

A couple called Mudde or Sludde are visiting D. today. Ned came at 8.oo a.m. to collect her backbrace.

Ned Ward is thirty-six to Christina's twenty-two. Alec Stone left his wife to live with another woman: such behaviour is 'frowned upon hereabouts', says Ned. As I fancy his liaison with Tina is frowned upon.

The year 1985 remains bizarre through the autumn: we had 'summer' in the month of October and on the eve of Oiche Samhna they were still saving turf in the West of Ireland. The chances of getting a bank of turf, being footed in the last week of October, to dry before the November frosts must be slim. The odds did not inhibit some cutters in Mayo. In places the struggle was to get turf saved earlier from sodden banks. Others found that turf 'lumped up' on the roadside, ready for tractors to haul it home, was sodden from the rains of summer. The October sun was not a great deal of help for it was a 'dead' sun with no back-up of drying wind to help evaporation.

31 December

Died this year: Shiva Naipaul in London, Italo Calvino in Rome, Axel Springer in Berlin, Simone Signoret in Paris.

At Chepstow races in wet green Wales the favourite Powerless was nowhere, while a rank outsider with the unlikely name of Pigeon came romping home at long odds. So ends this peculiar year.

All yesterday the phone rang persistently.

Someone is watching; someone is listening. A glow of fires along the hills and Shandon bells ring in the new year.

Not much of an obituary for Böll in *Die Stern.* He came before Grass and the Swiss

Frisch who had helped Grass to get published. What hope had a German writing in German just after the war ended when *Tin Drum* came out?

Böll was suffering from severe circulatory problems in the legs; on returning home to the Eifel Hills after visiting hospital he died just hours after arriving. Böll was sixty-seven. Fortieth anniversary of Los Alamos tests in New Mexico.

Died this year: Heinrich Böll, Calder author, aged sixty-seven at his home near Cologne. I recall the big dome of a forehead freckled like a thrush's egg, pale-blue exophthalmic eyes staring from a clown's face; a walker in the hills. He had been correcting the proofs of *Gruppen Bild Mit Dame* (Women in Front of a River Landscape) just before he died. The Bölls had a summer cottage on Achill, had translated *The Third Policeman*.

Also passed away: Patricia Cockburn at her home in County Wexford. She understood the language of pygmies. And at her home in Galway Maine Ni Scollig died; how many years ago had I heard 'Eileen a Rune' on an old cracked 78 rpm, in Porchester Terrace?

All dead now, all the sweet singers gone into the world of light.

Dervorgilla Doran's symbol is a three-pronged fork. Cohabiting requires the nicest readjustments; as in the days of sail, tidal and wind shifts, management of sails, the chops of the Channel on a dirty night.

No smoking permitted in the salon.

The cup I was using was her favourite and could I please use another? Could I lend a hand with the garbage that was putrefying?

A breeze stirring the young pines disturbs the restless spirit of the dead Cooney. The wind blows through the wood; at night, tucked up in bed, I hear the sea pounding away behind the brake of pines.

Dervorgilla intends to let out the mobile home for an undisclosed sum this coming summer. The drains have already been dug and connected up with the sewerage system of the bungalow. The asking rate for Ballymona Lodge in high summer: £175 per week.

PART IV:

The Tomb of Dreams

The other day I came upon a diary I kept in 1977. That year I was the happy recipient of $7,000 from the American Irish Fund disembursed in some style at Arus an Uachtaran by the late William Shannon, the former American Ambassador, bald as a coot. It was a most timely subvention.

With Paddy Gallagher, the RTE cultural linchpin, as outrider and bell ringer I set out to scour the west in search of suitable accommodation. This is the Dublin part of that diary, the summer of 1977 in the time of the Provo killings.

– 44 –

The Trinity Professor

Dublin was infested with mice in the twelfth century. Dung-heaps, free-roaming swine, hog-styes, noxious stenches from the slaughter of cattle polluted the air in the thirteenth century.

In the mid-seventeenth century there were wolves in Wicklow. A public wolf-hunt was ordered in the ward of Castleknock, only six miles from Dublin.

There are thirty abattoirs in Dublin today. Slaughtering goes on at night and at weekends. In summer, in hot weather, two ladies in Rathmines keep their windows closed and avoid the garden humming with bluebottles.

The Trinity professor wears fishnet stockings, suspender belt and bustier, a Cupid's bow painted on the lips with the reddest lipstick and hair tied back with a scarf. He-she likes to mingle with the Ballyfermot rough trade drinking tea in the kitchen of the whorehouse and they have been told to call him 'Mary' and not to laugh at her in her fishnet stockings.

When he-she isn't mingling with the hard men in the kitchen she-he has to do housework, and the whore is strict. The house can never be clean enough with this sloven Mary sighing and scrubbing the toilet bowl with her bare hands, thinking of the hard men in the kitchen. But it won't do, it's not clean enough, not half clean enough for the mistress, who has no choice but to whip the arse off this slutty maid, the dirty thing.

The Trinity professor has not had a natural erection since he was systematically beaten as a boy by the Brothers who made him what he is, the sloven Mary in the whorehouse who crawls on hands and knees, in fishnet stockings and falsies, and cleans out the lavatory bowl with her bare hands, and is beaten by her angry mistress.

Never before such disparity between those who have and those who have not.

The Dublin pimp takes up his position. Hidden from sight in the deep hanging cupboard he unzips himself and applies his eye to the small peepholes he has bored at eye level and holds his breath.

In the bedroom under observation his whore-wife performs fellatio and unnatural acts with her grunting clients, unaware that she is under observation. She earns £700 a week. The husband in the dark watches, sucks in his breath, stands stock still, as the exiled Emperor at Longwood House on St Helena spied on the English watch coming on and off duty.

On the window-ledge outside the back bedroom at Emor Street, the weighing-scales fidget in the breeze. All night they fidget in the breeze and by morning the little pans are half full of rainwater.

Then the traffic on the South Circular Road starts and the early jets come in, whereupon the neighbour's dog howls. The mother spanks her little daughter. The child weeps.

The hidden pimp neither drinks alcohol nor smokes, but treats himself to expensive clothes, runs a Citroën. When his whore-wife goes off the game he beats her, plugs up the peep-holes with cigarette filters.

Two lapsed Republicans were shot dead in Dublin, as a salutary lesson for the rest. Seamus Costelloe, Chairman of the Irish Republican Party, had absconded with party funds from a train robbery at Sallins. When John Lawlor, the Ballymore Eustace haulier, revealed the whereabouts of hidden arms dumps to the police he had signed his own death warrant.

'Call me Gus.'

'I'm Imelda.'

'My pleasure.'

The hidden prompter couldn't believe his eyes or ears, no longer recognised his own bedroom nor his own wife, Milly O'Callaghan that was; both bedroom and wife had undergone a subtle transformation, substantial sea-changes, become film set and star for a porno movie.

'This is our new bedroom. Fancy a drink or a snack? Are you peckish, Gus?'

'Ah, now, Melly . . .'

The sleazy dialogue is spot on, the bedroom transformed, the bedclothes turned back, the curtains drawn, the door locked, the TV pushed aside, the carpet Hoovered, obese client and whore-wife already buck naked. Gus is blowing out his cheeks like a bullfrog, unsober enough to act brave and bold, outspoken about his requirements, gazing down complacently upon his own particular hairy grossness.

He lies on the bed as though it were his own, his greasy head resting on the pillows, gazing down, a glass of Paddy balanced on his hairy chest; a heavy-breathing adenoidal type with unhealthy skin white as ebony, matted curly black hair, a regular forest darkening the armpits.

'If I said I wouldn't come in your mout', Melly, I'd be telling a lie. You know, like saying the cheque is in the post.'

The hidden husband is rigid as a hare in its secret form. What did *abasement* mean?

In the hanging-cupboard he can neither blow his nose nor clear his throat and can hardly blink his eyes, riveted to the peep-holes. Oddly enough here is another Fergus, unless he is sailing under false colours, and using an assumed name.

'Ah now Melly.'

'Ah now Gus.'

Trousers about his knees, grasping a fistful of tissues and breathing shallowly, his eyes fixed on the action, the concealed pimp is tense and rigid as a hare confronted with a hound.

'Ah now Gus . . .'

'Blow me, Mel.'

How teasingly adroit she has become, his Milly, professionally tarted up, that is to say provocatively undressed to velvet black choker about the neck, one snappy red garter about the bulging thigh, false eyelashes, eyes heavily made up, rouged nipples, the works, and all to pleasure this slug with hands clasped behind his neck as if casually sunbathing on the Sandycove sea wall. The pimp-husband whose name is Fergal grasps himself and applies dilated pupils to the peep-holes, preparing to ejaculate with the client who now is reduced to uttering a series of great hollow sea-lion hootings as the kneeling whore-wife, stilettos sharp as daggers, works upon him. In the bedroom that seems to expand and contract he utters a great hollow staglike bellow, a terrifying mating call, and plunges both hands into her hair, fuzzed up, crimped and dyed black.

In a trice the Cork train has departed from Platform 2, sucked into the void. Imelda Lurcan will never be found.

'We Irish think thus,' *pace* Bishop Berkeley, the tar-water expert. We think as we do because we do as we think; but who do we think we are? My late philosophical friend Arland Ussher phrased it elegantly: 'As our forefathers thought, we act; and our descendants will act out what we thought.'

Tame perks everywhere in Ireland, dog agility courses, Ho Chi Minh (He Who Illuminates) walks, Crazy Prices, Chinese and Italian takeaways, dual carriageways to all points; golf ranges, heritage and interpretative centres, safe houses and dawn meets; perfect piggeries; a time-clock in every oven and a big fat bun in every one. A jumbo-fridge for the rich

O'Hanrahans and jumbo-jet to foreign parts for the nice Miss Kerrigans. (Client and whore-wife are buck naked as if about to try a few falls at all-in wrestling or undergo a medical examination; her fingers sink into his soft yielding flesh as into plump blancmange. Obese and hairy Gus wears only black socks, perhaps ashamed of hammer-toes or for some whimsy of his own, an act of pure bravado.)

The sudden shadow of a flock of wheeling pigeons crosses the patio of sunflowers, circles about Avoca Road and Orinoco Street, settles on the ridge of the roof of the City Building Suppliers opposite Mick's shop. The old lady scatters Marie biscuits in her cramped backyard fetid with their droppings. Two hundred and more of them line the roof above us, keeping an eye on the giving hand; you can smell them when the breeze blows in the wrong direction. The melancholy drone of bagpipes, like a giant sobbing, the blackbird singing *Aujourd'hui!*, the low shifting clouds; all tell you it's Dublin, shower or shine.

In Searson's snug opposite the humpbacked Portobello Bridge, behind coloured glass, tobacco fumes hang dense. Jack Yeats used to recuperate in the nursing home opposite, after an exhibition at the Waddington, and give the nurses hell. Now it's a region of saunas, massage parlours, whorehouses.

The antiquarian bookseller uses the snug as his office. He is on the phone to a client in Killiney. A thick bunch of keys depends from his waistcoat pocket. Now he replaces the receiver. Now the door closes behind him. A truculent young worker with lime-stains on his blue overalls is calling his mammy in a gruff, manly fashion:

'Hello, Mammy. I'm just after walken in this min-yute. Can you put on me dinner right now?'

– 45 –

Walking in the Dream

It is the last day of a curious year.

A grudging daylight already fading by three in the afternoon, a frugal grudging daylight leaking away, just as before, as I seem to recall from the days of my youth. It's this melancholy climate that makes the Irish what they are: Farsoonerites to a man.

The weather is neither good nor bad, an overcast grey day. Typical

Dublin weather, you might say. Sea-fog and rivermist mixed; turning to fucking drizzle in the late afternoon.

Turned fifty this year.

Basho's age when, ill again (dysentery?), he undertook that last marathon hike into Japan in 1694. A year younger than Jane Bowles (be good enough to move on three centuries) when she died of a heart attack in Malaga, Capital of Sorrow. In a snail-bar in the brothel quarter I came upon the ghost of Terry Butler (RIP) late of Shanganagh Bridge and Bologna (and never shabby in life) who failed to recognise Rodrigo de la Sierra darkened by long tramping in the Almijaras.

Tired of walking in the dream I have returned to the country where I was born half a century ago; it doesn't feel like the place I knew any more; it appears to be most dreamlike itself. 'In my dreams I wept,' Heine wrote.

Great grey-backed herring-gulls squall over O'Connell Bridge where thin itinerant children beg, as their mothers before them, as their mothers before them, theirs before them. So much for the waste and futility that is our world. The gulls release their heavy loads.

The Liffey hasn't changed much. Anna Livia smells as before, oilslick and Godknowswhat flow by the Corinthian Cinema, its neon-red lozenges reflected in the river are Rimbaud's 'Arctic flowers that do not exist'. Slug-gishly stinking she crawls on, dragging her effluent out into the bay. I am in Dublin again; everything tells me so.

The shabby buff-coloured city conveys the overall impression (a shrug of the shoulders) of 'Make the best you can of what you have, it's all there is, there's nothing more.' 'Feeling only so-so,' they used to sigh forty years ago; 'only fair to middling'. Reasonable health was very much an off-chance.

The environs abound with unpleasant innovations (piped Muzak in buses) as well as pleasing old familiarities: the illuminated Bovril sign over College Green has been taken down, but immortalised in Beckett's *More Pricks than Kicks;* Magill's remains in Johnson's Court.

Are the memories of things better than the things themselves?

The city has changed in my absence, you never know how these things will turn out. Within the airless precincts of the modern lounge in what was the Sign of the Zodiac is a man of double deed in grey suit and bow-tie, sitting on a high stool with drink in hand, smoking a cigar and immersed in *True Detective* ('I Tried to Make It Look Like Rape'). The lounge is ruthlessly modern in a chintzy way with metal scrollwork in curlicues, phallic beer-pulls with hunting motifs and LasVegas-type cash registers for ringing up the change.

Renaults, Cortinas and a Mercedes wait in the reserved parking lot of the Meath Hospital, with a surgeon's squash racquet thrown into the back seat of the Mercedes. The country-bred nurse shouts loud personal questions of an intimate nature, as though interrogating half-wits. Porters stand about in green smocks. A dead man is pushed in on a stretcher.

Wishing to be well, when not exactly ill. Wishing to be ill, when not exactly well, I want everything to be still and at the same time everything to be in constant motion. And I want both to happen at the same time. Can that be arranged? The cock always crows at one o'clock on the third day of March every year for me.

Nico's in the evening.

'Were you at the Curragh today?'

'I was.'

'Had any luck?'

'I had.'

Pause.

'Is Tom inside?'

'He is.'

Longer pause.

'Tell him Mickey wants Jewish macaroni. Macaroni from Jerusalem. Tell him that.'

Night approaches.

The bus crews are drinking quick pints in Agnew's of Anglesea Street near the quays. Spent cartridges in William Street gutters, shattered windscreen glass and clots of blood (presumably human) in Dawson Street opposite the Royal Automobile Association. The renovated Mansion House is like a Christmas cake with icing or a Christmas tree stiff with false hoar-frost; Yeats would have been pleased. No beauty but hath some strangeness in the prescription. The postmen and the garbage collectors are on strike.

The dead are all around; very dear friends all gone home. We cannot escape them, even if our memory retains only indistinct images of them. Death is a silent picture, a dream of the eye; such vanishing shapes as the mirage throws.

An old Pope died in the Vatican. The Pan-German, pre-Socratic thinker and proto-Nazi Martin Heidegger died in Messkirch, his home town, aged eighty-six years. He had been influenced by Parmenides, Heraclitus (flux) and Hölderlin (insane); arguing that being (*Sein*) cannot be thought but remains a question raised by thought. Farewell the old fart.

Also passed away this year: Cearball O'Dalaigh, having fallen off a ladder in Kerry, who resigned the Presidency on an ethical point, and whom I once heard speaking the most mellifluous Gaelic to issue from a man's mouth, dressed as for a safari in bushboots, a sand-coloured outfit, officially opening an alfresco sculpture exhibition by the Limerick sculptors in a field near the sea. Do not come down the ladder, Cearball, I have taken it away.

Also died: Dr Michéal MacLiammóir (born Alfred Willmore of Cork) whom years before I had seen prancing like Nijinsky's faun on the boards of the old Abbey stage, preposterously got up as Aleel in a daringly brief white shift short as decency would permit, in Yeats' no less preposterous play *The Countess Cathleen* ('Did that play of mine send out certain men the English shot?'). Thespian, playwright, painter, linguist and man of many parts, he was one of the rare sights of Dublin, passing through in heavy make-up, or emerging from one of the Gents in Stephen's Green; an emanation from a previous age, a dandy in war-paint, an alarming fairy. Once I had seen himself and Jimmy O'Dea, dressed as women and camping it up with eyelashes and pouts at a great Christmas panto at the Gate.

The bagpipes played mournfully all through one miserably wet afternoon in Emer Street near the South Circular Road in the Liberties, the gasometer sinking, the gulls squalling.

I ride through Time. Dead times and places return to life, the dead walk again. Two in particular, a man and a woman. Peter Allt was killed stepping on to electrified railway tracks somewhere in England, *en route* to academic tenure in Holland. Gerda Schurmann (née Fromel) was drowned in the Atlantic attempting to save her son Wensisclaus who had got into difficulties in the water off a Mayo beach.

I see them walking around Dublin with set faces, seemingly ashamed of themselves and as if under punishment, condemned in some way; averting their eyes they hurry by, never together, always alone. Had they met through me, when alive? *Defunctos* are everywhere. Whenever I pass, afoot or by bus, the new high-rise apartments in Abbey Road, Kilburn, London, I think of Gerard Dillon (RIP), who had lived in the basement of his mad sister's flat with a large gingery cat called Whiskey. He used sand in his paintings, worked as a night-porter in some West End gentlemen's club, toting baggage and stoking the boilers.

He moved to Dublin to begin his death, sharing a house with Arthur Armstrong, another Northern painter; and died of the third stroke that he had feared would finish him off, which it did, in his fifties, as two brothers before him.

Condemned, they hurry past with heads averted. Some of their *horror vacui* infects me. But then horror is perfectly natural. Our history is not as others know it. Never was; never will be.

On reclaimed ground at Ringsend near the site of another Provo 'execution' (in Irishtown Seamus Costelloe got it in the face with a double-barrel shotgun) the soccer players are struggling.

'Hurra, chaps, for the man who got the curly goal!'

'Clap for the north wind!'

In Grogan's of Castle Street an inebriated man shouts in mock-rage 'Fasschist baste!' A couple of hopeless cases sit boozily on the steps of a deserted house in Liberty Row, staring at their broken boots. The silver beech saplings dance alongside the canal near Paddy Gallagher's dream-house. He too gone to his reward.

Permanently worried and permanently watering pale-blue eyes follow the close print (at Shelbourne Park dog track the brindle bitch Glen Rock 'literally staggered' from the No. 2 box and failed to reach the first bend; urine tests had been taken; at White City in the English Derby, Glen Rock hit the rails).

Customers come in for loaves of Boland's bread and bottles of Lucan Dairy and Mick serves them absently, lost in the dream where Glen Rock is hitting the rails at White City or coming drugged from the No. 2 box. His big red-faced son is in the Gardai. His shop smells like a country shop in the country of my childhood (King's in Celbridge) when everything alarmed me.

Mick looks dead-beat. He lights up a fag, covers his puffy face with a soft stubby hand, the index finger darkly stained. MAN HELD FOR PUB MURDER declares the *Evening Press* headline. The Ballymore Eustace haulier John Lawlor had been shot dead by the Provos in Timmon's public house in Essex Street one lunchtime: summoned there by the hit-man ordered to 'execute' him and shot with as little compunction as the killer would have given a mad dog; Lawlor sipping the coldest pint he was ever to swallow.

Mick heaves a heavy sigh, licks his fingers, turns a page. Skies over Dublin, shower or shine; the subsiding gasometer, the ebbing Tolka, the filthy incoming tide dragging the weeds this way and that; skeletons of bikes thrown in, sodden bread, squalling gulls. So, so, it must be. *Es muss sein.*

– 46 –

Native Son

One grey morning in Timmon's didn't I fall into conversation with a garrulous returned Native Son who had lived for many years in a poor part of New York and was now back in Dublin where he had found employment in St Brendan's, formerly Grangegorman Lunatic Asylum.

In his high apartment he had paid sweeteners – bribes or protection money – to the Costa Rican garbage collectors. Otherwise your garbage wouldn't get collected, or they'd do something unpleasant with it. Speaking of garbage, he had thrown Tennessee Williams out of his place one night; Williams was very drunk, had come with one of his bum-boys. He thought that Brendan Behan was a shy man. I could have told him otherwise.

On another night he had to throw out an even drunker Burl Ives. He had seen Cassius Clay (Muhammad Ali to be) in the ring fighting Spinks. 'Clay took a punch from Spinks in the solar plexus that could be heard in Pittsburgh.' The story is repeated later, Pittsburgh becoming Phibsborough. He tells stories of suicides in St Brendan's, all true, 'as sure as you're putting that cigarette in your mouth'.

He feared for the world, the state it was in; a third world war would not happen; instead we would have world famine. Ireland had forgotten too soon.

Fifty percent of the Dublin phone booths have been vandalised and all the phone directories stolen for lavatory paper, the booths converted into urinals. Mick is out of briquettes. Six bullocks are being driven by two herdsmen in dungy Wellingtons, what the Germans call *Blücher,* into the abattoir in Swan Alley, for it's slaughtering time again. One of the herdsmen in a crushed hat, seen from the back, is a dead ringer for my late friend Paddy Collins.

A young bloodstained burglar was caught red-handed at three in the morning attempting to jemmy his way into Rosita's sea-green Morris Minor. She had thrown on a shirt and run out, armed with a bicycle pump, snatched up. The robber had a screw-driver in his hand and explained that he had been chased by a gang from Kelly's Corner. He was looking for the Meath Hospital. 'Well this isn't the fukken Meath Hospital; this is me fukken car,' said the Contessa in a great wax.

The bloodstained burglar was most apologetic and staggered off into the night.

On a television mast at least twenty metres tall a lone blackbird sings over Emor Street, above the home of the RTE producer Harris just returned from a short winter break in Benidorm. A deranged boy is breaking up the crazy-paving newly laid in his narrow back garden.

The Libyan wives are leaving Emor Street, baffled by the English spoken by the Irish, by Dubliners in particular, which to their ears sounds like some extinct foreign language. The computer-expert husbands will follow in a month with the Peugeots.

The student from Honduras is studying a book on venomous snakes in an effort to improve his English. A fellow over the wall three houses away practises scales on the bagpipes all through one long wet summer afternoon.

All the municipal dumps are closed; the nearest one in operation is out at Lusk. The number of tourists visiting the Republic is up by 14.5 percent, revenue up 32 percent.

Two-thirds of the rainfall normal for the month of August fell in the inner city alone; in several places there was thunder and lightning.

Eight inches of mud engulfed the Scout jamboree in Woodstock, Co. Kilkenny. Despite the mud and overnight rain the 4,000 parents and friends who visited the camp found the 2,000 Cub Scouts in good spirits and the Camp Chief danced with the Girl Guides from Vienna. French Scouts cooked crêpe Suzette, Ringsend Scouts dispensed cockles and mussels and some Dutch Girl Guides danced in clogs in the mud.

The the sun came out to provide a beautiful setting for an open-air Mass celebrated by Dr Birch of Ossory. Elsewhere archaeologists and patriots joined in a search for the grave of bold Robert Emmet.

All's well in the Liberties!

A discoloured sun sinks behind the brewery chimney. Leaning across the narrow deal counter, Mick the chain-smoker studies the racing form in the *Evening Herald*. Sunk in thought, the blue eyes water, following the print, the last third of a damp fag glued to a pendulous wet underlip. The puffy features are unhealthy, the body bloated like a toad, smoke gets in his eyes. Old Puffy Face, look forth! Not that Mick is old. He must be about my age, but he looks bad, a swollen caushapooka suppurating in damp aftergrass. Mick squints at the form sheet, his fingers stained to the joint by tobacco as if clipped in cowshit.

− 47 −

Down in the Country

It was the worst winter in living memory, the coldest and wettest in Connemara since 1840. We, the Contessa Rosita and Rory, arrived in Bealadangan in October to take up residence in a modernised cottage rented out by Johnny O'Toole for six months' letting. It rained non-stop for the first six weeks and we feared that the thatch would rot. The old postman cycled over the causeway and arrived swathed in oilskins like Skipper, rain or snot depending from the wings of his discoloured nose. It was impossible to keep the turf dry; snow and hail came after the rain, icy draughts poured under the door or blew down the chimney to put out the fire.

At night in the attic the rats cavorted, making no attempt to modify their antics or go about their nocturnal affairs silently as you would expect normal rats to behave.

In the cold winter kitchen we found claw prints on the dried grease of the frying pan. In the chill bathroom, rats' teeth-and-claw marks on the Pears soap. At night we heard them running rat races in the attic, enjoying rat hoolies in the deserted kitchen, come drunk from the skips of the pub opposite. An Hooker was a haunt of hostile Gaelic speakers in knitted woollen caps who shot pool: 'spots' and 'stripes' were their only English words. A few of them spoke English, but most reluctantly; the sad bachelor on an old and venerable bicycle who could name all the pubs on either side of Kilburn High Street. Sean Claherty the carpenter had returned after eight years working in San Francisco.

The late-arriving Gaels were known as Milesians in the Book of Invasions. The first Mesolithic Man reached Ireland at the beginning of the sixth millennium BC (6,000 BC) across the narrow sea. Even at the end of the Mesolithic Period (*circa* 3,000 BC) there may have been only a few thousand inhabitants on the island. The laws were not committed to writing until the seventh or eighth century, or thereabouts; one cannot be more specific. The gap of 'world pain' was a blank in Irish history; without Renaissance or Reformation, let alone Auschwitz caesura; the Irish were nonparticipants nonpareil with a hey-nonny-nonny no.

Out of the medieval darkness that stretched back into a Gaelic infinity came the first public lighting to Dublin in 1689 to a population of around

40,000 souls; gas lighting followed in 1825. But before that came the Norsemen out of the dark sea with their battle-axes, helmets and devil's horns, great hewers-off of simple Irish heads, great lusters after fresh Irish maidenheads and pillagers of churches, despoilers and desecrators of holy things.

The natives, ever adept at learning a hard lesson, repaid the debt for dishonoured sisters and mothers with compound interest, blinding and mutilating in their turn quite in the rough and ready Norse manner. For oppression breeds craftiness and hones the native cunning, breeds ultra-cruelty in its turn; inbred cruelty the cruellest of all, the long-deliberated-upon vengeance of the long oppressed. No greater oppressor than those who have been long oppressed and woe betide those who fall into their clutches.

While Belfast gets roasted by fire-bombs, Connemara is drenched by Force Ten gales.

The old grievances take on a new reality here; Cromwell mounted on a black stallion chases Pearse Ferriter on foot through the bogs, dispatches him with a sword-thrust through the fourth rib.

The corner-boys of Carraroe and Costello Cross no longer go to Mass but stand sullenly in the lee of the newsagent's shop, pawing the nude model-girl who smirks back at them in flaky colours from the front page of the *Sunday World*.

Granite boulders in which are embedded feldspar and pink potash are scattered about Costello Cross as if pitched there in the giants' battles of prehistory. They loved fighting amongst themselves down there then, bedad they did; first mythical battles, then real ones. Sufficient to say, the scroll of Irish history, with its quota of misery, blood and bluster, is still unfolding and unwinding.

I left Connemara and the weeping Contessa for a pueblo in the foothills of the Sierra Almijara in August; into the hottest Andalucían summer in living memory. In Malaga the thermometers registered 110 degrees and the birds dropped dead in their cages. No rain fell in months and the vines perished. The children took me for a Frenchman. In Connemara with my superior accent I had been taken for an Englishman and as such became the butt of Gaelic-speaking young pups disguised in their own language as in the folds of an enveloping cloak, muttering 'Up the Republic!' at the end of a chill bar in Carraroe, that sullen, misshapen village without a centre.

In the chilly pubs of Galway an obsession with maggots and worms prevails: the cheeky curate in the bar spoke of Herod's maggoty corpse and in the open vegetable market I encountered the double-negative interrogative when a raw-faced woman tried to sell me a stone of potatoes.

'Ye wuddent be wanten a stone or tua spudds, I don't suppose woodja??'

One final word from the Gallows Bar, Galway.

Brisk dialling of taxi rank.

Punter (a Mr John Small): 'Hellew there . . . wouldja send a taxi to the Gallows please?'

Taxi rank: 'Where?'

Punter (patiently): 'The Gallows.'

Taxi rank: 'Where?'

Punter (resigned): 'The Gallows.'

Taxi rank: 'What's the name?'

Punter: 'Small.'

Taxi rank: 'Right you be, Mr Small. I'll be right there.'

And he was as good as his word. It was pouring with rain on Eyre Square as usual.

Ireland is the most westerly country in Europe. It is twice the size of Switzerland but not itself a part of Europe, geographically or in any other way; one more step and it would have been into the Atlantic. It's as far out as the wind that dried your first shirt.

Of the four fertile provinces of Ireland, Connaught is the least fertile but the most westerly; and Connemara the most westerly part of Connaught. As is well known, the Protector (no protector of things Irish) tried to confine the entire Irish race therein, like pigs in a poke. He thought he was dealing with aboriginals, heathens, and acted accordingly.

Ireland is in many respects a melancholy place. Melancholy is the projection of a psychic state; in this case brought on by the centuries of occupation, a fixed subjugation. The sun is low there in winter, the days are short and weak daylight fades away in the afternoon, the nights long and black as a skillet. Day breaks reluctantly again, the low clouds dripping rain; high water and floods everywhere, swamped fields, the snow melting slowly off the Maumturks, the bars closed, the corner-boys clustering in the lees of walls, the toilets overflowing. A sheepdog trots by on the road, watched by the marble eyes of drenched sheep high up on the slopes of the mountainside. Seaweed drying on the fretwork walls, a *pucán* rotting in the harbour, the moon down behind the Maumturks, the wind getting up at four in the morning, the sycamores trembling.

There are signs (someone laid out the seaweed) and sounds (a donkey-engine meliorating out in the bay) of human habitation, of the humans themselves there is no visible sight.

Is this the essential charm of the West, under the flying clouds? Its emptiness. The skies over Mayo would make you dizzy.

The whole country is flooded. The lock is in the door. The bog is wet. Con is growing. The place is cold but wholesome. Never leave your country. God is generous. Con is blind. Una is young. A man can't be in two places at once, unless he's a bird.

'There is no beauty but hath some strangeness in the prescription,' wrote Lord Byron with his quill pen; and he is a lord, a man who knew of what he spake. Strangeness. A hundred square miles of island-studded water, haunt of mallard and widgeon, ptarmigan and cormorant, moorhen and gulls, swans upended in tarns of lapis lazuli. The strangeness of the known.

The gently rolling hills of Iar Connaught where romantic scenery abounds around every corner! Eyes of a bullfrog straining, veins in the forehead swelling, ceili music and set dancing, guided walks ('Corkery's Hills'), tame perks and much tomfoolery, learned lectures ('Corkery's Watercolours'), the twittery beat of the banjo, 'The Rose of Tralee' sung at closing time. And then?

'They do live on maggots.'

'Cockroaches an' lizards an' . . . schnails.'
　'Whassaaa – *schnails* is it?'
　'A small little fella altogether.'
　'*Scchnaills*?'
　'Slugs is all right.'

'I'll not take anudder wan . . . oh God no.'
　'A fine big duck now . . .'
　'Turkeys' eggs . . .'
　'Ho-ho! the bluddy buggers!'
　'Starten to lay now . . .'
　'Dark it will be until dis night is out.'
　'Turnen out bad . . .'
　'Getten very windy.'
　'That was the time you'd fly home by nine o'clock.'
　'An' still they were happy. There was nature in the people den.'
　'*Scchhhnaills*, is it?'
　'Are ye goin?'
　'I yam.'

PART V

Ballymona Lodge, 1986

− 48 −

Brittas Bay

Weak January daylight cannot harm the fragility of the Turner watercolours on display for one month in the National Gallery by the terms of the Henry Vaughan Bequest. By pure chance I walked into the room of Turners years ago. In an adjacent room the entire *Liber Studiorum*.

Constable observed Turner on varnishing day at the Royal Academy: 'Turner has been here and fired a gun.' It was his second visit. He studied his canvas – 'a grey sort of affair'. After staring fixedly at it for some time he added a dab of red and instantly a red lead circle converted itself into a mooring float. Turner cleaned and wrapped up his brushes and went home.

John Constable had a sick wife ('I do not contemplate a happy old age') and has been painting the same subject for fifteen years; a state occasion to mark the opening of a bridge over the Thames. Homage to that peerless recorder of that day on the river; a crowded barge, flags flying, clouds scudding, hats waved, a festive occasion, huzza, huzza! How many times had I passed by Constable's house in Well Walk, Hampstead, coming to and from the heath? 'Beauty lies in the eye of the beholder,' my mother used to say. 'Good bones will tell; breeding will out.' She was a great snob and fancied Anthony Eden in his homburg hat and pinstripe suiting. The Suez fiasco finished him.

Fine buildings, bridges and piers retain their dignity even as ruins and can improve with age; whereas advancing years do us humans no favours. What woman, an acknowledged beauty in her prime, can hope to keep her looks as an octogenarian weak in the pins, with false teeth, going deaf, the gloss gone from the skin as the sheen from the hair? Let alone as chapfallen crone of ninety winters, deaf as a post, balding, memory going, mind in ruins, a sorry spectacle wrinkled, grey and foolish. The raging beauties strip down to skeletons; they are no longer recognisable as the persons they were before, the cruel years having worked upon them, done irreparable damage.

Baroness Blixen eaten away by tertiary syphilis, a wedding present from Blore Blixen, Hemingway's gun-bearer. Djuna Barnes with her multiple ailments, aged ninety in Patchen Place. Louise Brooks aged ninety. Gloria

Swanson, an old hag.

More snow on the back ranges of the hills lit by weak mid-morning sun, presently vanishing into the mist. Pork fillet unfrozen and now under fan oven heat; bottle of Spanish plonk chilling in fridge. Cash Murphy and dishevelled friend padded by on foot, up to no good I'll be bound. Overcast all day; miserable aspect without cheered by crackling of wood fire. Hard dry oak and yew are rejects from Ned Ward's hurley stick factory, brought by Ned in his wheelbarrow. He also brings me gifts of lamb chops which I cannot eat, and river-trout in season, small and quite flavourless. His father was a great hunter and trapper who kept the Ward family going during the war, in Roscommon.

Wednesday, 8 January
Weather cleared and weak sun shone by one o'clock, thermometer steady at 45 degrees, cold persisting. More snow fell on back ranges of hills during the night. Twenty or more cars passed the gate heading in the Wicklow town direction; a funeral, but whose? Sodden rowan leaves and windfalls rotting on gravelled driveway. Depressed by bank statement that shows £3,000 reduced to £1,500 within two months. In pitch darkness I hear firm footsteps passing by on the road. Who? Slept ill. Difficult to rise.

Nine years before I knew him Ned Ward had the near-fatal accident on the Loughlinstown Road. He was driving his wife and baby Nelly back from the nursing home when a Jaguar travelling at high speed went out of control and ploughed into them. Ned was crippled for life, baby Nelly thrown free. The other driver was killed; no relatives of his called on the injured couple in hospital.

Ned Ward and friend out shooting pheasants or rabbits. His girl rents a flat above Ann Lait's office for £20 a week. It's unheated but not cold, a bargain at the price. Ned's brain-damaged wife has been in hospital under observation these ten years, reduced to the mental age of ten. She has become childlike.

The wife's relations disapprove of Ned and Christina cohabiting. He can lure young foxes out of hiding, breeds gun dogs, is mad about hurling and, I dare say, Christina, and visits his wife regularly.

'Spread out, Glenealy – you're all bunched up!' howls a supporter at the hurling.

Re-reading Yeats' *Autobiographies,* an almost merry book, as Ussher thought *Ulysses.* Yeats himself compared the opening chapters to that of a playful tiger.

One suspects that the sober Senator did not get much beyond the opening.

I saw Shelagh Richards taking a bow as the producer of *The Playboy of the Western World* at the Gaiety with Siobhan McKenna as Pegeen to Cusack's Christy Mahon.

Shelagh Richards's Sandycove bungalow was up for rent; I had phoned from Santa Cruz to Patricia Collins who told me that it was too late, Shelagh Richards was ill and probably dying, I should try elsewhere.

Today in St Anne's Church in Dawson Street a Requiem Mass was celebrated for the repose of the soul of Shelagh Richards, the original 'Nora' in *The Plough and the Stars,* the last of the last.

She was married in the same church to the playwright Denis Johnston, and may even have been christened there. A son and grandson carried the coffin.

Her closest friend Siobhan McKenna read I Corinthians, 13, Though I speak with the tongues of men and angels. Des Cave of the Abbey sang 'Nora', many wept. Hugh Hunt flew in from Wales. Among the distinguished mourners were the painter Patrick Scott and Ulick O'Connor in a snapbrim velour hat. The committal was held at Glasnevin Crematorium. *Irish Times*

Early March

Up bright and early, showered and breakfasted, offer of lift ('throw on your coat') to village by Biddy. Her son Laurence aged six has lost appetite, has a dry cough and spots (pink) behind ears. Dervorgilla consults Dr Spock and says it's measles.

Getting into her car Biddy informs me that vandals went on the rampage in Arklow the previous night and smashed windows; we should be prepared for them tonight. She had found a large black spider in the bath.

Biddy calls on a friend whose baby (one of twins) died stillborn; to find out the time of the funeral today. Then she decides not to go, because of Laurence and the danger of contagion. She drops me at the post office at 9.30 a.m.

I post a letter to Anthony Kerrigan in Palma. What's the Spanish for 'retained semen turns to poison'? *por favor.* Bought grey two-tone reefer jacket in Connolly's haberdashery for £28. The bright lad who serves me says jauntily that he is 'headin'' off for the 'Big Apple' soon; jobs were there for the asking. No work permit needed? Not to worry, it can be arranged. Irish Mafia.

As I stand before the long mirror in my two-tone reefer with many pleats and side pockets, the child's funeral cortège passes slowly behind the hearse carrying the small coffin and the townspeople bless themselves and remove their hats. I am told that the little twin sister is just surviving.

The people of Wicklow town have a great fondness for funerals. In winter hardly a week goes by without a cortège passing through to the cemetery, with pedestrians stopping in their tracks, doffing hats, shedding tears.

With his backside to the courthouse and the mangy Provo bar the pikeman stands aloft on his stone pedestal, caught in mid-stride like Paavo Nurmi, brandishing a non-existent pike, stolen by late-night revellers from the Periwinkle Bar.

— 49 —

To Arms! To Arms!

Remote villages along the Connemara coast are rough as their own rocks, or a Red Indian reservation near Spokane during a Republican convention.

Hereabouts the youth are ever in a chronic state of flux and all on fire with poteen and Republican frustrations, thwarted ambitions and hopes mixed up with sour disgruntlement with their own unhappy lot; which is passing strange, seeing they are taking home wages hitherto undreamed of in their wildest dreams, the pay packets from Japanese fish-canning factories and the sea-farming of mussel and oyster beds.

In boulder-strewn Drim in the far extremity of the western seaboard the solitary pub remains open until two in the morning and mighty is the imbibing there where none dare leave sober, where few even *arrive* sober.

Ancestral anti-English prejudice thickens the air even further. It's a form of perverted patriotism, like running a car on gas instead of petrol, as happened during our 'Emergency' (quaint Irish euphemism for World War II, which apparently was none of Ireland's business).

The cowboys or apprentice Provos see themselves as a daring combination of vigilantes and Community Alert, with the menace of hardline Ku Klux Klan, dangerous in their cups; i.e., most of the time. They do not like to hear the sound of the English language.

Hotheads such as these, seething with ancestral wrongs, real or imaginary, against all things English forever and forever, would have no compunction at all in obeying orders to shoot Captain Naric out of hand or butcher the luckless racehorse Shergar, both perhaps buried at night, subsumed back into the Irish soil. (The land itself, never a spent force, is in its turn the instrument of a remote past.)

I have seen their opposite numbers in Derry and shuddered. As savages of the jungle paint their faces for tribal celebrations, or football supporters daub theirs with the colours of their teams, shake rattles and howl abuse indiscriminately at rival supporters and referee, so the Orange enclave of what used to be called Ulster, in a similarly provocative fashion paint their gateposts, gable ends and even the pavement coping-stones of the streets with the colours of the Union Jack. When a Protestant Unionist salutes the flag he salutes more than his own glorious past; he salutes his great good fortune to be born a Protestant in Ulster, salutes the Boyne victory and his God-given and granted tenure on the land, salutes himself as the potent reincarnation of all this grace and goodness.

Thus envenomed sectarianism is incorporated into the rich fancies, the heated faces, the faciae of buildings and for all I know the very faeces of these embattled bigots, these rampant Orangemen to whom the green, white and gold is as a red rag to a bull.

Swift claimed that he could tell a Whig stool from a Tory's; but the men of destiny (obstinate as nippers resisting potty-training) incarcerated in high-security prisons and held on serious criminal charges not excluding murder, would deny all; deny even the Court's legitimacy and right to try them in the first place, abrogating to themselves the God-given right to make a mess where and whenever they choose, and proceeded to smear the cell walls with their own excrement, hot and steaming.

> It is a miracle, we may suppose,
> No nastyness offend the skillful nose;
> Which from all taint, with peculiar art,
> Extract savor and essence from a fart.

To us Irish the figures of the past, our ancestry, have the reality of fixed destinies; with historical themes our dialogue is formed by our awareness of them as *fated beings,* invisible but alert and out there somewhere, the calamitous Catholic defunct (the faithful who by definition need no conversion).

'A people lost in the Middle Ages refound and returned to Europe. A free Ireland, a world nation after centuries of slavery' was how the patriot Sir Roger Casement phrased it, sailing for Ireland with arms for the uprising in a German U-boat loaded down with sanitary pipes.

In the frozen forecourt of the Hotel of the Isles in deepest Connemara in the depths of a freezing winter, the solitary palm tree shivers. In the poor empty bar a frugal coal fire dies miserably in the grate.

In a warm conservatory at Kinvara, Garry Nally sits snug. In the tidy living room of his neat Georgian house there squats a curious love-seat painted powder-blue, cornflower blue; it's Lady Augusta Gregory's bath-tub with one side removed and some cushions thrown down for the lovers. We the pseudo-lovers, the Contessa Rosita and Rory, sit there and drink Jameson poured by a liberal hand. An aged Pomeranian wheezes on the thick carpet at our feet. On leaving, we are given bunches of grapes from the conservatory; it's real old-style Irish hospitality, the dram of whiskey, the kiss on the back of the hand, may the road rise with ye. We depart from Kinvara in good fettle.

One pale washed-out late November day in the Maum valley beyond Screeb I saw the white forms of distant sheep grazing on the steep slopes of the mountainside, reduced now to the size of lice.

A fierce dog the colour of a grizzly bear tore open a plastic garbage bag on the boreen to the beach. A single yellow court-shoe lay on its side on the sea road to Carraroe.

An injured Saint Bernard dog limps about the hall of Hyland's Hotel, its back broken by cruel boys. An aged sheepdog sleeps in the backyard. We drink in the deserted bar after midnight; the trusting owner says to leave tabs, pay when we leave.

The howling dogs of Castleconnell give collective tongue when the aged bell ringer hauls on the rope and the church bell tolls the hour. Has this been going on for centuries? The dogs start getting uneasy five minutes before the hour and assemble in the middle of the road; they begin to howl as the bell ringer hauls down the rope for the first loud clang of the bell. They howl loud and long, a most mournful sound.

An infatuated couple are glued together in an endless kiss near a wet wall in pelting rain on the drenched outskirts of Kilkenny town. Scores of hooks are screwed into the ceiling of a pub in Rearcross from which gumboots hang, as I speak to dowser and mystic Jim Armshaw who asks me my personal opinion of the Astral Body. The name Rearcross means nothing, it was a marking error on the Ordnance Survey Map, a cross to indicate a hamlet. Up to 1820 there were no roads; to 1887 no church, which was shipped from Scotland. The old IRA burnt down the barracks.

A winter butterfly emerges trembling from the woodwork of the bed we have dismantled, sluggish as a moth, all aquiver in the weak sunlight that penetrates into the chill bedroom.

A rainbow arches itself over the boggy land on an extraordinarily still November morning with the snow-capped Maumturks reflected upside down in the estuary. Someone is hammering on a roof, the sound meliorating off miles away into the still valley where the sober bachelor comes wobbling on his venerable bike, affecting to be pissed. Then a bout of brisk sawing; then absolute silence but for the distant cries of curlews, the air dense and quivering with cold.

Now the Maumturks are reflected inverted into the blue estuary where Johnny O'Toole (RIP) thirty years ago saw fifty hookers with sails set entering the little lagoon beyond the bridge where today two seals hunt mackerel, the bull driving the shoal to where the cow waits, hidden, pretending to be seaweed or a dark hole.

Their speed is astonishing in the water as they fire themselves at the shoal that scatters, frantic to escape those deadly snapping jaws.

The two seals go hunting for mackerel below the bridge where we watch; as the tide begins to flood in again. The wind cuts through the struts of the bridge with a vibraphone effect; down in the silence of the bright inlet the two seals hunt to kill with vibraphone effects.

The purple grape-coloured and violet glacial mountains are reflected all atremble in the estuary now. Silence of the cemetery where great age improves the headstones and the Celtic crosses; mildew and weathering have reduced the pomposity of the gravestones under which lie the last remains of several octogenarian males of the region.

One morning we surprised a hare sunning herself behind a boulder on the beach. The causeways and the little granite docks were built as relief work in famine times when Gorumna, Lettermore and Bealadangan were islets of the estuary, when the fifty hookers sailed past. Who is it speaks of the void eternally generative, of occurrence as part of an infinite series? Nietzsche?

I recall the Lake of the Blind Trout, the hare on the beach, the court-shoe on the road to Carraroe, the huge men in the pubs and their barely hidden animosity.

You could throw a stone across the little lake, really a pond fringed with bulrushes; we swam across it in the nip, sat on a flat boulder warmed by the sun. The inlets and tarns turn from cobalt to lapis lazuli as the sun moves behind clouds and the wind rises and the colours darken and the last leaves flutter from the copse of trees and the Maumturks huddle together for the only possible, to materialise and vanish, uncannily freakish, as if playing games with the observer.

Reality is concreteness rotating towards illusion, or vice versa,

arsyversy; illusion rotating towards concreteness. The Irish were Picts
before they were Celts, Picts covered in feathers and crippled with strange
superstitions but perhaps happy in their way. The world (the earthball
rotating in space) is much older than we had supposed. The smaller the
island the bigger the neurosis.

− 50 −

The Old Flame

Encountered whom do you suppose in a month of Sundays but the Old
Flame resolutely crossing Butt Bridge to Tara Street station. Her car
was parked in Dun Laoghaire to avoid the city traffic congestion; she
offered to drive me home. Her lending library books were the new Graham
Greene and Ben Kiely. She wore a summer frock and chattered, delighted to
see me. The train was packed with bawling babes that made her testy; she
said she was crippled with arthritis, in America she had to ask them to turn
down the thermostat, in restaurants she froze.

Her car was parked by the yacht clubs. She drove like the wind, aged seventy-one years, past her old home in Dalkey where as a breezy young thing
she had dived off the rocks and gone to school at Loretto Convent, never gave
cheek to her teachers, was a dutiful daughter to aged parents, was a good girl
long before she met me.

We flew by Dalkey Island where we went for a picnic one hot summer long
ago, took photos of the goats slaughtered since, saw a condom on a boulder,
were rowed back to Bullock Harbour. She was thirty-nine, I twenty-four; she
said she was a baby-snatcher.

Punnets of early strawberries were for sale by the roadside, getting
progressively cheaper all the way into Wicklow, famed for its strawberries as Aranjuez for its asparagus. Thirty years before we had eaten a
punnet of strawberries in a field at Swords before visiting some relative
put away in a mental home. We pulled in at a roadside fruit shop run
by Spaniards; the mother was at the check-out, one daughter *hablar*-ing
away in Spanish on the phone to Madrid, in a thoroughly Spanish ambience.

After Earl Grey, strawberries and cream, the Old Flame strolled in the
garden and took cuttings, chattering away to herself. She used to say that
when she talked a lot it meant she was happy. She was not an observant

person, nor had much intuition about others, living alone, widowed, not greatly changed from the person I had known thirty years before.

– 51 –

The Far Horizon

Friend Kluger phoned from Berlin to say the city was very hot and humid. The boss of the Berlin Zoo was a great admirer of my novels.

He (Kluger) wants to come here late August for a trip West. Storms in Leitrim cause the River Bonet to burst its banks and sheep are swept away in floods at five in the morning. Grass of the uncut lawn beaten down by wind and rain, the rats in the outhouse digesting their poison. Mist and drizzle obscures the nearest hill, miles off on the far horizon.

The coal is damp, the wood won't burn, the rats are all poisoned, Dervorgilla away foreign. Only a Spanish station comes clear as a bell on the airwaves, male announcer going on about '*nueva perspectiva*'; then some expert explaining the Aztecs in the language I love but cannot speak.

Mid-July drizzle of perpetual rain, awaiting arrival of orange mail-van seen speeding into Binnions's yard, with Blackie wagging his tail, preparatory to attacking postman. Pigeons cooing in Cooney's wood, wind rising, as I am handed the letter. A sweet missive from the Fruitcake, that variable lady born under the sign of Balance, the wonky scales, my ex-wife.

Front room: new rugs on floor, black lino paint around the edges, the books gleaming, inviting perusal, I hope, to those chaps.

Bornholm with Schocken. Favourable short review in *Publishers Weekly*.

Konrad's wedding in country. Maze of woods, marquee in clearing, garden full of summer people & summer children. A gracious figure came towards us with straw hat & gloves – mother of the groom – leading us straight to the marquee where none other than Kit Horner hoary & ancient stood. Looks as if you could blow him over. Overcome, watery-eyed at the sight of the three chaps . . . Soon there was wrestling on the lawn.

Very nice when most had left & the evening light slanted through the trees . . . Horner overstayed his welcome as usual, became incoherent. Rather frail figure, swaying across the lawn to have a piss in the trees.

I'm off to Boulogne this weekend with my boss Jackie Ennels. Back on Monday evening (4 days). Merry weather here with trees frisking about in the sun. A fond embrace.   J.

A small neat handwritten note on a cigarette (Old Holborn) roll-up gives an address near Barcelona:

> Valldoreix,
> Paseo del Romero 65.

Indicates the present whereabouts of Sean V. Golden, who gets about. In a briar patch in County Wexford some children out blackberrying found a leather-bound first edition of Carolan's harp airs. The *Cork Examiner* reports a 'spate' of moving statues of the Blessed Virgin, at Ballinspittle and in Kerry.

A Jewish jeweller comes down from Dublin for two months every summer to his bungalow near Ned Ward. They have lameness in common. The neighbour's foot was caught in a combine harvester and had to be amputated just below the knee. Ned refers to him as 'the Jew-boy' without any malice aforethought; and this the same good Christian (Ned) who arranged for a pauper Dane who died penniless in Dun Laoghalre to be given a decent burial in Glenealy among Protestants in the Protestant cemetery. Sven the Dane used to drink in Healy's pub and Ned Ward made a collection there and got them out to attend his funeral. Was that not the act of a true Christian? Yet he can call his lame neighbour a 'Jew-boy'; as he might call a Negro a 'nigger,' or a spade a 'spade.'

Cold morning shadows eerily slant from the side of the bungalow seen at an unusual hour, early for me, unaccustomed to warmed houses. Nescafé well laced with Jameson to hand.

Cycled to Wicklow by back road.

Arms of the harbour open to northeaster, pile of timber on quayside, little traffic going through, Healy pub closed induces a feeling of unreality peculiar to Wicklow port. The heart sinks.

Bought my vegetables from Fallon who used to sell stationery and typewriter ribbons. A box of greens for £5.50 and Anna singing as she makes out the bill, Michael (who formerly worked in a bank) whispering on the phone, organising contraband vodka. Crossed the bridge for gin and tonic at Leitrim Bar. Three fellows in black leather at snooker, Clifford Dowling (former butcher's boy) in one of his sullen moods. I hear fukken dis and fukken dat as I phone Sadie for a taxi.

Serene blue day with outside thermometer registering over 60 degrees. Clumped out in heavy Wellingtons across the Carmelite grounds by Stations of the Cross, no teasy novice lingering on rustic seat, no owl roosting above the path, no poachers gliding through; an old nun stares down from an upper window. A branch blown across the path by Hurricane Charley, a feeble game of tennis in progress on the hard court, deep rainwater pools on the path to the sea by the mucky farm, cattle bellowing in the byre.

I cross the meadow and over the dunes on to Magheramore beach to find the stream has changed course, now runs deeper and straight into the sea, too deep to wade across. I climb across the boulders on to Silver Strand. Sunbathers stuck into deckchairs outside summerhouses, transfixed in rigid poses of the sun-starved Irish longing for Benidorm. A little swell and collapse of waves on beach.

Scudding high clouds all day and sun going down behind distant hills in stupendous sunset, a mongrel sitting on kennel roof next door howling at it. Subside into armchair, push open sliding door: Hussar vodka and fresh orange juice on cubes of ice, what could be better. Rereading *The Periodic Table,* still mystified by the chemistry.

Biddy Doran has ambitions for her children, would have them talk nice, have nice manners. I hear them on the swing.

'Whin I ring the clock yiz must stop.'

'Now hold yer legs in or you might hurt dim.'

'Be nice an quiet.'

'Keep yer head down now an keep yer legs as well!'

'Goin roun an roun, dizzier an dizzier.'

'Ah GOD don't be holdin yer legs out!'

'Gimme a push. Give us a swing! Push me round about, fukken EEEeeejit!'

Dunganstown East, visit to Ye Moncken Holte.

Stella shows me the stiff yellowed pages of an album devoted to faded persons. Light thickens and the crows make wing to the rocky wood. My brother's fondest loves: Henry Williamson's *Chronicle of Ancient Sunlight* (in old Penguins) and the documentary films of Humphrey Jennings.

— 52 —

Stardust

W'ait here. I won't be long.'
        Taking an empty petrol can from the boot my brother set
        off into the night.
An hour later he returned to Lil Doyle's to say he had had no luck; walked
five miles in the Arklow direction and found no garage open. What he proposed to do now was to walk in the Dublin direction where there must surely
be a garage open, even on Sunday night.

'I'll be back in a jiffy.'

Off with him again into the black night.

An hour later the pub closed up and the lights went off. I sat on the wall
outside, smoking roll-ups and looking at the stars. In a while my brother
arrived carrying the empty petrol can: there were no garages open in Co.
Wicklow on the Sabbath. My brother had driven over an hour before closing
time and suggested a nightcap at Lil Doyle's. The Mini had run out of petrol
just before the Barndarrig crossroads and we had coasted into the car park;
where now we left the stalled car and set off on foot for Dunganstown.

Walking the back roads on the moonlit night my brother remarked on the
movements of the moon, how she raced across the night sky in three hours,
then vanished over the horizon. Where did she go to? What was she up to?
He thought it was passing strange. And why so fast? And what about the
Dark of the Moon?

'An assignation?'

My brother said again that he didn't understand Aristotle any more than
he understood the movements of the moon. In previous centuries it was
dangerous to travel on the roads; coaches were held up at pistol point and
pedestrians set upon by footpads and cut-throats.

'Look at London in Dickens's day.'

He marvelled at the difficulty of obtaining fresh fish on an island (Ireland)
surrounded by salt-water seas full of mackerel and fresh-water rivers full of
salmon. He and his wife had been vegetarians ever since Stella had been put
off meat by the stinks in a butcher's shop, from the days when pigs' carcasses
hung on hooks and bled into the sawdust. They had enjoyed a very tasty herb

omelette in Paris and decided then and there to become vegetarians, and had remained so ever since.

The moon went scudding behind trees into the clouds and then out the other side. My brother and I as lads had walked the front avenue at Springfield, puffing Craven A, passing along the road and up the front avenue past the lodge gate where the Keegans slept. We walked across Mangan's long field on stiff frosty grass and saw glinting moonlight reflected on the dormitory windows of the Collegiate School where forty or more Protestant orphan-girls slept, dreaming away the night. We now walked to Dungan-stown heights where my brother brought out an antiquated rusty Raleigh to take me the five miles home, giving precise instructions how to get there. Having walked five miles from Barndarrig crossroads, my perambulating brother would have covered some twenty-four miles in all, without a drink. And without finding any petrol. The car remained all night in Lil Doyle's car park. Could he not have borrowed a pint or two of petrol to get him home?

Not him.

− 53 −

Lammas

Up at 8.00 to thunder and lightning, overcast and drizzle followed by downpour. A heron flying by, changing direction from hills to sea, outside thermometer reading 60, down 10 degrees from yesterday.

Sunday Miscellany on RTE radio, a long-running arts programme old as the hills. Old-timer Big Ben Kiely, himself a reincarnation of Finn MacCool, the anecdotalist in the ingle, tells of a man aged forty who in his lifetime had lost forty-four overcoats. Ben himself will never see sixty again, drinks with the crypto-Fascists in the back bar of the Clarence Hotel on the quays with Brian Fallon of the *Irish Times* and the Austrian Ambassador; has a charge-account lunch preceded by a few drinks downstairs. After brandy and coffee and more tall tales, Ben noticed that his own new overcoat was missing from the coat-rack.

A brother is as easily forgotten as an umbrella (*pace* Mr James Joyce); but what about overcoats?

Telephone crackling as lightning strikes.

A grey crow on the fence-posts preening its feathers; line of silvery rain-drops like mercury along the black handrail of drenched patio. Dread of the Chinese gentleman arriving from Kyoto, a Mr Steve Sakuma visiting Arklow 27 June to 6 July, with accommodation arranged. Letter from a Mr Steve Jusick of Indiana, USA, requesting a signed photo or a few lines written by my hand from 'your great Scenes from a Receding Past'. Odd calligraphy. A Special Favor. An autographed collection of noted twentieth-century liter-ary figures. Thank you for your very kind consideration. Your friend Steve Jusick 8212 Rutledge Mersill, Ind.

This occurred on Sunday, 29 June, being the third Sunday after Trinity, the Trinity term in the law sittings coming on to Lammas.

1 August (Lammas)

Appropriately enough a *slim* letter from publisher to say 'royalties are still being made up', a thumping lie I'll be bound, with a familiar ring to it. *Balcony* sales of 'nearly 3,000 at last accounting' from presumptuous first printing of 10,000 remaindered and sold off at cost price to collectors.

Invitation to sup at Sutton across Dublin Bay with Cantwells. Sunrise 5.25 a.m., poor class of a morning, hung around waiting for phone call that never came, set off on foot at midday, given a lift to Wicklow by English-sounding fellow in broken-down car, claiming to know Cash Murphy.

Walked from bar to bar, none too pleasing, then gin in Grand Hotel. Double of Anthony Burgess in Wellington boots drinking Scotch and water. Took Wexford bus from outside hotel, sat on sunny side, boiling behind glass all the way to Bray. Made out £2.50 cheque to Dart, return to Sutton. Walked about Sutton looking for St Fintan's Road. Passed two Suttonites (male) out exercis-ing two dogs (mongrels), then a single male pedestrian (dogless) who threw me a look askance, as if he knew me. He hesitated as he passed, then stopped.

'You wouldn't be Rory of the Hills by any chance?' said he.

'A piece of him,' said I. 'You wouldn't happen to know the whereabouts of Eamonn Cantwell? St Fintan's Road.'

'I do. I'm his brother.'

Dined on spaghetti and home-brewed wine, up talking until 2.00 a.m., slept like log in spare room. Rose betimes and crept out, not leaving note (impolite). At 6 a.m. snuck past Elmcot on La Vista Avenue in a cul-de-sac, the residence of novelist Banville, his back to the sea as Heaney's desk faced a wall. Six in the morning not the time to pay a surprise visit; let sleeping novelists lie.

Roamed about harbour deserted but for wandering dogs like myself. Took first Dart out to Connolly station. Harbour full of trawlers in from Friday's storm that sank a Spanish vessel. Sphinxlike enigmatic Oriental woman seated in stationary train, obviously a character from the novel Banville is writing. Doors whoosh shut, Tannoy stops announcing imminent departure, and the train leaves for Bray.

Bray station is like old times. A Greystones connection in three hours. Decide to hike over the Head.

Greystones has become a home for dogs, fouling pavements, assembling in packs, snapping at strangers. Dined alone in Magritte Room (*Tiens!*) at La Touche Hotel formerly the Grand Hotel in my parents' day, where Sam Beckett (probably in the bar) heard the news that the Nazis had invaded Poland and decided to make his way back to Paris. Dined on half-bottle of Bordeaux and breast of chicken, small Magritte Room empty but for German couple near me. The loud confident male German guffaw that Beckett would have heard at the Closerie de Lilas at the close of day. Decided to overnight in Burnaby Hotel; retired early, stunned by air and hiking, slept the sleep of exhaustion.

– 54 –

James

Grand morning turns to gloomy afternoon with a wintry drizzle and cold rain blowing the birds about. While bathing my eyes there came a heavy thud against the front door. No challenge given, no word spoken, no loud abuse, and I with no weapon to hand but for Dervorgilla's trusty Turkish blunderbuss hanging on the wall. I waited for the door to burst open but nothing happened.

I waited, then drew back the safety locks and flung open the door to the light of a murky morn. No postal delivery van with engine running, no pale loiterer at the gate. I returned to bed with palpitating ticker and found with amazement the alarm clock in it. Who had put it there?

Almost dozed off when I was made to spring up again by a thud against the french windows. Took up heavy police torch, staggered into front room, found nobody there but a note in Dervorgilla's hand on the table which said 'Welcome home'. Flowers artfully arranged had already faded. Stale odour of unaired rooms after my few days' absence, signs of her careful occupancy.

Know your neighbourhood; someone is watching. A heifer bellowing in the mist, fingers of rain scratching on the roof.

My son writes to me from London: 'For me the present is full of fear & uncertainty of what will happen to me. Salud para todos. Cuidate y escrib- ame en tus ratos perditos (spare time). Canino de su hijo James.'

I have invited him over for a week.

His old drinking buddy at the Baird, Alex Diggs (Scotch and splash) for- merly of the International Brigade, has been cremated in Golders Green Cemetery. Why does he prefer friends either much older or much younger than he? They probably spoke Spanish together.

James is myself all over again, both troubled middle sons. The true misery began for him in Berlin, when I took up with Hannelore and the family began to split apart; classes in German after classes in Spanish. He attended the Nerja school in a white smock like the others, spent long hours in class, learnt nothing from Señor Pepito, a sort of Spanish Pickwick clapping his hands, ringing a bell, calling Jaime.

In Berlin, aged eight, he asked me: 'How did Jehovah ascend to Heaven in his bodily form?' Later he wrote of his *Mutti:* 'Her anger weakens me.'

Fathers don't see their sons. Not after the sons have grown up; the sons have begun to withdraw. I gave James 1,000 pesetas for his twenty-sixth birthday and he cashed it in a Torremolinos brothel.

Blind Hamm, the son, asks Nagg, the immobilised father: 'Scoundrel! Why did you engender me?' Nagg: 'I didn't know . . . That it'd be you.'

I don't see this thin middle son who stands six feet two inches in his bare feet, the whited extremities of an El Greco martyr, doing a Charles Atlas for the bathing girls of Brittas, gorging himself on Dervorgilla's raspberries and free-range chicken from the Belton farm; rather I see (a) a stocky confident child aged four standing on the upper bunk in a Ranelagh bedroom to recite something he had memorised for his granny, grandad and Uncle B; or (b) browned by the Spanish sun, aged six, the child who stood for hours by the stream behind Burriana to watch the water-bugs and frogs; or, hands clasped behind his back, the child who watched the palm trees being pollarded on the *paseo.*

His manner: slyly watchful, chastened and yet brash, uncertain yet per- sistent, contradictory, bilingually scatter-brained. He makes me sad.

Aerogramme love-letters wing their way to all points of the compass, for he is always in love, believing (wrongly) that in a carnal Paradise full of geishas he will be liberated.

'What do you call it?'

'A cove.'

'An alcove?'

'No, a cove.

'A cove can be a person too?'

'Yes.'

'How?'

'As a term of affection. They say "bloke" in London, here it's "your man".
A cove is a bloke, also an inlet, a little bay. As this one.'

His light streams out from the mobile home, parked illegally in the paddock, with an owl on the roof, he, being a great reader in two languages,
reads late. He is reading *Great Expectations,* picked out from among Dervorgilla's few books. The owl Minerva perched on the roof of the mobile
home, and another (or the same) on the telegraph wires humming with
gossip and hot scandal as we walked below on the first night he came
from his job as night security guard in a rundown hotel or whorehouse
on the Holloway Road. I noted in my diary: 'I am six months here. 70
degrees by midday. Many flies dart to and fro in the humid air, Blackie
kennelled.'

I recall the large puffy somnolent barn owl asleep in the telegraph wires
and the glitter of moonlight on the sea off Brittas and the pleasure of having
James with me, that I could show him an owl asleep.

He naps on the sofa after I have fed him, complains that the chops
weren't brown enough, a little colour coming into his face. Feed the starving. Free-range chicken, tinned salmon and salad, tomatoes and onions,
bacon, two brimming plates; he does not eat enough in London or eats the
wrong sort of food. He needs sleep, having outgrown his strength; the air
here is soporific.

Supper of cheese omelette, bacon and rice, slices of ham. James in armchair, plimsolls removed, El Greco toes clenched, writing to Marina.

He has found some clip-joint in bashful Wicklow town and returns at
three in the morning; I hear his plimsolls creep by on the gravel, and then
his light goes out.

He says he loves Wicklow (already, quick to love) and prefers the Nuns'
Beach to Burriana any day. I enquired how it had gone at the club. He drank
water, was approached by a queer, 'heavy hints were made', he walked home.
Hearty breakfast, toilet seat splashed with piss.

5 August

James departs, with country gifts for his mammy: dozen free-range eggs, jar of honey and apple pie from the Belton orchard, all good natural homegrown food for the family. James with glow in cheeks from walking, swimming, fresh air, changing punts for sterling, £20 plus £5 for the crossing. Sadness of his going.

For a week in July he was here with me, slept in the mobile home, walked the beaches, drank with me in the pubs, posed pectorally for the bathing girls, the lovely Brittas bathing girls, gorged himself in the raspberry bushes, lunched on mince curried in sherry, carrots and tomatoes, rice and raspberries and cream, reluctant to make eye contact (in case I should read his dirty thoughts?), retiring late to bed. 'Jane Austen has a habit of saying more than is necessary.'

Sun slanting through the young pines in Cooney's wood shines through the slats in the venetian blinds, reaches my table. September on the way and the days becoming perceptibly colder, though still preferable to the asphyxiating August heat of Texas – 'degrading', Eudora Welty called the New Orleans heat – those burning mornings when I left Palm Springs Apartments for the campus and my two classes. Sickening heat on Guadalupe Street aquiver in the early morning haze. Fresh orange juice and natural yoghurt with coffee and croissants at Captain Quackenbush. Relax at Quax. Tar-black grackles croaking rustily in the thorn trees, the fountains dry.

Sunday, 10 August

A wren on the fence in the rain; inky clouds passing at sunset, a white breast-feather fell from the sky. All signs are omens, the cruel old Romans believed, auguries. A cunty smell of fish in the clean bathroom, both impossible. Could it be kipper grease or roes of herring? I am alone again. Dull throbbing pain in left eye. Anguished epistle from James who is in correspondence with José (*El Jardin de Allado*) Donoso.

Dear Papa,

I returned safely, a weary journey on the train. This is not love but a sort of sick, lost longing of desire. Marina moved into squat. I have changed too dramatically since I met her.

I find I can only confide in you. You are my consolation, your presence. Will look for job, soon, soon as I get myself straightened out. I am weak, weakened from it all. Rory, tell me what to do, serious stern sensible advice is what I need.

I don't love her. She can have an affair with Claudio who she's going to share the squat with. Dear Rory, mind your way & take care of yourself.

Cuidate, J.J.

No sooner in the door than he began sending aerogrammes to Marina, whoever she may be; SOS signals, alarm flares, messages corked in bottles thrown into the sea. I too, at his age, was always besotted with someone, seeking salvation through love, itchy for response, any response.

James was ever a dreamer and a bit of a mystery, not least to himself, whatever about his estranged parents oft well-nigh demented with worry about him, the troubled middle son, which of course he played on as on a xylophone.

He was a baffling mixture of irreconcilable contradictions, charm and awkwardness, resourcefulness wedded to helplessness, forthrightness to fur-tiveness, flighty yet sagacious, simple yet devious. He read and spoke Span-ish, drank Budweiser, was alert with a desperate *joie de vivre* – an inept boxer who keeps coming on for more punishment: night-guard duties in that dark building of ill repute on the grimy Harrow Road.

'Will you ever forget the time Uncle Dodo came down from Largs to visit us?'

'I won't,' said I; 'not to my dying day.'

The turdy old bollicks had come good at last; some years after his visit he had invited James to be his guest at Largs. A friendly fisherman had taken him out after mackerel in a rowing boat, and his silent uncle had cooked gigantic steaks for supper.

Henry Williamson, my brother's old favourite (his dog-eared and 'foxed' Penguins), was aged twenty-four when he published *Life in a Devon Village,* the same age as my middle son when he had visited Ballymona Lodge. Wil-liamson had spent seven years in a Devon cottage with the barest necessities and two pet white owls for company when he wrote his Devon Village saga and began assembling material for *Tarka the Otter,* which he would rewrite sev-enteen times. It was our favourite book, read to us many times by Mumu.

Williamson was a lover of nature, the great outdoors and its creatures; his favourite noun must have been 'estuary', his favourite place Ventian Sands in Devon. 'Every hour out of doors is an hour of immortal life,' he wrote; a sentiment with which my brother would concur.

During the war he ran a nudist camp in Devon, taking German female nudists, tall Fraus and Fräuleins, which did not endear him to the locals.

As an old man he had visited Professor Burns at a house he had rented for a year in Battle main street and told him there was a three-week-dead shrew in the hedge. What a nose! I had come off an early train from London to Old Church House and Alan took me round the garden, told me of Williamson's wonderful nose.

It was the same Private Williamson who had crept close enough to the Boche lines to hear them talking, and flitted back to his own lines again, invisible as a poacher in the night.

'Every hour out of doors is an hour of immortal life'; Synge or David Thoreau could have written that, or John Clare.

I remember him standing on the upper tier of the bunk bed he shared with his brother in the garden flat at No. 47 Charleston Road in Dublin, reciting something he had learnt and memorised for his granny and grandpa and Uncle Bun and how he repeated all of it and would not be gainsaid because he thought he had had an indifferent hearing the first time. They all laughed at him but rather marvelling too, at his early sternness, a plump child on a bunk bed.

Or again behind Playa de Burniana staring for hours at a stretch into the irrigation stream at the Jesus bugs and the frogs.

Or again, with his hands clasped behind his back, studying the livestock in the yard of our apartment at Calle de los Angustias, a mule and a pig and fowl; studying them for hours as I came and went, unseen, on the balcony above.

In a very gloomy pub in north London (could it have been the Clissold Arms that was like the lounge of one of those liners sailing to India in the 1950s full of dull English people?) he had told me in great detail of a battle Cervantes had been in or had written about or had invented, he himself now long and lean as the Knight of the Rueful Countenance. Where had the plump child gone to?

Ezra Pound was ashamed of his parents when they visited him in London, ashamed of his daughter (whom he had abandoned and sent to foster-parents in Bavaria) when she visited him in Venice, perhaps even ashamed of himself in the traitor's cage in Pisa.

And I? I'm not ashamed of my son; wish him every happiness in his life. Sometimes he seems so *desolate;* he is myself over again, and yet not; it makes it harder for me to touch him. Why is that?

— 55 —

The Roscommon Fairies

I called on Ned Ward and found him working the power mower. The carroty Joe Junior, one of seven redheaded brothers, was scuffling the gravel; it was the brother whom Ned trusted least and he liked to have him where he could see him. Christina was ironing clothes and the TV on full blast; the setter bitch and her straying pups were reunited in the wire cage by the gate.

I said I'd call back later and we might have a drink at Mac's.

John Stamp had piled up a fierce turf fire in the open hearth under the stuffed fox. Pint in hand, Ned was disposed to speak of his childhood in Roscommon. When the parents were out Aunty Peg looked after young Ned. One evening as he was preparing for bed a strange fiery light flooded the bedroom. The Aunty blessed herself and said oh glory be to the God the fairies are moving house and you mustn't look at them. The Aunt would not let him go to the window to watch the fairies moving house. Lights were flickering along the path in the dark and the dog became hysterical and began barking and running round and round the house. The Aunt took out her beads and kissed the cross and told young Ned to say his prayers quick.

'A fairy breeze went by. I got back into bed. A fortnight later didn't a brother take bad and die in Birmingham.'

(Who was that Taffy poet who would not venture out at night for fear of the fairies? His name escapes me. When he took to walking in the hills he felt himself to be a *different being*.)

The stuffed dog-fox in the inglenook had a melancholy glazed look in its eye as though it had suffered a painful death in a trap and been cut open, dosed with preserving liquids and fixed up with a pair of glass eyes lifeless as marble, then sewn up again by the incompetent taxidermist and wired upright on a wooden plinth. On long spindle legs it resembled one of the lean timber wolves that incessantly patrol their outdoor compound in the Dublin Zoo all winter long; as though by persevering a gap might be found in the high fence and the captive break out past the polar bears.

Ned Ward had lured a young fox out of a ditch by imitating a rabbit's death throes. He had come upon a dead stag in a ditch and sawed off its head, softened it up in a bath full of water until the stink almost drove him from the house. A friend was mounting the head and span of horns on mahogany; it would look well above Ned's trophies for marksmanship.

Ned drove us back to Ballymona Lodge; when his girl Christina retired and Ned joined me for a nightcap. I took out Dervorgilla's school atlas and showed him Mahón on the Island of Menorca and told him I would get there one day. Sand from the Sahara blew into the living rooms of high apartments.

Ned Ward and his two brothers were given huge meals of steak and spuds by a kindly Mrs Coffin in their Birmingham digs when they were working on the building sites from 8 a.m. to 8 p.m. He put in overtime, did extra work, bought himself a motor-bike, ate huge meals served up piping hot by the kind Mrs Coffin. He put money away. At the end of the day he was knackered, dog tired.

He tells me this over a Chinese meal in Bray. In the headlights of his car we see a vixen fox trotting home, and a mile on, her cub, who gets confused by the light. Ned slows, the cub disappears into a weedy gripe.

Taking a drink in the Forge one day I heard a voice say 'the hay bogey', and later, 'in the haggard', and it occurred to me that soon these terms would be lost like Atlantis, words that had gone out of use, for things that no longer existed. Like the last Manx street-crier ringing a handbell, selling or buying junk, on a float drawn by a sad horse in Douglas on the Isle of Man. Extinct as the Manx language itself.

Pasture and paddock; were they the same?

'I cried all night,' a voice said. 'I cried my heart out.'

– 56 –

Big Mick (Ned's Racist joke)

Big Mick of Cahirciveen was the tallest and strongest man on the building site but when he had the drink taken he would get out of hand and offer to fight the best man in the Eireann Go Brawl pub where they drank in Birmingham.

The lads got sick and tired of this and didn't they go and hire a gorilla from a circus, chain it up in the pub cellar and the next evening when big Mick got stroppy and started to throw his weight about didn't six of the lads lay hold of him, roaring and bawling, and fling him down the cellar steps, shouting out: 'Down with you now, Mick you big fucker and fight your match!'

Then a hurly-burly and almighty set-to began below in the dark (the lads having removed the electric bulb) with thudding uppercuts and piledrivers and deep gorilla grunts and hollow groans and the sounds of barrels and bottles fucked about and the stuffing being knocked out of somebody with thumping haymakers in the breadbasket, with blows landing loud and resonant as the big Lambeg drum being lambasted on an Orange parade that could be heard at Killybegs; then one final awful blow and dead silence.

The lads set down their pints and stared at each other. Gob, had the gorilla laid out big Mick? They were getting set to rush for the door when it blew open and there was big Mick in a lather of sweat, with the shirt torn off his back.

'That's the trouble with them black lads,' says he. 'Give them a fur coat and they start gettin' grand notions about themselves.'

The Afrikaans version of that joke goes something like this: unsober Afrikaner farmer is sitting drinking outside bar in Pamplona during the running of the bulls. He swallows his drink, spits on his hands and steps out into the street, takes hold of one Almighty powerful Maura bull by the horns and throws it over on its back.

Amazing, said they; such valour, such strength, to throw a bull over on its back.

'*A bull!*' says the drunken Afrikaner. 'Is that what it was! Och min, I thought it was a bleddy Kaffir on a bike.'

– 57 –

The Screaming Horrors

On a voyage to Lisbon George Borrow saw a sailor fall from a cross-tree in a sudden squall. A boat was launched but the men couldn't save him. They saw him below with arms outstretched and sinking ever deeper, and as he sank his life came up in streams of little bubbles. It is not an easy death, suffocation in salt water, but akin to swallowing glass. Borrow is the man who wrote about the screaming horrors.

It can be brought on by downing a plurality of pints followed by cold tea, which induces projectile vomiting. I have had the screaming horrors thrice myself, the last time in an old friend's house in Palmerston Park.

A female hand waved from the kitchen window and the little house-devil Scutty the dachshund began to bark, announcing my arrival. A sister was visiting with a grandchild and Granny was puffing black cigarettes and bully-ragging her daughter who was thinning out baby food and testing it with the tip of her tongue. Then the Granny seized the infant's pudgy arms and went Guuuugggguuu! to distract the pet as the mother shovelled the food in and Scutty, naked as only a German sausage can be, spun around.

When they had all departed my genial host came beaming in with a primed tumbler of Paddy in either hand and behind him in the indigo glass of the conservatory I watched the darkness coming in the garden where we had unsoberly trimmed a bush until nothing remained of it but a stump.

Between the putting down of the glasses on the low table and reseating himself and resuming whatever subject he, the keen yachtsman, had been covering when he interrupted himself to fix the drinks, I had an unpleasant vision or visitation.

A company of six or seven Taoiseachs, the quick among the dead, sat stiffly upright in the conservatory which had broadened out and extended itself to twice and thrice its normal size to accommodate them. All were dressed in drab sagging snuff-coloured suits worn in the 1950s, Burton's off-the-peg that made them stiff as effigies in Madame Tussaud's. And there they sat silent and woodenly posed as for an official group photograph: Lemass, Lynch, Haughey, Fitzgerald, Costello and Cosgrave still as statues or lifeless figures in a waxworks.

There for a moment, silent and in sharpest focus; then they vanished, evaporated into thin air, and the indigo panes had perceptibly darkened and full night fallen on the garden, the garden had been wiped away and a distant voice was addressing me by name (Rory) and a hospitable hand held up a tumbler and for a blue moment of pure terror I didn't know who I was or where I sat; knew only the horror of non-entity, that which Proust recognised in the passing chambermaid's eye in the hotel at Combray or was it Balbec? It was like being wrung out.

I had *silent* screaming horrors when I landed myself in Clonskeagh Fever Hospital with a temperature over 100 brought on by malnutrition and scarlet fever that caused black spots to dance before my eyes when I was removed in a stretcher from a friend's flat in Northbrooke Road and read off a stone inscription on a gable-end: ASYLUM.

The screaming horrors of Palmerston Park came and went silently too. I lifted my glass of Paddy. The dark wings had flown away. I saw the shapes of bushes in the light that spilled out into the garden and the architectural plans laid out under the Anglepoise and I was calm again. I knew where I was; I had come back to myself; I was among friends.

The Spanish screaming horrors are more sensational and more terrifying, and control is totally lost. I had had a heavy intake of Fundador cognac over an extended period in the great heat of summer in Andalucía, up in the hills in Cómpeta and was sitting on the roof watching the sunset when the attack arrived. It came with the strike of the bell from the church in the square below. I felt it winging through the warm air, aimed at me. Each stroke of the iron clapper was the blow of a bullwhip on my bare back and each stroke laid on with a will by an invisible tormentor. I screamed with pain; each time it struck I howled like a dog.

Could this be Wilde's 'sudden shock' in Reading Gaol, as set out in that long poem of his with its insistent umpahumpah metrical beat? Kin to the short sharp shock recommended by penal reformers, thundering Tories and heated Whigs all the way back to the shameful stocks, the bawling of perspiring OTC drill sergeants, cold baths, Queensberry rules and all that bluff camaraderie of sodomy and sadism. Wilde, a 'varsity man himself, would soon have got the hang of it: certainly Lady Wilde, decking out her pet in frocks and frills, had shown little interest in making a man of her little darling. And now came Conal Cullinane, scion of an illustrious line of patriots, bearing tumblers of Paddy on a tray. He was of the pure stock of the most Irish of the Irish, set as a bolt into its socket or a crossbar on two upright goalposts, rigid as a fundamentalist in his lifelong beliefs (prejudices and bigotries); prey to the heartfelt conviction that of all the countries in the world Ireland was the best and the Irish race uniquely fitted to occupy it.

His father before him had also been a patriot, took up arms to free old Ireland, went on his keeping, conducted his courtship of wife-to-be in ditches and barns, a true patriot and an Irishman through and through, down to his very combinations.

The Bruiser himself had been a fearsome breakaway forward in his Bective Ranger days. He still retained the yachtsman's rolling gait but now in retirement took restricted exercise, knocking buckets of golf balls on the nearby driving range. Intakes of Paddy gave him a paunch and a jowly look; he liked to have his meals on the table at set times, could be testy if crossed. Formerly he had resembled Ernie O'Mally, hero of the Easter Rising; but now he more resembled Sir Isaac Butt. Conal's face was potato shaped, jowly with a burly burgherish fullness (could it be the fierce intake of Paddy?).

There was a hint of brusqueness behind the regular affability, a hint of anger in the *suffused* look. The committed gaping at the TV screen was part of an indulged life; it had made its mark. The Bruiser was a big-beamed, well-set-up, barrel-chested manly type who claimed kinship with Cuchulain, and spoke of bygone times and friends – the Baa Keegan, the Yak and Eskimo Nell, a big American blonde who had caused a stir among the UCD hearties of rugger field and rowing club. The Bruiser's jaw jutted like Dan Dare's.

He watched the RTE news with rapt attention as though World War III were imminent. He liked regular meals in a well-run house where he was boss; was still an active member of the Bective RFU board. Dr Tony O'Reilly, the Heinz bean King and newspaper tycoon, he revered this side idolatry; that an Irishman could perform so brilliantly in an international market appealed to his sense of values, his moral sense of what was what, Irish of the Irish.

Beaming fit to burst he approached bearing two stiff Paddys on a tray with a jug of water for form's sake.

'Get inside this, Rory bach.'

Palmerston Park with its secluded walks, mature pollarded pines with chattering magpies and its flowering magnolia was a popular cruising ground for Dublin gays dropped by the No. 12 under the great spread of horse chestnuts at the terminus. The CIE conductors refused to take their fares, fearing herpes contamination: the gays had free rides into the city centre designated *An Lár.*

I was carried in a stretcher into Clonskeagh Fever Hospital and put to bed.

A beady eye had regarded me from the little judas window set into the door behind which a red night-light glowed. Who was that sick bearded person in the bed with just the head showing? If I was anybody, I was a middle-aged woman afflicted with some troublesome female problem.

Assume nothing.

– 58 –

Titanic

Two months of relentless pelting rain preceded this Indian summer in September and the patio walls show a greenish tinge where the floodwaters receded. Almost three months have passed since Dervorgilla's departure into Bavaria, but she is expected home from Zug tomorrow. The house is spotless. Giving a last wipe to the mantelpiece Biddy heaves a sigh. 'The first ting Dervorgilla will do is stand at the winda and say "Lord save us!"'

Clinton Binnions, a shadowy form aloft in the cabin of his fast-driven agricultural machine, thunders by a few times, spurning the slopes, fumigating the land, and keeping a close eye on any movements in or around Ballymona Lodge. The word had spread: Mistress Dervorgilla is returning.

Mist obscures the valley below, drifting over the Japanese fence that defines our lot. Lowering itself in the middle as if 'making a leg' or genuflecting, the fence follows the contours of the land, reaching now into the spotlessly cleaned modern bungalow with all its mod cons. The hunt once came this way, a riderless horse galloped by, farting and foaming at the mouth. Sliding doors and both windows are thrown open to the *tic-toc* of little wrens. Summer came in September.

In August five-hundred miles south of Newfoundland, at more than 13,000 feet deep, nearly upright on the frigid Atlantic floor, the *Titanic* was found with all its Edwardian bric-à-brac intact. The pianos had broken loose, eight cases of orchids were still there; no sunlight had rotted anything, no heat had formed algae or parasites to disturb its long rest. The passengers had in the course of time been devoured by the denizens of the deep, all 1,513 of them, a banquet in Davy Jones's locker.

On 14–15 April 1912 it had gone down fatally gashed on its side, red and green running lights still aglow. It was estimated that to sink two-and-a-half miles to the ocean bed would have taken two hours. And what if some sleeping passengers survived in the dark cabins, awoke to total silence, no human voices; or perhaps only the deep gurgling of its slow passage down? What a terrifying end: to be entombed in the fastness of the ocean deeps, alone, a fate worse than suffocation in the submarine *Thetis* that sank into the mud of Liverpool Bay with a whole ship's company that couldn't be raised, to the great horror of my mother, who was claustrophobic.

On Monday, 1 September Blackie chose a bad day to go roaming and was run over near Blainroe garage. Cash Murphy called in person to convey the bad tidings that 'poor Blackie was kilt'. He had thrown the body into a gripe.

'When Dervorgilla hears this she will do her nut,' Biddy said. The smell of damp Labrador haunted the porch until long after Christmas.

Cycled into Wicklow one Wednesday morning to find a drab line of townspeople with their backs to the wall by Delahunt's and two Gardai on duty directing traffic through.

'What's going on?' I asked a beaky-faced father holding the hand of his roundy-faced son.

'A funeral.'

This melancholy news was imparted in appropriately sepulchral tones. They speak of bad weather here as if it were unusual and not the norm. And here comes the slow black hearse and the mourners with hands clasped.

To Grand Hotel for lunch of turkey and ham, a glass of Bordeaux. Home the back road, passing surly gum-chewing youth who did not return my salute. Connemara motorists salute pedestrians and passing cyclists by elevating one finger from the steering wheel and tilting the head fractionally to one side.

Dervorgilla gave a weak gasp when told the sad news of Blackie's demise, conveyed with relish by Biddy on the phone. The claw-marks remained on the half-door where he had vaulted out, the sack of Spratts lay in the shed until sold to the Dutchman by penny-pinching Dervorgilla.

We had seen the last of poor Blackie whose remains would begin to decompose in the gripe and be ingested by rats and carrion crows. His powerful pong lingered long in the porch.

Henry Valentine Miller aged eighty interviewed on Radio 4. American intonation of a committed Gauloise smoker, married five times, arrived in Paris aged forty, played ping-pong all his life; plummy actorly voice.

Hushed voice of vain twittery old aunty turns out to be Lawrence (Larry) Durrell, longtime former admirer, the Brit who went to Greece. Effusive praise for *Tropics*, likened to *Lady Chatterley's Lover,* that deeply absurd novel.

Alexandria Quartet sags on the page in a redolent prose limp and pregnant as overripe plums. *Balthazar* in paperback among Dervorgilla's few fictions.

Henry Moore passed away last week, aged eighty-eight. As a lad was much affected by Michelangelo's unfinished statue of slaves; praise for M's *monumentality* of vision. Only Blake can speak of vision without causing us embarrassment. The two vain Henrys took their status as Artists very seriously indeed; but only bad ones harp on the fact of being Artists. What is one to make of those big holes cut in monumental blocks of stone? A quite unnecessary complication of the ordinary. Time will do it, an Ice Age; prehistoric standing-stones in a field become scratching posts for cattle, for dogs to piss against.

Teeth paining, gums inflamed, tongue seeks source of pain, capped teeth loose as before treatment, all seething, on fire. Up at 2 a.m. for Anadin. Combine harvesters working in the dark with powerful headlights. Glow of stubble burning in the fields, smoke swirling up; a nocturnal Turner.

7 September
Morning nausea, unable to focus eyesight. Found that left lens has dropped out, resultant head-staggers most unpleasant, Bay of Biscay turmoil; difficulty of finding lens with only one eye. Teeth begin to pain again, joining in worse than before. Very dark stilly night.

8 September
After post set out walking to dental surgeon in Church Road. Empty waiting room. Matthews drained front upper incisor of its poison, extracted pus and blood with powerful finger pressure, a golfer's grip. He is off this weekend for a golfing break near Liverpool. His English friend down with food poisoning. I came at the right time, it could only have got worse, and he would have been away. Prescription for penicillin.

To Old Court Inn for double gin that does not taste of gin. Dowdy bar-girl transformed by new hairdo, and bursting out of her jeans; the sordid old Periwinkle Bar a thing of the past. Renovated premises attract a new type of clientele; gone the boozers of the dark corners, now clean pine surfaces, a reader over from the lending library perusing Rushdie's *Shame* through a monocle, ordering up coffee.

Looked into Taw Shay, thought to be a Provo bar, found an *Independent* reader but no sign of service. The Bridge Tavern gutted by fire. Arson?

Walked home on back road, all uphill. Outline of dead dog on tarmac. Six miles there and back.

My description of my condition had omitted the pain. Matthews drilled a hole into a dead nerve. The pressure building up, he said, penicillin alone would not have cured.

Poor night's rest, no appetite, bottle of white wine. Stillness and darkness of these dry nights.

22 September
Fifteen-mile hike to Greystones by Kilcoole sands, the ghost of Philippa. Took train back, observed by hairy O'Hills the switch-thrower high in his signal-box. Cycled to Barndarrig for gin and tonic with chicken sandwiches at Lil Doyle's. Return mostly on foot, pushing bike, dehydrated, so home

more dead than alive, sixteen miles there and back.

At dark the glow of fires in the barley stubble announces the end of summer.

23 September 1986

Guttural foreign (German?) voice on phone this morning announcing that Metz will be in Palma on 27 September, which signals Dervorgilla's imminent return and the end of peace. Who is this Metz? Mistah Kurtz – he dead.

– 59 –

October Footing

In a dead man's clothing should be the last person in the world to criticise Colum O'Hills's sartorial get-up. We may speak in the singular, for his clothes never vary, summer or winter, constant as a crow's feathers. My earliest memories are of him dressing. It's a style that came in when clothes rationing went out, in the days of duffel coats.

The Dote that was a worried child has grown into a worried man. Every Sunday he motors down to Mass; no longer a Latin Mass, alas.

The trusty old hacking jacket with single or double vents, pens and pencils protruding from breast pocket, Neolithic trews affording sorry glimpses of blue-white skin like plucked fowl ready for the pot. Down-at-heel brown brogues that have been through miry places, plashy ground. He who detests waste in any form speaks again of his inability to make a garden. The weeds come up again every spring, the *same* weeds that he had uprooted in the previous winter, the *same* stones removed last year are back again this year, apparently burrowing upwards. Gardening books offer 'hundreds of suggestions that are impossible to follow'.

Similarly with the unfinished house which he has been working at sporadically for ten years; it will never be finished; never will he rid himself of all the incompetents; a month's work produces 'an infinitesimal effect'.

My brother's gardening trousers with their layers of scales and perforations call to mind something very old and loved, of imperishable lineage: the old bridge at Mostar.

All the fish introduced into the waters of the West are infected with disease, and sugar beet and wheat with a virus.

Offaly defeated their arch-rivals Galway at Croke Park in the All-Ireland hurling final. Both counties on either side of the Shannon had been under six inches of water all summer. The excitement was so intense that under one Galway stand (full of priests) a rude toilet collapsed into itself, the Offaly supporters were in stitches.

The Shannon basin is flooded; root vegetables get scarcer and dearer as the fields become wetter and wetter; frogs sleep under every leaf. Fat rats cavort in Dervorgilla's vegetable patch, nearer home; Biddy lays out poison in the outhouse, in a saucer.

– 60 –

Dusky

Blackie had a younger brother Dusky who had been given by the Dutchman Verveen to the Dorans who rent out Herbsts' gatelodge to act as guard dog and pet for Biddy's children. His tenure here on this earth was to be even briefer than his brother's. Dusky made the mistake of *barking too much*. He barked at all who passed on the road, barked at cattle, dogs, passing cars; at the beach he barked at seagulls and at the surf. He barked day and night; chained up in his kennel he continued to bark. He was boisterous in play, barking with excitement, Lara the sly minx setting him on.

One morning Biddy was hanging out the clothes and was sent flying by Dusky; after that his days were numbered. The Quiet Man was told to get rid of him and this he did unobtrusively. One day the kennel was empty. No doubt Dusky had ended his days in a gripe, as his brother before him, both subsumed back into their original elements, bone and gristle become $H_2PO_4 = (OH)$ 20, phosphoric acid and trihydrogen phosphate, hide and teeth become roots and grass, potassium and potash, coal-black Labrador of two years (Blackie) become Anubis, one of the tutelary guardian spirits of the Underworld, become one with Nature.

Had Blackie lived . . . ah. No more would he vault the half-door in the back porch, snore in his dreams, go for the nervous postman who had to make a rapid delivery with Blackie snarling and snapping at his heels; whimper in Sadie's taxi, scorch after me when I cycled to Brittas or Wicklow, upset all the butchers, challenge a fierce billy goat tethered on a long chain near the Black Castle during an egg-throwing contest, dribble on the leatherette seat in the Ancient Manner.

Two wild-looking mountainy men in dungy Wellingtons had appeared at the back door one morning. One looked at Blackie with a twisty eye and pointed a dirty finger. *Datsa de dogge! Datsa de black lad!* He had followed the killer all the way from the dewy killing-field to the kennel at six in the morning, and was accusing Blackie of running lambs and killing a ewe. The bloated farmer stood foursquare on the gravel and looked sideways at Dervorgilla and stated flatly that the dog would have to be put down. Nonsense, Dervorgilla said, Blackie would never kill, and sent them packing, with a flea in their ear.

Enclosed in the back porch and more persistent when the door was closed, the all-pervasive hum of excited wet Labrador persisted long after the demise of Blackie; that strong heartbeat was stilled and his parts decomposing in a gripe near Blainroe garage, by now well digested by rats and carrion crows. That's how matters are settled in the country.

– 61 –

Grey Days

October the 7th was a grey day.
I awoke as if drugged from deep sleep. Ned Ward came early to collect Dervorgilla's backbrace and wooden horse from Turkey, her exercise horse.

A classic grey October morning you could say: sky and land as one, Friesians strolling on to the field, clean as if hosed down after the mechanical milking, clean as Peugeots in a Cork car-wash, presently conveying the impression of being airborne, afloat on the milky transparency of an early mist.

On such a morning in Dublin how many years ago had my eldest son (begotten and born in Johannesburg under the fire sign of Cancer) run home, terrified by rough-spoken labourers up to their necks in the drain, laying sewage pipes outside our garden flat in Ranelagh. He had been waiting at the gate for a No. 12 to take him to Miss Kerr's kindergarten in Rathgar when they arrived with their shovels and picks.

He was saved by a sweet girl on the way to her office who took pity on him and brought him in by the gate. Seeing me watching at the narrow window she made a moue to convey, 'I bring him safely back', closing the heavy gate and off with her on her high heels. It was most prettily done and I have never forgotten it; she was so alluring and so kind. Wet grass from overnight rain was trembling in the front garden of 47 Charleston Road; the same blades of grass all atremble in the morning dew, keen as whetted knives when my middle son James was born on Shakespeare's Day.

It was on the same sort of grey overcast October days, if you go back thirty-three years, that I walked a mile to the Mercy convent in Celbridge, with satchel and school books and sandwiches, tuppence in my trouser pocket for a Granny Smith, my mother patting the pocket to make sure the coin was there. So down the avenue and past the front lodge, Colum and I, getting our education from the none-too-tender mercies of the nuns with their straps and rulers and ear-pulling.

Why does the Bishop give those he confirms a stroke upon the cheek?

On such a grey morning we sailed from Galway on the *St Edna* for Inishere before the three boys were born. Such overcast days come to remind us of life's brevity and impermanence, how our time here on Earth slips away. The cold Atlantic heaving and gulping with its immense tides, the clouds passing in the sky, all imply it: this endures, wayfarer, but you pass.

One such morning a shabby off-white Mini that had never been through a car-wash came crunching over the gravel, no longer to set Blackie baying. Colum, come to enquire whether I would care to accompany him on a business trip to Laragh to look into a case of suspected arson in the Vale of Caragh. A Cork publican's summerhouse had burned down or been burned deliberately by the owner on the banks of the Dodder, a little fast-flowing brown stream.

The blackened beams of the two-storey house gutted by fire were open to the elements; planning permission was sought to build a new house. But had the rich publican burned down the old one, the sod?

'Is the water moving?' Colum asked.

'We could have a look.'

I dropped in a twig and it was carried away.

'It's the kind of river that fish like, running over pebbles,' my brother said, standing on a tussock and staring down.

There were no fish in the shallow fast-flowing brown stream. On an ash tree by the overgrown driveway a sign said FERRETS SOLD.

Driving back at breakneck speed as always Colum remarked upon the strange yet typical greyness of those autumn days. Days that seem to turn one inside out. 'Typical' was a strong word in his vocabulary and could work both ways, conveying either mild approbation or severe censure. For such a patient man, he drove like a maniac, impatient to get from one point to another with the minimum of time wasted, for he hated wasting time, of which he seemed to have so little not occupied by working, generally overtime.

So we went hurtling along the narrow lanes. Were he to hit anything, going at this speed, we were goners, pulverised.

'And herself, how is she?'

'Stella doesn't believe in breathing.'

Stella was way out. One of her speculations was: Do we breathe the same air as the air in Julius Caesar's time?

'That's bad. We have to breathe.'

'I know.'

'I saw a nun walking backwards up a hill the other day,' I said. 'Walking very slowly backwards up the hill. What does it signify?'

'I don't know. Indigestion?'

'Is Stella still reading Eudora Welty in the clothes cupboard with the cat?'

'Oh yes.'

'And the jackdaws – how are they making out?'

'They all died.'

Stella doesn't believe in breathing. Can you beat it? Time arrested is the stillness of nature. Stillness helps thought but thought itself is helpless. Arthur Miller, uniquely self-pervaded, is having *Death of a Salesman* done into Chinese. 'I won't take the rap' will be rendered into Chinese as 'I will not carry the charred cooking-pot on my back.'

Turkeys are fed and thrive on dandelions on the Beltons' farm. Chickens absolutely love dandelions. You can tell the eggs laid by hens fed on dandelions. Wednesday is killing day.

The bullfinch has become a protected species under Section 19 of the Wild Life Act of 1976.

– 62 –

Verveen

One day I was in O'Connor's buying slices of turkey and stepping out who did I see but Franz Verveen the Dutchman standing under the Mona Lisa's smirk and invited him to step into Healy's pub that was conveniently adjacent with its door hospitably thrown open.

So in with us for a few jars.

In the dim convivial atmosphere Verveen lost some of his ceremonial Dutch reserve. He was not a man you would care to be overly familiar with, nor could I ever imagine myself addressing him as Franz. He borrowed some of the sheets I had just run off at the copying machine. He bred Labradors; Blackie and Dusky had come from the Verveen kennels. I questioned him about Jan Cramer. I told him I had worked with the puppets in Amsterdam and indeed had met the famous Harry Tussenbruck, the doll-maker. Imagine that, now. I knew the famous old repertory cinema with the impossible Dutch name there by the canal and had drunk Bols gin. As a Piscean I could not but love a small city with so many canals running through it. We got along fine, Franz Verveen and I. Later that night I phoned his number and the wife answered.

'You don't know me from Adam,' I began diplomatically.

'Oh but I *do* know you from Adam, Mr Rory of the Hills. And what I want to know is, what have you done with my poor Frow? He has retired to bed with a most thick head on him. He wishes to convey a message. He liked the pages you showed him and suggests you offer it to the *Wicklow People*.'

Time does not exactly fly in Ballymona Lodge. Two months of driving rain gave way to an Indian summer in September and not a dry day since St Swithin's prior to that. A great Soviet-style grass-cutting machine with shadowy driver aloft in his high cabin spewed out silage in the Carmelite Missionary grounds in an August infested with flies. Time passes as it must have passed for the Good Fairy in the Pooka's pocket.

Many old walled gardens have snails. For this you need a pair of hedgehogs to sort out the snails; the patient crunching of snail shells hour after hour on a soft summer's day has been going on for fifteen billion years. Think on that, browsers.

— 63 —

The Mangle

I was a skinny child, a faddy eater, timid, afraid of my shadow. Notoriously faddy at home in my own habitat and in familiar surroundings; away from home I was impossible, the despair of my parents, and had to be coaxed to eat anything, could hardly be induced to swallow a mouthful.

'Now we'll have no more of this nonsense!' would give way to 'Leave the

child alone, don't *nag* at him'; but neither threats nor cajoleries worked. I was
a neurotic wreck, fearing bouncing girls as I would soldiers in uniform; Dr
O'Connor prescribed a tonic, iron. I would not eat butter.

Luncheon with my parents and the Dote in the Royal Hibernian Hotel
was an ordeal of the first magnitude that began at the revolving door with
uniformed flunkey in white gloves saluting us as we walked in. I felt completely at a loss; the aromas of the Grade A hotel ambience were as unsettling as incense at Benediction and a bishop chanting in Latin; it turned my
stomach. I wanted to go home and get behind the mangle where I felt safe.

Stiff and awkward in my best suit and new shoes and hair stiffened with
conditioner at Maison Prost in Stephen's Green I felt ashamed to speak, too
timid to eat or even attempt this display of unfamiliar dishes. Secretly I said
to myself. What are we doing here?

'Ma,' I whispered. 'I don't like it here. I want to go home.'

'Nonsense, dotey. This is a lovely place,' my mother replied in her richest,
plummiest voice, smelling of cognac and tobacco.

When we were all seated, after the Removal of the Overcoats, and my
mother's fur all drenched in perfume, her hat and demi-veil removed, we were
faced with a huge menu in French and the *maître d'hôtel* to explain the mysteries,
familiarly addressed as Charlie by my parents. The waists of the young waitresses were cinched in by shiny black leather belts which made their bottoms
stick out and they wore maids' white caps with ruffed black bands like garters
inverted coquettishly on their nodding heads. They swayed on their feet as
they approached, bending over the table to spoon soup into our plates from a
great tureen, their made-up faces set stiff in artificial smiles from lips that seemed
to bleed.

I scarcely recognised my parents in their posh city clothes, my mother's
voice up a pitch, my father's down, when they spoke to Charlie or 'our' wait-
ress, but between themselves they murmured in soft asides, commenting on
the diners around them. I picked at what was put before me while the Dote
ploughed through his meal.

'I want to go home, Ma.'

'We'll be out of here soon, pet. Your father has to settle the bill. We'll go
to Combridge's. You'd like that.'

'I want to get in behind the mangle, Ma.'

John Sibley, a benevolent portly man, owned Combridge's in Grafton
Street and sold books there; he played left-handed off a handicap of eight in
Greystones and was known to my parents, who seemed to know everybody
in Ireland living and dead. His hands were strong and stubby and fragrant

with cologne, the nails clipped short. He set the book in the centre of the wrapping paper, shot his cuffs, squared it off neatly, smiling a tight smile, a magician about to perform a conjuring trick, then he brought the overlap down in two v's, tucked them in at either end, sellotaped the parcel, tied it up with string which he broke with a quick jerk and handed the package to me with a wink.

'Don't we say "Thank you"?' my mother asked.

'Thank you,' I whispered, mesmerised by this jugglery.

In the art shop at the corner of Molesworth Street and Kildare Street I chose some Winsor & Newton brushes and watercolours in tubes (Hookers Green No. 2, Burnt Sienna, Cobalt Blue) which my mother again paid for. I was much too timid to ask prices or pay for anything I bought.

The heavy mangle stood in the kitchen between the tall cupboard and the window under the clothesline. Blocky as a medieval torture instrument oozing black grease it stood foursquare in wrought iron on its castors; the space between it and the wall was used regularly by the cats as their lavatory, the old messes growing fuzzy hair. When the stink became unendurable old Mrs Henry, our cook, cleaned it out with buckets of water and Jeyes Fluid.

When I hung on to the mangle for dear life I felt safe. Nothing could get at me in there, skinny as a skeleton.

– 64 –

A Hanging

Aged about ten I dug a hole six feet deep in the soft soil of the cleared potato patch in the garden and then spread and raked the earth tidily about the hole, opened out the *Evening Mail* and held it tight as a drum with bricks at four corners. Then I bet my younger brother sixpence that he couldn't jump on it without tearing it.

'You're on! It's a cinch.'

Brother Colum, the Dote, two years my junior and already a very serious person, removed his boots, peeled off jacket and pullover to make for the lightest of landings, light as a feather, even executed a couple of 'soft' trial jumps on the raked part as rehearsals for the unimaginably soft landing that would earn him the tanner.

I threw the silver coin down by the hidden pit and stood back with folded arms.

'Go ahead, chump. Let's see you then.'

With a look of intense concentration my brother jumped on to the centre of the innocently spread paper. The winner's smirk was wiped from his face as he landed and descended and descended; his feet told him there was nothing there and down he went, accelerating horribly, as the felon swinging on a rope, a plumbline dropping vertical into unheard-of depths, down into the very bowels of the earth itself.

The fixed expression of pure shock was indeed striking. And a muffled cry came up from below where I had packed straw.

'Not fair!'

– 65 –

On Cuesta del Cielo

Some years before and Rory of the Hills was living at Nerja, first on Calle Carabeo and then on Calle de las Angustias, at forty-eight the father of three bouncing boys; and had taken to tramping the grand asphodel-clad valleys between there and Frigiliana with Augpick and Kit Horner with his Jew's harp and bush boots and wine *bota*, three fellows hairy as Mormons, bearded to the very eyes.

And later again with Augpick when we moved to Cómpeta up in the foothills of the Sierra Almijara and together walked the logging trails that led back into the hills, never finding the legendary fish-trail to Granada. These I declare among the pleasantest times I spent anywhere at any time with anybody ever.

Augpick had broken his under-jaw, the inferior maxilla, when being driven, a 'trusted mechanic' at the wheel, to a fancy-dress party in Halifax. The car overturned on a tight corner. Augpick was encased in a suit of armour like a small sardine in a tin; when the helmet snapped shut away went poor Cyril's lower jaw.

Thereafter the jaw gave him a permanently pikelike undershot truculent look, which he played up to with snooty Danish door-keepers, Spanish major-domos and *maîtres d'hôtel* whom he treated in the most high-handed manner imaginable.

Augpick would call at seven in the morning and we had coffee and *anis seco* at the bar at the end of Calle Carabeo and then down with us on to the dried-up Rio Chilar for the walk to the electrical power station and from there on to the lower aqueduct for easy walking on aqueduct walls a foot-and-a-half wide; an hour's walk took us to the upper Morisco viaduct that meandered back off into the hills. Booster *Bustaid* was sold at the *farmacia*, and two of these would set us off, inhaling joints or taking hash on bread to send us merrily on our way. By midday we would be back in the high hills, taking tuna and tomato lunch on a high corner of the viaduct in the breeze among pines, the *bota* chilling in the water, the breeze blowing up from below.

We went as far as we could on a day's march, turning for home in the cool of the evening to the sigh of the breeze in the pines and the tinkle of the goat-bells below, the unseen goatherd clacking his tongue at them; to reach Frigiliana as the light faded in the sky, to sup in the plaza near the church. And then the last leg by road by La Molinetta to reach Nerja at nightfall.

Often we walked to the deserted village of the copper miners, just the walls standing, in the shade of a great palm tree. Kit took a 'short-cut' and Augpick and I lost him down in a valley of young pines, then in the remote distance we saw a tiny figure on the skyline and heard the distant Jew's harp; Kit twanged it and crossed over into another valley, coming off the higher aqueduct.

Often, drinking on the Nerja *paseo* at the Alhambra or Marissal, we spoke of climbing Cuesta del Cielo. It was no more a climb than ascending the Big Sugarloaf in Co. Wicklow; but a long hike upwards to the summit over 2,000 feet high. So one day in winter we did it.

Kit Horner, Cyril Augpick of Halifax, Nova Scotia, Old Parr and Rory of the Hills set off early on foot past La Luna shrouded in early morning mist. Some hours later we approached the summit. The ground cover of rosemary and thyme and tussocky scutch grass that scented the air gave way to scree and bare sandstone outcrop that stank of sulphuric acid when broken off. When I stepped across one such tussock something halted me. I knelt, parted the grass, looked down into a hole dark and evidently bottomless. A stale, spent muggy air blew up from the innards of the mountain.

'Hear me! You hear me down there?' I called down into the great dank silence and darkness below.

I felt the cool breeze blowing off the summit and my sweat turned cold and I held up my right hand like a traffic cop and said 'Stop where you are!' to Old Parr who was labouring up the mountainside with the sweat fairly pouring off him, Moses toting those heavy Tablets of the Law, my call halting him in his tracks.

'What is it? A snake? a fairy rath? an apparition?'

'A turd?' suggested Kit Horner.

'A hole,' I said.

'A *hole?*'

'A hole 2,000 feet deep,' I said.

'Ah-hah.'

I must have stepped over the ventilation exit of the long-abandoned copper mine; the miners had not thought fit to seal it up, an air vent so small and so high up on the side of the mountain where no one walked. I found a round rock the size of a cannonball and dropped it into the dark maw open wide as a man's shoulders; it fell away as if suddenly sucked down into the blackness below that seemed to breathe or to hold its breath, waiting.

After an interminably protracted silence – for it was still falling – we heard the reverberations 2,000 feet below as the projectile struck the floor of the mine, echoing up from a great dank deserted chamber long abandoned by the copper miners.

'Ehhue,' snickered Augpick who was kneeling beside me. 'That's fukken deep, man.'

We moved on up to the summit, the sweat drying on us. If one, not looking too carefully, had stepped into it, the fall would have been ghastly as a hanging; that eternity between the hangman's grunt announcing the springing of the trap, when the poor hanged bugger's weight carried him abruptly downwards with a remorseless gravitational pull that severed his spinal column. This ghastly fall would have taken longer. The luckless rambler howling as he descended would be scratching and tearing at the sides as he was sucked downwards.

We sat about a cairn of cut rocks on the summit and rolled joints and brought out the tuna, tomatoes and bread, and the chilled vodka and orange juice from the *bota,* and we disposed ourselves there at our ease.

'*Mejor no hay,*' declared Kit Horner, inhaling deeply until he was cross-eyed. '*Hay no haya novedad.*'

He stared wildly about him with that manic look of his, the trapped animal look you encounter behind bars in a zoo.

'On a clear day I dare say you can see Africa,' said Old Parr, the Grim Old Grouser. 'The tops of the Atlas.'

It's difficult to embarrass a Spaniard but it can be done, Jim Parry told me once. I had embarrassed Placido Espejo by attempting to speak of abstract matters when in my cups; but for an Andalucían the abstract does not exist; only the concrete is real. *Realidad* is a rock, all else presumption.

It is clearly impossible for my brother to suffer humiliation; for his Taoist patience and reserve puts him beyond that. Once in Kensington Gardens near the monument he had his hand on the door of an unoccupied phone-booth when an angry drunk tore it from his grasp and shouldered him aside, and my brother with a weak smile gave him best. It was the same sheepish, deferential smile he had given the haughty horsewoman, asking was her mount nervous. 'No, but it's a spooky kind of day,' the lady said.

We are what we seem to be. The man from Halifax, Nova Scotia; the man from Hounslow West, home of howling dogs; the man from Murri in India; the man from Michigan, USA, making church pews from pitch pine in a garage near Crystal Palace, with power-line plugged into the mains. And Rory of the Hills.

– 66 –

The Road to Aranjuez

The distance from Cape Cod to Jaffa is
terrible – and yet not so great.
Jeremiah Stone

The car was a grey-blue BMW about 1970 vintage, an intermittently sound two-litre model with 100,000 miles on the clock (another 2,000 would be added after the journey from Garratt Lane to Cómpeta and back, or near the distance from London to Moscow) which Parry had procured for a modest price, deviously arrived at, from Pablo the Asturian, an economist from Barcelona now working for Lloyds Bank International and living in Saffron Walden.

The trip began at the Jolly Gardener in Garratt Lane near the Crystal Palace with the BMW parked outside, ice melting in the gin and tonic balanced on the bonnet, and Parry's soiled plimsolls sticking out under the chassis as he patiently tinkered with a faulty king-pin on the sunny morning we set off for Spain where the consummate auto engineer would spend much time on the flat of his back under the engine with never a word of complaint from him.

We just made it to the Dover ferry.

Then the great engines were churning up mud and seaweed from the harbour and the clumsy vessel nudged away by tugs was reversing out of Dover harbour, when a wit remarked 'They're trying to raise Lord Lucan.'

We fasted across the Channel and down through the cheesy centre of France and all the way to Hendaye with our useless pesetas, except for three Mars bars on credit in a garage somewhere near Parthenay.

The BMW kept breaking down and Parry was on the flat of his back again. As a non-driver I took the passenger seat and stayed awake, attempting to keep the driver alert and diverted. Old Parr, foodless for two days, was grumpy as a sea lion; Parry fast asleep on the back seat, worn out by hunger, long stints at the wheel and more and more spells on the flat of his back, tinkering with the engine. Somewhere on the long straight *carretera* south of Madrid the engine mounting broke when we drove off the road.

Both of them were reliable drivers, and now it was Old Parr's stint at the wheel, while Parry slept in the back seat. Getting no response from some witticism, I glanced at the driver: both hands lightly touched the steering wheel, the BMW was going at a fair speed down the motorway, the driver's chin on his chest and his eyes closed, fast asleep.

'*¡Cuidado!*' I whispered.

But now he was elsewhere, sound asleep; the BMW holding its level course. If my blood had run cold before, it froze now, for approaching us at high speed was a mighty pantechnicon coming on heavy and dangerous as a battletank going into action, the driver's face just a blur aloft in his cabin behind the bug-smeared windscreen, staring down aghast as the BMW left the road and Old Parr was instantly wide awake. The BMW plunged into a boulder-strewn gully fortunately clear of boulders for some way, with the huge pantechnicon – I saw a blurred *Huesca* – roaring alongside, releasing mighty air-brakes; we rode up the gully for a moment of pure terror and then Old Parr regained the *carretera* and presently brought the car to a trembling halt and Parry wide awake now was asking what the hell was going on.

It was not the first or last time that death had stared me in the face in the company of Old Parr, who was becoming more and more irascible as the years rolled on, the old fart.

That was the night when he went sleepwalking and spoke in tongues – Urdu or Punjabi. The Grim Reaper who had touched him lightly on the shoulder somewhere south of Madrid now bore him backwards into the first language of his childhood in India before the Parrs sailed for England, carried him back to a time when as a toddler he had prattled in Urdu.

He spoke to me in that tongue, handing me a heavy key, laughed a light skittering laugh fit for another language, a strange tongue, and I seemed to hear bare feet pattering across a hot courtyard, the monsoon blowing in the tamarinds and a dark servant bowing obsequiously to the Sahib.

I put him to bed, still tittering and muttering to himself, safely tucked up on his foam mattress bed in Calle Rueda above the hill-village overlooking the cemetery whose columbariums gleamed white as bones in the moonlight under the scudding clouds.

(Later reports of the Missing Lord had it that he was alive and well and now resident in Ontario, Canada, after brief sojourns in Australia and Botswana.)

Some years previous to this I was in the passenger seat of a seat hired from Pepe Angel with Old Parr again at the wheel and Kit Horner, never the most reliable of drivers, snoring on the back seat. Alert and wide awake our nerves were ajangle, as nerves tend to be after an outing with Kit; for we had been walking around Granada in teeming rain, drinking great quantities of vodka and shooting pool until the early hours of the morning; now we were on our way back to Nerja.

We seemed to be passing through an illusionary landscape on the way to Malaga in pouring rain with earthen embankments collapsing on both sides, little or no traffic passing either way, an unearthly desert Eke the sequences in negative film stock in *Orphée* where black becomes white and vice versa.

For quite some time I had been seeing white rats flitting across the washed-out road, coming from the earthworks that had been softened up and fallen into the road; they came mostly from my side and disappeared under the wheels. I did not mention these rats to Old Parr, who drove in silence.

It was the silence in *The Turn of the Screw* movie announcing the appearance of the dead Quint on the battlements. All nature had become woozy and shapeless and had fallen silent and into this we glided slow as glue, as ahead of us the white rats flitted, ignored by the driver wrapped in thought.

We rounded a sharp turn and there with Madrid number plates was a long black limousine half off the road, suspended in the void, the front wheels – a daring cinematic touch – still turning, the headlights probing the valley across which heavy rain fell in torrents, bombarding our roof.

Old Parr sucked in his breath and pulled in some way ahead and we walked back without a word to where a shadowy form – male – slumped over the wheel.

Old Parr pulled open the door on the driver's side, no doubt preparing himself for a grisly sight; but the car was empty. The headlights were on and the wheels turning; behind the outline of the shiny black car the murky sky was lit up by the light of the city we had left, backed by the snow-capped Sierra Nevada.

– 67 –

Saul Bellow Reading at TCD

12 October

To Dublin by train with Old Parr to hear Saul Bellow reading a paper at the Edumund Burke Hall in Trinity. Bought Penguin *To Jerusalem and Back* – Bellow's only non-fiction – at Hanna's for the author to sign. Hall packed, seating 400. Proceedings start on time for a change. Professor Thomas Kilroy of University College Galway leads the distinguished American guest on to the podium. Bellow dark-visaged, smaller than anticipated, formally dressed in suit, looks younger than his seventy years and cannot decipher some of his own notes dashed off in flight with maybe a stiff drink to hand. 'The Mind of the Reader & the Expectations of the Writer in America', a fine rolling title.

The great minter of punchy phrases is in splendid form. He speaks of words going home – in the sense of hitting the bull's-eye – of psychobabble (did he invent this term?), of 'the dark menace of complexity'. He is an expert fielder of awkward questions from the floor; cranes forward to listen carefully with manic half-smile; Saul Bellow does not cosy up.

Applause goes on and on at the end, but Bellow and his minders retire to a back room. Old Parr would not hear of me going there to have my copy signed, and a chance to shake the great man's hand, having read everything that Bellow published since *Dangling Man* of 1944. Penguin New Writing had published an article on young American writers attending some conference where Mailer, Baldwin, Updike, Terry Southern and Styron had pontificated. Bellow – a pale face with pimples, long-suffering Talmudic eyes – had remained with his buddies in a corner, telling dirty stories. I had liked the cut of his jib even then; but I never got to meet him or to shake his honest hand. An abstracted Banville went out with his wife among the press of Bellow's admirers leaving the lecture hall.

I took Old Parr to my father's speakeasy in Lower Georges Street, the Long Hall, to drink some fine old malt, on which subject – fine malts – he was an authority. And so back to Ballymona Lodge with pork chops on the evening train by the tossing sea.

– 68 –

An Incident on the
Road to Pontoon

O nce in the August twilight near Lake Cong with a corncrake calling in the valley below us Rosita and I filled with Jameson and illegal poteen liberally bestowed by the Roche brothers and it hid in bottles in a hayshed and we were put on the wrong road on hired bicycles by the younger and wilder Roche brother and found ourselves going hell for leather on a switchback Mayo back road white and dusty in the moonlight and becoming trickier and trickier as the swooping descents gave way to steeper and steeper ascents one giving impetus to the other until I applied the brakes and found there were none and then came a steep descent followed by an even steeper one followed by a sharp turn and no longer listening to the corncrake I skidded into a western wall surmounted by rusty barbed wire and almost went through the wall or it through me and had I been less sozzled and incapacitated the wall or the barbed wire together might have done me serious injury but the skid helped to modify some of the impact but fucked me into the barbed wire anyway.

Rosita cycled back to disentangle me from the barbed wire and helped me into the homestead in Pontoon fortunately not far off, I bleeding profusely and put to bed with the fleas that made a night of it, sucking the blood of the wounded cyclist

Next morning Rosita cycled to the hotel at the head or end of Lough Cong for a bottle of Jameson and called on Dr O'Leary.

I was sitting up in the flea-ridden bed in extreme discomfort with nose and left kneecap swollen to twice their size when the younger Roche arrived in his green postal van to say he had a telegram for himself, stained like a Redskin with flea bites and camomile lotion and iodine swabs. The telegram from London said: CONGRATULATIONS YOU HAVE WON THE AMERICAN-IRISH FOUNDATION GRANT WORTH $7000.

Old Parr was to join us later in teeming rain, sharing one modernised cottage with thatched roof, later gutted by arson, a grudge against Johnny

O'Toole by a local Borstal Boy had it in for him. This would have been in 1977 or thereabouts.

Old Parr was the very man who had unsoberly, following our bout of wine-imbibing with Nagenda, driven his Citroën Diane into a wide deep hole dug by road-menders directly outside the police station at Clapham junction; I again in the passenger seat, with Old Parr's wife's baroque cello (1792) wrapped up like a mummy and propped against the back seat, a shrouded louring presence guarding us.

'Mr Parr, we are not disputing whether or not the hole was lit or signposted; we are considering the fact that you were breathalysed and found to be twice above the normal limit I am fining you £50 and withdrawing your licence for one calendar year. Case dismissed. Next.' So spoke the Beak.

Old Parr, I may say, ate humble pie. This would have been a couple of years earlier, around '75.

– 69 –

A Walk to Greystones

Something is always happening in Binnions's long sloping field; or beyond in the valley, or along the skyline. The living room changes with the seasons, as does the valley outside; freezing produces Japanese snow effects on the glass. Sunlight then gives bathyscope luminosity of summer sunlight refracted on ceiling when filtered through batten curtains and double glazing, shadows of rowan saplings dance on ceiling, producing those seabed effects, spurts of deliquescent transparency. Added to if anything when hungover, seen from sofa, shivering *nell' intracta foresta*.

27 October

To dispel hangover I walked the fifteen miles from the Murrough or plain-by-the-sea along the railway line to Greystones whose cosseted canine population is growing. To Burnaby Hotel for foaming pint. Last swallows of the year flit over Gents' Bathing Place, sans diving board. Saw bullfinch in bush. Grim Protestant ladies of advanced years and stern deportment out stalking behind small yapping dogs that befoul promenade. The ex-racing driver (Isle of Man) Manliff Barrington seen darting into newsagent's for his *Irish Times*. A wedding reception in full swing at La Touche Hotel, Eire Nua strongly represented, excited bridesmaids being photographed. Priest displaying social ease with hands in pockets. Bemused horse standing by a dead horse at Blacklion crossroads. Full tide in harbour. Fishermen asprawl on boulders.

16 November

Chill clear November day. Sickle moon, lights of Dunganstown west across the valley, Ballinaclash beyond, Rathdrum.

Knorr vegetable soup with dash of sherry topped with dab of cream. Cheese omelette and Mateus Rosé, Mouton Cadet. We do ourselves well in Ballymona Lodge.

− 70 −

An Official Visit:
Garda Reynolds

22 November

Sweet sounds of early morning in the wood, a pheasant's choked-off cry, a ship's siren out at sea. Postal van at nine, sound of letters arriving, my limited contact with outside world. Slow procession of grey clouds over horizon; Basho image of thoroughly Japanese snow mountain in the far distance serenely bathed in early afternoon light. Preparing supper. Pork fillet tenderised with judicious blows of rolling-pin, bombarded with seasoning, garlicky and ready for fan oven, mashed spuds rigid with garlic, G&T appetiser, claret at the meal. Orson Welles, peerless trencherman, said the way to appreciate food was to eat it alone and think about each mouthful. Pass the salt.

Sky is similar to October Cómpeta sky, mussel-blue shapes clearly defined, reddish distant hills, evening star shining bright in damp clear air. In half an hour all will change.

Friday, 28 November

Biddy in her element this morning bringing authentically tragic news. Had I heard what happened in the night just over the hill? I hadn't? Well, hear this. A mother and daughter were raped and strangled, or vice versa, strangled and then raped the almost naked mother in the living room and the daughter, aged twenty-four, dispatched in the kitchen, the Nolan family wiped out.

In the shed the rats had taken the poison and were now dying in convulsions in the foundations. The louring afternoon brought a rare visitor in the shape of a well-fed Civic Garda with notebook and pencil and some queries about my movements in the last few days. Garda Reynolds.

I invited him in. He sat on the edge of the sofa alongside his cap, getting me in a good light, refusing Nescafé or tea or a drink, all patent bribes. He hoped I didn't mind him putting some questions, it was only a formality. My movements now (licking the point of his pencil, arranging his great posterior): would I mind telling him what I was doing on Tuesday, on Wednesday at such-and-such an hour, where was I, could I say now?

I cycled to Brittas on Wednesday to Cullen's shop and spoke to Una. And returned when, and who saw me and who talked to me, if anybody? I saw none, none spoke to me, I said.

The large phlegmatic presence fills the room to overflowing. I had a drink at McDaniel's and spoke to John Stamp who served me. Back when? Just at dark. That would be (shooting cuff to check wristwatch) 4.30? Right. And didn't stay long? No (no light on bike). Don't mention rat poison, as I was tempted to do, in the way of tittle-tattle; don't mention bike without light, don't pick up heavy fire-dogs, don't fiddle, sit perfectly still, look innocent, I picked up the heavy fire-iron and laid it down again with a sickly smile. The Garda licked the point of his pencil. Had I seen anyone acting suspicious?

I wrote books bedad, had I by any chance any of them here and could he see one? I had three sons, had I, and a wife in London? Now he is reading the back flap of *Balcony of Europe* listing *Last Exit to Brooklyn, Cain's Book, Tropic of Cancer,* all dirty books brought out by Calder and all banned in the Republic. Had I written any of these? Now he is dipping into *Balcony* as though sifting incriminating evidence, licking the lead and frowning. It's not looking too good.

He has been stationed here eight years. No, no leads yet. Mrs Nolan was a widow aged sixty years, a widow eight years. After aeons of agonising time, slow time, the Garda put away his notebook, thanked me and took his leave.

The squad car was parked up the road. He had come on foot with his cap on, wearing his stern official face.

On 12 December the *Irish Times Anthology* launch was held at the Castle Inn on Lord Edward Fitzgerald Street above Dublin Castle, attended by all the hoi polloi among whom was Liam Miller of Dolmen Press, Kavanagh's widow seated in a corner, Maeve Binchy smiling amid her crush of admirers; seen prominently too was the undershot pike's jaw of Francis Stuart of *Black List H* fame, instantly recognisable for what Bellow wickedly called 'the cynosure flush', applied to some mobster. Among the contributors was Rory, instantly set upon by a furious woman who lit into him because of some remark let drop some sixteen years before in Berlin. I had no recollection of this furious woman or that indiscreet remark; how tenaciously we Irish hang on to our grudges!

On the following morning I happened to be passing through Chapelizod *en route* to the bar by the bridge and coming out of the newsagent's with a copy of the *Irish Times* found myself in bearded profile on the front page. Rory of the Hills at Castle Inn.

It was the very day on which Fortune, the murderer of the Nolans, was brought to trial. Perpetua in a froth of excitement phoned Dervorgilla, screeching down the line 'He's on the front page of the *Irish Times!*' Was her sister harbouring a double murderer? The report of the brief court hearing was below the picture: bearded pard in foxy profile holding a dirty roll-up in one murderous claw. Dervorgilla had kittens.

The *Wicklow People* was sold out by midday. YOUTH ACCUSED OF MURDERING WOMEN, ran the restrained headline in a news-sheet more accustomed to reporting cow winched to safety, having toppled off a cliff.

Meanwhile Rory was ordering up a half of Guinness and a Jameson chaser.

Barman Stamp very smart in a new red gansey pulled half a pint for me at McDaniel's that same afternoon and said 'Hanging is too good for that fucker.'

'What about half-hanging him?' I suggested. 'You know, *half-hang* him. Then cut him down, bury him, leave him under for a bit, to meditate on his crimes. Then dig him up and re-hang him. Like marinating snipe.'

John Stamp's eyes blazed.

'Now by God you're talking!'

'Or do the job properly. Give him the works. Crucify him. That's a gorgeous gansey you've got on.'

Tommy Cullen, a decent sober man, at age fourteen picked up a detonator at the Arklow mines to have it blow up in his face: he lost the sight of one eye. Years later, now married, a one-eyed father, he was to lose a much-loved son, buried him in the ground.

Storm wind for a few hours, then dying out. Fire in living room dying out, wood and coal mixed. Gunshot at dusk. Two figures hurrying across Binnions' field now empty of Friesians.

All stations jammed, only Spanish clear as a bell, thermometer reading 55 degrees, biting wind, crows blown hither and thither, gulls tossed about in clear blue sky before sunset; fire long dead in grate. A rake of drunken tinkers were boozing by the stream that runs past the Forge pub. A drunken male attacking an even drunker slut.

The skin of the murdered daughter was found in Fortune's fingernails, Doran the bus driver informs me; now how does he know that? How the news gets around.

– 71 –

Halley's Comet

A re the Chinese a shy race? What do you suppose?' Stella Veronica speaks in suddenly inspired *non sequiturs;* she exists on a different wavelength to you and I.

'Shynese,' Colum titters.

They had been married thirty-six years. Their nuptials were celebrated in Brompton Oratory in winter; a fellow thirsting for the sacrament tried to shoulder them aside and a moth trapped in a candle flame was immolated on the spot. Her three ravishing sisters were bridesmaids. The newlyweds lived in Ludlow Road out Ealing way, like so many Irish before them.

They were very formal with each other. She was most withdrawn; deeply withdrawn within herself, and a past-mistress of the nubilous aside. As for my brother, you would suppose the next wind would blow him away.

I recall a man with baby-blue eyes in the Prince of Wales in Highgate who introduced himself as the grandson of Douglas Hyde. Just behind us in Pond Street was the summer residence of Oliver Cromwell.

In a snug in Castlebar in Mayo run by two dumpy old women who crouched in the window-ledge like Rhode Island Reds on their perch, observing movements on the road, the corner-boys clustering and catcalling; the two old ones now and again retreating into a dark recess in the rear. A small fierce old man with crutches by his tall stool sipped Jameson and kept watching me, at last addressed me, asking the one question to which there is no satisfactory answer: 'What do you do?'

'I write books actually.'

'What classa books?'

'Books that don't sell.'

He had driven a cab for years in the Bronx and advised me to go there and study the low life, there was plenty of it in the Bronx. Later, looking for the Gents, I entered a room full of shelves packed with biscuit tins, the man from the Bronx was sitting on the edge of a camp-bed in carpet slippers, preparing to retire.

'We're all in a glasshouse now.'

Where was I?

And where am I now? What do you do when memory begins to go? As soon as I'm fitted with a bridge my potency will begin to go. Seas, rivers, lakes, great bodies of water always in motion will no longer stimulate me. Formerly woken by an erection (the cock that is the herald to the morn) and now thank God hardly a stir down there. The pictures on the wall have taken a slide.

I spend too much time looking back into the past; and the past that I know is no longer there; it has taken a slide, God knows where. I too have taken a slide.

'Time flies when you're enjoying yourself' Biddy called out the other day, bringing her household chores to a triumphant conclusion. 'Throw on your jacket and I'll give you a lift into town.'

Lara is just like her ma, with the same taste for the melodramatic.

'Herbst's bull broke out!'

'Mammy can't go to Spain!'

'Laurence is lost!'

Halley's comet, now at its closest, is coming around again, returning in the time-span of one human life, and will be forty million light years away in March when I turn fifty-nine on the 3rd.

As it whips past the sun it discards ice and stardust, dragging a peacock tail seventy million miles long. Its mysterious icy heart is said to hold clues to the origin of our solar system.

It was seen by Julius Caesar, aged seventeen, above Gaul in 87 BC. And the infant Eudora Welty was carried in her sleep to the window of her home in North Congress Street, Jackson, Mississippi, by her father Christian Welty to see it. She was always waked for eclipses and grew up to the striking of clocks. Her mother had been born left-handed and stuttered; in her family were five left-handed brothers, a left-handed mother and a father who could write with both hands at the same time, also backwards and forwards and upside down, different words with each hand. He had a telescope with brass extensions to find the moon and the Big Dipper.

Was Halley the clever savant who pulled or pushed Tsar Nicholas backwards and forwards in a wheelbarrow through a hedge in the garden of some English lord when the Tsar visited England (useful footnotes to history), unless I confuse him with another?

A chilly winter here as in England where the bats have miscarried along the Somerset borders. The Shannon has burst its banks at Athlone.

– 72 –

Dervorgilla at Home

No tenemus nada . . . Yo soy nada.
Honduran proverb. (We are nothing; I am nothing.)

In a brown dressing-gown drab as a Benedictine shroud Dervorgilla prepares to retire for the night after a good long souse in the tub, the bathroom being the only room in the home unreachable by phone. She asked to see the story I had just finished, one well calculated to set feminists' teeth on edge. She would take it to bed with her; it might send her to sleep. Next morning I had her comment.

'People sometimes ask me what kind of writing you do. I tell them "Writing without beginning, middle or end." It *still* has no beginning, middle or end.'

'By the first third of the next century, which will be loudly pictorial, writers may become extinct,' I said. 'As the dodo, the corncrake, Steller's seacow, bell ringers and town criers, our trade will be as extinct as falconry.'

Yeats in his old age wrote: 'I am a crowd, I am a lonely man; I am nothing.' And again: 'In a little time places may begin to seem the only hieroglyphs that cannot be forgotten.' A prehistoric standing-stone in the middle of a field in Kerry used by cattle to scratch themselves and for passing dogs to piss against.

The young and precocious Seamus Heaney wrote of *the climate of a lost world;* 'a covenant with generations who have been silenced'. My refuge was behind the mangle, Heaney's the top of the dresser: 'The top of the dresser in the kitchen of the house where I lived for the first twelve years of my life was like a Time Machine.'

Ebbing time; time ebbs away.

The crabby old woman stumbling on Belton's Avenue was not mother Noelie but daughter Varna, who is half her age, her bloom reduced by incessant labouring, the endless chores of running a farm. Slaughtering day is Wednesday; Pa Percy is seldom seen.

Belton's free-range chicken wrapped in silver foil in the fridge, a bottle of Rioja on the sideboard. Seen through double-glaze glass: the frisky Friesians coming into Clinton Binnions's long field, the pasture as if tilted down to receive them; boom of rising wind in the chimmey; rowan saplings scraping against the outer wall with winching seafaring effect. Hills receding into the distance, rain on the way, large live spider in the bath, dead bluebottle on the window ledge. Biddy busying herself at her chores, three hours twice a week to leave the premises pristine. Three hours paid for are three hours earned; the dignity of labour means 'no cutting corners'. Now I am being charged for lifts into town, so much per mile. Her old banger needs constant servicing.

Biddy begins in the bathroom and when she comes out half an hour later the place is sparkling. Living room, kitchen, Dervorgilla's bedroom are Hoovered and swept, every object lifted and every area dusted and polished. My room comes last – the smoking area. I step into the transformed living room, the long window wide open on Binnions's field of grazing Friesians being chivvied by Ned's white setter running them and barking, the hills gone further away, the rain nearer.

A glimpse of 'The Ascendancy at Home'.

'A glass of Jameson for the gentleman who just came in!'

Great-hearted Mertull won the Tralee Steeplechase on a track so sodden that the exhausted winner collapsed and died after the race.

When Dervorgilla was in residence the last act of the day, generally a busy one, was to carry the telephone into the bedroom for a good long gossip with a female friend in Ballinaclash; whereas my first act of the day was to kneel in the bathroom and attempt a silent piss into the toilet and then have a stool in the toolshed which had a convenience and handbasin among Dervorgilla's riding and ski equipment, tennis racquets and golf clubs, a sack of Spratt's. Fox covering its tracks.

– 73 –

The Eye and Ear Hospital

By the morning train along the coastline to Dublin and walk to the Eye and Ear Hospital in Adelaide Road, afflicted with not one but two suppurating cysts on the right eyelid and as a natural consequence partially sighted on the right side and feeling queasy and lopsided as though I'd been well and truly hammered in the ring by a merciless opponent.

After the obligatory wait of one hour and a half in the waiting room amid the halt and lame, moving from bench to bench as if awaiting confession in the company of others with eye trouble, I was at last admitted to the inner sanctum where a matronly roly-poly head nurse took charge of me.

I was seated and assured her that my cysts were thoroughly ripe and ready for the knife. Presently in came a brisk young surgeon, a redheaded man hardly thirty, to wash his hands at the basin, humming under his breath.

'Close your little eye now dear,' murmured the matronly nurse and I felt the needle prick, the puncture and the anaesthetic fizz. Take a deep breath and marvel at what you see.

The pasture gleams and blooms, scadoo, scudoo, 'neath bilious clouds that scatter and amass . . . The young surgeon's breathing fanned my face as he probed and probed.

Think on. Deep in a sunlit grove a dragonfly hangs, scudoo, scudoo, like a blue thread loos'd from the sky, scudoo. Without saying a word to me the young surgeon dug out two ripe cysts from swooning eyelid. 'That will do nicely, nurse.' The matronly one washed and bandaged the inflamed eyelid, winding the bandages about my head like a turban.

I left the hospital feeling weak as a house-fly in midwinter and made my way to a low-beamed old pub in the purlieus of Leeson Street bridge for a steadying half-pint of Guinness and a shot of Jameson.

Then I made it to Merrion Square and the Arts Council office, where I was not expected, for the scheduled function, to which I had been invited, was taking place in the Arts Club in Upper Fitzwilliam Street, whose noble premises I had already passed, twice, moving in a daze (ever tried walking about Dublin with wan blind eye?). I felt queasy but walked on and saw lads playing cricket against a cemetery wall near Tara Street station, from where I had so oft arrived and departed when living in Greystones.

I would take the Dart to Bray and wait for a connection to Wicklow. I would retire to Ballyhara and take it easy.

Two brudders, wan wiff a bad eye.

I stood on the platform at Tara Street and looked with one eye at the hoardings. Tara Street station was still Tara Street but the other terminals were renamed after martyrs who had shed their blood for Ireland. Amiens Street station had become Connolly station after James Connolly; Kingsbridge station had become Heuston station after Sean Heuston; Westland Row (through which I was now passing) becoming Pearse station after Patrick Pearse the patriot; all executed in Dublin Castle in the cause of martyrdom and bloodstained shrouds. And presently there was the sea again on the left and Sandymount Strand and the house of Heaney out of sight beyond where philosopher Ussher many times stood abstracted on the tracks at the level crossing.

– 74 –

The Year Ending

Though the weather forecasts warn of night frosts and first snows have fallen, the mid-November days remain mild. The birds have plenty of food and no need to repair to the feeding tables.

A drenched hawk fiercely tears out the gizzard of a field-mouse on the dripping fence. The valley lies vague in misty haze, Cooney's wood ashiver after a fall of rain.

Yesterday I heard a single gunshot there and asked my authority on things of nature, Ned Ward. Yes, it was he, was him with the high-power rifle putting down a useless dog. 'Poor things,' my brother says, reserving all his pity for dumb creatures. Trying to sleep the other night he heard the crunching of little bones; one of the Russian cats eating a rat or jackdaw.

He is taking his wife to *Pale Rider* tonight.

'Would you not like to come with us?'

But my days of movie-going are over; American movies alarm me, I find the stereophonic sound excessive. After ten minutes I walked out of *To Live and Die in LA*.

The apple tree bare but for a few leaves. A few apples remain rotting on the boughs. Conversation overheard behind partition in the Ancient Mariner:

'I hear she's blind.'

'Ah *course* she's blind. Whaddya tink?'

'Dey cudd'na kilhm!'

Quintessentially gloomy are the Black Castle ruins subsiding into the sea. A billy goat on its long tether nibbles the tussocks near the broken wall. This is one end of town; funerals leave at a slow pace out the other end.

I heard a ship's siren one morning; then a pheasant's alarm call; post being forced through the letterbox and falling with a soft thud on the carpet where Stella Veronica left muddy footprints. Snow on back ranges of the Wicklow hills lit by the dead sun. Nescafé laced with Jameson to make the hackles rise. Rory's middle period: 'From Numina to Nowhere'. The pheasant goes blundering off through the close-packed young pine wood. A distant dog begins barking.

My brother heard RTE news of a drunken farmer who fell on his back in the midst of his pigs who devoured all but the boots with the feet in them. The pigs were slaughtered and buried with the boots and feet. A perfectly preserved clump of pine roots 3,500 years old and hard as iron has been dug up in Glasnevin, County Offaly.

My brother is reading Thomas De Quincey the opium addict whose brother put to sea. Thomas sailed to Ireland, saw the poverty, the brawling, and the rich going by in carriages. Stella Veronica's legs are getting stiff 'Do I suffer from arthritis?' The pair of them cycled into Soviet Russia to see Leningrad, the great River Niva, the Hermitage, assailed by mosquitoes big as locusts.

My middle son James is today the same age (twenty-four) as Henry Williamson when *The Sun on the Sands* was published. Williamson rode a Norton motor-bike into Devon. Colum reads and rereads Williamson.

The Mayoress of Glenealy wearing her chain of office and medal strides about at the tug-of-war contest. An irate contestant bawls 'Yurra bollicks!' into the face of the flinching referee. Ned Ward and his girl Christina puck a ball about. Darkness falls early; we retire to Kane's pleasant pub in the village.

In the Swiss Alps Dervorgilla swung at the end of a rope. The clouds parted and she looked down. Far below the small and tidy fields of Switzerland were bathed in evening light. 'Lord save us,' breathed Dervorgilla.

26 November

Temperature 40 degrees, snow on hills, difficult to get to sleep, the bed warms slowly with body heat. Heard or imagined a car pulling up on the road outside and smell of cigarettes, rumble of voices planning robbery. The heating comes on at 8 a.m. with a stomach rumble in the pipes. Fresh orange juice and Nescafé laced with Jameson to start the day.

Dervorgilla had spoken of the snowstorm of 1982 and twelve-foot drifts, the icy wind blowing in from the sea and hedges vanishing when she walked the twelve miles to Rathdrum to teach in school.

'You can take down the pictures.'

So I did; and now have bare walls.

Died this year: actress Siobhan McKenna, in Dublin. RIP.

28 November

The Dublin Dunne gang apprehended in Brittas, Garda Superintendent Con Randles on the job. When you get criminal operators with big takes you also get informers. A plainclothes detective gave John Stone a nod and a wink. Notice anything funny about your Sunday clientele? The Dunne gang were sitting there, ordering up expensive drinks; two female Dunnes were caught in the Ladies when McDaniel's closed for the Sunday break. The squad cars arrived soon after. The Dunne gang trades in cocaine. John Stamp wouldn't tell me the Sunday take; but Alex Stone admitted to £5,000.

13 December

Saw sickle moon. Rabbit in fridge, Piat D'Or, presents from Dervorgilla. Gardening gloves from Texas, present from Anastasia, thinking of me cycling in the frost to Brittas.

31 December

House-flies expire on weak legs, mummified daddy longlegs swings all day on living room window, swayed by the breeze when I slide open the door that gives on to the valley.

Whenever I feel sad and miss Spain, the scent of pine trees up in the hills above Cómpeta, I put my nose in the hunting bag of the late Dick Suchman and am back there. Like a whiff of smelling-salts to a neurasthenic. The dry leathery smell of the bag proclaims España.

Would the passes be snowed up?

– 75 –

The Road to Arklow

For my last evening in Wicklow I suggested a drink at Lil Doyle's. After supper we drove there and had a good few 'jars' and were among the last to leave at closing time. Stella Veronica took her usual place behind the driver and I sat by her; the empty front passenger seat was for a phantom passenger, who would be riding with us that night.

The brother let in the clutch, or whatever it is you let in (I don't drive) and eased her out into the crossroads, still continuing some engrossing subject covered in the bar, keeping an absent eye fixed on the Arklow Road with little darting glances, but nothing was coming from that direction, or so he judged. But I saw otherwise: a black car shiny as a beetle came hurtling towards us from the Dublin direction; the brother still talking and sniggering, still pulling out, with little quick darting looks in the Arklow direction, in that dreamy state induced by the (for him) unusual pleasant euphoria of gin and lime; or perhaps he was thinking of my imminent departure and how it would be without me. At any rate his mind was elsewhere when the other car hit us broadside on and sent us whirling around until we came to rest by the far ditch, where the engine died.

I felt no brutal jar, no crowbar in the teeth, no fracture of the spine; only the tinkle of broken glass on the tarmac and the Mini groaning in all her meek metalwork. Beside me Stella Veronica sat still as a statue and the brother uttered no sound. The Mini groaning, glass tinkling on the roadway, the driver rigid and silent, his wife rigid and silent beside me, and I too, as we were whirled around and around – like hobby-horses with nostrils agape and swooning eyeballs, rising up and down to the jiggy oldtime music of the circus merry-go-round carrying the three of us away.

– Epilogue and Epigraphs –

Memory recalls shattered glass on roadway and on the seat, hubcaps by hedge, bits and pieces of bodywork strewn about on the road, bits that might have been human parts, the Mini being whirled around and the blue ambulance light revolving, and the Gardai flashing their torches in but no questions asked, no enquiries as to whether or not we were injured.

We sat there, the three of us huddled together in a strange dreamlike state that was not too alarming nor unpleasant as you might think, the euphoria before extinction, the famous lethargy that attends drowning or freezing to death in the Arctic.

The ambulance driver did not appear nor did the other driver whose black car was far down the Arklow Road, and the dumpy woman (not Lil Doyle) who was a dead ringer for our mother (deceased) stood in the lighted doorway of the pub alongside her tall son who had been serving us drinks, staring across at us but making no move, just staring at the wreckage scattered on the road and the car pointing in the wrong direction.

Then Colum was politely asked to step out and walked to and fro in a bemused way, his arm held by the Garda Sergeant who was murmuring into his ear and my brother was nodding.

Back in Ballymona Lodge I took a final steamy bath with Radox and in bed began to feel the stiffness of my neck, the difficulty of turning my head; slept well however on my last night and awoke to find myself surrounded by baggage packed, overflow of books in large cartons. In Ann Lait's office I was presented with a staggering final bill.

'Poor Rory is lying on the floor smoking a cigar,' she laughed down the line.

Poor indeed was Rory now. To Heuston station; stowed luggage on Cork train waiting on Platform 2. Took a window seat facing the way I was going; waited to be whirled away into another life.

The glass doth shew the face whyle thereon one doth look,
But gon, it doth another in lyke manner shew.
Once beeing turn'd away forgotten is the view.

Otto Van Veen 1608

It is singular, how soon we lose the impression of what
ceases to be constantly before us. A year impairs,
a lustre obliterates.

Byron, *Journal*

The Whole Hog

For dearest Zin,
again

Circumstances are never fully our own because they contain another person, we forget that. We thought of the other person as part of our perplexity: in reality that perplexity is part of the other person.

Djuna Barnes, *Nightwood* (variorum edition) (1936)

Why yes *he thought* it ain't a place a man wants to go back to; the place don't even need to be there no more. What aches a man to go back to is what he remembers.

William Faulkner, *The Mansion* (1959)

– Prologue –

Getting On

It began a long time ago, though it seems but yesterday. The lies, the notion of privilege, of being safeguarded by night, was ours in perpetuity; that at least was the notion put about by our loving parents.

But it wasn't so at all. Those were merely mother's lies, the lies you tell a child. The life we were to lead seemed to confirm this, declare it: that we were special.

But we we weren't, that wasn't true at all. What follows is the stark truth about those bare-faced lies. We were not special.

Good News for Pisceans

In order to achieve the best rhetorical effects a diary requires a ready readership of but one. Therefore a perfectly petrified readership – James Joyce's 'ideal reader in search of an ideal insomnia'. The diary is a device calculated to shut the average reader out. To shut him or her up.

This then is suitable for your specialists in doubt, subterfuge and confusion, sad wenchers, lost domainers, *flâneurs* and nightwalkers, midnight imbibers of Greek brandy at the Four Lanterns on misty Muswell Hill, the haunted hill of a black transvestite ('Call me Dolores like dey do in de storybooks!'), haunt of ambitious Greeks saving to return home to Naxos; haunt of retired minor criminals from Soho, long oddsmen and those reckless poker players who are prone to draw injudiciously to inside straights.

The Lost Ones

Those who believe in fresh starts never get around to it. A seaman in Brady's sordid Irish pub, frequented by National Front louts and head-butters at the Oval, is a widower, having lost his wife in Korea, to some disease. She was buried there.

He consulted a shaman as to the whereabouts of her immortal soul. The shaman consulted his oracles, then declared: 'At Number 6 Caldwell Street at the Oval, guv.' Cor blimey, it's his own address! His ghost-wife occupies the upper storey and can be heard at night, moving the furniture about and sighing deeply.

Pisces (20 February–20 March), my birth-month. Sensational planetary aspects have to be utilised to the full and not for a single second should you imagine that anyone can outmanoeuvre or outpace you. Good news for Pisceans everywhere.

PART I:

Only Family Matters

– 1 –

A Bit of Strange

Though my parents never made any money they knew how to spend it, spendthrifts both of them in their different ways. They watched the Irish Grand National at Fairyhouse every Easter Monday, motoring there very grandly in the Overland, my mother in a cloche hat with demi-veil and fur coat, my father gripping the wheel in pigskin gloves as though 'she' was getting away from him, though the Overland could not go faster than a moderate 40 m.p.h. because of a tendency to overheat.

Grogan the groom told me of the big stakes laid and won by the rich Aga Khan. He rolled in the hay with a local girl, who wore powder and lipstick, frizzed out her hair, and was our part-time maid of all work.

'Would you fight your match?' Grogan would ask, cocking his head to one side like a bantam boxer, striking a pugilistic pose.

He had bow legs and wore leather gaiters, hobnail boots and smelt of carbolic soap, though he washed his hands with axle grease, in a bucket. He said he would wear out Lizzie. He had a tense white face on him from the wearing.

In August my parents drove to Galway for the Galway Plate and put up at the Great Southern in Eyre Square. They drank whiskey and walked through the Spanish Arch holding hands and Mumu told me that the Arch was named after the Spaniards washed ashore in the Armada. The living ones were hidden from the English and the dead ones were buried by the Irish. Mumu and Dado arrived home next day in a not-too-sober state and went to bed early.

Mumu's gums were an odd colour, the colour of rubber, kept in a glass by her bedside, attached to false teeth. She drank a morning glass of lukewarm water and Epsom Salts.

My Uncle Jack was a great sportsman and sucked raw eggs; he won the Grand National with a horse called Workman (Tim Hyde up). Uncle Jack bred and trained racehorses and had better luck than my father, who preferred to play golf at Lucan and the Hermitage to attending sick livestock on his estate.

Mumu's younger brother Jimmy Boyd rode three times in the Liverpool National. He came in second; the following year he was third. The Dote and I sucked Bull's Eyes and shot birds with a Daisy air-rifle. Plum puddings hung from bags suspended on hooks from the kitchen ceiling, so we shot holes in one and it leaked and old Mrs Henry told us we were bold boys and she would tell Mumu on us, so she would, but she never did, so we stopped shooting holes in plum puddings hanging from the kitchen ceiling.

Dado dressed like a swank. A dark three-piece suit with display hand-kerchief in the breast pocket and handkerchief up one sleeve. Gorgeous tie and patent-leather pumps, relics from his dancing days. When the patent-leather pumps wore out he wore my cricket boots, with wads of newspapers as undersoles. The paper came out in shreds, he shed the stale old news that was just beginning to be forgotten: the stamp scandal, the fellow who had absconded with all the funds. When these functional undersoles protruded, Dado became Pegasus, the winged horse that caused the fountain Hippo-crene to gush upon Mount Helicon.

Springfield (Ideal Hunting Box or small Racing Establishment, suitable for Stud Farm) was sold. Another breeder, more methodical in his ways, took over the running of the farm that had never been properly farmed in Dado's day, the acres of lush grass let out for grazing. Other horses now exercised in the seventy or so acres where Ringwood Son and Cabin Fire flew over the jumps and Grogan (on One Down) had come down.

I left home.

- 2 -

Largo: Three or Four Miseries, 1956–85

Coppera (Rijeka Harbour, summer 1956)

An awkward squad of Yugoslav soldiers in baggy pants and ill-fitting tunics line up on the quayside near steps that descend into the still blue water of the harbour toward which a launch with some visiting dignitary aboard is chugging, its flag fluttering in the breeze.

A volley is fired and a small pompous figure on the launch offers a brisk salute. The launch draws in alongside the steps and a stout little man in a linen suit darts nimbly up to where a stiff squad of awkward soldiers come to attention as the white smoke of the gun salute drifts over the water. It is 6.30 in the morning of August 1956 and the Adriatic sun already hot in the port of Rijeka, in the long ago and far away when I went with my first wife weeping with exhaustion and vexation, on the way to Cavtat, Mlini, Dubrovnik, working as puppet operators and stage managers for John Wright's Marionettes, touring Yugoslavia, Austria, Germany and Holland, before embarking on *Die Waterman* for Cape Town.

When Coppera Hill (née Anders of King William's Town in the Eastern Cape) weeps she means it, and oh how she weeps; she is converted into a child again, becomes herself again in King. Everything has been taken from her, so the child understands, and is cast down.

It rends her to bits, so it does; she liquefies, weeps her heart out, for that's her way. Coppera's in tears again, hand her a hanky! Woe is me.

So it went.

Hanne (Grand Hotel de la Loire, Paris)

At 20 rue de Sommerard off the rue St Jacques downhill from the Sorbonne you'll find it, a hotel of narrow rooms used by students who sometimes use the toilet as a place for copulation. The owner wants to know when the money will come to pay the rent; we stay until it arrives, first not eating much, then eating nothing. We eat each other. We have begun to smell; an overwhelming longing for sweet white wine forces me to steal a noggin of Scotch from a shop fitted out with mirrors. I await an influx of funds from a Dublin bank, for reviewing work, but no deposits are being made. I walk in the Luxembourg Gardens, see Beckett striding past the line of statues of famous French dead, his hair stiff and erect like a cockatoo.

Dream: a high-ceilinged double room perhaps in Paris, with interleading doors open wide. On the parquet floor crouch shadowy listening forms. Squatting on the floor but a little apart from them Beckett is playing a strange musical instrument, half lyre, half washboard, with lead pieces inset but without any strings. How can he play a stringless instrument? Only Beckett could do it. He plucks this strange unknown instrument, head cocked, chanting to himself. Music and words are very odd, delivered at unheard-of tempo. In the darkening apartment Beckett plays and I, unseen, listen to this disturbing music. It's the music of snakes.

There are long silences to achieve effects. Now he rises, approaches. Someone whispers to me: 'Now he sings of Judas.' Beckett's high apartment is not far away, on Boulevard St Jacques overlooking Santé prison.

I have returned from Parc St-Maur with a bad conscience. Behold Judas, the betrayer.

At the Closerie des Lilas he had hardly looked at me, a few sharp mistrustful glances vouchsafed, then he left abruptly, up and away after three whiskies, hardly acknowledging my beloved Hanne. The blood-soaked sheets from her difficult menses are changed without comment or complaint by the Spanish maid, who cleans out fifty rooms every morning. Hanne, who has good Spanish, befriends her, is told her troubles.

After a night of twisting and turning in those sheets I am standing at the window looking down towards the rue St Jacques just before first light. As daylight begins to ebb into the street a fellow comes walking down the hill and stands outside the unlit Hotel Diana. All that side of the street lies in darkness. He stands on the kerb with hands in pockets and looks up. He appears to gesture. Out of the darkness of the hotel entrance she emerges just then, dressed in a red coat. They embrace and walk off together down towards the rue de Sommerard. I watch them crossing. Soon the butcher shop opposite will open; the pavement had been hosed down the previous night. The owner takes his first Gauloise outside the shop, under the awning. We have begun hallucinating now on the third day without any food; inhaling Gauloise makes the head swirl. No deposits are being made. The manager is very patient, but what else can he do? It's 3 January 1973.

Hunger had weakened us and misery had ground us very small. When we began to stink, we turned against each other. Three days without food and we were very strange to each other. Do you take us for utter fools? We were in flitters.

− 3 −

Forgive My Silence

A card of mourning, handwritten, came to me when I was least expecting it. She wrote:

Forgive my silence.

My sister is dead. I'm living in Rørvig mostly in this weeks. Kos journey suspended. My mother is near going mad. I don't know myself how to be normal again. I'm freezing in this lovely summer.

She committed suicide, flinged herself out from a tower. I'm sick, we are all sick, please write something to me. She was so lovely, so weak and lovely. Pisces.

Anna

No address, May 1978.

It was in North Zeeland, in Little Russia that I turned into a mare in a
lovely meadow there. Nearly all kinds of nature is there in Little Russia
– meadows, hills and certain kinds of wild flowers growing in dry
places where snakes like to be. It was ten days after my sister's funeral
and I was there with the painter chap that I told you about. I was mad
there, mad of unhappiness. I was dead of misery, wanting to be with
her, look after her, but she wasn't there.

I must say the painter chap was very kind; he just stayed with me
and said nothing. There was nothing you could say really. She was
buried, had gone away; I couldn't understand why she had done it. All
her clothes were there and the flat was the same, as if she had gone out
for a minute.

I was not myself; I had turned into a black mare prancing about in
the meadow. It was gleaming and I could see the sexual parts opening
and closing like a flower.

The painter chap was Torbin Thimm, a former lover who grew roses com-
mercially with his sister in Jutland. He had rented a studio across from Anna's
apartment in Østersøgade.

On the *Litfasssäule* by the Gedächtniskirche with its head blown off by a
Red Army tank, the piercing eyes of Beckett stare accusing from a poster and
follow Rory. *Nicht ich* comes to the Schiller Theatre annexe, a chilly place.

The convenience stood up as Teutonic as anything else in Berlin; whereas
the last Parisian *pissoir* behind Santé Prison was as Gallic as garlic or Gauloise.

Hannelore (Prinzregentenstrasse, Berlin)

Wasn't I very hungry, pfennigless, when Beckett's eagle eye hooded, found
me walking by the café patronised by Georg Grosz? It was a freezing day with
cold air from the Baltic Sea coming up Kurfürstendamm and I was thinking
of a currywurst bread roll garnished with pepper and washed down with one
of those heavy warming dark beers that the Germans drink in winter; but I
hadn't a tosser, not one pfennig. And there were the ravaged ascetic features
glaring at me from the *Litfasssäule* near the bombed-out Memorial Church.

February (German) 1974. *Nicht ich* running at Schillertheater Werkstatt.

From Berlin on 18 September 1971 she had written to me:

No telephone call, no little handwritten letter – awful silence. What about welcoming the New Year together? Christmas will be already quite dull for me without you – and then dearest, that horrible waiting.

I have put gin and vodka in the fridge instead of food. The first things for you, the missing things for me as I stated that my figure seems to concentrate in my bottom and my bosom although I have lost some weight. I become more and more restless. At night I hear my heart beating and my mind seems to work with a heavy uneasiness.

It's very cold outside. Yesterday I heard some birds singing in the Tiergarten and I thought that Christmas might be an error ... I'm doing a carpet to calm my nerves after I had made a blue and black cap.

I finish this little letter now because the sleeping pill I took seems to pull me from the chair.

[Written along margin:] 'All the time I'm painfully longing for you. Hannelore.'

But by 1974 when she was pregnant by me the gilt had worn off the ginger-bread enough for her to be understandably sour and snappish. Who was it said that when the Germans shut themselves up in their silent resentment they prepare a blow – Harold Nicolson or Count Ciano?

When she hitch-hiked with a plain girlfriend she never accepted lifts in cars that hadn't four doors; she sat in the back, with a *shiv* in her sock. Once a hairy truck driver stopped at a small beach and suggested they swim in the altogether. *Nein, danke.*

Her first boyfriend was French – Pierre, let us call him, who played the guitar quite well. She had met him driving through a mist on the road to Nîmes or was it Montpellier coming down off the Cévennes in her Karmann Ghia. They hit it off at once.

Her first German boyfriend was, oddly enough, a replica of Pierre; let us call him Hans. He didn't play the guitar but in all other respects he was a German Pierre: same port, disposition, voice, manners, as if a continuation of the same, except he had no French.

Then there was a long silence. She wrote to him but received no answer. Time passed. One day, months later, her mother handed her a letter, an official notice from a hospital, to say Herr Hans so-and-so had died during an operation on such-and-such a date. He had gone in to have an operation to change the shape of his nose. The letter was handed over months later.

Who was in the right – the vain boyfriend trying to change the shape of his nose, the mother trying to protect her daughter?

> Finding is the first Act
> The second – loss,
> Third, Expedition for
> The 'Golden Fleece'
> Fourth, no Discovery –
> Fifth, no Crew –
> Finally, no Golden Fleece –
> Jason – sham – too.
> Emily Dickinson

One morning in our perambulating around Krumme Lanke we saw a heavy-set, hairy he-man swinging from a liana bullock naked with a big loaded cock semi-erect; and she had pretended not to see him, as she had averted her eyes from certain explicit nudes in the Neu National Gallery.

Flora (Connemara, winter 1985)

There's no use pretending that there are no constraints; naturally there are, must be. There was Flora Rossiter who had married a man called Jessup, so now she was Flora Jessup but wrote under her maiden name of Rossiter.

I said: OK, by all means let us live together but no hanky-panky, and she had agreed to that, and found a modernised cottage for us to share in deepest Connemara, across the first of three causeways joining up Annaghvaughan, Gorumna and Lettermore. It was a thatched cottage in a group of four or five, later torched by one of the local disgruntled lads who had been refused employment by our kindly landlord Johnny O'Toole, owner of the cottages and landlord of An Hooker pub opposite, where he slept with his wife Lucy and a shotgun for protection. Against arson and grudges of course he had no protection, in a remote place where grudges were assiduously cultivated.

We drove to Galway town in her green Ford for provisions, washing, Gauloises and spirits, and it rained for six weeks without stopping. The old postman came cycling over the causeway to deliver damp parcels of books, with a permanent drip depending from the tip of his old discoloured nose and I offered him morning shots of Jameson, fearing he would otherwise never make it back to the PO.

We were to share the cottage for the duration of an honorarium paid out on condition that I live in my own country for ten months and engage in a work of fiction or biography; but when the honorarium ran out in the ninth month I returned to London, found it impossible to live there and left for Spain. Flora wrote to me, on a postcard.

Emor Street
17 October 85

Dear Rory
Would you ever write?
I find I'm so upset and confused all the time. I can't understand what happened after a time of so much closeness and nearness and now nothing. I felt so strongly that we would be together, I don't know, some very deep gut feeling that what we had was so good and you telling me to rely on that and not be impatient and ever since you went to Spain this numbing awful silence. What changed so drastically for you? We're so good together in every kind of way – I feel as if the whole thing was a farce now. I know it will be hard for you to try and explain but I feel as if I'm going bananas. Please write, hey? Much love – Flora xxx

– 4 –

The Genesis of *Langrishe, Go Down*

For the son the first hard loss is the loss of the mother and there never will be another loss like it, for later losses are partly of one's own devising. Wasn't it Gertrude Stein, that heavy Red Indian totem, who said fathers are depressing. Mothers may not be cheering but they are not as depressing as fathers.

Well, one can bear the loss of a father, but what unmitigated anguish is the loss of a home! You have only the one home, the one you were born in; but the break-up of the family means that you have lost it forever. As one day (for the son) comes the first involuntary erection and emission, so one day there goes the last, so too for the daughter when menopause follows hard upon the last menses.

My younger brother swore that the very stones which he had dug out of last year's potato patch had come up again this year. 'The constant renewal of nature is impressive in contrast to the necessity to renew the man-made, with an evidently opposite tendency to decay,' he informed me in a letter. The balanced antithesis was worthy of Ruskin himself, a suggestion of fussy overshoes, whaddyacallem . . . galoshes.

The ultimate privacy is to be found only in the sleepy stagnancy of the grave. Even if that privacy is an illusion, upon our becoming a part of the multitudinously teeming subatomic microbe life that exists underground, now with all vanity obliterated.

My first novel, *Langrishe, Go Down*, was about the death of a house and the break-up of a family. It took me two years to write, two more for a dilatory publisher to bring it to the public eye; the final editing took twenty-four hours non-stop (but for dinner in Jammet's) and I stayed up all night, wearing out two copy-editors. *Langrishe* sold just over 2,000 cloth copies in the first fort-night after publication in September 1966, after which sales sank to a dribble. And it has consistently sold in a dribble ever since, in five or six European languages. Beckett called it 'literary shit'.

Later, move on thirty-three years please, another publisher com-missioned a sort of sequel; and this was finished in two months. Were I a painter of the stamp of Magritte, I might have suggested the decline of the Higgins family in one significant image: Virginia-creeper leaves from above my father's room now blown into the gutter of the small balcony above the long windows, one opened about a foot at the bottom for fresh air. The leaves would change colour from spring into autumn, first green, then scarlet, then orange, then purple, then dark-plum coloured, blown about the little balcony by various winds, then clenched together in a ball by frost, reduced to the size of a clenched fist, now the teak colour of Tollund Man dug out of the Danish earth.

The narrow room must have once been a changing room for the big bed-rooms on either side, and here my father, the narrow fellow in the grass, the great sunbather gone the colour of rhubarb, then the livid red of a turkey-cock's comb, had withdrawn when my mother withheld or withdrew her favours or had tired of sharing a double bed in a large echoing windy room with rattling venetian blinds (for Mumu was claustrophobic) or the embar-rassment of using two chamber pots drawn out at different times from under both beds; this narrow room commanded a view of the Dublin hills with Buck Whaley's Hell Fire Club on the summit, where at one time the smoke of the steam-driven Blessington tram must have made pretty patterns over towards Hazelthatch station and Baldonnel aerodrome.

*   *   *

I have always been troubled by the strangeness of strange places. The otherness of places I didn't know, assailed by their smells and strangeness, announced along the Dublin quays by a sulphurous stench rising off the river at low tide, suggestive of loss of control and God knows what else, as we waited with Dado for the single-decker bus (bound for Birr) to take us home. The sulphur stinks and the sickening Virginia cigarette fumes from Gold Flake and Player's and Sweet Afton were the prelude to a bout of vomiting. As effective as the mixture of a haircut at Maison Prost's with stiffener that made the scalp go rigid, and a large-size sixpenny ice-cream wafer at Woolworth's that produced splitting headaches, as the preliminary states of discomfort and stomach upset, before the wild stinks of the monkey house and lion house in the Zoo put the kibosh on it, with more vomiting. On the bus home I always vomited, and sometimes even on the gravel before the house. The visit to Maison Prost in Suffolk Street was followed by a visit to Woolworth's in Grafton Street and then the Zoo regular as clockwork, for Dado was at a loss how to amuse 'the lads', who were then taken to Eason's in O'Connell Street or Combridge's in Grafton Street, to buy books: Baroness Orczy and Rafael Sabatini, then Sapper and Leslie Charteris.

The unfamiliar was always threatening – fresh-ground coffee aromas outside Bewley's suggested Africa, heat, wildness; for which the methane fumes mixed with slag and coal around the Kingsbridge goods yards gave fair warning. The warning whistle of the Great Southern and Western steam train puffing into Kingsbridge Station made me want to throw up, as did the seaweed and sewage stinks around Dun Laoghaire, when we went walking along the pier with Dado.

Dado had parked the Overland some way down the front avenue at Killashee and in the back seat with curtains drawn we consumed the cakes and buns baked by Mumu with all her love. Sundays were visiting days but the Overland seemed strange to us with its rabbity smells which reminded us of home and what we were missing, and the knowledge that it would soon be back in the garage there made us sad. Under the care of the French nuns, La Santé Union, or later under the Jesuits it was the same sadness of departure for us both; the nuns were all Irish but the sadness was the same, the same sadness when Dado had departed; the visit was soon over, the cakes eaten, the newspaper cuttings collected, and Dado drove away.

Premonitions of this oncoming loss were conveyed in a subtle way by Mumu when she read Grimm and Hans Andersen to us, those terrifying tales of the overgrown castle with the sleeping beauty within, the dank and dripping cellar through which hurried the cruel queen, the woodland house made of sugar where the witch lived, the giant's castle above the clouds, the old woman who lived in the shoe; all were premonitory hints of that first ejection from the home and intimations of the places and the ordeals to be encountered later.

The strange house the Dote has found so hard to finish was perhaps another such dwelling found only in dreams and fairy tales. The house that he couldn't complete was the house that didn't exist, the home that wasn't there; no more the abode of parents long dead and gone; say rather one of Piranesi's fanciful ruins.

He whom we call the Dote was no doubt a singular fellow of undeviating probity, positively Quakerish in his austere ways and grey functional clothing. Faithful to his religion through the Latin Mass and after; faith was proven in work, a spur to morality; right-doing was just part of one's duty. As altar boy he had served at Mass, rang the little joined bells to make them chime prettily at the Consecration, rotated the thurible to send out puffs of incense.

A nature indentured to work gave him a settled distrust of flamboyance; solely on the evidence of *The Guermantes Way* volume two, which was in the study at Springfield, the Dote preferred Ruskin to Proust, who was too neurotic and rather too purple for the Dote's taste. He was as set in his ways as an Amish quilter. Sometimes when exasperated by him, Mumu said he was thick; obdurate meaning obstinate.

My brother Colman was first called the Dote in his infancy, because he was the last, and then (as a lad) the Dowd. The Dote, the Dowd, the Scholar, the Architect, the Town Planner and now (alarmingly) the Litigant.

The *litigant!* A bit of something strange all right.

− 5 −

Ordeal at Mealtimes

When summoned to table by gong or handbell with dishes getting cold, little Rory's face fell and his little heart sank into his little boots (size 12) too, and with what laggard step he made his weary way table-ward! Indeed he brought a sinking heart to the table, where he preferred to take his meals in reverse, not from soup to dessert but the other way around, *pari passu*, starting with what he liked best (jelly or trifle) and working his way back to what he liked least, the soup, which was frequently refused. And Mumu indulged him in all this, sneered at by brother

Bun for being too lenient and accommodating, he himself, ever a hearty and not particularly fastidious eater who, it was said, would eat *anything.*

Monday meant mash again that smelt of mouse droppings; then came Tuesday's corned beef, Wednesday's soggy dumplings; Thursday was greasy mincemeat day and with it the week declined; when Friday came around again, it brought with it some really smelly fish whose purposeful pong would turn your stomach, and for sure young Rory had one fastidious stomach. He was forever throwing up whatever didn't agree with those queasy insides of his; so much disgusted him; *too* much, I'd be inclined to say.

'He's a true Hill anyway,' murmured Mumu as if speaking to herself, proudly and possessively, munching on those loose dentures of hers in that way she had. 'At least he's no greedy-gut.'

Young Rory was no greedy-gut, but a real Hunger Artist. At best, meal-times at Springfield were onerous occasions; at worst, penitential.

'Don't you want to grow up to be a big strong man like your father?'

'No I don't.'

Brother Bun, poker-faced, kicked Rory under the table.

'Bun just kicked me, Mumu.'

'Nonsense! Pure imagination. just eat up what's put in front of you. Cook has taken great pains with this.'

'This' was streaky silverside of beef with valves sticking out of it and gnarled tentacles that seemed to writhe in agony on the plate.

'This thing's still alive . . . ah feck it.'

Dado's fork was already snaking out for the tasty portion, 'I'll eat it.' Mumu showed me a face frozen with disapproval and brother Bun kicked my shins harder under the table, looking innocent as pie.

Truth to tell, Dado was a small fidgety bantam cock of a man, vain as any peacock, who was sometimes mistaken for this or that famous jockey, as happened once outside the Monument Creamery in O'Connell Street. 'Aren't you Morny Wing?' A big stout woman had stopped him in his tracks. Vanity pure and simple.

His cramped sleeping quarters was a narrow chamber of trapped ambient air stilled by Dado's scorching farts, for he had a heavy hand with the emetics and was forever dosing himself with Milk of Magnesia and Eno's Fruit Salts to clean out his stomach and bring his guts – much referred to – back into proper working order again.

'Ah Rory, the old guts are killing me.'

If it wasn't that, it was stabs and darts of appendix, which excused him from the pumping chore ('The old appendix is at me again'). He was tricky, evasive, sly, my father.

Dado was probably now letting off sly farts under the bedclothes, his nostrils arched free of the quilt, his eyes closed like a dead man's.

'What kind of a day is it out? It's a bit stuffy in here. Throw open the window, there's a good lad.'

I did as I was bid, waded through the miasmal scorching air towards the window that opened out on to the little balcony, the view of the Hell Fire Club on the summit of distant Dublin blue hills in the distance beyond Baldonnel aerodrome.

In Mumu's big bedroom alongside Dado's, the windows were always thrown open and the venetian blinds flapping inwards, and there were many flowers in vases, to make the room fresh, like Mumu's flowers in her tiered arrangements amid the burning candles on the high altars at Celbridge and Straffan churches. You'd almost expect birds to be flying around Mumu's head in the gusty swirl of the bedroom.

'The days are getting a great stretch into them, thank God, aren't they?' murmured Mumu, propped up on great mounds and escarpments and embankments of pillows. She was reading *Flotsam*, a dirty book translated from the German, lent to her by Helen O'Connor, who was as voracious a reader as herself. It lay now face down on the upended orange crate that did service as a bedside table, her place marked by a hair-clip. Mumu surfacing from deep sleep, casting aside sheets and quilts and emerging to take deep breaths at the beginning of another day, was like a whale blowing.

If she was badly overweight then Rory was grievously underweight and Dr Sheehan gave his professional opinion that what I needed was iron to build up my bones, Metatone or Virol to bring the roses to my cheeks when feeling not up to it and 'peaky'; and that was the way I generally felt. Worse still, I was 'looking pasty-faced', which meant constipation and dosages of herbal remedies to bring about a 'motion' or stool; and all little Rory's stools were hard, hard, hard.

'Get him to eat bananas,' Dr Sheehan advised Mumu; 'lots of bananas. Feed him up with Fyffes, ha ha ha!'

'Oh doctor, he's terribly faddy about his food. He won't *touch* bananas.'

'Oranges then, lots of oranges. Fill him up.'

So I was given lots of oranges which Dado peeled with his penknife all in one knacky revolving peel, before handing the slices to me and drying his hand on a large pocket handkerchief.

When he cut an orange for himself, he bisected it and sucked away part; the rest he threw away; as he always left a few Player's No. 3 in the discarded packet.

For he was wasteful and extravagant by nature, never having had to earn a living by the sweat of his brow, nor done an honest day's work in his entire life.

By not eating, by refusing this or that dish lovingly prepared by a mother's hand, by flatly refusing to eat what is put before one, the mother's love is tested. For sons have that power from a very early age; from the time the difficult child has been weaned, ceased to be a suckling, the mother can be controlled.

The child can refuse titbits offered as bribes. Judge of the poor mother's mortification and discomfiture when her little pet, previously so tractable, so manageable, now declines to accept whatever goodies are placed before him and begins to bawl! Or a flat refusal to accept any such bribes, with an aplomb as upsetting and deadly as the power of veto. Now the mother must beg and grovel before her small tyrant.

By refusing tasty morsels and little treats, the brat, embryonic tyrant that he is, finds himself in a strong negotiating position, with a bargaining strength to obtain what he wants, that which he can hardly name, not yet able to talk; and the mother, weighed in the balance, has been found wanting.

Little Rory, the famously faddy feeder (fff), the picker at food, the *more* than fastidious eater, refused eggs and butter (the latter associated with womanly flesh and early superior strength) and had to be coaxed to drink milk. Sago that resembled frogspawn or semolina pud with a skin or scum on it enlivened with a dab of raspberry jam were 'sweets' not enjoyed by the skinnymalink fusspot who sat next to the silent Dodo, silent but for the methodical chomping at his food. Rice puddings and bread puddings and nice spaghetti puds were tolerated, brown sugar was spread liberally on soda bread and a red-hot poker laid across it to produce the consistency of glazed marzipan, crystallised fruit, angelica and ginger.

Woe betide the cook who offered butter or eggs in no matter what form. Meat had to be cooked until carbonised before I would consent to touch it. ('Don't pick at your food, Rory, there's a good boy!')

As a consequence, I weighed no more than four stone, give or take a pound, by the age of six or seven. Four stone avoirdupois, if that, a thin shivering shank of a child permanently anxious: witness the living skeleton of Booterstown Strand captured in the Box Brownie *circa* 1933 with matchstick legs and rickety arms when stung on the forearm by a wasp that must have mistaken little-meat Rory for some half-starved mongrel stray.

The Hill family table, the great groaning board, was indeed a battleground and the meals served up were occasions for skirmishes and strategies for survival ('*Don't* pick at your food, child!').

Dado, who had the palate of a dog, once accepted dishwater lying on the pan for gravy. Pulling back from the table and crossing his legs as a signal that the 'sweet' (trifle or stewed apples from the orchard, served up with Bird's Eye custard) should be brought in, he gave his opinion, picking his teeth with a spent match in lieu of toothpick, that you would hardly get better gravy at the Shelbourne or the Gresham than the dishwater on the pan. 'What's wrong with it then? The lad is too fussy altogether.' The lad had refused to accept it; when it was poured forcefully over my tiny portion of carbonised silverside of beef by the irate Dado, I had pushed my plate away and burst into tears.

'*Now* what's got into him?'

Old Mrs Henry, our cook, said that my stomach must be one mass of worms, full of sugar and jam and sweet things.

Sometimes, to emphasise the point he was making and bring it home sharply to Mumu, Dado struck the edge of the table with his clenched knuckles, as a court beadle might strike the floor of the chambers for silence; or as the judge, clearing his throat, might rap the dais before him with the gavel, before pronouncing sentence.

Dado referred in most disparaging terms to 'that mincing two-faced bitch' whom we know to be none other than Miss Pasty-Face Dermody who had once called uninvited, come over the fields, but only once and had never presumed to come again in her tight home-made tweed skirt that demonstrated how tightly laced she was into a corset.

You might suppose that the Dodo had a second stomach, as cattle have, for he masticated his food in a slow methodical way just like a cow, moving his lower jaw from side to side. He had some theory about digestion, ways and means of extracting the best possible nutritive results from the food consumed, subjecting every blessed morsel speared on the prongs of his fork to the most exact scrutiny at close range, before bringing it to his lips, hesitating, then popping it into his mouth to begin grinding from side to side, eyes closed, a bovine 'Fletcherising' guaranteed to extract the maximum of good from his meat, brought to the kitchen door in a butcher's basket by the Bowsy Murray himself, smelling as usual to high heaven.

It was as though he (the Dodo) suspected that his meat might be spiked with nux vomica or cyanide. He ate in silence. But sometimes, when some remark tickled his fancy, he emitted a high-pitched witchy cackle; otherwise he ate in stoic silence. Never a word of praise had he for the food put before him; never a good word for the cook, old Mrs Henry or Mumu.

'What's this thing, then?'

He was holding it up on his fork, peering at it.

'That's cauliflower, dear. Don't you like it?'

'Not much.'

'Then we won't have it again,' said Mumu, always ready to defer to his wishes.

The Dote and I were very much in awe of him. The eight and ten years that separated us made him appear a very senior brother, already fully vested in authority, a stern prefect to reeky fags; it was an awesomeness which he did nothing to modify. On the contrary his silence at table seemed to make it clear that he thought very little of us, a wormy pair.

Seldom did he speak and when he did it tended to be either dismissive or outright alarming, and always the imperative ('Hey, you!' risen up suddenly to tower above us, down in the ditch, remorseless and heavy as lead – the *Golem!* – 'Hey, what's the big idea?').

The strained silence that followed was indeed strained. The Dodo was rolling the whites of his eyes ceiling-ward and then fixing his napkin into its silver ring, preparing to leave the table.

We sat frozen in embarrassment. It was all for some innocent question the Dote had put to Dado, which the Dodo had taken as cheek. We were the pups from the convent with thick provincial accents (mudder, me brudder, dis, dat) who fraternised with the snotty-nosed Keegan boys from the front lodge who used the plantation as an open-air latrine, for the Dodo to tread in and bring into the house.

It was as though he and brother Bun were the true sons of their father and mother and Springfield was their true home and Clongowes Wood College was their rightful Alma Mater and their airs and graces were the only possible attitude to adopt towards the brats (the Dote and 1), who were just worms to be trodden into the ground.

Giving cheek at table, making cheeky remarks, from the likes of *that* (the Dote reduced to the size of nothing) was no better than *lèse-majesté,* 'Infernal cheek!'

We saw ourselves as a humble, ignorant pair at garden parties given by Helen O'Connor, at Dr O'Connor's residence near the National School (which we would attend for one day), or at Springfield with the wild relative who joined the Royal Navy and played very rough games involving barricades and repeating air-rifles, stumps as swords and pads as bucklers, bamboo canes as pikes, and pellet slugs. We were sons adopted by fosterage, taken from a poor family to be brought up as little gents, but gents never accepted by our elder foster-brothers, who described us as whelps. We would have to watch our Ps and Qs.

If he (the Dodo) was the stern prefect with power to punish, set lines and use the cane, we were the shivering wretches with bums bared awaiting punishment, a cruel punishment meted out with an impartial severity which made it all the more cruel. He was never a big brother to us.

Maybe it was some idea he got from his reading – *Teddy Lester's Schooldays* was a sort of Bible at Springfield, and Mumu had read it to all of us in turn as we grew up. Slapton School, where Teddy Lester was the hero, was run on Sandhurst lines of military strictness, a reign of terror with heavy caning in the dorm.

We had no option but to grin and bear it; take our gruel like a man, bent over a chair, for the Dodo to lay on with a will, grunting at every whack.

The Dodo, padded up, school XI cap down over eyes, collar up to the nose in the Sutcliffe manner, stands at the crease and defies the umpire (Harrison of Notts, the school cricket coach) to give him 'out'. Up goes the finger and the Dodo snaps to attention, rams the bat under his arm (subaltern with swagger stick) and retreats to the pav with a slowness intended as silent comment on a poor decision. But no matter how cruel and unjust the punishment, the heavy caning in the dorm, no matter how great the sadistic pleasure in those inflicting it, it simply wasn't done to peach on a fellow. Certainly not in Slapton School, where we learnt many ways of the world, of which we had previously known nothing. Through Arthur Digby (fullback on the Slapton XV) we learnt of true English grit and bulldoggishness, tenacious loyalty, endearing thickness.

A very curious England emerged from these pages; perhaps useful to us later when we discovered the real England for ourselves. Slapton School seemed to be run on sadistic lines, the Beak in a wax again, cane in hand; rites of passage occurred in playing fields and dorms. It prefigured the drill grounds of later military academies. The pallor of Teddy's complexion worried the Dote and me, for we knew him as our friend; in the background perhaps was a weak mum deferring to her authoritarian husband determined to make a man out of unpromising material and who gave short shrift to lily-livered sons.

This brave but pallid youth and the stern father were to us (the Dote and Rory) as quintessentially English as the Eton wall game, being sent to Coventry, the Windmill (naughty theatre) and chorus girls scantily attired, the Changing of the Guard, rough and ready executions in the Tower, the bloody end of Mary Queen of Scots, pig-sticking in the Punjab, running the gauntlet, the Royal Navy and its strict regulations, foaming tankards of ale quaffed by the Lubber and his cronies in a local hostelry before visiting the bookies, with a nod in the direction of the bursting beer belly of the ogre-monarch Henry Tudor, who got rid of his several wives as soon as they tired him, callous as Bluebeard; all this seemed as familiar as the roast beef of old England and we cried out in a rhapsody of fond memories, 'The day of the big match dawned fine and clear!' For we seemed to have been there, cheering on Slapton School.

There were complications, naturally.

The dorm prefect, a betting man, was in the hands of the village book-ies; this fact is discovered by the school bully, the Lubber, who puts it to his own nefarious uses by forcing the betting prefect to cane Lester and 'the little yellow chap' Ito Nagao, the white hope of the school XV as scrum half, Lester and Nagao are given the father and mother of a caning in the dorm on the night before the big match, which memorably 'dawns fine and clear'.

Lester and Nagao, crippled by the heavy cane used, cannot give of their best, and take the field half crocked. The illustrations in colour show the Slapton XV in loose-fitting drawers and collarless rugger singlets of shocking pink. The Slapton team appear to be running in on tiptoe like stage fairies waving wands in an end-of-term masque. Were they apprehensive of the outcome? And, sure enough, they lost. This was somehow endearing, like the inaccuracies of old oil paintings in the time of Stubbs that showed a long-bodied racehorse with a small head, never with all four feet off the ground in a gallop; this had to wait until the invention of photography and the neat hand of the dandy Degas to get it right.

We were worried by the paleness of Teddy Lester's face. But we learnt of drill, of class, swotting, flogging, paper-chases, ritual punishment taken for granted, meted out and executed and accepted in stoic silence, the heavy cane rising and falling, the beater grunting, the others watching from their beds. The unutterable strangeness, the unspeakable, unforgettable *foreignness* of all foreigners, particularly those of another pigmentation living in paper houses in their millions thousands of miles away on islands scattered about the Sea of Japan (where Ito Nagao hailed from), which was the home of Ito the nippy Nip, scrum half of the Slapton XV, the famously plucky halfbacks Lester and Nagao. We were for them; we were madly cheering them on the sidelines.

'Will you call your brother and tell him his meal's on the table?' cried Mumu from the depths of the kitchen. She was banging pots and pans about and sounded flustered.

We went out with a torch, the Dote and I, passed under the yew tree's spread of branches and stood by the sagging tennis net, waiting for the Dodo to make an appearance on his never-changing exercise path alongside the beech hedge. The Dodo, who could wear away the patience of a saint, had worn a smooth path there, worn away the gravel surface and superimposed his own path upon the existing one, by incessant marching up and down, methodical as his mastication of food at table.

There was no sign of him. We doused the torch but stayed put, for Mumu had told us to tell him that his supper was ready, that it was getting cold, he should come in at once, so we stayed at our post and waited patiently.

Then the astounding figure burst forth again from beyond the flowerbeds and the small orchard of young apple trees and the heavy bush of Scottish thistles. He hove into sight, moving like an automaton or a soldier on sentry duty, arms pistoning, marching robotlike, his head thrust forward, taking short choppy strides.

When he had reached the end of his outward march by the rose bushes, he would turn on his heel and resume his inward march, and there we would lose him until he appeared again.

The Dodo took short fussy steps as if constricted in a tight skirt and corset, heading for the far end of the garden by the potato drills that were diminishing as the winter proceeded, there by the plum trees.

'Ma says your supper's ready!' we screeched in unison and ran for our lives, laughing and flashing the torch beam into the old yew tree that spread its great branches all about, not waiting for a reply or any acknowledgement that he had heard and understood, only the wart-hog grunt of assent to tell us that he would be on his way.

He was, if that were possible, even more terrifying at close quarters at table, where we were too timid to open our mouths except to put in food; watching him go through the exact and precisely unchanging ritual that began with him sitting down, the thoughtful removal of the napkin from its silver ring, engraved upon it his initials, D.B.J.H. Esq. and the circumspect spreading of double damask linen napkin on the stout thigh, his lap.

Then began the secondary ritual with knife and fork and the sighs of resignation when the fare wasn't up to scratch and always the peremptory ducklike nods and mouthings of the sign language deployed to get what he wanted, the salt, the pepper, the gravy boat, bread (the staff of life).

Fastidiousness of manners and deportment had been instilled into him by the nuns at Killashee prep and made him ultra-finicky and obsessional; witness his constant manicuring of fingernails, running his fingers along the emery board with an anguished expression on his face like the great American cellist Steven Doane playing Bach.

I thought later of another figure perhaps closer to the Dodo in his seclusion: Rudolf Hess trapped in the Spandau exercise yard, draped in his old military cloak, pacing up and down stiff as a board, not speaking to the guards now, wrapped in silence, grimly serving out his life sentence.

Some days he seemed to us dank and evil-smelling, as if the Bogey Man had hauled himself up the cellar steps, smelling of dampness and mould and decay, come to take his rightful place at the family table and gratefully accept whatever food was placed before him.

On other days he was heavier, slow-moving and monumental as if hewn from stone, from granite, even more silent than before, withdrawn deeply into himself or into whatever it was that troubled him, for assuredly something *did* trouble him, something was eating him. Sitting there as impassively as the Golem, and so heavy he might break the chair he sat on, seated between Mumu at the foot of the table and myself, the Faddy Feeder, the picker at bones, to his right hand.

Dado and Mumu in turn addressed each other in coded terms which we only partially understood and had to make some shift to decode; references to a mysterious Mr K and a Mrs B and the unforgettable Miss D who had called once but never again, and Charlie Twybell and the Ruttles and the Dempseys and youknowwhat and youknowwho and youknowwhere, and a certain Mr Curiosity Box, which I took to refer to myself, all ears at table, or hiding under the long table, hidden by the drapes of the tablecloth.

My parents were constantly glancing out the long windows as if these coded parties were massing on the front drive and coming on with much chattering and shouting to trample all over Dado's recently scuffled gravel, leap up the front steps and burst into the dining room where we sat at table, all risen up appalled.

Hey, what's the big idea?

Don't play with your food, dearie.

Latterly, in the darkness of the confessional, the priest would murmur behind the wire grille, 'Don't play with yourself, child.'

I was the ever-so-thin little monkey in the cage of the Dublin Zoo absently squeezing pawpaw rinds in tiny simian hands, goggling out past the bars with flaming orange eyes, apparently without any shame living amid his own dirty excretions.

For as the lost monkey will masturbate himself all night long in the darkness and seclusion of his stinking cage, in the extremity of his loss (his lost forest home, the wilderness, the swaying treetops) at night in the Zoo when all the gaping humans have departed; so Rory played with himself in the darkness of the dormitory, pulled his wire into oblivion, from the beginnings in the Third Line, through the Lower Line and on into Higher Line, for so was the school divided into three, like the three persons of the Blessed

Trinity; from Grammar through Syntax into Rhetoric, Rory played himself out. As likewise did some three hundred other pubescent schoolboys approaching manhood and a job in Esso Oil or the Bank; and Revd Father Perrot, SJ (nicknamed the Michaelmas Daisy), and Father Meany, SJ, and the oozy Father Ffrench (who had a bad stutter), hearing of this sin whispered into their inclined ears in the semi-darkness of the confessional, in turn urged me not to play with myself.

'Don't play with yourself, child.'

'No, Father.'

So I received absolution and said my penance.

The Dodo, who never got to bowl for the school XI, for no skipper had ever asked him to 'turn his arm over' and try a few overs from this end, nevertheless put in hour after hour at patient practice, bowling into a long net erected on the tennis court in early summer by Tommy Flynn. One stump stuck in the ground to mark where he released each grunting delivery, another twenty-two yards away which he attempted to knock out of the ground and into the net; pounding in heavy and truculent as Voce of Notts; throwing both arms up like Bill Bowes when the ball missed the stump by a millimetre. The Clongowes purple and white tie was knotted about his portly waistline as a makeshift belt, in the fashion of a previous age, adopted maybe by Dr W.G. Grace himself, who had set the fashion, like Edward when he was Prince of Wales knotting his tie in a certain way, a style to copy.

The Dodo sent down thousands upon thousands of deliveries, the white shirt clamped to his back with the sweat of his exertions, undone several buttons down. He set off from the gravel path on to the tennis court, six strides to where the arm went over; then the march down the crease to collect the ball, the rubbing against his flannelled thigh to bring up a shine and leave a mark as though he were bleeding; then the thoughtful march back to the rockery wall, against which he sometimes urinated, splashing like a cart-horse below us, for the Dote and I had climbed on to the greenhouse roof and hid behind the tall chimney where the jackdaws had made a nest and brought up their young, diving down to feed them worms; it was from there were heard the Dodo pissing and sending down his thunderbolts, the tail of his shirt now out, the studded cricket boots much in need of Blanco.

These practice sessions went on for hours, for he had limitless patience. When at last he gave up, the stump stuck in the net, pullover about his shoulders, he sat himself on the garden seat outside the summerhouse and gazed down past the sundial and the palm trees and the pergola, thinking no doubt of the great bowling feats of his heroes.

Once the Dote and I, at a tender age, had escaped from Nurse O'Reilly, who was running a bath for us, and come down from the bathroom, scuttled downstairs and out on to the gravel, naked as the day we were born, and about to run around the house and into the garden when who came from cricket practice with all their cricket gear but our two elder brothers, with caps on their heads, carrying bats and pads and pullovers about their shoulders in the style of Test players quitting the field at the end of a gruelling day.

'Hey, what's going on here?' cried the Dodo in his high soprano voice.

He opened the innings for the school; he was a stonewaller difficult to remove. Having dug himself in, he occupied the crease as though he intended staying there forever, perfectly satisfied to make few runs, refusing to take quick singles. D.B.J. Hill had to be *pried* out.

Nurse O'Reilly, who was taking a quick puff in the porch, called out that we would certainly catch our deaths of cold, and we should come into the house at once.

'Would you ever run out like good boys and tell your brother that his meal's ready and will be getting cold? Muffle up well.'

So, well muffled up and armed with the torch (its batteries failing, shining weakly on the garden door), obediently we sallied out into the pitch-black night of winter when the earth had already begun to harden with December frost and underfoot the grass of the tennis court was now stiff as astro turf and the net (never taken in) snagged and torn and tangled up with its supports and the sundial just a greyish blob by the palm trees shuffling their stiff sodden fronds and the summerhouse with its clapboard walls and climbing roses (finished now) just a dark thing on its elevation and the cold wind off Mangan's big field soughing through the bare branches of our great beech tree, oh!

Would you ever call your brother? Never never would we call him by his Christian name, Benedict. D.B.J.H. Never never never ever would he call us by ours, Rory and Colman George. Why he hardly seemed to see us, never adverted to us; we might as well not have been there at all. We were like the bell that summoned him to the table, functionally useful at times; at other times, playing games, getting giddy, a curse he had to put up with. D.B.J.H. Esq. The *q* had a curlicue tail to it that soared up and away, the swirling pretentious signature of a fop. He was named after his father, who had the makings of a fop.

Could the rapidly perambulating one, whose footsteps we heard hurrying towards us, see like a cat in the dark, then? Hardly; but years of incessant path-pounding summer and winter had worn away the gravel surface, as a decayed tooth is worn away to its exposed nerve, and the hard earth underneath shone with its quartz like a stream, upon which he resolutely marched.

The stiff familiar figure hove into sight now, pounding the path by the tall beech hedge, swinging its shoulders, head thrust forward from the trunk like the figurehead on a ship sailing before the wind, sails filling with the wind, turning upon itself and then as it (or he) swung around on his heel we recognised the oncoming Dodo, ready for the return march, and called out together in our shrill trebles, 'Ma says you're to come to supper!' as if that would stop him in his tracks; and ran off screeching with laughter. The pair of us good little brats ran off laughing fit to burst.

Benedict!

– 6 –

Mainly Semantics

On their holidays from Clongowes, which after all stood less than ten miles away beyond Clane village and the jolly Farmers (the lights shining like an ocean liner sailing through Kildare, over fields and low ditches sparkling in the frosty nights), the Dodo and brother Bun seemed to have changed; certainly they spoke a different language to ours, dis and dat and mudder an me brudder and me fawder.

They favoured a strange tacky talk of obscure and puzzling references to unheard-of rituals that took place at the pool and in the three dormitories that segregated the three Lines. They spoke knowingly of the Yak, 'Baa' Keegan, 'Shanks' Lowry, Eskimo Nell (an American girl who came once at visiting time), 'Daisy' Maloney, 'Dog's Hole' Maguire, 'Horny' Ward (the science master), 'The Dog' McGlade, SJ (Classical Greek), 'Spud' Murphy and Father 'Spike' O'Donnell (who parted his black hair with a central parting like Mandrake the Magician and was said to have an ungovernable temper), Father 'Razz' O'Beirne, who discarded his dog-collar and bloodied the nose of a Communist who spat on him in Salamanca.

Not to mention pandies, cockers (on the bare bum), twice nine, sleeps, sods, spooning, sowing, sneaks, tacks, snogging, sucks, Square Johnnies and Refectory Johnnies.

'Bags first go!' they cried in fluting voices.

'Crikey, I'm creased!'

Little Micky Kelly, SJ, was Father Minister, a sort of liaison officer between the parents and boys, much sought after by the loving mothers, much deferred to by the awestruck daddies, walking with him around the Higher Line track or about the castle (formerly country seat of the Wogan-Brownes) or down in the pleasure grounds.

He had a soft small appeasing voice and handshake and he was the authority you appealed to for 'Sleeps' which got you off night study, swotting up prep for next day's classes.

He presided over meals in the refectory thrice a day aloft in a wooden rostrum like the pulpit in St Audoen's in Dublin, with some narrow steps leading up. A nimble little hop on to the first step and then up hand over hand; he threw back the wings of his soutane and seated himself aloft on his throne and twinkled at his subjects below, watching to see that no billet-doux passed from table to table, for the three Lines were divided again here, the Third Liners as far as possible from the Higher Liners, all hoping for a touch, to 'get their hole' before leaving.

The other Father Kelly was Father Brendan Kelly, SJ, back after years in a Jesuit house in Australia to be Higher Line prefect and coach of the school XV; a tall, bucktoothed, quick-striding man whom you attended for easy pandies, unlike the Prefect of Studies, who sat in his office with the door threateningly open. If he heard you creeping by with a punishment tag in Latin, he called you in, whipped out his pandy bat, and would take the hand off you, panting as he struck.

Father Brendan Kelly was an equable sort of a man who coached in sports, track events, field events, relays, cricket and rugby. On Saturday evenings he sometimes took Declamation, a kind of pep talk to the Higher Liners assembled in the games room that got you off study. He asked the Higher Liners to open their dormitory windows at night because it wasn't so fresh in the morning when he came in at 6.50 to see that his charges were dressing in their cubicles and going down to Mass. He asked the Higher Line to desist from defacing the square (the toilets with cubicles called boxes presided over by a square Johnny to see that no hanky-panky went on, no passing of notes under box doors or soliciting messages on the backs of box doors, or bunking over the barbed wire to swim in the Liffey) with graffiti; though he understood the inclination and had heard that the walls of Pompeii were similarly defaced, so someone who had been there told him.

Finally, the local country lads of Clane and environs served at table and were called Johnnies since ages immemorial. Father Kelly said it would be kinder to call them by their given names, Johnny and Micky and Kevin and Paddy. We knew their names and it was rather demeaning to be called Johnnies, all of them. We were given privileges and should not abuse them. That was about all he had to say.

— 7 —

An Unwelcome Visitor Calls

O ne fine summer evening about six we were all sitting about the study table taking our supper or high tea (ham and salad with chopped tomatoes, hard-boiled eggs for those who would have them, all but the ham our own produce, with a Swiss roll for 'afters') when a spry figure, undoubtedly female, flitted past the window and presently we heard a timid knocking on the side door which stood invitingly wide open.

The family sat rigid and mortified as stone: Mumu stared at Dado as though it were all his fault, the Dodo stared at brother Bun as if by staring hard enough he could compel the unwelcome Visitor to go away, the Dote stared at me in mild surmise: I was the one who wouldn't touch hard-boiled eggs or be persuaded or coaxed to drink a glass of milk.

'It's that one from Maynooth,' piped up the Dote, who sat facing the window, facing Dado who had his back to it. 'Miss Carmel Noseyparker Dermody!' sneered Dado, who had been 'getting a colour up' in the long grass of the orchard, stark naked on an oil-soaked rug, and was lightly dressed in slashed running shorts and sandals, his combinations or 'combs' cut short at the middle, and was hardly dressed for 'receiving'.

'Carmel Dermody, what a lovely surprise!' we heard Mumu's most dulcet tones in the hallway.

The Noseyparker, or Two-Faced Bitch in Dado's scornful appellation, had already entered, getting no response from her timid knocking, and was standing in the hallway outside the lamproom where the Aladdin lamps were kept and filled, staring at a great pile of coke that mounted to the ceiling, uncertain how to proceed further.

'It's that bitch from Maynooth,' Dado said in a strangled aside, staring at the Dote's innocent little face as if it were a burnished mirror wherein was reflected Mumu being gracious to Miss Smarty Pants in the hall, and now saying, 'Come in, come in! You must take a cup of tea with us. I'm sure you must be famished after your walk.'

And in they came; the family rising as one.

Mealtimes were always a little charged, what with the demands of the

faddy eater, the Dodo's silence and pointing and 'Ahems' for the procurement
of condiments out of reach, Dado's table-rapping with knuckles and coded
references addressed to Mumu; the meals, sometimes soon over, at other
times indefinitely prolonged, arbitrary as inter-parliamentary debates (but
here carried on in silence with innuendo and sign language, eye messages),
this person vindicated, that one damned. It would put you in mind of the com-
plexities of our unfair and lopsided Statutes of Kilkenny, the Codicils of the
Elders of Zion or the archaic and long obsolete Manx laws, procedures and
protocols to control an island less than a third the size of our own, the stocks
and the gallows barely dismantled, flogging still popular in sentencing.

'Yes indeed, Mrs Hill. I'm *famished*.'

She lived with her old cranky mother somewhere on the way to Maynooth
and had 'run up' three tweed skirts, after two sittings, lined and zipped, that
Mumu was so delighted with, she said she would order more. But calling
for sittings and calling unannounced was not the same thing; as long as she
knew her place (and stayed in it) socially she was acceptable at Springfield;
otherwise not. She had come across the fields to pay us a surprise visit, it was
such a lovely day for it and she loved walking; she wore booties and ankle
socks and the booties were yellow with pollen, and she never stopped talking,
the cup balanced on her lap and her little finger raised when she sipped in a
delicate ladylike fashion. She wore one of her own tweed skirts and under it
a corset that attempted to flatten her pronounced rump. The deep imitation
leather armchair bought at cost price from Jack Ellis, whom Dado called a
Jew-boy, was as awkward to get out of as the deepest bunker in Portmarnock
links and groaned deeply and embarrassingly every time she moved as if
involuntarily emitting wind, dry farts.

She sat sideways on, sipping tea and flattering Mumu, offering to my
abstracted gaze a disconcerting view of fleshy female inside leg and fat thigh
and she was asking Mumu where would she (Mumu) be without them (the
Dote and myself, the second-last born faddy feeder and the last-born who
'was no trouble at all').

'Run along now, boys. Go and play in the garden,' Mumu bade us in a
grand affected accent, as the chatelaine giving orders to a groom. 'Say goodbye to Miss Dermody.'

So we ran out into the summerhouse and did murderous imitations of the
unwelcome guest. Speaking in prissy tones and balancing an invisible cup
of tea on the lap, we were in turn Miss Carmel Dermody, the guest who had
called unannounced but would not come again; for behind all her gush she
had watched us, and saw us judge her and find her wanting. She was no fool.

'I'm not overstaying my welcome, am I?' the Dote asked, giving me a sly look. 'You have a lovely place here. How do you manage to keep it so clean?'

'I don't bother,' I said in the voice of Carmel Dermody.

'Your two manly little lads must be a real blessing,' the Dodo ventured boldly, and we fell about pissing ourselves laughing.

'Oh not a *tall*,' I gushed, 'we love to have you.'

'Do you know Dunmanway?' shrieked the Dote.

'I'm sure you must be famished!' I got in.

It was as good gas as the Gaiety.

'To tell you the truth, I *am* famished,' squeaked the Dote.

'You're really famished?'

'What a bummer,' said the Dote.

It was the new word he had recently discovered: bummer. Miss Carmel Dermody was a *real* bummer.

— 8 —

The Handbell and the Gong

To stay immobilised was the Dodo's dream, since all action was suspect, tarnished back to its source. As an opener who refused to open up he was most himself, forever standing guard, an emblem or graven image: Len Hutton of Yorkshire and England, obdurate and unflinching as Yorkshire granite.

Always at his fingernails, buffing, snipping, trimming, blowing on them; like one of Faulkner's devious rustics a-whittling slivers of wood on the back porch of Mrs Littlejohn's kitchen, whittling in order to disguise what he was thinking or waiting for the summons to food, 'Vittles is up!'

What was that imperious term he used?

I SAY!

The handbell rung vigorously by Lizzy told him what he wanted to hear, namely, that the food was in the oven awaiting his arrival. When the meal was over he rose, pushed his chair in and left as silently as he had arrived, at the summons of a gong. A gong for lunch, a handbell after dark. He never flew combat missions in the dark when he was serving in the RAF, and when the war ended he came back and was working in an office on Stephen's Green in Dublin, studying to qualify as a quantity surveyor, had laid out cartridge paper and tacked it down with drawing pins on the study table, brought in his

T-squares and rubbers, mapping pens and marking ink, HB pencils sharpened keenly as his fingernails, and set to work there every evening, before
Ovaltine and bed, cackling at Tommy Handley ('It's That Man Again!') on
faulty transmission from the BBC, as if the Irish Sea had got into the works
and Handley and his jokers were drowning. The family was obliged to eat
elsewhere and took meals in the drawing room, in the dining room empty
of furniture except the table and chairs, and even in Mumu's bedroom with
a view of distant blue Dublin hills, with Lysanders and Avro Ansons rising
up from Baldonnel aerodrome.

'Stay!'

The Dodo's poses at the non-striker's end were dramatic in the extreme;
he remained rooted to the spot, gloved hand rigid as the tall Civic Guard
who directed the traffic over Capel Street Bridge and along Ormond Quay
in both directions. None of your cheeky Compton creeping down the pitch
before the bowler's arm was well over.

It was an illustration of one of Mumu's favourite quotations (was it from
some novel by Brinsley MacNamara, whom she had known in her youth?):
'Wanted: a detective to arrest the course of time.'

The left forearm vertical and stiff from the elbow up, the palm (white-
gloved) extended to stop oncoming traffic; the right hand making an accommodating gesture of 'free flow', under the rigid left elbow as though paddling
the air, 'Proceed!'

All Civic Guards had to be six foot or over in those days, clomping down
in outsize boots from the training depot in Phoenix Park past where Gina
Green had taken the Dote and me to the Dublin Zoo, past where I went later
when playing cricket for Phoenix with Jimmy Boucher, who bowled body-
line, with Dick Greer and Brendan Fox and David Pigott, and crouched in
the leg trap with the Quinns, Frank, Brendan, Paddy and Kevin.

Boucher had once bowled out the New Zealanders. He kept his jock-strap
in a canvas bag used for small change, silver coinage in the bank, having once
worked in the Munster and Leinster.

You could hear the click of his fingers as he released each fiercely flighted
delivery that broke either way, after the high-stepping, chest-out bustling run-
up had the shiny red ball whipping off the pitch; the click was as menacing as
the Xhosa tongue-click; and the leg-trap that had been crouched behind the
batsman and to one side rose upright again. The six deliveries came buzzing
down the pitch like a hive of wild bees.

'Nice one, Jimmy,' someone murmured.

When Phoenix played the Free Foresters, both teams lunched in the

Dublin Zoo and a cheerful fellow who had been a British Army officer in Soviet Russia during the war said he had slept with a Russian woman and that it was like sleeping with a she-bear. But what was a British officer doing in Stalinist Russia? Were the Allies fools enough to share their Bletchley Park code-breaking knowledge with Uncle Joe?

The Dodo, as I say, was always at his hands, attending to his fingernails, buffing, trimming, clipping, pushing in the cuticles, blowing on his fingernails and holding them up for closer inspection with the quiet complacency that a cat, when engaged in toilet, gives its paws.

The Dodo was as one of those dandies you find in paintings by Carpaccio forever fondling one of those terrible little dogs called Tenerife, or as the butterflies that flitter about a Whistler canvas. Such vanity!

− 9 −

An Unwelcome Visit Recalled

Dado said that she was 'country cute' and he had a good mind to give her a flea in her ear if she had the neck to come calling again. The cool cheek of her!

'Underbred,' said Mumu with a dismissive sniff that put the upstart back in her place. 'But what more can you expect with parents like hers? A big thick cattle dealer and his big lump of a wife with no more social graces than a heifer. That sort of woman should *never* wear beige. The daughter is making sure not to take after her.'

So that's how it was.

As long as Carmel Dermody knew her place, and stayed in it, well and good; she was acceptable. Acceptable, that is to say, as a talented seamstress who could 'run up' skirts and blouses to order. She was most definitely not welcome as a casual visitor who dropped in uninvited for tea and a chat, wearing sensible brogues for walking across the fields and a powerful girdle that attempted to control that big behind of hers.

She was after all just the country-bred daughter of a big thick lug of a cattle jobber who had an unprepossessing wife and an ugly big house somewhere up there near Maynooth.

Neither Mumu nor Dado would seek or accept any reciprocal hospitality from the Dermodys; nor would Miss Two-Face attempt to offer any; that was clearly understood by all parties concerned.

The truth of the matter is that my dear departed parents were in some ways strangers to this world. Both had their own particular brand of ingrained self-centredness, a lethargy, akin to the apathy of the stars, the indifference of the galaxies floating away into space. They preferred to let things slide.

They were cast down twice, twice blew all their wealth away, all security, ending up in a damp underground basement fit only for rats. There they lived on the dole, and for four years on the money Rory sent them from Johannesburg.

When, through no choice of theirs, they began to go down, they went far down; finally they found themselves in a place where I couldn't reach them.

Inherited money, money for which you hadn't sweated, was funny money, hardly money at all. Dado had no compunction in asking for and getting large overdrafts to 'see him through', very condescending to bank managers and then cringing before the same official when the American dividends finally ran dry. Dado stopped picking his ears with a match and began poking up both nostrils with his little finger, letting off a barrage of farts, poised at some strategic point.

Mumu was no help at all, except at helping him to spend it, the cab at the door, Phoenix Park races, dinner at the Royal Hibernian and the Red Bank, Jammet's; the dividends rushed away. 'Keep it and you'll always have it,' Mumu said bitterly, her lipstick awry, her awful hat at an angle, like a ship sinking.

When they ran into debt (and 'ran' is the operative word), she protested that she was at her wits' end; now the bank manager was losing patience; stiffly phrased letters began to arrive. Dado, hands in pockets, was off, whistling to himself. Inherited money wasn't money at all.

Though Catholics were discouraged from holding a lease in the Burnaby, the most Anglican of enclaves within a mainly Protestant community, Dado found a small holiday bungalow up for sale on Kinlen Road on the extreme border of the Burnaby. Even though he was still nominally a Catholic, though no longer a practising one, he became a member of the Greystones Golf Club. In time, with the passing of years and schooldays ended, Rory joined him, proposed by 'Brandy' Ball and seconded by Simon Pettigrew.

Having lost or spent one fortune, Dado and Mumu began resolutely to throw away another. With the proceeds of the Springfield sale, for which Dado had got a good price, he bought 'Caragh' (Gaelic for 'friend'), and complacently saw it go to rack and ruin over the years.

The cycles of extravagance were repeated, the squandering went on apace, dinners at the Grand Hotel and the Horse and Hounds in Delgany, hacking on a hired horse, on a four-day whiskey binge with Captain Ball, and him with only one leg (the other he had left behind on Anzio beach). Until at last, for the second time, it was all gone again; but this time for good. There was no house to sell, just a load of debts; not even the furniture was theirs. They quit Greystones in ostentatious poverty. After sixteen years of ever-dwindling resources the American annuities dried up, their poor effects were piled up on an open wagon and they left for a new life in Dalkey 'like the Joads setting out for California', the Dote reported to Rory who was living in London.

Notions about social inferiors and betters remained with them: that was all they had left, their illusions. The American money dried up when the real estate (the Hill Building in LA) was sold.

When the herd of cattle that had grazed in the seventy-two acres at Springfield were sold and the land steward Tommy Flynn got his walking papers and returned home to Longford, the downward spiral had begun.

The farm was not worked, the fields lay fallow, were rented out for grazing, the idlest form of farming for gentlemen disposed to a life of ease. Dado did some light scuffling, did a few chores around the house and farm, counted the eggs laid in the mangers, occupied his days in unrelenting idleness.

After Springfield was sold, they moved to Greystones; after the Burnaby they moved to Dalkey; after Dalkey to Dun Laoghaire. Going down into the Haigh Terrace basement flat would 'do' for them both; and indeed it did, given time and enough dampness. A brain haemorrhage in the night did for Mumu; cancer finally caught up with Dado two years later. Their last years were not happy ones. They gave me my life and I should be thankful to them.

In Haigh Terrace (ominous mnemonic!) they were already halfway into the grave; Dean's Grange Cemetery wasn't too many furlongs off. Their mouldy underground quarters were situated midway between the Garda station and the spired church built by Italian POWs.

– 10 –

A Fragment of the True Cross

My earliest and fondest memories were of the Dote dressing himself on the thin strip of carpet worn threadbare by constant usage on the floor that separated our twin beds in the unheated nursery.

Solemnly vesting himself in a mealy-coloured woollen gansey knitted by his mother; applying himself to the task in hand with all the intense serious-ness that was habitual to him; for that was the way he was made, that was the way he was and nothing could change that. Never exactly 'the glass of fashion and the mould of form' but the cheap striped tie knotted about the neck so fragile, the shirt worn for three or more days slipped over the head; then on with the boots with turned-up toes and brassy eye-studs, dull clothes that proclaimed duty, duty, duty, before the slick of water to settle the quiff, the comb run through the parting. His everyday clothes were as keepsakes flung into a drawer and forgotten by this careful brother of mine who never threw anything away, whose earliest ambition, so he averred, was to be a crow.

A crow; cor!

Were not clothes 'weeds' for poet Edmund Spenser, as 'wonted weeds' were mourning apparel in Shakespeare's day? My younger brother would have looked neat and chipper if kitted out in silken knee-britches or half-hose, ruffs and powdered wig, the face powdered too, cheeks rouged and a touch of lipstick and eyeliner, in the time of Haydn and Schumann; to bring a touch of natural colour to anaemic cheeks, a sparkle to the anxious eye.

He had a nose on him thin and keen as the nib of a pen; not a fountain pen, mark you, not a Bird or a Waterman with little sac and clip, but a penny pen with disposable nib and a cheap wooden grip ink-stained and chewed with mental effort, frustration and long usage, dipped into the inkwell of Quink, giving off a whiff strong as chloroform or smelling salts; in order to attempt joined-up writing, copying out the adage set forth on the top line of the exercise book. A penny pen in First or Second Infants of the Holy Faith Convent hidden behind the walls of Celbridge in the care of the nuns in the time not long after the Eucharistic Congress of 1932.

Now divesting himself of his drawers and pullover (stitching had already run along one arm), rumpled shirt and combinations (his 'combs'), the day-wear; to climb into his nightwear, crumpled pyjamas as bedraggled as the items he had just discarded and folded neatly at the end of his bed.

Pulling the shirt over his head with arms crisscrossed in a fussy way that never failed to irritate me, his face – when it appeared again – screwed tight and anxious in a purposeful scowl as though caught in the act of somersault-ing headlong over a vaulting horse or 'pulling off' some daring trick of the loop which contrived to whisk the gymnast back the way he had come, arms now outflung for applause, before running off, vanishing like Harry Houdini over the fearful fall of Niagara in a barrel.

Well, it takes a worried man to sing a worried song. The finite is ever trapped within the infinite. All good things must come to an end. It never rains but it pours.

Abhorring laxness, the sluggishness that leads to backsliding, the Dote was ever his own man. When he applied himself to the task in hand it became a mighty serious matter, an act of single-mindedness. Firm and even-handed in his dealings with others, he was as honest as the day is long; his character had been formed early and nothing would change it. Humanity is its work in itself, our daily bread can only be earned – and we have this on the very best authority – by the sweat of our brow. When he pulled the ganzy over his head the face that reappeared was an Aztec or Mayan mask of suffering.

He drove me from the Holyhead ferry in his beaten-up Mini Minor through Wales and across England via Stratford-upon-Avon where a company of merry Spanish bakers was working in a bakery at six o'clock in the morning, from whom we bought a loaf of warm bread. And off via Edgehill, site of a famous battle. Coming at last with swollen feet to the two-storey semi-detached house sublet to slutty hippies at 18 Ludlow Road on the way to those sad-sounding places, Ongar and Hounslow, home of howling dogs.

My poor brother was distraught and all but in tears when he saw what havoc the hippies had perpetrated against his house somewhere off the Great North Road, amid the onward-spreading sameness of the great urban sprawl.

'LYNN WAS HERE!!!' haggishly screeched one wall, daubed and besmeared with what looked like menstrual blood. 'HIS 'N HERS!!' was splashed slapdash in runny purple humpy lettering athwart the defaced headboard, roughly as evacuations voided on counterpane and sheets. The cramped rooms were livid with shrieking psychedelic colours, porno magazines crammed into the overflowing privy, its cistern blocked with nameless filth. All the signs of hanky-panky were there, as though the rascally subtenants had just departed, leaving their foulness and smells behind. All the never-ending mess of other lives had been toppled pell-mell over my now thoroughly confused and upset brother, so careful in his own way; his privacy and security had been breached, torn apart.

Didn't Wordsworth have some scatterbrained theory that houses should be the same colour as the land they stood on? In some primitive cultures human dwellings are glued together with excrement.

In Stieglitz, West Berlin in the years of the Berlin Wall, the former 'brown district' with many of the grim Nazi villas still standing aloof behind their high protective walls, there lived Walter Waldmann in deep seclusion, a 'scraper' by profession; that is to say an illegal abortionist.

In Andalucía on the coast, the walls of the fishermen's cottages are precariously put together with rubble masonry, rocks, driftwood off the beach and sea-sand in the cement likely to 'give' in heavy rain; as happened the morning Trevor Callus drove back from the Málaga nursing home with his Norwegian wife and newborn daughter Camilla in his DKW. My wife and I were passengers. We had hardly turned the key in the door of our house when we heard the rumble of one of the poorer cottages opposite collapsing into the street down which the rain was pouring. Calle Carabeo in Nerja always had a high pong of sewage, human waste, which delighted Callus, who liked to quote statistics of what *caca* was flushed daily into the Hudson in New York.

An old-fashioned taste in clothes was part of the Dote's habitual reserve, of not drawing attention to himself: socks pulled up over trouser ends for cycling; shabby woollen gloves in need of darning. One thought of Freya Stark travelling through the Arab lands with riding-shirt buttoned up to the throat, woollen stockings covering her head, shirt worn over riding britches, making her way through Bouzai Gumbad into Bistritza and on over the Parmirs.

Colman was transparently honest, honest as the day is long, incapable of cheating, notorious for never accepting bribes, straight as a die. As they say nowadays, he 'hung in' there tenaciously, a person of set habits fixed as his formal attire, reticent by nature, even secretive – to every nook its cranny. Conscious of his obligations and set in his ways, he had long ago put himself in order. In his view we had not been put on this earth to enjoy ourselves; think rather on frugality, on decorum.

The unchanging ritual of dressing was as mannered and composed as Colman's way of saying his night prayers, when whispering into joined hands as he prepared for bed just across from me; enacted with the same ritual care that he used when vesting and divesting himself as an altar boy serving Mass, careful with cruets and thurible, immensely slow in measured genuflections, solemn as a crow digging in a potato drill.

Behind all this there was something obdurate, fine and unflinching, as true to form as a splinter from the True Cross. Colman, donning surplice and soutane in the sacristy at Clongowes, holding the paten under the chins of communicants with their eyes shut tight, was as solemn and subdued as a convict donning prison garb in preparation for serving out a stiff sentence; the clothes themselves were the token of bondage, a penitential vesting correctly meek, a humbling investiture.

With eyes lowered, he invoked the Scourging at the Pillar in the ritual he was partaking in, marking the progress of the Holy Passion. He himself, the humble altar boy, the suppliant, a veritable pillar of rectitude and correctness, robed in red soutane to his ankles, verily washed in the Blood of the Lamb. In the fringed white surplice stiff with bleach and ironing, he became the Lamb Bled White.

The little white puffs of incense sent out of the perforated thurible boat sedately swung by my brother, told in Latin, *Castitas! Castitas!* Be chaste, sin no more, Heaven is nigh. A whiff of that stuff assailing my nostrils caused my giddy head to reel.

Hands joined at breast level, eyes downcast and pale as a sheet, Colman moved slowly and gravely as in a trance, for himself and for the other altar boy from Second Syntax, preceding the celebrant priest – and this morning it was to be Father Eamonn Diffilly himself, republican and Gaelic revivalist – through the arch of the sacristy door, moving together in a phalanx towards the high altar as the school of over three hundred boys knelt as one, a field of growing wheat ruffled by a sudden breeze.

He was by nature a *kneeler.* He liked to get things right, liked to obey; it became him. In retirement in his later years, free time became a burden; he fed the half-wild moggies, worried about the weeds, began to be a little autocratic in shops, bossing shopkeepers about, keeping them on their toes, glad to serve Mr Hill (no informality please) who had been a big noise in the Planning Department of the Wicklow County Council. He ordered wood and milk, took in the *Irish Times,* was (I suspect) somewhat of a tyrant in the home.

The half-finished home had all the chilly ambience of a Bavarian *Kursaal* out of season, water dripping on to deserted landings, the phone ringing and no one there to answer.

His wife Stella Veronica didn't answer back, didn't give any lip, seemed contented enough to live in the past, with her memories of Greystones, which after all wasn't so far away.

The ugly cats glided about, were fed regularly. They had been found lean and starving on some building site and taken back and fed and had lavished upon them all the love that couldn't be lavished on the children that hadn't come. In that sense their life together had a certain shape to it, though admittedly an uncomfortable shape, as the lives of others always seem to have; the chill of nothing much.

For so frail a being he seemed to carry on his back an enormous freight of irresistible sorrows, as *der buckelige Männlein,* his hump.

Sincerity was the *sine qua non* of his existence, that which propped up the whole shaky edifice and kept it standing. When duties were respected and honoured, as they should be honoured and respected, then the emoluments would flow; how could they not?

This I sensed in the stink of the swirling incense that drifted back from the altar; but Catholicism for me was like the lukewarm milk Colman fetched in old-fashioned bottles at a certain shop in Wicklow that sold newspapers and processed 'turf', known as briquettes. That was the Catholic Church on its wobbly foundations, a leaning tower of Pisa seen in the incense fumes and the two altar boys robed in red, kneeling and genuflecting when the priest came to the altar rail holding the ciborium with the hosts in it and the altar boys suddenly sticking out their tongues at the priest and then swallowing the blessed oval dissolving on their tongues.

That to me was all humbug, like the hand-shaking and the Pope prostrating himself on the tarmac of strange airports, purporting to kiss the ground, a lowly and unhygienic act. The Blessed in Heaven in their serried ranks, supposing they were observing this malarky, must have been in stitches.

Now wasn't it typical of my brother that his lowly dwelling should be nameless? That veritable Crusoe stockade of his was 'The House With No Name', Ye Olde Moncken Holt, haunt of coot and hem, abode of otter; which went with the subdued genuflection, meek mien, the serving. 'Lurkyne in hernes and in lanes blynde,' (Chaucer).

Not for Colman such grandiose notions as Frank Lloyd Wright's Falling Water by a river cascade in the woods of Pennsylvania or the Robie House in Chicago; not the dwelling place that Luis Barragan had designed for a rich client in Mexico City; nor the stupendous eighteenth-century wooden chalet where Balthus hid himself away in the Swiss Alps; nor Gaudi's gaudy edifice in Barcelona – a witch's house built of sugar; nor Branson's grandiose Caribbean hideaway, an island retreat fit only for high-flyers such as himself.

It would certainly be more subdued and darker, along the lines of the Roman villa built for Alberto Moravia (born Pincherle) by an architect father in a small thickly wooded garden somewhere behind the Hotel Excelsior; a darkened abode purpose-built, suitable for a melancholic at his own depressing dinner party.

Pliny the Younger owned summer and winter villas, Malaparte and Dali had their exotic Mediterranean belvederes and eyries built to puff up their own vanity; but a whiff of Bauhaus simplicity and austerity would better suit my brother's spartan taste.

Nabobs like Maugham and Berenson owned palaces with Lamborghinis and Astra-Romanas stashed in spacious garages, with gardeners and droves of servants at hand to gratify every whim; but my brother was having none of that. Maugham, the milk-drinking nonagenarian mulitimillionaire, was irascible as a stoat, staring down the table at his uneasy guests dining off his silver plate; the host convinced that they were hatching schemes against him; while his French servants, having already devoured his dogs, had proceeded to rob him blind. Riches didn't amount to much under such circumstances; or at least hadn't produced happiness.

The luxurious homes of the very rich, private pleasure domes of the Côte d'Azur battlemented and buttressed and with flag flying that announced the owner was in residence, once the property of some duc or vicomte but now more likely owned by a film star the likes of Rex Harrison; these were fortresses of wealth perched on a hill.

The benign old codger Berenson paced gravely about the manicured grounds of I Tatti and all's well with the world; at least so believed the not-so-decrepit Rex Harrison in San Genseio at Portofino.

– 11 –

A Rude Country Habitation

The House With No Name in Dunganstown West was hidden behind its protective escarpment of earthworks and cramped weed-choked ramparts and had already a dilapidated look, even before completion. The Dote had taken to heart Mumu's bitter axiom that you can't have too much of a good thing. She had a repertoire of such old sayings: what was sauce for the goose was sauce for the gander, a little learning is a dangerous thing, a little goes a long way, it never rains but it pours, you've got to be cruel to be kind.

Eat every scrap, she bade us at table, confronted with reheated beef and dried-out swedes, stewed apple and custard after school; and we would again be reminded of the starving millions in China.

The House With No Name, the unfinished home, was duplicated on another scale in the drab clothes he wore and seemed to prefer above all others, the trusty Balbriggan surtout as snug a fit as feathers on a Rhode Island Red, the pens and pencils of his profession protruding from his breast pocket, the jacket so well worn (worn seven days a week) that it already had a reach-me-down second-hand appearance soon after he had bought it off the peg in some old-fashioned Talbot Street, Dublin haberdashery away from the fashionable quarters; duplicating the jacket just discarded, a herringbone tweed in mustard twill. No question of taste; taste didn't come into it. Appearances didn't count, after all, didn't amount to much; for behind all fiction loomed the undisputed fact. As behind Citizen Kane's Xanadu stood Hearst's real foursquare San Simeon, the stately pleasure dome erected with no regard for cost on the deserts of the Gulf of California, just as Branson's men had dynamited the crest off a deserted Caribbean island to build his House on the Hill (Necker), his bailiwick seventy-four acres of sun-blasted scrub and cactus and screeching seabirds. As behind Sutpen's Hundreds (Faulkner's fancy) stood the remnants of some honest-to-God antebellum Mississippian mansion with shadowy colonnades fit home for the loon bird and the coon; empty slave quarters somewhere decently out of sight, in that time and that place fragrant with wisteria and magnolia sweet and fresh, where Southern belles in hoop skirts did not walk but floated.

My sober, level-headed brother, set in his spartan ways and normally so sparing of praise, declared that a good two inches separated every word in Scott Fitzgerald's 1925 novel, *The Great Gatsby,* one of those American moralities on the theme that wealth does not buy happiness, which came out the year before I was born.

But hold your hearses, Golubchik, wasn't 'Jay Gatsby' already an assumed name, a disguise for 'Jimmy Gatz', and the mansion built there on West Egg in the great wet barnyard of Long Island Sound with its marble swimming pool and forty acres of rolling lawns just as much an invention as the vast palace faked by Welles's small ingenious models as conceived by his special-effects man Vernon L. Walker and executed by his Art Director Van Nest Polglase?

The grandiose mansion was itself a surrogate, an imitation of some grand hotel de ville that the rich but alcoholic author had once seen like a drunken vision and had tabulated and stored up in his acquisitive and retentive writer's memory for later use; to be there, immutable, transfixed as a figment of the imagination, a dream.

A stranger called Lou Harrison built himself a house on a high spit of land overlooking the Pacific, because he couldn't stand the constant din of the metropolis. 'The thing roars all day long and there's no getting away from it. There are no woods to go to. Too much turbulence, too many goddamn people, too much noise.' He found a safe retreat in the Mojave Desert, where he built his house entirely of densely packed bales of straw fixed to cement foundations, with soundproofed rooms.

Charles Olson thought that he had recognised the origins of the mosque dome in the curvilinear tents of the nomads pitched by oases, and the form of the minarets in cypress trees. These, to frequently drugged eyes and brain, were indeed deceptive likenesses, beguiling in their winsomeness as certain imaginary ruins found in Venetian Masters depicting parts and relictae, broken monuments of dead generations, roofless ruins and the dust of ancestors, perfect parts of an impossible whole.

I remember the holy old man who had built himself a corrugated iron hut away from the sea, held down with wire hawsers and sods of earth on the roof, near the sand dunes at Baltray golf links when I played in the East of Ireland Golf Championship and bought a set of irons off the pro, Mick McGurk. Dado had been incautious enough to give me a blank cheque signed by his own fair hand. I made it out for £20 and traded in my old set of woods and irons.

The hermit had returned home after spending a lifetime herding cattle in Canada. His step was long and slow and when he said 'Praise be to God' (the weather was fine) it was like seeing a feather dropping off an angel's wings. He put in time chipping old gutta-percha balls on to the greens with hickory-shafted clubs. A little girl came across the fairways with a pail of fresh milk every evening and a plume of blue smoke that rose straight up from his make-shift chimney informed her that old Barney the holy man was at home.

I called on him once but, on hearing the drone of the rosary within, left him to his devotions. He was a reflective self-contained man with skin the colour of old parchment, from his years on the prairies; he kept himself to himself. I never got talking to him.

In my mind's eye, the eye in the back of the head, I imagined or thought that I saw a stone house standing by itself on a desolate headland facing an immense ocean that lay to the west; and where on earth could it be but a plot of land at Carmel Point on the Monterey Peninsula to the north of Big Sur – the house that Robinson Jeffers built with his own hands, hauling granite rocks from the shore with strong horses and pulleys.

In the pavement outside the front door of Tor House was inset a piece of Yeats's Thoor Ballylee and fragments of George Moore's ancestral home in Mayo that had been destroyed during the Civil War.

Gift-stones were cemented into Hawk Tower and in the wall of the court-yard (as a small blue unmarked casket containing the ashes of Orson Welles were cemented into a wall on the bull-farm of his *amigo* Antonio Ordoñez outside Ronda); these were fragments from the Great Wall of China and the Great Pyramid of Cheops, toted hither by the hawk-faced man who, as a

lad of seven years, had Latin slapped into him by a severe father, a minister
of the United Reformed Church, a gifted preacher and pastor, a student of
German and French, a scholar of Greek, Latin, Hebrew, Aramaic, Syriac,
Arabic, Babylonian and Assyrian, a professor of Greek and holder of various
chairs in biblical and ecclesiastical studies.

Colman, two years my junior, believed in work as a God-given duty and
obligation; not for him any platitudes about work being a curse, soporific
or negative reality: to my brother's way of thinking, that just didn't wash.
He was as sound as Galusha Grow himself, the homesteaders' champion,
member of Congress and defender of the prairie farmers who had built their
sod huts sans foundations and sanitation on the windy western plains, where
every man was his own fertiliser, and every woman too. Every man had a
right to as much of the earth's surface as was necessary for his support and
well-being, even a plainsman of Nebraska.

Well do I recall the little tits and wrens in their ovoid nests of moss and
twigs and sheep's wool and leaves with their false entrances and tiny
unseen fledglings twittering within; and weaverbirds that built their basket
nests daringly suspended over the Orange River outside dusty Vryberg,
an Afrikaanse township in what is now Nomaqualand, and their colony
of nests that weighed down the telegraph poles on the borders of the Kala-
hari Desert, seen when touring with the marionettes out of London on a
two-year tour of South Africa and the Rhodesias in the time of trouble for
the downtrodden tribes of Africans, the time of apartheid, with Colonel
Spengler and the *swak van du bloed* ranged implacably against them.

Those ingenious avian architects had contrived their habitations with a
makeshift perishable look to them, swinging out over the water, casual as
tinkers' encampments; sagging loose as spiderwebs over the river, intimating
that time and fate and the turning seasons would deal harshly with them.
And in my brother's unfinished house, I had had that feeling too.

The parsimonious deployment of building materials, the exposed brick
and timber, the mounds of rubble in tarps on the ground, the gaping holes
for absent front door and outlines of missing windows, the whole unsightly
and unshapely pile seen against the darkening sky across which passed a scattered assembly of raucous crows returning from their feeding grounds; all
this put me in mind of nothing so much as the Temple of the Crossed Hands
at Kotosh at the headwaters of the Huallaga river in Peru; of the adobe – and
thus perishable – city of Chan Chan built by the rulers of the ancient Kingdom of Chimor and later levelled by stout Cortes in his meteoric passage of

destruction across Mayan territory; of legendary Cuzco of the Inca Empire in the fastness of Peru.

I thought too of the children given to be sacrificed in Mayan times, whose tender lives were not to be spared, the little innocents led in procession to a place where they would be put to death by the priests; to reappear the following spring as flowers, placatory emblems to the sun. And I recalled the hideous beasts that destroyed Nineveh in the prophecies of Zephaniah.

It (the darkly speculative outline of the house-to-be) seemed all interstices, all its insides falling out, like the quarterings of some carcass with interior exposed by the butcher's knife; a skinned beast hung up for butchering purposes, suspended on the hook and already beginning to subside, pulled downward by its own dead weight, crawling with bluebottles. There in the falling darkness it appeared as an unwieldy structure, something dark and undefined, wavering as if underwater.

In the raising up of it – and my brother was ever-sceptical of any rash venture undertaken without sufficient forethought, raising expectations that were bound to be dashed, running ahead of all reasonable hopes; for such failure was inherent in all human enterprises – that failure was already evident, as intimated in the sad sag of the rafter beams off true and the dejected appearance of protective sacking thrown over mounds of stuff drenched by downpours of incessant rain, for the place was sited in a double rainshadow. Here too I detected only stages of dereliction. He was going to have trouble fitting windows.

Not much daylight was admitted. It was a shabby place of stale spent air and awkward angles. This sanctuary was a chosen haunt, a final retreat. The sadly sagging bed, a sorry spectacle, appeared to subside, supported by piles of yellowing outdated newspapers and magazines packed tightly together, supporting the bed-sag, holding the whole miserable contraption up. The bed, mother of all hiding places, was an unsurpassable hidey-hole. For, as said before, all was perishable here on earth, so my brother understood; certainly we were not put here to enjoy ourselves. Earthly Paradise was not for the likes of us. He was quite capable of not saying anything, when he wanted to (and if that house was mine, what part of me was buried in that grave?).

Dervorgilla Doran's cottage *ornée* was as true to herself as anything that remains true to itself, as neatly aligned as her Japanese-inspired fencing to its ground. Don't change a thing, darling Derv; it's *you*.

Of course the perfect fit, *vis-à-vis* landlord and rented property (whatever about awkward sub-tenant) was and is a myth: it may look grand (Dervorgilla graciously serving Earl Grey tea, sipping the brew, little finger elevated as in the painting, *Five O'clock Tea,* by Mary Cassatt) but is as false as the fit of frontal dentures in bridgework that tends to induce a frightful grimace when a winning smile was the effect intended. (All that had happened ten years ago. Now the Grand Hotel is up for sale, now Dervorgilla is a mother, by a German.)

*   *   *

Dressed as if in cast-off clothes, apparel of beggars, my brother and his wife had appeared by the door with the suddenness of an apparition and the exhausted look of nomads on the march. The *noli me tangere* look, veiled with suspicion, the look askance of those perpetually on the move, begging, the shifty look that will not engage your eye, was here made manifest. Then they made their way shyly and circumspectly across the breadth of the Grand Hotel lounge bar as if crossing tundra or shifting ice-floe, approaching where I was seated by a fire of great logs, gin and tonic to hand, and Werner Herzog's *Of Walking On Ice (Von Gehen im Eis),* which I had picked up in an Austin bookstore in the degrading heat of August in Texas.

Pastoral nomads came to mind, tent-dwellers, Bedu of Donakil footing it down the *routes horribles* known to Rimbaud burnt black by the sun, or Sanburu cattle herders of northern Kenya, the denizens of the Empty Quarter where I had never been. That, those there, or the spring migration of the elusive and backward Bakhiari; or the Kaffirs of the Hindu Kush.

A decayed and moth-eaten wolfskin coat (similar to that worn by Brossette, the chauffeur of Octave Mirbeau) would not have looked too amiss on Colman's back. Casting anxious looks about them they came on, making their way down the crowded bar through the press of people that ignored them, uncertain smiles frozen to their bloodless lips, frozen to the bone. How thin and ethereal were those evasive vegetarian smiles hovering on anaemic lips as if too timid to declare themselves as true smiles, any gladness of heart at seeing me; no, merely appealing ghosts of smiles, vapoury, sepulchral smiles. The motto *Horreur de Domicile* was their true blazon; it suited them down to the ground, for no house would hold them.

'Long live the living!' I cried effusively, rising. 'Success to sailors' wives and greasy luck to whalers. Take a pew. You both look frozen, as if you've come a long way. From Alaska or Archangel, I fancy.'

'Timbuktu, actually,' breathed my brother with a lost faraway look in his eye as he lowered himself cautiously into his seat.

'My, my! A body does get around.'

'Quite.'

They had seated themselves opposite me, the guarded semismiles still hovering about their lips but already melting away in the great heat thrown out by the fire; doubtless too by the warm anticipation of potent spirits about to be ordered up.

'Never throw a stone at dogs in Timbuktu,' said I, seated now. 'What'll it be? Your pleasure, Mistress Stella?'

She had the timid and reserved manner that went with demi-veil and fluttering fan to hide blushes and cover any embarrassment, now squinting up at the ceiling as if at *trompe l'oeil* angels with bare bums blowing cornets or little trumpets along the pediment frieze that ran about the entablature.

'What are you having yourself?'

'Gin and tonic.'

She said that she would try that.

Hadn't I once seen them walking together in Wellingtons along the muddy road that led to St Kevin's Church and the pub there, appearing to float inches above the ground, wobbling as they advanced, their centre of gravity imperilled, the next puff of wind certain to blow them both away?

Off with the pair of them now wibbleywobbley in their clodhopper boots wading awkwardly forward along the road, stiff as penguins tottering along the ramp of the Dublin Zoo, in their bluchers, top-boots, gumboots, waders, galoshes or whatever you care to call the damned things, wobbling wraith-like on down to Laragh, not linking or laughing. Not looking around nor yet stumbling, not talking, together and apart; and the thin shanks on them weak as gruel.

Theirs was indeed a strangely tripping and vacillating tread; not so much wobbling as toppling.

– 12 –

Brother Bun and the London Labour Mart

Brother Bun never had a girl.

Never rolled in the hay nor put a bun in any oven. Never took off for foreign parts nor travelled much in any direction except in a dead straight line that led direct from London to Dun Laoghaire via Holyhead once a year for his 'holliers' with his 'buddies', the lifelong chum Doran, or was it Dolan? As if to atone for privilege, his slang was scrupulously down-graded and low. 'What class of caper is that?' He spoke of 'buck' privates, once had tried to enlist as a private in the Irish Army. Dado sent Civic Guards out after him to drag him home; but his flat feet had already disqualified him for any military career.

His travels had been as circumscribed as Poldy Bloom's. A long streak of religious and racial bigotry (which we must touch upon presently) was a very Irish bias and came from our common progenitor's mistrust of strange people resident in remote climes and speaking in unknown tongues and all too familiar with strange customs and unnatural practices, doing strange things to one another at odd hours of the day and night, gabbing away in funny voices at the latter end of the world.

A strain of melancholy befitted the affrighted misogynist. The lonely bach-elor who lusts privily after hot female flesh, the Other whom he is too timid to approach, is surely doomed to disappointment and disaffection. His racial prejudices were merely the unacknowledged half-hidden fears of those other strange parts into which he had never dared venture, whose wholly unfamil-iar currencies were drachmas, rupiahs and ringgits, bahts, the Brazilian *real*.

(Fearing to have a goitre lanced by a surgeon in a white smock, carefully brandishing a scalpel, the young Dado had hatched his plans for escaping and did so in the classical manner, knotting bedsheets together, and so made good his escape to freedom through a third-floor hospital window, as do cowardy custards and those who cannot face very much reality – to which category my dear father-to-be assuredly belonged – to the great annoyance and chagrin of the nurses and the Ward Sister when all at once they came running to discover the bed empty, the window open and the bird flown.)

So when brother Bun awoke one day to find himself in a strange hospital bed surrounded by several 'darkies', coal-black medics from Barbados with shiny faces on them as black as tar and jabbering away in their own dark lingo, one with what appeared to be a snake – an adder? – draped about his neck and all gathered close as carnivores about a kill, grouped about his bed with the curtains drawn, he knew that his hour had come, the death knell was surely nigh.

What was it he lacked, apart from life? He lacked bottle.

He was surely now in Hell, out of which there is no escape, and about to receive fit punishment for a dilatory lifetime of self-abuse, beer-swigging and futile longing. When strong black fingers undid his collar and dug into him to commence the auscultation they were as red-hot pincers and he let out an almighty howl and began to fight for his life in the arms of the black men trying to pacify him.

But he saw no National Health internees from Lahore, Madras or Bombay with clipboards in hand, nor an Indian doctor with stethoscope about his neck, nor the black nurse, all white teeth and glittery eyes fixed steadfastly upon him, nailing him to the hospital bed.

What he saw were gutta-percha black pricks fully extended in the monkey house, as gruesomely active black capuchins sprang from branch to branch and began bouncing off the bars of their cage, glaring impudently down upon him with his little bag of nuts.

And he saw black men squatting on high sand dunes laughing at the antics of the brazen brown-skinned girls darting about like snipe, quick as quails, and nude but for the leis swinging about their necks, flashing horny grins and making lewd niggery gestures, wobbling their bums at him, giving him the come-on with thin double-jointed wrists and prehensile hands, inviting him to join them for a bout of jig-jig in the sea or make out with their screaming sisters splashing about buck naked in the surf, apparently all running amok.

All this he perceived in a flash of revelation, or imagined that he saw, before his reeling senses began to slip away from him again, dropping him into a bottomless pit of darkness unfathomably deep.

The dark singsong voices uttering incantatory words intended to be comforting and make him easy in his mind had no such effect but on the contrary terrified him out of his wits. All the more so for brother Bun, not understanding one single syllable of what was being said or rather chanted; hearing only voodoo incantations and wicked spells and niggery maledictions and sorcery thrown his way.

While being thus roughly manhandled and abused by the jabbering nignogs, brother Bun attempted to let loose one last almighty howl but all that issued from his mouth was a bloodcurdling, unmanned soprano scream, a castrato's unhinged shriek, the expiring babble and dribble of exhausted civic dementia; the true cream of the White Nightmare.

As with the migratory habits of birds of the air or the unseen passage of fish through the deep channels of the sea, compelled upon some course whether they wist or nay, so too some centrifugal force or compulsion (necessity?) propelled brother Bun across the Irish Sea by mail boat, the *Princess Maude*, sailing from No. 2 pier in Dun Laoghaire bound for Holyhead and thence whisked by train to London Town, to be rushed by Tube to Ealing Broadway at the end of the District (green) Line where a manifest destiny awaited, as it had awaited many another such Irishman, like him or as unlike as it was possible to be (men of the pick from Blacksod Bay to the Glen of Imaal); of those who had found themselves at the end of the same line, to be marooned in the great English Labour Pool, ever churned up afresh by new arrivals and dispatched hither and thither, whether it be into drainage ditches, man-handling heavy JCBs or hung aloft in the swinging cabins of crane lifts above mucky building sites from Kensal Rise to Kensington where a numerous and ever-renewed Irish workforce found itself to be positively indispensable with shovel and pick, every man jack of them as good as (if not better than) the man before him, or the man next to him or the man coming after him; until along came a true giant from Carraroe in Connemara, six foot six in his stockinged feet, to beat the bejasus out of every man jack of them, every fucker before him.

In this mighty subdivision of a largely ignorant semi-skilled migrant Irish workforce, in a movement akin to the compulsive migratory force that impels birds and fishes about their business toward specific destinations, the seasonal urge that carried them from one habitat and feeding ground to another, so innumerable Irish passed across the Irish Sea singing their doleful songs, orange visages now gone green, then white, all the colours of the trico-lour, and puking black draught Guinness into the quaking passageways and thence through British Customs, distraught and already feeling homesick, in great distress, in flocks and shoals.

Some ended up in the Liverpool area, some were headed for Kilburn; for others (among whom brother Bun and after him Rory) it was to be Ealing in Middlesex on the outer perimeter of Greater London, flushed hence out of the King's Cross labour exchange.

Brother Bun found himself 'quids in' there and settled into a 'cushy number' (his the dated slang of a previous era) in an office job connected with the film library of the BFI at their Greenford branch. Once in the course of his years there, until its premature closure, he had spoken 'on the blower' to none other than the famed film director Tony Richardson of *Saturday Night and Sunday Morning* fame, who had been most obliging and indeed courteous to him, Bunny Hill of 16 Windsor Road in the borough of Ealing, London W5, who had a Polish landlady, Krystine Szynanska, to look after him.

After the closure of the film library, brother Bun had found employment in the vicinity near the Hoover factory at Perivale where eventually he was 'put in charge of a roomful of gabby women', whom he could boss about to his heart's content, or not, as he saw fit.

He found digs for me near the Tube station beyond Ealing Common on Fordhook Avenue. The two-storey semi-detached was kept as neat as a new pin, all chintz and floral motif and polished banisters and cut flowers in the hall, run like a ship by a retired French couple, a long-suffering worried pair who feared that the end of the world was nigh – this was 1952 – with a rain of atomic bombs falling on Ealing.

They spent most of their time in the kitchen, listening to the news, venturing out now and again for necessary provisions. They were a sweet pair.

Much of my free time I spent soaking in a bath in the spotless bathroom, immersed in a copy of *Lilliput* (a Douglas Glass photo of a nude girl sprawled in the surf) which I had found in Kevin O'Sullivan's room. I had played many rounds of golf with him over Greystones and Delgany; he was red-haired with gingery hair on the backs of his hands; now he was working shifts in the motor factory at Acton Town, blowing up outsize tyres for the African market. Presently he was to vanish into Canada.

It was a beginning, the froth on the dream. At least it was *my* beginning. Although now it seems like someone else's life and about as remote in time as the Crusades; it would have been the same for many another migrant Irish labourer in light and heavy industry before and after me, until I made my escape into South Africa and found work in Johannesburg.

The centrifugal force, I have heard it said, is really inertia. When brother Bun, eager to defend his country against all invaders, had joined the Local Defence Force during our Irish 'Emergency', he went marching off on his flat feet down the avenue past the lodge (then unoccupied) and Killadoon (seat of the infamous Lord Leitrim) back gate, in his field-green LDF uniform proudly worn with forage cap set at a rakish angle and brown boots and smart puttees highly polished; he was proud as punch, marching off to defend his country, even if unarmed (arms, in the form of Lee Enfields, last used at Arras and Mons, were promised), off to drill at Straffan Town Hall facing the Catholic church with the legless and armless Christ in the polychrome stations.

He wore the determined *Weltschmerz* expression befitting one in uniform, a compound of sadness and resignation. The face that he would surely have worn had *Wehrmacht* paras come floating down on to neutral Irish soil, to sweep all before them. Then his goose would have been cooked for sure.

Meanwhile the Dodo was undergoing training at Cranford for RAF night-fighters, going into the West End on leave to see Pat Kirkwood at the

Coliseum, very leggy and toothsome in fishnet stockings, belting out 'Oh Johnny, oh Johnny, how you can love!' He saw Terence Rattigan's *Flare Path* and probably some naughty stuff at the Windmill ('We Never Closed').

Neither brother Bun nor Mumu was exactly the type for route marches. Both of them moved badly. Overweight and top-heavy, Mumu advanced awkwardly as if walking on broken glass or fire, or crippled with corns. Her long period in bed had left her in a semi-comatose state.

All his life brother Bun had the indecisive broken gait of an old man, catching his breath, puffing if he exerted himself, snoring when he slept, Guinness his preferred tipple. He died one Sunday in October 1998 of liver failure in Ealing where he had lived for most of his life under the care of Mrs Szynanska, thirty-two years after his mother died, twenty-nine after his father's death. Now they have all gone away.

None of the three surviving brothers had attended his funeral. The Dote stayed where he was in deep retirement in County Wicklow. I stayed put at World's End. The Dodo was thought to have settled thousands of miles away in Tasmania, home of the pademelon, the quoll cat, the possum and the Tasmanian Devil.

Mumu had died first, of a brain haemorrhage in the night, and went hence to Heaven. Two years later Dado followed when galloping cancer carried him away.

Then there was a pause, to allow the graves to settle in Dean's Grange Cemetery, then brother Bun followed unobtrusively into Ealing earth, slipping out of life without much to-do.

Sixty or more mourners attended his funeral in Ealing Abbey and someone read Yeats's 'Four Ages of Man' over the mortal remains of my brother who had never 'walked upright' in his life, being sorely afflicted with wicket keeper's stoop. He walked with a sort of waddle or shuffle, with toes turned out as though wearing snow-shoes, humpbacked as Humpty Dumpty.

The mourners were mainly the members of St Benedict's Club, buddies of my brother. St Benedict of Nursia, shortly before his death *circa* 547, looked up from his prayers and saw in the darkness outside his window that 'the whole world appeared to be gathered into one sunbeam and thus brought before his eyes'.

The last time I saw brother Bun was when we invited him down to Kinsale. Most of the other passengers disembarking from the Dublin train had dispersed when he slowly emerged on his flat feet from the Gents at Cork railway station, with no particular expression of welcome on his face, no offer of handshake or fraternal embrace, no backslap, God forbid; for we were never a demonstrative lot, and nothing had changed between us in a long interval.

That night at the Blue Haven bar when he was in his cups, he addressed a total stranger standing next to him, threatening (as once before in an Ealing bar) to 'sort me out'. He was still the elder brother.

'I'll soon put manners on that fellow.'

Me, Rory.

All three had died in winter and all three are in Heaven now, above the clouds. No, they have all gone into the world of light, become one with their grandparents and great-grandparents before them, the leavenings of the Hills (not to mention the Higginses) and the Boyd clans from Carrick-on-Shannon and Longford and Granard. Isn't that saying enough?

– 13 –

Ancestral Voices

The perennial myth of the Great Irishman is as old as the hills. Old and hoary as the beard of the Patriarch himself, dim holy man and humble sheep-farmer of Anglia who was reputed to have slept all over Ireland, generally in the open on exposed hillsides, as frequently as Queen Victoria had slept in ornate four-poster beds all over England.

The heroes who belonged by right to the renowned generations, the powerful strong men of the past, Finn McCool, Brian Boru and Cuchulain, have deteriorated into Dan O'Mahony the wrestler from Ballydehob who invented the Irish Whip, a throw in wrestling; and the heavyweight boxer Jack Doyle, who had famously bedded and wedded the movie star Movita, renowned for her knockout beauty; he himself perhaps more famous still for a proclivity to being knocked out cold in the ring. At least so he was mocked by the cartoonist Tom Webster.

The Horizontal Heavyweight became an all-in wrestler, the Gorgeous Gael, who then deteriorated into a song-and-dance man at the Theatre Royal in Hawkins Street off the Quays, appearing with Movita in *Something in the Air* with the Royalettes chorus line high-kicking; then deteriorated further still to become a bouncer at Mooney's pub in Notting Hill Gate, lounging at the counter, wearing an eyepatch like Peg Leg Pete.

Some years after that he died in a London hospital, and sure enough Irish obituary notices referred to him as a Great Irishman; sometimes with the rider that he 'had lived life to the full'. The English obituary notices tactfully refrained from mentioning the many times he had been knocked out in the ring, but all agreed that he had lived with *zest*.

The Great Irishmen who had died with their boots on tended to be minor celebrities known throughout the land. Such a one was the actor Noel Purcell, who in a long and undistinguished career on the Dublin stage had appeared in everything from Christmas panto with fake snow, tinsel and reindeer in the Olympia, that gilded emporium of rococo, to one-act O'Casey knockabout farces at the Gaiety and, then, in one final plunge downwards, was given bit-parts in English movies with small budgets.

He sported a long white beard like Santa Claus, or God; possibly in an attempt to conceal his ineptitude as an actor, by typecasting himself as the tall gauche nincompoop with the thick Dublin accent for whom nothing worked out. It was the same strategy adopted by Hollywood in order to broaden the available talents of Joan Crawford, enlarging her beautiful eyes by surgery to extend her range of expressions; give her at least the opportunity to convey more than *one* expression.

Noel Purcell pulled terrible faces, exposed his great horse teeth, caused his eyebrows to fly up, huffed and puffed, shambled about the stage. I saw him dismantle a stage room in O'Casey's *The End of the Beginning*. Finally, being pulled up the prop chimney, still blathering and protesting, the manic head first to disappear, then the awkward body and long legs, the boots last of all, blustery protestations still audible in the flue when the corporeal presence had disappeared. He was the Great Irishman personified. In the end he was only fit for bit-parts, the rear end of the panto horse; that's all he was good for finally. He was definitely a bits-part man, a fit-up artiste.

'When beggars die, no comets fall,' as brother Bun was fond of quoting.

Purcell's cockney counterpart was Alfie Bass, who held down small character parts in British movies and carried a hod in the Francesco Rosi movie *Christ Stopped at Eboli*. When Bass died he got more flattering and longer obituaries and news coverage than the distinguished movie-maker, Carol Reed, though none thought to describe him as a Great Englishman.

Alfie Bass was the prototypical footsoldier of the old wars, fought in the mud and finished in a day by Nym, Bardolph and Pistol, rough-spoken sods of soldiers. A blocky root of a man with a permanently worried expression, a bulldoggish frown on features as wrinkled as a prune; a racing tipster, small-time gangster or London barrow-boy in our times.

'The more one sees of him, the more the wonder grows.'

I saw Jimmy Bruen once in the dusk of the evening hammering off practice shots with a long iron from a raised tee on Portmarnock links, digging great divots that came slowly back to earth again. A playful giant was sending off cannonlike projectiles up-soaring into the gloaming towards a distant caddy, who was busily recovering the much-bashed-about Dunlops in a bucket.

It was the Hibernian Wonder Golfer himself getting in some practice, Jimmy (The Loop) Bruen of Muskerry in the County Cork. He would have been up in Dublin on insurance business. When a son was born unto James J. Bruen, former Connaught Ranger and bank official who stood well over six feet tall, little did he know that the child of Margaret Bruen would grow up to be a golfing prodigy who won the British Amateur Championship at Birkdale, defeating the great American Sweeny in a titanic final.

The old codger Bernard Darwin, doyen of English golf commentators, had declined to describe the fabled Bruen Loop, the famous whiplike flailing action that sent the ball in a high trajectory to a distant green three hundred and fifty or more yards away. It was something outside our ken, like the Angel Gabriel looping the loop; but was in fact probably an adaptation of the hurling puck, the same whiplash swing of the body that dispatched the *sliotar* far upfield, or over the bar.

It was a shy sportsman who inspired those rhapsodies of praise; and like all true legends he was to die young, in his early fifties early one May day at his home in Cork, of a heart attack, leaving six children fatherless.

But leaving behind the great legend of his doings, the prodigious shots, the records, for us to marvel at all the more; the fierce crack of the contact and the Dunlop 65s soaring away! Great shot, Jimmy!

Bursting free from the chrysalis and imago of his living fame to become yet another of the Imperishable Ones in the legions of our illustrious dead.

Eily Arnopp, of Kinsale, born and raised in Barrack Street, was the mother of nine children by a taxi driver who predeceased her; she is famous in Kinsale as being the only person to have lived in the same house in the same street all her life, and died there. Obituaries in the *Southern Star* said she had lived life to the full. You said: 'Most of the Arnopps are either grossly fat or painfully thin.'

Irishwomen by and large, no matter how gorgeous they had been in their prime, like Lady Eleanor Palmer or Hermione, Duchess of Leinster or Daisy, Countess of Fingall, would never be great Irishwomen unless they became champion horsewomen like Iris Kellett. The moulded forms were of Mother and Martyr – sometimes the terms were synonymous – the beauties had become haggard eccentrics, frowsy widows with their wits astray, lost women, old hakes. The lovely girl (notoriously fast) who loved to slide downstairs on a tray via polished banisters, wearing pink tights, had become the immensely old and frail dowager Duchess of Desmond who fell to her death from an apple tree at the age of one hundred and four, some said one hundred and forty, but much too old to be climbing apple trees. The Connaught Queen Grainne Mhaol, the Pirate Queen, Grace of the cropped hair, who had it all her own way once, sailing her vessel up the Thames to speak to Elizabeth I as an equal and what is more, in Latin, died in penury in rocky Connaught. The ladies who had lost their looks and their wits now turned into Shan Van Vochts and Sheila na Gigs; Cathleen ni Houlihan with a pained expression (as though she had a pain in her hole) became the womanly model on the punt note. Yeats's earlier moth, the lovely Maude Gonne, became a harpie, following in the footsteps of the Countess Markiewicz who had entered Irish politics, that muddy carp pond. The best option was to die young as did Hermione, Duchess of Leinster, chatelaine of Carton in its heyday, with hunt balls and outings to Punchestown races, doing it in style.

– 14 –

Harry Allen, J. Pierpoint Morgan and Luis Buñuel

The hooded figure, known to be a woman and a murderess, a husband-slayer condemned to death by a named judge on a date already specified months before, wearing a smart outfit and with her face carefully made up, fell heavy as a sack of earth into the pitch darkness below; accelerating as she fell, faster than Rousseau's bastards went down the chute of the foundling hospital, her last terrified scream smothered by the hemp rope that gripped and snapped her spinal column.

She was spared further ignominy and shame, what ensued after the loosening of uterus and sphincter muscles, the gruesome descent of the prison doctor into the bowels of the execution shed to disarrange her clothes, her decency no longer protected, the nice ethics of how men should behave with women at their mercy, taking out his stethoscope to auscultate her and pronounce the woman dead.

Ruth Ellis was the last woman to be hanged in England. Justice was seen to be done down there in the gloomy shed. No one would ever be killed that way again, though the hangman slept like a babe. Gravity had almost pulled her head off, falling as from an immense height she voided herself.

*   *   *

Our dear mother, one of the Boyds of Carrick-on-Shannon whose father had been Peace Commissioner of Longford, was ever a snob. The French finishing school at Parthenay had done it, had finished her.

She never referred to the people in any charitable way, but always disparagingly, looking dismissively down her nose at the common people, at individuals, 'dreadfully common', the sweaty nightcaps, the *canaille,* not much better than common tinkers, who came begging with their numerous noisome progeny, stinking up the front porch into which they crowded; to be told to wait, she would see what she had for them (the Master was in, upstairs in his study, forsooth); and then out came the cast-off clothes, the bags of apples, the stale soda bread, the fistful of coppers, a sixpenny bit, received with both hands, and the chorus of 'God bless your ladyship, but you wouldn't happen to have—'

The front door closing on the renewed chorus of entreaties and a scrofulous babe, wrapped in a dirty papooselike shawl, held up like the Host elevated in the clasp of the golden monstrance at Benediction in rising clouds of incense; the door finally closing once and for all on the stinks and the pained look on the face of the Mistress.

I've heard that they left a sign near the gate – a stone turned a certain way – to indicate a house where they were given alms. Such entreaties recurring at irregular intervals (Mumu rather suspected that they used a system of secret signs) must indeed have been music to her ears, for it confirmed her innermost belief that she was not of the common stock, but a superior being, a lady of means.

We were brought up to see ourselves as a cut above the rest, an elitist band of rural nobs, the Higginses of Springfield, all four sons educated at Clongowes Wood College, of parents who dined royally and regularly at the Royal Hibernian Hotel. Mumu was the chief instigator of this fantasy, the elevated status claimed as our birthright and one that characterised us as above all others; so what choice had we, her four abashed and shy sons, but to believe her: that we were indeed out of the top drawer? She could be very sharp when such presumptions were discovered in others, the social upstarts who were 'stuck up', putting on airs and graces that did not become them: they needed to be taken down a peg and shown their place. The note of condescension and quiet superiority I heard a lifetime later in Berlin, in the mouth of a youngish Prussian *Frau* who spoke so proudly of *'mein Mann'*, overtly pleased with her husband and *'alles in Ordnung'* simmered like something rich and good cooking on the Aga.

Having myself turned seventy-one, par for the course plus one extra stroke, with hand on heart I cannot truly say that I have quite shaken off this grandiose notion, implanted so long ago by our mother, who wanted only the best for us.

Seventy-one was Buffon's (Georges-Louis Le Clerc's) age when he finished his great treatise *Histoire naturelle* (1749–67), concluding that the earth would eventually freeze over and all life thereon become extinct. He was then a shade under five feet five inches and afflicted with gallstones, fifty-seven of which were removed from his bladder at the autopsy when he died at the ripe old age of eighty.

At the age of seventy-one Harry Allen, the public hangman, was interviewed by the *Daily Telegraph*. 'It may be eighteen years since I last hanged a man, but even at seventy-one, I'm perfectly ready, willing and able to resume my duties,' said the ex-hangman, flexing his biceps. 'Since the rope was scrapped, discipline has gone right out of the window.'

In his time of tenure he had attended or conducted over a hundred hangings. He appeared at the gate wearing one of his multicoloured bow-ties, so that anti-hanging demonstrators outside the jail would take him for a doctor or lawyer.

'After breakfast I always used to return home, have a bath and go to bed. I slept like a baby for the next eight hours. I've never been bothered by dreams and nightmares.'

Somewhere in the north of England, off the beaten track, don't you know, he had run a quiet pub called Pity the Poor Traveller (or was it Poor Straggler?) Our 'arry was the publican and genial host. Before you could blow the top off your pint of Thwaites real ale, he'd have 'topped' his man. Pulling pints or hanging felons was done with the same aplomb. He sounded like a married man. And children too? Had he topped Ruth Ellis?

Harry Allen had succeeded Albert Pierpoint as chief executioner in 1956, and conducted his last public office in Britain in August 1964, just a year before parliament abolished the death penalty for murder. Ruth Ellis was hanged on 13 July 1955, nine years before the abolition of hanging, having killed her husband to end an intolerable situation. For her husband had subjected her to years of indignity and abuse. A friend showed her how to use the gun, before he decamped to Australia. She shot the husband dead outside the Magdala pub near Hampstead Heath, one of a range of quiet pubs in that area patronised by Rory, walking over the heath from Muswell Hill. Michael Morrow had a room up the hill from the Magdala and, if not exactly witnessing the killing, saw the effects, the husband's brains spread over the pavement 'like ice cream'.

Did the sentencing judge, donning the black cap before pronouncing the dread words, feel that justice had been done? Did the hangman, putting the hood over Ruth Ellis's head, tell her that it would be over soon? Did they sit down thereafter to hearty breakfasts, each satisfied that justice had been done? A pot of hot tea, kippers, toast and coarse-grain marmalade, kedgeree or split pulse, onions and condiments served piping hot for the hangman, and the judge in his chambers.

Did the hangman let her go in silence? Or touch her shoulder, she already hooded, straighten his bow-tie and murmur, *Be a brave woman. It'll soon be over,* grunting as he hauled on the switch? One way or another, he let her go.

Harry the hangman died on 17 August 1992 at the age of eighty-one.

J. Pierpoint Morgan was seventy-four in the summer of 1911 when he took up with Vita, the illegitimate offspring of the Honourable Lionel Sackville-West. She was nineteen to his seventy-four; each had something the other wanted. At Princes Gate he was chairing a meeting involving a loan to some Chinese, but when he received her message he quickly left the boardroom to see her: 'In he came like a whirlwind and crushed me.'

Rory was fifty-nine years of age when he met his nemesis in the shapely form of the gentle lady Alannah who was some twenty and more years his junior, divorced wife of Pedro Sanchez of Mexico City, a failed photographer who had ambitions to be an architect.

When Sanchez went up, he went up, when he went down he went down, and carried her with him. After a while she had nothing to say; they separated, she left Mexico City for Cuernavaca (where eighty-four vultures circled over the Rancho Pico, casting slow-wheeling shadows on the lawns, they moved slow as bluebottles over the carcass of the dead horse, sinking down and settling at given intervals and then rising again, joining the flock above, wheeling at different altitudes, their eyes fixed on the corpse) and then left Mexico for London, and returned to Ireland, drifting sideways towards her fate, Rory of the Hills.

Twenty-one years previously, in 1970, you were nineteen years of age, weighing just under eight stone and got up as Juliet Greco with kabuki doll's white face masked in make-up, Nefertitian black eye outline, eyelashes inches long, dark hair down to your waist and a skirt brief as decency would allow, bolero waistcoat with dazzling baubles and Aztec-style pendant earrings. You were certainly 'with it' in the free-for-all fashion of the swinging sixties, living in Mexico City and working as a freelance photo model wedded to Pedro Sanchez.

Together these two fine love-birds, holding hands and exchanging fond looks, called for payment due to them in an advertising agency near Reforma, on the eleventh floor of a modern skyscraper, much of it occupied by other advertising agencies, fashion outlets and film production companies. Still linking, like Siamese twins, they stepped together into an elevator, accompanied by a friend called Juan, who was in the movie business.

A third man stepped quickly into the elevator and stood behind Juan who had his finger on the button for the eleventh floor.

'¿Que piso?' asked Juan politely.

'Cinco, por favor,' said the stranger in a tough gangsterish voice out of the side of the mouth.

The belted beige gabardine gave him an exotic European touch; leastways it was an unusual mid-morning get-up for Mexico City. He seemed to have no face, only threatening surfaces angled at them. (Was he carrying a piece?)

Even with his back turned to the Sanchez love-birds holding hands, he had presence. The beige gabardine was loosely belted, the epaulettes stood up like wings, the coat collar was upturned, the trilby worn down over the brow, the gangster's voice was as rough as Georg Grosz, that of your habitual cigar smoker, the menacing glint that emanated from the dark sunglasses shadowed by the downturned hat brim, was alarming. This fellow was obviously not to be trifled with, a louche figure from *film noir*.

They rode up together in silence, not exchanging a look, the stranger standing there impassively, not fidgeting, hands in the deep pockets of the gabardine, eyes fixed on the flying digits of the little screen as they rose swiftly.

When the elevator had shuddered to a pneumatic halt on the *piso cinco,* the door slid open and the gangster slipped out. The air vibrated a moment and he was gone, gone to see his money man and producer Oscar Danziger, no doubt.

The elevator gulped air, released its brakes, and sailed upwards. Juan was gobsmacked as one might say, rendered speechless, swallowing his spittle, white-faced as though he had seen an apparition; at all events he said nothing until they reached the eleventh floor. Backing out of the cage he marvelled: '*Subsimos en el elevador con Luis Buñuel, el Maestro de los Maestros del ciné Mexicano, olé!*'

'Luis Buñuel!' chirruped the Sanchez love-birds in unison. 'Luis BUÑUEL!!'

La Voie lactée (*The Milky Way*) had been released the previous year; now he was preparing *Le charme discret de la bourgeoisie* (1972); ahead lay *Le Fantôme de la liberté* (1974), and *Cet obscur objet du désir* (1977).

Luis Buñuel, at eighty-three, sat in the bare study of his house in Mexico City surrounded by high monastery walls crowned with broken glass.

The great Mexican gasbag Carlos Fuentes, tireless in his pursuit of important connections, 'names', last saw Buñuel in February 1984 in the company of his wife and two sons, and said: 'I'll see you in October.'

'No you won't,' said the old movie-maker. 'We'll never meet again, *amigo.*'

And they never did. What went up came down again, but whatever went down never came up again. Never, never came up again.

$$-\ 15\ -$$

The Monk in the Cornfield
(Where There Was Nobody)

Beau comme un large champ d'été . . .
Henri Michaux: *L'Espace du Dedons*

Since there seemed to be nobody about, I crept like a thief into the lamp-room where formerly the Aladdin paraffin lamps had been stored but which was now used by the Dodo as a reference library, generally for sporting matters. Tidy mounds of magazines and newspapers were arranged in alphabetical order along the shelves, a morgue of out-of-date newsprint yellowing and smelly that still retained some things of interest for the Dodo, the rugby and cricket records. Also photographs of English royalty, the little Princesses Elizabeth and Margaret Rose in decorous manner presenting bunches of flowers to other smiling eminences, all that ritual royal bowing and scraping; here an interest that he had inherited from Mumu, always a great admirer of British royalty.

A cat had also found its way into the sanctum, for there under the lowest shelf was an ossified mound of cat-cack that had solidified and grown a stately carapace of heraldic fluff on a crack of the paving stone, awaiting the attention of Lizzy who would come and scrape up the mess with pan and bucket of water and Jeyes fluid.

And here were the London *Daily Mails,* the *Dispatches,* the *Wisdens,* the *Illustrated London News* and *Tatler & Sketch,* the *Irish Times, The Field, Good Housekeeping, Home & Beauty, Lilliput,* and *Herald Tribunes* from America, back numbers of the *Evening Herald* and *Evening Mail,* with cricket and rugby teams in their correct club colours and blazers painstakingly rendered in watercolours by the Dodo.

What was of abiding interest to me were the *Lilliputs* on one shelf low down, for they contained photographic studies of nudes in black and white, by Douglas Glass, showing off English models without a stitch, alone on the seashore. Choosing one of these, I ran for the open fields, through the side plantation leading to the big wheatfield towards Griffinrath, to take the model for an outing with an Irish boy after months of being cooped up in the stuffy study.

These Douglas Glass studies of nudes in woods, seashore and field were my *Wald und Weise* movies; in that respect *Lilliput* was as good as a private viewing of blue movies, better than the naturist feature of nudists supposedly enjoying themselves in a camp somewhere in England, seen later at a cinema in Oxford Street, filmed in a very peekaboo manner that contrived not to show any pubics.

What Churchill and his War Cabinet called World War Two and what Dev and his Dáil were calling 'the Emergency', an elusive Irish euphemism if ever there was one, was a time of strict censorship of films coming into the *Saorstát.* Hollywood productions, already prudish and reserved before the Hayes Office, were trimmed further for Irish audiences, who were kept even more in the dark as to what exactly was happening in the world.

Betty Grable might bat her false eyelashes, pout her luscious lips and expose a certain amount of sheer stocking above the knee, but only so far. Rita Hayworth could ruck up her skirt with both hands and twirl about in *Gilda;* but that was about all permitted. The Hayes Office was there to see that she went no further, also the Daughters of the American Revolution and Mother Machree, for wasn't Rita herself half Irish?

Grable was an emblem on the fuselage of a Boeing 707, part of the war effort, like selling war bonds, when Irish bread was getting darker, rationing of a sort was in force. It was a time before such scandalous blockbusters as *The Outlaw,* with Jane Russell sprawled in the straw, or *Duel in the Sun* with Jennifer Jones darkened up and poured into a towel; before the later permissiveness, of explicit nudity and full frontals, animal grunting in stereo sound not to be heard even at Wimbledon or Flushing Meadow, and the attendant bad manners (McEnroe); all that came later.

What arrived from across the water were Regency romps from Gainsborough Studios, Margaret Lockwood with permanently wet underlip, a beauty spot, the deepest cleavage imaginable and leather gear, brandishing a brace of horse pistols in *The Wicked Lady,* with James Mason offering to horse-whip Phyllis Calvert.

Then there were Celia Johnson and Trevor Howard carrying on in *Brief Encounter,* but forbidden to Irish viewers, because it was deemed to encourage adultery, strictly forbidden by the Irish Episcopal See, though *Spring in Park Lane* (Michael Wilding and Anna Neagle) was considered innocuous enough to be distributed in Ireland.

The young wheat stood a good three or even four feet high in a field of five or six acres protected by some scarecrows leaning sideways at drunken angles, with faces of straw swaying in the breeze as if it was the wind blowing over a body of water into which the randy Rory sank as into blessed surf, a continuation of the rapture that began with the sharply pleasurable experience of the first nude dip in the cattle trough at the ring-pump, when the mossy sides became a substitute for the female pubic parts, obligingly parting, opening for Rory.

Undressed in a trice, Rory spread out the nude model before him in her Cornish wheatfield as a playful sunny companion, and was soon ejaculating for dear life into a pocket handkerchief spread out.

In Killashee they called it 'pulling your wire', and the priest in confession called it 'playing with yourself'. Well, look here will you now, that was how I pleasured her, when she pleasured me in a hidden wheatfield, without a word exchanged, without a touch; without seeming to be in any way loose or wayward, Dorothy Lamour in a sarong led to lewd thoughts; lewd thoughts led to lewd acts. Not with this one. Dance, pretty lady, dance!

Beau, comme un large champ d'été,
Beau l'espoir!

Henri Michaux

This would have been *circa* 1944 or around the time Mussolini had fallen
from power and I had turned seventeen, an indifferent scholar in most subjects in the class of Third Syntax in Clongowes Wood College where the
wind always blew coldly around the old castle walls and the Dote (in a class
above me) and I had come to learn at first hand all those slang terms that
had seemed like another unknown language when spoken by our two elder
brothers.

On a fine summer's day when none seemed to be about, I stole like a felon
into the study and, in the blink of a wink, had made off with her.

It was one of the Dodo's life studies from Kildare Street drawn by that
industrious copier, a roll of stiff cartridge paper drawn upon with graphite
or a hard pencil to give no smudge effects and held in place with paperclips,
one taken from a pile numbered and entitled in a corner.

The blind was rolled down to the limit, casting a strawberry-red light into
the narrow room that smelt of oils. A study of 'The Boy with a Rabbit' was
propped up on the table, half finished and looking if possible even deader
than the original; the flaccid white hand clutching the lettuce leaf was stiff
and moribund, the true hand of a cadaver.

Now I was gliding down the stairs with the stolen roll held casually under
one arm and making my way across the hallway, down eight steps to ground
level and like a redshank past the lamproom, out the back door and round
with me into the yard and via the harness room up the stairs and through two
empty lofts until I had reached the third one and pushed open the groaning
door.

In two quick spells of bending, I was already naked and had unrolled the
cartridge paper to reveal the round and somewhat chubby model quite nude
and seated on a rostrum with stiff folds of cloth shadowed in the classical
Roman manner, the nude herself without any suggestion of pencil shading,
just the outlined white body seated on an art school rostrum with hands
clasped behind her neck to make her breasts stick out (which they certainly
did), the back likewise arched to throw them further into prominence (which
indeed it did) as likewise the rear cleft, the near foot flexed and its fellow artfully 'at point', like a ballet pose.

The angled pose (difficult to hold for any length of time) served to hide
from view the part that was most desired and thought of but most *verboten;*
to wit, the twat. The bush of hair betwixt the legs was hidden away; the coy
model had also shaved her armpits for the pose.

Moving now with purpose and precision, I had her laid out on an old copy
of the *Evening Herald* with four stones at the four corners of the cartridge paper

to prevent it from rolling up again, revealing now at close range my abject state of tumescence brought about by the nudity (mine as well as hers), but mostly by her own close proximity.

'Nymph, in thy orisons be all my sins remembered!'

I slid home the wooden bolt to secure privacy and with simian agility mounted the door frame and clung one-handed to the first rafter, then both hands to the second rafter, then the third, until I dangled directly above the nude spread out below. With both hands locked, I began to swing; and it seemed now that she moved with me, bestirring herself a little from her pose (as flick pictures convey an illusion of movement when the pages are clicked); so, in a white blur of apparent participation, she seemed to gather herself and go with me, as I swung gasping above her, my eyes fixed steadfastly upon that lovely nakedness outspread below.

'Oh if'n I haddana . . .' groaned randy Rory. 'If I cuddana . . .' and dropped lightly on to the floor covered in hayseeds and swallow droppings, and hunkered up alongside her.

'See what you done to me,' I said, and scattered my seed splashily as Onan himself, though careful not to splash her, as if holding a hose.

Now the worst ignominy would be my father calling out from below: 'What's going on up there?'

Dressing myself hurriedly, rolling up the cartridge paper, clipping it up again, spreading the *Herald* over the semen, I unbolted the door and fled down the stairs into the front yard, and so by the garden gate around the corner of the house and in by the front door, up the front stairs like jack rabbit (spent buck) and back into the study.

I replaced the roll where I'd found it, closed the door, leaving no fingerprints. Dance, daddy longlegs, dance!

When Rory was twenty-five years old and into single figures as a playing member of Greystones Golf Club among the grey hairs and suffused features of retired British Army officers, Captain Parsons and Captain Pettigrew and Major Stone and Rory's *bêtes noires,* the Right Reverend Riversdale Colthrust and the Honorary Secretary, Colonel Howard Cornwallis Lewis of the Gloucestershire Halberdiers, the last of the bulldog breed, gallant Rory was hotly pursuing tail in the shape of the adorable Philippa Phillips. A Montessori instructress from Leeson Street convent, hotly pursued by the salad-green and inexperienced Rory with a more or less permanent erection, as a knight of old might have brandished an escutcheon, glove or stocking as a lady's favour. But all to no avail.

Rory then took to banging brassie shots from beside the third green over the guarding bunker, off towards the fourth green, besplattering it with Dunlops and Warwicks, lost balls recovered by the caddies and sold again at discount, the practice balls slashed by the irons.

So what's so strange about that? you may ask. Well, on nights of full moon in winter I wore socks and clunky golf shoes with spikes and nothing else, banging the balls away from beside the third green (par 5) behind which I had undressed. That's how I got my only lonely satisfaction, with a hey-nonny yea and a hey-nonny no, punching wood from semi-rough and all around me the cuckoo spits and the wormcasts and the song of the nightingale soaring. *Mi ne frego.*

– 16 –

Ah, Those Moonlit Revels!

Thwhackk! Th-thwhackk! Th-thwhackkKK! went Rory the hammer hurler, fairly laying into them, thumping the very skins off the Dunlops, all dispatched on a low trajectory out of the already stiffening clumps (for it had set in to freeze); with the regularity of a metronome, every contact in the fat of the wood another sweet shock to the spine, carried through with a full swing of the hips with stiffened member standing up rigid as a poker, the arms held high in the follow-through, the left as though braced against a shield; a monumental male nude figure emblematic and stark white as on the Parthenon, besplattering seed like dewfall on the grass and all the grass glistening and sparkling with the fiery sparkle of quartz and mica in the frosty night air, with distant objects brought close and close things far removed; so that the glossy bulk of the hill on the eleventh seemed to pulsate in the increasing cold, expanding and contracting.

And the crows, disturbed by something passing below, had risen up squawking from the rookery above the Delgany road, stridently aroused, and the moon too was risen up over the hill; spread and above was the Milky Way and the Plough all around the hubbub of subatomic invisible insect life and the remote stars singing in their constellations and small white clouds sailing along were beginning to disperse themselves (and Rory, out of sight behind the mound guarding the third green, was hurriedly dressing himself in order to recover twenty Dunlops scattered like mushrooms around the fourth green).

The best shots had felt like cloth tearing, ratteen or stiff canvas. It was perhaps an uncommon way and occasion (a moonlit night with frost in winter) for conducting practice sessions in the nude; but Rory off a three handicap had felt the shock of each shot travel up his forearms and into his teeth as if he was holding ball bearings in his mouth that became as soft as dissolving snowballs. With every smash-shot that smote the Dunlops away, Rory felt as though he were eating snowballs.

Now, having collected the scattered shots, with brassie under oxter like a gamekeeper, or a poacher leaving a forbidden wood, pockets bulging not with game but with Dunlops, Rory made his way home to Kinlen Road, gliding imperceptibly in by the back way.

– 17 –

Roll On, Ye Mighty River, Roll!

I am attempting to find a trail of wet footprints leading from the rectangular cattle trough under the hawthorn where the wank in the tank occurred, the first temptation succumbed to; and find where the wet telltale prints of naked male adolescent are leading; soon to be joined in the dance by a neat naked female print; and so toe to toe and heel to heel leading this way and that with all the formal delicacy of minuets, bourrées, mazurkas and gavottes; whatever about the entangling and entwining intimacy of the tangos so despised by the high and mighty Señor Borges of Buenos Aires, who was blind.

At our first assignation in the cavelike dimness of the bar Montes (now a bank) I had asked Anna: 'Do you find me feminine?'

And she, as though responding to a password, had answered with another question: 'Do you find me masculine?'

I thought her very feminine, despite her tallness, despite the smallness of her bust, of which she was very conscious, coming from the land of Suzanne Brugger and Anna Lindesgaard. What did the size of parts of her matter to me?

Since the time I was bathed in all innocence by my mother, just escaped out of diapers or free of the clutches of Nurse O'Reilly to romp on the gravel in my pelt with the Dote screeching and pissing himself with excitement to feel the air playing over our skin, I have swum and capered and dipped and cavorted and fornicated and frisked, wallowed and soaked and sodomised with a fair few sirens, some of whom would as soon use the back door as the front, some of whom seemed paragons of virtue yet were veritable engineers of lust ('Is it all the way in?') along the lines of insatiable Messalina, hereunder listed provisionally for the benefit of the more lecherous reader, following incandescent signs that speak volumes to him or her in the dark, burning still, burning bright, winking like the red traffic sign that bids you STOP.

When a woman says 'Stop!' she may mean to convey quite the opposite ('Go!') and is so understood by both parties eager to get on with it and not too particular about splitting hairs; but in order to oblige the lady, one must abide by the formalities.

With Anne Marie in the shower at No. 12 Calle Generalissimo Franco (afterwards Calle Pintada) in Nerja, twice or thrice.

With Hannelore on numerous occasions in the showers of various Berlin hotels, a hotel in Michelangelostraat in Amsterdam, many dips in May in the aqueduct above the Fabrica de La Luz on the Rio Chilar (dried up) outside Nerja.

Showered with Harriet at 20 Granite Creek Road, Santa Cruz, California.

Showered with Anastasia at her place on Oakmont Boulevard, Austin, Texas and swam in the Colorado River (leave your guns at the gate).

In the nip with Philippa in the Irish Sea at Kilcoole, County Wicklow (cf. *Dog Days*).

In the nip with Flora in the Lake of the Blind Trout at Pontoon in County Mayo and in a hot bath in Johnny O'Toole's (RIP) modernised thatched cottage later burnt to the ground in a vindictive arson attack; in the nip in the nippy Liffey beyond Straffan Bridge, County Kildare, on one day of a summer long past.

In the nip with Coppera in the pools of Juanero on the logging trail out of Cómpeta that led into the hills.

In the nip with Anna in the Arcadian pools below Canillas beyond the stinking dump you called Gehenna.

Swam with Erika on Playa de Burriana at Nerja and in the Stambergersee on the opposite shore to where Mad Ludwig drowned with his doctor, in Bavaria.

And what about Hannel? Last seen by Anna (no friend) 'looking haggard', walking through the King's Gardens in Copenhagen. Perhaps she was not the swimming or dipping type, ever plagued and bothered by an irregular menstrual flow.

In the nip with Hannelore in Krumme Lanke and Schlachtensee in Berlin by night in summer and in a hot bath with Mary at 63 Grand Avenue, Muswell Hill, north London; but hold your horses, who is Mary? Why Mary Mildwater, she whom my former wife Fruitcake nicknamed 'Hotwater', was and is a Piscean like myself. Will you ever forget the day you spoke to three men, all of them Pisceans, sitting cool as you please about a table at the Alexandra pub near the police station and the flower shop where the sexy girl worked who wore an ankle bracelet? The Alexandra was one of our thirty-six 'locals'. All five of us in the bar were Pisceans and none too sober, least of all Mary Mildwater; which must tell you something revealing about Pisceans.

All five of my heart-scalds have similar names and identical or near identical initials: Harriet, Hannelore, Hannel, Anna and Alannah.

The first time I saw Alannah, she had come from swimming a hundred lengths of Acton's hotel swimming pool and she seemed more otter than woman, with fish scales or drips of water like sparkling jewels in her dark hair. And when she moved, she moved. I had met up with a Norwegian sailor, Sven Johnson, in the bar, who spoke of his father, the trout tickler. He had a bone-crunching handshake; I was given it, and then Alannah, who didn't flinch.

Sailorman Sven, who had sailed the seven seas, had the right hands wrung off us. We went around the corner and into the Shipwreck, aptly named, where we were served up a most unappetising meal. Both the owners have since died in Spain, where they had opened a bar called Dirty Dicks; no apostrophe where none intended.

The name I adopted was Rory of the Hills, the prototypical homeless one. Some Russian writer took to looking back to find the source or cause of his archetypal Russian sadness, his sad Slavishness; it wasn't his work, nor his wife, nor his previous girls, nor his parents. At a very tender age he was already sad. Why was that? Then he remembered: as a toddler he had ignited a match in his mouth and burnt his tongue so badly that he had howled, and his frightened pappa and mamma, his babushka, had come running.

As a Piscean, my first memories, after the amniotic fluids that laved the unborn and unchristened Rory in Mumu's stomach had drained away, would be watery ones; and, right enough, in 1933 the Liffey flooded the village. I was six, two years before Mussolini's modern Army and Air Force attacked Abyssinia defended by naked warriors carrying spears. The water came up as far as Marlay Abbey, flooding Flynn's bicycle shop. The penny farthing bike that hung outside looked as peculiar as a giraffe standing on dry land surrounded by Zambesi flooding.

My first feeling was one of fear, fear connected with floods and attendant omens presaging watery ends, rampant flooding and even more ominous omens, for hadn't the river Anna Livia, normally the most tractable and easy-going of well-behaved rivers flowing between narrow banks not half a mile from Springfield lodges, burst and overflowed her banks?

Nurse O'Reilly, a headstrong Cavanwoman with buckteeth, a great one for laying cautious bets (a shilling each way on Royal Braide in the 4.30 at Fairyhouse) now could lay no bets because the turf accountant was unreachable there opposite the forge, unless of course he was out in a rowing boat collecting bets all over the village.

We tink of Dee . . .

I sang discordantly with the other little lads of my class, the girleens being off to one side of us, singing out of key as always; the gravel was biting savagely into my bare knees and I thought of St Patrick driving the sharp point of his crozier through a convert's bare foot and he, the injured convert, bleeding like a stuck pig, thinking it was part of an initiation ceremony, never said a word. I wore shorts, kneeling with the others at the May altar to the Blessed Virgin on the gravelled driveway before the Holy Faith convent surrounded by young yew trees bending this way and that before the freshening breeze, the nuns holding on to their coifs when genuflecting piously.

> *We tink of Dee*
> *An whaw dow art,*
> *Dye majusteee, Dy stay-ate,*
> *An I keep singing in my hurt*
> *Imma-kul-late, Imma – KUUL – late!*

But I wasn't thinking of any such thing, her beautified and serene self up there above the clouds in a remote and distant Heaven unimaginably far away. I thought rather of the cold roast beef in the larder at Springfield that old Mrs Henry would bring out and slice up and put in front of me on a plate to take well salted with garden peas that tasted even better cold. And old Mrs Henry would ask me how the sodality had gone, and how the girls had sung; and I would reply that all had gone well.

But did I care how the girls sang, the big girls with their chests heaving, smelling of stale sweat trapped inside their frocks, and the excitement of boys with their mouths open, staring at them, getting fresh? Not I.

I thought rather of the Devil who was my true playmate, Señor Satan with all his suave works and pomps, who wandered through the world for the ruin of souls. He was close enough to touch, though himself invisible, like sin itself. Sin was just something you wanted to do, maybe with one of the big girls who sometimes sat with us in the back of the class and put us through our Catechism, and then you would get the girl-smell; the pong of sin. Satan was always urging me to do the bad things I liked doing, such as touching myself, the priest in the darkened confessional told Rory not to touch himself, not to play with himself. And Rory, abasing himself, low as a slug and just as mean, said, 'No, Father' and 'Yes, Father', whichever way it was; because he was always doing something wrong, something that was said to be sinful.

But Satan was very clever and closer to me than my Guardian Angel, who was said (by the nuns) to be always there but invisible, as my constant counsellor and conscience. I named mine Batty.

What do we do here, eh Batty? He never told me anything, but I could feel him invisibly present, his mouth set in a severe line, his brows drawn down in disapproval, for I did much that Batty would have to disapprove of, if he (it?) was a true GA, wherever he was, with his mouth close to my ear, advising me: *Don't do it!*

I had real trouble with the Holy Ghost. He was the third equally divided part of an everlasting confederacy of goodness and holiness and sanctity that betokened a true divinity split three ways, like signposts pointing off in different directions to Birr and Athy and Edenderry; a tripartite divinity that could divide itself into three equal parts without any bother, like Mumu dividing up a Swiss roll into three equal parts for brother Bun, the Dote and myself.

I saw the Holy Ghost only as the wings of God, torn off and put to one side, not part of the divinity at all but floating away light as a feather, apart and still invisible. These, the priest told us and the nuns agreed, were 'revealed truths which we cannot comprehend'. I thought of them as something kept in a special great chest in a sealed room in the Vatican to which only the Pope had access, the key, or keys, for the great chest with the secrets in it was always kept locked and only Pope Pius XII knew what was in it, and his lips were solemnly sealed.

I sang with the others, with more conviction now, the cold beef and peas close enough to smell. I sang with half my heart in it at least. I sang piously in falsetto:

> *Deep in dye wounds, Lord*
> *Hide an shelter mee;*
> *So shall I nivver,*
> *Nivver part from Dee!*

'Don't you try and get fresh with me, Mister Man,' warned the big girl staring hotly at Rory, who looked as if butter wouldn't melt in his mouth. At Rory who, as a matter of fact, didn't eat butter.

'Don't you *dare!*' warned the fiery girl and her warm breath fanned my face.

When Molly Cushen walked slowly on to the bridge, I watched transfixed by Breen's Hotel. She moved very slowly and then stopped to lean on the arm of the bridge, dissolving in tears.

I had never seen a girl weep her heart out like that; she wept as though she was being torn up inside, and the insides of girls were to me a total mystery.

Nor did she become ugly on that account, crying so bitterly; she became, if that were possible, more beautiful than before, as though by weeping she had drawn closer to me. And I thought to myself: That must be real love; that's the price you must pay for beauty.

She was the prettiest girl in the convent, with her pale oval face almost Chinese, with round cheeks and long black hair and dark eyes, all pupil. She had a low voice and was in the class behind me, so I did not see much of her except in the playground, where she was sedate and moved about by herself, watching the other girls yelling and screeching as they raced about.

It was the voice that got to me, glottal; sooner or later she would have to get her tonsils out. Intimacies confided in that resonant voice would indeed be womanly intimacies; the voice of Molly Cushen seemed to come up out of the ground, not up out of her stomach. Her mother had died and would be buried next day in Donycomper Cemetery. The nun told us that we should be kind to poor Molly who had lost her mother. They had been close, the nun said.

Now she was dissolving in tears.

A wind blew downriver from behind the ruined mill and blew strands of black hair across her face as if she wore a mourning veil and she stopped; on the hump of the bridge as if she couldn't go a step further, because it was closer to Donycomper Cemetery which was just up the hill on the Lucan road. Now she was racked with tears, weeping convulsively, her shoulders heaving. This was real crying, those were scalding tears; she wept as though her heart was broken. A shadowy form was holding her, shaking her; that was her mother in a shroud come back from the dead to comfort her daughter. I thought: That then is true love; it must be hard indeed, love.

I remembered the blood-flecked bowl that stood on a table in the changing room where the girls kept their coats. After harsh dentistry for the whole school, called out class by class for extractions, the girls who had had teeth pulled out spat into the bowl and walked about with chalk-white faces, handkerchiefs pressed to their mouths and their white smocks also bloodstained. They walked slowly about, grimacing, as if in purdah, as if by walking slowly about, the pain would go away. That then was real love: the pain that wouldn't go away.

The white suffering face of the young girl on the bridge was a face 'washed by all waters' as the Germans say. A dark-haired, white-faced pretty girl weeping her heart out on a humpbacked bridge, missing her mother who had been dragged away to her death, that too was certain, a token of love, of not forgetting, holding in the heart that which had vanished. Love had to do with a humpbacked bridge with five arches which took the traffic that moved slowly in two directions, coming and going. Horse-drawn carts and turf wagons drawn by little donkeys moved in terrific slow motion over the bridge, up by Gleason's shop and down past Green's open door, the dark maw of their hovel. The shell of a mill long out of use, a breeze blowing downriver, the beginning of love.

– 18 –

Black Bucks Vain of Their Dicks

A t the Bray Head end of the north beach at Greystones, where the trains came out of the tunnel, it was possible to swim nude, far enough from preying eyes on the harbour wall. The nearest humans were the fishermen some way out at sea, pulling off around Bray Head.

One sultry day in August Rory, horny as Pan, sprinted starkers from the cold embrace of the sea and threw himself like a thunderbolt upon the warm inert vaguely female form, compliant, soft and wet, made from the topsoil that had parted company from the cliff above, now supine or prone, featureless with the suggestion of gigantic thighs.

Into this engulfing bride didn't the bold Rory embed his prick as into a steamy big seaside girl with her chubby legs wide apart, and shagged all the shapelessness and seaside silliness out of her, gasping and panting at the size of it, the strength of it. Then he cleaned his member and dressed in a hurry, just shirt, trousers and sandals, hoping that none of the fishermen out in their boats, hauling in and letting out nets, had seen him shagging the mud pile silly, as though it were a big soft lump of a girl. They would stand up and shout something obscene for sure. But none seemed to be interested, concentrating on their tasks, lost out in the haze. The sea was still very cold in August and the mackerel were running.

Half-hearted attempts to pick up girls down from Dublin sunbathing and oiling themselves on the harbour wall came to naught. Rory asked a girl, who was brown as a nut, if she would go swimming with him on the south beach;

he was on his Raleigh with one foot on the railings above the beach near the ice-cream hut and she had appeared alongside him; he had been watching her for weeks. She went about with her mother; walking from her home near the crossroads on the way to Delgany. She was rarely alone. Rory didn't know her name.

'I can't swim,' she said, staring at the sea.

She had brown eyes, with nice hands and hair. She was lovely.

'I'll teach you to swim.'

'Will you?'

Silence. She stared at the sea; Rory stared at her profile. They would lie side by side on bath towels near where the little stream trickled out into the sea. He might suggest Kilcoole beach where one could sunbathe without togs, perhaps together now on one towel. He would urge her to enter the sea naked with him, would teach her the breaststroke. Read Herrick to her, oil her back.

'How you disturb me,' I said.

Meaning: oh I fancy you, brownie.

'Then you should go to the other end of the beach,' she said with invincible female logic.

Kiss your opportunities goodbye. Such chances come rarely. Rory changed into his togs all of a doodah by the rocks and waited for her to appear in the striped costume he had seen on her when sunbathing; but she did not show up. She didn't like his crablike approach; she had walked off.

One had to make fit submission to the Great Female Principle. And what was that but immersion in the sea, in a state of total nudity in that fulsome embrace, bracing while powerfully and undeniably feminine?

The semeny odours of the foreshore spoke of the male-female union, as did the clams stuck so obstinately fast to their rocks, little sister clams to big brother rocks, as did the rock-pools and bladderwrack, the fishy tang of cunt, the cunty tang of fish, the mackerel gutted and thrown on the beach by the point, flung out of the boats coming from beyond Kilcoole, given away free at dusk, as well as the general shifting about of sand blown by the breeze, the sucking and gushing and sibilant whispering that went on all the time, the sun scudding into the clouds, only to reappear again, and the beach suddenly in shade and then wiped clean as the sun burst forth again; barnacles clipping and kissing and the little waves rolling in on their sinuous rills, every seventh bigger than the preceding six and the mussels puckering up their slobbery drippy lips and all the ceaseless activity that goes on every day on the beach (even when there is nobody there, just the sand castles subsiding and the lost towel and the paddle as signs of former occupancy). It went on anyhow; life as ceaseless agitation.

Could her name be Molly? Hairy Molly, the dark brown one, the *morena*. Mightn't she be Molly? My Molly. Might not she be my *morena,* if only I could shake off the mother? Stranger things have happened.

Water is the great aphrodisiac for Pisceans. Feared at first (forceful ducking), then accepted, then indulged in, then forgotten, as potency waxes and wanes, as the moon goes around.

I have always thought of bodies of water, no matter how big or how small or agitated (Anna) or tranquil (Philippa), whether in perpetual motion (Harriet), as rivers and mountain streams, or at rest (Lough Dan, where Philippa appeared to be decapitated, up to her neck in dark mountain water), as feminine.

The tang of seaweed has always seemed to me a cunty tang ('salt swoll'n cunt') and something to fear; as the chilly embrace of seawater is calculated to shrink the flinching member, first seizing the balls in a sudden rough grip and presently up around the neck; until one casts off buoyantly into another free element (the one we came out of, when we were fish) that bears one up, miraculously on the surface, a female grasp of male matter (the member getting acclimatised to the cold of the underwater and the nibbling minnows). Trust in the female (what Herr Mann calls *der Andere*) is what keeps the apprehensive and wincing male swimmer afloat and free of his own uncertainty, in this supremely female element, the sea.

So Rory, at first a non-swimmer though born half a mile from Anna Liffey, always saw water, whether hot or cold, harbour or open sea, precocious Mediterranean shore or freezing Atlantic, from taps or coming naturally, whether in thermal springs or in spas with noisome emetics, vile concoctions said to be good for you, to be essentially a *female* element, in its chill deeps holding his male member in its frozen grip, a clutch well calculated to unman Rory.

Rory feared fast-flowing rivers with tricky currents and bends with deep holes, around which the current swirled as if to say *Steer clear, me hearties!* There was the sloping gravelled hole down the slope of which the Dote had once stumbled until the water was up to his nose; another inch and he was under, choking, but fortunately for him the pool levelled out and he walked out the other side, watched by myself and Gina Green, gone pale as sheets on the riverbank.

Then Rory feared deep water, the tidal sea, the befouled Liffey with filthy effluents discharged from the city, flowing out under Butt Bridge and off into the snotgreen scrotum-tightening sea referred to by Mr Joyce, himself a great water man, that was Dublin Bay where every summer someone drowned.

Rory feared all this just as he feared the ramshackle rusty hulks from foreign parts, *Valparaiso* and the *Straits of Magellan,* that were moored at the dockside there with moody, dirty-looking crewmen lounging about on deck. He sometimes thought of offering his services as a deck-hand, like the young Conrad or Lowry after him; but never did, could never pluck up enough courage to hail one of these lounging lascars. Just as well perhaps. They would have shagged poor Rory overboard as useless cargo somewhere off Rockall. What happened out there was very remote from the boy and girl stuff.

The movies that came my way and seemed to reveal something of that threatening strange life, the life that other people led, the lovers who *went after* each other like carnivores after their victims ('Studio *Vingt Huit* high up on a windy street in Montmartre in the full blasphemy of a freezing Sunday,' wrote Cyril Connolly of *Un Chien Andalou,* where Pierre Batcheff and his Spanish-looking girl 'patter after each other like stoats in search of blood'), were

> *Un Chien Andalou*
> *Extase*
> *Blood and Sand*
> *Bahama Passage*
> *The Brothers*
> *The Lady from Shanghai*
> *The Outcast of the Islands*
> *Knife in the Water*

Women are not the best judges of women, nor of their special appeal for specific men, those watchful, horny, thorny lads. 'Can't see what you see in that one,' Stella Veronica told Rory. 'The gommy-looking one,' she called her, Rory's nut-brown maid. In those days all Irish girls were virgins; if for no other reason than they never escaped from their vigilant mothers' ever-watchful eyes. They even dressed like their mothers, wore the same make-up, or none at all. Nude sunbathing would have to be done on the sly, for the mother would notice the Bahama complexion.

But, having taken another look at the sunbather on the harbour wall, Stella Veronica was ready to concede that the gommy-looking one wasn't so gommy-looking after all and was in fact a good-looking girl. A real good-looker, if a bit on the dark side.

Some girls are greedy for it already before their time. What about the one in a pack of screeching schoolgirls running out of the sea and sitting on boulders below the Eden Temperance Hotel in the small stony cove blocked with seaweed? She was very red in the face from excitement and sat in such a way that her uniform school skirt of dark blue serge, rode up to reveal her dark declivities, for she wasn't wearing knickers or hadn't bothered to put them on yet and didn't seem to notice Rory, very thoughtful, walking below, getting an eyeful of her charms, as though he had lost something, say his watch (he never wore one), in the shale.

Hannelore had spoken to me of the nudist camp at Bastia in Corsica where she went with her dancing teacher and Dr Hans Borken, and of the black men 'hung like horses' who were very sportful in the surf, showing off what they possessed to the laughing girls. Their members glistened black as ebony and the girls couldn't take their eyes off them.

She and her friend undressed in the hut and walked out into the sea where the black men were shouting and cavorting and ducking one another. It was a small act of female consideration. Dr Borken followed them a little later, a bit shamefaced about his pale white nudity.

Hannelore had always contended that women were stronger than men. The men dressed up as soldiers and went off to war but the women did something more difficult: they stayed at home and fed and cared for the children during the bombing.

Prone on a towel, not yet having 'gone in', waiting for the sun to come out, immersed in the *Essays of Schopenhauer* and apparently impervious to distractions (Monsieur Gool's handsome son, a French Resistance fighter, had that morning walked on his hands into the sea, to the delight of those watching the upside-down legs advancing deeper and deeper into the sea, like the Manx symbol of three whirling legs or Brueghel's Icarus drowning), the pubescent Rory now being treated to the arousing spectacle of a young wife, no doubt sexually voracious, down for the day from Dublin on her own, drying herself after a dip and kicking off her wet clinging togs now itchy with sand, allowing the bath towel to slip from her hands to take the sun (which had come out again) just as she is, giving Rory a chance to fully appreciate her unadorned charms, stood up just the other side of the bathing box by the railway line.

The sun goes in again; she wraps herself in the towel; Rory runs into the sea. Culvert one hundred and sixty yards seaward. Lap dissolve. Iris out.

– 19 –

Roryamours 1956-99

Dostoevesky married his stenographer, Anna Grigoryevna Snitkina;
he was twenty-five years her senior, a fitful epileptic and survivor of
a Siberian labour camp.

In the highlands of Cuernavaca, in the state of Morelos, the air is like
wine. At dawn, in the Rancho Pico, the two black-and-white cocks crow with
the bright clarion-call of bugles.

The later, appealing roughneck, Ernest Hemingway, boasted that he had
given 'Mr Scrooby' fifty-five times in one month to his fourth wife, Miss Mary.

My former publisher, Calder, boasted to another potential conquest that he
had had three hundred women in his time. Rory doubted if he himself had had
more than twenty, being a late starter. But why diversity? Five of the twenty he
had surely enjoyed more than three hundred times.

You have to begin somewhere and you must end somewhere. Jack Trevor
Story boasted that he had but ten loves in his life and his trouble was that he
couldn't forget any of them. I, being choosy, have had rather less than ten,
and I too cannot forget any of them.

Chronologically then, here they are, sauntering out into the ring: my first
wife Coppera Hill, née Anders, was born in King William's Town in the
Eastern Cape of South Africa; we lived together as man and wife for twenty
years and more and have three sons, one of whom has given me four grandchildren, one a girl (Hi, Yanika, my sweet!): that long union came to an end
in an unforeseen manner like a house of cards toppling.

Then there was Mrs Harriet Deck of San Francisco; Hannelore Schmidt
of Berlin; Hannel Vang of Copenhagen, a sort of sob-sister to Anna Reiner,
also of Copenhagen, that quiet port on Kattegat. And then there was Alannah Buxton-Hopkin, who was born in Singapore of an English father (Dr
Denis Buxton-Hopkin, who had been a voluntary POW staying with his
patients after the fall of Singapore) and an Irish mother, one of the Foleys of
Summercove. We were married on 20 November 1997 in a Dublin register
office.

She is my last love, the love of my life. When I hear the toot of the Peugeot on the one-way narrow street below, the horn tells me that she is near, returned from Castletownbere or Castletownshend or even Ballydehob, visiting the cheese people or the English bird couple, the Foxes, or the art people who are everywhere in County Cork; when not out riding in the riding schools she assiduously attends. She has her rituals.

– 20 –

The Hoax that Joke Bilked

My brother's unnamed house, even in an unfinished state, was a peculiar domicile for an architect to conceive, let alone design and build for himself and his wife. If your dentist, upon opening wide his mouth exposed horrors, dental decay run riot, rotten roots, missing teeth, wouldn't you be taken aback?

The uncomfortably narrow stairway led upwards to the narrow sleeping quarters, the rat races in the rafters, and down to narrow rooms crowded in upon themselves. The whole dusty ambience was forbidding, veiled in dust; it was like entering a house shut up for years, the air stale, the surfaces dimmed by lack of daylight.

It was as unlike the house that Charles Eames built, afloat on the air at Pacific Palisades, as you could well imagine. My brother would have maintained that pleasure is *not* useful; we were not put on this earth to enjoy ourselves, so why quarrel with beastly circumstances? You would not get the impression (the feeling of a loft with its habitual cobwebs and scuttle of unseen mice and stale trapped air) that my brother was ever touched by the uncommon beauty of common things, which had touched Charles Eames; certainly not by his architectural forays. All I remembered was an uncompleted shell, the narrow bedroom like the set from *The Cabinet of Dr Caligari* with Werner Krauss oozing out of the plywood wall.

Brother C. took against me for the way I had portrayed him and his wife and their unfinished house in *Dog Days,* perceiving only jeers and sneers where I had attempted to portray him as a heroic Dostoevsky character, a mixture of Dimitri Karamazov and Prince Mishkin. I had to portray tsarist-style Russian squalor and of course the *dacha* half-finished, an oversight, in the face of other more pressing concerns (the soul).

He didn't like it, didn't get the joke, thought I was ridiculing the neighbours, for whom he would always be Pan Hill, the big boss, the Town Planner. Can you see it? Can you beat it? The style of it!

Now it's as if I'd put a curse on the still nameless house finally completed without any flags raised at cornice or roof to announce all was ready for human habitation; and what remain are blackened beams and owls roosting in the now distinctly chilly and uncomfortable bedroom, the cats running wild; everything now in disarray and the voracious growth of weeds proliferating and obscuring the shapes of the deserted habitation.

Frater, Brüder, hermano, it wasn't ever my intent to belittle you. I have nothing but respect for you. Long ago when we were chisslers, I could have injured you badly or broken your neck on the road from Lough Dan going downhill like the hammers of Hell when the front wheel of my heavy Raleigh locked with your back wheel (boy's bike) and pitched us both on to the road.

Once in the loft above the garage some highly combustible film stock caught fire, surrounded by petrol leaks and full tins and lofts full of hay; we could have burnt the place down, might have suffocated, but managed to put it out. Do you remember that? I was the elder one, I should have known not to play about with celluloid and matches.

There were times when I could have blinded you when we played the Wilhelm Tell game and I shot holes with the Daisy air-rifle through the apple balanced on your head – you were the fall guy.

How do brothers survive brothers? And was it some sort of joke you were making, some point you wished to make, by building your own ruin and folly for all to see and admire on this island crammed with ruins and follies, not to forget the hidden graves of those murdered by the Provos in the night and buried in secret places in Wicklow, in this sometimes wholly delightful Vale of Tears? Was that it? I'll die laughing, if so.

One thing is sure: once your mind is made up, it's made up for good. The account is closed; I know that.

– 21 –

The Anaya-Toledos of Mexico City

Carl, my eldest son, split up with his Mexican wife, Carlota Anaya-Toledo of the Jardin Balbuena, a grandiose name and address that was, like much in Mexico, disguising a mess. When the marriage didn't work out, the love didn't work out either. Thanks chiefly to the father, Adolfo Anaya-Toledo, who, as a Mexican gentleman of means had on his word of honour promised them a flat and Carl a job and when neither was forthcoming the marriage was already on the rocks. Carl couldn't find a job without the official papers Adolfo had promised to secure. The ignorant wife sent her putative son-in-law to consult a *bruja*, a soothsayer, or witch.

There was a long and painful parting. Carl left Mexico and returned to London, was given back his old job in the Odeon projection box. Carlota threatened to follow, would not agree to a divorce.

Years later he found love again in Hemel Hempstead when he took up with a pale girl by the name of Sally, who had a rough father. By Sally he had the long longed-for child he never had with Carlota, a daughter whom he dearly loved in the short span of life allotted her, for she was only granted a few days in winter.

So, she (Elizabeth they christened her) died and was buried in a little casket in a wood in Hertfordshire and Grandmother Cappera read an Emily Dickinson poem in lieu of a prayer. Carl was the romantic who believed in all-out love, like Byron, in the reckless way that the late unlamented Dr Goebbels had believed in total war. Carl was for loving blindly, giving all without any reservations, which is a sure prescription for failure. It was the same terrible medicine that Dr Goebbels had prescribed for the *Volk*, with such disastrous consequences. Carlos was for all-out love. Well, that's unwise. Who was it wrote that 'to love without reservation is to be betrayed'? Djuna Barnes?

– 22 –

The Shapely Flanks of Rita Hayworth
(*The Lady from Shanghai*)

i

November 17 of 1946 was a cloudy day in Acapulco with an oppressively overcast sky holding down the heat. Twenty miles out coxswain and famous cocksman Errol Flynn of 'In like Flynn!' fame, stood at the wheel of his yacht *Zaca* (*Circe* in the movie they were about to shoot, a month after Orson Welles, the director, had begun scouting for locations) in choppy seas, trying to hold her on a steady course.

Lawton the cinematographer held the filter to his right eye, waiting for a break in the clouds. In character and dressed for the part, Welles ('Black' Mike O'Hara, who had throttled a man with his bare hands during the Spanish Civil War) and his former wife, Rita Hayworth (Elsa Bannister, *femme fatale* and murderess, unsatisfied spouse of the famous criminal lawyer Arthur Bannister, crippled in both legs), had rehearsed the opening scene of the shooting on the aft deck and were ready for the cameras to roll.

The Acapulco sun blazed forth, the mixer hollered 'Speed . . . Take One! Let em roll!' and Welles, holding a beat, spoke his first line. His Irish accent was priceless; but there again his contact with the noble race had been largely confined to working for the two famous pederasts, Hilton Edwards and Michéal MacLiammóir at the Gate. It was rich and strange, a veritable verbal purple vestment. The shooting of *The Lady from Shanghai* had begun. It was a movie already doomed to fail on many counts, for Welles, for Harry Cohn, the president of Columbia Pictures who wanted to bend Welles and *The Lady* to his will, laying on the terrible theme song 'Please Don't Kiss Me', which was as corny as they come, and obliging Rita Hayworth to sing it out at sea, adding another $60,000 to an undertaking already costing plenty. And how could she refuse? She was under contract; he had her over a barrel. She was appearing as a favour to Welles, who was slow to pay alimony. Their daughter Rebecca had turned twelve and there were school fees, dental fees, God knows what fees, to be considered. When filming was over, Welles planned to vanish into Europe.

In the meantime (back on the *Circe-Zaca*) one of the camera crew, working without a hat, collapsed and died of a coronary thrombosis; to be sewn up in a duffel bag and thrown overboard. 'Sail on, *Zaca!*' sang out Flynn, whose spirits could not be suppressed. He spoke in a strange clipped English accent to match his wispy moustache, and was in awe of Welles. He must have had his own ideas about Rita Hayworth too. His own wife was heavily pregnant, aboard with the crew and cast; the two lawyers, Bannister (Everett Sloane) and Grisby (Glenn Anders) seemed more like criminals; and O'Hara's sidekicks (one was Bud Schilling) turned out to be half-wits. Even the judge (Erskine Sanford, the fuddy-duddy old editor of Kane's newspaper in *Citizen Kane* seven years previously) seemed loopy. Well, everybody is somebody's fool. Flynn had his rapacious eye on many things; all that moved and was female was his potential prey. All that was female and good-looking moved him; he was swayed by beauty, always greedy for it.

The location shooting would be extremely arduous, not counting the corpses thrown overboard; Welles was up to his neck in what he preferred to do: show ambition thwarted, women disappointed and turning on their men; evildoers at their evildoing. He had run up a huge bill at the Hotel Reforma in Mexico City; he and Rita Hayworth had been received off their flight like visiting royalty. Flynn was jealous of him, not least because of his apparently effortless success with women. And what women! Hayworth and then Dolores del Rio, whose underclothes must have cost a fortune.

'Rita couldn't take the heat,' they said. She had to make two dives from Morro Rock. Temperatures soared and Rita collapsed on camera. Orson was most solicitous, he couldn't do enough for her. She was carried down into her cool cabin and Orson stood guard.

The shooting went on, using understudies, shooting the back of the head, moving shadows, the shifty ones, the lawyers who acted and looked like bad criminals. The unctuous theme song was poured like molasses over everything by Cohn, still trying to bend the great director to his will. Sharks swam in the lukewarm water. Rita said she was finished. Flynn's eyes were permanently bloodshot; now he had taken up with an Amazonian giantess with teeth missing and not a word of English; she spoke the language of the night, grunting and groaning under Flynn, who was insatiable.

When Cohn saw the rough cut he exploded, offering one grand to anyone who could explain the story to him. There was no plot, there were no close-ups of Rita. He decided to plug 'Please Don't Kiss Me' into every nook and cranny, like Muzak into Macey's, penetrating even into the toilets.

'The only way to stay out of trouble is to grow old,' Cohn said, snipping the end off a huge cigar; quoting from the wunderkind's obnoxious script. And his executives seemed to agree with him. 'Hey, fellas, concentrate on that.' They hooted with hearty laughter by the door. 'If you kiss me, don't take your lips away!' Cohn was in stitches. The studio hack composer, Heinz Roemheld, whose orchestration of the tune had snored away on the strings, was summoned to the office and congratulated by the president on doing a great job. Welles of course had hated the song; a long and abusive memo had come in. Rita sued him for a goodly sum to cover child maintenance; but Orson-Black-Michael-O'Hara-Welles was no longer there.

'He never was,' Cohn said bitterly, unaware that he had made a witty joke. He could kiss his money goodbye, *The Lady from Shanghai* wouldn't make one red cent; Rita could kiss her alimony goodbye too. It was a crying shame, Cohn said, choking on his long Cuban cigar.

'We used Acapulco just as we found it,' the wunderkind had told him. 'No more, no less, Harry.'

ii

She had come a long way since, aged seventeen, she had danced in *Dante's Inferno*. And yet, not so far; for she was ignorant as pay-dirt. 'Orsie' (her pet name for Orson) had her reading Plato, Cervantes and Shakespeare, but all that quick culture went in one ear and out the other; she wasn't made for it. She was a dancer, and when she danced her body spoke volumes and in many languages. She was not in control of it; her beauty escaped her; went out to all the men sitting with hard-ons, silently in the dark, smoking like furnaces; their spouses uneasy beside them, rustling like wheat in the wind, the womenfolk knowing that they had lost their men who had run off after Rita.

And then there was her former co-star Victor Mature, a dense fellow who wore trousers two sizes too large for him, and had the mouth of a carnivore. They had met on the shooting of *My Gal Sal* and the relationship had prospered quickly, so gushed the gossip columnist Hedda Hopper. The coupling of cheesecake and beefcake appealed to the romantically inclined gossips and vulgarians of Hollywood. Hollywood *wanted* this marriage.

But it was not to be; her destiny lay elsewhere. Soon her mad Orsie was sawing her in half for the Mercury Wonder Show and cutting off all her long mane of red hair (Margarita Carmen Cansino had Irish and Spanish blood coursing through her veins) for *The Lady from Shanghai* where she undertook some serious man-killing after all the floss and flicker of *Gilda* and *Cover Girl*.

Cohn was fit to be tied. 'Rita, honey,' he implored, 'you gotta stop doin' this ta me. You gotta listen now. Listen good. We *own* you, sweetie, bag and baggage, body and soul. You're ours. Columbia owns you. There's the contract. Now behave yourself. You ain't gonna work for this nutcase no more.' Or some such palaver; Cohn was incensed.

So Rita came to heel. How could she not? She was a contracted star earning real money; it wasn't peanuts. Her great public adored her, servicemen everywhere wanted to get down on her.

The swell of bust was duplicated behind in the swell of proud calf, noble flank and buttock, on the screen in Technicolor. It flowed in all directions. Her curves duplicated the contour of rich coastlines, of good real estate for the seriously rich from Point Conception to La Jolla on through Baja California along the lines of latitude just above the Equator. These were her outstretched and noble flanks in fishnet stockings and mighty high heels, her dancing kit ripping my dreams, something cruel there, with the flaming tresses the urgent frou frou of skirt lifted in the dance, the big pouty lips red as cherries, the show of brilliantly white teeth – infill condition, *asperges*, plenty, America! Nutrition, privilege, dollars, security, blaze USA!

When they saw Hayworth or Betty Grable (an even riper peach) dance, the thoughts of all good red-blooded Americans flew to Belmont Park or Saratoga Springs or Aqueduct, all the racetracks and the great fillies and mares that ran in the fifth and the fourth and the third race; the thoroughbreds pounding by had the bodies of supermodels; at every stride the tipsters cheered and waved them on with race cards, binoculars clenched in their hands.

Betty Grable was of course *all* curves. Single-handed she had won the Battle of the Bulge. Her body on the screen was worth two or three divisions in the field.

Cohn, in a black mood, gnashing his molars and armed with clippers, cut and hacked away at the finished film, trying to make it an acceptable vehicle for the masses, cutting it down to eighty-six minutes, holding up the release for a year, releasing it into the second half of programmes, hoping few would notice it. Few did. Orsie had had his scissors out too; he'd sheared off Rita's lovely long red mane, made a peroxide blonde out of her, filmed her in the San Francisco aquarium, wouldn't even show them (her and Welles) embracing, much less glued together in a *beso*.

iii

It was the one movie I always wanted to see again.

Betty Grable, all lips and legs, was just part of the American war effort on the home front; akin to selling war bonds. Her image was stamped on the fuselage of Flying Fortresses where she exposed as much of herself as the Hayes Office would permit; a low-angle shot of the famous come-on look as though she were lifting or thinking of lifting up her skirt to show what little she had on underneath. Years later this would spawn the shot of Monroe standing astride the grid above the subway, in *The Seven Year Itch*.

The heavily insured legs and horselike flanks assured the servicemen and flyers that Democracy was indeed worth dying for if Betty Grable, with her skirt torn off by a great wind, represented it.

There was too much strangeness in the Welles movie for Cohn. Try as he might with his scissors and 'Please Don't Kiss Me', he could not eliminate the erotic strangeness. I saw the film first in the Adelphi in Dun Laoghaire, where I had also seen Abraham Polonsky's *Force of Evil* with Philippa. The slagging picnic, the sequence in the aquarium, the clinches that never came, or came and were never seen; the whole movie was full of unsaid things: innuendoes, portents of unspeakable things. It was the sort of movie that Philippa detested, full of 'suggestive' images, a very strong Catholic taboo word in those days.

The wank in the tank led forward through all the years to the dim aquarium where Elsa Bannister (Rita Hayworth) and Black Mike, two killers, do not embrace, absolutely do not embrace each other, though evidently dying to do so.

It led to the revolving barrel of water where she of the luscious underlip, permanently damp, revolves in *Les Enfants du Paradis*. The nude Arletty, who had a Nazi lover, a Luftwaffe colonel no less, during the Occupation, swoons in the tank, as though male arms are urgently reaching out for her. She says impudently, '*J'adore la liberté.*'

It led, after some teasing, to the naked wife crouching on the yacht in *Knife in the Water,* a sight to which we in the dark cinema are privy, with the blond young Polish hitch-hiker, but not the husband.

It led to Madeleine Carroll and Sterling Hayden, two stoats on an island where the sun shines all day under the sea, in *Bahama Passage*.

It led to the permanently drenched native black girl of Carol Reed's *Outcast of the Islands* who can speak no English, and is seen showering; she is half otter, all stoat.

It led to Patricia Roc bursting out of her cleavage in *The Brothers* and swimming naked in the sea somewhere off Scotland.

All led back to Hedy Kiesler (who went to Hollywood and was turned into a waxworks figure) in *Extase,* swimming naked in a Czech lake, after undressing behind a bush as provocatively as Madeleine Carroll had removed her stockings behind a screen, with her stoat Hayden watching, in a skyscraper in New York. And all led back to the cattle tank at the ring-pump at Springfield in the long ago.

PART II:

Foreign Faces and Places

− 23 −

Voyage

We plunge over the Equator. Flying fish sink, porpoises rise, and evening after evening the sun goes down in formations of cloud, furnacelike, dramatic as anything in Doré's illustrations of Dante. The approaches to a new continent. Such lovely leewardings! They must lead somewhere.

Undersized dining-room stewards – Malays – traverse the decks banging out the same tune on their dinner gongs. I've grown tired of the repetitive meals, the same dull company – it's a kind of prison.

The passengers for the most part are Dutch, German, or Afrikaners returning to their homeland. One tall Afrikaner – von Lieres – is returning to Vanrhynsdorp in the Cape after several years studying engineering in Germany. He tells me that in some South African families they send their sons into the police force for a year or so to toughen them up before they take up a career. Before they take up a more respectable career? I ask. He gives me a blank look and smiles; we do not make jokes about the police in South Africa. On the first lap of the tour we will run into him again. I share a cabin with two young Germans – also engineers. Going to German South-West Africa. Strategists.

Among the German contingent is a family from Berlin. The parents sit close together on deck, stoutly perspiring, handkerchiefs over their heads, calling for beer. They have one son of fourteen; it's mainly on his account that they are going to South Africa. Germany is not for them any more. Two wars in one lifetime is too much.

What is it they fear? Communism, militant Communism? The Tartar tank crews with their slit eyes and Mongolian features, the strange leather headgear of the Red Army spearheads that entered Budapest to crush the Hungarian uprising, finished them. Emanations from a nightmare. It is this they fear. Soviet tanks manned by Asiatic crews.

So off, then; *pis aller!*

The wife hopes to take up her old profession in Johannesburg: orthopaedics. The husband too will work. Both have done so all their lives, worked hard; they are not young any more, but they will work for the

535

future of their son.

The small *Fräulein* in Coppera's cabin has her wedding dress and trousseau with her. Though hardly more than a child, she is going out to German South-West Africa to marry a man she has never seen except in photographs. She is a war orphan from Hamburg. It's an arranged match.

The first sight of Africa low on the horizon on the port side, a dim white skeleton coast; a mirage that goes.

Walvis Bay, in South-West Africa. A barrage of heat. Offal from the ship's kitchen floating astern. Seagulls squall over it, their whiteness reflected in a rainbow trail of oil. From the stagnant greenish waters a stench of putrescence rises, sharp as sulphuric acid or rotten eggs. A squat white bird, resembling a penguin, paddles round the stern and one of the crew – an idle Malay – takes pot-shots at it through a porthole down by the waterline.

Empty deckchairs, inert in the heat, creak in the sun. The wan-looking bride-to-be is taken ashore on a tender with some of the pale young Germans.

On shore, a collection of shacks faces the sea, the sun shooting fire on corrugated iron roofs. *Die Waterman* out of Amsterdam, a decaying wharf with figures of African dock labourers parading on it, and beyond them, an excessively long rusty-plated terra-cotta Russian tanker from the Bering Strait – on these the sun, from almost directly overhead, brings to bear its fierce and implacable rays. Baked littoral and saffron dunes, a reflection of a decayed wharf swimming in mid-air, with figures walking upside down on it – all burn and tremble in the sun.

A local flat-boat comes alongside, and into its capacious and dirty hold black men dressed in rags, with bright-coloured bandannas about their heads, begin offloading cargo, while others wait in the hold. The passengers, laughing, throw them apples and oranges, as if into a bear pit. The oranges explode down in the hold. Some of the remaining sallow-faced young Germans come with jackets under their arms to gape at the coal-black dockers. After a time the flat-boat sails, laden with cargo, grey-black smoke pumping out of its stack. That side of the ship now seems deserted. Leaning over the rail I imagine I can see sand, fathoms deep, and the reflections of a double tier of bored passengers staring down. Their shadows go shuddering into the deeper green of the sea, where a shoal of voracious red cannibal fish, like mullet, swim up out of the stench against our kelpy side. They come in dense, resolute shoals. When a fishing lime, unbaited, touches the water, they take it and one by one are yanked on deck. They lie twitching on the boards where one cannot walk barefoot; quite soon their vivid colour goes.

This desolate place with its heat and smells, the hyena and lion reek of old Africa – this is Walvis Bay. Sidgewick, author of a beginners' book on astronomy, lived for a time with his girl in a cave up in the hills, and died later of coronary thrombosis on a boat on the Seine.

At last this jaunt is nearly over. Tonight we lie to at Walvis Bay.

A storm before Cape Town. All the ports bolted; the woodwork groaning. The Cape rollers begin. Black sea and waves at night. Nausea. We poor sailors turn in early.

In the morning the storm has blown itself out, though the sea is still running high. We are into Table Bay, *Die Waterman* approaching its berth. A blinding glare comes off the sea. During the night one of the vague young Germans, wandering about the ship, fell down a companionway, had a heart attack and died of it. The body lies now in his white cabin. No one knows anything about him. He is to be buried in Cape Town. A collection is started.

Table Mountain looms over us, balancing on its summit a single cloud. It's a hot day in high summer. The passengers crowd the rail. A beauty in a black dress, wearing sunglasses, stands alone on the quayside and waves to someone standing beside me.

Prancing airs of the Cape of Good Hope. It's 20 December 1956.

On 24 December, two engines pull a long line of carriages through the Blaauwberg Mountains, on the Garden Route, travelling from Cape Town to East London in the Eastern Cape. Wheatlands go right up into the lime-blue foothills of the mountains. The horizon seems very far away, bright and luminous. Everything is on a grander scale here – even the swallows are bigger. At Mossel Bay, on an island, a lady in a picture hat paints at an easel.

Blossom, Le Roux, Zebra, Power, George, the Outeniqua Mountains, the beaches of Wilderness, the inland sea of Knysna, the thick green grass of the ostrich farms, an engineless grain train pulled into a siding and Africans in broken sunhats unloading sugar cane.

For a whole day we travelled through this landscape of grey-blue militant cactus with no other vegetation, no house, the whole face of the land covered with these things, and nothing else as far as the eye could see, scarcely a blade of grass.

– 24 –

The Jacaranda Street Nudist

W e toured South Africa and both Rhodesias through 1957–58. After outfitting and rehearsing in a theatre in Cape Town, the tour started in somewhere like Paarl or Worcester in the Cape Province, and we toured via Nelspoort as far as Windhoek in South-West Africa, and then looped back via the Transkei, Orange Free State and Transvaal until we reached Ladysmith in Natal, then over the Limpopo at Belt Bridge in floods and rain, a delay of two days, on into Southern and Northern Rhodesia, as they were called then with resolute political incorrectness, for the republic had not yet come to pass.

We 'did' Odendaalsrus, Kroonstad, Volksrust, Nylstroom, Warmbad (we swam at night in a pool made by Italian POWs) until we reached Louis Trichardt; and thence to Gwelo or do I mean Gweru before Victoria Falls; and then Wankie, when we were at our last gasp, did us. We rode alongside the driver in the high cabin of a pantechnicon rented out by the National Theatre, Wright made notes, Brink drove, old Madge went ahead and arranged bookings; the puppets and stage were dismantled and packed and had to be reassembled and set up; the African 'boys' were in a hutch at the back; and in this large uncomfortable contraption we travelled thousands of miles over two years and contrived to put aside £200 (old currency) in hard-won savings.

We ended up in Johannesburg.

Coming from the terminus, a merely facultative stop somewhere near Observatory golf course, the No. 11 bowls along Isipingo Street, a pretty street planted with rows of jacaranda trees, stopping just past our flat (Mount Willmar, where the fifth or topmost floor finds us), conveniently enough; and so into town via Netherley House (a home for the indigent old male whites), a fivepenny ride via Gundelfinger & Weinraub, the Ord Tie Factory, Kahn's Pianos and the municipal tennis courts where a bored coach in flannels and a peaked cap lobs brownish tennis balls over the net to an uninspired novice; hence via Long Street to the offices of the J. Walter Thompson advertising agency. That would be after temporary employment at 66 Loveday Street in the Constantia Bookshop; before I found final employment at the junction of

Market and Kruis on the sixth floor at Filmlets (SA) under general manager Pax Moran (emphasis on final syllable as in 'also ran').

Consider this. Two queers are quarrelling bitterly on the landing near Ruth Levy's apartment in Hillbrow. It's a bitter business, a lovers' tiff; but before you could invoke the lizard or utter the charmed word 'Bozy', one draws out a gat and plugs the other three times in or about the heart and takes to his heels down the back service hatch used by Africans *(nie Blankes)*. Arriving for one of Ruth Levy's drinks parties, Adamczewski is an impassive witness of the consequences. The dying queer crawls along the ground, blood oozing through the back of his shirt, moving his legs slowly sideways, his fingers in the cracks of the cement. He seems to be 'fornicating with the cracks'. Adamczewski hears the footsteps of the murderer escaping down the stairs. It's a day in late November 1958 in Johannesburg.

In the Adamczewski rented quarters at Samedo we play weekend poker on green baize with new-cut decks of cards bought in the Portuguese convenience store on Isipingo Street. Adam, the host, Callus and Crossley from advertising, and Rory; we drink Smirnoff vodka and play for moderate stakes. Mrs Fiona Adamczewski (née Doran, daughter of a Dublin doctor) had staked out something else on the accommodatingly expansive sofa with the Israeli paratrooper who happened to be passing by. Callus notices a telltale stain on his flies and raises the bidding. The room is as long as a refectory, breezes blow through, the green baize table is far away; around it sit the figures of the avid gamblers. Figure me there.

In this city, which claims the highest suicide rate after West Berlin, forty persons die every week from unnatural causes. One double locks at night with a deadlock and lies awake listening to the howling of the watch-dogs. It is a city of watch-dogs, howling in unison by night, when the murderers are about.

Simmonds Street, Marshall Street, Hollard Street, Syfret's Trust (Johannesburg Stocks and Shares Brokerage), the Chamber of Mines, Marshall Square know Rory.

The uncertainty of beginning again. Thin high cirrus masks the sun, but soon it's blazing forth; blue skies and warm air of the high Rand, this marvellous winter climate.

Nu-nite Nitewear, Kahn's for pianos, morning haze. Cold mornings on the sixth floor. The dry fug from the electric fire. In the resounding canyon of Kruis Street below us furniture is being dragged across the pavement and into new premises with a harsh grating noise like the roaring of lions. McGraw buffets open the window with the heel of his soft fist to stare out at Mosenthal's clock to check the time again and admit more blasts of cold air.

But who is McGraw?

My workmates, and what strange colleagues, come and go at the whim of Pax Moran's moods. I believe he hires advertising scriptwriters as he would collect freaks, for freakish we surely are: weepy De Wet, anxious McGraw, silent Hill, and the twitchy Bagley. In appearance the Scenario Department resembles some nihilist cell in times of the Tsar, a desperate group sporting Trotsky goatees, all except the clean-shaven McGraw. However there's nothing even vaguely sportful about this department.

'I *think* I'm hip,' says McGraw, 'but I suppose the young people of today would consider me hopelessly square.'

Another prodigiously watery yawn engulfs him and his weak, red-rimmed eyes fill with tears. He wipes his eyes and nose with the corner of a Kleenex plucked from the extra-large box by his foot; pulling down his albino eyelashes. I am witness to a boredom scarcely to be tolerated, witnessed or endured; I pity the sufferer but he makes me suffer too. McGraw's spongy feet, hacking cough (he coughs for company), damp damp hands, watery stare. He has his eye on the tight rump of the Afrikaans switchboard girl.

'Chaps, do you realise that this time ten years ago I was burning archives in the gardens of the British Embassy at Liège? The tenth of May?' peering myopically at his desk calendar.

McGraw sucks or rather *grinds* boiled sweets throughout the working day, for the good of his nerves, for tyrant Moran is within reach via the intercom on his desk and likes nothing better than upsetting and terrorising the nervous McGraw. He visits the Gents (*Europeans only*) fifteen to twenty times a day, for an incontinent bladder, tiptoeing past the GM's open door, a bunch of Kleenex in his damp hands, dabbing his wet forehead.

O. Rubenstein, J.B. Pain, the Mental Health Society of the Witwatersrand, African Underwear Manufacturers, these names in turn are revealed to me in the rackety old elevator ascending wheezingly to the sixth floor.

The streets, the evening light and heat; then the pleasant bus ride back to Isipingo Street. Evenings on the back balcony with Kensington mine-dumps in the distance. Danish blue cheese and Gordon's gin, what repeal, what peace! Coppera six months pregnant with our first son, to be named Carl Nicolas after her father and Nicolas of Chamford.

Going to work in the morning in drip-dry shirt and tie, tweed jacket from Horton's of Wicklow Street, sauntering along Kruis Street, and whom do I see before me but a familiar bearlike figure shambling along on his spongy feet, progress by locomotor ataxia – McGraw *en route* to further humiliation.

We like to walk from the jacarandas of Isipingo Street to Observatory golf course, for the scents of pine, pepper-gum and eucalyptus all along the way. The wind is warm, the eucalyptus has a dry clean, hygienic scent, wafted through the warm air. A memory of Cavtat in Dalmatia where we began with the puppets. We have a child now, a little boy; he cries out with delight when he notices the eucalyptus branches flowing away before his newly opened and astonished eyes, above the stroller.

On the hillside above the golf course, where Harold Henning is the pro, the African Zionist sects are singing and parading; it's a very energetic religion, they march and counter-march among the trees, appearing and disappearing near the Benoni road. The deep choral chant of the bearded priests comes to us, the deep voices raised in prayer, promises, invocations and objurgation. The female supplicants respond with their thin banshee wail. A canticle of psalms by the brotherhood and sisterhood of the bushes, the voice of Africa at its lamentations.

A multitude of insects rises over the grass. It's evening time, the sun going down over the hill. The insects show up palely luminous and agitated; the golfers are going home.

The singing and the insects rise together, the golfers neither hearing the one nor heeding the other. We drift along with our child, pushing him in the stroller; he brandishes his fists and woollen booties, smitten by some vision, laughing at the departing golfers, the risen insects, the balmy air all around us. We dream of living elsewhere: on St Helena or in the Seychelles. Endless life; endless choice.

The pedigree dogs in the ornate suburban haciendas along Urania Street bark at us, as they must at all intruders. The dark Daughters of Jerusalem are showing off their brown legs. The sprinklers revolve and revolve on the green lawns, widening their skirts of spray. Peaceful days in Johannesburg.

The brunette's morning exercises in the nude still go on; a resplendent bare white figure exposed in the morning sun, a white goddess burning behind glass in an apartment across the way. Juno's loveback and mesial groove; sure I must perish by your charms unless you take me in your arms.

One fine morning, on taking my seat upstairs in the No. 11 bus, I recognised her below the Canterbury-bell–shaped jacaranda blossoms, standing in the queue. Sardines always swim towards the sun, we are told; to catch them you must go to the east of them in the morning and to the west of them in the afternoon.

At the bottom of Jeppe Street a Bantu boy on a butcher's bike cycled along-side us. I looked down into a deep butcher's basket and a severed bullock's head, with goggling eyes and protruding tongue, glared up at me. Bristles stood up about the severe mouth, as if it had known the extremity of pain when being dispatched; the eyes were as though gouged out with a red-hot poker, and what a fury of resignation about the flayed mouth! A striking death's head.

Unsoberly attempting to alight, an old white ('European') man topples off the platform of an outward-bound No. 11 at the stop before Mount Willmar in Isipingo Street, and lies twitching and helpless on the flat of his back, star-ing up at the blossoms of the jacaranda tree, an assembly of bell-shaped blue flowers. Some of the passengers reach out as if to help him. Those who are alighting make as if to jump over him. He lies there, holding his heart, his chest heaving. He has hurt his head. 'Oh, oh. I have lived too long,' says the old drunk who lies on his back on the pavement, staring up at them. 'Let me die.' He blinks up at them. 'I am too old.'

'Oh no you're not,' says Coppera, extending a helping hand. Coppera's old man, Jonathan Carl Anders, is immensely old, as old as the hills, pale as parchment, deaf as a post; still putting in six and eight hours as a practising lawyer in King William's Town, still shouting out indiscretions, a man with a heart of gold.

The old man gives his name as Mr Allen, a habitué of Netherley House round the corner. He has alighted a stop too far. Seventy-six years old.

They take him there, Coppera and the kind helpful man from the No. 11 bus. The patio of Netherley House is some way back off the road and oldsters can be seen hobbling about in the gloom. Ferns droop from pots, a turkey-cock is scratching its wings on the cement floor.

'It's like looking into an aquarium,' Coppera says.

I too have my aquarium. Every morning of a working week the sun rises again over the mine-dumps of Bez valley. Regular as clockwork or cockcrow I am already at my post by the window, shaving gear before me, the kettle on the boil, stark naked.

Greenish and brilliantly lit by the risen sun of the high Rand, she drifts into view at the second-floor window opposite across the darkly shadowed intervening ground. Sharply defined morning shadows lie in the gardens separating Mount Willmar from the block across the way.

Morning after morning the sun shines on a second-floor bedroom. Morn-ing after morning a figure appears at the window to exercise in the nude after showering. Dark-haired and pale-skinned, she raises her arms to expose dark axillary hair. The husband, a shadowy figure appears occasionally in the background, standing and watching, dressed in pyjamas.

Irma La Douce is showing at the Brooke Theatre where we rehearsed and set up the show; *Wedding in Springtime* (Princess Margaret and her swain) at the Coliseum. *Killer Ape* showing at the Bio-Café in Rissik Street. The Black Sash ladies assemble outside the town hall.

But one grows weary of the long sameness of the days here; the only variety offered being the tropical storms that recur punctually at five every evening, refilling the swimming pools; but even of these one grows weary.

On endlessly dusty roads the quacks and commercial travellers with their sample cases go in large dusty limousines. Dr Rex Ferris is a specialist in *natuurgenesing*. Beware of:

> *Swak longe*
> *Breuk*
> *katar*
> *Swak hart*
> *Slegtesukalasie*
> *Abgesakte maag*
> *Stinkasem mangels*
> *Hardlywigheid*
> *Hare watuitval*
> *Blindedermonsteking* . . .

all bad things to be afflicted with, in Africa.

As might be expected in a continent so vast, so tightly held by the rotten system with such extremes of want separating those who have too much and those who have too little or nothing, much credence is given to quackery and faith healing and spirit mediums and the raising up of the dead.

The manufacturers of quack medicines do a roaring trade in Sloan's Liniment, purity of blood being of prime concern in the land of apartheid.

When a woman is doing her face in the mirror, she seems to be narrowly watching herself. Certainly she is coolly observing, seeing how the new effects work as they are applied, tweezers to eyebrows, trimming hair, watching fascinated as the Fast Little Number becomes metamorphosed into *une femme genete* ('troublesome'?), shedding the years.

Watching a woman making herself up in a mirror when she thinks she is alone, constantly touching unattractive spots and striking poses to catch herself off guard in the best light, catch herself unawares, is fascinating. That's one thing; but what of a woman who, aware of her attractiveness, walks naked about her dressing room, unaware that she is being observed from across the way, at the window darkened because the sun is behind it, flooding into her wide window?

Naked she sits at the mirror, applying unguents where needed, moisturising cream for body tone; rising and moving out she begins to dress herself, wearing only a bra as she glides about the room, soundlessly, light as gossamer.

Clear as an oxygenated well-lit aquarium tank in which swim fish of all stripes, exotic ones as rare as orchids found high in the Himalayas, the wide span of window showed the mysterious depths of the room as a secret chamber, the innermost sanctum of the pale nudist who moved about there in perfect sang-froid, towelling her hair, the dark axillary parts showing. The naked woman came and went, at her toilet, as though no one was watching her; profoundly alone and silent and undisturbed, in her own time. She passed by in her tank, her clear glass room, come wet from the shower, undulantly ripe in her movements, her style; as an exotic fish might swim to and fro in perfect isolation and silence, neck throbbing, fanning the tail, causing the eyes to bulge a little; until some stir (husband flushing toilet?) distracted her and in a whirl of fins and bubbles (seemingly expanding, unless this was an optical illusion caused by her quick change, or by a displacement of the water, the uprushing bubbles disturbing the former perfect composure of the scene set and fixed, the voyeur's delight) she has suddenly gone. Only to reappear ten beats of the heart later, come from another side of the tank, moving sedately into sight again, still stark naked, the dark triangle flaunted: so the naked brunette strolled to and fro in territory that seemed preciously close and yet very far off, as though a breath would disturb the clarity of the tank and frighten off the beautiful fish.

To say that this image (recurring five times a week just before eight o'clock in the morning, the sun risen on the high Rand regular as before, lighting up the room as if it were a stage set) was profoundly disturbing would be putting it mildly; my eyes were out on stalks. It was the most electrically jolting sexually charged image I had seen (and watched more of) than any since Hedy Kiesler took off all her clothes behind a bush somewhere in Czechoslovakia and the watching camera got an eyeful of her big bum as she waded into a mountain lake in Gustav Machaty's disturbing old movie, *Extase*. It was before Hollywood changed her name to Hedy Lamarr and made her a waxwork figure of little interest to anybody, young or old. As the sexually frustrated wife she had been rather chubby with puppy fat; the coldly embracing water was a masculine embrace for her; it had always been a feminine embrace for me. Seaweed and seawrack, the briny tang of the foreshore, the withdrawn foreskin of the swimmer entering the female sea, the taste and tang of sex.

Was she by any chance the siren Antoinette Botha, a great attender of art galleries frequently photographed in the Johannesburg *Star*? Could that have been the dark-haired one dressed in a smart black outfit and sunglasses who stood alone on the quayside and waved to someone (the lover) beside me on D Deck when we were berthing at Cape Town, sailing from cold Amsterdam on *Die Waterman* near Christmas some four years previously?

*   *   *

The train went by New Brighton on the Xwartkops river outside Port Elizabeth in the dusk of the evening, the lines and lines of mud hovels gave way to the arid land; an internment camp sprawled featureless in the evening dusk. Destitution is the irreducible minimum, below the breadline. From it nothing can be taken away, an African shanty town made up of line upon line of huts, as forlorn as Belsen or Auschwitz, baked dry by the cruel sun. Through hides and skins hung on poles, lean cattle wander about near open drains, with mangy curs and ghosts, presenting a most mournful aspect. Where the huts ended the barren land began again.

And in the twilight I watched naked children brown as monkeys stretch out monkey paws towards the lighted carnage windows that were gliding slowly by, the dining car festive with Christmas decorations. The kids reached out, chanting, 'Hippy, hippy, hippy!' Happy Christmas in South Africa, grim land of apartheid.

On 25 December 1956, 1 awoke on the upper berth to find that the long train had been standing motionless for hours out on the veldt. Warm air came through the carriage windows and all along the track the crickets were crackling like wildfire. Then the train began to move again with much banging and colliding of bumpers.

Onward from Hex River, Mossel Bay, Plettenberg Bay, to Port Elizabeth, East London, to the end of the line at King William's Town, Coppera's birthplace under the Amatole Mountains. King, arrived at in the gloaming with her aged parents waiting on the platform for the returning daughter and her newly acquired husband, was like a night scene from Zoltan Korda's *The Four Feathers,* the troops marching to a band, about to embark for the Sudan War. Had no one told them that the war ended years ago? South Africa, and perhaps the whole sleeping continent, was in a time warp. Africans with blankets draped about their shoulders moved about in a dream, stared with dull eyes at the white folks disembarking from the long train.

Death is a silent picture, a dream of the eye; only such vanishing shapes as the mirage throws. We had left Europe (where every grain of sand has passed through innumerable dead bodies killed in wars) four years before with affrighted Germans fleeing after the Hungarian uprising; we would be returning to Europe with affrighted Belgians fleeing the Belgian Congo. We sailed into Table Bay to the lilt of Cole Porter's 'Night and Day' played merrily over the tannoy, and the Rhodesian train driver, a large beefy man, was still cracking his feeble jokes; and then I spotted the beauty on the quayside, coming closer and closer as the tugs moved in to push us against the quayside.

Was that Antoinette? Ask Achim. Were all the silent sirens we had ever lusted after, whether blonde or brunette, always the same, the one-and-only? The only one for me; but all reducible to a single form, provided she was my type (pretty ones working in flower shops in Durban, frisky *Fräuleins* up ladders in male haberdashery shops in Schwabing). My interest was merely the process of reducing a substance to another (simpler) form. The alchemist's quest and the lecher's keen interest were similar, both intent on turning base metal into gold.

In cookery you reduce by boiling off liquid, turning down the flame in order to intensify the flavour; in much the same way (to mangle the metaphor further) as the conquest or subjugation of a town or fortress is 'reduced', is conquered, so the dream girl is reduced to manageable proportions, becomes seduceable; 'Antoinette Botha', the lovely Afrikaner, waved to someone standing beside me. Naturally it wasn't me she waved to, it was the pretty brunette who had run trippingly in high heels across a Munich street between streams of traffic and threw me a look of unambiguous intent that reduced me to a jelly in the blink of an eyelash. One had to comply with the *visu*, the hot look that subjugates with the finality of a branding iron establishing ownership of a beast.

Apparently my type was the leggy brown-eyed sulky sort of girl who gets you into trouble; trouble before and even more behind.

— 25 —

The Sharpeville Massacre, 1960

21 March 1960. Anti-pass law demonstration in Vereeniging. The police, with Saracens in support, fired on and killed 56 African demonstrators, men

and women, wounding 162.

24 March. Smell of sickness in the deserted Sundowner Bar. Later the regulars drift in. The subdued brandy drinker orders another Commando from Richard, as he has been doing for months, years, on end. Beginning to show in his face. Soon immersed in his *Rand Daily Mail*.

Of the 162 wounded, 38 are at Vereenigning Hospital and 124 at Barag-wanath Hospital; over seventy percent of the wounds were in the back and so terrible that it was thought dum-dum bullets were used by the police. These wounds were in fact caused by 'tumbling' bullets sprayed from Sten guns firing continuously, without pauses between bursts.

On one of the ominous days after Sharpeville, a time of dire portents when the long-threatened seemed about to come at last, a rumour was circulating to the effect that a mob of Africans was marching from the shanty towns on Johannesburg. The old woman, Anna, our washer-woman from Orlando, I knew was in the flat with Coppera. I decided not to phone, and went back to work.

Moran, who prided himself on his fair treatment of his own African servants, had an automatic pistol out on his desk and some rounds of ammunition. 'If I have to go,' he said, mock-histrionic, 'I'll take some of them with me.' 'Oh, Mr Mor-AN!' pleaded his secretary and scuttled from the office.

The rest of that peculiar day: the feeling that we were on the brink of civil war, that one might perhaps not live beyond tomorrow, that Coppera and Carl would die, lay on my heart like a hand of ice.

After work the city cleared fast, a rapid exodus to the suburbs, leaving the centre of the city deserted. African newspaper boys were flying through the streets on their bicycles and flinging down the late editions at the feet of the remaining white 'European' bus queues, with the swagger of insolent pages come from the enemy lines with bold ultimatums.

But the *Star* reported nothing of an undisciplined horde marching on Johannesburg, no picture of the bloodied head of the Princess de Lamballe stuck on the end of a pike. It reported only common everyday occurrences. The beautiful Miss Antoinette Botha was photographed at the pottery exhibition of Henk Jacobs and Harry Duys.

21 April. A month after Sharpeville, and the bloodstains are still on the road. I ask Lewis Nkose, 'What kind of man is this Colonel Pienaar?' 'Pienaar?' he says. 'He's a butcher. He's got the face of a butcher.'

Nkose speaks of the sweetish smell of blood after the shooting. He was there. The police chief was Colonel D.H. Pienaar.

The air is full of flying mine-dust. I have an inflamed throat and retire to bed before nine, feeling wretched. Mourning air of forgotten childhood mingled with premonitions of one's last end. Evening Benediction begins. Night falls, out of the craters rises the mist. Knowing nothing, believing nothing; live a little longer, if you can. I dream a disturbing dream.

I am flying in the Alps with six others. We are dressed as for skiing. Our arms extended, like gliders we fly about in the rarefied air, our shadows following us below on the virgin snow. High up in the Alps, I am drifting about. Someone calls 'Feel the snow! It's like fire.' I sail down and kick up some with my bare feet. Yes. Like fire. There is a high escarpment that no one can clear. I attempt it, but it is impossible, the face is too steep.

In the Alpine hut one of the party has cut himself by accident. There's not much blood, but nevertheless he says he must return to base. He leaves immediately. A pair of scissors lies on the table. I take them up and cut myself deeply on both wrists. Great clots of blood stain the walls and the snow near the door. I have severed an artery; the blood goes on pumping out. I am weakening; it is I who have done this, yet I seem to be standing outside myself. I watched 'myself' do it: 'him' I take for myself.

Coppera brings in John Wright to see the feverish invalid sitting up in bed reading Spengler's *Decline of the West*.

A Johannesburg *Star* photograph of the 'weapons' used by the African insurgents at Sharpeville. In 40-45 seconds of firing, so many killed, so many wounded, so much blood. A pile of knobkerries, sticks, stones. Like what? Windfalls in a winter wood.

Nineteen fifty-nine was a dry summer in Jo'burg. Torrential rains came with the autumn and every day the pictures slid a little more off-kilter on the walls, following another fall-in down in the mines. The greatest fall-in occurred in January 1960 the year of Sharpeville, when 435 African miners were buried alive at Coalbrook Mine with six European supervisors or gangers; none was ever recovered.

On 3 March 1960 I was thirty-three years old and beginning to think of myself as a writer, for Calder and Grove Press had contracted to bring out the first stories, *Felo De Se*. In sixteen recently made independent African territories eighty-five million new black citizens had also begun to think differently about themselves.

As and from tomorrow the British flag will be run down and the new flag of the free Republic run up in its stead. The national anthem becomes *Die Stern*. 'Out of the blue sky' sings the massed choir of black and white, or brown and scorched pink.

Seated on a dentist's chair on the sixteenth floor of an office building in the centre of Johannesburg, I command a fine view of flat rooftops and washing blowing on lines, a flagpole with the Union Jack flying in the breeze that has been blowing since the siege of Mafeking (the tattered original flag is preserved in a glass case in the town hall where we performed with the puppets), and on a distant mine-dump away towards Benoni a white scarf of dust is blowing off the rim.

The telephone rings. Dentist Gavronski's former wife, Nadine Gordimer, is on the line and wishes to know the meaning of 'being on the threshold of pain'. Dentist Gavronski tells her all he knows about the threshold of pain. The air of Johannesburg is a wonderful refining air blowing out of the bluest of pale-blue skies; such a pity the system is rotten to the core. The system stinks; and it's not a country one could live in, much less bring up a child in. We toy with the idea of living in the Seychelles, a windy French possession away from the beaten track; or St Helena, a thousand miles into the North Atlantic. An islander whose grandfather sold macaroni to Napoleon, then serving time in Longwood House, advises us against it. We decide to return to Dublin.

– 26 –

The Lazy Azores, 1960

21 July 1960. Last day in Johannesburg. Main railway terminal. Train for Blaney and East London. We sail from there on the 28th. I read of ten Africans killed and four injured, three seriously, in a faction fight between Mbonos and Ngulubenis at Maritzburg.

The taciturn soldier in my carriage has little to say; the train passes by Kliptown, Midway, Lenz, the locations out of Johannesburg. A week's holiday in King William's Town lies ahead. Coppera had left ahead three weeks before to show our child to her parents.

Kidd's Beach, Eastern Cape. We rent a house near the beach. The breathing of the cattle at night. Generally deserted beaches. The coloured youths dancing like dervishes naked on the dunes; their swaying stallions' erections. Two African girls coming in their city finery. They all go swimming together. Scrummages in the surf. Their whinnying cries.

The lagoon. Deep coughing of the baboons among the laurels. Days alone there. The dog swimming in the estuary early in the morning. The Bantu girls coming with their fancy-men. Putty-coloured skin of the Cape Malays, with deformed features, like lepers. In the evening we buy brandy, for fifteen shillings a bottle.

Coppera's dream: 'It's a big hotel next to the railway lines. My mother and I have a big room on the second floor. I'm trying to pack but she keeps on emptying the suitcase. She is distracted with worry and moves fretfully from room to room spreading the clothes about.

'On our side of the building and directly in front of the hotel four oil tanks stand, delicate quadrupeds with their four big balls on the top standing about a hundred feet off the ground.

'There's a revolution in the city. The first oil tank is set on fire above our heads. It explodes in flames. There is a great hullabaloo in the hotel, with guests screaming out of windows and running through the rooms. I run to my mother, but she is so petulant she doesn't care. I look everywhere for the suitcase. She's hidden it. I ask her where it is. She says she doesn't know. I hear people running past the hotel and shouts outside. Then I find the suitcase. I begin to pack in a hurry. My mother keeps taking the clothes out and petulantly throwing them on the bed.

'The second oil tank is now on fire. I hear the roaring of the flames and black particles of steel and ash are falling past the windows. Try as I can, the suitcase always remains empty. Outside, we see the flames going straight up. There is a man down there. I knew he was there. I shout to a friend to go and help him. There are two of them after him and I can see him clearly lying on his stomach under the third oil tank, which he is about to set on fire.

'As he reaches up, he is shot from behind through the back of the head. Dying, he goes on making the futile gesture of pulling a lever, but it's someone else who moves his hand.'

28 July 1960, East London docks. The *Warwick Castle* berthed. After an easy Customs check we go to a small cabin, uncomfortably so with a collapsible cot installed. Telegrams from Johannesburg are on the bunk. We will be cooped up here for the next eighteen days, with decaying fruit and damp ammonia-smelling diapers. Sailing via St Helena and Ascension Island to Tilbury, England.

Port Elizabeth. A liner, pearly-grey hull, entering a harbour early in the morning. A seaweed-covered breakwater, a sludge of fog, a liner sounding its horn, and in the dampness on the mole fifty Muslims in red fezzes standing waiting, like diver-birds grouped on a rock. Suddenly handkerchiefs appear in their hands and flutter above their heads. The silence and vastness of the liner making its way slowly into the harbour. Its tiers of deserted decks; chill of the hour, just before daybreak.

Cape Town. The Muslims in full regalia posing patiently for amateur photographers on D Deck in a thin drizzle of rain. The ship's bossy nurse orders them about. They are Cape Coloureds, returning to Cape Town after a nine-month trip to Mecca.

Low cloud over the city, Table Mountain invisible; smoke rising from the business quarter, joined up to low-hanging discoloured clouds – like a city after a bombardment. The persistent thin rain. Two tugs pulling the *Warwick Castle* off its berth. The harbour turns round. The tugs cast off. Music over the ship's loudspeakers; the wake stretches out behind. Now we leave this continent; now the ship sails. Feeling of elation.

A day out and the Cape rollers begin. Vomit on the companionway mats, the dining room half empty, the Belgian Congolese children running wild, yelling: '*Malade! Malade!*'

Two days out and already bored with shipboard life. St Helena in the morning. I wrote to Mr Solomon (or Solomons) there.

St Helena. Volcanic cliffs, then the valley, and Jamestown, with boats coming out. We are to stay here until evening. I see a high waterfall, white water spilling over the rim of rock, and more boats putting out from the island. Festive appearance. The islanders come on board to sell trinkets. I talk to one of the young men. He herds sheep; he brought some from the back of the island at five this morning. His singsong voice. Biblical scene.

The young men are leaving the island, he tells me, to work on the American air base on Ascension. They made an airstrip along the ridge of a volcanic mountain. They can double their wages there, working in radio. The jute factories pay little. Those who stay are attempting to start a trade union movement – the first in the island's history. They load jute into the hold. It has a bad smell. Some of the older islanders are going into domestic service in Scotland. A butler and housekeeper. He is small, scorched black by the sun, his English difficult to follow. He sounds Welsh. Did Welsh missionaries come here?

I go ashore with another passenger – a white-haired, stout, elderly Chinaman, polite and formal. Mr Johns is courteous, neatly dressed in a blue suit with a white shirt and dark tie, a raincoat over one arm, a rolled umbrella in his hand (tell me, what Chinaman would ever go out without a rolled umbrella?). He carries an expensive attaché case – as an emblem of caste? We introduce ourselves. He tells me that he was born here on St Helena but left it as a young man to seek his fortune in the USA. He worked for fifty years as a traveller in the bible trade, married an American lady from Boston,

Mass. and is now retired. He is through with the bible business. He had hoped to spend his last years on the island, but his wife does not care for it – not enough social contact, too many white ants, insufficient refrigeration. They had originally planned to live on the island for three years, in a sort of trial retirement. But his wife couldn't stand it; they are leaving again in the spring. He himself would have preferred to stay, but he will do whatever his wife wants; never would she be happy there. They plan to return to Boston.

I make an arrangement to meet Mr Johns later with Coppera (who has stayed on board with Carl); we are to take a taxi and visit Longwood House. I take leave of him on a small humpback Chinese bridge, surrounded by white blossoms, with the sound of water trickling in the irrigation streams. No sound of human voices in this quiet backward island retreat a thousand miles from anywhere. I take a walk up the valley. The relief of being off the ship, away from the passengers.

The *Warwick Castle,* much diminished, lying offshore about three-quarters of a mile out, seen between two converging cliffs. Terraces sown with peas and beans, warm dry air, hot sunshine, peace. An outdated greeting to Princess Elizabeth and Prince Philip painted on a hillside. A rustic England of the early nineteenth century is perpetuated here with an annual rainfall of 36 inches, a very temperate climate; 1,700 feet above sea level in a temperature of 70 degrees all the year round.

Longwood House in the afternoon. Napoleon's last resting place, a long way from the frozen rivers and corpse-strewn plains of the lost Russian campaign. The cold names of the rivers that flow into the Baltic, Vistula, Niemen. Niemen-on-the-Ice. Bonaparte getting into a closed carriage with his mameluke at Smorgony, defeated and on his way back to Paris. 'Halted at Jaffa at the western entrance to Asia, and halted at Moscow at the northern gateway to the same continent, he was to go and die among the seas bordering that part of the world where mankind and the sun were born' (Chateaubriand).

In the billiard room, the pockets are rotting from the table, the green baize turning white with age; the billiard balls in their wooden frames rest behind glass in the hall. Chipped antique objects – the Emperor's cannons. I take one in my hand. Napolean used to throw them around; his small hand once touched it. Touching it now, I touch lost history.

The smallness of his bed; its green canopy – a child's bed. His death mask, cast in bronze, stands on a pedestal. Effigies of him in every room and in the hall. Vain as Voltaire.

St Helena lies between the two poles. 'At the extremity of our hemisphere,' says Tacitus, 'one can hear the sound made by the sun sinking in the sea:

sonum insuper immergentis audiri.' When Napoleon went out, his spirits low, he passed along stony paths lined with aloes and scented broom.

In the narrow valley, known then as Slane or Geranium Valley, and now as Tomb Valley, there is a spring at which Napoleon's Chinese servants, as faithful as Camoens's Javanese, used to fill their pitchers; weeping willows hang over their spring; green grass, studded with champacs, grows all around. ('The champac,' say the Sanskrit poems, 'for all its colour and perfume, is not a sought after flower, because it grows on graves.')

Napoleon liked the willows by the spring, but everything saddened him under a sky beneath which life seemed shorter, the sun remaining three days less in that hemisphere than in ours. Towards the end of February 1821, in his sixth year of exile on the rock, he was obliged to take to his bed ('How low have I fallen! . . . I who have stirred up the whole world, and I cannot lift my eyelids!'), and he did not get up again. He was being systematically poisoned by his English captors and part of the Royal Navy swung off the island, watching and waiting. His end came soon. He died in Longwood on 5 May 1821. 'He sleeps like a hermit or a pariah in a valley, at the end of a deserted pathway,' wrote Chateaubriand.

In 1840 the remains were brought home to France – he had come home to be buried in the grime of Paris. Bonaparte passed through the tomb, as he passed through everything else, without stopping.

Vague feeling that he did live there once; pined away and died there; written of by de Segur, Chateaubriand, latterly Kafka, fascinated by the horrors of the Russian campaign. Suffered from migraine, dysuria (retention of the urine).

Murat, Ney; carnage at Borodino, blood-soaked fields. He had drilled peepholes in the window shutters to spy on the English soldiers going on and off duty. At daybreak here, forgotten. Never forgotten.

The lazy Azores; three miles of sea below us. The English clergyman's anaemic full-grown son in the dining room. 'Oh of course they're not trustworthy as pets.' Finicky English voice – that strange, slight talk which governed the British Empire. 'I never take liberties with an Alsatian.' The English ladies opposite us; their movements, talk, complacency – their security. Lily Briscoe. Walking on the upper deck. Beginning of an overcast day. The jet fighter out from Ascension, island of ashes, a pinpoint, then directly over the mast, then four miles out to sea.

The Canary Islands; Las Palmas. One can smell it approaching: the stench of colonial Spain.

Generalissimo Franco causeway. The taxi ride. In the cathedral the old waxen-faced priest high up in an alcove reading his office – an image from Goya. The confessional stained black about the grille; sins (bad breath?) of generations of humble penitents. An island of bad teeth and halitosis. Smells of cheap Cognac and wine gone sour in the bars. A vegetable market, white colonnades and green trellis, all the charm of Spain.

Fish-tinning factories; the Coca-Cola factory under construction on the hill. An island inundated with Japanese-made merchandise with falsified US trade marks. Populated caves in the dirty hills above the town. The well-dressed tout offering us a Parker pen made in Osaka; another in the cathedral shows us the manuscript Vulgate of 1614.

Hot idle days. The tourist-class swimming pool with two feet of water, Belgian Congolese children splashing in it, screaming snipe. Shrouded cars on the foredeck with Belgian Congo registration plates. Exodus from the troubled Congo.

Circular intimations of calamity: 'The contemporary of Napoleon conceived his completion of European philosophy as the fulfilment of a primary undeveloped origin: whereas the contemporary of Adolf Hitler conceived the identical history of the European spirit as the gradual epiphany of Nihilism' (Hans Magnus Enzensberger). So what of Father Adam and his teeming billions of posterity? Do not come down the ladder, dreamers, for I have taken it away.

The weather turns foul: heavy seas, troughs of grey waves. A porthole, a stretch of harbour, docks of Las Palmas, a boat loading up alongside the *Warwick Castle,* a view of burnt hills, already only a memory.

Two portholes; slothful slop and wallow of the waves striking the side of the ship; grey-green sea choppy all the way to the horizon. Staring before her with empty eyes. Baby Carl crawls in the playpen, we crowd into our small cabin. Soon it will be over.

The tarpaulin-shrouded cars on deck. Hardly any place to exercise now. The English Channel.

We reach the mouth of the Thames in the late afternoon, but cannot get into Tilbury. There is a dock strike on (also a printing strike). England is on strike; nothing has changed there.

When we wake up next morning, we're in. Through the portholes we see English bobbies standing about with their hands behind their backs on the wet dockside. It's raining in grey Tilbury. Naturally it is. Naturally so.

PART III:

Nerja in the 1960s

– 27 –

Ominous Auguries

Afreshening offshore breeze made a kind of inditing on the surface of the water, innumerable diamond-shaped points of light glittered over a wide area, leaving the rest serene. The Mediterranean and its little mirrors, the dance of the little mirrors of the Mediterranean, with everything trembling, constant little tremblings, junctions, disjunctions, nothing still, no, never for a moment still. A calm day out at sea.

Two boats were fishing far out, working well apart, half lost in the haze. On the horizon three or four bigger vessels were hull-down into the glare. I watched the archway – more than my eyes watched it – but there was no sign of her. Instead of Harriet came now a rumble like thunder, but unmistakably not thunder, a long shudder from over the water I felt now under my feet, hard as iron. It passed through the palms, the plaza and on through the village, a pulse, a gust blown in from the sea. Among the wisps of cloud over the ships a puffball of flak appeared, lead-coloured in the centre, turning septic yellow, spreading out innocently enough, as a small white cloud.

I looked up, listening for the sound of aircraft, but none were flying over the area. Nothing in sight at all events, nothing had banged through the sound barrier. Were the ships shelling the clouds to try to disperse them? Was it firing practice? Or had war started? I listened, with more than my ears. Nothing.

Nothing. Only a stirring in the palms, a faint breeze on my face, a voice murmuring *You are done for,* and a few small dun-coloured birds flew away.

Then a second flak ball joined the first at precisely the same altitude. The reverberation rolled in thick and dull, and from over the horizon – a chain reaction – came the spreading rumble of answering fire. Heavy-calibre naval guns were letting go their salvos down near Gibraltar. Baron Gerhar's grim prediction came to mind; the mad Finn thought World War Three was imminent – the final war. Had it started? The last. How could we get back to Ireland, or back to Aran, and would we be safe there? Or, if it came to that, could I give Coppera a 'massive overdose' of sleeping pills? Or would Harriet come to me and say, 'If I have only one more day, one more hour to live, I want to spend it with you.' As I knew I wanted to die embracing her.

My old *amigo*, Harry Calnek was hurrying from the Marisal. The hunched-up figure rapidly crossed the plaza. Hands deep in pockets, caught up in the ardour of narrative construction, Calnek was returning to his trusty typewriter.

No sooner had he left the plaza than a third flak ball appeared alongside the other two. White at first, then turning yellow – and the third ponderous detonation followed; the stiff palm fronds above my head shivered and the last of the dun-coloured birds flew away.

A triple blast of destruction had blown in from the sea. Above me among the palm fronds outstretched like arms, skeleton features grimaced, announcing the opening movements of another war. World War Three had started on the site of the old Peninsular War.

The bell of San Salvador at this precise moment sounded the half-hour: 10.30 a.m. I had not heard the hour strike. The single stroke hung in the hot and luminous air. *You go*, the bell told me sweetly; *I stay*. Half-past the hour. A slick of heat on my back. Nothing stirred. A lick of heat, a tongue of flame.

The white puffball with its sickly centre, human pus on cotton wool, hung like a sign in the sky over the motionless ships. I waited for the final blast to blow me off the plaza, off the face of the earth.

The informer was going back into his kiosk, shaking the last drips from the neck of his watering can. Then, always taking me by surprise, the second stroke, like an overtone, sounded calmly from the church. Or from another belfry? But there was only one belfry, one church, one God, one true religion, one winter cinema (but two summer ones to make up a trinity), and fifty tavernas for a population of ten thousand souls, the population of Guernica before the bombing. Iron on iron, hammer on anvil, one questioned, the other replied, and real life was over.

She broke away from our long embrace as if caught up by the wind, with a light step ran quickly down, hearing someone approaching, or so she imagined, someone quickly entering from the street by the open doorway below; perhaps it was her husband or Coppera keeping tabs?

But no one came up. She smiled at me from below. I went down then to embrace her again. A sort of fluid glow emanated from her skin. Everything about her disturbed me, inside and outside, her mouth and unfathomable Nile-blue eyes, the Jewish weight of her sorrowful heavy eyelids, her quickened respiration – I had put my hands over her breasts that rose and subsided with her rapid breathing – the scent of her Sabine-rape blonde hair the colour of wheat.

I was holding another woman in my arms and allowed to intimately touch this forbidden body, hearing voices through the door but unable to make out the words. Calnek and his Canadian girl Sharon Marcus were on the roof above, clinging vine, mimosa spray. We went down and out into the shattering sunshine of no thought, Harriet to their apartment on Calle Generalissimo Franco to 'fix' their lunch, Rory proceeding the other way, towards the bridge. She was to meet me there in an hour's time, to pledge our troth in a cane plantation as the tick-ridden burros hee-hawed, flicking their stumpy tails, tormented by the flies that would eat them. Faith, unfaithful wife kept him falsely true.

John Deck sat on a cane chair on the mezzanine of No. 12 smoking a black cigar. His shirt was open to the navel and he was unshaven; his bare shins showed between rumpled canvas pants and worn canvas sneakers. The cotton pants were tight about the crotch and he seemed all ponderous head, Negroid upper lip and lobeless ears. I sat on the red divan and Harriet stood facing us. She had raised her skirt to expose a discoloured bruise the size of a 50-peseta coin high up on her brown thigh where the panties gripped. Since she sunbathed for two hours every morning in the nude behind screens in their patio, she glowed with health and well-being, a ripe-thighed temple-dancer. She shimmied her hips and looked brazenly at us.

'See here, messmates.'

I looked at my darling's wounded flank but prudently made no comment. Drawing deeply on his cigar John stared at the guilty-looking bruise and then at her face. Was she exposing one of his own love-bites or what?

Who had done this thing to her? What apelike paw had marked her so? Her pose had been a cajoling one, part of a tango that required snapping castanets. One of her most endearing and characteristic movements began as a shudder in those ardently engulfing hips; a beautiful gentleness glowed from her skin. Now, watching her husband, she dropped her skirt.

'What do you make of that?' she challenged him. 'If anything.'

Deck tilted back his chair until it stood on two legs, and allowed cigar smoke to issue from great flanged niggery nostrils.

'Are not health and corruption said to be incompatible? So thought the ancient rhetoricians, and they knew their stuff.'

We had nothing to add to that.

'On a streetcar in Hode, Arkansas,' Deck pontificated in a Negro preacher's almighty drone, 'I glimpsed the exhausted. But, sure, anything's permissible and possible in a world in which no one any longer believes in anything. But don't despair. Study groups among the Pennsylvanian Elks, after extensive Bible poring, revealed that in fact the Second Coming had already occurred, unnoticed by anybody. In 1837, to be exact, with the Kingdom of God established "invisibly" a few years later – let's say about the time that flatulent old bitch Queen Victoria planted her mighty arse on the throne and made herself Empress of all India.'

Harriet laughed a provocative laugh and sailed across the room, very well 'gathered up' as the Spaniards say of horses cantering, *muy recogida,* when tearing along at full speed. Going downstairs now with only the upper part of her body showing with much brown bare back, she called back tauntingly, 'OK, I'll let both you guys do it into my behind!'

Rare, rare, her pierced beauty. The heavy musk of falling hair. In a field of force, the uncoiling honeycomb of forms, the golden wheel of love.

Some nights later I was drinking beer with Calnek in a small bar in Calle Cristo. It was Good Friday and we found ourselves in the middle of a power cut, plunged into darkness, a regular occurrence in those days. Candles were then lit along the bar counter and looked very pretty. The bar was empty but for us.

We heard a scratching sound outside and a whispering in conspiratorial tones and the slap of espadrilles and stood in the open doorway to watch a silent company file past, bearing the semi-naked Saviour covered in veils that rose in a night breeze to expose the braced white chest, the terrible wound in the side caked with dried blood.

The mourners filed silently by, softly as ghosts, hurrying Him off somewhere as if ashamed. We went back soberly to our drinks.

'What do you make of that?' I said.

Calnek looked owlishly at me through his heavy bifocals with his afflicted Jewish eyes.

'That guy wasn't carrying no Cross. He was trying to hold it down.'

Christ's five bleeding wounds *(cinco llagas)* are perpetuated all over Spain, sculpted over church porches like bunches of grapes. St Paul writes somewhere in his Epistles of Jesus as the image of the invisible God, and Alfred Jarry wrote somewhere that God is infinitely small.

> *The world of the Jew*
> *Is the world of the Jew*
> *And yet*
> *And yet . . .*

Colourful expressions of Harry Calnek: 'Old Sharon would talk the scrotum off the statue of David.' And: 'Cold as a gravedigger's arse.'

– 28 –

Mrs Harriet Deck

S ome mornings when she came down on to the *paseo* she wore her morning face, having come straight from bed to me. Or, having overslept the hour that we had agreed to meet, had come straight out, her face still marred by sleep, by the sheet, by strands of hair. She brought, as a gift, the face her husband saw every morning when he opened his eyes and she opened her legs for him again. Ah, how sad is the sound of the horn winding in the depths of the wood!

She had come straight to me in this manner: her direct way, from the most distant county there is; brought her brightness unimpaired, even if her voice was slurred, she brought some of her sleep with her, offered something of her secret (wifely) self to Rory of the Hills.

When the brown hand with the symbolic ring of gold made an intensely private gesture, my heart missed a beat and turned over with the movement, as if we were locked together in a kiss and the sheet had fallen off and we were naked, clinging together, hearts beating in unison.

She touched her hair and pouted out her dry lips.

'I must look awful.'

She perched herself on the high bar-stool and asked Miguel Rojas for coffee, crossing one leg over the other. I saw the inside of her thigh, that intimate region of give and take, hide and seek, as she spoke of her past, that sure sign of trust, of love, to offer to the new one (Rory) the old one's (Deck's) perquisites. She was travelling towards me now, her hair streaming in the wind. (Deck, who took his conjugal duties seriously, had threatened a Mexican groom who had ridden off with Harriet, coming home an hour too late with buttons undone, covered in dust and sweat. 'I shudda horse-whipped the little Mexican fucker'.)

They had come east on Route 66, from the bottom of California, the legendary coast. At night, tired of the road that never ended, they came to a township in the back of beyond, some Red Indian reservation hardly marked on the map, maybe Winslow in Arizona.

She said she wanted to spend the night there; but her cautious young husband was having none of *that*. 'Those are mean bastards, Dilly. You don't fuck around with Indians. We gotta push on.'

So they pushed on, she staring with a vacuous glare through the windscreen all smeared with the guts of squashed bugs. They sailed out of New York harbour on the SS *Klek,* a Yugoslav freighter bound for Tangier, saw the incoming and outgoing flights circling over Idlewild and landing every three minutes. It made them feel good to be Americans, flying the flag and proud of it.

The ship's doctor was as handsome as they come, dressed in white duck, face the colour of teak. He spoke of Ljubljana in Slovenia where he came from. He was homesick and fancied Mrs Deck something awful.

They walked the decks together at night. John was a poor sailor and spent most of the voyage below, puking his way across the Atlantic.

Dr Vuc Eisen was certainly handsome.

'I guess he fancied me.'

This carefully imparted aside was accompanied by a dip of her knee so that more brown thigh was exposed, tender flesh, as she sipped coffee in a prim ladylike way.

'Did he try anything on, this fresh fucker Eisen?'

'Oh sure' (this was Harriet the Hardboiled City Girl). 'We were after all on the high seas. Every licence allowed.'

I ground my teeth. Miguel busily occupied himself wiping the steaming coffee machine, understanding nothing of what was being said or implied, observing us covertly, for were we not meeting there three or four mornings a week before anyone was about and the *paseo* was deserted. With long travel, smart city girls suffer changes of heart; isn't that true, most times?

'The great romances in life and in literature imitating life, as it's apt to do, have never been between husbands and wives but between husbands and *other* people's wives,' Deck pontificated, at his most mocking and mock-oratorical, 'as I need hardly tell you. Look at Irish and English history from the time of let us say the Norman invasion up to Edward VIII and that American wife so erring in her ways, Mrs Simpson. Consider the known high content of adultery in world literature. Look at Emma Bovary. Where would we be without adultery, I ask you. We'd be where Jacko put his nuts: in somebody else's bed. Think of that gamekeeper, whatshisname buggering Lady Chatterley in the bushes.'

They were awaiting the arrival of Dr Jorge del Bosque who was giving them Spanish lessons. What the suspicious husband meant to convey to erring Rory, who was certainly sending signs to Deck's young wife, was: now

I know what you're up to, Mick. And I'll go along with it for form's sake. I'll tolerate it, up to a point. You are, after all, old enough to be her father. I know that Ilium had to burn, as well as Helen, in order to create the *Iliad,* but . . . But. *Don't touch her, she's mine!*

I lifted the knocker and let it fall.

The sudden sound reverberated through the house. It appeared to be empty, with that curious airy emptiness peculiar to Andalucían houses (a window or door was open upstairs), with their bare floors.

I waited for some response, lifted the knocker again, let it fall. The heavy lumpish sound reverberated through the house once more.

I waited, lifted the knocker again, let it fall. Then I pushed the door. It gave inward; I entered. Ferns hung from wire baskets supported by chains under a nondescript chandelier sprouting light bulbs like branched fruit, bunches of grapes. A heavy maroon felt cloth covered the table and in the centre of this lay an air-letter with the chevrons of Old Glory addressed in a swinging female calligraphy to:

> Mr and Mrs John and Harriet Deck
> 12 Calle Pintada
> Nerja
> España

conveyed to Numero 26 Calle de la Cruz by the obliging Correos, no doubt interested in the unfamiliar stamps. I turned it over on its back and learnt that the sender was a certain

> Miss Mimi Fagg
> The Museum
> Nigeria

Well I never. An empty hallway led to the empty stairs of their empty flat. I knocked on their door, knowing there was no one there. No one answered; they were out, perhaps on the beach, or taking a drink on the *paseo* and talking to Miguel in demotic Spanish, swiftly picked up from the ever obliging Dr Jorge del Bosque, who himself (let it be whispered) rather fancied the charming Mrs Harriet Deck. And who did not?

I was alone. Solitude – one knows instinctively that it has benefits which must be more deeply satisfying than other conditions, states of elation aside. I let the knocker fall again, in case the old woman was there. *¡Oyenos!* Quite empty. I walked towards the *paseo*, bore that empty feeling away with me. *¡Oyenos!*

'I'm not gonna help you no more,' John Deck said, avoiding my eye. 'No more pimping.'

He was half turned away from me, leaning on the bar counter, looking sourly into his glass of lukewarm Victoria beer, his shoulders hunched up. His cheeks bulged out like lugs, swelling as though he was suffering from *dolor de muellas;* his lobeless ears gave him a Germanic degenerate look – Himmler's ears. I swallowed some beer and stared out the door, where the warm wind was blowing the dust along.

'You were helping me. This is news indeed.'

'Sure I was. I was pimping for you. But not any more, buddy. Anyhow, you wouldn't have gotten very far with her unless she'd strewn a few roses in your path.'

The half-demented one went by on his ruined feet, bound for the bar down the Calle; he could imitate the bawling of a burro to the life.

'And Callus?' I said, producing the name as stealthily as if I was soundlessly withdrawing a sword from its scabbard.

'Callus! what the fuck has he got to do with it? You must be mad. Callus means nothing to her. I know her well enough to say that. You need fear nothing from that quarter.'

I said nothing to that (was he pimping for me again?), ordered another beer for him, stealthily.

We were in the Calle de la Cruz in one of the old bars that served lukewarm Victoria beer in bottles and low-grade wine, rough Cognac and anis, *seco* and *dulce,* as favoured by the fishermen.

And who was this Callus, the Troublemaker, not to be confused with Palos, the one who bedded his own mother and invented the saw? Not Philoctetes either; was Callus (born in Malta of a sergeant major in the British Army) related to Talus, who was one of those impetuous and liverish Mediterranean divinities like the freak fire-giant created by Hephaeotus in the story of the Argonauts? Was it he? Maybe it was.

He had a mountain forge at Etna beneath the earth and Minos as guardian and protector of his patch, the Cretan coast. Thrice a day he strode around the island and never stopped for a siesta. If strangers landed, he ran up the hill and jumped into the furnace. Steaming and red-hot, he rushed down upon them, beshitting themselves in their haste to get back into the boats.

None but Medea dared to confront him, one vein filled with liquid fire. That was Callus. Mad as a brush.

The wild man of Borneo was for climbing staircases in Montreal, shinning up the side of a house in Calle Nueva by the wrought-iron window guard, his head appearing at balcony level to a shrill scream from Sonya Hool, Callus climbing over the balcony rail and bursting into the room, putting the wind up the Hools, chatting to an American friend peaceably within.

'*Surprisingly* hairy,' Harriet said.

– 29 –

A Child's Funeral

Entre las flores y la nieve ocultarán el Cristo.

A funeral was passing along Calle Pintada (Calle Generalissimo Franco), the coffin lid not in place: a little corpse was being carried away in flowers by young boys. I stood on the balcony of No. 12 with Harriet and looked down into the open coffin, and there in the midst of the flowers was the infant's peaceful face upturned to us, a little girl being carried past the wrought-iron dog-heads spewing rainwater, hardly ushered into life before being carted out of it again.

The colour of the dead face was the colour of my dead mother's face on the third day of her dying: off-white clay gone grey-putty colour, rock returned with thanks to the hands of her Maker.

The small white coffin was bedecked with flowers, exposing only a section of the *caja-fuerte;* with the lid off to the dead eyes open in the waxen face and that slightly asymmetrical stare peculiar to the very young, an unfocused look directed past us and the dog-heads at a remote Heaven above the clouds.

The boys bore her along at a brisk pace, as if anxious to reach the *cementerio,* followed by a smaller object that was also covered in flowers, a babe perhaps, carried by two other boys. But no. The coffin lid!

In amongst the flowers a small chromium-plated Christ lay with chest braced against the hard death on the Cross that awaited. Between the snow (winter) and the flowers (spring) they buried Him, hid Him away in the tomb.

Behind this sad entourage walked the stricken father with eyes lowered, hands clasped behind his back, wrapped in sad thought. He was followed by a cortège of little girls dressed in their Sunday finery; and behind them paced the young priest reading from his breviary.

From her deepened breathing, I knew that Harriet, who had a daughter, had been affected; it had affected me, who had no daughter but had three bouncing sons. Suffer us and our offspring not to perish, oh Lord! The grieving *padre* would return the crucifix to the bereaved *madre* who had mourned at home, as was the custom; no weeping women were allowed at the cemetery. The young hurrying coffin-bearers held the *caja-fuerte* low, like a battering-ram, and all along the way to the *cementerio* women stood in the doorways with folded arms and said *¡Qué guapa!* which was manifestly true: the dead child was beautiful, or death had beautified the clay. The cemetery was outside the town, near the brickworks and the football field on the Maro road.

It was an odd place of some distinction, this home for the dead. 'Deadsville', Trevor Callus named it, quick to invert brand names and plugs from his years in advertising. 'Endsville'. He liked to stroll about there near the grassless soccer field, hands clasped behind his back, smoking a cheroot to the sound of cheering, the sight of a black and white object being the ball rising above the dead wall and falling back into the field of play.

A narrow short avenue of cypress trees gives on to a high whitewashed wall into which is set a heavy black wrought-iron gate. In the first part of the cemetery lie the well-to-do defunct in ostentatious family vaults, with weighty embossed iron double doors sunk into a cement bed and held secure against tempests.

This leads into a larger enclosed area beyond the mortuary chapel where banks of coffins rest in the columbarium proper. There are no cypress trees here. The effect is not sombre, however, but functional, along the lines of bakery furnaces. The inscriptions for the rich dead are suitably engraved in marble or stone by Carlos Clu and Co. of Málaga; while the common dead have their names and dates, when born and when expired, cut by inexpert hands on cheaper material like slate. But whether rich or poor, all are dead and can no longer put on airs, and the pleas addressed formally to their Maker are modest and restrained.

The best flowers of the year bloom through October and November as though mindful of the dead ones, and during these two months of the year the cemetery is full of flowers and presents a festive appearance, with chrysanthemums set in the little arched niches. Above the walls the sierras rise, white with snow, in the distance over the river, making a pretty picture. The sierras are the washed-out blue of distemper, a whey-blue haze, Mary's colour.

Children are buried in the centre plot, without headstones. There are no gravediggers as such; the caretaker digs the children's graves, breaks open the white ossuaries with a pickaxe to admit another young cadaver and generally spruce up the place.

At an Andalucían internment there is always the merry sound of hammering and the breaking down of walls for a last look at the petrified face behind a porthole of glass, then more hammering and possibly a burst of song as the coffin lid is nailed down. I liked to walk about there unmolested and address silent prayers to my dear departed mother. Here in a few years' time came the skinny remains of Miguel Lopez Rojas, the tireless *camarero* who worked in the Bar Alhambra from nine in the morning until two and three o'clock the following morning and never had any free time to call his own; he died on 3 December 1964, worn out.

Is it on the night of the *Festival de Todos los Santos* or the *Commemoración de los Fieles Difuntos* that candles of remembrance burn all night in the *cementerio* and visitors behave informally, as if visiting friends, the men smoking and strolling about at their ease, hands in pockets, and the women (never short of something to say) calling out to each other, happy to be there, with all the candles sailing in pans of water and burning down and going out? No kneeling in ostentatious prayer with the lips moving (a most disgusting sight, like lips moving when the finger moves under a line of print) or telling beads; none of that damp Irish mourning, but loud jolly gossiping and the emptying out of dead flowers. Never the deep unfestive gloom of damp cypress ride and Celtic cross awry and mossy ways bemired, matching the hushed and reverential tones deemed suitable by my fellow countrymen on these occasions, which brings the morbidity of their natures to the surface; the women adopting the soothing and mollifying cadences of priests and nuns, those professionals at funeral practices, going about the execution of their sad duties.

The Nerja *cementerio* down its short avenue of evergreens was as unlike Deans Grange as day is to night; of Prospect I cannot speak, where the Protestants were buried near the Botanic Gardens at Glasnevin, where I liked to walk in the curvilinear glasshouses in the subtropical heat. Outside the walls on the riverside there was a dump intended for the bones of those whose term of occupancy had terminated, to be chucked out as *rejecta membra*. It was all done on a very decent human scale.

I stood with Mrs Deck on the little wrought-iron balcony of No. 12 and watched the cortège go on up the hill. A stout woman standing in the doorway opposite stared after the priest. Presently rain began to fall. Mr Deck was out in his espadrilles fetching Bisonte *con filtro,* his wife's preferred brand. Now he was sauntering down the hill in the rain, hands plunged in pockets and shoulders hunched, whistling. Sometimes he acted like the narrator of *Our Town,* kicking imaginary pebbles, a free man in Winesburg, Ohio, or wherever he was in America.

'Here comes the Señor. Let's go in and sit down,' I suggested.

So we went in and sat down.

'They seem to love the dead here,' Harriet Deck said. 'One does, of course. Love the dead, I mean.'

I had nothing to say to that. Was it a Jewish thought? Threads flex, hues meeting and parting in whey-blue haze.

– 30 –

Moody, Fenning, Kramer and McCracken

It must have been Christmas Day 1964 when the Decks came dressed formally, as they would have dressed in San Francisco, John in a dark seer-sucker suit, snowy white shirt, slim-Jim necktie and black boots; Harriet very smart indeed in a sort of half-length housecoat and black tights, *Strump-fhosen* that clasped her about the hips. They bore presents with them, flowers and a bottle of JJ from Málaga. We sat about and drank the whiskey. When Coppera pleaded exhaustion and retired for her siesta around two o'clock, we sallied out.

It was a strange day of fierce Andalucían sunlight splashed on white-washed walls and Nerja seemed deserted. We ran into Exley roaming about and invited him to join us for dinner, drank some *Cuné* in Antonio's bar, spread ourselves out, praised the wine to the jovial patron who moved skittishly on the duckboards behind the service hatch, batted his circum-flex eyelashes at us, saying 'Aye, Rory, aye?' without one word of English. And then back unsoberly to the Christmas dinner, to which Harry Calnek was invited.

Adelina had been waiting for us at the top of the stairs, beaming like the Queen Mother. She served up the first course and left. The tougher parts of the chicken were in a *paella,* the tender parts fried in oil with garlic seasoning. Exley did not complain of the toughness of the chicken but threw the bones about, affected by the Jameson. Calnek was subdued, spoke little and left early. We sat around the *brasero* and finished the whiskey. Deck spoke of his time in Korea.

He was second radioman, radio operator and titular gunner on a seaplane, having enrolled in the navy so as not to be drafted into the infantry; he spent a good part of his enlistment in training schools.

'You could buy good whiskey tax free in the NCO Club. I'd gone to an electronics school in Memphis and was assigned to Crew Nine. I learnt Morse Code and was given a chance to fly. It meant extra money and an easy life. Air crewmen stood fewer watches and did less work. Blues, peacoats, winter hats, fall-ins, fall-outs, friction, leaves, pick-ups, occasional women of the looser variety, fuck-ups, that was the Korean War,' Deck said, sprawled at his ease, smoking a thumping big Cuban cigar. 'We were enlisted men. When I was fighting for democracy over there, flying about in old PBMs, stubby-winged and heavy to handle. The bloody things couldn't land on four-foot swells, with none of the grace of the more famous PBYs, we patrolled the east coast of Korea, the Tsushima Strait and the Yellow Sea, in an anti-submarine outfit.

'The port of Wonsan,' Deck intoned. 'Barbershop music and college songs. It was Christmas 1952. The sea was icy. If you dropped into it, you wouldn't survive long. One of the seaplanes came down with thirteen officers and men. None survived.

'Those goddamn kamikazes, feasted and shaven to the pluck, climbed into a kind of flying chicken coop made out of fenceposts, orange crates put together around a bomb, and in these things they'd set out looking for an American destroyer. Some of them never made it. They'd explode somewhere off Wonsan. Desperate men. It was generally known that the Chinese used the Korean War as an extension of cadet training.

'The seaplane ramp,' said the sailor-aviator, warming to his theme. 'We flew out over the strait, a short gravy hop during which we photographed shipping. I was not at all prepared to die.

'The brothels were paper-thin,' said he, puffing like a steamboat. 'The whole joint shook when some of my buddies were hammering a job, polishing their knob. The bar hostesses were perfect. They were human and gentle and they needed us. I have never been around a collection of young, pretty, intelligent girls who needed me – not as a civilian and certainly not as a sailor. It was a blessing, a whiff off a dream, and another eloquent argument against worry. I knew I wasn't going to cream it.'

Leaning back in his chair and puffing on his *puro*, the husband studied his wife. The swollen lip my ardour had given her was back more or less to normal. And what better proof than a cut lip can a woman want, proof positive that a man has her on his mind?

'American service girls seemed a bit coarse in comparison,' Deck said. 'A big perfumed WAVE took me on her capacious thigh as if I were a cigar and she was rolling me. She dandled me up and down but nothing came of it except that I was keenly embarrassed, enough to bring tears to a man's eyes. She explained to me that it was all she could manage, because it was her "difficult" time. A period like lava flow, I should imagine. Glad I didn't have to perform. She'd have swallowed me up.

'You don't fuck around with a shipmate's girl or wife,' John Deck said. 'Jim McCracken, Joe Moody, Pat Fenning, Kramer. Get this: Fenning laid another man's wife and the husband got wind of it, beat the shit out of her, then got *him* drunk one night in a bar, laid him out with a bottle and then began stomping him and kicking the shit out of him good and proper. Sure as hell ruined his good looks. It was the last time he polished his knob there, I can tell you.'

I got the point.

– 31 –

The Way She Walked

The way she walked away from me that day, the day of our first assignation, first intimacy, heading for the brickworks and the cemetery, walking with that aura of hers, that short chopping stride, *pasa fina,* with the certainty of being seen and admired. Women feel it in their backs when they are being watched and admired.

The road, the *carretera,* bore her along on its boily back away from La Luna; the conviction of her own allure carried her along. She turned without stopping, sensing me watching her, saw that my eyes still followed her. I was a little below her on the cinder path that went branching off at right angles; it led over the tableland towards the sea, a route for the passage of goats at morning and evening, with much agility leaping across by stepping-stones as the sun came up or went down. Her lemur paw waved. I waved back. Without breaking her stride, she went on. She was my bit of stuff on the road.

Like most women, and all attractive women, she craved the touch of flannel. Was that the last time? If it was, I did not know it then. It was the first time and the last time, the only time, and I was going to establish my alibi. If you are going to tell lies you must be consistent with them, no divergences into the truth. Swimming, dearest. Not waving but drowning. *L'âme adore nager* – what Frog wrote that? I suspect Michaux. The soul adores swimming.

Mrs Harriet Deck was returning with her own no less plausible lies to tell her waiting husband; though what she thought to tell was true enough up to a point; up to the point where the lies began ('Lie in your teeth'), that is. She would not feed him an outright lie but her omissions contained falsehoods, modifications of facts, evasions of the truth; her elisions were masterly. Out walking for two hours, dear, saw a black sheep, spoke to no one, had a cold beer at La Luna.

So she went jauntily down the road, no doubt still feeling me inside her, as I felt her within me, being permeated with her, gripping me deep within. So she knew what it was like to be out of her depth, gliding away, knew the wonderfully dangerous intensification of feeling that comes with lying and cheating in love. There is no prescription against voluntary things, women as forces of nature; it is against *form*.

So she went swaggering away from me down the road and I watched her go, the soldier's girl on her way home. Hers was not the broad prudent seat (*pompi*) of rumpy Gerda Rhodes; nor yet the spare flat deflated seat of Sonya Hool, nor the tresses and hanks of dark hair proper to a Jewess – Gerda's Brillopad thatch, Lilly Lowen's orange golliwog locks – the appearance ineradicably Jewish, an Alexandrian effluvium of torpid female Hebrew flesh. No, she reminded me of none of those ladies. She was my spare-time, fair, loving, Polish-American-Jewish light-of-love.

She had not that narrowly determinable view of her race and the places occupied by that race, the spurious and obsessive concept of nationality that so many Americans have; she was American, sure, but she was surely Jewish too.

Was there something that said *Juden* in those blue eyes of hers? Some knowledge or sadness dredged up from God knows where; or was it merely the power that certain beautiful women have, of suggesting and invoking landscapes? (Cheever called it the dark plains of sexual experience where the buffalo still roams.) Their eyes gaze if not into then at least towards a landscape no man has ever seen, much less penetrated into; that small woman, that Jewy woman who so detested the term 'Jewess'.

When she was depressed and down in the dumps, she was really down; those dumps of hers were profoundly, Jewishly, deep. The guarded look she threw at me then conveyed something along the lines of 'Now am I neither happy nor sad. Now I am what I am.'

I'd think: How well I know you, Harriet, and yet I don't know you at all. You belong to your husband, not to me. I get the scraps.

A sullen wife and a reluctant mother sat all day in silence by the fire. I thought then: This is and is not the Harriet Lipski of Delancey Street that we heard so much about. Was it not profoundly Jewishly Jewish, this dolour, this impenetrable gloom? I can't say, I don't know; maybe it was. Some relative had told her once that she had Jewish eyes 'just like Uncle Ibn's'. But Uncle Ibn ('a loud-mouth with five grown sons in trade') 'definitely had Jewish eyes'. So she preferred not to believe it.

'Look,' said she (standing up close to me and widening her eyes so that I could study them, gaze into them and inhale her Cointreau breath), 'do you believe that I have Jewish eyes?'

'Yes,' I'd say, 'you definitely have Jewish eyes.'

'No, I have Italian eyes.'

'Well then, you have Italian eyes.'

Harriet was honest but in a very feminine way. She came to our apartment in Calle de las Augustias to tell me that she couldn't show up for our very first assignation. 'I can't do it. I wouldn't know what face to wear,' she confessed when Coppera was out of the room.

A partial failure some of the time, semi-successful part of the time, that's how it was for us then. It was passing strange, that winter, and the termination of our intimacy in the spring. Say around May Day.

– 32 –

Callus, Alas!

. . . a lover set out with all his equipages and appurtenances.

It was chilly in the Alhambra bar, like a dairy or a morgue, at nine in the morning when Miguel came on and began again tending his coffee machine that no one else was permitted to touch. There was snow along the sierras, cloud on Cuesto del Cielo that Old Parr had climbed with Calnek, Callus and Rory. We were alone there. Miguel diplomatically served us, did not ask of her husband nor of my *esposa*, did not see us, had come to no conclusion about what we were up to but knew we were up to something; else why look so *engaged*? Even transformed; and did we not see each other every day? And why these furtive meetings so early in the day? On these imponderables no doubt Miguel had pondered and no doubt come to some conclusion; but he wasn't telling anybody; mum was the word.

When she crossed one black-stockinged leg over the other my heart turned again with it. I heard a child crying upstairs, or maybe it was in the *retrete* where the *gitanos* cut the throats of the little kids brought there on the carrier of a beaten-up bike. A child was crying, Harriet was sipping black coffee and Cognac. The *retrete* was just a hole in the cement, the stink-sump of Iberia. How did the ladies manage crouching over it in ammonia-reek powerful as chloroform, and be able to rise again? The ladies could manage many difficult things.

Sometimes she dominated me with her eyes, the blue shafts of her eyes, at other times it was the sight of a brown thigh; but more often than not it was her voice that dominated me, and then again (she seemed abstracted, not knowing how much she was showing) it was the brown thigh that dominated all.

She spoke of the past, the time before she had known me, and Miguel, monkey-faced with the leathery skin of an outdoor worker, served us, '*Si, Señora*', moved away, the paper napkins in the glass like pennants in the breeze, in the morgue we sat in, the *Fundador* warming us.

Miguel saw nothing, heard nothing, said nothing; heard all yet understood nothing. His lips were sealed.

I watched her face, her teeth, eyes, mouth, a touch of apathy, burning lips. She looked at me without saying anything, her eyes somewhat charged.

When she was younger, she had kissed a naked and hairy chest in Chicago. Then that one disappeared out of her life and another took his place, there was always going to be another, because she was a pretty blonde lady and they all wanted her. This one shot squirrels, going about naked with a rifle in the woods; he was a theological student who read Oscar Wilde. Naked in bed together they ate grapes and he read her 'The Nightingale and the Rose'. He gave her a present of *A Shropshire Lad,* because she was his rose-lipt girl. 'Kinda innocent,' she laughed at her lost innocence.

She inhaled Bisonte, remembering the theological student walking about buck naked in the woods. Then there was another; there would always be another (her Byzantine nose had become more pronounced as she recalled the past, whitening across the bridge), because she was attractive to men. Would she remember all her old lovers? Would I too have that immortality?

I thought of the Albanian wood-cutters, white with the dust of the road, I'd seen passing like princes through a market in Sarajevo carrying Bronze Age saws, come on foot out of Ethiopia. And, by extension, I thought of Trevor Callus, god of misrule, cutting logs in Canada, grunting at each hefty stroke, the axe buried in the wood, a true woodsman, pulling it out again, panting at these exertions.

Callus burning the tyres of his Combi, heading for the Laurentians. He had spoken of a grey period in Montreal. The centre of the city was a cemetery, Mount Royal, where the dead looked down upon the living. Ville Marie was a settlement for missionaries and Place Royale was a fur trading post, and before that again it had been Hochelaga, an Iroquois Indian village.

He had once seen a girl undressing near a lighted window, and he had later accosted her in the street. The turreted roofs and outside stairways of old Montreal were an outright temptation to adventurous libertines like himself, the stairways were useful for assignation purposes since, in many cases, they led directly to bedrooms on upper floors. With a red rose clenched between his teeth and his amber eyes blazing with anticipatory lust, Callus climbed upwards, a lover set out with all his equipages and appurtenances. He liked high game on the edge, good sticky cod from Newfoundland waters; he had whom he pleased.

That was a strange madness of his – to be forever waking up in an unknown bed. A true *carpe diem* type, his days were filled with vital cravings and satisfactions attempted; all the glut of life available would hardly suffice. Consorting with Montreal whores, he had caught a dose of the clap.

Soon enough he and Harriet would cuckold Rory, for Harriet thought that Rory had seduced Anne Renshaw, a blonde Englishwoman, said to be insatiable: Harriet wanted revenge.

Callus concerns us here. He who enjoyed life as a cannonball enjoys space, blindly travelling as aimed and spreading ruin on the way. He was a true Scorpio, the dangerous ones who kill themselves in a ring of fire. His arms were tattooed with the lime-blue shapes of entwined hearts or vessels in storm, cannons belching fire and smoke. From his army and forestry background came the puce needle diggings. Callus digging with a rutter in Cumberland, grunting down in an open drain, avoided by his fellow workers who feared him, his recklessness and awkwardness, his doomed quality.

'A fast river cuts a deep trench,' he told me. 'A slow river cuts a shallow trench.' Munge was morning-mouth, apen armpits, ullage was something else, and he knew the word for false axillary hair worn by chorus girls, which for the moment escapes me. When we passed an open drain in Calle Carabeo, the stench was enough to make your hair stand up. He inhaled deeply as though smelling flowers.

'Shit, I can't get enough of *that.*'

Not bearing to be quiet, not able to abide still at home. Now abroad, now in the streets, now lying in wait at corners, that was Trevor Callus. 'You dig the soil to get something out of it and you have a woman for much the same reason,' said he. Digging with his thick tool in a trench in Cumberland, he knew he was finished if he stayed there. Another maddened forester flung a hatchet at his head, but he had one of his intuitions and ducked in time. The wet weapon had slipped from the other's grasp, or so he claimed. 'Sorry, mate.'

A perishing wind blew down from the Grampians. He had to get out. Callus struck with the hatchet, pulled it out, hit again, grunting at each blow; sweat poured off him. The bulge at his crotch became pronounced; everything 'turned him on'. No more sickness or excessive evacuation. The sun went down over a hill.

'He's changed,' Coppera said. 'He was different in Johannesburg, steadier. There he was a man.'

'With an excreta phobia,' I said. 'He was never steady. And now here, what is he?'

'Now he has become a chimpanzee.'

Wisdom of Coppera Hill: 'A woman's heart is like a room filled with pitiable stuff. Dancing with another woman is like drowning.'

– 33 –

Can After Can . . .

Can After Can . . .

Can After Can . . .

'S he sure as hell was white,' said John Deck. 'The winches were white, the anchor chains were white, the covers on the lifeboats were an unsurpassable glossy white; the plates, the hatch covers, all alike were spotlessly white.

'Peer into a vent and the shadow was white. The sand in the fire buckets was as white as the smoke belching from the stacks. Look into the paint locker; can-after-can-after-can-after-can of white paint!

'Sailors in white singlets, and officers in spick-and-span white uniforms pace the white decks. It was the whitest, brightest small freighter in maritime history; the SS *Klek* of Yugoslavia. We crossed in her.'

I saw the radiant Harriet walking the decks at night in the company of the ship's doctor, the handsome Dr Vuc Eisen. She told him all about herself. She looked brilliant, indeed dazzling. A mixture of honey and sun, matt skin, burning lips (*and* roving eye).

'Sunset followed sunrise as regular as decanting wine,' said the Deckman lugubriously, giving a flare to his niggery nostrils by taking a deep

breath, deepening his voice, really laying the accent on thick. 'The boredom was absolute, man. Changes of current, tidal shifts, the wake of passing vessels, garbage bobbing in the wake, the diver-birds diving, the flying
fish doing what flying fish do, the islands, oh God, the *islands!* Where would
we be without islands? I can't recall which ones we stopped at. They all
looked the same to me. Perhaps we stopped at them all? No matter, the
sweet winds were blowing from the horse latitudes to the doldrums.'

'And the ever-attentive Dr Vuc Eisen?' Rory inquired slyly. 'What was he
up to?'

'He sure as hell charmed the pants right off her,' Deck agreed. 'Once in
our cabin he gave her an injection up the ass.'

She lay facing her husband on her bunk and the handsome ship's doctor
prepared the hypodermic. 'This may hurt,' he said. She was ready for him,
smiling at her husband, her skirt riding up, she was ready for it, biting her lip.

'Walter Pater spoke of two things which penetrated Leonardo's art and
imagination beyond the depth of other impressions – the smiling of women
and the motion of great waters,' said Rory the Everready.

'We cut loose,' Deck said, snipping the end off his cigar.

− 34 −

Kampen Nact-Strand

'Y ou should see Brigitte Winkler in a bikini,' Coppera said. 'She
wore a red one down on Torrecillas today and looked ripe
enough to eat. There was a young German chap with her and *he*
looked as if he was about to eat her. You'd think you had the whole picture
when you see her in a bikini, but not at all. She was showing us some photos
of herself taken in the buff at Sylt, where the Berlin nudist girls go, and
there she was in all her glory. There was a hairy naked chum crouching in
the shallows, devouring her with his eyes, whom she described as a 'good
friend'. She really is startling, nude. The female shape undressed is so bla-
tantly avid and sexual, so hungry-looking; I wouldn't like to be a man.'

'Sardine become shark,' I said.

The odours of inlets and creeks. Brigitte Winkler had those great simple
limpid eyes that stared at one appealingly. Medea the wife of Jason, leader
of the Argonauts, must have stood so in all her beauty alone on the Cretan
shore. The good ship *Argo* stood some way out to sea; the Argonauts in it

were tired and hungry, fed up following the Golden Fleece.

'What about her golden fleece?'

Private parts tend to become public, if not outrightly pubic, along the shores of the Costa del Sol in season. Franco was hardly cold in his grandiose sarcophagus in the Valley of the Fallen before young *Fräuleins* were diving into the sea in smaller and smaller bikinis, with no tops before King Juan Carlos had well settled onto his throne.

Harriet, who liked to talk horny, asked me what it was like to have one. 'It must be great to feel it there between your legs, to feel the weight of it dangling down.'

Harriet Deck talked dirty like one of the mouthy, fancy-free young wives in Webster or Congreve, a bold reincarnation of Lady Bracegirdle ('I'll let both you guys . . .'). Come-ons were her speciality, her cloak and dagger work, her language as rough as the rasp of a cat's tongue ('lemme talk to the cunt') or loose as a longshoreman; female or not, she wanted to be cock of the walk. Queen of the castle.

'Strewth, Milady, you find yourself in the wrong century and probably the wrong country at the wrong time. Franco's Spain could be puritanical in its own funny Fascist way. In Sir Walter Raleigh's day the gallants bolstered their codpieces with bombast, to make their proudest possession look bulgy and heavier. You'd have me wear a codpiece.'

'Sure.'

She herself preferred sanitary towels to Tampax because they gave her the feeling of an equivalent weight to the missing testicles and tool.

'What about your breasts and hair?' I said. She gave me a look, her eyes somewhat bloodshot from sea-bathing; they had been to Carabeo beach that morning.

'Sure, to feel one's breasts, the weight of them. To let one's hair down, feeling it on one's naked back, that's a good feeling, like slipping nude into bed. That's good too.'

Her own hair was long and oily, as long hair tends to be, particularly in hot places. Oily hair gives a better feeling of abandonment; a hairless Venus would have no power to charm the manly heart.

She'd go for that all right, passionate but a little envious of the male, the ordained taker, the cocksman; and what worse devil hung betwixt their hirsute thighs?

*   *   *

'She wants you to come over for supper.' Her husband conveyed the invitation, laying a diplomatic hand on my shoulder. 'Coppera's coming. It's all fixed. She told me to say a place will be laid for you. She's preparing something good for you. So you gonna come, Rory, hey? . . . *¿Que desea usted? ¿Prefiere usted la carne al horno, a la parilla, hervida o guidada?*'

'Thanks. I will,' I said.

Through that other loved body, the other adored flesh that one craves to enjoy, all that is most appealing in that other person is continually fêted, yet continually being withdrawn. Love, that most despairing of grips; the cruel fabled bird that pinches like a crab.

She was all of that for me.

− 35 −

Harriet

The potent smell of blood must have assailed Harriet's nostrils where the Decks sat on *tenido*, six rows up above the barrier on the *sol* side, roasting in the afternoon sun near the dark corral, out of which the bulls rushed blindly to their deaths in the arena all watered and raked for them to bravely perform.

'We were sittin' right on the bull-gate,' she boasted. Wherever she sat was *ipso facto* the best seat by the mere fact of her occupying it. When she entered a room, she caused a stir. Wherever she found herself, *that* was the best place to be. She deserved the best seat and special attention; she expected it and got it. The two stout *guardia de noche,* Manolo and Fernando, adored her.

'Queens,' her friend, Anne Marie, said of the Jewesses of San Francisco. 'Jewish queens.' Their besotted husbands saw them as queens and treated them accordingly. It was something that grated very much on the white South African sensibilities of Coppera.

On that Sunday in the Málaga bullring most of the working of the bulls and the subsequent blood-letting took place right in front of the Decks. Even without binoculars I had spotted them across from us on seats lower down nearer the sanded arena which the *monos* in collarless claret-coloured dungarees raked religiously after each kill, dragging the corpses out on litters pulled by mules at a gallop, dragging them away to be butchered under the stands. This was performed as impersonally as zoo attendants might clear up dungy cages.

But soon another fresh black bull came galloping in with tail erect, and shortly after in clanked the picadors with their lances raised, and the whole bloody business was resumed: rush, push, lean over, gore, gore, push; and now the blood pouring in dark gouts from the great hump raised up in fury, for the bullish spirit had to be brought down, lowered considerably before the gadfly could sting him lethally with the razor-sharp curved sword that found its way past the horns and into the lungs and soon had him coughing up his life's blood.

All this Harriet witnessed, with her low blood pressure and her high, bright expectant look, down there in *tenido* that must have reeked of bull blood, after the scuffles, the heavy lancing, the bull wearing himself out in futile rushes, the blood jerking out of him, so that he arrived all weary and bloodied for the *coup de grâce*.

What Frenchman contended that women are not clean because of their menses? It sounds like de Montherlant. But wouldn't the monthly flushing out of impurities make them cleaner than men, so fixated on blood sports, on killing, like Hemingway?

Rory remembered the child Molly Cushen in the schoolyard after the attentions of the barbarous dentist, the bloody spittle she spat out delicately, the blood-smeared hand, and of the disturbing prepubescent beauty of the young Elizabeth Taylor as Jane Eyre's little friend who cuts off her hair and walks in the punishment circle carrying flat-irons in a heavy fall of studio rain, standing by the deathbed with eyes downcast, and her slurred voice with glottal stops, suggestive already of the coming pains of love.

When Rory saw Harriet Deck after a lapse of twenty-one years she looked like a ghost, standing in the arrivals lounge of San Francisco International Airport to meet her old admirer off the internal flight from Houston and drive Rory to Santa Cruz in her powerful car.

She stood among the others waiting, not waving or calling out, just standing there so that I could see her plainly among all the other strangers. The Rubicon of the years had been crossed and some of the bright lights accordingly doused, though enough remained for Rory to see the old flame undiminished; she was much the same as before.

Rory kept his hand on her warm thigh as she drove and she did not object. Out there in the breathing dark was Berkeley's campus. It was December 1986 and they hadn't seen each other since the Decks visited Dublin in 1965.

In the time when we were apart I had written to Harriet for a swatch of her hair, from head, axillary and pubics. Those intimate parts of her were sent by airmail from Copenhagen to Málaga in a stout manila envelope, with the pages of her letter sellotaped inside, and this was carried in a Correos sack by bus in the twisting and ascending road that went around some two hundred curves, climbing into the hills like a medieval messenger on horseback bearing gifts; eventually to be delivered on foot to Calle Rueda by the unreliable and rarely sober postman, Laureano.

Rory had got the idea from reading Byron. The hair on the head of the former beloved, long separated in time and space, that makes a stone of the heart, is no longer thought attractive, smitten by the passing years, by general wear and tear; the living hair dies, becomes dead hair on the head, like animal hair on Halloween masks of monster faces sticky with glue at the back, eye sockets empty, as on a waxwork or a mummy in a dusty coffin; hair found on the horrid masks that were intended to frighten children.

Once on a winter night flight from Seattle to Heathrow the Boeing had picked up passengers from LA. A pretty darkhead took her seat in front of Rory. Then morning light was leaking in through the oval windows and the darkhead now with hair combed and water glistening on strands of hair as she was having her breakfast, and then she was rising up and collecting her stuff and walking before Rory out into the arrivals lounge at Heathrow, moving into a different climate, but all intact, having crossed time zones flying at 33,000 feet above the clouds, the proximity a sort of intimacy, surrogate intimacy, pseudointimacy, like seeing Harriet again after a lapse of twenty and one years, and finding that Santa Cruz was another sort of Nerja.

Who was it wrote that love is Time and Space made perceptible to the heart?

The loved one's mere presence transforms the very climate of a place, *her* place in the world around us, the world at large, which falls away from us when the loved one again appears, offers herself to Rory again, saying 'Take me, for I am yours today.'

PART IV:

Berlin Divided, Munich *Mordfest*

− 36 −

Im Doll

Rory liked to walk around Im Doll, liked the name, because it was where Hannelore had walked about as a child with Pappa and Mamma Schmidt, until the Red Army sharpshooter drew a bead and shot the horse dead between the shafts. Another was quickly harnessed up and the housekeeper had the foresight to bury a valuable ring in the sugar canister and they left Berlin behind in a hurry and with it her childhood.

Then Berlin fell and the world came to an end for Germans. It was Rossellini's *Germana, Anno Zero* for real, which was very surreal indeed, with the black market and profiteering and the bartering that went on when there was no more money available, the sharp dealings proceeded in whatever valuables desperate men and women could lay their hands on, a cut-throat survival business where only the strong survived and Uncle Hans was pushed to his death from a train and Hannelore had no more use for dolls.

A city of ruins stood there as dire warning after the bombing raids had brought the people to their knees down in the shelters and the sick Führer, in his deep bunker permeated with bad smells, was preparing his last will and testament, getting ready to do away with Eva Braun and himself. Loyal unto death, Eva would be Frau Hitler for only a short time before he shot her, finally wedded to the death she wanted. The nuptial feast would take place in Valhalla, to which neither Goering nor Himmler would be invited; nor would any of Hitler's defeated generals. *Nein!* The death mills had all been closed down; the city laid waste around the Chancellery. His last face, the features of the vegetarian with stomach cramps, was a face of iron, his true face, implacable.

The man of humble beginnings, who had made himself master of Germany and most of Europe, was a strict vegetarian, a sipper of vegetable soup; he blamed the *Wehrmacht* and the *Volk* for letting him down; they had not shown their true German steel, in his view, and forthwith blew himself away.

– 37 –

Some Places She Took Me

When the Havel froze over, we took to walking on the ice. She would only consent to go so far in an easterly direction because marksmen with long-sighted rifles were hidden in the bushes on the GDP bank and those frontier guards had itchy fingers and were quite likely to squeeze off a round at anyone foolish enough to venture on to Soviet soil, the reclaimed land won by the Red Army. Trespassing on Soviet soil was a capital offence, instantly punishable by death, delivered at long range; and midway across the Havel the FRG ended and the GDR began; the West, technically speaking, ended out on the ice, beneath which the Havel still flowed in the direction it had always flowed; namely, east to west, following the contours of the land, abiding by the direction decided upon long ago by the old river.

She did not relish the idea of venturing into the Grünewald by night, for some couples never came out again, or the girl was raped and the man was set upon and done in. She would not sit demurely on the sandy banks of the Schlachtensee or Krumme Lanke, because dogs befouled the area; nor would she consent to swim in either of these tributaries of the Havel lakes, because they were dirty. On moonless nights and even on nights of full moon, the waters looked very Grimmlike and black, full of nameless awfulness, among which might be numbered the bones of the aircrew of a Lancaster bomber that had been shot down in the war.

To none of these excursions would she agree; but soon all resistance was overcome and she succumbed in the fastness of the Grünewald on the blackest of nights and swam naked with Rory in Krumme Lanke and told him he had the face of a fox, a swimming fox heading for the hen coop, that was Rory to a T, as the hen coop was surely the nudist Hannelore laved by the lukewarm waters of Schlachtensee.

Since they were hitting it off so well, she said she was ready to do whatever he wanted. So Rory, having had the fill of her frontwise, and the full enjoyment thereof, asked her to turn over and then had the fill of her backside which was large and shapely and if possible even hotter than her cunt, which was saying something. All this in the depths of the Grünewald where there were none about to see what was going on, what hogs were rooting for what truffles; except in the daytime when a mezzo-soprano from the Opera House, walking in the rides, exercised her voice at the full pitch of her lungs.

For a fact, some of the places where she took Rory were, I suspect, not her own choices, but choices made by previous admirers, of all of whom she spoke frankly, the four or five in her court.

Such a place was a student dive in Wittenburgplatz where we consumed a great quantity of cheap red wine and plates of sardines all standing upright with eyes and mouths open as if they had died of fright. We frequented a Polish bar and were adopted by a queer barman ('How are the young lovers tonight?') who served us vodka in little goblets with ice and snow about the rims, that was like drinking fire; this somewhere near the burnt-out ruins of the Soviet Embassy about which she made the widest circle and never referred to, as if it didn't exist, something shameful standing in Berlin as a monument to what must never happen again. On rare occasions, when in funds, we dined at Hardy's am Oper and drank expensive Hungarian Tokay; but more often it was an Italian restaurant, Rusticana, patronised by off-duty British Army officers in mufti. Hotel Bubec in Mexikoplatz was lovely in the snow, drinking vodka again, and the dome of the S-Bahn very Russian and the place overheated, so that we were reluctant to leave. Then there was a Greek place.

When Germany played in the final of the World Cup, we were the only couple in Berlin who not only weren't even looking at the television screen, but didn't know who was playing whom; the only loving couple in all Germany who had never even heard of Pele, the wonderworker.

— 38 —

In a Strange Sort of Time

You'd think to yourself. 'It'll never be the same again. *I'll* never be the same again.' But to be sure nothing essentially changes; as the importance of the other diminishes and falls away as love wanes, you return to yourself once more. You are yourself again; and she presumably returns to herself, too; whoever she may be; the loved one of that time and place, that place in Rory's anxious heart.

You say to yourself. 'One day, a day like today, a day that has become unlike any other day.' And it happens. You asked for it and it's been given to you, and all is changed.

That ferocious Frog Jean Genet, the princeling of language who turned himself into a real toad, wrote of the sheer pleasure of betrayal; betrayal in love, that is. A betrayed man's face is terrible, he says. But isn't it even truer of betrayed women's faces? Look at Picasso's *Woman Weeping*. Dora Maar weeping tears hot as molten lava, becoming wedges of thick, shattered glass, forced out of her eyes at the thought of losing Pablo.

On the days when I escaped from Coppera and the kids, she liked to arrange them in the windows like the heads of a hanging jury, as the mother made abusive catcalls after the fleeing one who had run up a quick omelette by way of lunch and was now hurrying for the train.

I had an assignation with Hannelore at Podbielski station. It was the day Zbigniew Herbert chose to call on us, walking down from his rented mansion at the end of Beskidenstrasse, a cobbled street with a pharmacy and bakery within easy reach.

I crept away unobserved and was soon out of sight at the Joachim Klepper Weg and hurrying across by the sunken meadows, the Rehweise, by what had been an anti-tank gun pillbox during the war, and approaching the station where Albert Speer, coming in his Mercedes from his Wannsee home, had noticed a crowd of Jews on the platform as he flashed by, not giving them a second glance or thought.

Zbigniew Herbert burst his Polish trousers and had to return home to change, but returned to take Coppera and the kids out boating on Krumme Lanke, knowing something was wrong with the Hills.

As I walked past the stalls of the open-air market that was held on a Thursday, the very air changed to match my mood of elation, as if I was a merrymaker in one of Zille's graphics of a beery Berlin in a happier time. I was so happy that happy is not the word, lucky happiness, *Glücklichkeit,* a happiness with a kernel of sadness (for my betrayal of wife and letting my children down) like a curry that is salted, or a gate vaulted or some hard handicap overcome.

I was leaving the zone of duty and faithfulness that belonged to Coppera and entering the zone that was Hannelore's, the free zone where rights no longer applied; the former's rights ended when the doors of the train that swept me to the latter sighed shut, in a strange sort of time that was both melancholy and monochrome, an illustration from Grimm.

− 39 −

The Giantess and the Guardsman

Rory had noticed (how could he not?) the truly amazing giantess strolling along the wide plane-tree lined pavement near the Spanish bar; pantherlike she patrolled the area, making it into a jungle clearing.

She had moved serenely past the two Greek *Gastarbeiters* deep in Greekish confabulation, who hadn't even noticed her, hadn't cottoned on, as she threw them a swift, lethal *visu,* clutching at them like a grappling iron seeking purchase, the lovelorn look that entraps and entrances. But they had ignored her.

As soon as she had accosted the tall English grenadier, they understood how the land lay and how the wind blew and came running with their tongues out for it, but already too late.

She could have taken on the pair of them in tandem, sucking off the warty cock of the one while his pal attempted congress from the rear, a Greekish variant very popular in the Levant. Her high posterior proffered invitingly for his gratification, with garter belt and fishnet stockings dragged down, love-knots dangling, stilettos discarded, buckles and bridles hanging loose as from a richly caparisoned charger, a bay mare with hair swinging like a mane or tail raised, miring.

That was surely one stupendous broad. The randy little Greeks would have had their work cut out to make any impression on her, let alone mount that peerless German mare.

He was exceedingly tall, well over six feet, reared on All-Bran and as tall as an English guardsman on parade, snapping to attention, deploying the swagger-stick, correctly attired with shoulders back and chin in; he carried himself as an officer should.

His elegant light-blue linen suit had all the lickety-spit and polish of the parade ground. He was close-shaven, well shod and pomaded, knew a good barber, and was just taking an evening stroll along the Ku'damm.

So was she.

The big whore Karen Schnell, Mistress of SM, was as tall as he; six-inch stilettos gave her a slight advantage. She was all absolute stunner. Her manner was brisk, business was business, she didn't believe in beating about the bush. She was sauntering along the west side of the the Ku'damm, on the lookout for likely clients. Then along came the tall guardsman as if he were strolling in Kensington Gardens. She stopped abruptly as he came opposite her and he stopped too.

'You wenna get laid, big boy? Get inna my pants' – pronounced 'paints' – 'Or fuck Karen up the ass?'

The guardsman raised his eyebrows: this was sharp talking. Karen Schnell spoke an obsolete American-movie slang never heard in brown Bronxville nor Schenectady, in a nasal intonation learnt from Barbara Stanwyck.

'Won't try an' buck you off if you wanna ride. No time like the present. My pad's just round the corner. If you wanna quickie, Karen's hot to trot. Don't care how long you are.'

An elderly sandwichboardman with mouth agape stood at the entrance to a side street, ringing a small handbell to advertise the strip joints. The evening parade of Berlin whores had begun. Traffic roared up and down the Kurfürstendamm. The threatening head of a big Alsatian dog with lolling tongue hung out of the wide-open window of a speeding BMW. The Mercedes-Benz sign revolved over Europe Centre, in a city split in twain, where rigid Russian-style Communism crept along Stalinallee right up to the wall at Potsdamer Platz; this side was committed to hedonism, the good goofing off, getting stuffed and getting laid – life with a zing in it.

Like ball bearings rattling in oil, the hurdygurdy man began grinding out an old Berliner tune on his antiquated machine (they had stood toe to toe and eye to eye, her breath fanned his face, she thoughtfully fingering his lapel as if to test the quality of the expensive cloth, absently touching the lapel in an intimate gesture as if presenting him with a rose for his buttonhole); at which they turned as one, of one mind, certain of what they wished to do and just how they would set about it.

'You do rather *arouse* me,' the tall guardsman admitted.

They turned as one in the movement of a formal dance, a dance they had danced before, maybe long ago. They linked arms in a familiar manner (as if they had once been intimate but had separated and now had met again in a city where neither of them had dreamed of ever meeting the other, but they had and were overjoyed, and he was looking forward to servicing her again).

She leant forward on her high heels, tipping her head towards his until they almost touched and whispered hotly into his ear some invitation of unambiguous intent, nibbling an earlobe that had gone purple with embarrassment.

'Would you care for a ride, sir? I'm quite free. My place is nearby. Come!'

And then she made that unforgettable gesture: a quick point over his right shoulder, pointing away behind his back the way she had sauntered out, looking for the first client to come within her orbit. A quick dabbing gesture that an archer might make with one gloved right hand as he released an arrow towards its mark, heading for the bull's-eye with all the fierce suck and pull of a powerfully sprung bow behind it. Or the gesture a surgeon might make after a coronary angiogram operation has been successfully performed and he removes surgical gloves preparatory to washing his hands, with a sort of nimble mimed wringing of all the fingers. Or (to strain the simile yet further), say, the perfectly timed punch that only travels a few inches, and catches the opponent flush on the jaw, moving into the blow, and drops him cold, settles his hash.

'You an army man?'

'No, no, nothing particularly like that. I'm an insurance broker, actually. Different racket altogether.'

It was a gesture made in all innocence once, by a young Dublin woman *en route* to her office, by which she had sought to comfort or anyway reassure me, Rory, that is, the father, to her just a face peering out of a narrow window at 47 Charleston Road, hearing the damn gate creak open again, for her to usher in his son, an excitable anxious child of seven, eight or nine at the time, whom she was sending back in again unhurt, after some rough workmen in an irrigation ditch had shouted something at him, shouted obscenities that had alarmed and frightened him, sent him weeping home again. No, he had stood at the bus stop, weeping, and she had seen and heard enough and had brought him back safely home.

The protective maternal gesture was the gesture that Picasso had caught in the painting of his young wife, Jacqueline, and their two children, Paloma and Claude. The figures of children and mother with arms about them are outlined in heavy black, like the lead holding a stained-glass window in place. The protective motherly gesture of enclosing and enfolding the two children was repeated, once more perpetuated. Almost a throwaway gesture, refusing any show of gratitude for a gift made with the heart, a free gift from the heart; the moue she made with her mouth expressed that. *Bah, it's nothing. Forget it!*

But her I couldn't ever forget; neither have I, Rory, forgotten that unsolicited act of kindness.

The Greek and Italian *Gastarbeiters* and the others from poor Balkan countries were cooped up in their compounds and out of touch with what was going on, never bothering to learn the language of their German employers, the *Deutsch* that might have saved them mutilated limbs from machines plastered with safety precautions, all set forth in script like orders barked out; saved them from electrocuting themselves on power lines designated *VERBOTEN! ACHTUNG!*

What did that mean? Free for a few hours they wandered about the city, window-shopping, gaping in blank amazement at the priceless furs in the windows of the fashion shops. No price tags gave fair warning that they shouldn't attempt to enter here; for it was far, far beyond their means. Those who didn't have funds didn't shop here but at Peek & Kloppenburg.

In any case most of their pay cheques went home intact. They seemed lost, wandering about the sinful city, gaping at the rich goods in the windows. Girlie shows proliferated. Nude playmates besported themselves, splashing about in shallow pools surrounded by tables set for dinner. Red candles glowed on the tables and were reflected in the windows; and the silent *Gastarbeiters,* sadly gazing in, saw the waiters moving about briskly, setting places and taking the first orders from stout patrons who seemed to overflow their fragile chairs; saw the nude playmates, narrow-waisted but big-busted and with big behinds, constantly smiling and aglow with health, tugging playfully at the neckties of smiling male customers sitting alone at tables, inviting them to join the other nude playmates in a frolic. Flashbulbs exploded and the *Gastarbeiters* gaped in wonderment at what they were getting up to around, and then in, the pools. Photographs of previous cavortings were on display, set out beside the mouthwatering menus on the triple-glazed windows.

Ah, but who could aspire to all that flash and glitter? The flesh of the nude playmates seemed incandescent, as if they were about to ignite as part of the floor show, the tie-tugging and the wanton invitations and urgings and splashings were a far cry from the paternalistic hardness of their own grim, goaty land, be it Sicily or Sardinia. What was this – bordello or zoo? The Berlin Zoo was near enough; that was about all they could afford.

Did one go out to eat or to be eaten by these female piranha fish? It was most confusing, never was it like that in old Sardinia.

The giggling girls were asking a real brute to get his kit off and join them for a good splash, to get his appetite up. There he was drawing down his trousers and the nudes were clapping. It was a riot of fun.

The *Gastarbeiters* slouched off into the night. They had seen enough. They would order a beer in the Augsburger Keller under the arches of Bahnhof Zoo and return to their compound. They could not stay up all night like these sex fiends cavorting around the pool.

– 40 –

Sommerspiele:
September 1972 in Munich

Red of anther, hush of autumn, tread of panther.

Nothing upsets Bavarians more than the Föhn, a devious Italian wind that slips in over the Alps and whistles through the Brenner, whispering Latin things into German ears. Possibly repeating what Court Ciano had told *Il Duce*: that Germans were dangerous because they dreamed collectively.

Be that as it may, when the Föhn blows, surgeons lay down their knives and publishers' readers cast aside typescripts, both knowing their judgement to be impaired. Remote objects, such as church spires, draw closer. The good citizens of Munich – where I happened to find myself in the Black September of 1972 – like nothing better than to sit for hours on window-seats or out on small balconies, staring into the street below, observing life passing.

In Jakob-Klar-Strasse in Schwabing the retired boxer takes up his position early, and is there all day, fortified by mugs of *Bier* handed out to him by an unseen *Frau*, become just a brawny arm.

A positively Latin feeling for blueness prevails. *Lividus* bleached out to the delicate washed-out blue of the Bavarian sky over the Englische Garten, also in the watery eyes of the citizens, in the flag fluttering in a breeze, on Volksbier labels. It's München blue.

Ciao! the better-educated ones cry out on parting; though in the old-style shops the *Grüss Gotts* ring out right merrily. Misha Galle called, then Volker Schlondorff with his wife Margarete von Trotta, for *Tischtennis*.

From Riem Airport into the city the way was festively prepared with huge Olympic flags. My taxi was driven by a woman. I offered Prinzregentenstrasse Fünf as my address, a Freudian slip if ever there was one, and was driven smartly up to Adolf Hitler's old address. I redirected her to a number in Schwabing. The Isar seemed to be flowing the wrong way – a disturbing hallucination.

Once again I began losing my bearings on the wrong side of *Der Frie-densengel,* walking my feet off in this city of fine girls and spouting fountains. Greek goddesses with Bavarian thighs, eyes closed against the inevitable, supported on their shoulders heavy pillars pock-marked by bullets fired from afar. The great stone goddesses were protecting the bridges over the Isar, traversed at set intervals by a villainous low-slung black limousine packed with what I assumed were Italian gangsters, who turned out to be Irish government leaders. *Der Friedensengel* balanced precariously on one foot, hopefully extending a palm branch. Across the plinth an activist had squirted in white aerosol LIEBE DEINE TOTEN!

Preparations for the Games had intensified throughout summer, with Police Chief Schreiber's men out in waders cleansing the old Isar of a detergent overflow from a factory. On 28 August the *Süddeutsche Zeitung* reported that sportsmen and politicians were fascinated *(begeistert)* by an opening ceremony without military overtones. Lord Killanin was in control. Aged Avery Brundage had flown in from the United States. The fire, too, had come from afar: Greece. Whether this was a good augury or not, few were willing to predict. The American traveller and cynic Paul Theroux would write later that the Games were of interest because they showed a world war in pantomime.

But something more disturbing than the Föhn (causing double vision) had slipped into Munich with false papers on 4 September when Rory arrived via Air France from West Berlin namely, Al Fatah. Their target: the Olympic Village. More particularly, Israeli coaches and weight-lifters, the heavy innocents stall-fed on milk and T-bone steaks, who were soon to lay down their lives in the German slaughterhouse prepared for them.

Cauldron of Blood was running at the Outpost Cinema for occupying troops whose regimental motto had a threatening ring to it: 'Have Guns Will Travel'. And fuck syntax.

As bubonic plague, the Black Death, entered Europe as a flea on the body of a rat, so lethal international terrorism, late twentieth-century style, entered Germany from the Middle East in the person of Muhammad Daoud Odeh (code-name Abu Daoud), probably travelling on a forged Iraqi passport. He was to remain there, undetected by the police chief Schreiber, throughout the impossible ultimatums – the terrorists tell German officials that more than 200 Palestinian prisoners in Israeli jails must be released by 0900 or all the hostages will die. Arab intermediaries helped to arrange a further extension until 1300. New deadlines were extended to 1500 and 1700. Regard the carnage that followed, the self-immolation, the capture of three terrorists at Fürstenfeldbruck military airport.

It was Föhn weather, Sharpeville weather, the girls out in summer clothes one day, scarves and coats the next. Police and ambulance sirens never stopped in Luitpoldstrasse, the dogs barking after the fox has gone. In a mossy fountain, somewhat magnified in the water, small white eggshells broken in halves seemed to tremble. Shabby men were reading discarded newspapers in a public park protected by high hedges. Trams clanged around the steep corner at Max-Planck-Strasse, clinging to the wall.

The black limousine was back now, strangely flying the Irish colours on bonnet pennants, with CD registration plates, still traversing old Munich. The Irish Tao-iseach, Jack Lynch, was conferring with Willy Brandt in the country. Buttercups grew along the grass verge on Thomas-Mann-Allee. A woman wearing leather gloves was gathering red berries. Near the Englische Garten two sailors asked the way to the archery contest, one of them drawing an imaginary bow. Men in shirtsleeves were out. I walked by the embankments, saw the skyline drawn and painted by Klee and Grosz; two brown beauties in bikinis were sunning themselves near the weir where terns were wading. It was a lovely September day.

Two workmen in blue denim overalls sat silently at a table on which were arranged some empty beer bottles with the remains of their lunch, under trees buffeted by the wind; a most peaceful scene, one would suppose. But on Luitpoldstrasse, leading to and from the Olympic Village, sirens never stopped wailing; it was difficult to distinguish police from ambulances; destination lock-up, hospital or morgue. The call was for law and order; but what is that but disorder with the lid clamped down?

Why was an Irish Embassy car packed with Italian gangsters? Riddles. One handsome terrorist declared that he would have preferred death with his comrades who had blown up victims and themselves with hand grenades flung into the helicopter.

A sombre choral work, then, to be expected in Munich. A style of killing had been set by terrorists who looked more like movie actors than political activists, acted and spoke like them too, in German and broken English, chain-smoking.

The leaves were turning when the killing began. In shop windows now the signs read HALLO HERBST! DU WIRST CHIC. The yellow press yelled MORDOR-GIE! The headlines screamed MORDFEST! *The Times* put it more diplomatically, more Britishly: 'Storm grows over what went wrong at Munich.' *Der Spiegel* of 11 September stated bluntly: DAS MASSAKER VON MÜNCHEN!

'The XXth Olympic Games resumed yesterday after a 24-hour suspension while Munich mourned the eleven members of the Israeli team who died at the hands of Arab guerrillas.' The sexy songbird, Mireille Mathieu, was driven around the marathon *Sporthalle,* standing in a white open-top Ford Capri, belting out *'Ein Platz an der Sonne fur jung und alt'.* Pope Paul VI, not to be outdone in outrageousness, was photographed in Venice standing precariously upright in what was described as *eine Prunkgondel,* solemnly blessing some Venetian sewage, a clotting of flowers and scum. To the rear of the precarious vessel stood what appeared to be Roman centurions.

The Schwabing flat had been cleaned and the rugs had their colours renewed. Framed on the walls were strange tortured viscerae, possibly human, in monochrome. A single flower, richly red damask, with streaks of sunflower yellow at its heart, hung in a small blue vase. Red of anther, hush of autumn, tread of panther.

We went swimming in Starnberger See – my Munich friend Erika, her boyfriend Wolfgang, and Rory. Out there in the blue, insane Ludwig had drowned with his physician. The wooded hills rolled away. On Saturday, the *Süddeutsche Zeitung* obituary notices face pages of movie advertising of an unrestrained lewdness. Marie Garibaldi was showing her all in *Amore Nudo*. *'MEIN TREUER LEBENSKAMERAD',* the obituary notice declared with melancholy certitude. The dead could no longer cavort with the lovely Marie Garibaldi. Hitachi advertised, 'I am you', with Oriental guile. It was time for MacBaren's Golden Blend. It was time for *Volksbier.*

Müller, the player with two left feet, had scored again, and was being ardently embraced by his captain Beckenbauer. *Tip-Kick Fussball* brings competitive fever *(Wettkampfstimmung)* into the home. A modern German family was shown in the throes of 'Tip-Kicking'. Charles Bronson was appearing in *Brutale Stadt,* Jerry Lewis elsewhere, a black detective appeared in *Shaft ('Der Absolute Super-Krimi!')*. The girls of the GDR ran away with all the track and field events; a splendid example of specialised breeding and expert coaching achieving good results within three decades. An exhibition of early Bavarian folk art was showing at the Staatliches Museum.

Germans togged out for golf are indeed a sight to behold. They go in for overkill, armed with *Golfschläger,* but cannot laugh at themselves, unlike the English, who do it tolerantly all the time. Nor can they endure their own Germanic incompetence. A game without visible opponents disturbs; and at golf you are your own opponent, even in matchplay. How the Germans suffer! They *detest* losing. By the eighteenth hole, none are on speaking terms.

I played with the Wittys and their elderly female friend on a woody links in the Bavarian Alps above Chiemsee. The lake itself was invisible below in the haze. I spent most of the round searching for lost balls among trees; the lovely Hannelore (another Hannelore!) flushed and peeved, saying 'Shit! Shit!' between clenched teeth. Back to Munich by train with two ancient, leathery-faced, well-preserved mountain hikers, man and wife in deerstalker and *Loden*. A relief to be off the *Golfplatz*. Watch them tearing up the rough, cursing blind. It is a game unsuited to their temperament. Back in Munich again, Rory was passing *Oktoberfest* tents and stalls being erected.

Prone to a certain kind of spiritual narcosis with which the entire race is afflicted, and more so than most races, the Germans must *suffer* themselves. Your average Bavarian is a baleful mixture of sentimentalist and brute. Herr Martin Kruger (long absent) had his trouser legs shortened by a Herr von Bismarck, Munich tailor, who asked him on which side he wore his shame.

It sounded grosser in German. Intemperance, fist-fights, puking, in those lovely Ember Days. Stay clean. Tripper and Raptus were on the rampage. Dominguin had been badly gored at Bayonne; the *carneada is* always the fault of the *torero*. Nature abhors a vacuum. *Neu! Ajax mit der doppelbleiche.*

Chelpolizist Schreiber negotiated with a terrorist whose head was covered with a woman's stocking. Itchy-fingered *Sturmkommandos* were dressed like frogmen in athletic tracksuits; they watched privily from their hiding places. *Omnipotenz, Super-Helden!*

The aneroid temperature registered somewhere between *veränderlichkeit* and *verstörung,* or something between distraction and bewilderment. The cover of *Der Stern* displayed a corn-yellow blonde in the act of peeling off a corn-yellow T-shirt, her only article of clothing; stamped most poshlustily on her backside were the joined circles of the Olympic symbol.

Clouds drift over the roofs of Munich; a blue evening falls. The ex-boxer points down into darkening Jakob-Klar-Strasse, amused by something he has seen below. There are moments when I am able to look without any effort through the whole of creation *(Schöpfung),* which is nothing more than an immense exhaustion *(Erschöpfung),* wrote stout Thomas Bernhardt. *Schicksal* all too soon becomes *Schnicksal,* in Germany at least.

Gusty *stürmisch* wind-tossed weather; then a warm sunny day in Munich. The face on the screen, on high hoardings, walks the streets, the violence is let loose. Hands were constantly feeling and touching, groping and tapping. Fingers parted the long hair of a troubled Jesus-double, touched noses, brows, the bearded lips rarely smiled, the looks exchanged were severe or merely sullen. Hands were never for one moment still, compulsively pulling and picking; plucking at the backs of leather seats, tearing paper, agitated, never still, the eyes restless as monkeys in the zoo.

In the capitals of the West the same feature films were released simultaneously: *Little Pig-Man* [*sic*], *My Name is Nobady* [*sic*]. *LIEBE* was sprayed indiscriminately over walls. *Amerika Haus* was riddled with bullets. The riot squads sat in paddy-wagons behind wire mesh and bulletproof glass, parked in back streets near universities, out of sight, played cards, bided their time.

A judas grille opened and a baleful eye observed us. In the heated bar the tall lovely unsober teacher Barbara König was swallowing ice cubes, pulling faces, charming the pants off Rory.

Ach ach; tich-tich. We cannot stop even if we want to, have become voyeurs watching atrocious acts. The lies are without end because the hypotheses are without end. It has become suspect to 'think'; all adults occupy the thrilling realm of moral dilemmas (civic inertia), political drama; *Strassentheater.* Dangerous blindness with a dash of singularity. Angels, for the man who cannot avoid thinking about them, wrote the pessimist Cioran, certainly exist. *So sitzt es mir im Gemüt.*

On the large screens of colour TV sets in the windows of banks the Olympic Games went on, in silence, in triplicate. The high pole-vaulter in the briefest of shorts lifted herself on unseen springs, collapsing in slow motion on to a large bolster. The GDR female athletes were pouring over the 100-metre hurdles, elegant as bolting deer fleeing a forest fire. From the rapt, tormented expression of the long-legged high-jumper, one knew that track records were now being broken in the head. The athletes on the podium were crowned with bay, gave clench-fisted salutes as their national flag flew on the mast.

*   *   *

In West Berlin at midnight, in the small white flat of a pregnant Hannelore (the *real* Hannelore), the phone rang, the ringing tone muted. A hidden voice, a Basque voice (not a Berlin accent) whispered into her ear: '*Es wird noch kommen!*' It vill come . . . It still vill come. Out in the Olympic village the twenty-five hostages were still alive. The ultimatum was that one would be killed every two hours, beginning at 15 *Uhr* – 3 p.m. Central European Time.

On Kurfürstendamm, advertising an empty cinema, two enormous Sapphic heads regard each other steadfastly with frantic blue-tinged eyeballs across an illuminated movie façade. Something funny is going on between those two. On high hoardings opposite Marga Schoeller's bookshop, the braced bodies of huge nude females proclaim a stressful poshlust, *luxuriante.* A nude female crawls into a tent, hotly pursued by a nude male on all fours. Above the murderous traffic that runs all night, a cut-out of the slain actress Sharon Tate looks over her shoulder at the human clotting below, as into a temporary camp in a jungle clearing. Pigs! her murderers had scrawled on the Polanski door: Manson's tribe. Disordered thoughts, *Chaos oder Anarchie* in the here and now. Karl Kraus had defined German girls: 'Long legs, obedience'; not any more.

All strove for a dissipated appearance; many achieved it. Sunglasses were worn indoors, even in ill-lit bars in the depths of winter. Insane seers and mad putative leaders sprang up, were applauded, discussed, shot down, wiped from the scene. Graffiti abounded. The young revolutionaries sprayed aerosol everywhere. ANARKI ELLER KAOS!, as though the terms were not synonymous. The garbled message hardly varied. In the La Rouche district of Paris it ran: LIBEREZ HESS!

An underground disco pulses redly: the Mouth of Hell. The pace is set for hedonism, gluttony, the here and now. Frantic with betrayal, two inverts copulate near the Spree in the headlights of a parked car, in the falling snow. The woodcock, wily bird, is said to dress its own wounds. Partridges sleep with one eye open. The Chinese, more observant than most, maintain that the rat changes into a quail, the quail into an oriole. The female muskrat, as everybody knows, is the mother of the entire human race. That is, unless I am thinking of the Umquat's Sedna. Muskrats are barren when born in captivity; if they breed, they devour their young. A young Munich veterinario blamed stress induced by crowded conditions. Or, more likely, the fact of being under constant human observation.

In West Berlin (population 2.2 million) every second citizen is over forty years; more than twenty-five percent are over sixty-five. Thirty-nine thousand die each year, with thirteen thousand more dying than are being born; every third citizen owns a dog.

Frau Meinhardt likes to curry-comb her two Airedales on the balcony, and curly orange hair floated into our morning coffee. She drove to Malta in a green Karmann Ghia, a nice change of air for the nervous bitches, mother Anya and whelp, a classical allusion. There was no shade in Malta; it was bad for the dogs.

She, the war widow, never referred to her late husband; the fine house in Niko-lassee was all that remained of that lost life. The old heart of the city was dead – Unter den Linden. She owned a house in Wiesbaden, let out the Berlin property; demonstrated how to work the vacuum cleaner, a *Walküre* model, adding on tubular parts and a rigid snout. When devouring dirt, the bag swelled, set up a strident whine, began snarling, all snout and stomach. A true German machine.

Tall beauties paraded on Kurfürstendamm, displaying themselves in tight stone-washed jeans, which advertised a worn but not yet threadbare look; that was the fashion. Their manner implied: 'We belong to the streets'; and by analogy – false – 'The streets belong to us'. *Strassentheater.*

Freedom marches followed protest marches, the squatters occupying empty buildings. They were untouchable, in a way. They, too, were in the dream, living the dream. They occupied the streets, seemingly at home there, some living a hand-to-mouth existence, squatting before lines of trinkets, the twisted metalwork. Wearing sandals like gurus and holy men, or going about barefoot; footloose as Rastafarians, Reb stragglers from the American Civil War, fuzzy-wuzzies from Abyssinia, Tibetan monks with shaven polls. The females were even more lightly dressed, as though in perpetual summer (*'La naturale temperature des femmes'* whispers Amyot in a sly Gallic aside, *'est fort humide'*), their extremists more dangerous than the males. Baader-Meinhoff. In West Berlin the Black Cells, the Anarchists, went among the passive resisters like hyenas among zebra.

Insistence on the unique and particular had spawned the microbe Duplication. The face on the screen was in the street. The violence there was let loose here, in the open, the dream gone mad. They were actors and actresses playing bit parts in a continuing series. The face on the hoardings walked the streets. The Individual as such was disappearing, had disappeared; remained in a disordered milieu grown ever grubbier, more dangerous by the minute. The world's capitals had become *pissoirs*.

On the summer evenings, in Málaga and Athens, Copenhagen and Munich, long cinema queues waited to watch a violent surrogate existence run on huge screens, the sound monstrously distorted. 'To learn is to have something done to one.' But why bother about Bach if a saxophone riff gives you some idea of eternity? Their own life had ceased to interest them. Huge hoardings displayed a Red Indian brave naked from the waist up, advertising a brand of shampoo. Rock cellars throbbed, their lurid entrances leading down into an inflamed red throat, out of which screeched and bellowed the *Schlagermusik*. *Schlagermusik* in *Luftwaffe* slang was the staccato rip of machine-gun bullets tearing at the underbelly of a Lancaster or Wellington bomber bound for Berlin.

Hungarian camomile, asafoetida gum, aeroplane grease, cola nuts, Syrian rue, fly agaric, horsetail, skullcap, yohimbine, these were popular. In Absurdia the poor drank the urine of the rich to get their 'high'. Informed heads, *Tagräumer*, trippers, might tell of the so-called Jackson Illusion Pepper, with a hole bored at one end and a cigarette at the other end through which the entire contraption might be smoked to provide colourful and elaborate hallucinations.

Road hippies on endless round trips sold their blood to Kuwait; took overdoses, observed the 'way out' regions inhabited by the teeming poor of the miserable Third World. Lost ones blew their brains out. A huge organ was playing at noon in a department store heavy with controlled artificial air. Shoppers, passive as fish, stunned by pumped Muzak, ascend and descend by escalators. Overpriced commodities were sold by ingenious advertising campaigns in an all-out psychological war not on want but on plenty. Everything was oversold, overstated, overheated; fraternity too had gone to Hell. The cities were splitting up from within, supermarts and car parks replacing cathedrals and concert halls. On fine summer evenings the long cinema queues waited silently in the north. To flee the world and dream the past was their intent; a sourceless craving now externalised, brought close. For them it would always be *Sperrmüll-Tag:* Throwing-Out Day. Say rather, Throwing-Up Day.

Alcoholic professors taught their own version of history. The students were apprehensive about leaving the campus. In the surrounding woods maniacs prowled all night, whistling. The young kept to their dormitories, debated much on their 'development', always making schemes. Schedules were drawn up, considered, amended, then abandoned. Believing that life goes in steps, exclusively concerned with drugs of one sort or another, hard politics, India-Buddha teachings, claptrap about 'freedom', their future was grim. But the protesters went marching anyway. They were lost in the dream. Their own parents belonged to an irrecoverable past.

On which side do you wear your shame?

Faina Melnik in athletic hot pants was displaying the Popo look, said to have been imported from Japan. The discus was thrown an unlikely distance by an unlikely-looking female. The huge Israeli weight-lifters were all dead, blown to kingdom come. The Games had gone on. The so-called Day of Mourning had been nothing less than hypocrisy; too much money was invested, too many interests involved; national honour had been at stake. The word had come down that the terrorists were not to leave German soil with their victims. The terrorists themselves had shown less hypocrisy; they were not interested in deals or (even) human life. The *Rheinischer Merkur* had its *Mordorgie*. 'Aroused Prussia' was a lard factory, a *mortadella* mincing machine.

RUSS MAY BEEF UP NAVY IN MED spoke out the *New York Herald Tribune*. BODIES OF SLAIN ATHLETES REACH LODZ, FLOWN FROM MUNICH (America Speaking). Lodz Airport, soon to receive its own baptism of fire from Japanese kamikaze terrorists. *Falsche Spekulation der Luftpiraten!* Art, 'progress' (towards what?) comes from weaponry, hot from the kitchen. The arms of the footsoldiers, peasant conscripts, were no different in kind from their primitive work tools. Art and progress came with the finely decorated swords and pistols and tooled leather-ware of their mounted officers. Horses for courses.

Der Bomber (Müller) scores again.

In the Neue Nationalgalerie in West Berlin hang two paintings commemorating the student uprising of 1968 in Paris: Renato Guttuso's *Studentenumzug mit Fahnen* and *Barrikaden in Paris*. To the sad cliché of the street barricade, the hero with flag unfurled, the brave corpses, must now be added the Faceless Male Terrorist in Female Bodystocking.

Leni Riefenstahl's extraordinary *Fest der Völker* was showing at the Arri (8 Woche). The XIth Olympiad at Berlin in 1936. In the old recruiting documentary, the plumes of smoke swirling densely black around the imperial eagle might have come from Hell itself. Wagner shows me a world that I'm not sure I would wish to enter.

Hermann Goering, the cocaine addict, grossly corpulent, was shaken with helpless laughter. Hitler, leaning forward, rubbed together his cold political hands. Hess, his putative son, all eye-socket and jaw of Teutonic Tollund Man watched Jesse Owens (assuredly no Aryan) run away with all the track events. A cinema full of war widows watched in an uncanny silence. You could hear a pin drop, the projector's whirr, the collective indrawn breath, suspense building for what would come next. What was one to make of the spider in the web, before the credits rolled, and the scalped athletes running stark naked around a Berlin lake, maybe Schlachtersee, through an early morning mist? No symbols where none intended.

Misha Gallé had been permitted an interview when Leni Riefenstahl, who was still a handsome woman, had learnt that Misha's father had been a Nazi judge. She told Misha Gallé that Herr Hitler had been a good man 'led astray by bad companions', The homosexual Röhm? The war widows, all dispersing silently from the Arri, had set their mouths in grim lines and, separating for *Kaffee und Kuchen,* baring their gums, were offering no comments.

Two months later a Lufthansa flight into Munich was hijacked and the three terrorists sprung from three high-security prisons sixty miles apart. Brandt had been obliged to do a deal, otherwise more terrorists were coming back. When interviewed, they chain-smoked, spoke in broken English and were reported to be of 'terrifying' niceness. They had the rugged good looks of Eddie Constantine and justified their actions at length. Deals had been struck; Brandt's hands were tied. Somewhere in the world ravishing girls eagerly awaited their safe return.

In February 1973, Abu Daoud, now passing himself off as a Saudi sheikh, was arrested in central Amman by a Jordanian security patrol. His 'wife' was a fifteen-year-old girl carrying a handgun and ammunition clips, which, on being arrested, she dropped. Abu Daoud's forged passport showed him to be the father of six children. His own father worked in Jerusalem as a labourer for the Israeli City Council.

On the last day of the XXth Olympiad, all the shops were closed and Rory walked through the Schwabing's deserted streets. It was a dead day. Misha

Gallé played *Tischtennis* with Wolfgang. On the huge Olympic board the last farewells; AVERY BRANDAGE [*sick & stet*] for all the world to see. Twenty *Grad* of *Bodenfrost* on 28 September. *Das Ende der Saison.*

Meanwhile the super-rat, immune to all poisons, had arrived unannounced in Rio. Six dead. Abu Daoud, where are you now?

— 41 —

One Thrust and He Was In

One sunny late September or early October day in the fall not long after the *Mordfest*, Rory went walking in the Bavarian Alps with Karen Reece, who translated porno novels from German into English for the Munich branch of the Olympia Press. Erika had departed into Tuscany for a vacation and Rory had a notion to proposition her good friend Karen, a dark-haired beauty who lived in Schwabing not far away from Erika's flat where Rory stayed. Karen had helped him post off eighteen large packages for the University of Victoria in British Columbia: the drafts, notebooks and final typescripts of *Balcony of Europe,* a broken-backed novel he had been working on for eight years and which was now finished, awaiting cutting and editing by John Calder in London.

They had chilled beer in a *Bierstube* and walked up a logging trail, smoking joints and talking of this and that. It was a lovely warm sunny day in Bavaria and lines of tall fir trees blocked out every horizon.

'It's not fair,' Karen Reece said; we were smoking joints far up the logging trail. 'You talked all day. I never got one word in.'

It was the marijuana talking; it made Rory (normally taciturn) garrulous. One thing reminded him of another thing, and so on and so forth. She was a lovely lady, it was a lovely day in Bavaria; the swallows flew low.

Even before he had kissed her, Rory was consumed with jealousy of her former never-seen loves. They came down to a cove by a river in the cool of the evening and stopped in another *Bierstube* before driving back to Schwabing. With some little persuasion Rory was permitted to spend the night with Karen, who drove as recklessly as Erika, one arm out the window.

Later I heard from Erika that Karen had returned to the States, not to her husband, but to join some religious sect; that was the last I heard of her. She was the one who got away, the lost love, the silver trout that escapes the gaff.

Her apartment was also a replica of her friend's in Destouchestrasse, down to the furniture and fitments. Karen was very neat and collected; the only messy thing about her being the fact that she had married an American called Dick Reece and the marriage hadn't worked.

She retired to the bathroom to prepare herself for Rory and bed. On a cleared table stood a large manual office typewriter. In it a sheet of typing paper. She had stopped (to go out with Rory to the post office) working with one line neatly, barefacedly typed on the top line of an otherwise blank page. With eyes narrowed and heart thumping in his chest as though rummaging and examining the variety of her underwear in cupboard or closet, Rory read, aghast: 'One thrust and he was in.'

Rory sprang back as though stung by a bee as Karen emerged from the bathroom looking positively radiant in a silvery shivery robe. Rory, ever the perfect gent, asked permission to use the toilet.

'*Natürlich.*'

When Rory came out of the bathroom, the page was gone from the manual and Karen was in bed, still in her robe. Rory undressed himself and got into bed with her. Rory removed her robe and proceeded to fondle and kiss her.

But that, sad to say, was the end of his progress into uninhibited night-time Schwabing *Liebe* with a lovely and compliant youngish *Frau* with a thick dark bush and complementary herbiage in her armpits. For Rory couldn't make love for all the tea in China, cuckolded by a ghost who had slipped between the blue sheets and, before Rory could well bestir himself, the heavy gross intruder without even an '*Entschuldigung bitte!*' had pushed him aside and boldly mounted.

'If you can't, it doesn't matter . . . just lie by me,' she whispered. Karen Reece was most accommodating. One thrust . . . oh sting-a-ling of salt-lick pan! Oh *pachanga!* Oh peaches and cream! Oh, Lord Rochester!

Meanwhile, hidden amongst the books, the most torrid lovemaking or rather free-for-all fucking went on apace in the most boggish vernacular German imaginable, in the porno novel that Karen had discreetly put away along with the shameful almost blank last page, the page she had reached in her valiant efforts at translating grunts from German into vernacular English. Almost but not quite so; like a venomous smelly jet of spit from a yak, spat stingingly right into the eye of the beholder peering through the bars of the cage at the yaks grazing in their compound.

The unseen former lovers of Karen, a numerous company of accomplished lechers, were clustered around the bed, making most offensive remarks in guttural German concerning the upstart *Engländer* who couldn't get it up.

In the morning Rory tried again, with no better result. He resigned himself to being just a good *Freund.* That would have to do.

PART V:

Danish Blue

Copenhagen in the mid-1970s

− 42 −

On the Rørvig Ferry

Sunday evening
6 July 1975
Copenhagen

My dearest,

Copenhagen is very hot in this weeks. Steffen has taken care of Petrushka all the weekend, I needed very much to be alone, have been busy with idiotic things the last weeks, everything at home was one Big Mess, not a clean plate, nothing clean cloth. I've been in one of my eternal recomming depression periods, when it is extra difficult to pretend effectiv – I'm far-off, cannot get out of my own figment imagination, the same themes turn and grow and change but are still the same, a kaleidscope of inner confusion. Now I am through the outside mess and have used the rest of the weekend to try to make fair copy of bewildered notes during the week and it became definitely bad: a row of high flown inexact words, neither prose nor poetry, without genuine sensations, a row of old fashioned assertions which do not hit. I am very depressed. If I never learn to write properly I cannot nothing in this world. I am clever to nothing, nothing at all. It is all approats, giving up, making dreams, useless dreams, hoping a little again . . .

I complain. I promised myself never to complain to you and especialy not about this matter. Now I have done. Now I have been a native woman thrown out of white man's tent because of bad manners.

In a way I remember you so well. Your brightness. Is anything called that? I can't stand to use the dictionary all the time. My only force is to make guess, hope they fit somebody, something. Thinking things over they disappear to me. Intellectual thing at least. They must come as a cut or they vanish as you say. You give me new words, too, I could fall in love in english. Sometimes I'm going to do. When I'm thinking over feelings they don't vanish. Oppersite, they crows. Because you don't think feelings, I guess. How can I live my life? Who is paying for dreams? Why do I need food? Why do I need things? (that damned things). Why do I not live on a greek island? Why is the world so sluggish a material? Down again:

Why can't I make it light?

I am ashame to complain. Will do it again and again. Tell me to shut up.

10/7: You say nothing about I Ching? Nonsense for you? (Old stuff hanging over Anna's head). Steffen always laugh when I absorbed (dictionary) of that kind of matter. But contempt me too, think it is a complicated and childish 'stage-setting' (dictionary) or rather depriving (dictionary) of an obvious reality, understandable for a child of five. Same Steffen get me to laugh so heartily and painfull (in danish: *hjertaligt og smerteligt,* a thorough-fucked-wordpair) the other day when he said; when you feel your thoughts to collect to complaint then beat your head into the wall. I'm beating my head into the wall now. Again. Oh I miss you. Again. Forgive me my love that I miss you so much. Just red your mad letter again, long parts without rest, I think I mean stop, pause, long breath, fading out and starting again, long breath from a love which wants to empty both body and mind. How can you write like that, how can you do it against us, how can you make me suffering that much? Sometimes I'm catched by a great anger to you, to demand, no to give the feeling of present but still you are not here, to prevent me to live here by keeping me there, I am longing and prevented, I am kept in imagination and must drown myself in home-made wine and over-excitement, sometimes I'm catched by a great anger to you. Then it disappears and I must laugh to myself.

[unsigned]

– 43 –

Rørvig

Petrushka and I go to Rørvig about every second weekend. First we take a normal inter-city train, then a little provincial train to Hundested (meaning Place of Dogs) (??) which is a little harbour town on the coast of northzeeland. To get out of the train in Hundested is every time a lovely surprise, the air is clear, the sea as always, the harbour modest.

Then we take a ferry, clumsy as a clog, to Rørvig. I always feel cruising among the Greek islands. Petrushka talks. She always does. In Rørvig my parents are waiting. They are glad to see me, I am glad to see them, Petrushka is very glad. The journey takes a little more than two hours.

We walk home (10 minutes) to the little summerhouse, about forty years old, dark trees, window-boxes even if we are in the middle of nature. ('Im Freien' lovely piano pieces by Bartók.) Rørvig is a holiday center, lovely nature, victims little butter-hole, the innocence's last chanal to a little reality, a little plants, a little owner-feeling. Very much like my parents are, very well-selected. The beatch still has its wildness, is very beautiful and pure. I use the weekend to wash and iron, wash hair, talk with my parents, sleep, cut the grass for my father, go to the beatch with Petrushka on my father's old high bike (why bar on gentleman-bikes?), look at television in the evening, go for walks with Petrushka and drink a beer at the inn (which is placed by the main road). My parents would die by annoyance because of the extra money, one could drink that beer at home in the garden . . . well, they don't see the pleasure in a polished pub-glass and a perfect temperature of beer and the easiness of being in a public place out of the home, the sacrosant home. I talked very much with my parents, never lie to them, tell them 'everything' but edit my reality.

[unsigned]

– 44 –

The Ancient Moats

'Every day in Denmark is different' is a roundabout, not to say tortuous and evasive, way of admitting that one was once infatuated with an enchanting Danish siren.

Or, put another way, 'In the woman who overwhelms us there must be nothing familiar'; a *mot* wrested from a James Salter novel. (Giacomo Meyerbeer frantically attacking the piano keys while Franz Liszt looks helplessly on.)

International airport lounge waiting time, bad-air airborne time, agenbite-of-inwit time, nail-chewing time, doctor's surgery time, railway station time – none of these strange times can be said to be normal time as we know it, in the boredom of living, but time as torture, atrociously stretched to infinity, as if with chewing gum or potent industrial glue, a fixative to fix for good and all.

So too with infatuation time, the most intolerably stretched-out time of all, when you venture with a new inamorata into a new love, into strange terrain; which generally involves *more* airport-waiting, *more* waiting at railway stations and nail-biting and may even involve more of the doctor's surgery. Duration is prolonged and takes on a new keenness when one is subjected to this anxiety, this perplexity. First love, then the *Pharmacia*.

In August 1851 the hirsute gentleman farmer Herman Melville in his newly acquired house (secured on a loan from his father-in-law) near Pittsfield in the Berkshire Hills of west Massachusetts had completed *Moby-Dick, or The Whale,* full of scattered last-minute revisions.

In London in the autumn of 1889 the thirty-one-year-old Joseph Conrad (born Konrad Korzeniowski in the Ukraine) lived in furnished rooms in Bessborough Gardens on the north bank of the Thames near Vauxhall Bridge, where he was putting together the component parts of his first novel, *Almayer's Folly.*

When the landlady's daughter had cleared away his breakfast things, Conrad noted in his diary the ever-changing colour of the sky over the Surrey docks, where Callus would later moor his canal barge. Conrad wrote:

> Opaline atmosphere, a veiled semi-opaque lustrous day, with fiery points
> of flashes of red sunlight on the roofs and windows opposite.

In Marseilles Conrad had become apprenticed to the Merchant Marine; had he strode up the gangplank of a French boat instead of an English vessel he might have written his novels in French, and English letters would have been the less for it. He certainly had no high opinion of *Moby-Dick* and declined to introduce a World's Classics edition. 'It struck me as a rather strained rhapsody with whaling for a subject and not a single sincere line in the three vols. of it,' he wrote testily to Sir Humphrey Milford.

Galsworthy of Conrad: 'The first mate is a Pole called Conrad and is a capital chap, though queer to look at.' Who was it described Conrad as 'a certain Pole with a wild look under the skin of his face'? Was it joker Joyce?

Conrad had a poor opinion of people, that was his way.

> I sit down for eight hours every day – and the sitting down is all. In the course
> of that working day I write three sentences which I erase before leaving the
> table in despair ... In the morning I get up with the horror of that powerless-
> ness I must face through a day of vain efforts.

> (from a letter to Edward Garnett)

'Words blow away like mist, and like mist they serve only to obscure; they make vague the real shape of one's feelings.'

Conrad must have thought this in Polish, if not French, written out as a precautionary adage to himself in English. Are not our feelings shapeless, sometimes shameless, uncontrollable, not ours at all? In Berlin in March 1930 Cyril Connolly wrote:

> In this stillness I wait for the first sound. In this blackness I wait for the first image – a cough, a motor-horn, the scratching of the dog's leash on the floor. Doors banging in another house, in another country, *Sète*. The dog fidgeting; the wind rising; the image forming. *Sète* at midnight on the way to Spain. The sleepy ride to a hotel near water. *(The Condemned Playground)* The Fascist Curzio Malaparte wrote in Italian The Volga Rises in Europe: another evening we dined by the water in Potsdam. A hot and beautiful night; we had a table by the trees on the edge of the lake . . . The candles lit up the polished table, the dark glow of port, the lighter one of brandy in our glasses. The night-air smelt of lake-water and of smoke from our cigars.

In a collection of essays published as *Myself With Others* (1988), the vain Carlos Fuentes wrote in Spanish:

> It was a hot, calm evening on Lake Zurich, and some wealthy Mexican friends had invited me to dinner at the eleagant Baur-au-Lac Hotel. The summer restaurant was a floating terrace on the lake. You reached it by a gangplank, and it was lighted by paper lanterns and flickering candles. As I unfolded my stiff white napkin amid the soothing tinkle of silver and glass, I raised my eyes and saw the group dining at the next table.

(Three ladies are seated with a man in his seventies whom Señor Fuentes recognises as Thomas Mann.)

> This man was stiff and elegantly dressed in a double-breasted white serge suit and immaculate shirt and tie. His long, delicate fingers sliced a cold pheasant, almost with daintiness. Yet even in eating he seemed to me unbending, with a ramrod-back, military bearing . . .
>
> I left Thomas Mann sipping his demitasse as midnight approached and the floating restaurant bobbed slightly and the Chinese lanterns quietly flickered out.

Well, in Denmark every day *is* different. You must take Anna's word for it; she was born in Copenhagen, married a Dane who wrote Dada-type short plays and she had a child by him. They lived in a coal-hole infested with rats some years before she met me.

She had changed her name from Olsen to Reiner when she began publishing poetry. When I knew her, she had a rented flat on Østersøgade overlooking what she called 'the ancient moats'. We were separated for four years and during that time she visited Greece.

During that time her sister had also committed suicide by throwing herself from a high place.

Anna ('my' Anne) was standing at the window of her apartment, a sort of attic on the third or topmost floor overlooking the artificial lake, no doubt thinking her own sad thoughts ('Mad of unhappiness') 'glaring out' (she wrote to me) at the ancient moats, as she had stood and looked ('glared') so many times before, at the scene she knew so well, when her sister was alive, that had now changed radically and become another scene in another time; or else something had changed within herself.

She had seen all there was to be seen, when the clouds parted and a sudden spurt of sunlight poured down on a golden church dome which she had never seen before. She was trying not to think of her sister's hard end, how she had flung herself from a high place down to a sudden and terrible death. Most terrible for those who had to clean up. Anna had come 'like a thief in the night' to her parents with the news that she had to break as gently as possible. Her sister had been a Pisces.

I had flown from Seattle to Heathrow where there was an eight-hour delay before the flight to Kastrup, and from there I had taken a taxi to Østersøgade, and found her apartment empty. I entered an empty flat below and looked at some of the notebooks and it wasn't her handwriting; her apartment was the dark attic at the top of the house. When you were in it, it was all windows with a view of the Østersøgade. Her landlady, Mrs Andersen, was half-mad, certainly unhinged, and wholly uncooperative.

I kept walking about the streets leading to your flat; at ten o'clock I phoned your number and you answered at once. You had just come back from Helsingor, where Hamlet had chased about after the ghost of his murdered father. I booked out of the hotel and took a taxi around and you were waiting at the door.

– 45 –

But Why Kandinsky?

Kandinsky told me that his grandfather had come trotting into Russia on a small steed studded with bells, from one of those enchanted Asian mountains made of porcelain.

Jean Arp, *Kandinsky the Poet* (1912)

People in their local costumes moved about like pictures come to life: their houses were decorated with colourful carvings, and inside on the walls were hung popular prints and icons; furniture and other household objects were painted with large ornamental designs that almost dissolved them into colour. Kandinsky had the impression of moving about inside one of his own pictures.

Will Grohman

As the snail carries its house on its back, so Wassily Kandinsky carried Russia about with him in his heart. By 1909 he had abandoned his legal career in Russia to move to Germany where he lived with the painter Gabriele Münter in a house known as Russenvilla in Murnau. He did not become an art student until he was thirty.

When Kandinsky had left Russia and was living in Germany, looking back he must have seen his lost land as a picture or series of pictures composed and coloured by his own hand; his paintings of Russia, his memories of Russia and he himself a part of the painting, trapped in the paintings. His work shows you that Russia of his childhood in the time of the tsars just before the Revolution; and that dead Russia springs to life again, in the same way that you can hear distinctly an earlier Russia of circus tunes and carnival music and fairground sounds in the work of Stravinsky, in *Firebird* and *Petrushka,* even in simple piano compositions.

You can hear that Russia if you cease thinking of Stravinsky as the experimental modernist of Paris who worked with Nijinsky and Tamara Karsavina for the impresario Diaghilev and composed *Le sacré du printemps* which caused a riot that was the making of Stravinsky. But he was a Russian composer dealing with that folklore before he was anything else. Kandinsky was a superb colourist, as was Paul Klee.

The colours were bleached out in mist and fog. Above the path on the steep slope of the hill among the small olive trees, some animal was struggling in its death throes. It cried out; a sudden screech of terror and then a whole series of gurgles becoming fainter as the predator dug in, dispatching it. It was Monday, 21 April 1980 and 9.30 p.m. in Cómpeta, two-thousand kilometres up in the foothills of the sierras. It seemed to be the killing time.

We rose at nine in the evening, having spent the day in bed 'solacing our existence', as Stendhal has it, and sallied out into a clinging mist that had swallowed up the pueblo.

If it was a scene from a French movie, then she was the Danish actress Anna Karina who appears in the inexplicable and dull movies of Godard; or, better still, Elsa Martinelli dressed in black poncho, brown cords, Hungarian riding-britches, pink cheesecloth shirt with wide leather Russian-style belt, a black high-neck pullover, boots, hair worn long, glistening with mist. I carried a walking stick *and* an umbrella. She (Anna, Nina, Elsa or whatever you care to call her) cried out with delight at the turn of the path by the forge beyond the *cementerio:* 'Uuuuuh, it's a French movie!'

The village had vanished; we were the lost lovers in one of those mysteriously inconclusive French movies by Claude Autant-Lara that seem to lead nowhere.

Well, all women are actresses at heart; I know that, as all men who have mothers know that. Not all women can be Helen, though all women hold Helen in their hearts.

*   *   *

When we walked arm in arm through the Tivoli Gardens late one day in winter, the place was almost deserted. She wore a flannel jacket to the hips and a dashing matelot hat in matching flannel, the clobber which Albertine might have favoured in Danciers. She had strong coarse hands which became delicate when she took something up, a pen or knife or paper or a fruit, as a surgeon's strong hands in protective gloves become delicate when performing some operation successfully. For me she represented the past, a living emanation of that European past, come from the old part of Copenhagen.

We walked through the clinging mist to the Biscuit King's place, the Villa de Chino, to dine there, but found it locked up; and so back down the avenue on to the lower road and past the bus terminus, tall as giraffe or elephant house in the Berlin Zoo, and up the ramp by the concave mirror to help ascending traffic into the plaza and up another ramp and into the Bar el Montes and so to the back room where a long table was set out for the Alcalde's party.

A couple of women with heads close together were gossiping and sipping Schweppes tonic at a table in the window embrasure, which we moved to when they had paid and left. When we sat down we were subjected to a series of hard inquisitive stares from the Alcalde, a bulky man among chatty wom-enfolk; the hard stares from the Alcalde becoming more persistent, as though he couldn't believe his eyes. Two bananas were brought to us on plates and our order taken; whereupon we patiently waited for more than an hour sipping white wine before the food appeared, two cheese omelettes with fries.

It was raining outside, umbrellas passed by the window going towards the *paseo;* we heard the rain pattering on the plaza. We drank not very good white wine, unchilled, and I was as happy there as ever I could be anywhere, stared at by the Alcalde, subjected to that implacable regard whilst listening to your voice telling me what you wished to say. You told me about your small walk-up apartment in Copenhagen on Østersøgade, the lake that was seven-teen feet deep in the middle, and of your unhinged landlady Mrs Andersen. You told of a Russian icon with a bullet hole in it and parts missing, torn from a well during the Russian Revolution; and of a pewter candlestick and a Chinese scroll. You didn't travel about Copenhagen by bus, because of the stinks of the commuters in damp clothes; instead you cycled about on your old trusty bike.

Anna's ex-brother-in-law, the homosexual sea captain, has a flower shop in Copenhagen, where his friends come for beer and arguments. Anna can hold her own there. The apartments of Copenhagen gays are always full of flow-ers. The sea captain throws out roses just past their prime.

She pleads, 'For Hell, do not!' She takes thirty roses on her antiquated bike, cycles to Østersøgade, barely visible behind the bank of sweet-smelling roses.

She spoke a sort of archaic Tudor English with Teutonic roots that evoked valour and escutcheons and banners flying and the neighing of frightened horses in the hairy olden times; and this was so charming to my ears that I never bothered to correct her. She said: 'The cold of hot countries is absolutely poignant.'

She said: 'I never played little girls' games when I was young and that is my unfortune.'

Unfortune!

She said: 'I talk in showers and then I am sad.'

She said: 'The sounds of the south are louder than those of the north.'

She said: 'The Danish forests are so lovely – they are so leetil compared to real forests. Uuuls aff karse. [Owls of course.] All these are leaf-tree forests of a good standard; they are most beautiful, I think. Most *bee*autiful! The Danish forests are full of flowers and birds and underwood [undergrowth] that in the springtime are nothing less than a pure *dreeem*.'

She said: 'You only have to look at nature to see how amazing nature is. Nature lies under God's protection and the Devil has no power there' (quoting the suicide Swede Edith Sodergram).

'Hell is the Devil's Paradise,' I said, quoting Tomi Ungerer.

– 46 –

Borges and I

Borges as a boy in Buenos Aires spent a great deal of time indoors. Little Jorge Luis and his sister Norah invented two imaginary companions, the Windmill and Quilos. 'When they finally bored us, we told our mother they had died.'

One of my own mother's many sisters had lived for most of her life in Buenos Aires, where she and her husband brought up a family. Was that Aunt Ida or Aunt Ada? Rory was unfamiliar with his many relations.

Borges's blindness began to come upon him by 1927, the year I was born, following no fewer than eight eye operations.

One rainy morning in June 1930 Borges met Adolfo Bioy Casares. Between them they invented an imaginary third man Honorio Bustos Domecq who emerged and 'was to take over and rule with a rod of iron'. Between them they created the comic detective saga, *Six Problems for Don Isidro Parodi*.

Borges thought that Copenhagen was among the most unforgettable cities he had seen (with his defective eyesight), along with Santiago de Compestela, Geneva and Edinburgh. Berlin he thought ugly, the ugliest city on earth. He was pro-English, with Northumberland blood on his grandmother's side.

Jorge Guillermo Borges, father of the author, was philosophical anarchist, lawyer, teacher of psychology in the School for Modern Languages. He gave his courses in English and wrote a novel, *The Caudillo*, published in Majorca in 1921, since lost.

> One night in Salto, Uruguay, with Enrique Amorim, for lack of anything better to do, we went around to the local slaughter-house to watch the cattle being killed. Squatting on the threshold of the long low adobe building was a battered and almost lifeless old man. Amorim asked him, 'Are they killing?' The old man appeared to come to a brief and evil awakening, and answered back in a fierce whisper. 'Yes, they're killing! They're killing!'
>
> (J.L. Borges, *Commentary on the Man on the Threshold,* translated from the Spanish by Anthony Kerrigan)

In late May or early June, the swifts return to Kinsale to reoccupy their old nesting places in the eaves opposite the Stony Steps. Clinging with their primitive feet, they launch themselves out and away, hurtling over the roof-tops; their screeching announces the arrival of summer; they are the last to come and the first to go.

Swifts are continually on the wing from the moment they leave the nest. In a lifetime of eighteen years they fly four million miles, to the moon and back eight times. They consume twenty thousand insects daily, travel six thousand miles on their migratory courses. The young are much pestered by bloodsucking woodlice in the nest.

Between Alannah and me, joined in matrimony in a Dublin register office in November 1997, there is a yawning gap of twenty-three years. Twenty-four years separated Dostoevsky and Ann Smitkina, twenty-five years separated King James II and his consort, Mary of Modena.

The years pass, flit by; the giddy lad becomes the staid old codger; the nipper has become the very old guy; and both are Rory. But there again, who has not sometimes felt a stranger to themselves?

Henry David Thoreau wrote over two million words in his lifetime, at the rate of ten to fifteen thousand per day. Working fourteen hours a day he completed the thirty-six volumes that were to make up the greatest treatise on natural history ever written; to die at the age of forty-four.

W.B. Yeats at the age of seventy-one wrote to Lady Dorothy Wellesley on 8 November 1936: 'Over my dressing table is a mirror in a slanting light where every morning I discover how old I am. Oh my dear, oh my dear.'

Borges, aged seventy-one, wrote: 'I have even secretly longed to write, under a pen name, a merciless tirade against myself.

'Since our only proof of personal death is statistical, and inasmuch as a new generation of deathless men may be already on the way, I have for years lived in fear of never dying.'

Nevertheless he died of cancer of the liver on 14 June 1986 in Geneva and is buried there under a fine tombstone honouring this gallant Argentinian sceptic, blind as Milton and James Joyce before him, in the rotogravure of time passing, taking all of us away with it.

– 47 –

In a Swedish Forest

In Aurelio's dim bar female hands appear at the small serving-hatch, extending little plates of *tapes, lomo* and *cerdo* cut into cubes and chewy pulpo.

An inflamed sun is going down in the Costa del Sol advertisement, back-lighting the sultry bright face at the end of the long brown neck above a pair of sun-kissed pumpkins fairly bursting from the sea-drenched cotton shirt pulled open to the navel. A very outsplashed lady indeed is Annelise Lundes-gaard, the Danish wet dream who adorns this come-on, catch-as-catch-can advertisement.

It was the year when undressed Scandinavian photomodels began to catch on as calendar girls in the dimly lit hill bars, a year after the demise of the prudish or maybe prudent Generalissimo who had once been Señorita Islas Canarias; it was part of the opening up of Spain to the delights of democratic capitalism that would have made Franco pop-eyed, an eyeful of the ripe charms of Annelise Lundesgaard, who they said was yours for the day if you bought whatever it was they were promoting.

Girlie nudist magazines printed in Madrid were passed surreptitiously from hand to hand by pale-faced barmen drained by long hours and self-abuse in Málaga bars near the Alcazaba where the gays went cruising and on San Bou in Menorca an authentic nudist beach was opened in the Catalan strong-hold. Viewed with disfavour by the Caudillo, it was taxed accordingly.

My own *potencia* had begun to slip away from me, a leaky old vessel slip-ping its moorings and drifting out to sea. Hair sprouting in ears and nos-trils, withering away from hypogastric regions; sight, hearing and appetite going, insomnia coming on, backaches and various internal disorders, all too clearly announced the outward drift, the downward plunge.

Musil interpreted the waning of the libido as the absence of the will to live; a very Austrian notion, to be sure, for are we not all bound for Deathsville? Heidegger's arduous path of appearances had never looked so arduous.

Anna says: 'The Danes have used up their dreams of power. All Scandinavians believe aff karse [sic] in a well-run world. Not I. The very mean things are just as fine as the finer things. You can love a thing so much that you don't want to disturb it,' referring to *boccoroni,* the little minnows or sprats that had come browned and sizzling off the pan as *tapas.*

From the serving-hatch of the dark kitchen the hands reach out holding the plate imploringly.

The local strumpets have short stumpy legs and the wide hips and big bums of born breeders, with the oval features of Eskimos whom now we must call Innuit or some such name. The Scandinavian calendar girls are their physical opposites, with long legs, sultry expressions, narrow stomachs supporting upthrust bust with nipples already erect, the lips moistful. From the serving-hatch of the dark kitchen the hands reach out. 'I am not yet ready for a middle-aged love,' Anna says, moistfully.

We were in the back room with a wood fire throwing out good heat and the chimney-pots vibrating, shaken by the wind blowing down over the high escarpment.

'Uuuuh! The fire has fallen down into the gloams.'

The gloams!

'It's a difficult to think in a forest, the walls of trees keep out the sun. In a Swedish forest there is absolute silence, no singing birds there, even the uuls [owls] are silent. Can you just imagine? Uuuuh, that was a miss for me!

'This was a pine forest, very dark and very heavy, I don't like the Swedish forest much. The Swedish villages were all empty, because all the Swedes were away working, the men and the women. They were working very hard, very industriously, and then driving home very fast in their Volvos. They return in the evening and close their doors and that's it for the day for the Swedes. They don't come out again until the next morning.

'The main tree in the Swedish forest is pine; oak and beech forests would have a different feeling. It's very still there, very quiet. Aff karse you are thinking in a forest but a thought never finds its way to the end, as in the mountains or at the sea, and the silence there is really heavy. The Swedish forest is like a Shakespearian forest, no dead leaves but mossy underfoot, I was walking miserably there.

'Once I came upon an *elg* [elk], a cow, we glared at each other silently and not moving, with only the distance of a bedroom between us. It was a kind of opal grey, like the mountain flower you get here. Then it melted away into the forest without a sound.' She fixed me with her unblinking lynx eyes.

Her favourite colour was lilac, this was the colour of the wood that had frightened Petrushka in Rørvig near her parents' summer place; it was found also in the 'underwood' of Swedish forests. The 'Greekish' islands too had this colour in the evening; Anna loved the lilac Greekish evenings.

There were days when she could be awkward and broke things. She could be tender and she could be fierce. One day she broke, by accident, the blue-and-white eggcup I had found in Málaga, the last of a set. She had left it on the terrace edge and the wind had caught the vines and a branch had swept it over, to be smashed at my feet in the patio below.

'Uuuuuh, not my fault.'

I said nothing, collecting the bits.

'Called you out?'

'Silent as the tomb,' I said.

'Oh.'

In bed that morning after coffee she had threatened to hit me in the face. 'I would like to,' she had admitted, growling in her throat, stretching her strong jaw muscles, narrowing her lynx eyes; lifting her fist as if it held an axe. I saw the gleam of sweat in her axillary hair, and the threat in her green eye.

Sometimes she had a crazy look, had become the dark-complexioned moll of some København dockside hood, the tough face on the expired passport photo taken in her wild non-taxpaying youth before she had taken up with Karr and lived in the coal-hole. Her hands were not soft; she was a big strong Viking woman, most fierce. I held her arm. 'It's not so cold now. Let me just have a sniff on the rouff.' She tore herself free.

– 48 –

My Everyday

*The dreams of the night throw long
shadows in the late morning.*

The watch calls half-past seven. Every morning I try not to fall asleep again but use the time between half-past seven and eight to get the habit of life again. But often I'm very tired and fall asleep again anyway and wake up, confused, five minutes to eight. Petrushka is able to do nearly anything her-self, brush teeth, dress herself (surprising clothes together, and so much clothes . . . lots of clothes, taken off again later in the day, brought home from the kindergarten by me in a big paper bag). We have not really break-fast, none of us can eat in the morning. I paint my face, arrange myself, adapt myself so I'm half eat-able for myself and the surroundings. Without make-up I'm very rough, wild. I feel my own face more well-known with make-up than naked. In the moderated version there comes a tenderness which I also have. Indeed.

Then we drive, Petrushka behind on my cycle. When we are in good time we stop at a certain baker and buy two yogurt, just across Rosenberg Slot, we have a bench where we eat breakfast. People pass by, not many, and cars pass by (more) and maybe think that we don't belong to the slaves of time, but we do anyway.

Then Petrushka wants me to tell about Rosenberg Slot which is built by King Christian the Fourth in sixteenhundredsomewhat (renaissance Castle). He was in love with a hard and beautiful woman called Kirstine Munk, who let him down in his oldness, riding around with a guardsman instead and let the king die alone with dropsy in his legs. Petrushka doesn't mind me telling the same story, but I move longer and longer from the facts which are so unsure anyway. Beside that she will come to school once and have her learning made correct there.

Then I arrive a little too late at my work and drink coffee. The dreams of the night throw long shadows in the late morning. I do not quite awake until later. The post and the nervousity of the day arrive, a dubble nervousity, a real terror for having done – or not done – something irreparable (I neither own general view nor memory, there is lacks in my scratched intelligence) and another kind of nervousity, a secret excitement, an expectation which selden have name and face (but have it now) and which is laying, trembling under everything. The most of my days goes with hiding or re-establish that I'm never quite attentive, not even when I really try, that I always in one way or another are thinking of something else. When I'm working on my own things, other kind of horrors come in, doubt, hopelessness, incapability but never inattention. When I was with you I could sometimes be melancholy but never nervous, there was never this gulf between acting and thinking or what I did and what I ought to do.

I'm the best looking girl here, or rather maybe, that girl with most effect. (About my beauty you are talking: I know of course that I *look* like a beau-tifull girl, that I *seem* to be clever, but I know too, that . . . well). Because I look like a beautifull girl there is attention around me. That I enjoy in all its craching schizophrenia.

Eleven o'clock I'm mad by thirst and buy a light beer (without alcohol), a buying everybody percieve correct as beginning of alcoholism, still ashamed to be what it is. I'm moving very fast, forget my purse in the canteen and things like that. Half past twelve I eat lunch, sometimes alone at my office if the persons in the canteen look too dull but mostly I stay trying to charm my superior to doubt that I'm so incapable they all the time are just going to discover.

Between four and five o'clock I take my bike and go for Petrushka in kindergarten. Often we are both rather tired and rather hungry and sit down on a bench on 'Stroget' (the main walking street in Copenhagen) eating ice cream instead of making important buyings or we go to Steffen's terasse and let an hour crumble away. Everything are closing at half past five sharp. Only seldom I'm in time to what I ought, only I am behind in tax, toilet paper, dishing etc. When we are at home about 6 o'clock I make tea, doing house-things, making food. Half past seven we eat, mostly very simple; potatos, salat, sometimes bacon, milk for Petrushka, wine for me (I make the wine myself). In this weeks we are eating strawberry, lots of them, they are expensive but we love them. (Strawberry, oesters and an irish poet and I shouldn't complaint.)

After dinner I make Café con Leche, still missing the goat milk and the 103. In between these things I write to you or myself, it's the same, but Petrushka hates that. She wants to talk. Much banal chattering with surprises in between.

Yesterday she told me that angels had halos in order to find their way in the nighttimes when they are flying in the heavens. Also she told me newly: My mother is dangerous like a crocodile! At nine o'clock a long bed ritual starts, she doesn't sleep before about ten o'clock, had never belonged to the much-sleeping children.

Then I am myself with a daylong need for *wasting the time*. I have a very big need for wasting time. I sit down on my bed, neither read nor write. I'm looking out in the air and dream. The pictures, the situations are pouring in, mostly very banal, difficult to use to anything. I hardly can stop. Late, at 11 o'clock when I ought to be in bed, I'm free and laughing at the pattern I've been running in all the day and which necessarity cannot break only fulfill or not fulfill. In these hours I'm happy, filled with optimism, trustfull and believing in long chains of days of this color. Then I feel young again, that I'm just on the start of all of it, that I in the next moment 'around the next corner will be able to fly'.

That's me, my love. What do you say? – I laugh – No matter what even you (the most precious thing I have in these times) say: the things are like they are. No more than that.

[unsigned]

8 July 1975

For some weeks I cycled a detour while I was on my way to work. Not by the fifth watery quadrilateral, a pond in a park, our bench of the mornings between two churches. Then the old church Vartorv, then the Kanal, Amager Boulevard, the bridge over Stydhavn, cycling close to the water by the flowering chestnut trees, to Islands Brygge quayside. In fact I hadn't time, would be late and was it, but I was a little happy, didn't know why. The way I choosed is ugly: a dusty bypass way a little outside the centre of the town (Artillivej) with little dying factories, football-grass, workships, hutments from the time of war and allotments, insane in their care for flagstaffs and geraniums. The way end in a Clondyke.

Suddenly a miraculous stream of scent come to meet me and up from a high hoarding I saw roses, faint-pink roses, lots of kilograms roses, thirty metres roses hanging climing . . . scented releasted roses. I felt blessed and plucked three of them and put them in a beer glass on my desk. 10 o'clock a letter arrived, a letter from you, the mad letter, the letter which is one breath.

Since I haven't had time to bike that way, have put it off, thinking of it but not touching it. This day, this morning I turned, without knowing it, to the left and suddenly I was on that road again. The roses scented still more strong than before, many were died, the last ones overbearing. Carefully I took three again, put them in the glass. They scent scent scent and a half time ago your letter arrived, even my instincts you have given back to me.

Sometimes I have that feeling that we are writing or thinking the same things in the same days, that we are in the same moods in the same periods, a lovestory conducted not in fake-german but by somebody else. I feel how the transport of the letters brings a artificial shifting in a congruence (?) which is present. A letter arrived. A answer to my unmailed letter.

[unsigned]

– 49 –

On the Beatch with Petrushka

My ambitions groan.

Petrushka is naked, I've very little black bathing drawers, my 12 years old nephew's. I had forgotten bathing suit in Copenhagen, he has forgotten these in Rørvig. I adapt myself to the sand, preparing meeting you. You come slowly with little floating standstill in between. I don't go far into it, people around, Petrushka around, but it is difficult to stop. And difficult to go on to the absolute end. ('We didn't make love enough, far from . . .' didn't refer to something numerically but to the abandonment, the courage.) Petrushka is running around, they fits so beautiful, the sea and her. I try to keep the picture, not making any thinking around it. She is collecting shells in an empty Nescafé glass. She meets a boy. You know how children meet each other and stop, to the extreme watchful, super-animals, sniff with all the senses. Then Petrushka with an abrupt move casts all the shells at his feet and goes away. Sometimes I'm wondering myself, that Petrushka in one hand gives me so much but in the other I could leave her tomorrow, calm, if I knew she was growing well without me.

I went for a walk, alone, went on a narrow high levelled path through sand mountains with pines, brooms and wild roses. I was tempty to go down into the green valley but went on at the narrow path in assurance that something fantastic must be found by the end of it. I went carefully, I'm so clumsy, hidden tree roots under the sand (take care not to dream so you fall, take care not to fall so you must stop dreaming). The air was mild with cold streams plaited in, the bees was humsing; following the less resistance (can I assert that? Like that appeared to me). I felt awake and happy. – And yet I was disturbed by something, somewhat punctured the lovely picture, an unrest which didn't come from myself, and when I came to the end of the road I saw what it was: It was the limitation.

Nearly all over in Denmark you feel the houses with people just beside you, the houses are waiting just around the corner, voices turn up, you don't know from where and when and how many; but you know that only a limit area is preserved, only a quiet limit area have somebody in the city at a meeting decided to preserve – when innocence confuse with an unbroken hymen the point is lost.

I am glad friday evening when I arrive and glad sunday evening when I leave. Rørvig is a lovely place. Exploited, yes, summerhouses close together, but there is still a kind of innocence, a fragile middle-class innocence, open to rape I'm afraid. A holiday center. A place without necessity, without power of resistance. A hobby. Like my father, so kind in his stupidity and like my mother, so clever in her presentiments and so stupid in her fear, her denying. I love my parents, have tenderness for them. They are innocent.

My Rory – these are lines from the beginning of the sinfonie.

Never more I want to hear who you are fucking at the Third River with the deep smooth vessel. There are so many places in the world – why the Third River? I fling my sorrow back: Your amulet didn't break or turned into a blaze. I took it off. You are trembling by the thought of Coppera with him you call Wittgenstein? I understand that. Poor poor everybody to whom this happen. Was Coppera trembling when you left her?

Sorry you didn't like the pictures. I'm not surprised, they were postcards. An impossible situation with the pictures, so much trouble already, promiscuity in an odd way to hunt love-signs of yourself. Yes, the dark pictures are from the bleu heur at Steffen's terasso. I don't send the naked one.

Strange so often you mention Knud Andersen, your instincts are sure, you remind of him, the same limpid selfishness without any wickedness. He was blond with blue eyes, you are dark with green eyes, it gives the differens.

Your letter scared me. I know that it will scare me lesser in a couple of days when I've red it more times. But I know too, that the sight of you and the dream I dreamt after will be lying, always attentive, in the back of my head. However there is nothing to complaint, I knew it, had expected it, wondering who it came, I saw it in the very second in Pepinos bar. I saw in your eyes that point where longing and fear are meeting each other. Have a meeting.

Strange passionate over-used words. My scribbling is the same for the moment, I have no other words in this weeks, I look at my 'poems' and I'm paralysed by their impossibleness, ridiculousness. 'When they come back often enough they become careless.' You say yes. Like that it is. I presume. I don't know it, never reach that distance, am like a child, in it or out of it, burning or forgetting, absorbed or not caring. My ambitions groan. Oh yes. That also why I lived so well with you: I had no language to force you into my problems. I became only body and soul with you, no spirit. The difference between soul and spirit. 'Old stuff hanging over Anna's head.' I love you. I fear you.

[unsigned].

PS About Wrong placed longings. You say: 'they are not wrong placed for I have them for you too.'

Sweet Rory, a touching misunderstanding. That was exactly what I ment: we have towards each other, and that is maybe the mistake itself. I discovered once that the romantic way of thinking ('to long for each other') started exactly when the religious way of thinking stopped. And therefore maybe all this love feelings among modern feelings are misplaced (religious) feelings . . . do you not understand? How can you hear difference between floating (air) and flowzing (water)???

You can! I just invented a 'z'. but how do you choose?

According to the dictionary, which I love and hate, it is the same. English is to me a very Floating-flowing language. A bee hums and a humsing man does the same (when he sings silently). A nice word-game is lost by taking the consequence immediately and call it the same. Well, english is not floating here – I better stop criticise your language!

[unsigned]

– 50 –

Linguistics

Gorm the Old begat Harold Blue-Tooth who begat Sven Forkbeard who in turn begat Estre who begat Henning Mortensen who begat – Hold it right there! Is this by any chance *our* Henning of Calle Laberinto who makes lethal grog?

'The very man.'

Wisdom of Henning Mortensen:

'We have to make sense out of the pine. Live with the pine, make a circle of our life.'

'What's this pine, Henning?'

'The pine of living.'

He tells me a story about Jesus who somehow survived Golgotha and Calvary and fled the Holy Land, settled elsewhere, married and had a large family, lived to be 108.

He recites

Should old acquaintance be forgot
and never brought to mind . . .

and translates it into Jutlandic, which closely resembles Middle English and its sounds and rhythms, and the words too.

Anna says that English is a language of the head, a language without any kind of metaphysical overtones or undertones, a language from the neck up. 'English novelists are kind old aunts, innocent watchers, unconcerned bystanders, kind people who would never do you any harm, never hurl an insult. And that's the bad side of them, as novelists. They understand in a certain way nothing; a very tolerant people. I like them but I could never trust them.'

Graham Greene, a man of mystery, says the *Listener,* for Hell! Anna insists: 'Graham Greene is not in the *least* mysterious. He's just another old auntie, like William Golding and E.M. Forster and all the other aunties before them, back to Samuel Butler and Edmund Gosse and George Gissing, all the same ilk, all old aunties.

'When the life shrinks, the language must shrink too; one would be tempted to think that, since the available options are few and getting fewer, that it must be so.'

'Trousers' is a very rapid and almost coquettish way of describing this awkward garment. Many of the English sounds have no distinct masculine or feminine roots, as you get in Spanish or French, and might refer either to a man or a woman; no great distinction can be made.

'I heard Gertrude Stein's recorded voice,' said Anna, 'reading some of her stuff. A very clear head-language, I thought. I didn't understand much of what she was saying but there was a bit of smoke and whiskey in the tone of voice that was pleasing. This I suppose is typical old-fashioned high-level speaking. It is one of the most beautiful languages you can get into.

'In German you get the rough stuff, the naked women mud-wrestling. *Lederhosen* really has a filthy sound, a diaphragm tongue for giving orders, *issuing* orders. German is a language of the stomach, a fat language, *svulstig,* as when you have too much fat around the heart.

'Now if English is a language of the head and German a language of the stomach, what is French? French is almost all movement, you might say it's spoken by the hands and arms, all that shrugging they go in for; a very performance language. It is very pleasing to build up the French sounds.

'But wait. Danish more than German is perhaps a true *language* of the stomach – *mauve* is very much a stomach sound. We are after all a nation of farmers and fishers; and Germany has long had its eye on the little Danish butter-ball.'

Anna wrote a fine slapdash cursive dashed off at speed, an unusual mixture of straight lines and cursive, the upstrokes matching the downstrokes. She wrote quickly, always legibly, the letters of her signature squeezed together more than the rest, as though she were hugging herself

'Uuuh you make me lude! I always seem to have your preek in my mouth when we are in the mountains.'

('It melted away into the forest without a sound.')

It: the elusive elk in the forest that had stared at Anna. She said: 'In Denmark normally they are eating every three hours. My mother is just washing up from the lunch when my father is already boiling water for the teatime.'

Her parents, the Olsens, were small-sized and frugal. This Danish frugality made their daughter into a reckless spendthrift. Her background was Hungarian-Prussian-Pomeranian, an alarming combination. Günter Grass had a Pomeranian granny. Pomerania was somewhere beyond Poland, immensely old, older than Russia, possibly wilder, even rougher. Anna's Pomeranian granny, whom she probably took after, had been tall and austere, a maker of good soups, vegetable soups, nipping off the ends of beans. Anna's mother's maiden name had been Lemm, which means prick, the male member. Once at Christimo's crowded bar she had hissed: 'Unless we leave at wance, I'll lick all the preeks in this bar!'

In the Cómpeta shops she found herself standing amid the tiny and talkative hill-women whom she called the Waggada Waggadas. They had fallen silent when she, the Danish giantess, entered towering over them, to watch her ordering in dumb show, laughing and pointing. She felt herself to be gigantic. But she never held their diminutive size against them: 'The leetle people cannot do anything enormous and ugly.'

She says, 'Beethoven couldn't stand the piano.' When he was dying he reached under his bed, took out the chamber pot, drank off the contents, saying, '*Zu spät! Zu spät!*' Too late, too late. At his last gasp, Beethoven was a card. It was said of him that nature couldn't have taken another Beethoven; it would have been excessive and intolerable, as two Niagara Falls, or a couple of Grand Canyons.

She said: 'There's never a heavy moment with Mr Mozart.' Sibelius was greedy for the dirty stuff, always stepping into whorehouses. He was an enormous male chauvinist pig. 'I very much like his Violin Concerto – regarded by violinists as the most difficult you could be put into.'

She says that Schubert's *Death and the Maiden* has nothing to do with either death nor any maiden known to Franz Schubert; the title was tagged on afterwards. At the second movement, the second violin is leading, the first often betrayed into over-emotional flights, at which Anna laughs with delight. 'Here comes the bills through Mr Schubert's door.'

– 51 –

Such Delightful Copulatives!

Pleaseful, moistful, fleshful are her delightful copulatives; she speaks of 'smashed potatoes'. 'For Hell!' she cried. 'Certainly she perceived me as an uncultured updressed whore, an oldish fucked-up model.' This of Anne Ladegaard, an elderly Danish writer who lived with her brother on the outskirts of Frigiliana near La Molineta; a lady who surely did not perceive her in any such unflattering way.

She is thirty-three years of age, with long legs, a prototype of the photo-model Annelise Lundesgaard in the Costa del Sol advertisement. My fancy is to call her the young whore on the outskirts of a dirty city. Nina, the whore from Singapore.

Cómpeta, two-thousand metres up in the foothills of the Sierra Almijara, she thinks of as the past, everybody's past; as when she was young and dressed up in the fashion of the 1950s and went out to display her finery, and on returning home again was noticed by a boy loitering in a doorway. Or perhaps not even noticed, as she sauntered by.

The roof tiles of the north are concave, she says, conduits for rainwater to run off, whereas the roof tiles of the south are convex, like shoulders hunched against the rain.

I asked her to translate a page of Hans Andersen for me. It was about a sliver of glass found on a beach. She translated it from English back into the original Danish and then forward into Swedish; she thought it was better in Swedish.

I asked her how did the Swedes regard the Danes; did they feel superior? She said yes, the Swedes thought of themselves as superior to the Danes.

Once when she had stood between Sven Holm and Rory, Anna in shirt and bikini bottom and sandals, the gaze of Sven and myself was drawn to the line of pubic hair, neat as a clipped hedge or mown lawn. The Danish lawns are so lovely!

Cómpeta (pop. 2,000; alt. 2,000m.)

There are many doubles, or *doppelgänger* as they say in German, of the Caudillo living and working all over Spain, themselves unaware of the resemblance, being versions of the Dictator at various stages of his career. The face on the stamps is powerful; it does not age like the cautious old man with phlebitis.

In Cómpeta too there are some pseudo-Francos. Antonio the former post-man, who was sacked but will be reinstated in favour of the alcoholic Laurentio, is one such; with paunch and neatly trimmed moustache and pop-eyed look, he is a dead ringer for Major Franco Baamonde, the fearless one, who later became Miss Canary Isles, as Rudolf Hell became Fräulein Anna in Nazi days. He had a small grocery shop near the post office with its mountain of undelivered mail and the door always locked.

Antonio, the pseudo-Franco and ex-postman, was a keen chess player. He once sold me a pot of confection purporting to be greengage jam, 400 grams of it marked 'Ciruela'. As he wrapped it up, he favoured me with an antiseptic smile. It was the conspiratorial smirk of the diminutive Generalissimo when just about to assume full power, including the signing of death penalties.

The stuff proved to be tasteless, fibreless and more or less odourless, and I intend to throw it out. The pseudo-Franco with goo-goo eyes and military bearing plays a fast game of chess, swooping on the enemy when least pre-pared, hissing between his teeth before clearing the board. He runs his small store efficiently and manufactures soda water by night, for Rory heard the pump going in the small hours when he went about the town in the night.

– 52 –

A Málaga Morning

A huge rusty freighter in from Odessa was moored to the quayside. A ship's hand in white overalls dwarfed to pygmy size is painting out the blisters on the hull with a long paintbrush dipped in black paint.

Harbour guards in riot helmets with chin-straps, armed with squat automatic rifles, unlock a small green gate that one could skip over, admitting a series of Franco doubles in shabby suiting, who scuttle by carrying briefcases.

Stiff as a ramrod the guard snaps to attention to give a military salute. His sharp eye catches us watching from the window of the seafood restaurant by the harbour. He smacks the rifle butt, marches stiffly away, a broken smile for the lovely foreign girl amused by these soldierly antics. It must be some sort of naval depot towards which the pseudo-Francos are hastening.

At sundown the Spanish flag is ritually lowered, draped and folded, carried indoors by a guard of honour as though it were a baby being put to bed, tucked away for the night with 'taps' blown on a bugle by another stiff soldier.

We are drinking a very good dry white wine from Valencia, port of gesticulating statuary, with *tapas*, little squids. The handsome barman is pretending not to look at you but he notices you all the same, the tall brunette with green eyes from Scandinavia where morals are notoriously lax.

Thousands and even five thousand-denomination peseta notes were being flashed about by the very well-heeled clientele, the fast Málaga set of Scotch whiskey drinkers with model girls in tow, puffing Gauloises.

The gorgeous girl with the lynx-green eyes standing so tall at the counter was just casually remarking to her escort, Rory of the Hills: 'I am so witchful when it is hardening up, this egg. And now I can feel it split.' So, no intercourse; the hard business of life must go on.

– 53 –

Kronborg

Clouds drifted through the September sky as we walked again through Dyrehaven to the hermitage on the hill. The unwalled, unguarded mansion amid a copse of beech was where the widows of dead Danish kings lived out their retirement. No moat or castle keep separated it from citizens who passed on foot, or the horse-riders and pony-trekkers.

A stag was bellowing to its herd of wives near *Tre Pile Stedet,* or the Three Twigs, where a dumpy sweet-faced woman served you coffee and me red wine, calling out for 'Matthew' in an accent that you swore was pure Bornholm. We sat at a table outside. There you had come as a child with your parents. There you had sat as a child, heard the warning bell at the level crossing, saw the little red train rush through. Heard the hoarse stag-bellow at rutting time, felt the air move. There you were young once, an innocent.

In the flower shop run by your stepfather-in-law, a retired sea captain now working as a pimp for male prostitutes, you told a long witty story in Danish, and the pimp shook all over, wiping his eyes.

Copenhagen is a city of uneasy old people, who stay indoors, live on cat food and dog food, rarely venture out, hesitating at street corners, fearful of the wild young, the nudist park, the drug scene. The young are not much in evidence except by night in Central Station, bumming kroner for more beer, collapsing across loaded tables.

City of phantoms, of tired faces, of sailors on shore leave. Or German students returning from a trip around the harbour. The Master Race, you said, were still after the little Danish butter-hole. Granite port of *Belge brote, somner platte, frikadeller.* Singsong musical voices.

The sleepy Danes are modest in a reserved way; reserve with them being a form of arrogance. A public display of anger only amuses them. The music in the bars is muted. In the San Miguel bar the flamenco music was turned down. There is not too much laughter or high spirits in evidence. These drably dressed citizens of the north are warmly bundled into their lives. Babes with chronically disgruntled old faces peer critically from hooded prams. Headscarves are favoured by the young mothers who move about on high antiquated bikes. The long *Allees* open like yawns.

Elderly couples walk soberly in lime-green *Loden* through the King's Gardens. The males wear pork-pie hats and puff cigars, the tubby wives go sedately in warm little hats with feathers, dragged by a dog on a lead, as like as not. The feeling is of sedate bourgeois Germans in a German provincial town, but don't dare tell that to a Dane.

Flagstaffs are a feature of the island of Rørvig. Narrow Danish house-flags get entangled in the firs. The cellar under your far-sighted father's floorboards yielded up good home-made schnapps made from herbs, very potent. We dismantled two single beds and spread mattresses on the floor for the night. Then went cycling on high old bikes – pedal backwards to stop – from Helleveg, the way to the sea. A three-masted schooner appeared out of the haze, and a swan flew overhead, sawing the air creakily, as I took you in the dunes, in the cold, still feverish, still very feverish, in your heated arms.

One day I went by train on my own to Kronborg, to see the castle where Hamlet had 'run around after the ghost of his father'. There is nothing much to see at Elsinore. Shakespeare had heard about it from his friend John Dowland from Dalkey. A Swedish passenger-craft big as a street seemed to be dragging the houses down along the harbour. Minute passengers crossed over by a glassed-in overpass to the station.

An ashen-faced invalid in a belted raincoat, moving with pain on two arm-crutches, his mouth set in a grim line, closed the train window. Forget the fresh air. Now all the windows were sealed tight, an Airedale stinking of decay, no air all the way to Østerport, in the dog-stink.

I had some words of German, some words of Spanish, but of Danish nothing but *Skaak!* and felt a right Charlie in the shops where no English was spoken, going out in the cold morning, skinned alive at the corner by the North Sea wind, leaving you and little Petrushka together on the mattress trademarked Sultan under the duvet covers, two pairs of brown eyes watching me from the warmth. I, descending steps into the bakery, tore a ticket from the dispenser, waited for my number to be called. But what did 17 sound like in Danish?

Your language sounds more far-off than it is, its pronunciation is far removed from any known thing, to my ears at least. Your misnomers are charming: 'artist's cocks' (artichokes); 'corny cobs' (corncobs); 'upflung waters' (fountains); 'downburnt buildings' (blitzed London); 'ox' (braised beef); 'outsplashed ladies' (the nude models of Delacroix, with their 'fleshful thighs').

'I am uproared,' you said, meaning miffed. 'I'd jump into bed with Olof Palme.' You left *postillons d'amour* lying around. 'Sweetheart – gone for a little walk. The lunch is set for tomorrow instead of today. Kisses – home again soon. Anna.'

'I look into the mirror sometimes and don't believe what I see' (watching yourself narrowly in the glass). 'I think it's funny to pay the world a gleaming lie' (applying make-up but no lipstick, no scent, no earrings; the scentless perfume was 'Ancient Moose'). Much will have more.

Do you know why witches fly?

You prepared the 'squints' (squid) Bilbao-style in their own ink, following the instructions. Pull the heads off the squids and remove and discard the spines and all the internal organs except the ink sacs, which must be put into a cup and reserved. Cut off the testicles just below the eyes and discard the heads. Wash thoroughly. *Calamares ensu tinta a la bilbaina.*

Conkers split on the cobbles under the chestnut trees near the yacht basin where the 'damned' Little Mermaid poses so coyly naked on her bronze seat on a boulder there, and a plain girl in a loose-fitting blue T-shirt displays big wobbly breasts as she goes laughing by with her pretty friend, and a company of Danish soldiers in sharp uniforms, with long hair and rifles at the port position, go marching by the Lutheran church where your model friend Sweet Anya was wedded to Strong Sven, the translator of Márquez. It was snowing then. Mr Fimbal, the Danish god of hard winters, stumbled by with his single arm.

We passed again by a group of stone women all stark naked, tending one who appeared to be injured or in the tolls of childbirth.

'What is this?' I asked.

'The Jewish Memorial.'

Professor Tribini, top-hatted and villainously mustachioed, sporting a red carnation in his buttonhole, flashed his gallant ringmaster's eyes at you, all fire and sexual push, at Peter Lieps in Beaulieu, where the railway tracks lead back to Centrum.

Bakken had come before the Tivoli Gardens, you told me. There was the real rough stuff – randy drunken sailors on the spree and big strong girls wrestling stark naked in mud. It was slightly before your time.

You had been at a Gyldendal publisher's party there, had trouble opening a sealed pat of butter; your dinner partner did it for you. You took him home with you on condition that you rode his tall new bicycle. With skirt rolled about your hips and 'brown all over' and at your most attractive after Naxos, you took him home. It was a time I would never know. You rode slowly home, his hand on the small of your back, through the pre-dawn at Bakken, down the long avenue of trees where we had walked, watched by Professor Tribini, abusing himself behind an oak.

'I was somewhat exalterated,' you said.

'Oh, I am over-lewd!'

You served up an excellent Hungarian soup with sour cream and told me your radio story of Satan in the wood, based on a real lecher, my successor after the time in Spain. You sat opposite me, giving me the eye. You'd certainly been at the Cognac again, a couple of snorters before setting out.

We were in Spain again. You had been going on about 'Paulus of Tarsus'. We were in an olive grove below the logging trail and heard the damnedest noise rising up out of the valley, a strange inconstant murmurous belling, bleating and baaing.

Some time later, over a drink at Viento de Palmas, a herd of over a thousand shorn sheep and lambs went tripping past, with active dogs as outriders and rough-looking shepherds bringing up the rear. The din was stirring – bells, barking, bleating, baaing. The shepherds did not stop for drinks, heading on for new pastures.

Now freezing air leaks into the kitchen and you turn the gas low, open the oven door, light candles. The water in the lavatory bowl becomes agitated, as if we were at sea. Sudden gusts of winter air strike through the interstices of the cramped toilet and the floor seems to shift underfoot. The Danes were all secret sailors, you said.

The spiritual suffering of the Swedes (which knows no bounds) is said to be unmatched in any other European country, their suicide rate the highest in the world. By the end of the first quarter of the next century all Sweden would be in the custody of a few large companies, the suicidal sameness of all Swedish life then complete.

We passed the Jewish Memorial again, the naked women bound together in a lumpish humanitarianism. And once your dotty landlady Mrs Andersen passed us on her witch's black bike, sending a hostile look our way.

I write down the magic names:

Humlebaek	*Hellerup*	*Hundested*
Østerport	*Oster Sogade*	*Ordrup*
Klampenborg	*Kokkedal*	*Kastrup*
Kronborg	*Skodsborg*	*Vedbaek*
Beaulieu	*Rørvig*	*Bakken*
Nivå	*Espergaerde*	*Rungstedlund*
Dyrehaven	*Helsingør*	*Melby*

In Denmark every day is different; so the old books say. Blow out the light.

– 54 –

Ronda

I'm a big girl now. I've got a big pussy and I suppose a big *asch* too.'

Anna had all those splendid not-to-be-denied Scandinavian feminine attributes, in spades; and if her bust was a bit on the small side (as indeed it was), it was more than compensated for by the size of her shapely bum.

'Love perfumes all parts,' wrote Robert Herrick, himself ever a lover of wet pussy. The choleric clergyman who had taught his pet pig to down pints of ale like a gent must have been thinking of his Julia whose large breasts bursting out of a lawn chemise he had likened to strawberries half-drown'd in cream.

In the Hotel Polo at Ronda in a lovely quiet blue high-ceilinged double room with long blue drapes drawn from the windows, Anna ordered up breakfast in perfectly accentless English via Room Service, specifying what we wanted and when.

Presently a dark-visaged young *torero*, in a blue tunic and white flannels with razor-sharp creases, bore in a large tray of steaming strong coffee and all the condiments and got an eyeful (one of the undoubted perks of the profession) of the tall brunette in the white robe sitting up in bed saying *'Muchas gracias'* in Spanish that would pass. Soon he was backing out of the bedroom as though leaving the chamber of the Queen, his eyes steadfastly fixed on the vision in the bed, now pouring out coffee. And my Anna surely had the face and demeanour of King Juan Carlos's lovely Sofia, ever smiling sweetly on all public occasions.

'Don't move an inch,' I said, and left her arse in air, to fetch a wetted face-cloth from the fancy bathroom with its shower stall and faceted mirrors. In whose full-length mirrors she was to see herself nude for the first time since a babe in Copenhagen.

'Uuuuuh! but I'm lewd, aren't I?' I heard her say in the bathroom with its door open. And she had doubtless performed a little skip and dance for the big mirrors and admired her bum, which she had never seen before.

A champagne cork from a previous honeymoon lay behind the radiator. A great yellow building crane straddled a monstrous hole in the ground across from the hotel and its waving palms. We dressed and made ourselves respectable again, preparing to have another look at Ronda, a most pleasing place to be. It reminded me of certain undulating lovely valleys in Yugoslavia near the Austrian border where I had gone with the puppets in a new Bedford truck, just off the assembly line, though the land about Ronda is more like the colour of Africa, pelt of puma.

In an alleyway off a nameless street a bar is crammed with soldiers in green uniforms of Thai-like neatness, bleached out and worn with panache under tasselled forage caps. Ronda is obsessed with green things: lizards, uniforms, oxidised bells. And bullfighting. ¡PENA TAURINA ANTONIO ORDOÑEZ! groans the sign, as if choking to death. I see a line of hanged victims carved in stone.

In the neat pedestrian walks you see the finite gestures of bullfighters (Ordoñez, the great matador, the first one I saw kill five bulls, was born here), jackets draped over shoulders in matador manner. When the weather permits and the bitter winter sets its teeth into the narrow arses of those brave *toreros*-to-be whose thin shoulder blades protrude like flying buttresses. The pretty Ronda girls are rumpy as *rejoneadores*, flying on blood mares from the bull's horns. Mauve slacks are worn as tight as tight can be. A chess competition takes place in what once must have been a Moorish palace. *Pena: J.M. Bellon. Torneo Social Ajedrez.* For three days the Levant wind blew a half-gale.

'I haven't quite got used to being frustrated yet,' I said. *Todavia no me acostumbro estar frustrado* in the vernacular.

While modern Spain sprawls like a hopeless drunkard along the Mediterranean, busily going to Hell, the new road that grandly ascends to Ronda is as extraordinary as the southern approaches to Barcelona. Cut off from the ongoing sorry mess of the coastal 'development' and deep in the off-season (the only time to travel in style) Ronda (at 850 *metros de altitud*; 32,049 *habitantes*) offers herself as a kind of Sparta. A bullfighters' town; from here came Pedro Romero and the great Ordoñez. Sealed up in the wall of a well on the latter's bull-farm, sealed up again in an unmarked blue casket, lie the ashes of Orson Welles, this most secret burying place a last tribute to happy days spent in Spain when he was young.

The coastal stretch from Málaga to Marbella is as ugly as the urban development from Salthill to Costelle Cross on Connemara's frozen Atlantic seaboard, allowing the Spaniards slightly better taste.

Up here in Ronda men with wind-scorched faces speak intently of bulls and the money involved and of bullfighters. They are sage addicts of circles and all shades of green, very partial to chess, with the ingrained habit of contradicting, a Moorish trait. They are half Moorish in their thinking and feeling, wholly Moorish when very drunk. That extraordinary high screech the men emit when in their cups is a modified and secularised version of the muezzin call to prayer. We walk on the windy walls, Seaport Anna and her besotted fancyman Rory of the Hills.

Into Bar Maestro – just wide enough for you to turn around – twitches a grievously afflicted beggar, moaning '*¡Bbbbboooojijii!*' A posse of purposeful men with bursting bellies come roaring for *cerveza* into a long bar overlooking the plaza, to be presently joined by quiet men in expensive suede jackets the colour of jaguars, but with the swarthy faces of Iberian impresarios.

'In Ronda your thoughts fly upwards,' Anna said. 'To live here would be to marry a very strict but beautiful woman.'

A calm nun in a well-cut powder-blue habit is transacting some quiet business at the Banco Central. The waiter with the scorched face above his red jacket is acting in an old Simenon thriller; as is the lovely girl who sold me carbon paper in the *libreria;* as is the contrary old man sitting in the corner. A thin bronze bell is tolling. The bullring is the largest and thus the most dangerous in all Spain. The New Town is as great a mess as Tallaght in Dublin, a sort of Arab shanty town. A ring of towns with peculiar names face Portugal: Arcana, Estepa, Ecija.

'*Una iglesia muy vieja,*' I told the contrary old man seated in a shadowy corner.

'*No, no tan vieja. Solo doscientos años,*' he contradicts me flatly, referring to the *Iglesia Nuestra Señora del Socorro* just across the way.

In the Restaurant Jérez, very Germanic, near the bullring a distinguished grey-haired man arrives with a cane and arming a lady in furs. The noble-looking Frenchman in the neck-brace sits and looks about, hair a sable silvered, pulls up his expensively tweed-clad trouser leg to expose a male calf of corpselike whiteness to the lady in furs who bends forward as if peering solicitously through a long-handled lorgnette. Slowly removing her sunglasses she exclaims, 'Ouch, *chéri!*'

The squat proprietor, who seems to know Rory, hovers about our table and stares pointedly at me as if at a long-lost son who refuses to acknowledge his own *padre*.

Soon the whole eastern coastline from Estepona near Gibraltar to Gerona near the French border will have gone the way of Marbella and Torremolinos, the Sodom and Gomorrah of the Costa del Sol, and it will be left to hardy souls to move on Ponteverdre or La Coruña. American bombing colonels out from the air base at Moron de Frontera quaff Cognac as if it was beer.

Over Ronda hovers a most Moorish moon and never do I wish to leave it.

'Don't move an inch,' Rory whispered, carefully withdrawing his inflamed member.

'Your cock is afraid of my pussy,' Anna said when I couldn't perform, for she was ever a straight-speaking girl. 'And do you ever take a shit?'

'*Au contraire,* my cock adores your pussy.'

– 55 –

Petrushka

[Handwritten]

24 July 1975
Østersøgade

My dearest Rory

Yes, my flat faces the lakes. Petrushka and I went down there tonight, just across the Norre Søgade. She has bread for the ducks and a letter in a bottle. The time is near to 9.00, the darkness is coming but the lake is still coloured, the air is misty (hazy?) by heat and smoke – a bird, I don't know which one, flies by in quiet hurry, the strokes from wings are regular as morse signals.

I'm happy tonight, have this 20 minutes together with you. Here are not much people, some few bourgeoises with dogs and a group of children. The five shout after the sixth; 'Suckling, suckling!' Petrushka is upset. An old man pass by, stiffly and regular as when you are walking with ski, and draws an invisible and absolute straight line after him. He wears a white linen-coat, wide trousers and new-chalked shoes. His complexion is sickly and sun-burned. He reminds me of an asiat. I follow him with the eyes, turn the head and talk with Petrushka – about the five which tease the one. Then I look after the old man again. He is still walking but on the same spot as before. My reason tells me that he has stand still in the meantime, but if somebody look sharp on me and said: 'This is not a man but a sign on a Chinese cardemono', I would say: 'Yes, of course.'

[unsigned]

– 56 –

The Floating Trousseau

27 July 1975
Copenhagen,
Thursday night

Mein lieber Liebling, mein Kind und Brüderlein, mein Dichter und Wirklichkeit, mein Angst und Freude, my Rory.

Just received your letter. Sorry to hear about Martin's mother dying. Read my 'epistle' from Bornholm, remember my new name and understand that you have done it again, catched me in my heart, beating me in my stomack, taken the air out from my lungs. You called me Anna Bornholm.

You have done it again. You have seen me again, seen me as I am (can be), you have lighted me through again, you are a seeing person, seeing me anyway. Oh, Gott!

I love every word in your letter, letters. A psychoanalist would tear his hair because of your determining of erotic, your picture of me in this fixing-bath, your Big Tips. I've never met anything like that, you even surpass

Knud Andersen. I cannot quite recognize myself but if you see me like that, I may be like that, must turn to be like that.

Your smile made sense to me, help me so much. What a promise – I was never jealous of Hannel, knew all the time that you haven't loved her, that you had tenderness for her but she was a spare-love. Is it cruel to say? I knew she had been the wife of the Pastor and even in separated it hints certain limits in her. For Coppera I have blended feelings. I perceive her, actually, as very sympathetical, beautifull and intelligent too, but obviously wrong for you. As me in my Steffen, apart from that we are through the hate. But I am very jealous of her. You have had your youth together with her, you have been together with her on the impossible beds of your youth and have wished – more fervently than ever since in your life – to make love to her. You (R & C) have had the trust together about you as a famous writer and herself as a beautifull woman in company with gifted men, men who everybody saw was secret in love with her, Coppera Hill. And you have had the kids together. It alarms me that you still quarrel. Then a long way is left before you are mine. Yes, I'm jealous. Jealous so it hurts in my teeth, my teeth turn soft in my mouth of jealous.

When you say that the love for the two H's already disappeared when I was in Cómpeta you are lying indeed, my love. To yourself and to me. I remember so clearly myself asking: When did the lovestory with Hannelore end? And you answered, very fast and with a sharp sidelong look: Who says it is end? I remember that. One remembers when the whip gibes.

But I will not (do not dare) to say something about Hannelore and about what I feel in my bones – Your memories of us are too full of 'unreliablenesses' but mostly more true than the reality. But then again reality stands in no need to be true to life, according to Monsieur Boileau.

That I must type my envelopes shock me directly. If you told Coppera about me then she must know that I'm writing to you? Shall I put on a false name too? I have the address of Martin from a wrong addressed envelope; reserve it because I know you are fond of him in a special way, a voluntary way. It would actually amuse me to be Martin Lindermann (*en route* to l'Espagne) and then – in out-folded state – Anna again. Like a real fold-out girl as from a pornographic magazine. A picture only for your pleasure, a code which only you know the solution.

If I'm your breath then you are the very mystery behind the breath, you hit me in the middle, fling everything else overboard, I see terrified and delighted the fine trousseau (embroidered with the wrong initials) float on the sea ('the Rough') for a moment and then go down. Disappeared. After real manner of women I think that this anyway was make by fine linen, could be remade for other purpose . . . But you laugh – a bit satanic, quite frankly – against me with the remains of me between your teeth and my objection blows out of my mouth.

With what arrogance you ignore my laborious collected trousseau. Indeed you make me naked. Don't you fear at all my fury that day the love is worn out? I wrote something four weeks ago after reading 30 pages in Rørvig of Böll's *Ansichten eines Clowns* and your stories, indeed, often give me the same kind of thoughts. Try to translate it here (it was actually written for you, – as everything I think).

So many stories is about 'the lust of the flesh and the irreparable lone-liness of the souls'. You barely know the quotation, it's from a Swedish female poet from about 1900. Now it is only quoted with becoming ironical distance. So many stories are songs about men's loneliness, men's search for that picture of love which are only given by glimpses. I'm thinking of all the stories (suddenly it seems to me that I never red anything else) about men's effort, their enormous effort in order to give women gifts, to give them their world, builted up through the years of reading and sensations and meditation and coined in stories told in bed in Cómpeta or in a tower in Heidelberg or in a field in Ireland. All this you give away for a kiss.

But when a woman reads these stories she reads them in another direc-tion, sees another message too, she sees your presents (so tempting in their tenderness and beauty) as demands. This gifts demand her 'obliteration', she must follow the man in his world, let her be drowned in presents, follow the man in his dreams, make his dreams alive, turn herself into a dream. And she knows, she expects – from the very first moment in a new love-meeting – your anger and disappointment that day you see that your gifts weren't received in that spirit they were given. She knows your disappoint-ment, turned into contempt in order to be bearable for yourself. Women are stupid, greedy and self-asserting. Stupid because you, the men, have been thinking everything out, have created everything – greedy when they are not happy by that they are given and self-asserting when they demand their own diffuse univers accepted as real (banned into litter and sex as we say in danish, meaning that the ilegitimate children of a king are ennobled). – I'm mourning; for the love (the creating) that cannot endure. After that follows the loneliness only usable for telling at that time when the love was there.

Towards the loneliness (the disappointment, the end) we are leaded, as necessary as the community (the hope, the beginning). This cycle is by most women perceived as created by men, it is him 'to blame', she want to continue the creative of love, prefare to stay in the beginning. A day she sees that his touch was casual, that his gifts are not for her, that the love cannot be thought without its cessation, she understands that the love was a lever for something else, something in himself, not her business, something useful; a new present. From him. As he can give to whom he wish! Then the beloved woman turns into an un-loved woman: a fearfull sight, a fury, a witch or only a tormentor, an envious creature hacking with the rests of her love: the selfishness, the greedyness, the demands. She sees her contribution (the giving up of herself) swallowed, devoured and rised again as *something else,* something outside her. And she is seized by a deadly hate against this giver who used everything, who used her out.

The next time she is offered the love of a man (his world) she first sees the shadows from her dead sisters corpses – and turns into a whore, a suffragette, or very lonely. (Or the most scandalous, the most 'perverse' of all; a woman with the same purposes as a man – a woman excluded from love.)

All this, my dear Rory, I feel in a very strong way in the meeting with you. With Steffen I had not this 'problematic' (what a word); with him there was a kind of cease-fire, a conspiracy, a looking-at-the-world-together. With you there is quite another kind of life. And I want to live, I think I want it so much that I will die for it. I love you. I have decided to love you. You made the decision irresistible.

I know you prefer letters with concrete contents: stories, descriptions (best erotical), you want to fill them out yourself, yes, put colours on. I send you a new cart of Copenhagen with marks and hidden signs which you can follow with the nail of your finger like Job scraped his wounds with a potsherd!

Petrushka is not a bit like me, I'm sorry to say. She is all the family of Steffen. I am not talking always, I'm talking in showers. I like to have letters to my home address. It was not me waiting for hours on the steps, it was the letter.

I haven't the slightest idea of what the postman looks like. I'm waiting everywhere. And not for hours but always. I remember myself standing on the floor in your bedroom, trying to explain you something. I could not and took a pair of dancing-steps in order to show you what I meant. I remember how much it pleased you, this simplicity and joy we had together.

To have few words demands clearness in mind. To have many words demands clearness in heart. You easy grows wild. It struck me that in a foreign language you cannot hear if your words are ridigiously, you can only hear your own thoughts.

I've never met such a absence of barriers from a man before. You must have made your women mad of love when you have been like that to them, too. My Knepp was good, very impersonal, I was thinking of nobody, so natural as washing oneself, a ritual, childish nearly. I fucked with the chap twice, it was the bitterness, the bitter need he took. Then I stopped because he approached to me, approached *your* regions. Do you understand? The fucking only helped me for a very short time. I put on the amulet again immediately of course. How can you think I didn't I only took it off because of delicate reasons.

I meet you in another way than in my former erotic conceptions: lesser touch, more imagination. I tell you Rory, I imagine you so you would die from it if you were here. I feel you, you are with me, you are in me, you are alive in me (slowly and fast) and you die in me, you are flinged up in me, inside me and you stay there and get peace. I tell you, few have been so passionate faithfull to you as I in this months.

And I . . . I catch a sweetness so unbearable that I disappear to myself, I dissolve, the top flies off, the bottom out. On Bornholm I found myself on the bed (an afternoon I stealed – stold? – me into my room) laughing against the roof and with my face wet by tears.

It is this I don't dare on the beatch because even the smallest help-from-hand is excluded and any other signs form body. The feeling of love (or the lechery) comes in waves. From the floating flowing standstills the reservoir is filled slowly, the first power from the first wave kept, the next added. Addition. Addition until no more addition is possible.

If I permit you to place me with maximum charm (what a hidden phrase) in the hidden centre of your novel, I permit you everything. And I think you will love most of it. Maybe all. I permit you everything.

Anna

– 57 –

Diary, April 1975

I stand at the window of the Bar el Montes commanding a view of the main plaza which presents the usual fucked-up aspect – idlers, straw blown about, the church door open. I did not know what to expect: the second appearance is always different – the sauntering certainly a bluff. Through the window I watch you sail into view. You saunter across the plaza, taking your time, you want to show me yourself advancing. Your tallness surprises, the *nudeness* of your ears, your hair is up. You wear a white linen shirt, a flared skirt of pale colours, you stop outside Luis Perico's bar, bend to look into a parked car, using the glass as a mirror, watchful, tall and self-possessed. The idlers stare. I open the bar door a fraction.

You see the movement, see me watching you, you make no sign. You come on, unsmiling, up the ramp. I open the door just enough to let you through. You come in, the pure fragrance of melilot, the shape that sustains you, the breath that moves. The portable chess set is on the bar counter by my gin and tonic. You ask for the same. Larios gin is made from sugar cane, the cheapest crop in creation, and tastes vaguely of mouse droppings.

You had come from afar, had already spent five days in Cómpeta, were thinking of leaving, the bitch had given you a darkened room, to share with little Petrushka.

'Do you find me masculine?' you asked as if it were a code.

And I answered, 'Do you find me feminine?'

There it began. You had to sit to try and recover. Luis kept close watch from the kitchen, but for us the bar was deserted. You spoke in an accent unfamiliar to me, you were several women simultaneously, come from different directions. It was most disturbing beginning again.

Did I seem real to you, dearest? One day in error I'd call you by a different name, it wouldn't be your name, and all would be over between us. One day you would begin to turn away from me, I turn away from you, you leaving. I know no other life before you. Steffen Karr drinks all evening in a strange hotel. I take you again so that my existence in you can go on. It's a dream, love is invented, we have invented it anew.

Then: the curious long kiss, your head in the clothes. Left behind: the time alone, the dead stillness, bat and lynx faces amongst the cobwebs, stirrings and gnawings in the heat of midafternoon, the incessant drone of flies, a small bird suspended on the wire outside. With tight nerves drawn like elastic, I hear the bird fly silently away. The stirrings and gnawings resume.

Against the hill the kiln is fired, thick grey smoke gushes from the pyre, unfurling upwards, then rolling back over Cómpeta. A little girl, self-absorbed and phosphorescent, is dancing in the flames. (We 'was shaking like mads'.) Gunfire sounds over the next hill. We are together at last. Time runs out in a circle.

– 58 –

Last Letter

Østersøgade 254
8 Julio 1980

My dear

Your letter came one the second of July, a rainy Wednesday morning, and thank you for that my love. It is Monday evening now, it is warm, I have all windows open, I am alone. Petrushka is at Steffen. Sgftfujhklppeoam-bcbcaquapl – I don't know what to answer. I can tell you about the beatch yesterday (I was in Rørvig in this weekend the first of summer's).

The sea was light grey as the sand. There was a vague wind, not strong enough to create foam but enough for the sunlight to make small and jumping reflecs, – the almost unbroken seasurface is colourless, it underlines the impression of material, – moire.

As so often before when I arrive to the beatch it was nearly empty. But soon later there are several people – as usually mostly lonely gentlemen. Where are all their wifes always hiding? They are not at the beatch. I use your *djelaba* everywhere now, also at the beatch, I lay on it, take it on take it off, use it as a pilow and as a tent. It is rarely too cold and never too hot, it makes me feeling home everywhere, it's a kind of recidense. I am looking forward to the smell of warm sand when I go to sleep in nights.

Some strand-wanderers pass several times, especialy I noticed two, loudly talking, not exactly noisy but proud of the conversation subject (which of the towns of Bornholm are situated southernmost). There are some people to whom everything they touch automatically become enviable to others: Think only to be them . . . and to get those shoes – and those thoughts, and exactly that colour of hair. They don't boast to that they are too, nearly royalistic, contented – I will say they are almost discret comparing to their contentment.

My father got some of the same, but at him the 'royalistic contentment' is rather naivite. He still, in the age of 72, gets astonished that not everybody is like him. But his naivite has been wounded (or vulnerable?)

during the last years from my mother's knife-sharp grief. Now he marvels in an uncertain way, not in an enthusiastically. (But still he reads indifferent newspapers aloud even if you keep your forefinger on the spot in your own book.) I'm vaguely looking listening to Margot Fonteyn telling about 'The Magic of the Dance' while I'm writing this. I've discovered a kind of interest for the ballet during the last years. It is new to me – like my interest of green plants in my windows. Both of its spinster-interest (spinster – what a mad word). But I'm swimming too. And write poems. It is after all youngish?

I re-read the sentence of the strand. There is something wrong. How can there be reflecs when the material was colourless? But there was. Maybe I have told about it in the wrong order?

I wear a golden chain around the waist, also at the beatch, also in the night. Try to imagine if you would like the sign. Feel a little false to wear it when you are not there. Feel half excited, half shy because of the slavelike in the sign, the supple. I am attract but know it is all a lie: I am no slave girl.

Later.

Took my bike, went to my sister's grave (haven't been there since I last wrote to you). The flowers were full of holes because of all the rain, little snails lived in the white petals.

Now it rains again, the windows are open, it is difficult to find out what is the sound of the rain and what of the chestnut leaves.

[unsigned]

PART VI:

Contretemps at Cranley Gardens

Events Leading to the
Hill–Anders Divorce,
Decree Nisi and Absolute

Berlin,
1 April 1973

My Dearest,

After a long time of silence and then your letter and phone calls now a few
lines from me. Today the so-called April-weather started with rain and
storm and the sweetness of April seems to have disappeared, but the rain
will do nature very well.

Mr Kunoth has died a fortnight ago on a heart attack and Mrs Kunoth
dressed in black is doing the garden now in a rather sad manner. I can't
write much – my spirits are a bit low, but of my mood sometimes I can't
control.

It would of course be lovely if you could come for a weekend but it
would not be good for us to be together in my little flat over a longer
period as the narrowness would choke us again after a while and we
would feel like wild beasts in a cage who can't escape from each other.
We have made this experience not only once – on the other hand we
would wonderfully live in much more space when you don't feel bound
so strongly to your family any longer. You see I don't believe it when
you say: your family doesn't mean all that much to you. Once I had this
illusion – I mean once I believed it – but in the meantime I have (and I
had to) learnt the reality. The discovery was hard for me, but this has
re-established my own life and has given me back at the same time part
of my independence.

Nevertheless it has not changed my feelings towards you and when
you think I might be finished with you therefore I can only tell and reassure you that this will never be the case (proof of it in September last year)
as a considerable part of my heart belongs to you whatever may happen

(in good and in bad) – something eternal. I hope very much that you can understand the sense of my words expressed in such a poor English. I miss you very much, but I had to learn to live without you and to rely on myself.

Let me hear soon when you will come. *Je t'embrasse beaucoup.*

Hannelore

Wednesday, 12 April 1972

This morning as I was crossing the hallway I saw 'with fascinated horror' some sort of long official document being pushed and forced through the letterbox, for all the world like an elongated tapeworm being forcefully shat from an anus to fall on the mat with a plop.

These documents, like lawyers' writs and things that put you off, can easily attain eighty centimetres and more. Have court proceedings started in an attempt to expel us from these premises for non-payment of quarterly rent?

Live at the top of the tree of Tule; excrement to be expected lower down. The crack in the living-room ceiling extrudes a foul-smelling caca-like liquid that stinks of urine. The big white Chinese lantern, so pristine when we bought it in Liberty's of Regent Street, is now filthy; the air here is bad, petrol fumes rise from the broadway below. Five bars of dirt, like tidal wrack, mark the ceiling, painted in black and purple psychedelic stripes by the previous owners, given five or six coats of white emulsion at the start of our tenancy, that for Coppera would last more than thirty years, longer than our marriage.

The books are out of order and uncatalogued, ranged along the dado, leaning at a tilt. No flowers. The wine-stained Staunton chess pieces are ranged in order on the chessboard made by a friend of Hal Rice's.

The crack in the ceiling is before my eyes, the stench remains constant. Outside, a kind of tower, tilted at an angle, ready to fall into the stinking broadway below.

The refuse has not been collected. A mountain of shiny black plastic bags clots the pavements. The traffic converges from six different directions; double-decker buses wait in their corral below, big as elephants. The stench that rises from the hallway five floors below is formidable. Stench of Chingford Lock. No flowers.

The dark bar across the way has lost the last letter in its name: THE GREE MAN. Here the head-butters assemble, the karate kickers.

Sound of milk bottles being smashed at the dairy at the back, below the fire escape; a way of relieving their feelings? A sudden movement might prove fatal. We are looking at three hundred layers of domestic refuse. No flowers, no air, stink of petrol rises from below. Breathlessness. Reading Conan Doyle: 'The Resident Patient'. He offers a reassuring world, an England that could be controlled. Biddle, Hayward, Moffatt, the hanged man, the merest blind. The black plastic bags glisten in the polluted air, the stench rises up, breathlessness, no flowers. A woodland glade it is not. Like a better past gone rotten.

I used to think that Soho lay underground, populated by criminals and prostitutes. Is it true? Rory, let it be stated, frequents a bleak bar situated just off the disused railway line, now a nature path, patronised by part-time gardeners, long-distance Welsh lorry drivers, tired old sods and other miscellaneous riff-raff, laid-off lathe turners.

Who wrote of 'the confounding melancholy of ordinary conversation'? A small listless little sod is talking terrible garbage to another sad sod. One is drinking half-pints of Long Life, a disgusting brew, the other shots of Tio Pepe. The genial host grunts as he pulls pints. There is a dartboard, of course. A sign says:

> This bar is dedicated to those merry souls who make drinking a pint a pleasure, who reach contentment before capacity and whatever they drink can take it and remain gentlemen.

The name of this quaint hostelry? The Royal Oak. The Weeping Willow might have been a fitter monicker. Rory went there to wallow in its all-pervasive and curiously predictable gloom. An ill-lit place; you see eyes fixed on you in the gloom as you enter. It can be reached via the Dewy Dell along the overgrown railway line.

The stout owner pants like a pug dog, sweats like a pig, likes a game of darts with some of the dart-minded patrons. Drinking Long Life is like sucking off an old tree.

Saturday, 4 August 1979

Fay's birthday, thirty-four today. Rory's presents: two bottles of good German hock, to be shared. A book for her: Hemingway's *To Have and Have Not*. Watney's pub in the evening, in the pub garden under the trees, copper beech, a strong feeling of Berlin, or can it be the love-twinge that colours the place, makes it monochrome, the colour that always augurs happiness for Rory, the sojourner? The premises darken as evening falls. White Shield poured in cunning fashion, rolled cigarettes, speak of this and that, walked back. I cannot say 'home'. Cranley Gardens is her home, not mine, it will be impossible when Terence, her troubled son, returns.

Terence is a disturbed child, the prototypical modern child perhaps, no perhaps about it; the break-up of the marriage upset him and more so than he can well explain, either to his understanding mother with whom he lives, or his less sympathetic father, who lives elsewhere with another woman, to make it all the more complicated.

He wrote Fay a little letter. 'Daer Mummy, I am small like a ant. Kill me. I love you. Good bye.'

He was having trouble in school and in the divided, half-empty home; he had begun stealing, he told lies, seemed confused and unhappy. He stole money from his mother's purse to buy an expensive watch and wore it, flaunted it. Fay made him take it off and told him to jump on it. He did so. No more recriminations, and no more stealing.

The half-Persian cat Medea was crawling with fleas, always savaging its anus, leaving white fluff on the furniture. Fay wore scanty red bra and panties, permitted Rory a glimpse.

'Don't get ideas.'

Rory, clasping himself as though suffering from acute bellyache, already had ideas. He brought her presents of wine from the wine store, flowers nicked from the gardens around, he came bearing gifts.

'Do you like lamb?'

Fay served him Greek lamb for dinner, much wine, Turkish coffee, Disque Bleu, Jewish bread. She wanted love, would give herself away, she was a most lovable woman.

Fay's severest term of censure was 'Peasant!' hissed between protruding teeth before slamming the door in Rory's face, a meek smile bisected on the mat.

'Dry mouth,' you said, turning away; though not dry below, never dry there, for Rory. 'Eggs make you caustic.'

'But I'm always caustic,' Rory protested.

— 60 —

In the Woods

I saw her once hop forty paces in a public street.

i

'If you can't, why do you try?' Her gunmetal blue-black hair unbound, her clothes in disarray, she looked like one of the Sabine women. Rory couldn't let her alone.

An awkwardness with Fay:

'We needn't . . .' (do it), she said, short and defiant. 'We need,' Rory insisted. He was all for it. They did it.

She did not approve of 'cowering indoors', liked to slap on her war paint, slip into something fetching, go out on the town. Put a brave face on it. Step out.

She came from Plymouth but had little good to say of it; she was of Irish stock on her mother's side, the Foyles of Clifden in remotest Connemara near the bracing Atlantic seaboard backing on the Maamturks where rain poured down incessantly and the cattle bawled in pure misery in the drenched fields. She had graduated from Leeds University with better grades than Henchley the biker, her boyfriend. She was smarter than him; at least smart enough to leave him when their son, Terence, was still a child. She was married at the age of nineteen, too soon and to the wrong man. The chaps in the office did not appeal to her; they were all deadbeats.

She took the Channel ferry to Paris to see some art but found it was a holiday and all the galleries were closed. The captain invited her up to his bridge to admire his instruments, allowed her to drive the ferry. 'It was strange,' she said.

'Oh, you like a bit of strange?'

Evidently.

Coppera, fast as lightning when it came to picking up hints and evasions, detected palpable evidence of misconduct on the very naked body of Rory.

Claw prints and weals on Rory's guilty-looking back and pectorals suggested that he had yielded himself to the wild embraces of some uncontrollable she-beast who had inflicted heavy punishment, had torn, bitten and scratched lumps out of him.

'What are those marks I see?' Coppera inquired most silkily from the bed, watching Rory dressing himself, rapidly, guiltily, evasively.

'Someone was teaching me life-saving methods in the Hampstead Pond,' said the bold Rory most swimmingly. 'The water is very dirty and I bruise easily.'

'You lie easily too, mister,' Coppera said sourly, observing the maulings disappear into a shirt, a belt being resolutely tightened.

'If those are love-bites, then you are in very bad trouble.'

Rory slunk away, looking most abashed.

Hannelore had spoken of the enormous need for compensation that a working life demanded, and the more clerical the work, the more enormous the demand. Panting like a black leopard climbing into a thorn tree to get after an ape, she (Fay, in her home in Cranley Gardens) gouged and scratched and tore at Rory's back and squeezed his testicles at the moment of simultaneous climax as if squeezing the bulb of a scent spray that would squirt seed point-blank into her wide open and receptive womb. From these fierce encounters between the sheets Rory emerged all marked and bleeding as though he had barely escaped from the attentions of a cougar or puma and not the rather unrestrained embraces of one of Her Majesty's more able tax inspectoresses in charge of a department in the vicinity of Great Portland Street.

'This mustn't be any hole-and-corner affair,' she told her newest lover. 'I intensely dislike furtiveness.'

Rory's sons had babysat for Terence when his mother was out on the town. When she took a flying leap from the mezzanine into the kitchen, gun-metal blue hair flying, Rory thought he detected something both predatory and feline. Perhaps she was half-Persian cat herself? She was in the best of health, unlike the ailing Medea.

She had been a former neighbour on the second floor below, abutting on the broadway; was to be seen in biker's gear, carrying her helmet. Her husband was Syd Henchley, the biker who left his 'hog' in the hall below. When he rolled it out, Fay jumped on the pillion and off they roared.

Fragments of food adhered to her somewhat prominent incisors, akin to a cougar after the kill. She liked to drink wine, introduced Rory to strong potions in working-class public houses, this brewer's Strong and that brewer's

Brown. Rory took her to *Nosferatu* at Notting Hill Gate, where all the freaks in London had converged to see Werner Herzog's unnerving movie. She was a bachelor-girl, having thrown over Syd the biker, struck camp, was 'making out' in Cranley Gardens where Rory came calling with bottles of Rioja and flowers nicked from adjoining gardens. Sometimes she played the piano, to calm Terence before he dropped off to sleep.

She reminded Rory of those scatterbrained and fearless society girls racing about in the early novels of Evelyn Waugh – Agatha Runcible & Co. Crouch End, Finsbury Park and Barnet seemed not quite the places to take Fay Henchley, and certainly not into those pubs there.

The broadway, Muswell Hill, was a place of broken marriages; the corner block of flats bulked over it like a cliff face with monkeys staring down into the dirty pool below, that was the broadway with incessantly circling traffic converging from five or six lanes, leading to the West End and out past Barnet into the country, or what passed for countryside there, out Watford way.

Her hair hung down her back to her trim seat, referred to as her 'bureaucratic bum', in the manner of Juliette Gréco. She was petite. Coppera, who detested and despised all rivals, held her in low esteem, dismissed her as a nit-wit. Who else but a nit-wit would have married Syd Henchley?

Social services, such as baby-sitting and general neighbourliness, had led to sexual services; one thing led to another and before you could say Heloïse and Abelard they were at the game of the two-backed beast, as to the manner born. Lubricity on the sofa and glimpses of red underthings were followed by extended love-bouts in the double bed, commencing just as soon as Terence was down for the night.

Terence was a fair-haired quiet little boy. He had the reserve that the only child has; his parting shots could be devastating. One morning, leaving, he had encountered Rory arriving with stolen flowers and a two-litre bottle of Italian plonk. 'A bit early to start drinking,' Fay's most unsettled offspring remarked, 'Isn't it?' It was 10.30 a.m. Greenwich Mean Time.

She was rounded and ripened, with two of the roundest flanks, from nape to rump hung the longest shank of hair down to the very cleft of her bum; all womanly, of all sirens the most retiring, the moodiest; of all desirables the most modest. 'Nothing is more disgusting than a question'.

No pouting out of lips, no batting of eyes, nor eyelash flutterings, no bust or bum play, no come-hither looks. She was what she was, without deceitful ways.

'You empty me,' Rory (The Mighty Member) expostulated.

'You fill me,' Fay interpolated.

'Finished', pronounced Coppera with relish, ever wont to take wind out of sails, deflate presumptions, a deliverer of grim judgements and prognostications, a facer-up to unpleasant facts that had to be faced. It must have been Jonathan Carl's Calvinistic German blood coursing through her veins, diluted with Welsh pessimism on her mother's side.

There was more Taffy to her than German stoicism and fixity; you couldn't argue with her. Ever try and argue with Balance, the constellation Libra, the seventh sign of the Zodiac? Save your breath to cool your porridge.

We were through with each other, through with our marriage, we were finished with each other, all washed up, for it was impossible to go on. And yet we did go on, after a fashion, for a while longer, anyway.

ii

Anna wrote from Copenhagen:

'I've saved enough money for the journey I think, but the time of the year is wrong, I think; for a long & difficult trip, which Greece always are (is) – it must be spring or early summer, just like it must be morning or early day when you start a difficult work. So I ordered (booked) a room in the monastery in Jutland, I told you about once. I finished the first book there, an extremely calm and beautiful place.

'Again you are so distant even if you are in the middle of my memory. I can never place you in the everyday (In my imagination?) – it's always an island with sun and no money – and no work. I must be bored into the pain before I start to write.

'So, my late love, give sound – tell me constantly where you are and be faithful – as I am.'

I phoned Anna from Fay's place at nine o'clock one night when Fay was out and Petrushka answered in Danish. She had only two or three words of English: 'Actually, Mister Hill'.

Her mother told me what she had to tell me. She would go to Jutland to work on a book from 5 September to 20th and prepare a reading for the Danish Academy in Copenhagen in early October. She would like to fly to Cómpeta for a fortnight. Two weeks was the longest she could allow. Petrushka was in a new school. She had begun that day, she liked it. She (the mother) had to be miserable in order to write. Orslev Kloster, Orsleukloster 7800 Skive, Jutland, would find her.

She was working in a monastery (cloister).

'I have been kicked out of house and home,' Rory told Anna.

'Why?'

'For irregularity. Or do I mean inconsistency?'

'Uuuuuh!'

'Exactly, my thoughts in a nutshell.'

'What will you do?'

'I'll have to find another home.'

'And will you?'

'Who can say?'

After a rapid breakfast of Viennese coffee and Gauloise at Cranley Gardens, which was the only honeymoon that Rory ever had, he took her to a deucedly odd double-feature programme of Werner Herzog movies at the New Electric Cinema in Portobello Road, a 134 bus to Warren Street and a taxi (£2) to the cinema (ticket £3 each) where *La Soupière* (1977) was showing with *Heart of Glass* (1976). The first a documentary about a volcano that never erupted on an island from which 75,000 people were evacuated, the camera tracked and zoomed about an empty city of stray dogs and blinking traffic lights; thousands of snakes had come down from the mountains, alarmed by the ground heat, to drown themselves in the sea. The feature film seemed to be about demented German glass-blowers. Fay sniggered at the deadly seriousness of the amazing Krauts.

Sun under trees. You wanted to. The dogs. Walked to Baker Street Station. Italian coffee place closed. Health food place open. Waited for the Globe to open its doors. Stayed until darkness fell. 27 to Archway, 134 to Cranley Gardens, home not home, not for Rory but for Fay. Port, bed, deep penetration, peaceful night, raining, discussed women's liberation (lower case please) in the kitchen.

In bed you admitted that you had wanted it under the leafy trees, ash or maple in Kensington Gardens, when we kissed, you had wanted more, the whole hog.

The sun in the grass, the dogs cavorting by the pond. Walk by the water, Essex or Sussex Gardens, drops of rain. The night. Back now upstairs. The cat's asleep, Terence away.

The moon, scudding cloud, came from behind, you at first passive then passionate, claws. Port and Gauloise before sleep. Intimate odour. Tenderness. Touch. Silence.

'I feel reality is retreating from me' – here Fay glanced quickly with the clouded pupils of a Persian cat at Rory, who was fidgeting. 'Or I'm retreating from reality.'

With shoes off and knees under chin, tucked up in the window-seat, she was watching what was passing outside, a dreamy powder-blue Persian queen cat troubled by something.

Stilly crouches she! Hey, heartache!

Never in his life had Rory forced his attentions on anybody, man, woman or beast. He was in some ways a craven lover, an admirer of fine but *soi-disant* parts, a luster after vanishing tail.

Whenever he expedited a lady's lust (as soon as possible after his attentions have fastened on her), she took a venu under her girdle and swelled upon it. Rory said 'When I touch I then begin for to let affection in,' just like Robert Herrick, the randy divine.

For so had it came to pass for Hannelore, who had conceived with child in the course of a short London break at 29 Chandos Road, Willesden Green, NW2, and had it aborted in the Hague.

Similarly with Fay Foyle: conception in torrid bouts one August in Cranley Gardens, aborted of a five month foetus (a daughter-to-be for Rory who had always wanted one) in a London clinic.

As it had come to pass otherwise for Coppera, who had fruitfully conceived and brought forth a trio of bouncing boyos.

When Rory had obliged Fay Foyle by staying three nights in a row at her house in Cranley Gardens, in her double bed between her scorching thighs, he had burnt his boats and no error. For by obliging the one he mortally insulted and disobliged the other, her deadly rival, Coppera (Rory's legal spouse for twenty-four years and more); who now had him – *Le Vent Galant* – ostracised from hearth and home, threw the potsherds in his face, told him to push off and never dare darken her door (now it was all hers) again.

Rory of the Hills, the classically homeless wanderer, the lost sojourner heading west, now cravenly begged permission to occupy Coppera's Andalucían *hacienda* in the foothills of the Sierra Almijara, for a year, or for some unspecified space of time. This the very *casa* purchased with Rory's elastic funds, when he was in funds, his time and his signature.

And when his time was up there, on Coppera's sufferance, where would he voyage to? He would see. Time would tell. A way would be revealed unto him. One thing was certain: England was finished for him. Ireland would come to the rescue, and through the good graces furthermore of he who was to be Nobel Prizeman of 1995, Heaney himself, who wrote of Aosdána and Cnuas, all double-Dutch to wandering Rory, now fairly demented with worry, deprived of his family and unable to work, homeless indeed.

'Lies again, always your fancy lies,' snapped Coppera. 'You're telling lies again.'

'What would be the good of telling you the truth?' muttered the devious Rory, blinded with his very own lies, which he deemed to be his truths, the only hope.

'The kids are old enough now to be told the truth.'

Arguing with Coppera was like standing in the doorway and having the door slammed in your face, time and time again.

'I understand you,' Rory told Fay. Whereas even after more than twenty years of co-habitation he didn't understand Coppera. She was as much a mystery to him as the first time he had encountered her, at a party for South Africans in her top-floor room in Belsize Park, London NW3.

'I understand you perfectly,' he told Fay. And he did.

Phoning Fay

Emerging from the depths of Queen's Wood and darting across the road into Highgate Wood (where all the corpses of the Great Plague are buried) and making his way up the disused and overgrown railway track for a service that no longer served Muswell Hill, in the vicinity of Pembridge Garden Villas and the former residence of man-murderer Nielsen who had murdered and then dismembered his eighteen male victims and either flushed them down the drains or buried them in the garden, Rory presently broke cover to immediately disappear into a public telephone box where he dialled 88 77 44 and he could hear it ringing in Cranley Gardens, close enough to hit with a catapult, and the receiver repeated the number he had just dialled as if uttering the password.

'It's I.'

'You can't come?'

'I can come.'

'Well then come. I'm just out of a shower. Standing here dripping,' she snickered.

'I'm coming as fast as public transport permits.'

'Peasant!'

'More like a pheasant. I do live in the woods, you know, nowadays. Rory of the Hills, blood-brother to Wandering Angus.'

'You're still a peasant.'

iii

The Henchley-Foyle marriage was not made in Heaven, so few marriages are, and had begun to disintegrate as soon as the co-celebrants had shifted ground, come to the big city of London.

Something was wrong; Henchley felt he was losing ground, losing face. When Rory encountered him on the stinking stairs, putting away his hog in the hallway, removing his leather gloves and helmet, flaxen hair plastered to his skull with sweat, no greetings were exchanged. He could already sense the presence of another suitor for his estranged wife here, sniffing around. Henchley wore the cross, disgruntled hot expression that was habitual with him, as though he were worrying about an overdraft, or the hog wasn't performing right, or he hadn't gotten his oats; he was all fired up with resentment; hidden disappointments were devouring him from within. The thought flew through Rory's mind, 'God, she's brave or reckless to lie under this heap of resentment!'

Some hint of this disturbance of heart was in the flushed biker's face as he ascended the stairs to his supper, to more humiliations. Perhaps she had refused him her favours? Syd was lost without regular nooky. She had told Rory some of their troubles. He had followed her into the child's room after an argument that lasted from midnight until three in the morning, waking up the child with his voice raised in anger, and he had done an ugly act, the child saw it and vomited. He continued to perform the ugly act and the child continued to vomit.

That was the end of Henchley for Fay, the end of their marriage too. He was told to pack and go, take his things with him.

He had given her a last lingering look of pure hatred and stamped downstairs for the last time, hauled out the hog and went farting off through the broadway. It was good riddance to bad rubbish.

She was a lovely silky lady to be in bed with on a cold night. She liked port for a nightcap and smoked Disque Bleu, liked to play madrigals on the clavichord, seventeenth and eighteenth-century music, Monteverdi's *Ulysses*, read sheet music, which delighted the notoriously unmusical Rory, who preferred Jacqueline Françoise and Billie Holiday. Women do not relish getting old; Fay was afraid of getting into a rut. Change was everything, she said, change was indeed life.

'It's necessary to make a change sometimes. Getting old, being old (Rory was fifty-two), means you can't make it any more.'

It was necessary to make a change, seize the day. Having penetrated into the depths of Queen's Wood with Rory and two bottles of Guinness and found a mossy bank on to which the sunlight filtered, she would sit up and straighten her back, no sluttish compromising positions tolerated. In a little while she sat up; the interrogation was peremptory, peppery: 'Why have you gone all shady on me suddenly?'

In marriage, particularly marriage undertaken rashly at a young and tender age (Fay had been married at the age of nineteen), there is always the strong partner and the weak one. Fay was the strong one and Syd the weak, say the predictable factor, for the failure would be all of his own making. He would make a mess of it. It was only a matter of time before the contracted bonds were broken: they would acrimoniously go their different ways. For he had had something good and now he had lost it. He had only his hog to comfort him, his black leather gear, the lovingly polished Harley Davidson throbbing between his legs when he let her out on the open road, farting like thunder, to show his contempt, to display his waywardness; was he not a biker through and through? He felt tenderly about his hog. Christ, man, he *loved* his hog.

He had settled somewhere far from London, far from Fay, somewhere down the country found other employment out-of-doors where he could display his strength. Terence visited him from time to time. He inquired of Fay, asked how she was, kept in touch, spoke on the phone, the same surly bloke as before. He couldn't help his nature, God had given him that nature, it was what he was, Syd Henchley, late of Leeds.

Fay kept in touch with Rory now, spoke in low adenoidal tones into his ear, a cat-purring, did not identify herself, because Rory at once knew who it was; Fay uttered the code-word for the day, the password for strange places – today it was to be *Winchmore Hill.*

Did Rory know where that was? He did not; but he could find it. Precise instructions were issued. He was to leave immediately, take the 102 to The Cock, then a W4 or 23 or 29 to The Green Dragon on Winchmore Hill, where he would find Fay in the Lounge, sampling the brews.

He went there. And she was there, sitting up like a cat, feeling the fires, purring, a smoky Persian.

She had of course admirers. Pill One and Pill Two and Boris-the-Bad of Yugoslavia were mentioned. 'Pill' and 'pillock' were dismissive terms of contempt. Pill Two took her out to a pub where a fractious drinker had taken offence and wanted to sort him out, hitching up his belt and glaring at Pill Two who had gone white as a sheet.

'Are you a man or a mouse or what are you?'

'No, no, no, I'm a mouse,' Pill Two protested feebly.

Fay was much amused by this frank display of the weak submission of machismo. She tittered when she told Rory that her fine protector had feet of clay. Syd would have sorted him out all night. You don't mill it with a biker. Syd would have beaten the shit out of him, laid him out cold.

Boris-the-Bad had phoned from Yugoslavia. Every so often he liked to phone her in the middle of the night, cracking his whip to make her perform. 'Boris speaking! How is my little perisher?' Love was a dirty business of rape and rapine, women were abject slaves. He was in the carpet business, import and export. Rory saw him as sallow-complexioned, bluff and bossy, with a walrus moustache like Nietzsche. He drank black coffee, smoked thick cigars with the bands on, took no shit from nobody, nobody least of all a woman, least of all a pretty one. Fay was his little London quail whom he adored, in his own way, from a safe distance.

'How do you spell Ljubljana?' she asked Rory.

For some reason or other, nothing to do with reason, she reminded Rory of Molly Cushen. The same long black hair, silken presence, same adenoidal confidential dark tones that inferred some dark conspiracy, talk at a tangent. Fay Henchley-Foyle was the woman Molly Cushen might have become, had she left Celbridge to discover the big outside world for herself. She was also reincarnated in the Dublin brunette Anne Marie, who trimmed Rory's locks and beard in a Cork hairdressing emporium – Ikon, upstairs in Princes Street – the same unsettling presence, same clotted-cream voice, the slurred enunciation suggestive of a Persian cat purring, the same I-know-you look in the eye.

These were to date avatars for Rory, reminding him of the wind blowing dark tresses across a child's chalk-white face on a bridge so long ago.

Rory now found himself standing on what the Danes (they who abhor public rage, calamity, the unforeseen, all manifestations of public and private disorder, for they are an orderly people and without order there is chaos; unless it be Germanic order – *Ordnung* – and then you get a worse chaos) call *Livsfare Jordskred* or unsteady earth, a warning sign on a cliff that beetles o'er its base into the Kattegat.

It was a very bad place for a Dane to be; also for poor Rory, for whom it was Queer Street.

Cranley Gardens would be impossible for Rory when Fay's son returned from the country.

Rory dialled 88 77 44, a most improbable conjunction of matching numerals and Fay's voice answered, laughing as though she were in the middle of something.

'Rory here.'

'Oh, hello Rory there. Are you coming over? I just had a shower and I'm dripping wet. Why don't you just drop in for tea and trifle?'

'I'm on my way.'

The pubs they frequented were Dick's Bar on the Finchley Road, The Good Shepherd on Archway Road, The Rose and Crown in Highgate, The Woodman by the hill where the 134s turn up for Muswell Hill Broadway between the two woods. She wore a blue tunic, a sleeveless black leather jacket, high heels, an expensive leather shoulder bag full of tenners.

She spoke of a vacation in Simla after Christmas, £2,000 each, with her new husband or man who suffered (on reading her diary) from what she called 'recapitulative jealousy', a bad form of the disease, reading her account of her brief affair with Rory, in and out of the bars and the woods, and the Raoul Dufy exhibition at the Hayward Gallery. Ruddles Best Yorkshire Ale was her preferred tipple.

'Blossom' and 'Sunshine' were her London terms of endearment for Terence, her *muy nervioso*, only son. She was a good mother, concerned for his welfare. 'Sticky' was another of her prohibitive terms.

She was not the early Waugh society girl on a spree, she was not the naughty sixth former looking to lose her virginity in the tool-shed with the virile young gardener or the virile handyman or the virile and handsome ice-cream vendor who had his pitch at the school gate, with all three in order of preference; she was rather Cora, the torrid young wife in James M. Cain's *The Postman Always Rings Twice*, having it off with the journeyman who just happened to be passing through.

She had aborted the five-month foetus without a word to the putative father, Rory. She told him later, at what seemed an opportune moment, perhaps in bed, in the dark. 'Did I ever tell you . . .'

She received Rory at the door, hair wet, eyes sparkling, in loose-fitting housecoat and bare feet, naked under the housecoat, which Rory discovered at the first embrace when the housecoat fell off the wearer of its own accord and with eyes closed she surrendered to the tyranny of love. Was she the deprived child who had grown avaricious for what she wanted? She detested what she called 'routine', by which she meant Missionary-style loving. She wanted the unexpected, close attention to the matter in hand, expected and would get, sexual dynamics; that aroused her to ecstatic states when she capitulated to the attentions of a persistent brute who would take her just as he wanted her, the way she craved to be taken, now receiving Rory (the timid caller transformed) with a new ardour that was mutual, raking his back with her claws, for her claws were out for it, as he took her deeper and deeper, she in a kind of sexual stupor, whispering 'Sorrysorrysorry,' hardly knowing what she was saying or doing. She was Cora, drawing blood.

'Now you can go whistling back across the fields.' Talking was part of the loving and giving that might begin at 11 and end at 4 a.m. with the birds beginning to twitter. It had started on the window-seat with Fay, listening to the revellers going home from The Woodman, and then the long-drawn-out loving, whispering sorrysorrysorry.

> A shudder in the loins engenders there
> The broken wall and tower and Agamemnon dead.

'Don't force me to do something I don't want to do.'

She knew a thing or two about love.

She scratched and panted in the tolls of love as if in the clutches of a predator, whereas it was she who was the bloodthirsty one, growling in her throat, her jaw jutting fiercely, blue-black hair tossed, masking a face that had grown longer, hungry now; she was showing her sharp teeth.

Love had liberated her. In her Cora-mood from *The Postman Always Rings Twice* she would have eaten the postman coming with a package. Instead it was Rory, who had crossed from the heath to pass through Highgate Wood and Queen's Wood visiting the off-licence at the foot of the hill, plucking flowers from suburban gardens, who appeared at the door laden with rhododendrons. Fay drew him in with one prehensile claw. Terence was away with friends; they had the house to themselves.

'I wanna be penetrated,' she said in the provocative nasal whine of Gloria Graham in the movie *Crossfire*. 'I want you to penetrate me.'

She could not be more explicit. She wanted to be carved up on the kitchen table like venison. Pyrotechnics were needed here. She wanted to devour and be devoured, to accept pain and to inflict it with her bared claws on the groaning beast, the god Pan, half-beast, half-man, all god who lived in the woods and was about to start humping her good and proper, running with her to the bed and throwing her down. She wanted the works.

Pan-Rory pounded her liver as though her pelvic parts so tender and open were the mortar which his pestle or mighty member so assiduously pounded; as her breath deepened, her nostrils flared, exposing the stricken whites of her narrow cat's eyes, opening wide as if stricken with *petit mal*, blazed up at Rory.

'Hey, heartache, I'm just slipping away, slipping away.'

Once Rory had returned from Gatwick Airport, having left his wallet behind in the kitchen of Cranley Gardens, only to find a soft-spoken innocuous-looking *succubi* or rival already ensconced in the kitchen, sipping coffee.

'This is Gussy.'

'Oh, howdy Guss!'

The disgruntled Rory spent an uncomfortable night in a friend's pad near Wandsworth Prison and was away early on a Málaga flight, put to the expense of buying a further one-way ticket. Such was life in a pig's eye.

iv

Now Rory would have to begin thinking of 252 and environs in the past tense, for his life had finished there. In summer the broadway had reeked of sickening petrol fumes and the stale stink of uncollected garbage. When the stand of sycamores was cut down in the Patch, the cemented area where the kids played, there was that much less shade; soon it would all be cement and the United Dairy would close.

The kids, ours and others, played in the Patch below, calling out 'Last one up the fire escape is a lesbian!' Thieves crept up it by night and nicked clothes and football gear off the wire clothesline. The apartments were a place of broken marriages.

The front door of the decaying block of flats gave immediately on to the broadway, very murky in winter, very steamy in summer when the tarmac melted. But summer and winter, fall and spring, the place was petrol-fumed as though a lit match would ignite it, send it all up. All the double-decker buses would explode behind the public toilets where the dark youths practised karate chops and high kicks. On the top or fifth floor of the cold water walk-up apartment, Coppera heated water on the stove, filled a bath half-full and bathed the kids, all three in the bath at once, little seals in a rock pool.

In Cranley Gardens just down the hill before Crouch End cricket pitches, the O'Neills were next-door neighbours to Fay Foyle. They had a mongoloid son who wandered about the garden with an air-rifle and took pot-shots at a bottle. At night we heard the manic laughter and the *ping* of hits. The mother was up and about early, hanging washing on the line. The apple tree had a bumper crop. The neighbour beyond the O'Neills hated cats and children. His name was Anthony William Snapes. People can be strange, there's no accounting for some. Mumu would have described them as a low lot, common as dishwater. Perhaps they were; perhaps not; people were just people.

On Saturday 11 August 1975, some twenty-four years after the nuptials in the little RC Church of St Thomas More in London N10, the phone went unanswered at No. 22 Cranley Gardens, until, in exasperation, Fay lifted up the receiver.

'It's for you.'

'Who is it?'

'Coppera.'

Rory strode to the phone like the brave hero in the Dickens novel ascending the scaffold.

'Your things are being sent around in a cab. That's it.'

She rang off. Brief and brutal. Would women make good hangmen? Or should we say 'hangwomen'?

A morose, coloured cab-person came pealing the bell.

'Darby Hall?'

'I believe you're looking for me, Rory Hill, a common misunderstanding. I understand that you have my effects.'

'The lady up there said I was to bring your clobber down 'ere.'

We'd planned to walk across the heath to see Billy Wilder's *Fedora* at the Hampstead Everyman, but hadn't the heart for it. Went instead to the Ruth Ellis pub in the wood, the Magdala of infamous repute. Walked back across the heath in the dark after a session in The White Polar Bear. A bird never flew on one wing. Bought bottle of Schluck at wine store and so home hand-in-hand via the woods. Consumed Schluck in kitchen. Nothing to eat all day. Not hungry. Curiously stunned state, as if struck on head with club. Told to leave home. Fucked Fay silly. Darkness, deep breathing. Ending, ending here.

Without her clothes Fay was more mare than cat. The glossy pelt on her, the dimpled rump, the mane of blue-black hair that reached to the small of her back, the way her nostrils flared. Are you glad to see me? Will you miss me when you're in Dublin? Will you think of me there?

Rory promised that he would. Soon he would be phoning her from airports, flying about, looking for a place to land, a home-base.

The Fay Foyle affair was the straw that broke the camel's back for Coppera Hill. 'You've done it this time. You've let us down too often. You can stay in my place in Cómpeta but I think you should pay some of the bills here. That's only fair.'

When Coppera spoke of fairness and fair play, it meant that she was up to something, scheming; feminine wiles had come into play, or so Rory's naturally suspicious nature informed him. When she brought the children into any dispute and thrust them into the firing-line, it meant the gloves were off and the claws out. Coppera's claws served a very different purpose to Fay's. But all claws were the same when they scratched and drew blood and all women's natures were much the same, particularly when it came to defending their interests, with the weapons they were supplied with, the savvy and the savagery, modified to suit the occasion, or the man for whom allowances would have to be made. If you can't, why do you try? Do you like lamb? Will you miss me? I can I can I can, I do I do I do, I will I will I will I will!

Brace up.

PART VII:

Down Mexico Way

Mexico City, Cuernavaca, Acapulco
February 1998

– 61 –

Blood and Sand

In a handsome park in Acapulco stands a heraldic bronze male figure set up high on a granite pedestal and what is more wearing nothing but Bermuda shorts and sandals, brown-skinned as a medlar but bald as a snooker ball, his brow furrowed as if in deep thought, troubled by matters of state, mouth set in a grim line, the great hooded eyes partly closed. Can it be ennui or boredom or the tedium of office or just constipation? The statue is called 'He's Got the Whole World in His Hands'.

It is none other than Don Señor Alfredo Calles, grandson of the General and President of all Mexico in the troubled decade 1924–34.

There can be no other kind of time in Mexico but troubled time; no time there in that grim, goaty land can be other than troubled. The lovely engulf-ing air trembles as though the spirits of the superstitious Aztecs, fear-crazed and given to making placatory sacrifices to the sun on their blood-soaked altars, on a daily basis, virgins and children not excluded, still breathed in the living air that blew from Cuernavaca and in through the Cortés window of the Rancho Pico set most prettily in the uplands of the state of Morelos, setting the wind chimes atinkle.

The trembling air was Aztec air, like the brown prehensile begging hands of the women who begged around the Cuernavaca Cathedral steps; beg-ging, forever begging, their hands outstretched for baksheesh. The twin volcanoes were standing guard fifty miles off, across the undulating valley all was shivery Aztec air, just as much Mexico as the eighty-two (Rory looked up and counted them) buzzards that arrived from nowhere one bright morn-ing to circle slowly in a funeral pyre dance over the Rancho Pico, their shadows moving slow and sedately across the lawn and over the swimming pool, glaring down at the lone nudist doing lengths, Rory looking up at them, numerous as bluebottles and circling, silently, going down one by one to feed on the corpse of the horse killed by another horse in a fit of jeal-ous rage, involving a foal and a kick that killed; where else could it happen but in Mexico, in the state of Morelos?

The expiring breath of the innocents hung in the air. The buzzards were descending one by one or in twos and threes, an inbred courtesy perhaps,

the courtesy of the air, the good manners of the buzzards who had flown
from God knows where, far away anyway, sensing or knowing of the kill.
But how? Their sight was said to be phenomenal; by smell, then? But would
the pong of death carry that far? Yes, in Mexico it would.

We came upon them feeding in the dried-up marsh by the soccer field;
a preliminary rustling like old papers being disturbed by a wind or an
umbrella blowing itself inside-out announced their presence and then three
of them came stumbling out, bloated with bloodied beaks they use for slashing open cadavers that they fancy. Getting airborne again with some difficulty, coming out of the long grass where the mare was decomposing, they
brought with them the stench.

The stench was brutal. More than all the bad things that had ever happened in Mexico since the execution of Maximilian; a stench more terrible than words can describe. Blood had been spilt lavishly everywhere;
it was a fecundating agent, like sulphate of soda, quicklime, petrol to clear
weeds.

Rory's fastidious nostrils were assailed by a smell that would make a sickroom seem sweet, a lingering smell of dissolution that seemed to collect bulk
and breathing body of all the vileness ever ejected from sick bodies, from
middens, from the open holes of Mexican toilets where women crouched to
discharge menstrual filth. And it was more than that; it was the stink of a
Mexican battlefield, with the buzzards having a banquet. The smell made the
hair of his head rise up of its own accord and he was back in a flick sixty-five
years to Springfield again and was six years old and standing by the dead
sheep that the dogs had opened up in their savagery and now the maggots
were busily having a go at the black and purple interior of corruption with
a scarcely perceptible yet insistent activity, like cancer eating one up from
inside as it had taken Dado. The sheep lay on her side against the wall of
Mangan's field where she had come to die or been chased into the corner by
the dogs, who had her cornered then, as the maggots had her now and were
working on her with a will, poor thing. She was theirs. Is that what the Bard
meant by 'progressing through the guts of a beggar'?

And I thought again of Molly Cushen, who had been my first love even if
I had never touched her. She had shown me what love was, standing on the
bridge with the wind blowing, weeping as though her heart had broken, as
it probably had, for her mother had died on her and, who knows, maybe in
pain; love was weeping on a humpbacked bridge. Sorrow was eating out her
heart, as they say.

I thought too of Harriet seated with her husband above the hot sand of the bullring in Málaga, just like the old movie *Blood and Sand* with Rita Hayworth and Tyrone Power as the stoats pattering after blood. Tyrone Power had to swim across a river and in the blue moonlight of day-for-night photography fight a bull, so that he could ascend to the castle where Rita slept, and climb up the side of the creeper and enter, to find her preparing for bed, her wide mouth decorated with a slash of lipstick like blood, as if she were a vampire, which was all extremely exciting and mysterious when I saw it at the age of fourteen at the Savoy Cinema in Dublin. It was the movie that made a matador of John Fulton, born Fulton John Short, his Italian father, a house-painter, having changed his name from Schoccitti to Short, which Spaniards couldn't pronounce. He killed his first bull in Mexico in 1953, Rita's bleeding mouth no doubt still vividly in his mind when he (aged twelve) had first seen her and knew he wanted to be a bullfighter. She had made a man of him.

It was a day in April when the great Ordoñez dispatched with much valour and panache the five great beasts he had been contracted to slaughter, four black as tar and one the colour of a puma, not disposed to fight, least of all fight Antonio Ordoñez. I had been unfaithful to Coppera in the spare bed in the *casa* Harriet's husband, my good friend John, had rented in Nerja; the downward slide had begun. Harriet lied about the fat lip I had given her; she said a pumpkin had dropped from the patio roof. Her policy was to lie in your teeth until found out and then give in with as much grace as possible.

The smell of blood must have wafted up to her; but weren't women inured to blood and blood-letting, their own at least? They had to grow accustomed to it from the alarm of their first menses. It was in their nature, as love was too, submitting or desiring what you had to have, the chosen one, all that giving and taking; it made me sad to take Harriet, for it meant unhappiness for others whom I liked. That was the price of love, the result of cheating.

The statue of the bronze figure aloft on its pedestal stopped passers-by dead in their tracks. It 'got' to them, as the morons say today. A plaque set into the block of granite informed the inquisitive that the figure aloft was not a military man, but Humanoid Erectus Mexicanitis, Alfredo Alfonso Juan Calles, born in Acapulco and grandson of the brave General.

Known habitat: Mexico City, Cuernavaca, Acapulco. Carnivore and user of tobacco and other euphoria-inducing substances known to science. Under it the rubric:

> *He's got you and me, brother;*
> *He's got you and me, sister;*

HE'S GOT THE WHOLE WORLD
IN HIS HANDS!

Not a quotation form the Koran, the book without camels, that authenticated it as from the very hand of the Prophet, as some aver; no, these the freewheeling and outspoken lyrics of an old number that climbed the charts in the early 1960s in the time of Haight-Ashbury and Dr Timothy Leary and pot-smoking when such ill-considered dreams (and dreams they were) of racial equality and freedom for all had got rid of Martin Luther ('I have a dream') King as they had got rid of Medgar Evers, leader of the Civil Rights movement, shot by a sniper using a high-powered 1917 Enfield rifle in Guynes Street, Jackson, Mississippi. His dying words were 'Turn me loose.'

Such notions were being freely and flagrantly bandied about; it was in the air; for ideology is not acquired by faith, but by breathing the tainted air.

The statue was saying something; the pose was referential, enigmatic, almost lugubrious; an outflung imperious arm would not have looked amiss. Big Alf had a distinct look of Professor Tribini the Copenhagen ringmaster and impresario villainously top-hatted, striding about the ring in top-boots, cracking a bullwhip to make the lions growl. Or could he be the master of ceremonies in a bordello?

There was a twin in London: not in Kensington Gardens but in Madame Tussaud's waxworks just off Baker Street, home of Sherlock Holmes. Pablo Picasso was dressed casually in loose drawers and nothing else but the flip-flops that he had favoured at La California. His suntanned body was as dark as undressed teak; he scowled at the loungers who had come to stare at famous dead men.

Other waxen imagery of the famous *defuncti* posed, stuck in one attitude for all eternity or at least until this dead one went out of favour or the unthinkable happened and Madame Tussaud's waxworks closed. Famous politicians dressed in authentic but ill-cut Savile Row suits long out of fashion stood uncomfortably around, waiting for Churchill to say something grandiose and bombastic, so that they could laugh and move away, take a quick smoke outside. Constricted in their stiff collars and neckties, they held their heads high as if being garrotted, strangled in the Spanish manner, jutting their waxen jaws; they looked most uneasy.

Lord Nelson was there too, dying for all time on the deck of his ship, the ship that will never sail again, become part of the great waxworks that had been the British Empire; on whom, it was thought then, the sun would never set. But set it did. And then it was finished, had to be cleared away so that others could live, get out of their bondage; make way for a new and even more terrible England.

Like much that was pleasing in the land, the village green and mince pies, the national game had gone out of favour; no more sticky dog wickets, no more Hobbs.

The game was played at night now, as with other criminal activities, on a floodlit pitch with a black sightscreen and a white ball, the players dressed in lurid pyjamas with draw-strings; it was halfway to being American baseball in a ballpark in Pittsburgh; but played in a determined but joyless way in the chill English air. Next they would be playing games down in the empty mines. But in the meantime there was this nightmare game of cricket, by Jove! Spooky wicket.

– 62 –

The Aztec Look

Certainly he was a singular-looking geek, there could be no two ways about that. He appeared to be a little taller than he actually was, and however he managed that trick I cannot say, because frankly I don't know. He had the look of a despot.

Possibly he was a magician controlling optical illusions, using himself as a subject as he strolled along, shrinking only to become gigantic again, like Marcel Marceau ducking behind a prop to re-emerge on the Olympia stage now tall and elongated as Goliath, now shrunken to the dimensions of little David with his slingshot, looking chastened. (Not that Alfredo ever looked chastened, God forbid.) The master mime from Limoges changed sizes at will as you might don and doff clothes.

The great hooded eyes (armadillo or lizard, certainly reptilian) were unnerving: more so than before the operation, for they seemed to have only one expression, or maybe none at all, except haughty indifference. The stare or eye-probe went right through you and out the other side, without any cognisance of the party perceived; one (Rory) had become a thing; and *that* was unnerving.

As he buttered his toast at the breakfast table he liked to chivvy and bully-rag the little Greek who owned a chain of cinemas through Connecticut and was vendor for all the popcorn machines that supplied the movie buffs.

He had brokered some chair at Harvard, was a little sweet on Roxy; he was a very rich old Greek, very, who went in for long rambling inconclusive yarns as such academics are prone to do.

'Connecticut my arse,' Alfredo drawled with the weary lack of forbearance of a dictator signing another death warrant, and the great prohibitive blinds came clattering down.

Roxy batted her oynx-and-opal eyes at her former lord and master whose overbearing Mexican ways she was all too familiar with, remarking 'There go the lions again.' For one of them had roared out in his cramped cage in the little zoo on the island.

Honorio the houseboy, a married man long in the service of Alfredo Calles, glided to and from the kitchen where Maria his wife was preparing something good. He wore natty Bermuda shorts and a serious expression.

Big Alf was applying himself seriously to the matter in hand: what his plate contained. He liked to pile on what he preferred and start eating. In Denmark it is customary and good manners to dig in as soon as food is placed before you, and the men are demanding seconds before their womenfolk (who double as cooks) have sat down. The same custom probably obtains in the cramped quarters of the zoo, always lions before lionesses. I wondered if the expression of lofty indifference covered the fatalism that must lie behind all cruelty. Mexicans had an affinity with cruelty, because they were adepts at inflicting pain.

'¡Ah Pájaro! Pájaro!' crooned Alfredo in his most cajoling voice. He was King of the Castle, the White Elephant bought as a sure-fire investment a week before the peso fell. Now on the market for nine years, it was still unsold. It would have been just the eyrie for a reclusive movie director; Kubrick was still alive, living somewhere in England.

After breakfast we would all go down the hundreds of steps for a dip off the private dock. The old Greek had a bad leg. Alannah swam like an otter and could not be got out of the warm water. A trimaran with two employees from the Acapulco municipality came and collected any scurf that might have accumulated on the surface overnight and was floating there, one man to keep the engine ticking over, the other to remove the debris with a net. Alfredo called out affable greetings; the sea was being prepared for him as though it were a large warm bath. He accepted all that, as if it was his due. The sea was warm. Jellyfish floated in it, trailing their stingers.

He was aloof in manner, not exactly standoffish but apart, like the dying James Joyce, lord of languages. He kept himself to himself, as we Irish say in our fork-tongued, sly way, denying all.

He kept himself to himself at a right royal remove from common clay; the distance between yourself and the King, the *Rey,* his Reyness, is immense, boundless and immeasurable as a state of mind. And I should know, having once shaken the hand of a king, and a Spanish king at that. It's not in the eye but in the firm but distant grip.

He was a striking-looking man who moved about the city on foot. He didn't drive a Sunbeam nor a Chrysler but a small yellow Toyota that no car thief worth his salt would look at twice, the King in mufti disguised as a civilian. He was as bald as a coot.

He had begun to lose his hair at an early age and seeing it was going anyway, he bethought himself '*¡Carajo!* I might just as well lose it all,' decided to go the whole hog and have it shaved off, offering to astonished bystanders a noble brown dome speckled as an auk's egg in place of the former thatch. And why ever not? Wasn't he himself the grandson of a real bad egg, addled by Mexican standards, a right *huevo malo?*

For a full decade, Mexico found itself in the firm grip of General Plutarco Elias Calles, says the quaint history book which never tells the truth. The man from Sonora came from a poor background and when his term of office ended, his name stank in the fastidious nostrils of all liberal-minded Mexicans.

Big Alf had the face of an Aztec Eagle Knight without the helmet, or maybe the ringmaster in a circus who controls the animals and stage-manages the whole show with that face and that deportment that you associate with such apparently effortless mastery, even before you witness it in action. It was a look, a port, midway between contempt and indifference; we do not *try* to amuse and we are *not* amused.

He was a king in exile. His astrological sign was the Lion, images of which filled his house, with paintings of generously rumped ladies of easy virtue. Deprived of all hair, maneless now, he had become not less but positively more kinglike. He had been manager and owner of the night-spot Tiberio on the Boulevard Miguel Alemán in Acapulco; he puts us up in his odd apartment in Mexico City. It was the city of the future, highly dangerous, junglelike in its extremes of wealth and poverty, its ferocity. You had to keep your wits about you, otherwise you'd be clawed to bits in short order.

The lordly and lionlike Alfredo Calles showed us tenderfoots (Alannah had married a Mexican, had lived there; it was Rory's first and last visit) the place to have breakfast (The Biscuits), the place in which to have lunch ('all you can eat for forty pesos') the place not to go to (Sanborn's), the best bookshop (Casa Lamm) all on Colonia Roma, lent us his chauffeur (Don Cutberto), tried without much success to 'Mexicanise' Rory. But even a lion-tamer couldn't manage that. He couldn't do it. We should never carry passports or much

money about with us. He moved like a man who knew his way about: thirty
of his friends had been mugged, but not him. His manner was menacing.

But to tell you what Alfredo Calles (Big Alf) is like, I must first tell you
what he is not like. His son Alfredito (Little Alf) he does not resemble in the
least. They are poles apart in deportment, character, temperament, upbringing, favours. One is quite bald and lordly, the other is not. Big Alf (to further
confuse matters) has a double in the same building: a painter who unlocked
the door and stepped out carrying canvases and, seeing Rory's look of recognition, said 'I am not he' and crossed the road, laughing.

If I tell you that there is something in his dark Mexican eyes that reminds
me of a turkey-cock which seems to be permanently in a furious temper,
bridling, it does not mean that Big Alf in any way resembles or reminds
me of any turkey-cock I ever encountered; but in attempting to describe
the cross look in the turkey-cock's eye I seem to be describing the history
of Mexico, divided and subdivided by successive waves of conquerors, one
more rapacious and bloodthirsty than the other in its greed, from the time
of the Incas and the Aztecs to Pancho Villa and the President (deeply cor-
rupt, like the others) who succeeded Calles; to Lazaro Cárdenas.

As we crossed the great sunbaked plaza after viewing the Diego Rivera
murals, I heard a most joyful and tuneful melody coming from under the
shaded colonnade and who was it but a one-armed beggar playing a tune
by blowing on a thorn leaf as one might twang a Jew's harp or vamping on
a harmonica (Marzy dotes). Rivera had shown me a previous Mexico and
the barbarous cruelty of the Spanish conquistadors, and then the Americans
came with their cartels and their arrangements, their plans for Mexico, hated
by Diego with all his simple and trusting big heart, the man who had swallowed some of the ashes of his maimed woman, Frida Kahlo.

Not anything as grandiose as the Plumed Serpent, then, but more domes-
ticated and just as savage in its own way, the turkey-cock comes strutting,
lord of the Mexican farmyard, boss of the patio, whom even the dogs fear, its
fury, its ill-tempered ways, its contrary nature, warped and disturbed.

They are ill-natured creatures, the male of the guinea-fowl (*Numida
meleagris*), hostile to all, forever bad-tempered, gobbling at intruders, with
inflamed ugly wattles erect. As retrievers or pit bull terriers are bred for
specific purposes, so turkey-cocks are bred to vent their spleen, their bile.

They are choleric, expect no quarter from enemies; always expecting
the worst, and rarely disappointed in that. For a violent end awaits them; a
cruel fate has so arranged it. In order to live with any dignity they must sup-
press any instinct of tenderness within themselves, knowing that their fate

is to be decapitated by a cook with an axe in her hand. Or she is for hewing their head off with a hatchet on a block of wood, cursing them as ungrateful creatures. They have no love for their offspring whom they consume, purple with rage, in embryo in hens' eggs. They will gobble up whole generations, not bothering to distinguish one lot from the other, pitiless as Saturn.

Sometimes, livid with fury, wattles suddenly flooded with blood, they spread out their tawdry wings as though this were a general's bemedalled cloak, a cloak of glory, as if to cry out, but only to expose their dungy hind-quarters, the awful anus, as if 'mooning' or cursing their Maker, wishing they could fly. They feel lost in the evolutionary chain of being.

But Big Alf is not like that at all.

A disdainful, baleful look characterises the hooded eyes of turkey-cocks, protected by a flap of skin that hangs down rather like the leather windbreak before the western door of Málaga Cathedral. Their eyelids are permanently inflamed as with acute conjunctivitis and the hard-boiled gangster eyes have an oily sheen, adding to the menace of these farmyard creatures not quite as big and belligerent as buzzards. They seem to look down their beaks at you, their head level with your crotch where they could do much damage, had they a mind.

They have no respect for anybody. Fearlessness with them is a kind of vice. They could turn on you.

They have no graces. Their call is unpleasant, more caw or phlegmy clearing of mucus from a constricted throat. They are not particular about what they eat and disdain to clean their arses. They shit in unexpected places, knowing you will tread on it, carry it into the house with you.

With them the act of love is gross, a display of supreme power and contempt over those whom they despise (the clucking hens); with claws like spurs they spurn the cowering hens, putting their full weight down on them, drawing blood. They cackle like witches.

But Alfredo Calles is not like that at all.

History, wrote Octavio Paz, has the cruelty of a nightmare. Presumably he meant Mexican history. And who can gainsay that, seeing that there is nowhere a crueller history?

In a monochrome, slightly foxed, photograph taken during a banquet at the National Palace in Mexico City in December 1914, the waiters (male to a man) standing behind the distinguished company appear blurred and smudged as if caught in the act of fleeing from the dining room, leaving this dangerous assembly, for the President, Gutierrez (a monumental bulky presence), is flanked by the *pistoleros* Pancho Villa (to his right hand) and

Emiliano Zapata to his left, dangerous company for any sitting President. The eyes of Zapata glitter like topaz or, better, gleam like a tiger's in a thicket; possibly 'touched up' by a nervous photographer. You can see by the fixed stare caught by the nervous photographer that he (Zapata) has felt the finger of destiny rest on his shoulder for a split second, as surely as the cook came for the turkey-cock, or the Plumed Serpent for the unfortunate Cuauhtemoc whose very name sounds like a death-rattle.

A white silk scarf is knotted about the neck of Emiliano Zapata, lending a dandyish look to the reformer who crouches in his seat, hands on the table. Pancho Villa appears to have something in his mouth and he too crouches a little as if preparatory to catapulting himself across the table to have it out with whoever has the stomach to face him. Both are obviously outdoor men, with their scorched complexions and heavy moustaches. Anybody with a moustache like that is asking for trouble.

Attendants bearing plates of food are stationary for a second, caught in mid-stride. Glasses of what looks suspiciously like water are set before the diners, with no wine bottles on view, and a centrepiece of roses before *El Presidente,* who appears quite calm in the midst of these troublemakers and killers with scant respect for authority. The revolutionary fervour that burned in their eyes and hearts could not be quenched, could not be suppressed, much less put out.

Who was it wrote that thinking about something you know nothing about is not very helpful? When I thought of Mexico before I set foot in it I thought of a country askew, a great bony protuberance coming out of the USA and extending down to Guatemala and Honduras. The names of states sound like cries of pain: Guadalajara, Guanajuato (birth pangs for a big baby who was to become the pistol-toting pug-ugly muralist Diego Rivera), Oaxaca; sores and suppurations, acts of unbelievable cruelty, the brave Emperor with the impossible name from whom a cry could not be wrung.

I thought of congruences in no particular order:

Stout Hernan Cortés grown lean, the hideous syphilitic being in the angry murals of Rivera; of Cantiflas and colonialism; of hangings and insurrections; of those two feathered serpents, Maximilian and Carlotta; of figures hung on gibbets like crows roosting on a tree; of disembowellings aplenty; of *indigenismo* and *Chamools* (whoever they were); of Uxmal and Quetzalcoatl (whatever they were); of *insurgentes* and *tormentas* (lots of these); of Cuernavaca and Morelos; of fantasy and fact; of Rivera's Zapata leading on his white horse in the mural; of the courage and cool cheek of Frida Kahlo maimed for life; of Totonac and Huastec; of an open coffin and tears, idle tears (buckets of those); of rusty weaponry in a courtyard where the wind blows dust about; of men in huge sombreros cantering into town, brandishing revolvers; of Montezuma's revenge; of Cuauhtemoc being tortured and not uttering a cry, biting through his lips, and his torturers laughing at him; of David Alfaro Siqueiros and José Clemente Orozco and their terror-inspiring murals like big blisters that would never go away or be lanced or cured; of horses rearing; of obsidian-tipped spears.

Of the astounding spectacle that was the sudden twilight on the road (all tolls) from Mexico City to Cuernavaca, when Roxy drove like the wind and the little Greek counselled slower driving, or let Alannah drive. Of the cartoons of the great José Guadalupe Posada, a man of the people; of communal *ejidos*. I thought of a scorpion in a shower stall and how small it was; when I thought of Mexico, I thought of all that. I thought of much more, that must also be Mexico; how big it was, immense really, stretching away forever, and the two volcanoes bowing politely to each other: Popocatepetl and Iztaccihuatl like two kettles boiling over, lids hopping up and down, or two turkey-cocks fighting to the death.

When I thought of Mexico, where I will never go again (once was too much), I think of history immobilised, gone septic, much more immobilised than mere Irish history (history small and shrunken, scratching its sores); history as a hump on the back, a pain in the neck, an acute pain in the arse. I thought of Mexico, the whole of Mexico, the same grim, goaty land that Graham Greene had walked into, confronting his worst fears, his horrors.

− 63 −

The *Zaca* Sails Again!

What have Little Mo, Gorgeous Gussie Moran (famed for her frillies), Binny Barnes, Myrna Loy and Gloria Graham got in common?

They all reminded Rory of Roxy. She had that 'arrested' look that you get on the faces of pretty girls who know they *are* pretty and are excited by the prospect of playing tig and forfeits and hide-and-seek and blind man's buff in the shrubbery with the boys. She was 'it'. There would be hiding and running and much shrieking in an extensive garden with tall trees and food and soft drinks laid out on a long table and servants serving and the sun would shine, oh yes it would surely shine.

Her adult life would be a continuation of that game. She had looked into the mirror and liked what she saw. She had reached her goal in fast clever moves, like getting 'home' at tig. Modelling and what her daughter ungallantly called 'face-fucking' (using oneself as bait, like supermodel Naomi Campbell) led to the movies and they led to clothes designing, the rag trade, and then she was 'home'.

There was more to her than face and body flaunting. You might learn something of the mother by studying the daughter, but not much. Big Alf's pet name for her was apt, for she was birdlike, with thin bones and a beaky face, exotically tinted hair. You knew this little bird came from the tropics and had flown far. She was always alert, picking at her food, batting her eyes; given to sudden flights of fancy.

She was a somewhat confused Californian lady who read *Time* magazine and believed that the ETs or vegetable men from outer space had already landed on Earth and were living incognito in Baja, California; which may be God's truth for all I know. Stranger things have come to pass in our time.

I could see her as a daring *rejoneadora* mounted on a pure-bred palomino mare, galloping across the bullring just out of range of the bull's horns to rapturous applause from a great crowd that packed the Plaza de Toros.

Or as the scantily clad Lovely Juanita being hurled high from Ganjou brother to brother, from Bob to George and from George to Serge, twirling up like a spinning top in a bizarre musical act widely regarded as dangerous, performed to the strains of that perennial favourite, the Scheherazade Suite of Rimsky-Korsakov.

Nothing could be too extreme when it came to choices, provided these involved well-cut clothes or very few clothes and some pandering to vanity, theirs and hers, as was only a woman's right.

She thought that the pelicans that flew alongside the launch (ostentatiously hired by Alfredo, standing masterfully on his private dock; unobtrusively paid for by the Greek) were albatrosses. Like furry pets dreamed up by Disney's fun people, they flew alongside the launch, looking for scraps.

'¡Ah, Pájaro! Pájaro!'

She had never read a serious book in her life, or listened to classical music and certainly had never heard of Coleridge. Love between them may have gone cold but some affection remained, like eggshells in a nest abandoned. Pet names are a guard against loss, like primitive music – was that Dr Matthew Mighty-grain-of-salt speaking? One would have to take much of Roxy's fancies with a mighty grain of salt. One could almost see her being fired from the mouth of a cannon, wearing little gauzy wings like a butterfly, almost. She was, as they say, 'fun to be with', she *was* much fun singing mock-Wagner in a falsetto voice, in the dining room doorway of the Old Post House in Kinsale, her true home. From there she had shimmied down a rope, to be rowed out to the yacht moored off the Bulman in moonlight where a lover waited. She was full of life.

When we were taken out in the launch we may have passed the sea lanes traversed by Flynn's yacht *Zaca* so many years before, with Orson Welles and Rita Hayworth aboard; the helmsman, cocksman, rather in awe of Welles, rather fancying the lady. How could he not?

'Were this Dublin Bay, it would be chilly,' Rory remarked fatuously to the tall sunhat perched like a chimney-pot upon the noble dome that was Alfredo Calles at sea. But he was deeply inhaling his own 'pot' and had little interest in such tittle-tattle.

The launch slapped against the oncoming swells, splashing Rory, a poor sailor, now feeling repulsed.

'Well, we're not in Dublin Bay now,' breathed out Big Alf snappishly, with implacable Mex disdain, 'pot' smoke pouring from both cavernous nostrils as if the famous twin volcanoes had begun erupting again; gazing knowingly the while at the coastline that was passing by, the whited sepulchre of the sinful city of Acapulco, where he had once run a famous nightclub, sprawled out there in the sun. 'Thank God,' Big Alf, amended as closure.

Only in a school of draw-poker, playing for high stakes, where calling a bluff is a serious matter and the opponent (who may be holding a straight flush) either stares one out or scrupulously avoids one's eye, would you encounter such fixity of stare, probing and probing in a situation of knife-edge tension.

Rory stared at the city at which Welles must have stared, having scouted for locations. There was a hotel formerly run by Johnny Weissmuller and John Wayne, which they had grown tired of and given as a present to their doorman. Such high-handed acts were typical, it was something in the air, abruptly giving and as abruptly withholding, insulting.

Roxy was laid out in the bow, like Rita Hayworth on the aft deck of the *Zaca*, glamorously taking the sun. Now she was for everybody, the whole world wanted her; she was taking everything with great deep breaths as the launch cut through the waves, and the pet birds, Disney's furry creations, flew alongside, staring with their dopey eyes, close enough to stun or kill with an oar. The beer cooler was being handed around. Rory, quick to take offence, felt a proper yokel.

'Pass the beer forr'ad,' said the little old Greek.

'I feel just like a beer,' Roxy drawled at the sun.

'You look just like Rita Hayworth,' said Rory, all gallantry now.

'Tut tut.'

She was in harmonious accord with her surroundings, like those exotic movie stars who can only play themselves. They are not required to play anybody else, the Garbos and the Garsons and the Hayworths, by directors shrewd enough to pander to such vanity; it was hardly vanity, it came natural as breathing. (Here Rory smiled to himself, seeing in his mind's eye, the eye in the back of the head, Garbo's Scandinavian hockey-player's shoulders in a heated winter pool.)

She (Roxy that is) was a woman of the future, whereas Garbo was a woman of the past, a nineteenth-century figure or effigy copied from some magazine. The woman of the future was a cool granny who had a grasp of essentials; what stories she would have to tell her grandchildren, of 'face-fucking' in the wicked twentieth century! The ladies of long ago played tennis in long skirts and headbands; it must have been more like softball than lawn tennis, Helen Wills Moody and Kay Stammers, dainty as porcelain shepherdesses or ladies at the spinet.

Those ladies had long gone. Women's tennis was now a savage game, with lesbians grunting and swearing under their breath, imparting topspin to crashing services.

She had worked and face-fucked in Mexico City, New York, Bali, London and Tokyo, the immense sprawling cities of the future, dangerous and creepy as the city shown in *Blade Runner*. Her grandchildren, if she had any, would be the highly neurotic progeny of the future. And what worse (louder?) sound could come after rock? Something calculated to burst the eardrums?

Aldous Huxley, long gone, had envisaged a future, our present, as 'the laughter of demons about whipping-posts and the howling of the possessed as they couple in the darkness'. Why, it sounded just like a rock 'in-spot', a Berlin cellar. Berlin would be everywhere, the cities would all be the same – horribly similar in their cacophony and crime; crime would be common-place like sport. Sport would more resemble battle.

That would be our future, and I rejoice not to belong to it.

– 64 –

The Jogger on Coronado Shore

Whilst staying at the Rancho Pico, Big Alf's country seat, didn't poor Rory ingest a prawn that was 'off', bought at the French place Carrefour that sold everything imaginable; and by God he lived to regret it, spending three feverish days in bed, taking nothing stronger than milk and reading *The Radetzky March* from the peerless hand of Joseph Roth, a prey to nightmares.

'Montezuma's revenge,' mocked Big Alf in his pitiless Mexican way.

There was a scorpion in the shower stall. Tongolele (his brawny dog named after a nightclub *chanteuse*) had eaten the cat's (Max's) food. A heavy palm frond had fallen in the night. Mexico had lost to Peru in the World Cup.

Big Alf, grandson of a president of Mexico, was a past-master of the bluff disclaimer and short, sharp deflatory rhetoric; but his greatest weapon by far was silence. His silences were uncanny. Rory was baffled. It was the enigmatic silence of the ringmaster who throws open a door and points silently up at the tightrope suspended above, across which the novice is expected to walk.

Once, going upstairs to a family get-together at the Old Post House, Big Alf had poked Rory in the back, intimidatingly: 'Don't dilly-dally, son. Keep moving', as if ordering a menial about in the presidential palace. And Rory saw his features darken and lengthen like a mask of Montezuma reflected in a mirror as they ascended together into the social mêlée that awaited them. It would include Father Paddy from Glenstal, the pink aunt and daughter already seated, drinks in hand, all flustered yet already in full conversational flow, an unabatable flood of trivia, a torrent of talk, a river forever flowing backwards. Talk about the froth of dreams!

Alfredo had a distinctly lordly manner, walked as if brandishing a cane, distant and aloof, carried himself like a king, but a king who read *Time* magazine and went jogging in lurid tracksuits with goofy insignia, jargon and numerals, a joker in the pack.

He had a kingly manner of high disdain, knew how to treat his subjects; his generosity had the quality of a king's bounty.

Big Alf out jogging resembled a *palo* aloft on the shoulders of sweating bearers, one of the three kings who brought gifts to Bethlehem, in costly raiment: the disdainful features might have been carved in wood. He never became flushed because he was naturally dark-complexioned. Jogging didn't become him, he was naturally a sedentary type, naturally lazy, the President accustomed to issuing orders for minions to carry out. Big Alf was high and lonesome as the snore of Christy Mahon's da; abstemious with alcohol, high on hash, which kept him on an even keel. Quoting some Mexican statistic of astounding import ('*five million pesos,* my friend!'), he was King Melchior mounted on a camel, a dispenser of symbolic charity in the form of handfuls of sweeties flung down to shrieking *niños*.

His consort Roxy had a good figure, liked to keep in condition, liked to be seen in shorts showing off her Californian knees; possessed by that desperate fear that all American women have, of losing one's looks, one's husband, the fear of growing old; she liked to get a good 'burn' as though she were a Pratt and Whitney Boeing engine burning off fuel at 33,000 feet; that was Roxy's way, ever the mettlesome lass.

When they went out jogging together on the roads around Charles Fort or over the bridge at James Fort on the way to Ballinspittle, they were a sight to see; a terrific display of well-muscled thigh and tanned knee, gabbing volubly away as they went pattering by, very exotic and foreign-looking to encounter passing on a narrow Irish road, as if you had met the Emperor Maximilian and Queen Charlotte out for a stroll, taking a breather.

One day Roxy would be heard of in Bali, next day she was doing a deal in Tokyo, flew on to New York, was seen shopping in Chicago. She was next heard of in Cuernavaca, taking a short break at Rancho Pico; then she was in the condo on Coronado Shore, jogging on the private beach where dogs and vendors were not permitted to set foot. Then San Diego was left behind and she was in London or flying to Paris to take in the spring collection. Faxes flew ahead of her like confetti at a wedding. She couldn't manage joined-up writing. Roxy was a scream.

She wore shorts because she liked to show off her legs. They gabbed while jogging; animated chatting and jogging didn't seem to go together, as with chewing gum while singing arias from light operas.

An old love had died, a clockmaker named Christopher Stokes with a clock shop on MacCurtain Street in Cork, not to be confused with Sigismund, King of the Clocks. He had been buried in Douglas's Protestant cemetery. Roxy was devoted to the dead man and arranged for Alannah to lay wreaths at anniversaries. She was like that.

Loyalty was almost a vice with the Buxton Hopkins; birthdays and anniversaries were remembered, faxes flew, long-distance phone calls were made, the fat chewed. Good intentions were rampant here; the family must stick together at all costs. That was the big idea.

¡Oh Pájaro! Pájaro! The fat's in the fire.

In the cool of the evening, sundowner time in South Africa, and the time for imbibing of Lion beer and Oude Meester brandy, Acapulco was enjoying a stupendous sunset over the water, promising another such day tomorrow, with a young fellow monkeylike shinning up a tall Royal palm to trim off some of the decayed fronds with a machete. The stand of palms rose higher than the third floor of Alfredo's Palacio, with a view over the bay and the lighthouse beginning to wink on and off as a warning to mariners. We sat with drinks before us on a glass table, summoned thence by Tiberio himself, the message conveyed by Honorio the houseboy, padding silently along the corridor, barefoot and in Bermuda shorts, silent as though he had been castrated by order of the Emperor. Drinks on the upper terrace tonight and pot-smoking! So we were all assembled, and the little old Greek was getting the sharp edge of Alfredo's tongue in what passed as friendly raillery but wasn't quite, and Roxy and Alannah were murmuring together as two sisters should, and Rory was drinking gin and tonic in a tall glass as Rory liked to do.

The evening calm was rudely disturbed by the heavy grunting and honking and farting (drunkard barging into quiet room, hippo foraging in a marsh) of the love-boat making its leisurely pleasure-cruising way between Boca Chica and La Roqueta.

The love-boat *Acatiki* was out and about, fairy lights dangled between two masts, picking out the shape of the celebrated organ, seat of one's innermost thoughts and secret feelings, suspended between mast and mast, below which the snoggers snogged, close in each other's arms, the girls in thin frocks proudly displaying love-bites like tribal markings, the not-so-young dancing with the not-so-young, those past it, just as the sun went down, and Rory's own heart sank into his *espadrillos* for he hated with all his heart piped Muzak in public places and no public place seemed free of it. The love-boat went gobbling across the bay, the dancers danced, the music played, call it music.

'Some people's idea of tropical dance music,' murmured Roxy.

'Some people's idea of fun,' murmured the small old Greek.

Tiberio offered no comment. The great hooded eyes were closed, the blinds down; he was not at home, or he was sleeping. He was not saying anything. If he was a true Emperor Tiberius whose every whim could be gratified, why then with one imperious wave of the hand he could have all three hundred dancers chucked overboard, the worst offenders castrated, as he had had Honorio castrated, or, better still, flung off on the island and the Jardín Zoológico cages thrown open and the pleasure-cruisers fed to the lions, to implement their boring diet of horse-flesh. Sink the damn *Acatiki*; then all would be quiet.

Alfredo's house in Calle Valladolid in Mexico City was full of ceramic lions both rampant and *couchant,* little lions and large lions in different material; he was obsessed with lions. His own languid indifference was based, unconsciously, on the MGM lion logo, the one that roars briefly and looks away indifferently, bored to death with MGM.

The lions (or was there only one?) roared in their cages at sun-up and sunset on La Roqueta at feeding time; it was the Island Where Lions Roar. The jungle and the authentic wilderness have been dispensed with and all the

wild animals hunted to extinction, replaced by a fake substitute wilderness
for the amusement of tourists, created by clever ad-men, con-men; a sort of
chic wilderness made of cardboard where you wouldn't be devoured by wild
animals, into whose natural habitat seemingly you had been permitted, for
a reasonable charge, to stray.

The wildly gesticulating lewd statuary in bronze, of manly parts, gleaming
torsos and Olympic legs, had been arrested in a somewhat similar way; not
permitted to stray over into outright indecency, of provocative pose and outsize
bronze member fully erect; there was merely a suggestion of it, a hint. The male
torsos sighed mutely with a lover's insistence, *Oh touch me! O please do!* It was a Zoo
of Dreams. The architect who had erected the extraordinary house of mirrors
had been homosexual and also practised as a sculptor; the gesticulating bronze
parts were all his work. Alfredo walked about in flip-flops and shorts, as though
walking through the cloisters of a monastery, cool as a cucumber.

Banana boat rides were popular on Acapulco Bay between La Roqueta
and the Boca Chica. The yellow thing vaguely banana-shaped, a long phallus
that curled up at each end with enough seats to take eight or ten screeching
pleasure-seekers in life-jackets was pulled behind a speedboat with throttle
wide open, bouncing across the swells and wakes of other pleasure craft
plying between the hotel and the island, the screaming girls also bouncing up
and down and giving themselves risky orgasms and pissing themselves with
sheer excitement: riding on the swells, they skimmed across the surface of the
sea. In the distance, but approaching, could be heard the unmistakable farting
and grunting of the good ship *Acatiki,* she was coming around again.

Clam-divers swam out beyond the point into the open sea beyond, holding on to an inner tube which carried a lethal array of knives and machetes
for prising clams off the seabed; a flutter-kick carried them along, only head
and arms visible, like otters or beavers moving slowly through the water.
They ignored banana boats and the cruising love-boat with its fake heart lit
up, a sore gone septic.

One morning, swimming off Alfredo's private dock, with the beer-
cooler and the avocados stashed in the shade, Alannah encountered one
of these dark-skinned, silent otterlike clam-divers and engaged him in
conversation in the sea as she likes to do. He was pushing his inner tube
before him, flutter-kicking very slowly. Why was he returning so soon?
What was amiss? (Her Spanish is excellent.) It was a long swim back to
where he had set out, the place where the glass-bottomed ferries set off
for La Roqueta, the place where they return to at dusk.

'*¡Hay agua mala!*'

The sea was full of jellyfishes waving their stingers beyond the point, with more of them in the open sea; he wasn't going to swim through them, explanations were superfluous.

'They're not great conversationalists,' Alannah said, lolling about on her fun-tube in the sea.

– 65 –

The Martinez Couple

Don Alfredo Calles was the owner and manager of the very fashionable Tiberio nightery on the Boulevard Miguel Alemán in sunny Acapulco, *the* place for cool cats to divert themselves. It was a splendid night-spot done up in vertical black-and-white stripes like a zebra pelt or a painting by Franz Kline, and Alfredo himself was an exotic match for the fancy décor.

El Patrón favoured the casual look – all-white cotton jeans and shirt, no necktie but white silken cravat, embroidered white waistcoat, white loafers and white socks, very tanned, a way-out cool cat with one gold earring like a pirate, but more a ringmaster in a grand circus, dapper as Bryan Ferry of 'These Foolish Things' fame (haven't we all got 'em?); but a more kingly presence: Don Alfredo Calles was the Boss and no mistake.

It was a way-out place to be, the whitest, coolest place in all Acapulco night-life. It wasn't cheap. It was there that Yul Brynner (who *had* worked in a circus) complimented Alannah: 'Nice ass you got there, kid' were his very words. He had arrived with a Hollywood crowd of big spenders and show-offs. Elsewhere, at another time, Chuck Berry had a feel, as also Charlie Haughey.

Alfredo Calles was by nature an easygoing type who conveyed the misleading impression of inflexibility. I never heard him lose his temper or raise his voice; but this was part of the kingliness, he didn't have to raise his voice when he issued orders around the Palacio or in Tiberio.

His manner with the servants was that of a feudal lord. He liked to give long detailed instructions. The houseboy or *mayordomo* Honorio, the non-swimmer, the silent one who glided about the Palacio in Acapulco, looked after the place in the months when it stood empty, with the maimed German Alsatian dog that Alfredo had adopted; he, Honorio, took the orders nodding that he understood. He had security for life; the feudal lord would see to that.

The Martinez couple of the Rancho Pico below Cuernavaca were gate-keepers, lodge-dwellers, who swept the lawns clear of leaves, a veritable labour of Sisyphus, for the leaves always fell, and the breezes blew all around Cuernavaca. They used brushes made of twigs, rarely spoke to each other, and were a couple straight out of the Conquest as portrayed in the Diego Rivera murals in the Palace of Cortés.

You could see in the Martinezes how passively and with what fatalism the Indians had bowed to the will of the Spaniards; they were born slaves, but they believed that their time would come. It hadn't come yet but it would come, in time.

When Alfredo Calles was about to leave again for his office in Mexico City he issued detailed last-minute instructions to Eliseo, not standing as a servant might, submissively before the master, but seated alongside Alfredo by the swimming pool near the sauna under the tree that nobody knew the name of, they spoke then as equals might discuss the running of the place, the fowl-run, the vegetables, the upkeep of the long bungalow, the pair of them with their heads together.

Eliseo Martinez had his own car, his own house. One daughter was a nurse, his son Miguelangelo was studying to be an engineer, his wife Graciela could iron clothes like an angel: she was one of the pigtailed peons offering their produce to the raping and rapacious Spaniards. They might inherit the estate, in time.

When Alfredo came to Summercove for his vacation he brought something of Mexico City with him. He and Roxy mingled with the locals at drinks parties; they socialised, they were not 'stuck up'. Big Alf liked a pint of draught Guinness at the Bulman.

Señor Alfredo Elias Calles (baritone) of Mexico City and Acapulco and the Señora Roxy (alto) of San Diego and Cuernavaca – international guest stars of the Kinsale Opera Society – by popular request sang their famous Papageno-Papagena duet from *The Magic Flute* under the inspired baton of Frank Buckley, the local musical maestro.

Francis X. Buckley, the Kinsale *Kapellmeister,* was a veritable Fortunio Bonanova on the podium, which he occupied with the maximum dash and verve, sprightly and emotional with the baton, in smart dinner jacket and tails, swinging tails – Arturo Toscanini in style and swagger. This was very well received by the local cognoscenti, the music-lovers.

With his back to the audience, shoulders moving energetically, coat-tails swinging, he was as wild as the sorcerer's apprentice, yet meek as Little Sir Echo, odd as the performing seal in a circus.

With a rush of blood to the head, he had rocketed headlong into *Ruddigore.* His mother sat in the front row, astounded. She adored him, as did the choir, made up mostly of girls from Super Valu, who stood enthralled. Oh the sweetest man you would ever hope to meet in a hall full of half-wits was our Frank!

PART VIII:

How the Century Ends

The rath forninst the oak wood belonged to Bruidge, and
Cathal belonged to Aedh, and Ailill belonged to Conaing,
and Cuiline and to Mael Duin before them – all Kings in their
turn. The rath survives; the Kings are all covered in clay.

Anon., Sixteenth-century notebook

The Three Brothers

T'ree brudders . . . wan wit a bad eye

Below Ringenane bridge in a field tilted down towards Oysterhaven Creek stand three mobile homes mounted on breeze blocks facing into opposite corners like boxers between rounds or as the stone heads with two faces buried up to their necks on Boa Island, set and fixed solid in the earth for all time, staring off in different directions.

They seem to avert their eyes from each other, as do the three brothers who occupy them, long-term bachelors not on speaking terms and having no direct dealings knowingly with one another, as if in accordance with some Kikuyu tribal custom at a fly-blown *manyatta* where they pretended not to see each other. 'Doll's Eye' neither saw nor wanted to see 'the Belgooly Flasher', who never spoke to nor acknowledged 'The Fascist Beast', who neither saw nor spoke to either of the other two. This dour trio of lackadaisical dim-wits had long been unemployed and lived only for dole day, which fell every Thursday; it was their day for stocking up on provisions and getting pissed. The Belgooly Flasher, a lurker at convent gates, was a small-sized crafty-looking fellow who gave the impression of ever being caught in the act of departure, abruptly leaving, dressed for winter, pushing an old bike weighed down with provisions in plastic Super Valu bags hooked on to the handlebars. He sometimes passes by. We live in Upper O'Connell Street between the convent (closed) and the pie factory (closed) in the Guardwell. Below us formerly was Sheehy's auction yard and warehouses used as storage, since knocked down and replaced by a block of flats with its own car park.

You said: 'The town is simply seething with cousins.'

The Belgooly Flasher went by manhandling his push-bike, head down as if fighting against a north wind. You said: 'There goes the flasher . . . his flashing days are over, thanks be to God.'

The three brothers are still not talking in the field that slopes down to the river that for Rory would always be the curlew river.

I myself, having been born into a family of archly uncommunicative brothers who rarely spoke together, the two elder with the two younger, I mean, like lifelong enemies, in a previous existence down the country in the days of Aladdin paraffin lamps and horse-drawn hay-bogies, know these sullen silences only too well.

I rarely communicated with any of them after the family split up; the youngest has taken offence at how he and his wife are represented in the pseudo-autobiography preceding this one, the middle brother died in Ealing and is now beyond all communication. The eldest, I am told, divides his time between Largs in Scotland and Hobart in Tasmania, formerly the penal colony called Van Diemen's Land.

I never had much dealings with my eldest brother: more than ten years separated us and he was closer to brother Bun, younger by two years. They had been brought up together, as had the Dote and I. The Dodo had been inclined to despise me as a convent boy with provincial accent and awkward manners, who associated with the snotty-nosed Keegan brothers in the front lodge.

In boarding school special rules obtained for him. He couldn't be pandied or punished in any way for failing exams and spent much time confined to bed in the infirmary, laid low by psychosomatic ailments brought on so as to avoid classes, the subjects he detested, such as Irish. Special rules had to be made to accommodate his strangeness; he was given 'lines' as though he was in an English boarding school. He was a lifelong secret subscriber to the school magazine, the *Clongownian*.

The Dodo was opening bat on the college XI, a stonewaller who took no chances, refused to take easy singles. He was a great 'gardener', forever poking and prodding at the crease, awkward in protective gear, the box, the gloves with ridged rubber webbing, the outsize leg pads shackled his movements, always requiring nice readjustments, making running difficult.

He was a bundle of mannerisms, based on famous cricketers whom he admired; never having seen them in action (in the days before television), he had to imitate styles caught by the still camera or confine himself exclusively to defensive strokes or none at all, just occupying his crease, staying in and not scoring. It was the same strategy he used to get into the infirmary.

His defence was gritty, poking at the crease, calling 'No!' to a partner anxious to chance a quick one. He wasn't one for sneaking cheeky singles or attempting anything forceful on the leg side, sweeps to the boundary, rattling the picket fence. The school cap down to his nose, shirt collar up around his ears, the eyes watchful, the bat tapping, raised up as the bowler was about to deliver, he was a sight to behold.

Does he get a tickle? They've held him in the slips, the umpire's finger is

raised and off goes the Dodo, bat tucked under arm, gloves peeled thoughtfully off, slowly wending his way back to the pavilion, to scant applause
– 'Bad luck, Dodo!' In his diary will appear: 'Wrong decision.' *Nota bene.*
    Bizarre.

– 67 –

In the Long Ago

It happened in the time when sons feared fathers, as fathers before them
had feared their own fathers, their hard fists and exasperated ear-twisting
and royal rages reaching back to the black times of the forefathers, the
crusty old patriarchs themselves in their nightshirts and long white beards,
their hard ways and prohibitions ('Thou shalt not . . .'); sticklers for form,
their right hand resting on the good Book of Manners in two hefty great
volumes, the Old Testament and the New.

Then, as if to make up for the loss of the love of the father (for how could
you love someone who beat you?), didn't they go and love their mothers all
the more; they *adored* them with an anxious and longing love that reached
out and could hardly be appeased.

Looking back through the fully extended telescope that measured off the
three score years and ten allotted to human life, time appeared to contract;
and there was Mumu dealing out a hand of Pelman Patience on the study
table, placing the cards face down and palming the deck before shuffling,
wondering if it would come out right this time.

And Dado, who rarely if ever engaged in work about the house, once he
had come in, stood on the front steps in cast-off cricket boots, a handkerchief saturated in linseed knotted about his neck, rotating a safety match
in one ear, then the other, a vacant look on his face. His jaw had fallen and
his mind, ah his mind, a total blank, unless he was admiring the scuffling
job he had done on the front gravel.

At all events it had all begun a long time ago and as though it had happened to another person in another country in another time. Before rural
electrification had brought electric light as the greatest comfort into the home
in the late 1940s; and before the monster TV, the greatest curse, had choked
off the old life. When the elderly men had gathered at gates and leant on walls
to gossip at evening time, watching the light go. All that had gone too.

As for myself, now aged seventy-one and well advanced into the sere and yellow, why I can hardly recognise that other puny and positively emaciated male child with matchstick arms and legs and face squeezed up into what the family called the bear's face. A shy slip of a thing, nervous as a whippet, with that worried frown caught in the Kodak snaps gone sepia with age.

Mr Doorley of Monkstown by the sea, a Dublin dentist by profession, had invited Rory to his place for a holiday to 'fatten him up' and enjoy some healthy sea-bathing in company with his daughter Evelyn. Brother Bun was to keep me company, for I was too timid to go by myself.

So it was porridge and fry-up for breakfast, and Seapoint for a healthful dip, and a walk on Dun Laoghaire pier after lunch, and a glass of milk and Gold Grain biscuits before bed and 'Did you move your bowels today, sir?'

A human life, in the scale of boundless time that we are adrift in, is but the duration of one indrawn breath that is then expelled; the passage of Halley's Comet through 'everchanging tracks of neverchanging space' in its circuit about the sun, coming into sight and going away again every seventy-six years, a reasonable human lifespan; such is our time marked out in the sky.

The Dote and I had made a pet of an elderly hen whom we named Ma Duggy White. Her body feathers hung down like soiled linen, a dirty shift showing under a skirt, and her hinder parts were always clotted with dung. Scratching about in the backyard she made a sadly droaning regurgitative noise in her throat, the distinct sound that hens make when foddering, sad music on a descending scale. This we called 'Years-Gone-by'. It was the sad music of the passage of time, the very sound of its passing.

The great Parisian organist Messiaen had heard the call of an unknown bird in the evening, in Persia, and put the sound into his triumphant devotional work as the voice of God, a sound hardly audible, a very remote, distant clear and perfect call, as the sound of the sea in a shell held to the ear, thought to be the sea itself but is only pseudo-sound, a false sea sound, only the memory of real waves or surf breaking on a real shore somewhere, tidal shifts and changes, capricious winds, all that.

When the Birr bus passes the front gate, Dado knows that the evening papers have arrived in Celbridge a mile away, flung from the bus in bundles on to the pavement outside Breen's Hotel, and he can stop poking in his ears with a match. It's time to send one of the Keegan boys for the *Evening Herald* and *Evening Mail* and on Saturday, *The Field* and on Sunday half a dozen London papers, with a penny or tuppence to John Joe for sweets or Woodbines or himself.

The young masters, Dodo and the Bun, are off at Clongowes pursuing their serious studies, sending weekly letters home with reports of their progress or lack of it, tales of their prowess (or lack) on the playing fields.

I had been 'held back' two years so that the Dote and I could start as equals, so that he was big enough to walk to the convent a mile away in the village. In fact it was I who was never able to catch up with the steady and conscientious progress made by Colman, the exemplary student at all times, whether put through the slapdash educational methods of the Sisters of Mercy (who favoured the strap) for beating the Catechism into us, teaching us our tables and all the singsong lessons by rote. Or later at boarding school in Killashee with a French order of nuns who had their own punitive methods.

Madame Ita Magdalene stood you in front of the dais and cut at you with a ruler edged with lead that could draw blood, if you got French irregular verbs wrong. Her face within its shadowy coif lengthened like a horse's and all flushed darkly with blood, her dander rising and the great horse-teeth clamped together. 'You'll get this right if we have to stand here all day.'

A long rusty freighter in from Bilbao occupies the whole length of the loading bay, the claws of the grab dipping into the open hold and swaying back to release another load into the truck waiting on the quayside to carry it off to Good's Mill on the hillside above the town.

When the southwesterly wind activates all the burglar alarms in the vicinity of the yacht club and out to the new houses on Viking Wharf, it sets the halyards of yachts moored in the marina a-jingling and a-tinkling as merrily as wind chimes. No, not wind chimes or chattering teeth; more the sound of ice cubes striking against the sides of a long-stemmed good, quality glass three-quarters full of Gordon's gin and tonic.

A young and fully grown voracious jackdaw has its head halfway down the gullet of its mother, near where the RMS *Aycturus* is offloading its cargo of soya beans and pig nuts.

It all happened long ago, even though it seems but yesterday. A decisive battle was fought and decided in the mud and filth and gore in midwinter with much slaughter by the well-trained English cavalry. It was over in three hours, with consequences that would last for centuries. At sundown the battlefield must have presented a melancholy sight, worse than the Cork municipal dump, when flocks of crows and gulls came down to join the pillagers and feed off the corpses. We know less of this battle than we do of the first battle of Kursk or the slaughter of Stalingrad. Mountjoy's army of four thousand were outnumbered more than two to one by O'Neill and O'Donnell; we do not know how many Irish were slain or how few the English; of the Spanish none at all.

Don Juan del Aquila and his army of four thousand had been bottled up in the town for three months and food was scarce; they made sorties by night, spiked two cannon that had been annoying them. For days after the defeat they waited for news of the Irish, who had marched from the north in semi-darkness, marching sullenly, cursing their Maker. Mountjoy, standing on a slope of wetland with several Grand Mariners inside him, awaited the arrival of the drenched Irish army; he seemed to be able to read O'Neill's mind. He sent Sir Henry Folliott and his cavalry to engage him across the stream near the Ballinamona bog, caught him off balance, and the rout had begun.

O'Donnell was proceeding in a westerly direction to Millwater; his pike-men following too close, some dozing as they stumbled on to regrouping infantry and caused the frightened horses to charge into the men, who were now certainly awake. Whereupon, in the great confusion and much cursing, his soldiers left the battle and were fleeing to the west, not to enter it again except as corpses floating down to White Castle in what was to be called the Ford of the Slaughtering. For there was no waving of white flags or status as prisoners of war or seeking sanctuary; Wingfield's horses came on like avenging angels with drawn swords, showing no mercy.

When the Spaniards offered to parley and Mountjoy acceded they were given shipping and safe conduct and sailed for La Coruña with band playing and flags flying. O'Neill submitted to Mountjoy at Mellifont the day after Queen Elizabeth had at last expired. The three brothers up on the tilted field were still not on talking terms. The clan system hadn't worked.

But I ask you, Golubchik, did brothers ever hit it off since Cain and Abel? Has a brother ever been a good *amigo,* a pal, a trusted confidant and friend, since Damian and Pythias were steadfast buddies? A person close to one to whom one can open one's heart, as the saying goes, even if the different lives that you lead have long separated you, given you different interests, driven you far apart? The brother you knew in childhood has long since departed, tiptoed silently away, become a stranger, passed away, or died.

In heavy musty old family albums with immensely thick pages you see the face of the late mother or late father in the faces of the young grandchildren playing on swings. But don't I see my dead father's hands (those of a shiftless fellow, a born idler) duplicated in my own hands, the hands of a writer, even to the dark liver spots on the backs of the hands stretched out before me for closer examination, like the darker circular markings on a blackbird's egg (or am I thinking of the thrush?).

My three brothers fly away in the clouds, like the umbrella lost in Dublin that was found again in the echoing cavern called Open Hole on the Old Head of Kinsale, through which the intrepid Alannah once sailed in a small yacht.

What have we got here, then, amid the gall and wormwood, the floss and flurry, fact and fiction? The Goncourt brothers involved themselves exclusively with French writing, but did they see eye to eye? They did not. And the *Brüder* Mann, Thomas and Heinrich of Lübeck, how did they hit it off? They didn't. And the fictitious Karamazov brothers, what of them? And what about the boozy half-brothers Geoffrey and Hugh Firmin of *Under the Volcano*, who can neither stop drinking nor blathering ('They are losing the battle of the Ebro'), the latter got up as Tom Mix, able to neigh like a horse.

Then you had the far-fetched pair of brothers in P.C. Wren's fable *Beau Geste*, doing the decent and honourable thing, the elder joining the French Foreign Legion, followed by the younger brother; heroic fighters against the tribesmen from the Riff. The brothers, dauntless characters, true scions of the house of Brandon Abbas and her ladyship, were *white clean through*.

What about the beastly Bulkiah brothers, Sultan Hassanal and playboy Prince Jefri, who never did a stroke of work in their lives? Borneo was always bad. As in the olden times, all were at each other's throats: Guelph versus Ghibelline, city state versus city state, Florence versus Venice, Verona versus Bologna.

We know that James Joyce had a younger brother, as indeed did Willie Yeats. Sam Beckett had an elder brother Frank: he mourned when Frank died of cancer.

Henry David Thoreau had a brother who died of lockjaw.

A London merchant, one Francis Rogers, newly arrived in Kinsale from the West Indies in October 1703 'amid foul weather' wrote: 'The town lyeth on the River Banny [sic] which runs far up . . . we did not a little indulge ourselves, with very good French claret drunk in the taverns at an English shilling, Brandy at three shillings & sixpence & four shillings per gallon.'

There were two ships called *Kinsale* on the high seas at one time. HMS *Kinsale* was built in the Royal Naval dockyard where the present-day Trident Hotel stands. Master Shipwright Stacey and one Chudleigh the foreman were the men who put the work through.

There is also a place of that name (Kinsale) in Montserrat in the Leeward Islands.

– 68 –

The Great Battle

O'Neill had set off from the north, bringing the foul weather with him, crossing 'o'er many a river bridged with ice', to arrive in a poor state for fighting under such harsh conditions. His Spanish allies (three thousand eight hundred of them cooped up in the town) were also in poor spirits, having been bottled up in the harbour for three months and provisions low, finding it difficult to feed themselves, they had begun to hate Ireland and the awkward Irish.

Between the bottled-up Spaniards and the frozen Irish at Coolcarron there were approximately four thousand English armed and ready, stoking their fires, priming their weapons, biding their time, raring to go.

The hot-blooded Spaniards finding themselves on short rations were fit to be tied. Mountjoy had set up a battery some six hundred yards to the east of Cork Gate on high ground and coolly proceeded to land penalties from all angles, making the Hispanics throw up the supper they had missed. When the two severed halves of the Irish Army had eventually come together, six thousand five hundred foot and horse, they made early use of the 'garryowen' tactics, devised by inferior Irish rugby teams down the years from the time of Eugene Davy and the Mauler Clinch. In my day a back line of Quinns playing for Old Belvedere were still wasting possession, following up futile high kicks and hoping that something good would come of it, Paddy, Kevin and Brendan running like hares.

Skipper Hugh O'Neill was the Irish hooker. A great lardy lump of a man of some sixteen stone plus, hard in the tackle and an adroit tactician. A great man for putting in the boot, getting the head down and pushing, farting and cursing, grunting as he shoved, not averse to some eye-gouging in the close work. Up-and-unders were his speciality, the fabled high garryowen. 'Lots of garryowen today, lads. The wind is swirling. Hit them with all you have, knock the shit out of them!'

'Red' Hugh O'Donnell was the Irish stand-off half, erratic, dodgy in defence, but brilliant on his day; a safe pair of hands, with a devastating drop kick, he could sidestep like a stag.

The English, the old foe, played their usual game, the scrum tight as a drum, heavy as a Churchill tank. At once they sent in their two heavies, Johnson and Rodbar, men not lacking in bottle, adepts at taking out their opposite numbers, maulings that might land them in hospital, playing to the weak side of unsighted referees, their crash-tackles calculated to capsize a bullock. Mountjoy, the English captain and fullback, of Harlequins and England, read O'Neill's mind as if his battle strategy (supposing he had any) was sketched out clearly on parchment. The back line, the so-called line of attack, O'Donnell and the two centres, Des Thorpe the nightmarishly sluggish scrum half who seemed to send the ball out with glue on it; the two wings, all could have stayed in the Bective Rangers changing room for all their effectiveness on the field. Many a green jersey was torn from a brawny Irish back, or a skinny back (Brendon Quinn), on that freezing December day.

The very topography of the place, undulating and marshy, with pools six foot deep in places, seemed to throw them into dire confusion and disorder, as if it weren't their own ground. Ireland playing 'away' internationals at Cardiff Arms Park and Murrayfield in the centuries to come had recourse to garryowens and then more garryowens, and then still more garryowens.

The English were encamped on high ground, hitting the walled town with two batteries placed strategically to do most damage; they continued to hit and hit until put out of action by the crafty and now very hungry Hispanics, creeping out under cover of darkness on a daring night raid to spike the cannons. The English and Irish could see and smell the smoke of each other's campfires, hear their doleful songs. The poor condemned Irish sang of imminent death, knowing their bad time had come.

To join the Spaniards, their allies, the Irish had to cross low ground and break through the English lines at Campbell or Ardmartin where the ridge drops to the valley level at Millwater. The Irish had hoped to proceed along the ridge and creep unnoticed around the English and join the Spaniards in the town, with only a small English defence at Cappagh to overcome.

The Munstermen complained that there were too many Leinstermen on the Irish team, the Connaughtmen said there were too many Munstermen, and the Ulstermen thought there weren't enough Ulstermen; but in one way or another the Irish tasted defeat again, that bitter taste like gall to which they had grown so accustomed. The so-called clan system was finished, all washed up.

With one practised savage backhander, a swipe with a sabre as calculated as the stroke that sent the polo ball goalwards at a chukker in the Phoenix Park, the screaming head of the unarmed pikeman went tumbling into tussocky marsh, the truncated body with outstretched arms begging clemency to the last and still in the act of falling as the horseman thunders by, hallooing, flourishing his bloody sabre.

'Seventeen, sirrahs!'

The exultant cry came from the plucky leading trooper Walter Hurlingham of Hendon riding Vulcan from the stables of Sir Henry Wotting, a magnificent bay charger of some seventeen hands.

The trooper of Wingfield's Horse came on at a rapid canter, flourishing their sabres and hallooing. Hal ('Nut-Case') Hosty of Leeds, then Alex ('Crank-Case') Pringle of South Shields, then the trio of foul-mouthed swashers Burns, Bedford and Nye; then hell for leather, making up ground, massive Dugdale and Cornfield, with Egglington and Barnacle far out on the right wing, followed by Campbell-Goulding of Island Magee; coming on fast as if beating for hidden frightened hares, the troopers hallooing and laughing.

The Irish Army was running away. They were beaten all right. You could smell the defeated army across the fields sloping down to the river where many of them fled, discarding pikes on the way, but finding no mercy, no pity there, where death awaited them.

Hosty had cornered a pikeless yokel gibbering with fear, down on his knees begging for clemency, beshitting his pants and holding up the palms of his dirty hands. But the Nut-Case was having none of that, his face turkey-cock red with hard riding; he was about to let him have it. War was a messy business, but sharp lessons had to be taught and learnt well. Hurlingham, sweeping past on Vulcan, was ever loyal to his Queen; he served her with a loyal heart. Vulcan was farting like a two-stroke.

'Paste him one for me, the rogue!' he called out jubilantly. 'One for good measure, give it to him good and hard!'

'I'll paste him one all right, I'll do for this fucker.'

The high-pitched scream of the victim, the trooper's grunt and sabre thrust were instantaneous. Nut-Case cleaned his weapon on the flanks of the piebald, laughing and waving.

The pursuit went rapidly on as far as Dunderrow, chase and kill without much grace, and with no mercy shown. The Irish had buckled as soon as they engaged; O'Donnell had gotten his knickers into a hopeless twist; he was finished as soon as he came in. Mountjoy had ended O'Neill in double-quick order in the bog. The Irish – and so many of them! – were finished; the sorry butchering went on until dark. The troopers grew sick of killing; the tally was great, it was a square dance without partners. The Irish had simply withered away. Weak cries of a man dying were heard down in the river, and a trooper cursing him as he floated beyond reach.

The Irish were decimated as the sabres rose and fell; hack followed thrust. They would have to be finished off so that the Queen could sleep untroubled in her bed. They had no stomach for such hard fighting. They had come frozen into battle. The day had dawned overcast and chilly, with a cold north wind driving a murky drizzle before it; it was not good for riding. Any foul weather would do for fighting: it was better not to see some of the barbarities done on that day, better to keep your mouth shut about what you had seen.

Still the killing went on. The sadists were having a field day. Hurlingham himself was sick of it, but satisfied at what had gone on, how it had ended. English casualties had been minimal; the surgeons had a quiet day. The English had fought well, cannily, using their nuts.

You'd have to feel sorry for the defeated, to go into battle so ill-prepared, so badly organised, and there were so many of them, more than double the English Army, not counting the Spaniards skulking in the town. O'Neill had worked wonders with untried, untrained volunteers, who had little stomach for battle; perhaps it would frighten off further volunteers?

Now the way was clear, the Queen had Ireland on her plate to do with it as she pleased; offer parts of it to the victors. Peace was assured, the Irish will had been broken: that was all that mattered, in the long run.

These heroes, relatives of Nym, Bardolph and Ancient Pistol, would re-emerge in North Africa in World War Two, to begin to swing another way a war they were losing, the Head-Banger, Nut-Case, Fast-Forward and the others were now being broiled alive inside tanks. The place names they chalked up on the sides of their tanks were like citations of valour, good as medals – Benghazi, Wadi Halfa, Sidi Bel Abbès, Tobruk – telling of hard-won victories in battles fought in cruel heat in the Libyan desert, of pipers inflating bagpipes and going in before Scots troops. They had punched holes in Jerry's defences, knocking Rommel out of Africa for a six, so that they could go home again to Leeds and Birmingham and Bolton and Hull. They were Monty's men as surely as Nym and Pistol had been Prince Harry's men, as sure as Hurlingham and Cornfield and the others had been Wingfield's Horse, in the long ago.

In the plantation before the house where I had been innocently amusing myself, I slipped on a branch and split my nose on a forked holly bough and ran across the front meadow, blood pumping from both nostrils on to my jersey, bawling for my ma. The grass was high, it was a summer of the early 1930s before the war. I wade through it, weeping, bleeding profusely, calling for my ma.

Later on the threshold of puberty, one day in a game didn't I beshit myself with excitement and must have confessed as much to Mumu, who ran a shallow bath and told me to take off those trousers (shorts) and get into the bath. And when I stood up in it she washed me down and when I sat down in it she threw the big sponge to cover my privates. So how old was I then, if I was embarrassed to expose my privates? And was she too embarrassed?

One day when I had been guilty of some misdemeanour in the garden or in the front yard, or in the rockery, Dado ordered me into the house as punishment on that lovely sunny day: 'Get into the house, you little pup!'

He followed me in, his dander rising, as mine was too, and pushed me in the back with his fingers, jabbing.

I turned on him, as if to go for him, glared at him; and he was shocked, took a step back, lost his authority, blustered.

'What what what . . . did you say?'

I turned my back on him, gave him best, received a hard prod in the small of the back.

'Get up those stairs, you bold little brat!'

'I'll tell Ma.'

'What did you say, you pup?'

'Maaa!'

'No supper for you, my lad. Up with you!'

I mounted the stairs with offensive slowness, prodded and poked in the back. My father was fuming. I was bawling. All was in order. Mumu was nowhere to be seen.

– 69 –

Sir Walter Raleigh and the Cockadoodledoo

Sir Walt in Cork, the butter hairy, his troops strutting on the Mall, the native kerns deceitful, liars by necessity; not a virgin in the land.

Balcony of Europe

One grey Sunday morning in the bad summer of 1603, two years after the fiasco at Kinsale, Sir Walter Raleigh was taking his usual constitutional along Merchants' Quay in the sorry port of Cork;

he liked to perambulate thereabouts because all that pertained to the sea interested him, he being a seafaring man for most of his life. He walked on the balls of his feet like a black bear on a chain, his nose discoloured from much wine-imbibing; he wore dark grey hose and a half-cape of a lighter grey trimmed with ermine and, as behoves a gentleman, he wore a sword (to defend a lady's honour, should she be insulted). On his head a Highland bonnet of faded blue from which a single peacock feather depended, held in place at an acute angle by a garnet brooch. He was cock of the walk.

He had been presented with seventeen thousand hectares of confiscated Desmond estates following the Kinsale débâcle that gave generous spoils of war to Englishmen of good standing, which he had sold on immediately and profitably to the Earl of Cork who was ambitious and no fool. Raleigh himself therefore did not lack means.

He was disinclined to take up residency in Myrtle Grove, a much-banged-about Elizabethan mansion which was his freehold in the fishing village of Yawl (in Gaelic *Eochail*, meaning yew tree). Congreve the dramatist, who gave *The Way of the World* to the London public, had spent his early infancy there; but Sir Walter did not care for Yawl.

He was a true sailor in that he frequented Bankside bawdy houses *before* breakfasting on beer and chops, for he was a manly man high in blood, attempting to modify his bear's pace to accommodate a gross high-rise early morning horn that threatened to burst itself free of the containing and restraining codpiece in its hempen stitching and stirring like a weasel in a sack.

Towards him came two fresh-faced wenches with a little dog, out for an early morning stroll like himself. They were clutching each other and giving out peals of laughter while engaged in close and intimate feminine gossiping; their bright eyes sparkled and their nostrils flared when they spied who was advancing towards them with measured tread, a roguish rogering smile already beginning to play upon his lips; about to sweep off his bonnet and do the honours as befitted a gent and a highborn one who, moreover, had the ear of the Queen of England. With ballooning skirts furled about their hips and cheeks ablaze with rude health, they were blown towards him, surprising him in the middle of a most pleasurable reverie.

He was puffing away on his curlicue pipe bought in Barbados, with enough smoking tobacco to last him a year, and smiling fondly to himself at the recollection of a certain blushing but compliant lady-in-waiting to the Queen (Elizabeth I, the regal woman in the ruff with the glazed eyes of the bream, or a cod – when she was being skittish – or the wobbly eye of a doll when she had a drop taken), who was a real handful with her heaving milk-white bosom bared to the nipples, whose favours he had once enjoyed, standing her upright against the bole of a great beech tree that stood alone in the corner of the palace gardens. On a sudden impulse, then and there, he had positioned her as impatiently as a window-dresser might roughly manhandle a helpless female dummy.

The tall beech groaned deeply down all its mighty length as a freshening southeaster poured steadily into its top-heavy summer boscage, blowing steadily from beyond the London Mall, and brought into play a great rustling and tittering and general unrest in the mighty tree that towered above them.

As he pleasured her with a deep-pronged pleasuring, the flustered lady had groaned in unison with her impatient debaucher and the great deep-breathing tree that swayed to its roots; this during the intermission of a motet by Palestrina or one of the lesser Venetians, anyway a small string ensemble that was busily sawing away inside, to amuse their tone-deaf Queen.

Finding themselves conveniently alone in the great garden now being thoroughly drenched in a sudden heavy summer squall that had sent the rest of the gossips scurrying for cover, they had seized their chance there and then, or rather the bold circumnavigator had seized *her* and pushed her up against the beech and made it very evident that his intentions were dishonourable. Oh sweet Sir Walter! You undo me!

The rain fell pattering amid the huge straining canopy and press of leaves but left the ground they stood on dry as tinder. Sir Walter, at the peak of his ardour, had lifted the lady up in his arms, pronged her with his overmastering passion that could neither be (by him) controlled nor (by her) resisted; for that was the way things were.

Was this what is called happenchance? The summer breeze coming up the Lee brought that other summer breeze in its wake, brought back the avid lady-in-waiting (what was her name?) into his arms. The red-cheeked hussies were giving him a bold eye as they passed by. 'It's him, it's him I tell ye! It's Raleigh! Ship ahoy, up the jolly Roger! Lovely day for it, Sir Roger! Will it hold up?'

Will you look at the perfidious state he's in! No woman could feel safe on a sofa with the likes of that one! Morning, Sir Roger. Grand morning for it!

The choleric Queen was crying out testily, 'Where *is* Sir Walter? Where *has* he gone to? Bring him here *immediately*!' The Queen's every word was law.

– 70 –

Fisher Street and Environs

We are to be found in the second house on the one-way traffic system ordained by the Local County Council; in the second-last house if you come the wrong way by car along Upper O'Connell Street, the system terminating at Casey's Corner where the road dips down by what used to be the Fishermans' Recreation Hall but is now a private dwelling house with family already in residence, as you can tell from the toys scattered about the yard.

Directly opposite this stands Bruno's Tower, a brave renovation job by the tireless Breton from Pont-Aven, working from sun-up to sundown creosoting railway sleepers that were to be his rafters. The former architect and garden designer built his tower on the site of a previous lighthouse and it (the tower) sprouts out of the living room like aberrant growth on top of a clump of toad-stools. The heavy Breton cross set up on the wall was brought all the way from Pont-Aven and has already acquired its own growth of lush Irish ivy.

Bruno Guillou has installed an arched window to match the liturgical effect of the corresponding one opposite, the architrave much favoured by the roosting pigeons who leave their droppings below, as though the place had been there a long time.

Upper O'Connell Street, presumably named for the Liberator, is one of the cleaner and less dog-fouled of the streets hereabouts, the new pavements laid down by the municipality going as far as the bottle bank near the marina where the yacht *Cassiopeia* out of Corpus Christi, Texas, had been moored all winter.

The dialects of the fishermen here are distinctive, as if they spoke different languages in Scilly, World's End and the Flat of Town. The one-way systems and short interleading streets make the place confusing; you could walk out and come back to what seems a different town, depending on which way you re-enter; walks taken clockwise and then anticlockwise along the embankment to the new bridge below Folly House yield up quite different views, as in Lacan's famous mirror-distorting effect; studying one's face in a mirror and seeing a stranger staring back.

Mazzer, a retired nurse from a psychiatric ward (of whom more anon), drives her small white Fiat down the wrong way past us, sounding her horn, not quite in control of the car, down on its springs. She drives atrociously.

'Why shouldn't I?' she asks defiantly. 'Wasn't I born here, and my mother before me? There's nothing in the deeds of my house to tell me which way I can drive my own car up or down the street.'

Mazzer is a portly lady bordering on the outsize, a stalwart big-bottomed battering-ram of a woman built along the lines of the well-corseted Margaret Dumont, Groucho's imperturbable stooge, massive and commanding who can neither be browbeaten nor downfaced. Mazzer controls the street rather as did Chaplin's fierce, baton-wielding cop with autocratic circumflex eyebrows in *Easy Street*, bending street lamps to pavement level with his bare hands.

The other ladies who live in the street are rarely seen and then only as clusters of gossiping noddies with tinted hair. One noddy is always in full spate; the rest you never see, they seem to live indoors, like the Swedes, their doors rarely open. One of the elderly Arnopp sisters, of ancient lineage, is said to be poorly, having taken to her bed, and a coal delivery comes regularly. After their brother Piercy died there was no man to dig the garden. A retired butcher, he passed away last year; butchers from all over the country attended his funeral, butchers being close as Freemasons. They are not very neighbourly neighbours, the Arnopp sisters; dressed like a Russian peasant one of them tears at the weeds, visible over our drenched stockade. Is it Dora or Kitty? I never know which is which; but one had not been seen out for months, maybe a year; smoke curls from their chimney early in the day. Kitty or Dora is dying.

The walled garden of flowers and vegetables and rustic arbours abutting on St Multose Cemetery over the wall must come as a surprise. We have those quiet well-behaved Protestant neighbours, *los muertos*.

It poured rain all this winter and cattle died in the open fields. The farmers didn't get the prices they wanted, fodder became short, livestock bawling with hunger in the waterlogged fields, up to their hocks in muck.

Rain fell incessantly, coming down like a hard penance, and in court the accused perjured themselves, threatened witnesses, swore at the Guards. Strange and unheard-of crimes occurred in remote places, the consequence of drunkenness and disputes about land and property, and the foul weather.

A man trimming a hedge slipped and fell from a collapsing stepladder, slit himself from ear to ear on the opened clippers, crawled in his blood across a lawn, his face chalk white, expiring in his wife's arms.

The Pope was tireless at performing good works, flying far, kissing the ground, saying Mass for two million of the faithful in Mexico.

A new and horrible new Ireland had begun to emerge. Skulduggery was exposed in high places, but those concerned seemed immune, hard to nail down; protesting their innocence, they lied under oath, denied all their misdeeds, slippery as eels. Priests, formerly trusted friends of the family, part of the family, for God's sake, were found to be guilty of committing unnatural acts with children under their care; the finger was even pointed at bishops. Nuns went to bed with other nuns.

We have four butchers' shops, one turf accountant, two banks, two postal deliveries in morning and afternoon, letter post on foot, and parcel post by green van in the afternoon, the parcel (books) given into your hand by a surly fellow out of uniform who will not catch your eye, sour as though permanently out of sorts. Alannah said wittily that he might feel happier if he was working in an abattoir; hadn't his da, sour as the son, been a butcher?

The sounds that wake us in the winter darkness are not the downpours of rain sloshing into the yard nor the dripping aftermath but around 4.30 the sound of Concorde 'going supersonic' as it invades Irish airspace, heading out across the Atlantic for New York.

Shortly after that we hear the same early car (coming the wrong way down the one-way system) stopping outside the narrow block of flats to pick up a colleague heading off for the day shift at the Eli Lilly chemical plant at Dunderrow.

They work a twenty-four-hour day there, spilling drug effluents through the muggy winter air, and when the wind blows in the wrong direction the Beugs get it, and close their windows, having already lost four peacocks to a neighbouring farmer laying down poison alongside their land.

These are the sounds that wake us in the darkness, and in winter that means fifteen hours of night with no exultant cockcrow to announce daybreak as the darkness leaks away and a wan purposeless sort of daylight takes its place. Small wonder that the 'mere Irish' are a lethargic breed. As said before, 'the smaller the island, the bigger the neurosis'.

The low sun shines at an acute angle into Upper O'Connell Street, coming between Mary Lane's wine bar and Satin & Lace boutique, lighting up the lemon-yellow door of Spring Cottage, so named on a scrollwork of entwined flowers, where Mazzer sleeps and snores and holds sway.

Two baskets of flowers are suspended on either side of the door and two printed cards with the prohibition NO PARKING, to be repeated in other windows. Such prohibitions are catching. Don't do this, don't do that. This house is mine. This way is mine. Keep out.

A recurring annoyance in summer months is the passing drunkard who knocks on the door at 5 a.m. on his way home, sometimes pulling out flowers from hanging basket and trellis. Mazzer believes that this may be a retired bachelor postman who is unable to break the habit of early rising and therefore has time on his hands. She threatens to empty a full chamber pot on to his head from an upstairs window one of these days.

Fidgety crows balance themselves on the telegraph wires near Good's Mill and drop down to snatch spillage from the lorries that ply between there and the dockside loading bay.

Great herring gulls escort the trawlers into the harbour and take the scraps discarded over the side. An otter fishing from the dock clings to one of the car tyres lashed to the sea wall. Jackdaw and crows take the easy pickings from Mamma Mia's skips and sly cats are fed by an old nun at the gate of the convent now empty of students, foul-mouthed girls puffing fags, boasting of conquests and rebuffs. The clear voices call up – 'suck-off, blow-job, mickey'. Their whores' language is purple.

The Urban District Council has supplied hygienic wheely-bins and imposed a charge for the Thursday collections. Before that the resourceful rooks were slashing open the plastic bags with their sharp beaks and the dogs dragged out the refuse for the birds to devour.

Blackbirds, thrushes and magpies assemble about the French prison where in January 1749 fifty-four French prisoners suffocated to death in a fatal fire. The nocturnal whistler passes in the night, always alone, whistling melodiously with trills and grace notes and arpeggios, going on his way so tunefully and cheerful. Curlews overfly the house in the darkness, sending down their lovely liquid calls. A single heron flies over the garden in the daytime, cranking herself forward, legs stretched out behind, heading for some fishpond. In the lane below the Friary Church the bats flit to and fro in summer, hunting insects. There are few dogs on the loose and cats seem to stay indoors or use the hidden gardens.

Wrens too I have seen in the garden, though seldom, woodpeckers never; for a while a piebald blackbird came and went and then did not return any more, perhaps killed by the cats. It was more white than black, more odd-looking than a magpie, odder than an ape painted white.

Crows sound guttural as old fellows gasping for breath, throats rusty with catarrh. The jackdaws give urgent mating calls on the roof opposite us, the cock with trembling wings outspread, puffed up with lust; the hen hopping out of reach, affecting indifference; then he is upon her.

Mute swans paddle in the marina, passing the green hull of the yacht *Cas-*

siopeia; the trim yacht has been on its moorings all winter, the long foul wet winter that continued late into April, the swallows arriving late. The Earl of Orrery thought Kinsale in 1660 'one of the noblest harbours in Europe'. The old port of bond houses and sedan chairs, burgheresses and Kinsale hookers, Charles Fort and James Fort, the ramparts, Desmond Castle; reaching back to the days of Thurston Haddock and Norman de Courcey, Philip Roche and Andrew Blundus; 'where the Brinney meets the Bandon', is our home today.

All through this summer, the saddest summer of the century and the wettest on record, the swallows could be heard but not seen twittering overhead as in previous summers, the summers of long ago; now reduced to dots and spots caused by indigestion, blurs in the retina of the jaundiced eye of the beholder; just sounds in the air announcing the summer that had never arrived.

The nests of the swifts in the eaves of the other No. 2 at the top of the Stony Steps are no longer there, torn down by cruel tenants concerned about the limy droppings squirted on the footpath and doorsteps.

There is an old superstition in Kildare, that if the nests of these exquisite summer birds are destroyed, the milked cows yield blood. No longer was heard their high-pitched screeching as they tore through the air around the Stony Steps. Renowned for their spectacular aeronautics while feeding, every autumn they emigrated to Africa, slept on the wing: nobs of the air in their spotless white dickeys and midnight-blue jackets, nattily attired they had their own schedules, their small dark eyes missing nothing.

The birds of Kinsale were as the birds of the Ark, sole survivors of the Great Flood; they sang as though their last hour had come. On an overcast Sunday in early August the seagulls were crying like cats over the garden of No. 2.

*   *   *

Judd Scanlan was sent down for twenty-two years for importing drugs from Arnhem and Amsterdam via Rosslare and Ringaskiddy into Cork, hidden in Donaghmore and Nad woodlands. Profitable connections had been made in Brixton and Maidstone Prisons with the Columbian drug cartels. Barbara Berg was bereft; they had a daughter whom he adored. He would be seventy-one when he left prison, an old man. The Gardai thought that he wouldn't be able to handle it. If you played with fire, you got burnt. The man behind the murder of Veronica Guerin on the Lucan Road was imprisoned in England, reputed to be a very bad egg indeed.

Hit-men were for hire in Dublin: if the price was right anybody could be rubbed out. Killing was like any other business; drug trafficking was carried out like any honest business, but what business was honest? Every nest had its bad egg. Cocaine and Ecstasy were worth millions, the tobacco of the twenty-first century. The villains had appropriate nicknames for those who had done time in the nick: the Bodyguard, Seedy Fagan, the Penguin Mitchell. In the dock they all protested their innocence; they were innocent men, they said. They had been got at.

Transport managers were recruited to facilitate drug trafficking from the continent; the rich villains took their vacations on the Costa del Sol, showed films of their marked victims, jeered at Veronica Guerin, who was marked down for murder. Ecstasy and cannabis importers were into the big time. It was a lark.

– 71 –

St Multose Cemetery and the Commogue Marsh

In St Multose Cemetery abutting on our walled garden lie the Protestant dead. Dead husbands lie by dead wives, dead sons and daughters by dead parents, kinsmen and their dutiful womenfolk, all dead Anglicans assembled here. Those who had lived a long time and those whose lives had been cut short, with modest gravestones commemorating them in a grassy walled place within the arched gateway that leads into the church grounds proper, the Protestant enclave.

Here lie the Arnopps and the Copithornes and the Drapers and the Staffords and the Waltons and George Edward Stanley and Margaret Flaherty (a Miss Barrington had married a Catholic), Buttimer Byron, Newman, Kingston and Wing Commander Ronald Sivewright (*Per ardua ad astra*) and Robert Johnston and his beloved wife Peg (née Gregg) who died four years after, aged forty-seven years ('Abide with Me') and Gertrude Mather who lived ninety-four years, and Hodgkin the kleptomaniac who hadn't lived so long, and Heathcote and Crawford and Donald Dean Marleau (born in Canada) buried near the wall under the great yew tree, since removed to accommodate another block of flats, a youth hostel.

This is a Protestant redoubt in a republican Catholic heartland where Anglican Protestants intermarry and breed with their own, keep faith with those of their own persuasion and keep themselves to themselves: the Goods and the Grahams, the Lucases and Daphne Daunt keeping the bloodline pure, to worship in St Multose and sing their doleful Anglican hymns amid the monuments and memorial stones commemorating those brave soldiers and officers who had offered their services and given their lives to the English Crown.

It was the site of the great battle, a cannon shot away, in the dead of winter in 1601 when Protestant English put O'Neill and O'Donnell to flight, watched by Catholic Spanish from the inner harbour. It was an afternoon's slaughter.

The Catholic cemetery of St Eltin is out beyond Good's Mills on the road to Summercove, and there roil the mortal remains of Joe ('the Trapper') Revatta and little Billy O'Brien (not to be confused with little Willie O'Brien, publican of the Bulman) and those other brave hearts who have passed away in our time, going out from the Bulman bar one damp day and stepping into the afterlife, wherever it may be, free of all encumbrances pertaining to the living, with benefits and rewards that scorn profit and loss.

The layabouts and loungers lounge about the Temperance Hall, sitting on their idle arses on the public bench supplied or resting themselves against the walls, Dicky Rock (RIP), and gouty Garr, still with us and mad as a brush; from World's End, the Fish, beery O'Leary of Barrack Street, the loonies and wiseacres, gossips and tosspots of the town. I recall the time when elderly men gossiped all day by gateposts in Ireland; but the instant TV arrived they went indoors and haven't been seen since. These old knowalls who hung about gateposts at dusk, travellers in time who maybe never put a foot outside their own parish are no more.

'St Multose, and St Eltin, who are they when they are at home?'

'Our patron saint. They are one and the same.'

'But one is Protestant and the other Catholic, how can they be the same?'

'They are the same chap.'

'How come?'

'I don't know.'

'Well, I'll be damned!'

In Loving Memory Of
ISABEL DOROTHEA JAMES
Dearly Beloved Wife Of
JOHN NEVILLE ABRAHAM JAMES
Born Oleby

22nd November 1896
Died Kinsale 16th July 1977

On unadorned white marble headstones the names were cut. Cheek by jowl the James man and wife lay underground.

In Loving Memory Of
JOHN NEVILLE ABRAHAM JAMES
Dearly Beloved Husband Of
ISABEL DOROTHEA JAMES
Born Dublin 17th November 1891
Died Cork 25th September 1979

In Loving Memory Of
MICHAEL NEWMAN
who died 16th June 1928
and his sister KATHLEEN
Died 14th July 1965.
And of their mother
KATE NEWMAN
who died 18th April 1978

'BLESSED BE THE PURE IN HEART
FOR THEY SHALL SEE GOD.'

Late April pansies of russet and orange with black hearts nodded their heads to the breeze that blew through the little walled graveyard where the Newmans slept their last sleep, as Rory strolled by, took note of their names and the year of their decease.

The recently mown lawn of the little Anglican cemetery was carpeted with a profusion of daisies and dandelions, numerous as the fields of poppies that sprang up from the blood of slaughtered Serbs, become the red poppies that grow only at Kossova.

JPR (Russell) NORMAN
25–12–1923 to 1–1–1999

PERKINS
HOWARD AND ANN née BUCKLEY
1911–1997.
Christ Our Light.

In Loving Memory of My Darling Wife
ELIZABETH ANN RAYMOND
Who died 10th October 1974
and her loving husband
TERENCE GEORGE RAYMOND
Died 23rd January 1994
Resting Where No Shadows Fall

Happy and loving memories
GERTRUDE MATHER
Lived 94 years
30–8–1899 – 5–6–1994

A clump of dandelions below the headstone, that read:

In Loving memory of
BARONESS MC M.C.A. DIBBETS
Grandmother of ASTRID WILLIAMS
29th April 1963 – 13th May 1997
Beloved wife of TOM WILLIAMS & loving
mother of Thomas Neal? [undecipherable].

In loving Memory of my husband
DONALD DEAN MARLEAU
Born October 1939 in Canada.
At rest September 1988.
'Until We Meet Again.'

In Loving Memory Of
PAT HEATHCOTE
Born 6th September 1909
Died 13th March 1997.
Beloved wife of
FRED HEATHCOTE
Born 12th December 1908
Died 5th March 1991.
At Rest

In loving memory of
ADRIAN JAMES WENSLEY WALKER
Born 6th March 1932
Died 4th October 1996.

In the cement below the headstone was cut the name WALKER, above an unweeded headstone of black marble.

In Loving memory of
GEORGE N. BEASLEY
Born; Kent 5th December 1915
Died; Kinsale 1st November 1996.
At Rest

In Loving memory of
GORDON ALEXIS GOOD
Born 20th June 1926
Died 6th July 1987.
In Heavenly Love Abiding.

Below the proud running header COPITHORNE lay the dead Copithornes in their serried ranks:

In loving memory of
JAMES RICHARD COPITHORNE
Mullendonny, Kinsale. Died 12–12–85
aged 67 years.
The Lord is My Shepherd.

DORMAN
In loving memory of
HENRY HOBART GEORGE
'Raffeen,' Scilly,
Born 19th January 1906
Died 4th May 1991
And his wife
GWENDOLEN ALLEN
Born 13th January 1908
Died 16th March 1997.

'Love One Another.'

In loving memory of
our dear brother
GEORGE ARNOPP
Died 5th October 1989.
Also our dear sister
MARGARET
Died 18th September 1990.
Well done, thy good and faithful
servant enter the joy of the Lord.

In loving memory of
MARIGOLD SLOCOCK
Who died 24th May 1986
Aged 92 years.
At Rest.

In loving Memory of
THOMAS CHAMBER
Coolbawn, Ballinspittle
who died 7th September 1982.
His wife Mary, née Blennerhassett
Died 6th July 1991.
Forever with the Lord.

The curious names of villages and townlands are presumably Anglicised versions of the Gaelic originals:

Ardbrack
Ballinadee
Ballinamona
Ballinspittle
Ballynacubby
Ballynagrumnoolie
Bawhavota
Cappagh
Commogue (Creek)

Crossbarry
Currahoo
Dromderrig
Dunderrow
Knocknabohinny
Knocknacurra
Ringfinnan
Timoleague
Tisaxon Beg

Our ship's chandler John Thullier has itemised the fowl of the marsh at Commogue and the life thereon.

Little grebe and dabduck keep diving, turning over weeds and stones to feed, as do the turnstones. A flash of russet orange betrays the presence of the kingfisher. Golden plover fly in formation towards Timoleague, their favoured habitation. You know the shelduck by its pied plumage, the widgeon by its chestnut-coloured head, the mallard by its gorgeous vivid green. Oystercatchers, cormorants and tufted mergansers feed here, herons perch on the branches of alders; little egrets have come from the Mediterranean to take up residency on the south coast. Mute swans stay all year round, paddling by the dyke and the Dog Pond near the road to Dunderrow and the Doon. Greenshanks and redshanks occupy the right bank under Knocknacurra (these slender birds easily take fright), lapwings assemble in large flocks facing into the wind. The little dunlin feeds near the curlews, the godwits have upturned bills, ducks and waders feed from mid-October to mid-February, a grim time of year that gets longer and longer, wetter and wetter.

> The causeway across the marsh at Commogue was built 150 years ago. For thousands of years the river has been flushing tides into the open inlet. Sluice gates under the road allow salt water to mix with fresh water coming down from the streams that enter the marsh from the surrounding hills. This brackish water, together with an alder grove in the northwestern corner, provides a diverse habitat for various flora and wild life birds. (Thullier)

The Fella says that John Thullier, bearded like a sea-captain, is 'perfidious'. Treacherous and deceitful, they have fallen out over some small seafaring matter that would not trouble landlubbers such as you or me, hiding in the shadows of the rushes.

The upturned mallards show their arses when feeding upside down, unconcerned with such disputes that make life in the country what it is: medieval. Is it not so? We never had a Renaissance nor a Reformation; we never needed them.

– 72 –

The Gangrenous Hand

Scott of the Antarctic

He died amid the snow blizzards on his return journey from the South Pole and has been carried 35 miles from the spot where he recorded his last words.

He is buried on an ice shelf that is moving, so we can work out where the bodies must be today. Scott and his two companions, Dr Edward Wilson, the expedition's chief scientist, and Lieut. Henry Bowers, have been covered over with just a foot of ice each year, and are now 90 feet below the surface. Scott's final journey will take another 250 years.

Daily Telegraph, 9 November 1998

The will to live must have eventually left them, been drained out of them; for nothing could change the prolonged inertia until death had dealt his last hand, freed them; best to slip away in sleep and be carried off into unconsciousness.

The minute hand and the hour hand were both nailed to the clockface and time stood still, waiting for them to do the decent thing and die. They stood outside Time, it was finished with them, held captive in a dark place like miners asphyxiated in a deep coal mine out of which the oxygen is being drained, or blindfolded hostages held captive in dark quarters by terrorists or madmen.

If one roused himself to speak, the other two listened apathetically without any signs of emotion, heard him out in stupefied silence, huddled together for warmth, breathing their hound's breath into each each other's faces, emitting sour wind and sighing. The blizzards closed around them; the brown air in the tent was bad, the stink of putrefaction lingered, all that remained of Evans who had died six weeks previously of a gangrenous hand cut on sledge runners. Exactly a month before, Larry Oates had stumbled out of the tent on his frostbitten feet, after pronouncing the famous epitaph, never to be seen again, as if he had gone off the edge of the earth. Someone had blundered!

The moan of the Arctic wind rose to a psychotic whine, dragging at the guy ropes. Was it day or night? There seemed little enough reason to hope for any improvement in their miserable lot, no human voices carried on the wind and each night they prayed never to awake. They were already in the Nether World. They stank like corpses.

The blizzards blew themselves out but the rescue party never arrived. Snow fell silently on the tent, a great mantle of snow laid down gently layer upon layer, year after year, obliterating them.

The tent with its three bodies intact became a sarcophagus, a snow-covered, iced-up hearse with no mourners to accompany it to its final destination. Scott and his two companions had now drifted beyond the camp which he had failed to reach eighty-eight years before at the end of March 1912. They were on a moving ice-shelf carried along at a slow and stately rate of just under half a mile a year; the slowest funeral cortège in the world would take another two hundred and fifty years to reach the Ross Sea. They still had some way to go, buried ninety feet deep in the ice like flies in amber.

'Outside the door of the tent it remains a scene of swirling drift,' the cramped fingers had written. Wasn't it Yeats who wrote, 'Too long a sacrifice can make a stone of the heart'? Captain Robert Scott's achievement is considered a success, like the siege of Stalingrad, the retreat from Dunkirk, the London Blitz, the Windmill never closing, a tied Test match at the Oval: such rearguard actions and tactical retreats are proof of man's mettle, reveal the human spirit.

By December 1999 the tent had passed One Ton depot where the rescue party had waited six days to no avail. In about 2250 the frozen grave will break up into giant icebergs and the three bodies sink to their last resting place on the bed of the Ross Sea.

The Siege of Stalingrad

When the Russian winter descended upon besieged Stalingrad with its heavy tread the temperature sank by eighteen degrees and ice-floes began to build up and grind together on the Volga, buckling up and groaning deep groans. Crossing the frozen river, Beevor wrote, had become perilous as a Polar expedition. The Sixth Army awaited its fate in dugouts 'grouped together like a troglodyte village'. In their deep misery the steely-hearted citizens of the encircled city had begun to hallucinate. And to such effect that Stalin, their great leader, was seen stalking amid the ruins in his heavy military greatcoat, moving silently and stiffly as if already cast in bronze. He had come to comfort them in their hour of need in the suffering city named after him.

Starving mice broke into stationary Tiger tanks of the Panzer Corps and ate the cables off the power installations, effectively putting them out of action. When the city was retaken by Zhukov and his generals a great silence fell and the wind off the steppes whistled through the rusty skeletons of Sixth Army tanks put out of action by Russian mice.

The courageous Captain Scott had chosen to die in his own way, a fate no worse nor any better than suffocation with the crew of the submarine *Thetis* sunk in the mud of Liverpool Bay; or drowned amid the loose pianos and stiff-lipped gentry who had gone down with the *Titanic*, holed by a drifting iceberg off Newfoundland.

Towards the end, the last three breathing their last breaths, Scott, Wilson and Bowers, all equal now in misery, stinking to high heaven, with spirits flagging, they may have come around to the view that the whole sorry enterprise had been ill-judged, if not rank foolishness. What was the South Pole to them but a cairn of stones built in the Antarctic wastes by Amundsen and, as a final insult, the Norwegian flag limp on its pole?

They had come to detest the sight of each other, the awful proximity, the gloomy bulks looming in the cramped tent, their hoarse voices and insufferable patience; the courage to survive so obstinately in such squalid surroundings was demeaning, detestable.

Oh all the fishes in the sea that swam upriver under the arches of the Archdeacon Duggan bridge opposite Folly House (whilom home of the Simpsons) agreed:

Bass
Codfish
Codling
Conger eel
Dab
Dogfish
Flounder
Mullet

Plaice
Pollack
Whiting
Wrasse

all were in full agreement. As were the birds that wintered in the Commogue
Marsh:

Bar-tailed godwit and black-tailed godwit
Black-backed gull
Common gull and black-headed gull
Common tern
Curlew
Dunlin
Greenshank
Grey heron
Lapwing
Little egret
Mallard
Merganser
Oystercatcher
Peregrine falcon
Redshank
Reed bunting
Ringed plover and golden plover
Sedge warbler
Shag
Shelduck
Snipe
Teal
Whimbrel
Wigeon
Woodcock
Yellowhammer
Yellow wagtail

as itemised by ornithologist Damien Enright and limned by Steve Pawsey.

Consolation for the defeated is that all lost battles are considered (by the losers)
to be triumphs, moral victories on the field of sport and battle, defeat seen as a

glorious victory (the tryless draw at Lansdowne Road), in the cant of history. *Verti la giubla!*

– 73 –

Warning Shadows

Whenever I'm working well on a book, scorning the mundane, the humdrum and the norm; or say rather when it is working well on *me*; as one might speak of gangrene working in a wound or of a powerful prophylactic calculated to fire up the sluggish system – I might receive the summons from what Saul Bellow calls the Hidden Prompter (who never sleeps, always alert for messages) who now wishes to convey an urgent message coming direct from the unconscious, central recording communications system or CRCS: for me to rise up pronto, take up my bed and walk from even the deepest sleep (it could be 5 a.m.) and, on going upstairs into the living room (up from my sea cabin, my sea gown scarf'd about me in the dark, groped I to find), to find the room where I work, lit from three windows from two sides like some irrefutable point in Euclidean geometry, now bathed in the most extraordinary light imaginable.

You might say it was the ambient light found in the Dutch Old Masters with the Dutch darkness driven out of the sky to reveal an ancient amber light known to those circumnavigators who had come into a bay in the Dutch East Indies just at sun-up and found it flooded in this light.

Let me put it another way. A man is walking briskly through a city become strange to him at an early hour when normally he would not be up and about. Walking at a brisk pace through a Berlin emptied of traffic and pedestrians and become strangely silent, Vladimir Nabokov ('Sirius' the Russian novelist) makes his way towards the nursing home where his new-born son (nameless and still in the shock or stupor of birth) awaits the father troubled by the unearthly light that floods the sleeping city, familiar buildings casting strange shadows at awkward angles.

The shadows fall at such strange angles that Nabokov feels he has slipped or fallen between the gap of one day and the next, dropped into a no-place, into the *Neveneinder ineluctably.* That part of the city he now traversed walking briskly, perspiring and nervous, was doubly unfamiliar to the new father now approaching a still unknown, unseen, sleeping son; and to be sure already held under threat, by the sinister Prussian shadows cast across the unfamiliar narrow streets and by shadows that were positively UFA-like in their menace, as though awaiting the arrival of Werner Krauss or Conrad Veidt and give them (the shadows) veracity, to deliver their lines; as the babe (now awake and bawling to be fed) awaited the father, now breaking into a trot, the nursing home (a strange home never seen before, lit by an unearthly light) at long last hove finally in sight.

But, then, neither was it quite like that.

I'd come up into the living room that I had left in total darkness six or seven hours previously to discover it now flooded with an extraordinarily calm orange effulgence, certainly an unearthly light; as a yachtsman leaving the darkness of the cabin for the open deck after daybreak finds all about him a double light, so that the yacht seems to sail in the air, sea-reflecting sky and sky-reflecting sea become one light bearing up the yacht, gushing from beyond the horizon, announcing the arrival of a new day.

Something as marvellous as that awaited me in the living room in spring or summer at that early hour. In winter, of course, the room would be in darkness, a cat sleeping, the ashes cold in the wood-burner, the automatic heating not yet on. It had something of the strong purposeful Prussian daylight, sunrise light, known to me in Berlin when I had left Hannelore and had to kill time walking round and round Schlachtensee (Slaughter Lake) or Krumme Lanke (an old German song?), laden with guilt.

The colour that bathed the living room (the cat now awake and silently begging to be fed) was such an orange that orange will hardly do to describe it with any accuracy. I would have to say it reminded me of the truly phenomenal colour of the dead orchard that Calnek and I chanced upon in our marathon walk from Cómpeta in the hills to Canillas de Albaida; we never found the fish trail to Granada but at least we found this. The fruit unplucked on the small orange trees had rotted or been stricken with some blight or killing canker that left them black and hard and wizened on the trees; the useless last crop hung there in tatters like hand grenades that had not 'gone off', or rather had half gone off, enough to partly destroy the casing; the sections of the fruit that were not black with blight were this vivid orange, an infected colour, the freshness of the fruit thwarted of their natural growth. It was a peculiar place to be in; like something in Grimm again.

The light was already beginning to flood the village too. The sea to the southeast (normally out of sight for anyone standing at the window) seemed to have drawn closer, flooding part of the village, so strong was the reflected emergent daylight now pouring or streaming over the roofs of the houses where the sleepers still snored, for now smoke rose up from the chimney-pots, announcing breakfast.

This house, formerly in Fisher Street but now Upper O'Connell Street, was once the home of Creswell, who lost his wife and moved elsewhere with his children. I kept encountering him or his double at drinks parties at Folly House (home to Mary Alice and Howard R. Simpson, late of the American Consular Service at Marseilles) or at Ardnacorrig, on cosmopolitan and posh Compass Hill (where lived historian Robert Dye and Tessa, a Hawaiian princess by blood), and knew him at once, for he always stood in the same posture (sundial) in the same outfit – red-and-white striped shirt, tan slacks, shod in Hush Puppies, holding a drink, a third depleted (red wine) with a social smirk on his face, standing a little apart from the other drinkers, silently brooding, deliberating upon something. Then I'd sidle up to him and say, 'Creswell, I believe.' To which he would respond with the utmost gravity and politeness: 'You've got the wrong man again. I'm not Creswell.'

'No? Well, you're the spitting image of him.'

'Nevertheless,' said the man who was not Creswell, looking over my shoulder with a crafty smile, as though he knew I was having him on, 'I am not Creswell.'

We painted the front of the house white, installed double glazing in three windows overlooking the narrow street, put a brass porthole into the front door to lighten the dark hall, painted the door Commodore blue, put in window-boxes.

We are No. 2. There is another No. 2 halfway down by the Stony Steps. Below us is the Guardwell. What can it be guarding so well? Search me. More puzzles in the labyrinth of our life. Lift me up, let me see!

If you examine the house from the outside (in the narrow street dividing the Guardwell from Casey's Corner or what used to be but is now Bruno's Tower) you might be looking at any semi-detached two-storey *casa* in a narrow *calle* in Palma de Majorca, say Calle dos de Mayo, and the surprise continues in that the hallway leads directly to a sunken patio with whitewashed walls and hanging baskets of flowers, a throughway admitting daylight while it lasts and affords admittance to the walled garden beyond, a half-acre of lawn and arbours and flowerbeds and a crazy-paved path of flat stones from a beach near the Old Head, and three apple trees and a tall twelve-foot brick wall at the end, with Protestant *cementerio* and twelfth-century tower and weather vane (missing salmon) with Canon Williams's Anglican bell tolling beyond the nearer wall where honeysuckle has been trained against a trellis.

The interior developed in as arbitrary and haphazard a fashion, the hit or miss Spanish manner of adding rooms to accommodate new-born babes, with the bedroom downstairs off the hallway and the living room and kitchen upstairs, the kitchen more galley than anything else, behind a clapboard division that screens it off. The floor to ceiling window with sliding door has been enlarged to admit more daylight, with access to the deck and teak rail overlooking the herb garden and arbours. You climb upstairs via a narrow gangway without banisters into the living room where sunlight penetrates to the street wall and two windows overlooking the street. A Welsh window-cleaner puts up his collapsible steel ladder once a month and ascends, full of wind and fresh gossip (he had stayed in a Chicago hotel ninety-two storeys up), one of a company of Jehovah's Witnesses from Bandon. His previous and late confrère Higginbotham had departed into Ecuador where he died of cancer while presumably engaged in proselytising, not window-cleaning.

– 74 –

Countess Markiewicz and the Siege of Derry

... a great perturbation of sweaty heroes ...
watching the hurlers above in Kilmainham.
Samuel Beckett, *Whoroscope* (1930)

i

The gun, which had never really left Irish politics but had always been secretly there, under the counter as it were, used as a bargaining ploy in dirty deals, was back again. Ever since Sir Roger Casement had imported arms from Germany on a ship that had carried sewage pipes as legitimate cargo, the gun had been there. It was still being used for plea-bargaining in political deals that referred to the disbanding of a secret army that had no intention of ever surrendering its arms while any remnants of the British Army remained in Ulster, the Orange province that would always fight and would always be right. Their Green counterparts still prated of a free united Ireland, turning their backs on the grim reality that the Protestants, the Orangemen, were implacably opposed to such a scheme; for those who have had power once do not readily surrender it.

Provos imprisoned in Portlaoise had smeared the walls of their cells with their own excrement, as heated up as their politics, the dirty protest of babes and revolutionaries in arms. Others had taken hunger strikes to the limit, died for their convictions, now cadaverous and stinking in soiled sheets. Neither camp would budge an inch from the position they had adopted; neither had one iota of mercy for the opposition, no matter how gallant or foolish in their mutual efforts to infiltrate enemy lines, to annihilate each other and all that was theirs.

Captain Robert Nairac, purporting to be Danny from the Ardoyne, had given them 'The Broad Black Brimmer' and three other rebel songs at the Three Steps Inn at Drumintee. He had then been taken out, beaten insensible with fenceposts and whatever other implement came to hand. Nairac, with not much life left in him, was then shot out of hand like a mad dog and the sorry remains chucked into a meat-grinder.

The Provos refused to give up their arms, their dangerous toys; they scattered about the bodies of their victims as heartlessly as cannibals would discard human bones after a cannibal feast on some desert isle where they had repaired for a celebratory repast. They weren't admitting what may have happened to Captain Nairac. These facts could never be publicly known; the hatred on both sides was implacable; the dead were dishonoured, thrown into unmarked graves, not even graves, not even recorded; they would like to forget them, forget all that had ever happened, what they had done to Nairac, what they would do to others. The victims were dumped as casually as the Mob disposed of its kills in the marshes and wasteland beneath the Pulaski skyway, discarded like carrion.

The weapons sold to them by Gaddafi were brought in secretly and wrapped in oil-soaked coverings as if they were holy relics or the shrunken bodies of mummies in sweet-smelling preservatives; buried in secret places at night in woodland and bog, and records kept of their precious whereabouts. Those entrusted with such secret nocturnal burials were told to keep their mouths shut, if they knew what was good for them.

When the great day came they would be dug up, resurrected for the uprising that was to free Ireland, so long in bondage to the hated enemy, perfidious Albion, the bad neighbour, the masterly manipulator of political skulduggery down the long centuries when Ireland was in bondage.

The country was riddled with arms caches and now with dead bodies buried in shallow graves, grudged even the respect owed to the dead, but every indignity heaped upon them, cursed as they were put down, hidden away. The weapons got more respect than the dead enemies; no single reverence could be accorded them; they were as hated in death as they had been in life. The sacrifices had been too great; the fight had to go on.

Killing had its own price that had to be paid – the weapons were not cheap, transporting them was expensive, bribes had to be dropped. One paid for the other in the bigger calculations of a secret war, a war of attrition against civilians and informers, and wrongdoers who deserved punishment and would get it, knee-capping, all part of the unacknowledged legislation of dreams, deals and bonds sealed with handshakes, nods and winks.

And how could anything good come out of such dishonourable and mean-spirited and twisted activity, carried out at night, when the hit-men struck again, out of sight and hearing of honest people asleep in their beds, dreaming of a free Ireland? How could it?

Ireland didn't deserve to be free. Ireland was in bondage, had always been in bonds. Dreams of sudden wealth had come to certain citizens of another island – was it Mozambique? – of treasure buried by pirates and the exact place where it had been buried seen in dreams with enough exactness for the sleeper when awake to draw a rough map, sell up everything and buy digging equipment and start digging. Those benighted dreamers gave up their jobs and went on digging a huge hole and then other huge holes near the first one. They found nothing and were ruined, for all their savings and hopes of wealth had gone into the digging equipment, and now they had nothing, the fools, the fools, the fools!

I have seen a dog digging for bones in much the same frantic manner on a beach near Bundoran, firing the sand back through his hind legs like a power-hose. At least the dog gives up, quits the demented digging and leaves the beach. Not so the Provos; they have their own itinerary, their dreams that they will never relinquish. Every race to its own wrestling. Every race has its own particular craziness. And Ireland? Ireland is no particular exception; every dog has its own fleas.

ii

As a precocious youth of sixteen summers, Orson Welles had travelled through Connemara in a donkey-trap, painting scenery until his money ran out, then he acted for the Edwards-MacLiammóir company at the Gate in Dublin, as is well known. There he began to find himself, began to develop his prodigious talents.

In October 1931 he played the Duke Karl Alexander opposite Betty Chancellor in *Jew Süss* and received good notices. He offered Alexander Korda the outline of a satirical film; it was to be set in Italy, on the Mediterranean coast, in one of those mythical kingdoms the size of Luxembourg, a farce about capitalist imperialism. Two towns had hated each other for seven hundred years.

It brought to mind the true story that Flora Jessup had told me of the last siege of Derry and her small part in it. For she herself had been on the Derry walls during the famous siege, and was 'had' there thrice by three of the boys in the course of one night. Liverish and with the direct stare of puck-goats with stinking breath, they had enjoyed her favours, one by one, each unbeknown to the others, in different rooms, between patrolling the walls and coming upon Flora, dauntless daughter of desire, a Botticelli page from the fork down.

She may not have been the Countess Constance Markiewicz in her uniform of Citizen Army green, brandishing a heavy service revolver, but at least she was serviceable and one of their own, for was she not herself a countess of the Holy Roman Empire? She had some such distinction, bestowed upon her by the Pope in the Vatican.

The three heroes who had enjoyed her favours in the course of one night may have feared it was their last on earth. The third was Cathal Goulding himself, quartermaster of the 'official' IRA, who encountered her preparing breakfast and had her there and then, under the table. She was his porridge and his Holy Communion.

During the siege the lads grew beards; Flora had had a rash for days after their attentions but had offered herself up freely for Ireland. She was, after all, to be the consolation prize for a brave soldier ready to offer up his life for Mother Ireland.

The notion of an uprising had excited them and no two ways about it; the hard men, the renegades, had been looking forward to Easter, for wasn't it to be their time? It was woven into the very tapestry of our history; implicit in the national anthem ('The Soldier's Song'), repeated in the story of Casement's weapons concealed under German sewage pipes, the thirty pieces of silver, the crowing of the cock, Christ's reassuring words to the Good Thief. It was all there, and in their credulous hearts they believed it, every word of it.

The traitors and informers, the turncoats whom James Joyce said we would always have with us as part of our heritage and history (as Christ told us we would always have the poor), the ratters, big and little grasses, those who had been 'turned', or were about to be turned, were now all united, like a Churchman pack with twenty cigarettes (extra strong) intact in it, presenting one stern face set and resolute to the common foe, perfidious Albion.

English Anglicans, hard-boiled Protestants, in their credulity believe that Queen Victoria slept everywhere they were pleased to put her up in: hotels and the rich private houses of England suitable for their Queen. As we in our credulous Catholic way believe that Saint Patrick slept all over Ireland, generally in the open on the sides of hills that became places of pilgrimage named after him. We also believe that the Devil, Old Nick, dined out all over Ireland and was royally entertained.

At least that's what they used to believe in County Kildare and may still do, for all I know. Satan rode with the Killing Kildares and dined with Speaker Conolly at Castletown, now taken over by Desmond Guinness and the Irish Georgian Society.

– 75 –

The Americanisation of Old Ireland

'Have a nice day!'

i

The Americanisation of Ireland began with the baseball caps. After that came the shopping malls; then it was every man for himself, the pell-mell downhill race of the Gadarene swine. Let me tell you about it.

Of all the countries in the world to emulate, we had to pick the worst. Baseball caps with goofy logos and slogans were worn by young and old, often back to front. Old codgers wore them, as well as farm-workers driving slurry wagons. A general uniformity such as you get among soccer supporters ('Who do ya support?') was established. Then came the rash of shopping malls from Tallaght in Dublin to Crazy Prices in Portlaoise.

Then came the bypasses around Cork city, as the large provincial town was called; as though some city engineer had taken leave of his sense and built roundabouts everywhere he could, and also where he shouldn't, slavishly following some road system he had seen in Sweden and Portugal.

Cork and Cobh were trying to join up, arterial hands reaching across the Lee; new caravan routes were opened up and the gravy-trains converged on Cork from all directions; the besieged city under attack from its own clogged-up road system, as a virus can eat its way into sound tissue or what had been healthy tissue previous to the onslaught of this particular pernicious disease.

It was all part of our new opulence and greed. Cork believed in the Celtic Tiger with all the credulity of its easygoing provincial heart; the hearts of simple Munstermen and womenfolk shallow and commonplace as bedpans.

They believed in the Celtic Tiger in the same way as they believed in 'Jackie' Charlton, that honorary Irishman, moving statues (wasn't Ballinspittle just down the road?), proportional representation, the Immaculate Conception, the Mystery of the Blessed Trinity, Healy's honey, the Mass, Yeo Valley organic yoghurt and the Sam Maguire Cup.

When Cork was victorious on the field it (the cup) was carried in procession about the streets by coach Larry Tompkins who raised it aloft as though he were Buckley, Bishop of Cork and Cloyne raising up the monstrance to display the Blessed Host for the people to adore and venerate. They were only adoring themselves, the preordained correctness of being what they were, in Cork.

The slogan was a misnomer in any case, if not an outright crib, suspiciously close to the adman's 'Put a Tiger in Your Tank', just another catchphrase or 'sound-bite' like 'Guinness is Good for You' or 'You're Never Alone with a Strand'.

Tigers were threatened with extinction in India, except as sport for maharajas hunting them from howdahs mounted on elephants; rarely seen in the Dublin Zoo and not any more in Duffy's or Fossett's Circus. The old authentic Celts themselves would soon be as extinct as the tigers of the wilds, replaced by *amadáns* in pink and purple baseball caps worn back to front.

A tunnel had been cut to facilitate the flow of 'urban' traffic about Cork city and ease the great Dublin–Cork nexus, divert it elsewhere and give the city an 'infrastructural edge' in bringing in foreign investment. 'Road rage' was not unknown; next there would be talk of 'downtown' and the 'inner city'; whereas it was only a provincial dump, full of insistent beggars and citizens of all ages and stripes sucking ice-cream cones even in the depths of winter. Winter and summer were indistinguishable, were it not for the foliage. The riverside walks and the bridges were dreary; in Dublin at least you knew the Liffey was flowing out into Dublin Bay, and the Comb ran friskily enough through Galway, braced up by its keen Atlantic air.

An import-export drug business had been set up illegally between Cork and Amsterdam, and where you get big money easily come by, you also get crime and protection rackets. Cork was only imitating Dublin.

Tribunals had been set up in the capital to try to weed out malfeasance and skulduggery in high places; in the last quarter of the century High Court judges were found wanting and a former Taoiseach found himself in deep water. There was much talk of settlement and appeasement, the old wounds long open and going septic might still be healed. Miracles never cease.

Then the miracle happened. In Belfast, the very seat of the grievous infection, and on the twelfth or last month of the passing century, the Lion sat down with the Lamb. The jackal had consented to share spoils with the hyena.

A new access road was cut into Kinsale from Belgooly, haunt of contentious blacksmiths, a feuding family and Provo-sympathisers or outright Provos; elegant (the road, that is) as it followed the curves and twists of the Curlew River wending its way to the sea.

The local chief of the fire brigade was taken up by American entrepreneurs and flown out to California to be trained up as a caddy master, flown home and installed in the Old Head of Kinsale Golf Club and made for life. Green fees were steep, the course windswept and exposed on a plateau near Hole Open.

Only foreign golfers were acceptable. In a small shack similar to a Balkan border control point with armed soldiers checking passports, the former fire chief kept an eye on the elongated ruin of the Geraldine castle, in case of falling masonry, collecting dues from those prepared to stump up thirty bob for the privilege of walking on ground that had formerly been free. On paying their fee, they were issued with a ticket and let in.

The old de Courcey castle ruin stood crookedly on its base, sad as an old man's mouth with gums and broken roots of teeth; below it stood the Balkan customs shed or toll gate or ticket office manned by the gingery-haired caddy master for the rich Kerry brothers who were developing the links, so that Tiger Woods himself could play a round with Payne Stewart one misty day in July.

Tiger Woods meets the Celtic Tiger! The land was swarming with tigers. Girls in public utility services and shops, pharmacies and doctors' receptions were taught not to keep the customers waiting but to advance with a welcoming smile as fixed as falsies, as winsome as Kewpie dolls. They dressed stylishly and showered regularly, exposing more flesh in summer, even navels; the models here were the swinging Corr sisters from Thurles, a trio of songbirds very popular with the Irish young, our Fizz Girls. All were pert and pretty like rubber dolls, quick with the magic formulae taught them in business schools: 'No bother!', 'There you go!', 'Have a nice day!' even if it's pouring rain. 'No problem!' 'No *bother!*'

No longer were the tall green double-decker buses of the Dublin transport system malodorous moving places of Virginia tobacco fumes and rotting shift-straps. In the rapid Americanisation of Ireland, this was a point in its favour; Americans were as hygienic as Scandinavians. They strolled up and down Grafton Street and called out to their spouses: 'Gee whiz, honey. Hey, getta load of this, honey!'

ii

The things we do badly are public monuments, always too bulky or set in an inappropriate place on a pedestal too high and mighty for their own good: witness Nelson lording it over the Coombe; or the upended blue ploughshare on Wilton roundabout in the outskirts of Cork, or our very own monument in Kinsale, beyond the Sovereigns Inn, formerly the Sea View Bar, purporting to be a 'wave', in processed (corton) steel, with a small 'fountain' attached. It cries out for graffiti as a poor text cries out for the blue pencil. Or dynamite.

The only useful thing the Provos ever did with dynamite was to blow Lord Nelson off his pillar in the centre of the capital's main thoroughfare, O'Connell Street, formerly Sackville Street. The Irish Army engineers shattered every window in O'Connell Street when they in their turn attempted to dynamite the stump.

It may be said that the main thoroughfare is as uninspiring as Stalinallee in what used to be East Berlin, or the main road that runs through Prosperous, Swords or Newbliss near the border, as if anxious to be elsewhere. An architect has given his view that the only hope for O'Connell Street would be to paint it a uniform purple from end to end, from the Rotunda to the bridge, royal purple, the colour of fly agaric or a cardinal's cap that signifies sanctity, here intended only to signify a throwing in of the sponge.

Degeneration upon degeneration upon yet more degeneration was Cork's (Cark's) dreadful fate. O Lord deliver us!

Gaelic games as organised by the GAA are nothing but a form of apartheid in sport, no 'foreign' games allowed (meaning no English games). Bullfighting should be introduced to broaden the public taste; a corrida in Croke Park for Easter, *every* Easter, might get them baying for blood.

– 76 –

When Rory First Tasted Wiener Schnitzel

The involuntary striptease that had begun on a boulder below the Temperance Hall, aptly named Eden, when a brazen schoolgirl had exposed herself

for Rory's benefit, continued; the flush-faced schoolgirl had been a regular
Gerty MacDowell for teasing display; there would be others after her. Yet
more came later; the involuntary striptease was to be resumed years later in
another country when the Jacaranda Street stripper performed for Rory and
for him alone in Johannesburg, after the puppet tour was over.

It was continued, very briefly, years later in a street in Munich where a
handsome couple were walking, the tight jeans of the brunette wide open
to a glimpse of gossamer scanties through which dark pubics erupted; a riot
below the waist that belied the calm, beautiful, made-up face with the disdainful aloof expression.

Goldbronze panting, sighing, Lydia Douce and the famous smackbang
Sonnez la Cloche. Everything reminded Rory of something else; now it was the
cane-brake near the swimming pool at Rancho Pico; a gauzy furred miracle of
a Mexican butterfly, vivid blue and earth-brown, trembling on a leaf, unaware
of its beauty, its uniqueness, its aloneness; a rare species that one does not see
much of, because there are not so many of them to be seen. They don't care
to be seen; that's the way it is with them. They are so shy.

Today you can have me, I am yours today.

Was it in Berlin or in Cologne that I first tasted Wiener schnitzel? It was
winter, and we were touring with Wright's puppets in Germany, heading
for Holland, having left summer behind in Yugoslavia. We were going on
to tour South Africa and both Rhodesias with the puppets; it was to be a
two-year tour.

Ever since I have been disappointed in Wiener schnitzels, for I never got
as good a one as the first I had tasted with Coppera in some humble German
or Austrian eatery.

In Johannesburg I became friendly with Bernhardt Adamczewski. He
was the German-Polish second husband of Fiona, Coppera's best friend
from King, her home town in the Eastern Cape. Adam gave me the idea for
extending and widening out the novel I was working on sporadically. I called
him Otto Beck and included him as the catalyst and mediator between the
Langrishe (Hill: Higgins) 'sisters', who in reality were my three brothers
and myself in drag; wedged between an Irish past and the European present. Jeremy Irons played Adamczewski ('Beck') in the television production
directed by David Jones, where Springfield garden and the father and daughters resembled emanations straight out of tsarist Russia, life in a *dacha* there,
in that time and place.

Otto Beck was Adamczewski, his pedantry and his pipes, his past as a
shepherd in the Dolomites. He died a few years ago in London, having mar-

ried his wife's best friend, who had been kind enough to tell him that his daughter was not his own.

The Berlin I knew there in Die Brücke with Wright's puppets was not the Berlin I got to know later when I lived there with Hannelore. As the Málaga that I knew first when passing through with Callus at the wheel of his DKW late at night was not the same Málaga that Coppera and I had known later with the kids when they were growing up and their Christmas toys were stolen in the Alameda Gardens by old men lurking in the shrubbery.

One's first impressions of a place are always wrong. Foreigners speaking a strange language were always misleading; one got the wrong idea of them, although Dubrovnik continued to remain strange for me, the people having coffee at seven in the morning in the great heat of August.

The pretty brunette with long legs jay-walking across a street in Berlin, skittish in her high heels in summer dress, crossing the wide street to where I was walking on the pavement, threw me a quick look of unambiguous intent. She crossed the wide street that was free of traffic while the lights turned from red to green and threw me this look that reduced me to a jelly.

When Hannelore spoke to her *Mutti* on the white phone she had installed in the little chocolate-box flat in Prinzregentenstrasse, she spoke as a loving daughter should regularly once a week, and used the softest sweetest tones: *'Mammylein'* so softly, permitting me to listen to her mother's voice, such a frail neurasthenic voice speaking beautiful German, like a wind in the fir trees. Hannelore spoke the most intimate German to her mother, in a voice she would never use with me.

Rory found that he could bring dead people back to life. Even when treated in a fictional manner, they came back to life. He could bring them closer. Rory could bring my mother back, as long as I called her 'Mumu' and not Lil; and my father, as long as I called him 'Dado' and not Da. I had to turn my back on the real parents in order to evoke this other pseudo-anonymous couple who were more real than my real parents, Bart and Lil. I thought, not quite believing it, that one day I would write a book about them. Well, this trilogy is it.

There was a time in the early 1950s when the CIE rolling stock, on first-class non-smoking carriages, the suburban service from Dublin to Greystones, was almost as grand as the Trans-Siberian Express and grand ladies travelled in the first-class carriages, on their own or with a child, on the way to the Grand Hotel. One such covertly eyed Rory, immersed in a book, in the reflection of the window. Passing through the tunnels at Bray Head, the carriage became as intimate as a *fiacre* in the Bois de Boulogne.

Rory was reading, or pretending to read *Mademoiselle du Maupin*. The pretty fellow-traveller spoke and said: 'He isn't going to talk to me.'

And of course Rory never would. To have a real woman wouldn't be the same as an imaginary one; he wouldn't know how to take her; it was all dreamy stuff, all dreams.

The old puppeteer Wright had died in his bed in Islington, amid family and puppets and well-wishers; he died in harness. With his young wife Lyndie he had travelled to Hvar in Croatia, which smelt of lavender. The widow and his young children, the brother and sister, had scattered his ashes on Devil's Gulch on the slopes of Table Mountain.

Harry Calnek, my old *amigo*, did away with himself at Malaspina Road on the Powell River in British Columbia, after alerting the local police as to his intentions and the whereabouts of his remains. He had bad cancer, which had also killed Howard Simpson.

The century was ending badly, as badly as it had begun, with wars and rumours of more wars.

– 77 –

The Regional Hospital, Cork

'Just sit up now, like a good man, and let me take a quick peep at your heart and lungs,' said the nurse briskly.

On the night following my admittance to the Regional Hospital in Cork, the Cardiology Department, for an angiograph in BI ward (Surgeon Peter Kearney) I supped lightly on fresh orange juice, half a block of HB ice cream with wafers stuck in like sails and two peaches cut into segments, and retired to bed early, to dream again of Mumu.

Mumu transformed miraculously into what was no longer the deep fish Sedna, mother of all mothers, but reduced now to the dimensions of a slosh ball for Russian pool, the cerulean blue of a blackbird's egg found in the hidden nests I used to search for in Springfield shrubbery with the young bride Mrs Dilly Ruttle, my very first love or first inkling of what love might be. The blue ball struck delicately, a softly angled cue shot by a player who knew what he was doing, rolling slowly across the green baize to hover on the edge of the left centre pocket, before toppling in. The dream went on in absolute silence; what struck me most was the tender blue of the ball that had vanished, and I wondered was it something to do with Mumu's buckets of flowers, long-stemmed delphiniums, calla lilies (her Christian name was Lily), red hot pokers, daffodils in spring, taken in the Overland by Dado (for Mumu didn't drive) to Celbridge and Straffan Catholic church to decorate the May altars and the high altars for Mass and Benediction, which she would not attend herself, owing to claustrophobia. I was dreaming back thirty-five years prior to the heart-probe in a hospital on the outskirts of Cork city, watching the clock above the reception desk in Ward BI, and Nurse Elaine Walsh was smiling in through the glass at me, third in a ward of four male patients with heart conditions awaiting the gurney to roll us into the operating theatre where Dr Kearney awaited his quota for the morning.

– 78 –

Adieu in the Form of a Letter to Mrs Mary Alice Simpson (widow) of Chevy Chase, Maryland

Howard R. Simpson, RIP
US Consul General in Marseilles, 1974,
d. Chevy Chase, 1999

My dear Mary Alice,

Greetings from a far wet place. Stocks of Howard's much-appreciated Vietnamese pickled whole-grain high-class chillies are much depleted and will soon be gone, like Howard himself, gone with the wind.

But the blackthorn is out and its white blossoms very luminous, as also the gorgeous gorse very orange, all along the banks of the tidal Curlew River which you may never see again.

By mid-May the hedgerows give off the tangy scent of wild garlic; the perfume of hawthorn (which hits you on horseback) delicately fragrant is everywhere, and the elderflower in full bloom with an over-sweet aroma suggestive of the sickroom but suggesting too the fullness of summer.

I'll end as helplessly as I began seventy-two years back, with nothing to love with except the heart, the only reliable organ left; and that's not so reliable either, per the angiograph in the hospital that you know only too well.

Do I hear a dog barking in the corridor?

It's been a bleak midwinter in the months since your hurried departure for the new life in Chevy Chase, Maryland. The opening of the cricket season was delayed in England by snow at Fenners, but the *Novillaros* (not yet in their *trajes de luz* but got up sharply enough in tightly fitting well-cut grey uniforms like bellhops in five-star hotels) strode proudly into the Madrid bullring for the first corrida of 1999 as they have been striding since the days of Lope de Vega and Calderón de la Barca. Or Philip the Fair, whose corpse was transported about the dusty highways and byways of Spain by the semi-crazed widow, until the head of the departed one had turned as green as weathered bronze and shrunk to the size of a small pumpkin.

She buried him with some pomp, as befits a king, within sight of the convent she had retired into to pray for his soul. They were a strange pair. He died of drinking a glass of water following a hard game of tennis.

Death, then, is shrinkage, declining and wilting away out of life; no more ice-cold Margaritas at Folly House. Well, the years roll by, as roll they must. So, how are things in Gloccamorra?

Ever,

Rory

PS Gloccamorra or no Gloccamorra, how are you sleeping in nookshotten Chevy Chase? Something wakes me at 3.30 and I get up to work on this book I'm finishing, but I suspect my mother is writing it. She always felt that she had a book in her. Now it's coming out.

I took a break at 11 a.m. and searched high and low for my teeth (mi teef), the frontal bridge that produces such a winning smile (if I care to use it), compliments of P. J. Power, dental genius of Kinsale, without which (and whom) I am a sorry sight. The search proved fruitless, as lesser writers would put it. Guess where I found the teeth?

In my mouth.

– 79 –

The Old Moon with the New Moon
in Her Arms

Under the table are boxes of tissues, aerosol cans and Hargate roach spray, an oxygen tank and additional breathing apparatus, the Divibus pump for use thrice a day to control asthma. As the blood's impurities build up the other organs, particularly the brain, are poisoned.

Her attempts to write poetry get mixed up in grocery lists for Jefferson Market on the south side of 10th Street. Her bowels are not functioning properly, nor do her dentures fit; it becomes an ordeal for her to collect the mail two floors below. She has become generous with abuse, finding fault with everybody. Her friends, for the most part, are long dead or live far from New York, though she has a brother who is still alive. She no longer receives any magazines or newspapers other than the *TLS*. It was, as she put it, her Trappist period. A Trappist period for Djuna Barnes.

What went wrong with *The Antiphon?*

'Tis a very odd verse play involving incest in the Jacobean manner that she had worked at for nigh on fourteen years, wasted years, if wasted they were. It was a nagging obsession to do with the father, himself an American version of old Karamazov. It was a move in the wrong direction, moving into a bogus seventeenth century. She had to write indirectly of the horrors that befell her long ago. Wald Barnes, the father, was involved.

By right she belonged to Europe, was its frustrated chronicler along with Edith Wharton, Henry James and T.S. Eliot. To stay out of Europe was a mistake, hence her silence, the Trappist period; whereas Freya Stark worked on well into her old age, learnt Persian in her eighties. Baroness Blixen (1885-1962), though afflicted with amoebic dysentery and tertiary syphilis and an invalid for the last third of her life, yet 'found' herself in Kenya and wrote *Out of Africa* in English. She found a way out of her misery (the loss of the coffee farm, the death of Denys Finch-Hatton); whereas Djuna Barnes (1892-1982) had sunk down under hers. There were leopards about the farm in the Ngong uplands where the air was like wine; the Baroness shot lions and leopards,

made shift to learn native languages, loved the second son of the thirteenth
Earl of Winchilsea who by night shot two marauding lions while Karen held
the torch. She wrote of another daytime kill:

> I went right up to it and watched the light ebbing from its eyes; it was my
> first meeting with a lion and I shall never forget it. In their build, carriage
> and movements lions possess a greatness, a majesty, which positively instils
> terror in the human being and makes one feel later that everything else is
> trivial – thousands of generations of unrestricted supreme authority, and
> one is oneself set back 6,000 generations – suddenly comes to feel the mighty
> power of nature, when one looks it right in the eyes.
>
> Karen Blixen, *Letters from Africa,* 1914-31

February 1958, touring with John Wright's Marionettes

One night near Kariba Dam, still under construction, a lioness loped for a
quarter of a mile down the road, trapped in the headlights of the Bedford
truck. I sat beside Wright, who was driving, and watched it moving; it didn't
seem alarmed. I thought perhaps it was a donkey, from the movement of the
haunches; until it leapt off the road into the darkness and I saw it was a full-
grown lioness, very pale, almost luminous in the headlights.

Wright stopped the Bedford, killed the lights, and we stepped out. I stood
on the ground above the great river they were damming and I felt that power
that the Baroness was referring to: lions and lionesses were moving freely
about in their own native habitat into which we had trespassed; it was their
ground. The deep imprints of their great pads had marked the wet cement
of the tarmac on the new Kariba airstrip.

'She was a very private person and on more than one occasion called the
police to remove weeping women from her doorstep,' so wrote Frank O'Neal,
the last helping hand to reach out, since Berenice Abbott would not bring
herself to help.

Could Djuna Barnes have progressed beyond *Nightwood*, had she
remained in Paris, or lived in Berlin or Vienna? It didn't happen.

Wednesday, 12 October 1994, twelve years after her death, Derek
Mahon, Alannah Hopkin and I visited Patchin Place in Greenwich Village; then Patricia King drove us over the George Washington Bridge and
out along the west bank of the Hudson through a very lush land with the
verges mown all the way to West Point and the railway line and the road
narrowing, on a superlatively blue day in the fall, to Cornwall-on-Hudson

for lunch at Painter's. After lunch we visited the post office and Derek Mahon bought stamps in order to inquire whether there were any Barneses living there. No, no such family; so we went to the library. An aged female historian of the town was in the basement, we were informed. She grudgingly conceded that the Barnes family had lived briefly there, but the family was 'not respectable' and never considered part of the community. But Djuna Barnes had asked that her ashes be scattered in a dogwood grove on Storm King Mountain; she wanted to come back, I said. Well, yes, maybe, the aged historian conceded; so we left it at that.

It was a lovely blue day in Cornwall-on-Hudson. We looked for the Barnes house on the way to Storm King Mountain but couldn't find it. We never found it. Many fine houses stood thereabouts with balconies and porches and an almost Austrian look to them; wooden homes.

Djuna Barnes was born on 12 June 1892, ten years after James Joyce, at Cornwall-on-Hudson in upstate New York. She was to live for the last forty years of her life in Patchin Place, Greenwich Village, where she died on 17 June 1982.

– 80 –

How the Century Ended

I know that time is passing because I cannot walk any distance without discomfort and hills are fast becoming impossible. I know of the passage of time because the beech sapling from Springfield (planted for my grandson Paris) was about nine inches when planted seven years ago in the garden here: it is now twenty-two feet high, whereas Paris, at twelve, is five feet three. His ambition, he tells me, is to be an international rollerball champion. He was born to blade.

One sunny day in Bavaria so many years ago, I went walking in the Alps with Karen Reece. The Agatha Christie long-runner, *The Mousetrap,* is into its forty-eighth year and may be good for another half-century, a London cultural pilgrimage for Japanese tourists.

Alistair Cooke's *Letter from America,* begun when Rory was nineteen years of age, has been transmitted from the same BBC studio for fifty-four years.

Passed away in that time that is passing, some by their own hands, I remember

Bernhardt ('Adam') Adamczewski, who died in London.

Zbigniew Herbert, who died in Cracow.

Henning Mortenson, who died in Copenhagen.

Michael Morrow, who died in London.

Mike Poole, who died in Cómpeta, laughing like a jackass to the bitter end.

Geoffrey Rowe, who died in Greystones, having risen from his bed one Christmas morning, to fall dead at his wife's feet.

Brendan ('Brother Bun') Higgins, who died in Ealing.

Howard Simpson, who died in Chevy Chase, Maryland.

Anthony Kerrigan, who died in Illinois.

Not forgetting Gerard, Paddy and Philomena, all gone to their rest.

Rita Hayworth who died in Hollywood, at sixty-eight. She was prematurely senile; her looks and memory gone.

Madeleine Carroll who died in Marbella, where she had been a recluse since the death of her daughter. She was eighty-one.

Two of my lifelong friends did away with themselves when threatened by cancer: Donal Farrell, by an overdose in St Amour, and Harry Calnek, by hunting rifle in Canada. May they find peace, wherever they went thereafter.

Petrushka Karr would have turned thirty. On the last day of the century, the tides splash in and out twice a day in Copenhagen, Cork, Dublin, Cape Town and Amsterdam, going with the rollings of the earth ball and her moon through everchanging tracks of neverchanging space.

Ponting or Hobsbawm, or some such pundit, informs us that genocide has marked out our century. But before the so-called Holocaust, the Germans slaughtered the Hemeros in Africa. The Turks slaughtered Armenians; the Hutus slaughtered the Tutsis in Rwanda; the Croats slaughtered Serbians, then the Serbs went in for some ethnic cleansing of their own in Bosnia and Kosova. Predators pattered after victims like stoats in search of blood.

– Epilogue –

Past It

Age does us no favours. Advancing years do not bring serenity; our end is likely to be as untidy and messy as our beginning, when we came bawling messily into this world.

The carnal clinch can be left behind as an embarrassment. Eyesight failing. Teeth gone to pot, bridges installed; hearing only so-so, memory likewise, nostrils and ears sprouting hair, pubics offer scant cover; the metabolism getting into the swing of it before the final dissolution, the final descent into the grave, to be scattered as ashes about some favoured spot, tipped into some river, lake or sea.

The rotting metabolism, past it now, bursts in terrific slow motion from the coffin six feet down and goes rampaging away to join the other maggot-moved corpses, joining up with the teeming subatomic life underground.

The long red tresses of Rossetti's beautiful model Elizabeth Siddall filled the coffin to overflowing when it was opened, years after her demise, for the poet to recover a Morocco-bound volume that he had laid upon the dead breast of the beloved.

Human hair grows out of hand in the sleepy stagnancy of the grave, before falling off in fistfuls as the monitoring death-moths engender and come forth in force, probing and rummaging, having a field day. The skeleton scatters out of the coffin's last embrace in bits and pieces and goes wandering off. Coffin boards are removed elsewhere by busy termites, wriggling worms going at it; human bones scattered all over the place, appendages – eyeless sockets and hairless skulls – dropping off and devoured in our final dissolution into the teeming earth. We all roll with the earth's turning, asleep forever on its broad, deeply breathing bosom. Thinking of dead friends is the price we pay for our rest. Very dear friends all gone home. *Vale,* Harry, Donal, Adam, Geoffrey, Gerard, Paddy, Vera, Philomena. *Adieu, adieu,* Anthony and Howard gone from Majorca and Chevy Chase, Maryland, fled out of life.

In May of this year, a survey published indicated that 20,000 citizens a year were emigrating from the Republic, Celtic Tiger or no Celtic Tiger. The island called Ireland was still draining away like sanies into a bucket.

Happy New Year, all you suckers out there, preparing to set foot gingerly into the twenty-first century. Have a nice day! *¡Feliz Año Nuevo! Bonne Année! Glückliches Neujahr!* Give my love to the sunrise.

On a marvellously sunny late-May day in the new century with swifts screeching overhead and jackdaws guarding their nests in the chimney-pots there came a letter in a hand that seemed familiar and what is more from Copenhagen. It was from Anna Reiner, the old flame twenty-five years on. She wrote:

'Why do you call yourself Rory? And how can you be seventy-one in the year 2000 when you are born in 1927? Or more interesting where did you spend the lost two years?'

Za vaschyezdarovyie!

LANNAN SELECTIONS

The Lannan Foundation, located in Santa Fe, New Mexico, is a family foundation whose funding focuses on special cultural projects and ideas which promote and protect cultural freedom, diversity, and creativity.

The literary aspect of Lannan's cultural program supports the creation and presentation of exceptional English-language literature and develops a wider audience for poetry, fiction, and nonfiction.

Since 1990, the Lannan Foundation has supported Dalkey Archive Press projects in a variety of ways, including monetary support for authors, audience development programs, and direct funding for the publication of the Press's books.

In the year 2000, the Lannan Selections Series was established to promote both organizations' commitment to the highest expressions of literary creativity. The Foundation supports the publication of this series of books each year, and works closely with the Press to ensure that these books will reach as many readers as possible and achieve a permanent place in literature. Authors whose works have been published as Lannan Selections include Ishmael Reed, Stanley Elkin, Ann Quin, Nicholas Mosley, William Eastlake, and David Antin, among others.

SELECTED DALKEY ARCHIVE PAPERBACKS

FOR A FULL LIST OF PUBLICATIONS, VISIT:
www.dalkeyarchive.com

SELECTED DALKEY ARCHIVE PAPERBACKS

FOR A FULL LIST OF PUBLICATIONS, VISIT:
www.dalkeyarchive.com